Once More unto the Speech, Dear Friends

Monologues from Shakespeare's First Folio with Modern Text Versions for Comparison

Volume One: The Comedies

Once More Unto the Speech, Dear Friends

Monologues from Shakespeare's First Folio with Modern Text Versions for Comparison

Volume One: The Comedies

Compiled and Edited with Commentary by Neil Freeman

Applause Theatre & Cinema Books

Once More unto the Speech, Dear Friends
Monologues from Shakespeare's First Folio with Modern Text Versions for
Comparison: Volume One: The Comedies
by Neil Freeman

Library of Congress Cataloging-in-Publication Data
Shakespeare, William, 1564-1616.
  Once more unto the speech, dear friends : monologues from Shakespeare's first
folio with modern text versions for comparison / compiled and edited with
commentary by Neil Freeman.
    p. cm.
  ISBN-13: 978-1-55783-656-4 (v. 1)
  ISBN-10: 1-55783-656-6 (v. 1)
  ISBN-10: 1-55783-655-8 (v. 2)
  ISBN-10: 1-55783-657-4 (v. 3)
  1. Monologues. I. Freeman, Neil. II. Title.

PR2768.F74 2005
822.3'3--dc22

2005028249

Applause Theatre & Cinema Books
19 West 21st St.
Suite 203
New York, NY 10010
Phone: (212) 575-9265
Fax: (212) 575-9270
Email: info@applausepub.com
Internet: www.applausepub.com

Applause books are available through your local bookstore, or you may order at
www.applausepub.com or call Music Dispatch at 800-637-2852

Sales & Distribution
North America:
Hal Leonard Corp.
7777 West Bluemound Road
P. O. Box 13819
Milwaukee, WI 53213
Phone: (414) 774-3630
Fax: (414) 774-3259
Email: halinfo@halleonard.com
Internet: www.halleonard.com

Europe:
Roundhouse Publishing Ltd.
Millstone, Limers Lane
Northam, North Devon EX 39 2RG
Phone: (0) 1237-474-474
Fax: (0) 1237-474-774
Email: roundhouse.group@ukgateway.net

CONTENTS

ACKNOWLEDGMENTS

My grateful thanks to all who have helped in the growth and development of this work. Special thanks to Norman Welsh who first introduced me to the Folio Text, and to Tina Packer who (with Kristin Linklater and all the members of Shakespeare & Co.) allowed me to explore the texts on the rehearsal floor. To Jane Nichols for her enormous generosity in providing the funding which allowed the material to be computerised. To James and Margaret McBride and Terry Lim for their expertise, good humour and hard work. To the National Endowment for the Arts for their award of a Major Artist Fellowship: to York University for their award of the Joseph G. Green Fellowship, and to The University of British Columbia for their award of an canada Council SSHRC grant to help in proofing, as well as a Faculty Workstation Improvement Grant. To actors, directors and dramaturgs at the Stratford Festival, Ontario, especially Richard Rose and the late Michael Mawson; Repercussion Theatre, Montreal; Toronto Free Theatre (that was); the Skylight Theatre, Toronto and Tamanhouse Theatre of Vancouver. To colleagues, friends and students at The University of British Columbia, Vancouver; York University, Toronto; Concordia University, Montreal; The National Theatre School of Canada in Montreal; Equity Showcase Theatre, Toronto; The Centre for Actors Study and Training (C.A.S.T.), Toronto; The National Voice Intensive, Vancouver; Studio 58 of Langara College, Vancouver; Professional Workshops in the Arts, Vancouver; U.C.L.A, Los Angeles; Loyola Marymount, Los Angeles; San Jose State College, California; Long Beach State College, California; Brigham Young University, Utah and Hawaii, especially Craig Ferre and Robert Nelson; Holy Cross College, Massachusetts; Guilford College, North Carolina. To John Wright and Don Paterson, in their respective offices of Chairman and Associate Dean at U.B.C., for their personal support and encouragement. To Donna Wong-Juliani for her generosity and patient advice. To Tom Scholte and Rachel Ditor for their timely research assistance. To Alan and Chris Baker, and Stephanie McWilliams for typographical advice. To Jay L. Halio, Hugh Richmond and G.B. Shand for their critical input. To Frank Hildy, Director of the Shakespeare Globe Centre (USA) – Research Archives, and to Mark Rylance, Artistic Director of Shakespeare's Globe for their support and encouragement. To the overworked and underpaid proofreading teams who supervised the material from which this series books stem, Ron Oten and Yuuattee Tanipersaud, Patrick Galligan and Leslie Barton, Janet Van De Graaff and Angela Dorhman (with input from Todd Sandomirsky, Bruce Alexander Pitkin, Catelyn Thornton and Michael Roberts); Alexia Hagen and Samantha Simmonds for their work specifically related to the three audition volumes. And above all to my wife Julie, for her patient encouragement, courteous advice, critical eye and long sufferance!

SPECIAL ACKNOWLEDGMENTS

Paul Sugarman for initiating and supervising the production of the original material, indeed without his perseverance, patience, hard work well above the call of duty, encouragement, belief and friendship, none of the earlier material (*The Applause First Folio of Shakespeare in Modern Type* and the publication of the 36 individual plays under the collective title *The Applause First Folio Editions*) would ever have become a reality. Glenn Young, founder of Applause Books, for persisting with the first oh-so crazy scheme. Greg Collins especially (and Rachel Reiss) of Applause for their original struggles to turn other people's chaos into a practical and standardised reality. Shannon Reed – now a teacher and a burgeoning playwright, then of Applause – for suggesting the idea of a series of audition volumes and agreeing to and then laying in the foundations of this new approach; John Cerullo and Kay Radtke for supporting her; and especially Michael Messina and Brian Black (and designer Courtney Napoles) for taking over the project and sticking with it through all its trials and tribulations. And a huge thank you to the eagle-eyed proofreader cum editor Erin Herlihy whose exemplary diligence has saved me from many an embarrassing moment.

MASTER LIST OF SPEECHES

for titles and page numbers, see the detailed listing in front of each play

NINETY-EIGHT SPEECHES FOR WOMEN

Comedy of Errors (6), pages 29 - 46

- **Luciana** — Traditional & Today: young woman, younger than her sister Adrianna — #10
- **Adriana** — Traditional & Today: youngish/early middle age woman, older than her sister Luciana — #4, #7, #8
- **Curtizan** — Traditional & Today: a woman of the town, so attractive as to keep a young man away from his wife — #13
- **Abbesse** — Traditional & Today: since it turns out that she is the merchant Egeus' long lost wife and mother of both Antipholi; has and should be played as a woman of sufficiently old to have had 23 year old twins — #14

Two Gentlemen of Verona (5), pages 47 - 61

- **Julia** — Traditional & Today: young woman — #5, #6, #7, #8
- **Silvia** — Traditional & Today: young woman — #9

The Taming of the Shrew (2), pages 62 - 79

- **Bianca** — Traditional & Today: young woman, younger sister to Kate — #11
- **Kate** — Traditional & Today: young woman — #15

Love's Labour's Lost (7), pages 80 - 99

- **Queene** — Traditional & Today: young woman of marriageable age — #8, #12, #17
- **Maria/(1. Lady}** — Traditional & Today: young woman of marriageable age — #9
- **Katherine/(2. Lady}** — Traditional & Today: young woman of marriageable age — #10
- **Rosaline** — Traditional & Today: young woman of marriageable age, from the text slightly more experienced than the others — #11, #13

A Midsummer Night's Dream (16), pages 100 - 149

- **Hermia** — Traditional & Today: young woman of small stature & marriageable age — #13, #14, #15, #16
- **Helena** — Traditional & Today: tall young woman of marriageable age — #17, #18, #19, #20, #21, #22, #23
- **Fairie** — Traditional & Today: (usually) woman of any age — #27
- **Titiania/Queene** — Traditional: young woman or child; Today: (sometimes) woman of any age — #30, #31, #36, #37

The Merchant of Venice (7), pages 150 - 187

- **Portia** — Traditional & Today: young woman of marriageable age — #7, #10, #11, #13, #25, #26
- **Jessica** — Traditional & Today: young Jewish woman of marriageable age — #17

Much Ado About Nothing (7), pages 188 - 214

- **Beatrice** — Traditional & Today: young or very early middle-aged woman: — #1, #2, #3, #4, #14
- **Hero** — Traditional & Today: Leonato's young daughter, of marriageable age — #9, #10

The Merry Wives of Windsor (4), pages 215 - 239

- **Mistris Page** — Traditional & Today: married woman, with young daughter of just marriageable age — #2, #3
- **Mistris Quickly** — Traditional & Today: a gossipy woman of middle to advancing years, still attractive to Pistoll — #6, #14

As You Like It (11), pages 240 - 280

- **Celia** — Traditional & Today: young woman usually slightly younger than Rosalind — #5, #8
- **Rosalind** — Traditional & Today: young woman, slightly older than Celia — #12, #13, #14, #15, #16, #17, #22
- **Phebe** — Traditional & Today: young woman — #21, #23

Twelfth Night (11), pages 281 - 309

- **Viola** — Traditional & Today: a young woman, who disguises herself as the boy/eunuch Cesario — #3, #4, #5, #6, #7
- **Olivia** — Traditional: young woman; Today: sometimes a woman (slightly) older than Viola — #8, #9, #10, #11, #12
- **Maria** — Traditional & Today: youngish (or, dependent upon the casting of Toby, middle-aged) woman — #16

Measure for Measure (3), pages 310 - 328

- **Isabella** — Traditional & Today: a young woman, and a novitiate woman — #4, #8
- **Mariana** — Traditional & Today: dependent upon the age of Angelo, young or youngish middle-age woman — #13

All's Well That Ends Well (7), pages 329 - 347	
Hellen Traditional & Today: a young woman	#3, #5, #9
Old Countesse Traditional & Today: older woman, mother of Bertram, often referred to in the text as 'Old Lady'	#4, #10
Diana Traditional & Today: young chaste woman	#11, #12

The Winter's Tale (8), pages 348 - 377	
Hermione Traditional & Today: married woman with young child	#1, #5, #6, #7
Paulina Traditional: older woman of any age Today: woman of any age	#8, #9
Perdita Traditional & Today: a young woman	#13, #14
The Tempest (4), pages 378 - 404	
Miranda Traditional & Today: a young (teenage) woman	#15, #16, #19, #21

THIRTY-THREE SPEECHES (& MORE) FOR EITHER GENDER

for titles and page numbers, see the detailed listing in front of each play

Two Gentlemen of Verona (3), pages 47 - 61

Launce Traditional: clown male, any age **Today:** clown, any gender, any age		#10, #11
Duke Traditional: older male **Today:** any gender with adult daughter		#4

The Taming of the Shrew (2), pages 62 - 79

Servant Traditional: male, any age **Today:** any gender, any age		#1
Baptista Traditional: older male, parent to two daughters of marriageable age **Today:** with the age proviso, any gender		#2

A Midsummer Night's Dream (12), pages 100 - 149

Egeus Traditional: male, with teenage daughter **Today:** any gender		#1, #5
Pucke/Robin Traditional: young man or child **Today:** often any gender but, because of the mistakes made throughout the play, usually still young		#28, #29, #34, #35, #47, #48
Quince Traditional: male of any age **Today:** any age, &, if the name 'Peter' is changed to 'Petra' or 'Mistress', any gender		#39, #40
Snowt {Wall} Traditional & Today: character actor of any age		#41
Snug {Lyon} Traditional & Today: character actor of any age		#42

The Merchant of Venice (2), pages 150 - 187

Solanio Traditional: male, any age **Today:** any gender, any age, probably close in age to Anthonio		#1
Duke Traditional: older male **Today:** any gender, possessing great authority		#23

The Merry Wives of Windsor (1), pages 215 - 239

Host Traditional: male, any age **Today:** any gender, any age		#18

As You Like It (7), pages 240 - 280 {see also Duke Senior & Jaques}

Le Beau Traditional: character male, any age **Today:** any gender, any age		#4, #6
Duke Fredericke Traditional: older man of some authority **Today:** any age, and sometimes any gender		#7, #32, #33
1st Lord Traditional: male, usually young **Today:** any gender, any age		#29
Corin Traditional: older character male **Today:** any gender, usually middle age up		#31

Twelfth Night (2), pages 281 - 309

Fabian Traditional: male character actor, any age **Today:** any age, any gender		#14
Antonio Traditional: male, usually young or early middle-age **Today:** sometimes any gender, usually young or early middle-age		#22

The Winter's Tale (2), pages 348 - 377

Old Shepheard Traditional: older male character with a son of marriageable age **Today:** as above, any gender		#16
Time Traditional: male, often cast as 'Father Time' **Today:** any gender, any age		#21

The Tempest (2), pages 378 - 404 {see also Prospero, Anthonio, and Gonzalo}

Ariel Traditional & Today: any age and gender that can convey the (presumed) mercurial spirit of the character: any gender		#5, #8

ONE HUNDRED AND SEVENTY-ONE SPEECHES FOR MEN

Comedy of Errors (8), pages 29 - 46

Duke {Solinus} Traditional: older male , usually asn authority figure #1, #3
Today: with the above proviso, any gender, any age

Merchant (Egeus) Traditional & Today: older male (father of two 23 year old sons) #2a, 2b

Local Dromio Traditional: younger clown-style performer, usually well-versed in commedia #4, #6
Today: any age, gender, provided part of Egeon's speech #2 (which refer to the Dromio twins as being the same age/sex as the two Antipholi) is struck or rewritten, and the speech, though not necessarily the role, can be explored without the commedia skills

Antipholus V. Traditional & Today: young male approximately 23 years old #9, #11
Dromio V. Traditional & Today: as local Dromio above #12

Two Gentlemen of Verona (3), pages 47 - 61

Valentine Traditional & Today: young romantic male #1
Protheus Traditional & Today: young romantic male #2, #3

The Taming of the Shrew (11), pages 62 - 79

Lucentio Traditional & Today: young lover #4, #5
Petruchio Traditional & Today: young male #6, #7, #8, #9, #13, #14
Gremio Traditional & Today: an older male, listed as a 'Pantelowne', #3, #10. #12
viz. the Commed'ia figure known a 'lustful and avaricious old man'

Love's Labour's Lost (10), pages 80 - 99

Ferdinand/King Traditional & Today: young man of marriageable age #1, #5
Boyet Traditional: older male acting as both chaperone and possibly match-maker: #2
the character is described by one of the young women as 'Cupids Grandfather'
Today: could be played by any gender and probably any age, though someone older than the eight young people falling in love is usually preferred

Berowne Traditional & Today: young man of marriageable age #3, #4, #6, #7, #14
Braggart Traditional: older man, to separate him as much possible from the #15, #16
young woman with whom he has fallen in love
Today: usually the same, but can be played younger if the 'foreigness' is followed through to allow for the same distancing as described above

---

for titles and page numbers, see the detailed listing in front of each play

A Midsummer Night's Dream (20), pages 100 - 149

Theseus Traditional & Today: male of some authority #2, #3, #4
Lysander Traditional & Today: young man of marriageable age #6, #7, #8, #9
Demetrius Traditional & Today: young man of marriageable age #10, #11, #12
Bottome Traditional: a man of early middle-age on up #24, #25, #26, #38, #43, #44, #45
Today: man of any age
Oberon Traditional: usually a man of early middle-age on up capable of #32, #33
playing the Fairy King
Today: man of any age capable of playing the Fairy King
Flute {Thisbie} Traditional & Today: young man that has 'a beard comming' #46

The Merchant of Venice (17), pages 150 - 187

Anthonio Traditional & Today: man of early middle age, older than Bassanio #2, #3
Bassanio Traditional & Today: young man of marriageable age #4, #5, #6, #12
Morochus Traditional: a brash man of colour #8
Today: as above, the key to his failure and deserved mockery is his testosterone driven behaviour rather than his race
Arragon Traditional & Today: older man, of academic bent #9
Lorenzo Traditional & Today: young-(early ?) middle age man #14, #15
Clowne Traditional & Today: male of any age (with father still alive) #16
Shylocke/Jew Traditional: once a comedic figure, with a red wig #18, #19, #20, #21, #22, #24
the character has become, probably incorrectly, a figure of wronged dignity
Today: older Jewish male, with a daughter of marriageable age

Much Ado About Nothing (12), pages 188 - 214

Benedicke Traditional & Today: young or early middle-aged man #5, #6, #7, #8, #15
Don John/Bastard Traditional & Today: young or younger middle aged man #11, #12
Claudio Traditional & Today: a young man, hoping to be married #13
Don Pedro/Prince Traditional: male of some authority, often close in age to Leonato
Today: adult male of any age #16
Leonato Traditional & Today: older man of some authority, with a daughter #17
of marriageable age
Dogberry/Kemp Traditional: the clown figure, middle aged man
Today: a clown type figure of any age, usually male #18, #19

The Merry Wives of Windsor (14), pages 215 - 239

Character	Description	
Falstaffe	Traditional & Today: older and very corpulent man	#1, #7, #9, #10, #11, #13
Pistoll	Traditional & Today: man of indeterminate age	#4
Nym	Traditional & Today: man of indeterminate age	#5
Ford	Traditional & Today: male, usually middle age and upward	#8, #12
Evans	Traditional & Today: older character male	#15, #17
Slender	Traditional & Today: younger character man of marriageable age, not particularly bright	#16, #19

As You Like It (21), pages 240 - 280

Character	Description	
Orlando	Traditional & Today: a young man, youngest of three brothers	#1, #9, #11
Charles	Traditional & Today: male character actor who can wrestle	#2
Oliver	Traditional & Today: a young man, oldest of three brothers	#3
Duke Senior	Traditional: older man of authority, older than his brother Fredricke	#10, #28
	Today: any age (but older than Fredricke), and sometimes any gender	
Silvius	Traditional: young male would-be lover	#18, #19, #20
	Today: as above, but sometimes older	
Clowne	Traditional: male character actor, young to middle age	#24, #25, #26, #27, #30
	Today: as above, but any age	
Jaques	Traditional: older male, usually close to the 'sixth' age of the 'seven ages' speech (#37 below)	#34, #35, #36, #37, #38, #39
	Today: sometimes younger (early middle age on), and sometimes any gender	

Twelfth Night (11), pages 281 - 309

Character	Description	
Duke	Traditional & Today: younger or young-early middle age man	#1, #2
Andrew	Traditional & Today: a thin-faced character actor, young to young-middle age	#13
Toby	Traditional: older male, uncle to Olivia, brother to her deceased father	#15
	Today: as above, though the age range is often ignored	
Malvolio	Traditional: an older male, of, at least in public, a puritanical demeanor	#17/a & b, #18, #19
	Today: as above, but often the age range is more flexible	
Sebastian	Traditional & Today: a young man, twin brother to Viola	#20, #21, #23

Measure for Measure (11), pages 310 - 328

Character	Description	
Duke	Traditional: older male of some authority	#1, #9, #12
	Today: as above, though age range much more flexible	
Angelo	Traditional & Today: young to youngish middle-age man	#2, #3, #5, #6, #7
Claudio	Traditional & Today: a young man, brother to Isabella	#10
Lucio	Traditional & Today: a young or youngish-middle aged man	#11
Clowne	Traditional: older character male Today: usually male, any age	#14

All's Well That Ends Well (7), pages 329 - 347

Character	Description	
Parrolles	Traditional & Today: young to middle aged male, a blow-hard	#1, #2, #6, #8
King	Traditional & Today: older male of some authority	#7
Clowne	Traditional: male character actor, usually young or middle age	#13, #14
	Today: male of any age	

The Winter's Tale (11), pages 348 - 377

Character	Description	
Leontes	Traditional & Today: married male (often middle-aged) with young child	#2, #3, #10
Antigonus	Traditional & Today: middle aged or older male	#4
Florizell	Traditional & Today: a young man	#11, #12
Polixenes	Traditional & Today: middle aged man, with marriageable aged son	#15
Clowne	Traditional & Today: a young man of marriageable age	#17, #20
Autolicus	Traditional & Today: singing/acting male of any age	#18, #19

The Tempest (15), pages 378 - 404

Character	Description	
Prospero	Traditional: older male Today: occasionally either gender	#1, #2, #3, #4
Caliban	Traditional & Today: male character actor, any age, often young	#6, #11, #12, #13
Anthonio	Traditional: the younger brother of Prospero middle aged man and upwards	#7
	Today: sometimes either gender	
Gonzalo	Traditional: older male character actor	#9
	Today: sometimes any gender, usually maintaining the age proviso	
Trinculo	Traditional & Today: male character, any age	#10
Stephano	Traditional & Today: male character, any age	#14
Ferdinand	Traditional & Today: a young man of marriageable age	#17, #18, #20

PREFACE AND BRIEF BACKGROUND TO THE FIRST FOLIO

There has been an enormous change in theatre organisation in the last twenty years. While the major large-scale companies have continued to flourish, many small theatre companies have come into being, leading to

- much doubling

- cross gender casting, with many an one time male roles now being played legitimately by/as women in updated time-period productions

- young actors being asked to play leading roles at far earlier points in their careers

All this has meant actors should be able to demonstrate enormous flexibility rather than one limited range/style. In turn, this has meant

- a change in audition expectations

- actors are often expected to show more range than ever before

- often several shorter audition speeches are asked for instead of one or two longer ones

- sometimes the initial auditions are conducted in a shorter amount of time

Thus, to stay at the top of the game, the actor needs more knowledge of what makes the play tick, especially since

- early plays demand a different style from the later ones

- the four genres (comedy, history, tragedy, and the peculiar romances) all have different acting/textual requirements

- parts originally written for the older, more experienced actors again require a different approach from those written for the younger ones, as the young roles, especially the female ones, were played by young actors extraordinarily skilled in the arts of rhetoric

There's now much more knowledge of how the original quarto and folio texts can add to the rehearsal exploration/acting and directing process as well as to the final performance.

No matter how well prepared, no current soliloquy book deals directly with the bulk of these concerns. [1]

This series is intended to help you explore your audition pieces theatrically, so that you can discover the extra details of humanity that the original texts automatically offer. Thus they do not provide much academic or comparative analysis; rather you will find in the commentary to each speech details and full discussions of the devices peculiar to that speech's genre and the age and gender of the character, so that the particular idiosyncratic characteristics each speech presents can be **practically** explored in and of themselves in whatever way you wish.

In the series as a whole, there are over 900 separate audition possibilities, some of which have been created by adding two or more consecutive shorter speeches from the same scene

- 301 in the Comedy Volume
- 298 in the History Volume
- 304 in the Tragedy Volume

about six hundred more than in any other series.

At the beginning of each play, the speeches are coded as suitable for women, either sex, or men; and approximate audition time is offered, with speeches ranging from twenty-five seconds to three minutes.

Each speech is made up of four parts

- a **background** to the speech, placing it in the context of the play, and offering **line length** and an **approximate timing** to help you choose what might be right for any auditioning occasion

---

[1] Though offering sensible basic guidelines as to how to use the original material, the recent publications of Patrick Tucker show the First Folio text only.

- a **modern text version** of the speech, with unobtrusive symbols showing where editors have changed the original texts' sentence structure, capitalisation and spelling
- a **folio version** of the speech, with unobtrusive symbols showing where modern texts have intensified or diminished, added or removed punctuation
- a **commentary** explaining the differences between the two texts, and in what way the original setting can offer you more information to explore

Thus if they wish, **beginners** can explore just the background and the modern text version of the speech.

An **actor experienced in exploring the Folio** can make use of the background and the Folio version of the speech

And those wanting to know as many details as possible and how they could help define the deft stepping stones of the arc of the speech can use all four elements on the page.

THE FIRST FOLIO (for a list of current reproductions see Bibliography)

Late in 1621 or early in 1622 two men brought to the son of a somewhat disreputable printer an idea that was to change the face of literature and theatre for ever. The men were John Heminge and William Condell. The son, also a printer, was Isaac Jaggard. [2] The idea was to publish all the available plays written in whole or in part by the late William Shakespeare, who had died in 1616, and with whom they had been actors, business partners, colleagues, and friends for more than twenty years.

The end of 1623 saw the publication of the justifiably famed First Folio (F1). The single volume, published in a run of approximately 1,000 copies at the princely sum of one pound (a tremendous risk, considering that a single play would sell at no more than six pence, one fortieth of F1's price, and that the annual salary of a schoolmaster was only ten pounds), contained thirty-six plays.

The manuscripts from which each F1 play would be printed came from a variety of sources. Some had already been printed. Some came from the playhouse complete with production details. Some had no theatrical input at all, but were handsomely copied out and easy to read. Some were supposedly very messy, complete with first draft scribbles and crossings out. Yet, as Charlton Hinman, the revered dean of First Folio studies describes F1

it is of inestimable value for what it is, for what it contains . . .

For here are preserved the masterworks of the man universally recognized as our greatest writer; and preserved, as Ben Jonson realized at the time of the original publication, not for an age but for all time [3]

WHAT DOES F1 REPRESENT? [4] (the opening three bolded points being the most important considerations for this audition series)

- **texts prepared for actors who rehearsed three days for a new play and one day for one already in the repertoire**
- **written in a style (rhetoric incorporating debate) so different from ours (grammatical) that many modern alterations based on grammar (or poetry) have done remarkable harm to the rhetorical/debate quality of the original text and thus to interpretations of characters at key moments of stress.**
- **written for an acting company the core of which steadily grew older, and whose skills and interests changed markedly over twenty years**
- the texts having to be flexible enough to satisfy requests for private performances in the Inns of Court, private houses, and especially at Court

---

[2] William, his father, had had a somewhat chequered reputation with fraudulent printing of theatre documents: two incidents had involved his publishing works by Shakespeare to which he was not entitled, and claiming works to be Shakespeare's which most definitely were not: William, nominally the head of the house of Jaggard, was blind and died before the Folio was published.

[3] Introduction to the 1996 photostat of the First Folio, *The Norton Facsimile*, page ix.

[4] All of what follows is discussed in great detail in the first seventy-two pages of *The Applause First Folio of Shakespeare in Modern Type*.

- represents a writing career of more than twenty years
- presents thirty-six plays [5][6]
- spaced over two monarchs, Elizabeth and James, the second of whom allowed for a greater deal of examination of the personal dilemma of those in authority, and the questioning of their mistakes
- for at least two thirds of Shakespeare's career, written for one permanent company that enjoyed huge aristocratic and, eventually, royal protection, thus ensuring it was always one of the few companies guaranteed a playing space in London
- played in two widely different spaces: at the beginning of Shakespeare's career, outdoor theatres in the less salubrious parts of London catering per performance to 2,500 spectators from all strands of society; by the end of his career, to a wealthier and socially more

- acceptable group of 700 per performance in an indoor theatre in the better part of the City of London
- for an audience whose make-up and interests likewise changed as the company grew more experienced

The whole is based upon supposedly the best documents available at the time, collected by men closest to Shakespeare throughout his career, and brought to a single printing house whose errors are now widely understood – far more than those of some of the printing houses that produced the original quartos.

TEXTUAL SOURCES FOR THE AUDITION SPEECHES

Individual modern editions consulted in the preparation of the Modern Text version of the speeches are listed in the Bibliography under the separate headings 'The Complete Works in Compendium Format' and 'The Complete Works in Separate Individual Volumes.' Most of the modern versions of the speeches are a compilation of several of these texts. However, all modern act, scene and/or line numbers refer the reader to *The Riverside Shakespeare*, in my opinion still the best of the complete works despite the excellent compendiums that have been published since.

The First Folio versions of the speeches are taken from a variety of already published sources, including not only all the texts listed in the 'Photostatted Reproductions in Compendium Format' section of the Bibliography, but also earlier, individually printed volumes, such as the twentieth century editions published under the collective title *The Facsimiles of Plays from The First Folio of Shakespeare* by Faber & Gwyer, and the nineteenth century editions published on behalf of The New Shakespere Society.

---

5 Though appearing in an early quarto version (1609), Pericles did not appear in a Folio publication till the Third Folio of 1664. Three other plays attributed in whole or part to Shakespeare
a/ *Sir Thomas More*, finally collated from various manuscripts in 1911
b/ *The Two Noble Kinsmen*, the best regarded edition being the quarto of 1634
c/ the more recently proposed *King Edward III*, first attributed to Shakespeare in 1656
were never included in any of the first four Folios (1623, 1632, 1664 and 1685) and thus have not been included in this audition series. Similarly, though wonderful in and of themselves, none of the purely poetical works, e.g the *Sonnets, Venus and Adonis, The Rape of Lucrece* etc., have been included.

6 it is the only source for eighteen plays, the better source for six more, and co-source for a further two — i.e. valued for twenty-six of the thirty-six plays presented: for the remaining ten, though most modern editors prefer the quarto versions of the play in some cases (*Troylus & Cressida* and *Titus Andronicus*), such choice is by no means universal: the differences between the two sets of texts are not always substantive either in plot or language used, but more often in what most scholars term the accidentals (the spellings, punctuation, and capitalisation). In some cases the differences are minimal (an almost identical sentence structure and positioning of major punctuation in both quarto and F1 *Merchant of Venice* for example); however, in certain plays (*Romeo & Juliet* and *Othello*), differentiations in single word usage are quite marked, occasioning serious choice by editors and readers alike. What F1 rarely contains are the oaths and blasphemies so common to plays written prior to the 1606 Acte to Restraine the Abuses of Players — in effect the Acte caused every such reference in any subsequent printed work to be removed. Thus every quarto, which were all printed prior to 1606, contained offensive matter, all of which were supposedly removed before the printing of F1 — not always successfully, as occasional references in F1's Hamlet show.

INTRODUCTION

So, congratulations, you've got an audition, and for a Shakespeare play no less.

You've done all your homework, including, hopefully, reading the whole play to see the full range and development of the character.

You've got an idea of the character, the situation in which you/it finds itself (the given circumstances); what your/its needs are (objectives/intentions); and what you intend to do about them (action/tactics).

You've looked up all the unusual words in a good dictionary or glossary; you've turned to a well edited modern edition to find out what some of the more obscure references mean.

And those of you who understand metre and rhythm have worked on the poetic values of the speech, and you are word perfect . . .

. . . and yet it's still not working properly and/or you feel there's more to be gleaned from the text, but you're not sure what that something is or how to go about getting at it; in other words, all is not quite right, yet.

THE KEY QUESTION

What text have you been working with — a good modern text or an 'original' text, that is, a copy of one of the first printings of the play?

If it's a modern text, no matter how well edited (and there are some splendid single copy editions available, see the Bibliography for further details), and despite all the learned information offered, it's not surprising you feel somewhat at a loss, for there is a huge difference between the original printings (the First Folio, and the individual quartos, see Appendix 1 for further details) and any text prepared after 1700 right up to the most modern of editions. All the post-1700 texts have been tidied-up for the modern reader to ingest silently, revamped according to the rules of correct grammar, syntax, and poetry. However, the 'originals' were prepared for actors speaking aloud, playing characters often in a great deal of emotional and/or intellectual stress, and were set down on paper according to the very flexible rules of rhetoric with a seemingly very cavalier attitude towards the rules of grammar, syntax, spelling, capitalisation, and even poetry. [7]

Unfortunately, because of the grammatical and syntactical standardisation in place by the early 1700's, many of the quirks and oddities of the originals have been dismissed as 'accidental' — usually as compositor error either in deciphering the original manuscript, falling prey to their own particular idosyncracies, or not having calculated correctly the amount of space needed to set the text. Modern texts dismiss the possibility that these very quirks and oddities may be by Shakespeare, hearing his characters in as much difficulty as poor Peter Quince is in *A Midsummer Night's Dream* (when he, as the Prologue, terrified and struck down by stage fright, makes a huge grammatical hash in introducing his play 'Pyramus and Thisbe' before the aristocracy, whose acceptance or otherwise, can make or break him)

If we offend, it is with our good will.
That you should think, we come not to offend,
But with good will.
    To show our simple skill,
That is the true beginning of our end .
Consider then, we come but in despite.
We do not come, as minding to content you ,
Our true intent is.
          All for your delight
We are not here.
          That you should here repent you,
The Actors are at hand; and by their show,
You shall know all, that you are like to know.

(*A Midsummer Night's Dream*, speech #39)

In many other cases in the complete works what was originally printed is equally 'peculiar,' but, unlike Peter Quince, these peculiarities are usually regularised by most modern texts.

However, this series of volumes is based on the belief — as the following will show — that most of these 'peculiarities' resulted from Shakespeare

---

[7] See Freeman, Neil, *Shakespeare's First Texts*, distributed by Applause Books, New York & London: 2nd. edition. 1999.

setting down for his actors the stresses, trials, and tribulations the characters are experiencing as they think and speak, and thus are theatrical gold-dust for the actor, director, scholar, teacher, and general reader alike.

THE FIRST ESSENTIAL DIFFERENCE BETWEEN THE TWO TEXTS

THINKING

A **modern** text can show

- the story line

- your character's conflict with the world at large

- your character's conflict with certain individuals within that world

- the conflict within the character

but because of the very way an **'original'** text was set, it can show you all this plus one key extra, the very thing that makes big speeches what they are

WHY?

Any good playwright writes about characters in stressful situations who are often in a state of conflict not only with the world around them and the people in that world, but also within themselves. And you probably know from personal experience that when these conflicts occur people do not necessarily utter the most perfect of grammatical/poetic/syntactic statements, phrases, or sentences. Joy and delight, pain and sorrow often come sweeping through in the way things are said, in the incoherence of the phrases, the running together of normally disassociated ideas, and even in the sounds of the words themselves.

The tremendous advantage of the period in which Shakespeare was setting his plays down on paper and how they first appeared in print was that when characters were rational and in control of self and situation, their phrasing and sentences (and poetic structure) would appear to be quite normal even to a modern eye — but when things were going wrong, so sentences and phrasing (and poetic structure) would become highly erratic. But the Quince-type eccentricities are rarely allowed to stand. Sadly, in tidying, most modern texts usually make the text far too clean, thus setting rationality when none originally existed, as with

Shylock: in the famous 'hath not a Jew eyes' speech, where the original onrush of four (quarto) or five (First Folio) sentences, suggesting a tremendous release and lack of control, has been turned into at least fifteen (sometimes sixteen, even seventeen) sentences of tidy grammatical correctness by most modern texts. Thus the ravings and anger of the original Shylock have been turned into the calm debate of a noble rational creature, a tremendous difference and one which has created a totally different arc/journey/character than, presumably, originally intended (Comedy Auditions, *The Merchant of Venice*, speech #21).

King Henry: in a speech set only in the First Folio, where alone after spending the night with his soldiers, he wonders aloud about the burdens laid upon any monarch, the highly irregular opening line structure is a wonderful testament to the struggle within him — a struggle eradicated by most modern texts that restructure the passage to create poetically correct (ten syllable) verse lines throughout. (History Auditions, *Henry V*, speech #14).

Mercutio: in the famous Queen Mab speech, despite both the good quarto (Q2) and the First Folio setting the speech as a mixture of prose and verse — with some meanderings in the order of what he is talking about, suggesting a character not necessarily in full control of himself (already drunk before the Capulet party perhaps) — most modern texts reset the speech as pretty verse throughout AND restructure the order of some of the lines to reconstruct a Mercutio in their own image, logical and gracefully verbal. (Tragedy Auditions, *Romeo & Juliet*, speech #14).

THE SECOND ESSENTIAL DIFFERENCE BETWEEN THE TWO TEXTS

SPEAKING, ARGUING, DEBATING

Having discovered what and how you/your character is thinking is only the first stage of the work — you/it then have to speak aloud, in a society that absolutely loved to speak — and not only speak ideas (content) but to speak entertainingly so as to keep listeners enthralled (and this was especially so when you have little content to offer and have to mask it somehow — think of today's television adverts and political spin doctors as a parallel and you get the picture). Indeed one of the Elizabethan 'how to win an argument' books was very precise about this — George Puttenham, *The Art of English Poesie* (1589).

A: ELIZABETHAN SCHOOLING

All educated classes could debate/argue at the drop of a hat, for both boys (in 'petty-schools') and girls (by books and tutors) were trained in what was known overall as the art of rhetoric, which itself was split into three parts

- first, how to distinguish the real from false appearances/outward show (think of the three caskets in *The Merchant of Venice* where the language on the gold and silver caskets enticingly, and deceptively, seems to offer hopes of great personal rewards that are dashed when the language is carefully explored, whereas once the apparent threat on the lead casket is carefully analysed the reward therein is the greatest that could be hoped for)

- second, how to frame your argument on one of 'three great grounds'; honour/morality; justice/legality; and, when all else fails, expedience/practicality

- third, how to order and phrase your argument so winsomely that your audience will vote for you no matter how good the opposition — and there were well over two hundred rules and variations by which winning

could be achieved, all of which had to be assimilated before a child's education was considered over and done with.

In many ways this gave rise to what could be called the **ice-skating Shakespeare**, where you, as a speaker, awarded yourself points both for style as well as content

- with good content and good style you might give yourself a 100% score in each category, a perfect '6'

- with good content but boringly delivered you might give yourself 5.9 for content but only 1.5 for style

- while with poor content but excellently delivered, your score might be 1.2 for content but a triumphant 6 for style! — a fine example of audience-applauding-flim-flam-artistry at its very best!!

B: THINKING ON YOUR FEET : I.E. THE QUICK, DEFT, RAPID MODIFICATION OF EACH TINY THOUGHT

The Elizabethan/therefore your character/therefore you were also trained to explore and modify your thoughts as you spoke — never would you see a sentence in its entirety and have it perfectly worked out in your mind before you spoke (unless it was a deliberately written, formal public declaration, as with the Officer of the Court in *The Winter's Tale*, reading the charges against Hermione). Thus after uttering your very first phrase, you might expand it, or modify it, deny it, change it, and so on throughout the whole sentence and speech.

Several modern acting dictums will serve to explain how this works today, in any form of script

- from the superb French director, actor and mime Jean Louis Barrault — "acting is staying in the ever-changing present"

- from the noted Shakespeare director, and for many years the highly regarded head of the prestigious Juilliard School (U.S.A.), Michael Langham — "characters have to speak aloud to discover exactly what it is they know and feel"

- from Rudi Shelley, for many years the mainstay of the acting programme at the famous Bristol Old Vic Theatre School (U.K.)— who asked actors to ask once they've done or said something, "What happens next?"

• two wonderful acting truisms — "acting is reacting," and ask "**why** do you say it, **what** you say, **when** you say it, **in** the way you say it"

And from the poet Samuel Coleridge Taylor there is a wonderful description of how Shakespeare puts thoughts together like "a serpent twisting and untwisting in its own strength," that is, with one thought springing out of the one previous. Treat each new phrase as a fresh unravelling of the serpent's coil. What is discovered (and therefore said) is only revealed as the old coil/phrase disappears revealing a new coil in its place. The new coil is the new thought. The old coil moves/disappears because the previous phrase is finished with as soon as it is spoken.

C: MODERN APPLICATION

It is very rarely we speak dispassionately in our 'real' lives. After all thoughts give rise to feelings, feelings give rise to thoughts, and we usually speak both together — unless

1/ we're trying very hard for some reason to control ourselves and not give ourselves away. For example

• we want to ensure people listen to our arguments and are not distracted by any unnecessary emotion, so that they have to deal with the points we are making and cannot slough us off with the awful comment 'why don't we talk about this when you're feeling a little calmer/when you're not so worked up/when you're not so hysterical!'

• we simply have to control ourselves otherwise we'll lose face, or the way and/or the what of what we're talking about

2/ the volcano of emotions within us is so strong that we cannot control ourselves, and feelings swamp thoughts, and so, for example,

• we bellow with laughter
• we whoop with joy
• we scream with pain or fear
• we cannot contain our fury

3/ and sometimes, whether deliberately or unconsciously, we colour words according to our feelings. Think of Woody Allen in Annie Hall protesting his 'love,' 'lerve,' 'looove,' etc. for the character played by Diane Keaton, or the catch phrase or punch line of any TV personality or cartoon: while the spelling is horrific, the humanity behind the words so revealed is instantly understandable.

D: HOW THE ORIGINAL TEXTS NATURALLY ENHANCE/UNDERSCORE THIS CONTROL OR RELEASE

The amazing thing about the way all Elizabethan/early Jacobean texts were first set down (the term used to describe the printed words on the page being 'orthography'), is that it was flexible, it allowed for such variations to be automatically set down without fear of grammatical repercussion.

So if Shakespeare heard Juliet's nurse working hard to try to convince Juliet to set her sights on the Prince's nephew whom Juliet is being forced to (bigamously) marry, instead of setting the everyday normal

O he's a lovely gentleman

which the modern texts HAVE to set, the first printings were permitted to set

O hee''s a Lovely Gentleman

suggesting that something might be going on inside the Nurse that causes her to release such excessive extra energy.

Now the First Folio (and the second quarto too, for both well-regarded original texts set the text in exactly the same way) don't tell you, the actor, what is going on or how to play/say the moment, but the long-spelled 'hee's' and capitalised 'Lovely Gentleman' certainly guide you to where you might want to explore.

E: BE CAREFUL

This needs to be stressed very carefully: the orthography doesn't dictate to you/force you to accept exactly what it means (it could be fear of being fired by Juliet's parents if she fails to persuade Juliet to marry Paris; it could be fear of Juliet herself; it could be extra wheedling because she knows Juliet loathes Paris; it could be embarrassment at having to persuade Juliet to this second marriage when she was a go-between for the first; it could even be an attempt to comfort Juliet in an attempt to get her to accept the inevitable). The orthography simply suggests you might want to explore this moment further or more deeply.

In other words, simply because of the flexibility with which the Elizabethans/Shakespeare could set down on paper what they heard in their minds or wanted their listeners to hear, in addition to all the modern acting necessities of character — situation, objective, intention, action, and tactics — the original Shakespeare texts offer pointers to where feelings (either emotional or intellectual, or when combined together as passion, both) are also evident.

So everyone when speaking, even messengers who know what they are going to say, shows signs of reacting to what they say as they say it, and reveals feelings about it, as with the Messenger obviously furious with the English nobles whose squabbling has left their generals facing almost certain defeat in France (History Auditions, *Henry Six Part I*, speech #1), and the most objective attempts at neutrality usually fail, as with Exeter reporting the deaths of two of his closest friends (History Auditions, *Henry V*, speech #17).

PRINCIPLES APPLICABLE TO ALL THE PLAYS

EXPLORING WHETHER YOU ARE IN CONTROL OR NOT

PRINCIPLES, PART ONE: A SILLY GUIDE TO THE DIFFERENT SORTS OF THINKING WITHIN A FIRST FOLIO/QUARTO SHAKESPEARE SPEECH

(just the ideas will be discussed here, examples will be shown in the section **Practical Exploration**, page 18)

A: Now I'M IN CONTROL (something the modern texts always maintain)

This is easily seen, because though you are looking at an 'original' text

• the sentences appear grammatical (though not originally set with such grammatical niceties in mind)

• the phrasing is logical

• the line structure complies with the ten syllable pattern expected of 'regular' Shakespearean verse

TWO FORMS OF CONTROL MOST MODERN TEXTS USUALLY MAINTAIN

• the **expected I-am-in-control** character: the situation is normal, and you/your character appear to be handling it quite easily

• the **unexpected I-am-in-control** character: where, despite the fact the situation is anything but normal, you/your character still appear to be handling it quite easily – this is a fascinating one, because it suggests you have/your character has a wonderful sense of purpose or self-control, and should be truly applauded for remaining calm despite every provocation to the contrary

B: AND NOW I'VE LOST CONTROL – what the modern texts almost never maintain

You must be beware when modern texts alter the original texts' layout to be grammatically or poetically tidy (thus creating rationality which wasn't originally intended), not only because it ain't necessarily so but also because, just as maintaining control in a very difficult situation is of tremendous theatrical interest to your audience (and hopefully you), what is equally, perhaps even more, interesting is when the character does lose control.

In the 'original' texts this loss of control can be seen in four different ways

1/ THE SENTENCES ARE NOT GRAMMATICAL, BUT ARE

onrushed, i.e. ideas modern texts set as separate grammatical sentences F1 joins together in one longer sentence, connected by a grammatically incorrect comma, colon, semicolon, or no punctuation at all, as when Iago jams together in one sentence his hatred of Othello immediately onto the preceding seemingly casual discussion of cheating Rodorigo – a syntactically appalling conjunction most modern texts separate into two different grammatically correct sentences – creating rationality where the original text set momentary lack of control (Tragedy Auditions, *Othello*, speech #9)

or set as **very short sentences**, as if an idea is complete in and of itself without further elaboration, as with the opening five sentences of Constance's reaction to the appalling news that her son's legitimate claim to the English throne has been abandoned as a matter of political convenience (History Auditions, *King John*, speech #20); or Coriolanus' one word sentence of greeting ('Thanks.') to his fellow aristocrat busy with putting down a potential lower-class riot; or Edmund's exploration of his 'bastardy' as opposed to his brother Edgar being 'legitimate' (Tragedy Auditions, *King Lear*, speech #9)

2/ THERE IS SUDDENLY A HUGE AMOUNT OF EXTRA MAJOR PUNCTUATION (SEMICOLONS [;] OR COLONS [:])
suggesting that the mind is putting ideas together very explosively – and note this doesn't dictate how the ideas are to be spoken, for they could be uttered

with great control, as with Don Pedro who in order to punish Benedicke for challenging their mutual friend Claudio to a duel to the death, strips Benedicke of any illusions as to what Beatrice actually thinks of him (Comedy Auditions, *Much Ado About Nothing*, speech #16)

with much release, as when Falstaffe reveals plans to woo the two married women Mrs. Page and Mrs. Ford in order to gain access to their husband's wealth, (Comedy Auditions, *Merry Wives of Windsor*, speech #1)

3/ THERE ARE SUDDENLY A LOT OF EXTRA COMMAS (NOT SET BY MOST MODERN TEXTS)

as if the character needs either to split up thoughts into even **more tiny details**, as with Cymbeline when declaring opposition to Rome, even if it means war (Tragedy Auditions, *Cymbeline*, speech #25)

or needs the extra breaths **to control itself** before continuing, as with Rosalind when attempting to persuade Orlando of the foolishness of love (Comedy Auditions, *As You Like It*, speech #16)

4/ THE LENGTH OF THE VERSE LINE IS EITHER

longer than ten syllables, suggesting that the character's thoughts are running away with it as with Romeo, first seeing Juliet on the balcony, with both quarto/First Folio setting an exuberant 16 syllables

    It is my lady: O it is my love; O that she knew she were.

    (Tragedy Auditions, *Romeo & Juliet*, speech #21)

which most modern texts reset more politely as a regular ten syllable line plus a short six syllable one

    It is my lady: O it is my love;
    O that she knew she were.

shorter than ten syllables, suggesting that the character needs time to think or react, as with Lenox taking so many pauses in telling Macbeth of the peculiarities of the night following the murder of Duncan (Tragedy Auditions, *Macbeth*, speech #15).

THUS THERE ARE TWO FORMS OF LOSS OF CONTROL MOST MODERN TEXTS HARDLY EVER MAINTAIN

- once the situation is understood and seen as stressful, the **expected oh-my-gosh-I'm losing-it**-Shakespeare

- when the situation is understood and seen as fairly routine, the **unexpected oh-my-gosh-I'm losing-it-Shakespeare**

PRINCIPLES PART TWO: A SILLY GUIDE TO THE DIFFERENT SORTS OF SPEAKING WITHIN A FIRST FOLIO/QUARTO SHAKESPEARE SPEECH

(just the ideas will be discussed here, examples will be shown in the section **Practical Exploration**, page 18)

A: THE ICE-COLD SHAKESPEARE

this is when you and the character seem to be completely at ease with no excesses in capitalisation or spelling

the **expected** ice-cold Shakespeare is when you/your character are under no stress and can easily handle the given situation; everything is well under control — here the lack of excess reflects the ease of the moment e.g. most of the Sonnets

the **unexpected** ice-cold Shakespeare is when you/your character are under a great deal of stress, and the situation is proving very difficult to handle: unless you are very careful everything will spin out of control, and yet there are no excesses in spelling or capitalisation. This case suggests you are struggling to maintain an enforced calm in order to keep a lid on yourself/others or things in general, and succeeding, e.g., the just married Blanche in *King John* who speaks very carefully though torn apart by the impending battle between France and England (her husband is French and the uncle she owes fealty to is English).

B: THE EINSTEIN SHAKESPEARE

this is when you/your character's mind has to work very hard to come to terms with/fully understand the situation, or to explore the idea to its fullest, or to persuade yourself or others to a particular point of view — and in the text there are lots of capital letters, pointing to the key conceptual words you/your character needs defined, or understood, or acknowledged or explored.

the **expected** Einstein Shakespeare is when it is obvious your character has to work so hard because of the given circumstances, discovery, needs, or challenges facing it — e.g. much of Hermione's self-defence against her husband's unwarranted charges of treason in *The Winter's Tale*.

the **unexpected** Einstein Shakespeare is when despite the fact that the situation/circumstances/needs seem quite normal or even casual, nevertheless you/your character's mind is shown to be working very hard: (for those who enjoy their Monty Python, this could well be a case of 'my brain hurts, Brian') e.g. when *Romeo and Juliet's* Mercutio analyses Tybalt's qualities, both silly and dangerous, for a skeptical Benvolio.

C: THE RUSSIAN SHAKESPEARE

this is when the text includes lots of long spellings, allowing the stress to come into the words, thus revealing the emotions (good or bad) underneath: (why call it Russian? Just a tip of the hat to the wonderful releases of temperament associated with that great nation, i.e. when you're happy, you're VERY HAPPY! and when you're sad, you're INCREDIBLY SAD!)

- the **expected** Russian Shakespeare is when you/your character are under obvious stress, the text shows it, and the listeners on- and off-stage expect such excesses, e.g. when *Midsummer Night's Dream* Lysander plights his troth after being transformed by Oberon/Puck's charm into 'Helen's knight.'

- the **unexpected** Russian Shakespeare is when you/your character are under no apparent stress, nevertheless the text displays lots of long spellings revealing a surprising release of very strong emotions — e.g. the King's fulsome praise of Helena in an attempt to persuade Bertram to agree voluntarily to marry her in *All's Well That Ends Well*.

D: THE VOLCANIC SHAKESPEARE

this is when the text is simply swamped with both long spellings and capital letters and you do not/cannot control yourself — this could be because of the delights of joy, laughter, love or the pain of fear, hate (and love)

the **expected** volcanic Shakespeare is when the situation is so overwhelming (whether for good or bad, and whether because of the circumstances surrounding you/your character, or because of your/the character's inner needs/desires) the text is swamped with releases, and such releases are understandable — e.g. Octavius Caesar's ravings about Mark Anthony's dallying with Cleopatra in *Anthony and Cleopatra*.

the **unexpected** volcanic Shakespeare is when, despite the fact that the situation seems quite normal, or even casual, the text is nevertheless surprisingly swamped: here the excessive releases may not be what people expect, as with the 2nd Lord in *Cymbeline* listing the stupidities of the dysfunctional royal family, the effect of the unexpected can range from the appalling to the comic (indeed the wonderful book *The Craft Of Comedy*, by Athene Syler and Stephen Haggard, suggests much of the truly comic is based on the unexpectedly volcanic — viz. contrast, distortion, and surprise).

PRINCIPLES PART THREE: ELIZABETHAN/EARLY JACOBEAN CONSIDERATIONS MIGHT BE USEFUL WHEN EXPLORING THE ORIGINAL TEXTS

As discussed above in Elizabethan Schooling (page 6), the **plays are just as much about debate and discovery as poetry and emotion**. Thus no matter how purple the passage or how dense the text, there is always a reason for the complexity or simplicity in the characters' language and imagery. Thus it's important to **distinguish between the two strands that composed the English of the day, Anglo-Saxon simplicity** (single syllable words) and **European complexity** (multi-syllable words). Thus

Though you/your character can speak quite complex language, when you/your character speaks a line, or more, composed of monosyllables, as with Juliet's questioning of Romeo

> Doest thou Love [ ] ?
>
> I know thou wilt say I,
>
> And I will take thy word, yet if thou swear'st,
>
> Thou maiest prove false

(Romeo & Juliet, speech #23)

your questioning/exploration/discovery is so immediate that you have no time for indulging yourself in words — you are being direct and honest.

However, when the opposite occurs, when though you/your character can speak quite simply but indulges in some wonderful many-syllable words, it would suggest that no matter what the situation, you/your character have time to enjoy not only what you say but the way you say it, as with Falstaffe's talking to the audience about the horrors of being thrown into the river Thames, with a wonderful final phrase

> The rogues slighted me into the river
>
> with as little remorse, as they would have drown'de a
>
> blinde bitches Puppies, fifteene i'th litter : and you may
>
> know by my size, that I have a kinde of alacrity in sinking;

(Merry Wives of Windsor, speech #10)

After all 'I have a kinde of alacrity in sinking' could have been set as the more urgent and fearful monosyllabic 'a man of my girth sinks like a stone,' but the superb sound and sweep of Shakespeare's original phrasing has a much better ring to it, and smacks of the entertainer enjoying himself with his friends — here, the audience — at his own expense.

Of necessity, **your character has to be incredibly selfish** since scholars tell us

- there were only three days of rehearsal for any new play
- there was only one day of rehearsal for a remount
- the original actor was never given a full copy of the play, just their

'sides' (i.e. their character's speeches themselves and the cue line from whatever character preceded them and thus triggered/cued each speech)

Thus **the inner needs of your character are just as important as any other character on stage**, since that's all the original actor would have known. This means that

- in any two handed scene there are four different characters on-stage, the 'private you' and the 'public you,' the 'private other' and the 'public other,' thus

- when the 'public you' speaks, the next thought can reflect some sort of response from the 'private you' within

- this is especially marked whenever there is a solo speech, soliloquy, or aside.

- thus, your character must play its own needs and scene to the utmost and never play the other character's scene even if your character is subordinate to them status-wise: the scene is just as much, if not more so, about the messenger delivering the news as it is about how the leading characters receive it.

Overall, Shakespeare texts demand that an actor is capable of creating

- in the best sense of the word, a very selfish character capable of pushing its own needs to the utmost

- a character that can think quickly on its feet, constantly reassess what is happening to it, and respond/change direction, tactics, and argument accordingly

- a character that adores language;   after all, Shakespeare himself is credited with inventing a myriad of new words and a wondrous series of phrases and maxims that are still in common use today.

EXPLORING THE COMEDIES

DECIDING WHETHER YOU ARE IN CONTROL OR NOT

PRACTICAL EXPLORATIONS PART ONE: COMPARING THE TWO TEXTS

CLARITY OF THOUGHT: THE NATURE OF DEBATE

- which will become much clearer as you explore each separate audition speech

N.B. any words surrounded by square brackets [ ] point to a text difference between the original & modern texts

1/ FIRST, LOOK AT THE SENTENCES (the large-scale organisation of the speech)

AS A RULE OF THUMB

In general, the appearance of a period or full stop indicates that one idea has been finished with and you/the character is moving on to something new. And because every Elizabethan was trained to explore an idea to it's fullest, sentences as first set in the original texts are often much longer than their modern counterparts, suggesting a much more focused and concentrated exploration, expression, and release.

If they do, that is if the original has not been restructured by the modern texts, then it would seem that the Elizabethan rhetoric is matched by modern grammar and, as far as the organisation of thinking goes, your character seems to be **rational** and in **self-control**.

A: WHEN THERE ARE **MORE** MODERN TEXT SENTENCES THAN ORIGINALLY SET

If you are faced with sentence(s) in the original text being split up into smaller units by most modern texts, then, as originally set, you/your character can be said to be in a state of **onrush** — that is, your ideas are being piled one on top of another in a single, much longer release, than grammar would normally dictate, which leads to either

a fairly rational onrush: if, at the point where the new modern sentence has been created the original punctuation was a colon, semicolon, question, or exclamation mark, then your onrush can be seen as essentially rational, since the second idea, quite logical even if regarded as ungrammatical or non-syntactical by most modern texts, moves on with some control from the first — as with the just beaten-by-mistake Dromio's pained reporting to his mistress of her supposed husband's erratic behaviour towards him

I meane not Cuckold mad,
But sure he is starke mad:
When I desir'd him to come home to dinner,
He ask'd me for a [hundred] markes in gold: *
'Tis dinner time, quoth I: my gold, quoth he: *
Your meat doth burne, quoth I: my gold quoth he: *
Will you come, quoth I: my gold, quoth he;
Where is the thousand markes I gave thee villaine?
The Pigge quoth I, is burn'd: my gold, quoth he: *
My mistresse, sir, quoth I: hang up thy Mistresse:
I know not thy mistresse, out on thy mistresse.

(*The Comedy of Errors*, speech #6)

Most modern texts reset F1's two sentences as six, as the asterisks (*) show. Try reading the text as six separate sentences, and then as two, and you can feel the difference, not just intellectually understand it, for F1 suggests a much more ongoing build via a series of more intense and sustained onrushed releases.

a somewhat irrational onrush: if, at the point where the new modern sentence has been created the original punctuation was either a comma, or there was no punctuation at all, or the onrush is totally unexpected, then your onrushed connection is very fast, as the second grammatical idea springs almost unchecked from the first, and the effect or result is probably unexpected by your listener, perhaps even by you yourself — as when Valentine, the one-time-critic of romance, confesses he has fallen in love

is made much more personable with the rush through the first line (marked by the *), as opposed to most modern texts' much more grammatically correct yet far less impetuous

> I Protheus, but that life is alter'd now,
> I have done pennance for contemning Love,
>
>   *
>
> Ay, Protheus, but that life is alter'd now .
> I have done penance for contemning Love,

                                        (*Two Gentlemen of Verona*, speech #2)

B: WHEN THERE ARE LESS MODERN TEXT SENTENCES THAN ORIGINALLY SET

If several separate sentences in the original text are pushed together into larger units by most modern texts, then you/your character as originally set can be said to be in a state of **heightened analysis/debate**, in that your precise modification of ideas needs much more careful delineation than grammar will permit, or that, in some cases, you are working very hard and probably enjoying it. Thus there is

logical analysis/debate: provided that the shorter sentences of the original have some form of grammatical structure then you/your character can be seen to be proceeding rationally, if somewhat hyper-analytically or very carefully — as when sometimes a character is working just far too hard, such as Boyet's joyfully telling the Princess of France that the King of Navarre is obviously in love with her

> 1/   If my observation (which very seldome lies
>   By the hearts still rhetoricke, disclosed with eyes)
>   Deceive me not now, Navar is infected {,}
>   With that which we Lovers intitle affected.
>
> 2/   Why all his behaviours [doe] make their retire,
>   To the court of his eye, peeping thorough desire.

> 3/   His hart like an Agot with your print impressed,
>   Proud with his forme, in his eie pride expressed.
>
> 4/   His tongue all impatient to speake and not see,
>   Did stumble with haste in his eie-sight to be,
>   All sences to that sence did make their repaire,
>   To feele onely looking on fairest of faire :
>   Me thought all his sences were lockt in his eye,
>   As Jewels in Christall for some Prince to buy.
>
> 5/   Who tendring their own worth from [whence] they were glast,
>   Did point [out] to buy them along as you past.
>
> 6/   His faces owne margent did coate such amazes,
>   That all eyes saw his eies inchanted with gazes.
>
> 7/   Ile give you Aquitaine, and all that is his,
>   And you give him for my sake, but one loving Kisse.

                                            (*Love's Labour's Lost*, speech #2)

Each of the F sentences numbered #2-6 above adds an extra energy, delight, or focus to what he has observed, and now obviously relishes in the telling, building detail by detail with each sentence adding an increased energy to what was said before. Sadly, most modern texts remove the key to the build by setting F #2-6 as one long sentence.

illogical analysis/debate: when the shorter sentence of the original has no grammatical structure, or simply appears in the middle of an idea (and thus in the middle of a modern sentence), you/your character can be seen to be momentarily thrown by what he or she is discovering (the wonderful Northern English term for this is 'gob-smacked,' i.e. you/your character has been metaphorically hit in the mouth) — as with the middle of Theseus' attempts to persuade Hermia to recant her denial of her father's choice of husband

> Demetrius is a worthy Gentleman,
> . . . and in himselfe {Lysander} is.
>
> But in this kinde, wanting your fathers voyce.
>
> The other must be held the worthier.

Though totally ungrammatical, the last two very peculiar sentences underscore just how important Theseus regards the advice he is giving, since it is the only legal means by which Hermia can save herself from either life as a nun, or, as her father has demanded, death. Sadly, though not unexpectedly, most modern texts set the syntactically correct

> Demetrius is a worthy gentleman {,}
> ... and in himself {Lysander} is;
> But in this kind, wanting your fathers voice,
> The other must be held the worthier.

> *(Midsummer Night's Dream*, speech #2)

One of the finest plays to explore from the viewpoint of sentence variations (with most modern texts setting both more and less than originally set) is *Troylus and Cressida*. Also, it is well worth remembering that in most of the Comedies and many of the Tragedies the trend is for most modern texts to create far more sentences than were originally set, thus establishing character rationality and self-control when often the exact opposite was shown in both Folio and quarto texts.

2/ THEN, LOOK AT THE MAJOR PUNCTUATION (the connecting spine within each sentence and speech)

Logical Connections/Emotional Connections

AS A RULE OF THUMB
As pointed out earlier, the major punctuation of an original text is not so much grammatical as oratorical or rhetorical. However, modern texts' punctuation is grammar and syntax based, and often the two systems clash. As a result

- key moments of passion and debate as originally set in F1
- as well as ungrammatical emotional moments when the situation is almost too much for the character to bear

are often altered by modern texts, substituting grammar for potential moments of human excitement or strain.

Thus, since the Shakespeare texts are based so much on the art of debate and argument, the importance of the major punctuation of the original texts must not be underestimated – both the colon [:] and the semi-colon [;] mark a moment of importance for you and your character, either for yourself/itself as a moment of discovery or revelation, or as a key point in a discussion, argument, or debate that you/your character wishes to impress upon other characters onstage.

The far less frequent semi-colons (;) suggest, because of the power inherent in the point you/your character has discovered or argued, and no matter how logical that point may be, that the passion or emotional power of the moment causes you to become side-tracked, and you/your character momentarily either

- loses focus on the argument and fall back into itself or
- can only continue the argument with great difficulty

As such, the semi-colon should be regarded as an **emotional connection** — as with Julia's realisation of what she has done in tearing up Protheus' love-letter

> Oh hatefull hands, to teare such loving words; [1]
> Injurious Waspes, to feede on such sweet hony,
> And kill the Bees that yeelde it, with your stings; [2]
> Ile kisse each severall paper, for amends :

> *(Two Gentleman Of Verona*, speech #5, sentence #1 and throughout)

the first semicolon (#1) suggesting that she switches from the ripped up letter (the 'loving words') to attack her fingers (the 'Waspes'), the second semicolon (#2) leading her to a sudden irrational if totally understandable sensual and emotional response.

The more frequent colons (:) suggest that whatever the emotional power of the point discovered or argued, you/your character can continue with the argument. As such, the colon can be regarded as a **logical connection,** in that you/your character are not side-tracked. It doesn't mean suppression of emotion, just refusal to give in to it — as with Jaques definition to Rosalind of his 'melancholly' (what would be currently termed a 'bi-polar' condition)

If Musicke be the food of Love, play on,
Give me excesse of it : that surfetting,
The appetite may sicken, and so dye.

(*Twelfth Night*, speech #1)

Sometimes the connection is far more emotional, as when linked by the emotional semicolon [;] (see page 15) — as when the now alone, besotted Olivia recalls her conversation with the 'young man' Cesario (actually Viola in disguise), especially the essential point about 'his' status, in that since 'he' is a 'Gentleman' marriage is a possibility

Above my fortunes, yet my state is well ;
I am a Gentleman.

(*Twelfth Night*, speech #9)

B: CONSECUTIVE SURROUND PHRASES

As the number of surround phrases increases, so too the importance of what is being singled out for you/your character to say, whether light-hearted or serious (and here question-marks [?] can help create the surround phrases too) — as with Beatrice's total dismissal of her uncle's suggestion that she should marry

As for a husband that hath
no beard ? what should I doe with him ? dresse him in
my apparell, and make him my waiting gentlewoman ? he
that hath a beard, is more [than] a youth : and he that hath
no beard, is lesse [than] a man : and hee that is more [then] a
youth, is not for mee : and he that is lesse [than] a man, I am
not for him : therefore I will even take sixpence in earnest
of the [Berrord], and leade his Apes to the gates of hell.

(*Much Ado About Nothing*, speech #2)

C: OVERKILL: TOO MANY SANDWICHES — CLUSTERS OF TOO MUCH MAJOR PUNCTUATION

Of course, as with clusters of other devices (notably capital letters or of 'funny' spellings – see page 21 below), so occasionally there can simply be too much heavy punctuation crammed close together. As such, they can point to too much joy or too much pain — and it is obvious such an

---

I have neither the Schollers melancholy, which
is emulation: x nor the Musitians, which is fantasticall ;
nor the Courtiers, which is proud: x nor the Souldiers,
which is ambitious: x nor the Lawiers, which is politick: x
nor the Ladies, which is nice : x nor the Lovers, which
is all these :. . .

(*As You Like It*, speech #38)

Of the six F set colons marking his powerful and profoundly personal self-definition, most modern texts change five to the more syntactically correct semicolons (those altered marked as : x) which, had they been set as such in the original text, would suggest more emotion than control.

SURROUND PHRASES: THE LOGICAL AND THE EMOTIONAL SANDWICH (REPEATED MAJOR PUNCTUATION)

AS A RULE OF THUMB

The role of the major punctuation is important in the debate process, denoting that you/your character have reached some important idea within the overall scheme of things. Though such punctuation is usually lightly scattered throughout the text, occasionally a short passage of up to a line and a half [1] can be surrounded (i.e. started and finished) by such major punctuation. This suggests that the information so surrounded is of extra importance to you/your character, whether working out things alone in a soliloquy or discussing matters with others on-stage.

A: OCCASIONAL SURROUND PHRASES

Sometimes these all-important surround phrases are denoted by colons [:] and can thus be called logical — as with the very first words from both character and play, as Orsino fully abandons himself to his flights of romantic indulgence

---

[1] Admittedly an arbitrary length, but, for all practical purposes on the rehearsal floor, this does seem to work.

intensity of sustained release does not signify a mind at ease. Rather the repeated hammer-blow of such concentrated releases when taken to such excess could point to a possible brain-storm, even breakdown —

as with Falstaffe's dreams of becoming rich by wooing at one and the same time Mrs. Page and especially Mrs. Ford so as to get to their husbands' money, where there are at least twenty-five surround phrases in just twenty-four lines

and thou this to Mistris Ford : we will thrive (Lads) we will thrive .

(*Merry Wives of Windsor,* speech #1)

3/ FINALLY, LOOK AT THE COMMAS (the deft-dance & tiny details of the speech)

Extra clarity; Need for Self-control; Speed and/or Enthusiasm

AS A RULE OF THUMB

The first texts are not dealing with careful grammar. Rather, they show how quickly a character's mind deftly dances from one thought to the next, this quick light 'dance' being part of daily Elizabethan life.

The comma marks the smallest part of the dance, the tiniest thought. As such, each comma must be explored because it marks a moving on to the next moment of definition or redefinition you/your character is in the process of discovering.

However, when finally spoken, heaven forbid the comma be marked by an actual pause. All it needs is whatever small bending of the text may be occasioned by the new discovery or new thought the comma has created within you.

AS YOU SEE **MORE** COMMAS IN THE ORIGINAL WHICH HAVE SINCE BEEN REMOVED BY MOST MODERN TEXTS

Many modern texts omit commas because seem ungrammatical, but their value goes far beyond mere syntax into the very action of character and play. The importance of these extra original commas cannot be stressed enough, for they show where you/your character needs new 'breath-thoughts,' either

to make a meaning absolutely clear, as with Rosalind in her attempts to break Orlando's illusions of romantic love

My honest Lads, I will tell you what I am about .

{hears Pistoll's whsipered aside "Two yards, and more"}

No quips now Pistoll : (Indeede I am in the waste two yards about : but I am now about no waste : I am a- bout thrift) briefely : I doe meane to make love to Fords wife : I spie entertainment in her : shee discourses : shee carves : she gives the leere of invitation : I can construe the action of her familier stile, & the hardest voice of her behaviour (to be english'd rightly) is, I am Sir John Falstafs .

Now, the report goes, she has all the rule of her husbands Purse : [he] hath a [legend] of Angels.

I have writ me here a letter to her : & here ano- ther to Pages wife, who even now gave mee good eyes too ; examind my parts with most judicious illiads : sometimes the beame of her view, guilded my foote : sometimes my portly belly .

O she did so course o're my exteriors with such a greedy intention, that the appetite of her eye, did seeme to scorch me up like a burning-glasse : here's another letter to her : She beares the Purse too : She is a Region in Guiana : all gold, and bountie :   I will be Cheaters to them both, and they shall be Exchequers to mee :   they shall be my East and West Indies, and I will trade to them both :   Goe, beare thou this Letter to Mistris Page ;

Love is meerely a madnesse, and I tel you, de- serves as wel a darke house,x and a whip,x as madmen do : and the reason why they are not so punish'd and cured,x is that the Lunacie is so ordinarie,ₓ   that the whippers are in

love too : yet I professe curing it by counsel.

(As You Like It, speech #16)

The four extra commas (marked , ₓ) point to the incredibly detailed way she is explaining to the love-struck Orlando how things are in the real world, the extra thoughts implying not only hard work, but perhaps fun too.

or for you/the character to regain self-control or calm down, as with Hermoine when she begins her doomed self-defense against the preposterous charge of treason laid upon her by Leontes, at one and the same time her husband, her accuser, and her judge

Since what I am to say,ₓ must be but that

Which contradicts my Accusation, and

The testimonie on my part,ₓ no other

But what comes from my selfe, it shall scarce boot me

To say, Not guiltie :

(The Winter's Tale, speech #6)

The two extra opening breath-thoughts (marked , ₓ) perhaps suggest a physical and/or mental weakness — hardly surprising given that she has been hurried out of prison in her post-natal state and forced to defend herself publicly in a large trial, presumably in a virtually all-male and essentially hostile environment.

Sometimes both reasons, the need for extra details and the need for self-control, exist side by side, as with Anthonio making jokes at the point of his death, a pound of flesh nearest his heart to be legally cut away by the knife of the vengeful but apparently judicially correct Shylock

For heerein fortune shewes her selfe more kinde

Then is her custome.

It is still her use

To let the wretched man out-live his wealth,

To view with hollow eye,ₓ and wrinkled brow

An age of poverty.

From which lingring penance

Of such miserie,ₓ I doth she cut me off:

Commend me to your honourable Wife,

Tell her the processe of Anthonio's end:

Say how I lov'd you;   speake me faire in death:

And when the tale is told, bid her be judge,ₓ [2]

Whether Bassanio had not once a Love:

Repent [not] you that you shall loose your friend,

And he repents not that he payes your debt.

For if the Jew do cut but deepe enough,

Ile pay it instantly,ₓ [3] with all my heart.

(The Merchant of Venice, speech #3)

Of the four extra breath-thoughts (marked , ₓ) at least three attempt some form of, admittedly dark, wit — #1 leading to the word-play about 'cut'; #2 focusing on 'judge' (a reference to the proceedings about to unfold); and #3 a triple pun as to paying with 'all my heart' (literally, willingly, and out of his love for Bassanio).

B: YOU SEE FEWER COMMAS IN THE ORIGINAL, MORE COMMAS HAVE SINCE BEEN ADDED IN MOST MODERN TEXTS

Sometimes modern texts add commas where F has set no punctuation at all. This is usually done to clarify grammatical or syntactical relationships. The unfortunate side-effect of these extra commas is that they often slow down you/your character's speed of thought or argument from what was originally set — as with the unfortunate Charles the Wrestler explaining to the landowner Oliver how he will have to injure Oliver's youngest brother Orlando to save his own reputation

I came to acquaint you

with a matter : I am given + sir + secretly to understand, that

your yonger brother + Orlando + hath a disposition to come

in disguis'd against mee to try a fall : to morrow + sir + I

wrastle for my credit, and hee that escapes me without

some broken limbe, + shall acquit him well :

(As You Like It, speech #2)

The seven extra commas added by most modern texts (marked [+]) more than somewhat slow Charles' fast-paced opening to Oliver, his vastly social superior — a great shame given that this is his only major speech in the play and the fast pace opening could well indicate nervousness, awkwardness, and/or embarrassment.

PRACTICAL EXPLORATIONS PART TWO: EXPLORING AN ORIGINAL TEXT BY ITSELF

RELEASING YOUR THOUGHTS: i.e. SPEAKING WELL & MOMENTS OF BLURT

- which will become much clearer as you explore each separate audition speech

In real-life, as we speak, argue, and discover and as each new idea, nuance, or rephrasing of an already expressed idea hits us, our vocal pattern changes. Sometimes we are exuberant throughout a phrase or sentence or two; sometimes we are very restrained over the same time-frame. Sometimes a word tickles our fancy and we play with it vocally, either quite consciously, or without really thinking, stretching and exaggerating or even compressing how we make it sound. Sometimes we are very precise in our choice of words so that the other person understands exactly the point we are trying to make. Sometimes we are so emotionally moved (unconsciously rather than directly thinking about it) that we again stretch and exaggerate or compress how we make it sound, not deliberately, but as a gut reaction. And sometimes we are so moved that we both choose a word for precision and at the same time our subconscious colours our feelings as we release it.

To elaborate on what was briefly mentioned earlier, because of the enormous flexibility of Elizabethan and early Jacobean orthography, all of these things could be set down on paper without the tyranny of grammar and spelling accuracies and be recognised for what they could signify. This is not to say that Shakespeare always did this deliberately — it's much more

a matter of his artistic consciousness hearing a character intellectually moved, emotionally moved, passionately moved, in control or out of control, and, as he was writing what he heard, the orthography of the period (not constrained by rigid rules of spelling, capitalisation, punctuation, or grammar) allowed him to set down unconscious clues as to what was going on without having to think about it. And these unconscious orthographic clues would be automatically understood and responded to equally unconsciously (and perhaps sometimes deliberately) by his actors. [2]

By looking at this unconscious orthography (these, as it were, extra theatrical/human clues), what we might call **theatrical serendipity**, and working backwards (what deconstructionists might call 'decoding') we can gain some idea as to '**what**' state a person might be in when they are speaking — never '**why**', that is up to each actor/director/reader/scholar to decide, and not really '**how**' either, for, having interpreted whether your character is in control or not, your chosen reasons why that character is in control will colour how you play that control or lack thereof. In other words, the original texts offer your more wonderful stuff for your rehearsal exploration.

Thus, the following is not a manuscript which must be spoken a particular way. It is a map that offers you clues for your journey — leaving you to make the decision what to do with your discoveries once you have found them.

1/ ICE COLD SHAKESPEARE

DO THE WORDS LOOK NORMAL TO YOU? : i.e. DO YOU HAVE TOTAL CONTROL?

Here the words look exactly the same as if they had been set in a modern text — there are no capitals, no peculiar (to our eyes), long or short spellings. The words are being spoken without any embellishment or any extra release. In other words, you/your character is in a state of calm and is being quite quiet, though whether this calm is justified by the ease of the situation or is something you have had to force yourself into so that you

---

2 When I first started professionally in English weekly stock as an actor/director, experienced actors would term certain lines as moving, or standing, or sitting lines, and show me how the rhythm and sound of a particular line would lead them quite unconsciously to that action — and they were usually right.

don't lose control of yourself and/or the moment is up to each actor to decide.

The expected ice-cold Shakespeare is where calmness is deliberate or not particularly surprising — as with Olivia's unembellished naked love-plea to Viola, that is Viola disguised as the boy Cesario

> Cesario, by the Roses of the Spring,
> By maid-hood, honor, truth, and every thing,
> I love thee so, that maugre all thy pride,
> Nor wit, nor reason, can my passion hide :
> Do not extort thy reasons from this clause,
> For that I woo, thou therefore hast no cause :
> But rather reason thus, with reason fetter ;
> Love sought, is good : but given unsought, is better .
>
> (*Twelfth Night*, speech #11)

where everything after the first line looks just like a modern text. The words are unembellished for the next seven lines — an incredibly rare setting for any original Shakespeare text — suggesting that Olivia is taking extraordinary care in what she is saying (to ensure her heart's words are made very clear? in an attempt to preserve her dignity? so as not to frighten Cesario away?).

The unexpected ice-cold Shakespeare is where calm is present despite the disturbing circumstances — as with both Adrianna, about her gad-about, too-often away, perhaps philandering husband

> I know his eye doth homage other-where,
> Or else, what lets it but he would be here ?

and her sister Luciana, who has decided to scold the reprobate

> And may it be that you have quite forgot
> A husbands office ?
>
> (*The Comedy of Errors*, speeches #7 & #10, respectively)

Adrianna's quiet statement of what is wrong adds a moment of dignity (and audience sympathy perhaps?) amidst her litany of complaints, and Luciana's opening appeal (to the wrong Antipholus) shows great self-

control given the real husband's behaviour towards Luciana's sister Adrianna.

2/ EINSTEIN SHAKESPEARE

ARE YOU FINDING QUITE A FEW CAPITAL LETTERS?:   i.e. ARE YOU DEFINING YOUR TERMS AND/OR SPEAKING YOUR MIND?

Being the selfish character that you are — after all you only know of your needs and predicament (as explained in the Elizabethan acting considerations section, pages 11-12) — at times it is very important for you to define precisely for yourself, and/or the audience (in a soliloquy), or others in a group scene (i.e. at least one other character apart from you), how you understand and want to deal with a particular moment, idea, or situation. Hence the capital letters. So, when you find them in your speech, or in just certain parts of your speech, [3] it's a nice clue to ask 'why am I using that word here.' And this can even be asked when real names appear — after all you could have used an uncapitalised personal pronoun (you, he, she, they, them) instead.

The expected Einstein Shakespeare is where the situation demands careful argument and/or presentation — as when Hermione gets to the main points in her self-defense against her husband Leontes' unjust accusation of treason

> For behold me,
> A Fellow of the Royall Bed, which owe
> A Moitie of the Throne :   a great Kings Daughter,
> The Mother to a hopefull Prince, here standing
> To prate and talke for Life,$_x$ and Honor,$_x$ fore
> Who please to come, and heare.
>   For Life, I prize it
> As I weigh Griefe (which I would spare:$_x$) For Honor,
> 'Tis a derivative from me to mine,
> And onely that I stand for .
>
> (*The Winter's Tale*, speech #6)

---

[3] Since capital letters traditionally start verse lines, rarely are such capitals included in any of the discussions here or in the texts that follow.

The specificity of the capitalised words underscores both her worth and by what she chooses to be judged — the whole enhanced by the two extra tiny breath-thought details (marked ,ₓ) which are not set by most modern texts.

The unexpected Einstein Shakespeare is when an intellectual response is not the first thing the situation would seem to warrant, or a trait not normally associated with the character, or it suddenly kicks in out of nowhere — as with the normally impetuous Lysander's careful opening self-justification in response to Hermia's father Egeus having attacked him for enticing Hermia through witchcraft, where the whole speech shows just two long spelled words as opposed to eight capital letters (*Midsummer Night's Dream*, speech #6). Or, even more unexpected, as with the way Egeus asks for a terrible doom to be pronounced upon his daughter

And my gracious Duke,
Be it so she will not heere before your Grace,
Consent to marrie with Demetrius,
I beg the ancient privilege of Athens;
As she is mine, I may dispose of her;
Which shall be either to this Gentleman,
Or to her death, according to our Law,
Immediately provided in that case.

(*Midsummer Night's Dream*, speech #1)

Despite the enormity of his request, the fact that it is expressed with virtually no long spelled words (just two) but with six capitals suggests a surprising attempt at self-control by trying to stay factual/intellectual.

As a result, you will suddenly find moments during a speech when **the mind switches on or off**, i.e. there is a great deal of intellect which suddenly disappears or appears — as with Jacques in the famous 'Seven Ages of Man' speech, where after eighteen capital words in nineteen lines the speech suddenly finishes with many long spelled words but only two more capitals in the last eight lines

With spectacles on nose, and pouch on side,
His youthfull hose well sav'd, a world too wide,
For his shrunke shanke, and his bigge manly voice,
Turning againe toward childish trebble pipes,

And whistles in his sound.
          Last Scene of all,
That ends this strange eventfull historie,
Is second childishnesse, and meere oblivion,
Sans teeth, sans eyes, sans taste, sans every thing.

(*As You Like It*, the end of speech #37)

all of which suggests something other than intellect is affecting him as he voices the two less than attractive ages that end the human journey (something he himself is perhaps facing?).

Sometimes there is **swamping, i.e. clusters of/too many capital letters**, that is occasionally there are just far too many capital letters within a small part of the speech, almost as if you/your character's mind is working too hard or there are so many points to be made that the intellect is close to crashing. In processing so much information, there can be said to be a swamping of the mind and you/the character is about to drown in a sea of overwhelming ideas — as with Falstaffe's delight at the thought of finally engaging Mrs. Ford and Mrs. Page in an a long awaited illicit romantic encounter

The Windsor-bell hath stroke twelve :   the Minute drawes-on :   Now the hot-bloodied-Gods assist me :
Remember Jove, thou was't a Bull for thy Europa, Love
set on thy homes.
          O powerfull Love, that in some re-
spects makes a Beast a Man: in som other, a Man a beast.

You were also (Jupiter) a Swan, for the love of Leda: O
omnipotent Love, how nere the God drew to the complexion of a Goose :

(*The Merry Wives of Windsor*, speech #13)

and perhaps it's not too fanciful to think that twenty capital letters in just the first seven and a half lines of the speech suggest a mental brain-storm of hope, lust, and anticipation that all but overwhelms him.

3/ RUSSIAN SHAKESPEARE

ARE THE WORDS SPELLED 'FUNNY'⁴: i.e. ARE YOU RELEASING YOUR FEELINGS OR CHOKING THEN BACK?

Being the emotional beast you are (remember that the Elizabethan believed thought instantly created feelings or emotions, and feelings or emotions instantly created thought) and being excessively verbal, it's not surprising that your feelings sometimes spill over into words and phrases. This is where word formations can be explored, for sometimes you will find even the simplest of words set in a normal twenty-first century spelling ('she') and a moment later in longer formation ('shee'), as with Shakespeare's version of St. Joan, a character known as la Pucelle (see History Auditions, *Henry 6 Part 1*, speech #2). And sometimes you will even find the same word spelled in twenty-first century normality and then in a shortened version in the same sentence as with 'Country'/'Countrie', as when the Roman Volumnia tries to persuade her recently banished and now all-avenging son to spare Rome and Italy from the enemy forces he now leads

> For how can we?
>
> Alas! how can we, for our Country pray?
>
> Whereto we are bound, together with thy victory:
>
> Whereto we are bound: Alacke, or we must loose
>
> The Countrie our deere Nurse, or else thy person
>
> Our comfort in the Country.
>
> (*Coriolanus*, speech #23)

by the 'ke' and the end of the two words suggesting either an unconscious emotional release and/or a deliberate (conscious) witty delight for both you and your listener.

Shorter spellings suggests that for some emotional reason, your reaction to the word is such that you, unconsciously, cannot give it full voice, or, consciously, are deliberately choking the word back.

In many ways, the application of the modern dictum quoted earlier, '**why** do you say, **what** you say, **when** you say it, in the **WAY** you say it,' really applies here, for the shaping of the words themselves can add extra information to the rehearsal and performance process. Sometimes a single word (as the contentious 'Chaine' in *The Comedy of Errors*, initially bespoken by Antipholus of Ephesus for his wife, and then offered in a fit of pique to a local Courtesan) can point to a single moment of emotional impact. Sometimes the repeated placement of long-spelled words can suggest a flurry of energy at the end of a thought or idea (as with Sonnet #42).

But what is of even greater interest in the longer speeches (and thus in the audition speeches that follow) are those moments when suddenly a lot of extra spellings occur over a fairly concentrated passage.

The expected Russian Shakespeare is when the exigencies of the situation naturally lead to an emotional response — as when Lysander, recently transformed from his everyday self into a chivalric figure prepared 'To honour Helen, and be her Knight' overwhelmingly pleads his love suite to her, opening with

> Looke when I vow I weepe; and vowes so borne,
> In their nativity all truth appeares.
>
> (*Midsummer Nights Dream*, speech not shown in this book)

or as with Anthonio, whose disgust with Shylock's money lending practices bursts forth with

> Marke you this Bassanio,
> The divell can cite Scripture for his purpose,
> An evill soule producing holy witnesse,

AS A RULE OF THUMB

Essentially, **longer** spellings suggests that you/your character has been emotionally affected by that word enough to set up within you a flurry of emotion somewhat more powerful than usual — though how you speak it is up to you, and releasing it can be great fun — as with Oliver's suggestion to Charles the Wrestler that as far as Orlando (Oliver's younger and troublesome brother) goes, Oliver wouldn't mind if Charles were to '**breake** his **necke**,' the suggested extra (venomous? delighted?) alliteration offered

⁴ See Appendix 2, Part Two, for words that are so similar in their original and modern spellings that for the purpose of your explorations they can be regarded as one and the same.

Is like a villaine with a smiling cheeke,
A goodly apple rotten at the heart.

(The Merchant of Venice, speech #2)

with the seven extra spellings in the first four lines leaving no doubt as to the intensity of Anthonio's feelings.

The unexpected Russian Shakespeare is when an emotional response might be quite surprising, or unusually excessive given the circumstances or the relatively unemotional lead-up to this sudden release — as when the unmarried Antipholus of Syracuse expresses his shock at being very publicly and embarrassingly mistaken for Adriana's husband (in fact for his long lost twin Antipholus of Ephesus)

To mee shee speakes, shee moves mee for her theame;
What, was I married to her in my dreame?

Or sleepe I now, and thinke I heare all this?

What error drives our eies and eares amisse?

Untill I know this sure uncertaintie,
Ile entertaine the [free'd] fallacie.

(Comedy of Errors, speech #9)

with fourteen long spelled words in just six lines (five in the first line alone).

WITHHOLDING/CHOKING BACK

Of course, sometimes there are moments when you can hardly speak, and words seem to our eyes short spelled, suggesting **restraint** (whether deliberate or not). Perhaps it is **deliberate** when Rosalind attempts to control herself in her quarrel with her uncle, who is intent on banishing her on the grounds that she is daughter to (in his eyes) his troublesome older and more popular brother

So was I when your highnes took his Dukdome,
So was when your highnesse banisht him;

(As You Like It, speech not shown in this book)

---

the single underlined words being short-spelled (though, tellingly, her control begins to slip with the longer spelling of 'highnesse', in the second line).

Perhaps it happens **unconsciously** when the love-critical and anti-Beatrice Benedick unexpectedly refers to Beatrice's beauty even before being tricked into falling in love with her

There's her cosin, and she were not possest
with a furie, exceedes her as much in beautie, as the first
of Maie doth the last of December :

(Much Ado About Nothing, speech #6, sentence #4)

where there are five short spelled words in the first two and half lines.

4/ PASSIONATE SHAKESPEARE LEADING TO VOLCANIC SHAKESPEARE

A: WHEN THERE IS A REASONABLE BALANCE BETWEEN CAPITALS AND 'FUNNY' SPELLINGS

Sometimes, especially when moved or stimulated, we/you/the character are, at one and the same time, emotional and intellectual in our responses, and . . .

AS A RULE OF THUMB

. . . that's what can be seen when 'funny' spellings and capitals in the original text almost balance each other.

Thus there is expected passion, quite understandable given the circumstances — as with Toby's explanation to his fellow conspirator Fabian as to why he will not deliver Sir Andrew's challenge to Cesario (the disguised Viola) in its current ridiculous format, since the boy has obvious 'capacity and good breeding'

his employment betweene his
Lord and my Neece, confirmes no lesse.

Therefore, this

Letter being so excellently ignorant, will breed no terror
in the youth : he will finde it comes from a Clodde-pole.

(Twelfth Night, speech #15, the last line of sentence # 7 and all #8)

where the four capital words and five long spelled words in just three and half lines are vivid testimony to Toby's hardly surprising passionate dismissal of Andrew.

And of course there is unexpected passion when, perhaps after a relative period of calm, everything bursts through at once, sometimes in the most inappropriate circumstances — as with Olivia as she lists her beauty to whom she believes is the young man Cesario (actually Viola in disguise)

It shalbe Inventoried

and every particle and utensile labell'd to my will : As,

Item two lippes indifferent redde, Item two grey eyes,

with lids to them : Item, one necke, one chin, & so forth .

(*Twelfth Night*, speech #8, sentence #6)

After a lengthy period of relative control through the scene so far, Olivia suddenly releases five capital words and four long spelled words in three and half lines — the situation of being alone with (as she believes) a young man for the first time in twelve months, and talking of matters sensual, having an affect perhaps?

B: ARE THERE FAR TOO MANY CAPITAL LETTERS AND 'FUNNY' SPELLINGS: CAN YOU NO LONGER KEEP YOUR PASSIONS IN CHECK?

Inevitably, and especially in dramatic theatrical conflicts (at which Shakespeare was a master — both within a single individual, and between different individuals), there are moments (good and bad) when (we)/you/the character cannot turn the passion off, whether in excitement and joy or fear and disgust.

AS A RULE OF THUMB

In the original texts those moments are marked by far too many capitals and long spellings within a very short space of time, which of course leads to **the expected volcanic Shakespeare** where the verbal excesses (emotional and intellectual) are only natural given the circumstances — as when a deeply disturbed Leontes, unnecessarily fearful of his wife's chastity, attempts to be cheerful with his young son Mamilius, his one remaining pride and joy, while watching Hermione and the man with whom Leontes

believes she is betraying him, his long-time friend Polixenes. Leontes is undergoing rapid switches in focus with the first two lines referring to Mamilius' smudged nose; the next one and a half lines a tortured realisation that 'neat' is description often used of horned animals once trimmed and ready for eating — (a reference to himself as a cuckolded husband); the **'Still Virginalling'** a description of how Hermione is touching Polixines' hand; and the final sentence returning to tease his son)

They say it is a Coppy out of mine .

Come Captaine,

We must be neat ; not neat, but cleanly, Captaine :

And yet the Steere, the [Heycfer], and the Calfe,

Are all call'd Neat .

Still Virginalling

Upon his Palme ?

How now (you wanton Calfe)

Art thou my Calfe ?

(*The Winters Tale*, speech #2)

The eleven capital words and ten long spelled words in just five and half lines show just how deeply Leontes is being affected, especially when trying to tease his son (further underscored by the three of the four sentences being short).

And since excesses often come at the most inappropriate of times, **there is also the unexpected volcanic Shakespeare,** where the circumstances rarely warrant such an explosive reaction — as with Falstaffe's sudden prayer for a cool evening less he 'pisse my Tallow' as he prepares for his supposed assignation with Mrs. Page and Mrs. Ford

When Gods have hot backes, what shall poore men do ?

For me, I am heere a Windsor Stagge, and the fattest (I thinke) i'th Forrest.

Send me a coole rut-time

(Jove) or who can blame me to pisse my Tallow ?

(*The Merry Wives of Windsor*, speech #13, sentences #4+6)

Eight capital words and eight long spelled words in just four lines seem somewhat excessive — a sign of the fervent wish or prayer of an older man hoping not to let himself down by not being up to the event perhaps?

SUMMARY

BASIC APPROACH TO THE SPEECHES SHOWN BELOW
(after reading the 'background')

1/ first, use the modern version shown in the first column. By doing so you can discover

- the basic plot line of what's happening to the character

- the first set of conflicts/obstacles impinging on the character as a result of the situation or actions of other characters

- the supposed grammatical and poetical correctnesses of the speech

2/ then you can explore

- acting techniques you'd apply to any modern soliloquy, including establishing for the character

- the given circumstances of the scene

- the character's outward state of being (who they are sociologically, etc.)

- the character's intentions and objectives

- the resultant action and tactics the character decides to pursue

3/ when this is complete, turn to the First Folio version of the text, shown in the third column: this will help you discover and explore

- the precise thinking and debating process so essential to an understanding of any Shakespeare text

- the moments when the text is NOT grammatically or poetically as correct as the modern texts would have you believe, which will in turn help you recognise

- the moments of conflict and struggle stemming from within the character itself

- the sense of fun and enjoyment Shakespeare's language nearly always offers you no matter how dire the situation

4/ should you wish to further explore the differences between the two texts, the middle column, the commentary, discusses sentence by sentence, and often phrase by phrase, how the First Folio has been changed, and what those alterations might mean for the human arc of the speech

N.B.

Occasionally, seemingly similar words in each text will be bracketed. This highlights spelling differences, quite often vis-a-vis real names, both of places and people, e.g. 'Calais' (the modern version of the French town) and 'Callis' (the spelling often used at the time the Folio was set). Very rarely will the differences be noted in the commentaries, and it is suggested that actors or readers use whichever format appeals to them best.

HOW THE THREE COLUMNS WORK VISUALLY

SYMBOLS INSERTED INTO BOTH TEXTS

[ ] : set around words in both texts when F1 sets one word or phrase while modern texts, basing their choice on editorial glosses or alternative source texts (a quarto printed earlier than F1), set another

{ } : where some minor alteration has been made to the speech or the shape of an individual word originally set: this will only occur in a speech built up from two or more smaller speeches in the play, where, sometimes for clarification, a word or small phrase will be changed, added, or removed

{ψ} : again in the case of a speech built from two or more smaller speeches, this symbol shows where a sizeable part of the text has been omitted (e.g. before sentence # 2 in the Messenger's speech, the first in Henry Six Part One)

xxxxxxxxxxx : indicates where one speech or part of a speech has been joined to the one that follows

shaded text: indicates where modern texts have altered F1's verse structure (changes in prose are not shown)

SYMBOLS INSERTED IN THE MODERN TEXT

MODERN CHANGES TO THE FIRST FOLIO SENTENCE STRUCTURE

†: marks where modern texts end a sentence and start a new one, though F1 extends the current sentence beyond this point

◊: marks where modern texts have continued a sentence, though F1 ends the sentence here and starts a new one after this point

º: marks where an F1 hyphen, suggesting both words have equal spoken weight, has been removed (&, rarely, -º, where a hyphen is added, suggesting a greater verbal connection than F1 might have intended)

MODERN CHANGES TO FIRST FOLIO CAPITALS

Δ: marks where F1 has set a capitalised word which has not been capitalised by modern texts (the importance of the F1 capital being it suggests that the word has been deliberately chosen, which in turn suggests that the character is capable of intelligent/intellectual process no matter how emotional the situation): the symbol will also be set when modern texts (rarely) create a capital not set in F1

MODERN CHANGES TO FIRST FOLIO SPELLINGS

* (* set high): marks where F1 has set a 'long-spelled' word that has been standardised by modern texts (the longer spelling of a word in F1 (e.g. 'shee' instead of 'she' as used by Joan la Pucelle in speech # 4 of Henry Six Part One) suggests that, at the moment the word is said, the character is revealing some emotional feeling associated with that word (in this case, since Joan is talking about 'Gods Mother', her mentor, the longer spelling is hardly surprising)

* (* set low): marks where F1 has set a 'short-spelled' word which has been standardised by modern texts (the shorter spelling of a word in F1 (e.g. 'Tyrannie', 'perpetuitie', 'Skie', and 'Mortalitie', as used by Talbot ending lines 2-5 in speech # 6 of Henry Six Part One) suggests that, at the moment the word is said, the character is, in speaking the word, holding something back – either an emotion associated with that word or of feelings in general (in this case since the dying Talbot is talking to his dead son, the emotional withholding is hardly surprising)

SYMBOLS INSERTED IN THE FOLIO TEXT

PUNCTUATION REDUCED OR INCREASED BY MODERN TEXTS

since the Shakespeare texts are based so much on the art of debate and argument, the importance of F1's major punctuation must not be underestimated, for both the semicolon (;) and colon (:) mark a moment of importance for the character, either for itself, as a moment of discovery or revelation, or as a key point in a discussion, argument or debate that it wishes to impress upon other characters onstage

as a rule of thumb:

a/ the more frequent colon (:) suggests that whatever the power of the point discovered or argued, the character is not side-tracked and can continue with the argument - as such, the colon can be regarded as a **logical** connection

b/ the far less frequent semicolon (;) suggests that because of the power inherent in the point discovered or argued, the character is side-tracked and momentarily loses the argument and falls back into itself or can only continue the argument with great difficulty - thus, the semicolon should be regarded as an **emotional** connection

as such F1's major punctuation is not so much grammatical as oratorical and rhetorical: however, modern texts' punctuation is grammar and syntax based, and at times the two systems clash: thus key moments of passion and debate as originally set in F1, as well as ungrammatical emotional moments when the situation is almost too much for the character to bear, are often unwittingly altered by modern texts: hence the following key markings will be set

; **x** : indicating where an F1 (emotional) semicolon has been reduced or omitted by modern texts

: **x** : indicating where an F1 (logical) colon has been reduced or omitted by modern texts

; **+** : indicating where an F1 (emotional) semicolon has been set as something heavier (: , ; ? !) by modern texts

: **+** : indicating where an F1 (logical) colon has been set as something heavier (. , ? !) by modern texts similar 'x' or '+' signs will be used when question (?) or exclamation (!) marks or commas (,) are likewise altered

→ : indicates that, though the original text has set two short lines for a single character, perhaps hinting at a minute break between the two thoughts, most modern texts have set the two short lines as one longer one

PUNCTUATION OMMITTED BY MODERN TEXTS (usually commas)

x : set where modern texts omit an F1 comma (or other punctuation): many modern texts omit commas because they are ungrammatical, but their value goes far beyond mere syntax into the very action of character and play: the importance of these extra F1 commas cannot be stressed enough, for they show where a character needs either

a/ an extra thought to make a meaning absolutely clear, or

b/ an extra breath to calm itself down

in the commentaries, these extra phrases will be referred to as **breath-thoughts**

PUNCTUATION ADDED BY MODERN TEXTS (usually commas)

+ : set where modern texts add a comma (or other punctuation) where F1 has set no punctuation at all: most modern texts add such commas to clarify grammatical/syntactical relationships: the unfortunate side-effect of these extra modern commas is that they often slow down the speed of the thought or argument F1 originally established

PROBABLE TIMING

(shown just before the speeches begin, set alongside the number of lines)

the # before the period refers to minutes, the # after to seconds - thus 0.45 = a forty-five second speech

SYMBOLS & ABBREVIATIONS INSERTED IN THE COMMENTARY

F: the First Folio

mt.: modern texts

F # followed by a number: the number of the sentence under discussion in the First Folio version of the speech, thus F #7 would refer to the seventh sentence

mt. # followed by a number: the number of the sentence under discussion in the modern text version of the speech, thus mt. #5 would refer to the fifth sentence

#/#, (e.g. 3/7): the first number refers to the number of capital letters in the passage under discussion; the second refers to the number of long spellings therein

within a quotation from the speech: / indicates where one verse line ends and a fresh one starts

TERMS FOUND IN THE COMMENTARY (part one)

OVERALL

1/ **orthography:** the capitalization, spellings, and punctuation of the First Folio

SIGNS OF IMPORTANT DISCOVERIES/ARGUMENTS WITHIN A FIRST FOLIO SPEECH

2/ **major punctuation:** colons and semicolons: N.B. the following is taken from the previous page since the Shakespeare texts are based so much on the art of debate and argument, the importance of F1's major punctuation must not be underestimated, for both the semicolon (;) and colon (:) mark a moment of importance for the character, either for itself, as a moment of discovery or revelation, or as a key point in a discussion, argument or debate that it wishes to impress upon other characters onstage

as a rule of thumb:

a/ the more frequent colon (:) suggests that whatever the power of the point discovered or argued, the character is not side-tracked and can continue with the argument - as such, the colon can be regarded as a **logical** connection

b/ the far less frequent semicolon (;) suggests that because of the power inherent in the point discovered or argued, the character is side-tracked and momentarily loses the argument and falls back into itself or can only continue the argument with great difficulty – as such, the semicolon should be regarded as an **emotional** connection

3/ **surround phrases:** phrase(s) surrounded by major punctuation, or a combination of major punctuation and the end or beginning of a sentence: thus these phrases seem to be of especial importance for both character and speech, well worth exploring as key to the argument made and/or emotions released+

SYMBOLS INSERTED IN THE FOLIO TEXT (CTD)

DIALOGUE NOT FOUND IN THE FIRST FOLIO

∞ : set where modern texts add dialogue from a quarto text which has not been included in F1

A LOOSE RULE OF THUMB TO THE THINKING PROCESS OF A FIRST FOLIO CHARACTER

TERMS FOUND IN THE COMMENTARY (part two)

1/ **mental discipline/intellect:** a section where capitals dominate suggests that the intellectual reasoning behind what is being spoken or discovered is of more concern than the personal response beneath it

2/ **feelings/emotions:** a section where long spellings dominate suggests that the personal response to what is being spoken or discovered is of more concern than the intellectual reasoning behind it

3/ **passion:** a section where both long spellings and capitals are present in almost equal proportions suggests that both mind and emotion/feelings are inseparable, and thus the character is speaking passionately

SIGNS OF LESS THAN GRAMMATICAL THINKING WITHIN A FIRST FOLIO SPEECH

1/ **onrush:** sometimes thoughts are coming so fast that several topics are joined together as one long sentence suggesting that the F character's mind is working very quickly, or that his/her emotional state is causing some concern: most modern texts split such a sentence into several grammatically correct parts (the opening speech of *As You Like It* is a fine example, where F's long 18 line opening sentence is split into six): while the modern texts' resetting may be syntactically correct, the F moment is nowhere near as calm as the revisions suggest

2/ **fast-link:** sometimes F shows thoughts moving so quickly for a character that the connecting punctuation between disparate topics is merely a comma, suggesting that there is virtually no pause in springing from one idea to the next: unfortunately most modern texts rarely allow this to stand, instead replacing the obviously disturbed comma with a grammatical period, once more creating calm that it seems the original texts never intended to show

FIRST FOLIO SIGNS OF WHEN VERBAL GAME PLAYING HAS TO STOP

1/ **non-embellished:** a section with neither capitals nor long spellings suggests that what is being discovered or spoken is so important to the character that there is no time to guss it up with vocal or mental excesses: an unusual moment of self-control

2/ **short sentence:** coming out of a society where debate was second nature, many of Shakespeare's characters speak in long sentences in which ideas are stated, explored, redefined and summarized all before moving onto the next idea in the argument, discovery or debate: the longer sentence is the sign of a rhetorically trained mind used to public speaking (oratory), but at times an idea or discovery is so startling or inevitable that length is either unnecessary or impossible to maintain: hence the occasional very important short sentence suggests that there is no time for the niceties of oratorical adornment with which to sugar the pill - verbal games are at an end and now the basic core of the issue must be faced

3/ **monosyllabic:** with English being composed of two strands, the polysyllabic (stemming from French, Italian, Latin and Greek), and the monosyllabic (from the Anglo-Saxon), each strand has two distinct functions: the polysyllabic words are often used when there is time for fanciful elaboration and rich description (which could be described as 'excessive rhetoric') while the monosyllabic occur when, literally, there is no other way of putting a basic question or comment – Juliet's "Do you love me? I know thou wilt say aye" is a classic example of both monosyllables and non-embellishment: with monosyllables, only the naked truth is being spoken, nothing is hidden

SPEECHES IN ORDER	TIME	PAGE
COMEDY OF ERRORS		
#'s 1 – 3: The Duke and The Merchant		
1/ **Duke {Solinus}** Merchant of Siracusa, plead no more.	1.10	30
2/a **Merchant** In Syracusa was I borne, and wedde	1.15	31
/b **Merchant** A league from Epidamium had we saild	1.40	32
3/ **Duke** Haplesse Egeon whom the fates have markt	0.50	33
# 4: Mistaken Identity in General		
4/ **Local Dromio** Return'd so soone, rather approacht too late:	0.50	34
#'s 5 – 7: Woman in Waiting		
5/ **Adriana** Patience unmov'd, no marvel though she pause,	0.35	35
6/ **Local Dromio** Why Mistresse, sure my Master is horne mad.	1.00	36
7/ **Adriana** His company must do his minions grace,	1.30	37
#'s 8 – 12: Mistaken Identity and Love Complications		
8/ **Adriana** I, I, Antipholus, looke strange and frowne,	2.15	38
9/ **Antipholus V.** To mee shee speakes, shee moves mee . . .	0.25	40
10/ **Luciana** And may it be that you have quite forgot	1.30	40
11/ **Antipholus V.** Sweete Mistris, what your name is else I know not;	1.15	42
12/ **Dromio Visitor** . . . she's the Kitchin wench, & al grease,	1.45	43
#'s 13 – 14: Mistaken Identity's Effect on the Locals		
13/ **Curtizan** Now out of doubt Antipholus is mad,	0.50	45
14/ **Abbesse** And thereof came it, that the man was mad.	1.30	46

SPEECHES BY GENDER	Speech #(s)
SPEECHES FOR WOMEN (6)	
Luciana Traditional & Today: young woman, younger than her sister Adrianna	#10
Adriana Traditional & Today: youngish/early middle age woman, older than her sister Luciana	#4, #7, #8
Curtizan Traditional & Today: a woman of the town, so attractive as to keep a young man away from his wife	#13
Abbesse Traditional & Today: since it turns out that she is the merchant Egeus' long lost wife and mother of both Antipholis, she has and should be played as a woman sufficiently old enough to have had 23 year old twins	#14
SPEECHES FOR EITHER GENDER (0)	
SPEECHES FOR MEN (8)	
Duke {Solinus} Traditional: older male, usually an authority figure / Today: with the above proviso, any gender, any age	#1, #3
Merchant (Egeus) Traditional & Today: older male (father of two 23 year old sons)	#2a, 2b
Local Dromio Traditional: younger clown-style performer, probably well-versed in commedia / Today: any age, gender, provided part of Egeon's speech #2 (which refers to the Dromio twins as being the same age/sex as the two Antipholi) is struck or rewritten, and the speech, though not necessarily the role, can be explored without the commedia skills	#4, #6
Antipholus V. Traditional & Today: young male approximately 23 years old	#9, #11
Dromio V. Traditional & Today: as local Dromio above	#12

COMEDY OF ERRORS

#'s 1 - 3: THE DUKE AND THE MERCHANT

1/Duke {Solinus}   Merchant of Siracusa, plead no more.   1.1.1 - 25

Background: These are the opening lines of the play, and, as with most of Shakespeare's first speeches, they are largely self explanatory. Solinus, the Duke, speaks on behalf of Ephesus, his city-state, explaining how Egeon, a prisoner, may legally be put to death simply because of his coming from Syracusa, an enemy city-state. The one thing that could save Egeon would be the payment of a large fine (emphasising the money theme so predominant throughout the play), though it appears he has not the wherewithall to be able to pay (for Solinus' change of heart, see speech #3 below).

Style: public address to one specific character in front of interested observers

Where: court, trial chamber, or even place of execution   **To Whom:** Egeon, a 'foreign' merchant: older male (father of two 23 year old sons)

# of Lines: 23   **Probable Timing: 1.10 minutes**

Modern Text

1/ Duke {Solinus}

1   Merchant of Siracusa, plead no more.

2   I am not partial* to infringe our ᐃlaws* ;
The enmity and discord which of late
Sprung from the rancorous outrage* of your Duke
To ᐃmerchants, our well-dealing ᐃcountrymen,*
Who, wanting gilders,* to redeem* their lives,
Have seal'd his rigorous statutes with their bloods* :
Excludes all pity* from our threat'ning looks* :
For since the mortall* and intestine jars*
Twixt thy seditious ᐃcountrymen,* and us,
It hath in solemn* ᐃsynods* been'd* decreed,
Both by the Siracusians,* and our selves,
To admit no traffic* to our adverse towns* :
Nay more. if anv born* or Ephesus ᐃbe seen*
At any ¹ Siracusian* ᐃmarts and ᐃfairs* ;
Again* , if any Siracusian* born*
Come to the ᐃbay of Ephesus, he dies,
His goods confiscate to the Dukes dispose,
Unless* a thousand marks* be levied
To quit the penalty and to ² ransom* him . †

3   Thy substance, valued at the highest rate,
Cannot amount unto a hundred ᐃmarks* ,
Therefore by ᐃlaw thou art condemn'd to die.

First Folio

1/ Duke {Solinus}

1   Merchant of Siracusa, plead no more.

2   I am not partiall to infringe our Lawes ;
The enmity and discord which of late
Sprung from the rancorous outrage of your Duke,ₓ
To Merchants ⁺ our well-dealing Countrymen,
Who⁺ wanting gilders to redeeme their lives,
Have seal'd his rigorous statutes with their blouds:
Excludes all pitty from our threatning lookes:
For since the mortall and intestine jarres
Twixt thy seditious Countrimen and us,
It hath in solemne Synodes beene decreed,
Both by the Siracusians and our selves,
To admit no trafficke to our adverse townes:
Nav more, if anv borne at Ephesus
Be seene at any Siracusian Marts and Fayres : ₓ
Againe, if any Siracusian borne
Come to the Bay of Ephesus, he dies:
His goods confiscate to the Dukes dispose,
Unlesse a thousand markes be levied
To quit the penalty,ₓ and to ransome him:
Thy substance, valued at the highest rate,
Cannot amount unto a hundred Markes,
Therefore by Law thou art condemn'd to die.

Commentary

F's orthography reveals several unexpected traits in what is often played as a flat out death sentence.

*   the opening curtness of a short single line sentence
"Merchant of Siracusa, plead no more."
plus the opening of F #2 with the only surround phrase in the speech
" . I am not partiall to infringe our Lawes ;"
suggest that for whatever reason (boredom? anger? concern?), the Duke is determined to bring matters to an end

*   yet the onrushed F #2 (somewhat diluted by modern texts' splitting it in two), and its opening emotional semicolon suggest this may not be as easy a task as might at first appear

*   while F #1 and the first four lines of F #2 are essentially factual (6/2), the next eight lines dealing with the blood feud between Ephesus and Syracusa forbidding any trade – 'Who wanting gilders . . . our adverse townes:' – are highly emotional (3/11)

*   the startling explanation of that just to be seen in each other's city means death ('Nay more if any borne at Ephesus') becomes highly passionate (7/4 in just four lines)

*   however, in finishing, while remaining somewhat emotional and intellectual, Solinus seems to calm down a little (just 3/3 in the last six lines), with, as befits such a bourgeois play, the only two non-embellished lines in the speech (save for the final unit of money-measurement 'Markes') dealing with Egeon's lack of wealth which, had it been sufficient, might have ransomed him
"Thy substance, valued at the highest rate,/Cannot amount unto a hundred Markes,"

---

¹since Ff set a twelve syllable line, some commentators suggest dropping 'any' to create pentameter   ²F1 sets an eleven syllable line, F2 omits 'to' to create pentameter

2a/ Merchant   In Syracusa was I borne, and wedde   1.1.36 - 61

Background: Duke Solinus, having explained why Egeon has been condemned to death, has ordered him to 'say in briefe the cause/Why thou departedst from thy native home? /And for what cause thou cam'st to Ephesus'. The following, hardly brief, explains exactly why: **#2a/** sets up the initial circumstances, including marriage, becoming a father of identical twins, profitable and happy times: **#2b/** establishes the moments before a devastating shipwreck.

Style: public address to one specific character in front of interested observers

Where: court, trial chamber, or even place of execution   **To Whom:** Solinus, Duke of Ephesus

# of Lines: 25   **Probable Timing: 1.15 minutes**

First Folio

2a/ {Egeon as} **Merchant**

1 In Syracusa was I borne, and wedde
Unto a woman, happy but for me,
And by me; $_x$ had not our hap beene bad:
With her I liv'd in joy,$^+$ our wealth increast
By prosperous voyages I often made
To [Epidamium], till my factors death,
And {the} great care of goods at randone left,
Drew me from kinde embracements of my spouse;
From whom my absence was not sixe moneths olde$_x$
Before her selfe (almost at fainting under
The pleasing punishment that women beare)
Had made provision for her following me,
And soone, and safe, arrived where I was:
There had she not beene long,$_x$ but she became
A joyfull mother of two goodly sonnes:
And, which was strange, the one so like the other,
As could not be distinguish'd but by names.

2 That very howre, and in the selfe-same Inne,
A [ ] meane woman was delivered
Of such a burthen Male, twins both alike:
Those, for their parents were exceeding poore,
I bought, and brought up to attend my sonnes.

3 My wife, not meanely prowd of two such boyes,
Made daily motions for our home returne:
Unwilling I agreed, alas, too soone wee came aboord.

With the Duke's total change of heart from the death sentence of speech **#1 above** to the attempted (though hand-tied) sympathetic help offered in **speech #3 below**, it seems obvious that, whether consciously or no, the Merchant (Egeon) is a remarkably fine story teller: F's orthography clearly shows how.

• if the story itself were not enough, the single surround phrase
" ; had not our hap beene bad :"
is a clear indication as to Egeon's (the Merchant's) current state of mind and why the speech is so emotional throughout (4/27)

• and via sudden long spelling clusters, it seems that certain moments are burned into his brain (or, good raconteur as he is, he wants them burned into his audience's brain), such as 'my absence was not sixe moneths olde'; plus 'A joyfull mother of two goodly sonnes'; and 'That very howre, and in the selfe-same Inne/A meane woman was delivered'; together with 'My wife, not meanely prowd of two such boyes', and the doom-laden 'alas, too soone wee came aboord.'

• this latter point, the last line of this part of the speech, seems the most disturbing of all, for F sets it as an irregular (fourteen syllable) line: however, most modern texts reduce its significance by splitting it in two (a regular line of ten syllables followed by a short line of four), as the shading shows

• yet, in the sea of emotion, what is startling is that three key sets of story-telling details are presented totally unembellished
"Unto a woman, happy but for me,/And by me;"
"With her I liv'd in joy, our wealth increast/By prosperous voyages I often made"
"(almost at fainting under/The pleasing punishment that women beare)/ Had made provision for her following me,"
"And, which was strange, the one so like the other,/As could not be distinguish'd but by names."

Modern Text

2a/ {Egeon as} **Merchant**

1 In Syracusa was I born*, and wed*
Unto a woman, happy but for me,
And by me, had not our hap been* bad:
With her I liv'd in joy; our wealth increas'd
By prosperous voyages I often made
To [Epidamnium], till my factor's death,
And the great care of goods at randon* left,
Drew me from kind* embracements of my spouse;
From whom my absence was not six* months* old*
Before herself* (almost at fainting under
The pleasing punishment that women bear*)
Had made provision for her following me,
And soon*, and safe, arrived where I was. †

2 There had she not been* long but she became
A joyful* mother of two goodly sons* :
And, which was strange, the one so like the other,
As could not be distinguish'd but by names.

3 That very hour*, and in the self*-same ^inn* ,
A [poor] mean* woman was delivered
Of such a burthen ^male, twins both alike . †

4 Those, for their parents were exceeding poor* ,
I bought, and brought up to attend my sons* .

5 My wife, not meanly* proud* of two such boys* ,
Made daily motions for our home return* :
Unwilling I agreed . †

6   Alas, too soon*

We* came aboard* .

2b/ Merchant {In Syracusa was I borne, and wedde (ctd.)}: **A league from Epidamium had we sail'd** 1.1.62 – 95

# of Lines: 34 **Probable Timing: 1.40 minutes**

First Folio

2b/ {Egeon as} **Merchant**

4
A league from Epidamium had we saild
Before the alwaies winde-obeying deepe
Gave any Tragicke Instance of our harme:
But longer did we not retaine much hope; x
For what obscured light the heavens did grant,
Did but convay unto our fearefull mindes
A doubtfull warrant of immediate death,
Which though my selfe would gladly have imbrac'd,
Yet the incessant weepings of my wife,
Weeping before for what she saw must come, +
And pitteous playnings of the prettie babes +
That mourn'd for fashion, ignorant what to feare,
Forst me to seeke delayes for them and me,
And this it was: x (for other meanes was none) +
The Sailors sought for safety by our boate,
And left the ship + then sinking ripe + to us.

5
My wife, more carefull for the latter borne,
Had fastned him unto a small spare Mast,
Such as sea-faring men provide for stormes : x
To him one of the other twins was bound,
Whil'st I had beene like heedfull of the other.

6
The children thus dispos'd, my wife and I,
Fixing our eyes on whom our care was fixt,
Fastned our selves at eyther end the mast,
And floating straight, obedient to the streame,
Was carried towards Corinth, as we thought.

7
At length the [sonne] + gazing upon the earth,
Disperst those vapours that offended us,
And by the benefit of his wished light
The seas waxt calme, and we discovered
Two shippes from farre, making amaine to us: x
Of Corinth that, of Epidarus this,
But ere they came, oh let me say no more,
Gather the sequell by what went before.

F's orthography continues to shows how, whether consciously or no, the Merchant Egeon is a remarkably fine story teller.

• the single surround phrase in this part of the speech
": But longer did we not retaine much hope ;"
is again a clear indication as to Egeon's (the Merchant's) underlying state of mind, and why the speech remains so emotional throughout (8/30 overall)

• not surprisingly, the first three lines foreshadowing the doom to come are full of release, more emotional than factual (3/6)

• and, equally understandably, the remaining thirteen lines of F #4, describing their abandonment by the Sailors to a 'ship, sinking ripe', is highly emotional (1/12)

• and again via sudden long spelling clusters, it seems that certain moments are burned into his brain (or, good raconteur as he is, he wants them burned into his audience's brain), such as the opening three lines of this part of the speech; plus 'Did but convay unto our fearefull mindes/A doubtfull warrant of immediate death'; and especially the 'pitteous playnings of the prettie babes'; which 'Forst me to seeke delayes for them and me', plus the final, once more doom-laden foreshadowing of 'Two shippes from farre, making amaine to us'

• and, after the releases of F #4, as in the opening to speech #2a/ above, so Egeon manages to establish (enforced?) some sense calm
a/ the binding of the children to opposite ends of the mast shows little release (just 1/4 in the five lines of F #5)
b/ then, there is even less release as he describes them all floating on the mast towards Corinth 'as we thought' (1/2 in the five lines of F #6)
c/ the sunrise is a calmer recollection (0/1 in the first three lines of F #7)

• however, the about-to-be explained tragedy of two ships from different city-states making towards them becomes emotional (0/4 in just two lines), while the three line ending becomes partly intellectual for the first time since his story-telling began (2/1)

• and again, as in 2a, in the sea of emotion, what is startling is that several sets of story-telling details are presented totally unembellished
"For what obscured light the heavens did grant,"
"Yet the incessant weepings of my wife,/Weeping before for what she saw must come,"
"And left the ship then sinking ripe to us. "
"To him one of the other twins was bound,"
"The children thus dispos'd, my wife and I,/Fixing our eyes on whom our care was fixt,/Fastned our selves"
"Disperst those vapours that offended us/And by the benefit of his wished light"
"But ere they came, oh let me say no more,"

Modern Text

2b/ {Egeon as} **Merchant**

7
A league from Epidamium had we sail'd
Before the always* -wind*-obeying deep*
Gave any ^tragic* ^instance of our harm* :
But longer did we not retain* much hope,
For what obscured light the heavens did grant
Did but convey unto our fearful* minds*
A doubtful* warrant of immediate death,
Which though myself* would gladly have embrac'd*,
Yet the incessant weepings of my wife,
Weeping before for what she saw must come,
And piteous* plainings* of the pretty* babes,
That mourn'd for fashion, ignorant what to fear*,
Forc'd me to seek* delays* for them and me . +

8
And this it was (for other means* was none):
The ^sailors sought for safety by our boat* ,
And left the ship, then sinking ripe, to us.

9
My wife, more careful* for the latter born* ,
Had fast'ned him unto a small spare ^mast,
Such as sea°faring men provide for storms* ;
To him one of the other twins was bound,
Whil'st I had been* like heedful* of the other.

10
The children thus dispos'd, my wife and I,
Fixing our eyes on whom our care was fix'd,
Fast'ned our selves at either* end the mast,
And floating straight, obedient to the stream*,
Was carried towards Corinth, as we thought.

11
At length the [sun], gazing upon the earth,
Dispers'd those vapors* that offended us,
And by the benefit of his wished light
The seas wax'd calm* , and we discovered
Two ships* from far*, making amain* to us,
Of Corinth that, of Epidarus this,
But ere they came - ^O* let me say no more,
Gather the sequel* by what went before.

3/Duke   **Haplesse Egeon whom the fates have markt**   1.1.140 - 155

Background: Solinus appears to have been sufficiently moved by Egeon's story telling, (whether sincerely or no is up to each reader to judge for themselves), and though, as he explains, he cannot either pardon Egeon or waive the fine, he will allow him till sunset to range throughout the city to see if he can raise enough money for ransom.

Style: public address to one specific character in front of interested observers
Where: court, trial chamber, or even place of execution   **To Whom:** Egeon, a 'foreign' merchant: older male (father of two 23 year old sons)
# of Lines: 16   **Probable Timing: 0.50 minutes**

Modern Text	First Folio
3/Duke	**3/Duke**
1 Hapless* Egeon, whom the fates have mark'd To bear* the extremity* of dire mishap! †	1 Haplesse Egeon + whom the fates have markt To beare the extremitie of dire mishap:
2 Now trust me, were it not against our △laws*, Against my △crown*, my oath, my dignity, Which △princes would they, may not disannul*, My soul* should sue as advocate for thee: But though thou art adjudged to the death, And passed sentence may not be recall'd* But to our honor's* great disparagement, Yet will I favor* thee in what I can; Therefore, △merchant, I'll limit thee this day To seek* thy [health]* by beneficial* help*. †	Now trust me, were it not against our Lawes, Against my Crowne, my oath, my dignity, Which Princes would they + may not disanull, My soule should sue as advocate for thee : But though thou art adjudged to the death, And passed sentence may not be recal'd But to our honours great disparagement: x Yet will I favour thee in what I can ; Therefore + Marchant, Ile limit thee this day To seeke thy [helpe] by beneficiall helpe, +
3 Try all the friends thou hast in Ephesus; Beg thou, or borrow, to make up the sum*, And live: if no, then thou art doom'd to die. †	Try all the friends thou hast in Ephesus, + Beg thou, or borrow, to make up the summe, And live: if no, then thou art doom'd to die:
4 Jailer, take him to thy custody*.	Jaylor, take him to thy custodie.

Unlike the rational four sentence character most modern texts set, F's single onrushed sixteen line sentence suggests Duke Solinus is sufficiently involved in Egeon's fate for the grammatical niceties to be more than somewhat ignored.

• overall, the speech is both emotional and intellectual (6/8)

• the surround phrases establish the limitations to the Duke's change of heart from speech #1 above:
" : Yet will I favour thee in what I can ; "
but if Egeon cannot find the ransom
" : if no, then thou art doom'd to die : "
the first surround phrase is extra-weighted by ending with an emotional semicolon, the second doubly-weighted by being both non-embellished and monosyllabic

• two more non-embellished lines detail the restraints Solinus is working under
"But though thou art adjudged to the death,/And passed sentence may not be recal'd"
and if the longer standard British practice of spelling of 'honours' and 'favour' is discounted the non-embellished passage would be doubled by adding the two lines
"But to our honours great disparagement :/Yet will I favour thee in what I can;"

• unusually, eight successive lines (three through ten) are purely iambic, with all the details Solinus wishes both Egeon and those in attendance to understand clearly emphasised by falling on the five stronger beats of each line

#4: Mistaken Identity in General

4/ Local Dromio   Return'd so soone, rather approacht too late: between 1.2.43 – 67

Background: Unknown to anyone, the Syracusian Antipholus has arrived in Ephesus. He is the identical-twin brother of the tardy local (Ephesean) Antipholus, whose drinking and tom-catting are currently creating such problems for his wife Adrianna, (see speech #5 below). The local Dromio, sent out to bring the local Antipholus home, has in fact found the visiting Antipholus, who has just sent his companion/servant (the visiting Dromio) off to secure their money safely in the hotel where they will be staying. The trigger to this local-Dromio speech is the visiting-Antipholus' question 'How chance thou art return'd so soone.', having mistaken the local-Dromio for his own servant. The speech deals with all the horrors back home at Adrianna's over the delay in starting a rather sumptuous lunch.

Style: part of a two-handed scene

Where: unspecified, probably a public street   **To Whom:** the wrong (visiting instead of local) Antipholus

# of Lines: 16   **Probable Timing: 0.50 minutes**

Modern Text

4/ Local Dromio

1 Return'd so soon*! rather approach'd too late:
The △capon burns*, the △pig falls* from the spit;
The clock* hath strucken twelve upon the bell:
My ^mistress* made it one upon my cheek* :
She is so hot, because the meat* is cold* :
The meat* is cold*, because you come not home :
You come not home, because you have no stomach* :
You have no stomach*, having broke your fast:
But we that know what 'tis to fast and pray,
Are penitent for your default to∘day. ▪

2 I pray you jest, sir, as you sit at dinner . †

3 I from my ^mistress∘ come to you in post:
If I return*, I shall be post indeed* : ◊
For she will [score]* your fault upon my pate:
[Methinks*] your maw, like mine, should be your [clock] *,
And strike you home without a messenger.

First Folio

4/ Local Dromio

1 Return'd so soone, + rather approacht too late :
The Capon burnes, the Pig fals from the spit;
The clocke hath strucken twelve upon the bell:
My Mistris made it one upon my cheeke:
She is so hot + because the meate is colde:
The meate is colde, because you come not home:
You come not home, because you have no stomacke:
You have no stomacke, having broke your fast:
But we that know what 'tis to fast and pray,
Are penitent for your default to day.

2 I pray you jest + sir + as you sit at dinner:
I from my Mistris come to you in post:
If I returne + I shall be post indeede.

3 For she will [scoure] your fault upon my pate:
[Me thinkes] your maw, like mine, should be your [cooke],
And strike you home without a messenger.

Amazingly, no fewer than twelve of the sixteen lines are surround phrases - one of the most overwrought passages in Shakespeare.

• given the circumstances, it's not surprising the speech is so emotional (4/15 in sixteen lines)

• the non-embellished lines could suggest that at times when talking either about or to his supposed master (i.e. the local) Antipholus, he has to be very careful
"But we that know what 'tis to fast and pray,/Are penitent for your default to day."
"And strike you home without a messenger."

• and it might be that Dromio loves his food, for the only semicolon within the surround phrases points first to (the horror of) spoiled food
" : The Capon burnes, the Pig fals from the spit ; "
and then to a lament that the time for lunch is well past
" ; The clocke hath strucken twelve upon the bell : "

• F's ungrammatical sentences #2 and #3 are much more interesting than the modern syntactically correct rewrite, for with F #2 jamming together 'come home' because 'I'll be beaten otherwise' and the separate F #3 jamming together the breadth of the anticipated beating 'scoure . . . my pate' with 'please come home' shows far more of Dromio's concerns than the much more logical structure offered by mt. #2-3

#'s 5 - 7: Woman in Waiting

5/ Adriana

Patience unmov'd, no marvel though she pause,   2.1.32 - 41

Background: The married Adrianna is waiting with her unmarried sister Luciana to start the major meal of the day, dinner at noon. They cannot eat yet because, though it's way past the time Adrianna's highly social, not to mention philandering, husband should be home - he is still out drinking with his friends (though judging by the frequent comments made throughout the play about Adrianna's nagging, the fact he doesn't want to come just yet may be perfectly understandable) . Luciana, whose knowledge at the top of the play seems to come mainly from books and observation rather than direct experience, has come up with a somewhat bookish approach to explaining the necessary relationship between the sexes (women's rights groups please forgive her - she is very young and very inexperienced) . The following is the married Adrianna's practical direct experience reply to Luciana's rather apple-pie male-rightfully-dominating view of gender relationships.

Style: a speech, rather than dialogue, as part of a two-handed conversation

Where: in the home of Adrianna and the local Antipholus, who, unknown to anyone (including himself), is in fact the long lost infant twin for whom both his brother and Egeon are searching

To Whom: Luciana, her unmarried younger sister

# of Lines: 10   **Probable Timing: 0.35 minutes**

Modern Text

5/ Adriana

1 Patience unmov'd! no marvel though she pause -
    They can be meek*, that have no other cause*:
    A wretched soul*, bruis'd with adversity*,
    We bid be quiet when we hear* it cry*; ◊
    But were we burd'ned with like weight of pain*,
    As much, or more, we should our selves complain* :
    So thou, that hast no unkind* mate to grieve* thee,
    With urging helpless* patience would relieve* me;
    But if thou live to see like right bereft,
    This fool*-begg'd* patience in thee will be left.

First Folio

5/ Adriana

1 Patience unmov'd, + no marvel though she pause,
    They can be meeke, that have no other cause:
    A wretched soule + bruis'd with adversitie,
    We bid be quiet when we heare it crie.

2 But were we burdned with like waight of paine,
    As much, or more, we should our selves complaine:
    So thou + that hast no unkinde mate to greeve thee,
    With urging helpelesse patience would releeve me;
    But if thou live to see like right bereft,
    This foole-beg'd patience in thee will be left.

With no capitals at all in the ten lines, this seems a very genuine cry from the 'deserted' Adrianna. The humour lies in the logic being somewhat confused, and in the long spellings suggesting her reactions are somewhat over the top - a very different response from the modern texts' jamming the two sentences together in one litany of never-ending complaint.

• yet despite the emotion (0/10), an argument of sorts is still being made: F's two sentences allow Adrianna to discount the general doctrine of the pain of a 'wretched soule, bruis'd in adversitie' especially when 'We' are not directly involved - a definite dig Luciana who is not (0/3 in F #1's four lines): this then allows the greater emotional impact (0/7 in six lines of F #2) of Adriana suggesting Luciana would not advise 'helplesse patience' if she had ever experienced what Adrianna is currently undergoing

• the (enforced?) quiet underscoring the two unembellished lines 'Patience unmov'd, no marvel though she pause' and 'But if thou live to see like right bereft' point to Adriana's deep exasperation with her 'theory'-smitten sister

6/ Local Dromio   Why Mistresse, sure my Master is horne mad.   between 2.1.57 - 85

Background: Having been rejected and beaten by the visiting Antipholus, the local Dromio has returned to his mistress to report about the actions of his supposed (and incorrectly identified) master.

Style: as part of a three-handed scene

Where: Adrianna's home   **To Whom:** the two sisters Adrianna (his mistress) and Luciana

# of Lines: 20   **Probable Timing: 1.00 minutes**

First Folio

6/ Local Dromio

1 Why Mistresse, sure my Master is horne mad..
   I meane not Cuckold mad,

2 But sure he is starke mad:
   When I desir'd him to come home to dinner,
   He ask'd me for a [hundred] markes in gold:
   "'Tis dinner time, quoth I: my gold,⁺ quoth he:
   Your meat doth burne, quoth I: my gold⁺ quoth he:
   Will you come,⁺ quoth I: my gold,⁺ quoth he;
   Where is the thousand markes I gave thee⁺ villaine?

3 The Pigge⁺ quoth I, is burn'd: my gold,⁺ quoth he:
   My mistresse, sir, quoth I: hang up thy Mistresse :⁺
   I know not thy mistresse, out on thy mistresse.

4 Quoth my Master, I know⁺ quoth he, no house,
   no wife, no mistresse: so that my arrant⁺ due unto my
   tongue, I thanke him, I bare home upon my shoulders:
   for⁺ in conclusion, he did beat me there.

5 Am I so round with you, as you with me,
   That like a foot-ball you doe spurne me thus:
   You spurne me hence, and he will spurne me hither,⁺
   If I last in this service, you must case me in leather.

Modern Text

6/ Local Dromio

1 Why △mistress*, sure my △master is horn-mad* .
   I mean* not △cuckold mad -

2 But sure he is stark* mad:
   When I desir'd him to come home to dinner,
   He ask'd me for a [thousand]³ marks* in gold:
   "'Tis dinner-time," quoth I: "△My gold!" quoth he. ⁺

3 "Your meat doth burn* ," quoth I: "My gold!" quoth he.⁺

4 "Will you come?"⁴ quoth I: "△My gold!", quoth he;
   "Where is the thousand marks* I gave thee, villain*?."

5 The △"pig*," quoth I, "is burn'd": "△My gold!", quoth he.⁺

6 "My △mistress*, sir," quoth I: "△Hang up thy△mistress*!
   I know not thy mistress, out on thy mistress*" .

7 Quoth my △master. ⁺

8 "I know," quoth he, "no house, no wife, no mistress* ·"⁺
   So that my arrant, due unto my tongue,
   I thank* him, I bare home upon my shoulders:
   For, in conclusion, he did beat me there.

9 Am I so round with you, as you with me,
   That like a foot°ball you do* spurn* me thus? ⁺

10 You spurn* me hence, and he will spurn* me hither :
   If I last in this service, you must case me in leather.

- after the passionate opening short sentence (2/2, F #1), F's text becomes onrushed, as befits a character reporting he has just been beaten by his master, in such a way as to avoid being further beaten by his mistress: however, most modern texts do not maintain the onrush, instead splitting F #2 (the master's peculiar insistence on talking about 'the gold') into three; F #3's even weirder response to the 'Pigge' being 'burn'd' into two; F #4's reporting of the beating into two; and the final hurt dignity plea of F #5 also into two

- adding to the overwrought quality of the speech, the initial reporting of (the wrong) Antipholus' seemingly strange behaviours (F #2-4) is made up of an amazing thirteen surround phrases (only F #2's non-embellished lines two and three not so set) that suggest the weirdness and indignity of the situation are being hammered home (in an attempt to avoid a second beating perhaps?)

- F also sets F #4 in prose, as if the memory of the beating pushes Dromio out of the formality of verse into the immediacy of prose: most modern texts set the passage in verse as shown, removing this possibility⁵

- and despite all the seething emotions and needs running through the speech, a reader might be surprised that there aren't more excesses in the nineteen lines(4/15 overall): certainly F #2's last five almost unembellished lines (the monetary 'markes' and 'gold' plus 'brune' being the only exceptions)

   "When I desir'd him to come home to dinner,/He ask'd me for
   a hundred markes in gold :/'Tis dinner time, quoth I : my
   gold, quoth he :/Your meat doth burne, quoth I : my gold
   quoth he : /Will you come, quoth I: my gold, quoth he;"

and F #5's final

   "Am I so round with you, as you with me/That like a foot-ball
   …/If I last in this service, you must case me in leather."

seem to suggest that Dromio is attempting to stick to accurate verbal reporting rather than releasing a general unfocussed bleat of complaint - perhaps hoping the reporting might just help avoid the anticipated beating mentioned in speech #4 above:

³ F1 = 'hundred', F2 and most modern texts correct the figure to '1000'
⁴ since Ff set a nine syllable line, some modern texts add 'home' to create pentameter
⁵ modern editors argue since the speech was just three lines from the bottom of the First Folio column, and there was too much text for the space, the original compositor had no choice but to set the speech as prose

7/ Adriana   **His company must do his minions grace,**   between 2.1.86 - 115

Background: Adrianna's response to the Local Dromio's news of her (supposed) husband's outrageous behaviour in denying even knowing her. The speech is triggered by Luciana's comment 'Fie how impatience lowreth in your face.'

Style: as part of a two-handed scene   **To Whom:** Luciana

Where: Adrianna's home

# of Lines: 27   **Probable Timing: 1.30 minutes**

The usual approach is to dismiss Adrianna as a shrew who deserves what she gets, yet, in the following, nine short spellings ('merrie', 'homelie', 'mar'd', 'sunnie', 'enamel'd', 'beautie' twice, 'falshood' and 'eie') and ten unembellished lines, are more than enough to suggest that her unhappiness may have a genuine starting point (as is usually the case in most dysfunctional marriages). However, the final monetary logic of comparing her looks to a 'jewell' that has lost its 'beautie' and others beauty to 'gold' allows the audience to laugh at an expression of feelings again somewhat over the top, no matter how quietly she may be trying to express them.

• the silliness of this final analogy is enhanced by the long final onrushed F #11, where, after a series of legitimate complaints, she equates herself with love and money, undoing all the sympathy she might have hitherto earned from her sister and the audience: by splitting it into three, most modern texts attempt to give this emotional finale a much more rational base than was first set - much more than it really deserves

• the two surround phrases '; poore I am but his stale. ' and ' : I see the Jewell best enameled/Will loose his beautie : ', a reference to Antipholus' neglect of her, indicate from where her current unhappiness stems

• as is to be expected, at times the speech is highly emotional (2/25 in twenty-seven lines) but, with ten of the twenty-seven lines being unembellished, there are passages of (enforced?) calm broken up by sudden surges of release, notably
a/ about herself, 'th'alluring beauty tooke/From my poore cheeke?'; plus 'My decayed faire,/A sunnie looke of his, would soone repaire.' and
b/ about her husband's tom-catting around 'But too unruly Deere, he breakes the pale,/And feeds from home; poore I am but his stale.' plus 'a love he would detaine,/So he would keepe faire quarter with his bed:'

• all her unembellished quietness concentrates on how Antipholus has created whatever undesirable qualities she now displays
   "then he hath wasted it./Are my discourses dull?/Barren my wit,"
   "Then is he the ground/Of my defeatures."
   "I know his eye doth homage other-where,/Or else, what lets it but he would be here?"
and even the unembellished complex analogy still deals with his neglect
   "yet the gold bides still/That others touch, and often touching will,/Where gold and no man that hath a name, /By falshood and corruption doth it shame. /Since that my beautie cannot please his eie,"

Modern Text

7/ Adriana

1   His company must do his minions grace,
    Whil'st I at home starve for a merry* look* :
    Hath homely* age th'alluring beauty took*
    From my poor* cheek* ? †
                        Then he hath wasted it.

2   Are my discourses dull?

3   Barren my wit ? †

4   If voluble and sharp* discourse be mar'd*,
    Unkindness* blunts it more [than] marble hard.

5   Do* their gay vestments his affections bait* ?
    That's not my fault, he's* master of my state.

6   What ruins* are in me that can be found,
    By him not ruin'd?

7   Then is he the ground

8   Of my defeatures.
                        My decayed fair*,

9   A sunny* look* of his would soon* repair* .

10 But, too unruly ^deer* , he breaks* the pale,
    And feeds from home; poor* I am but his stale.

11 I know his eye doth homage other*-where,
    Or else, what lets it but he would be here?

12 Sister, you know he promis'd me a chain* ,
    Would that alone a'love he would detain* ,
    So he would keep* fair* quarter with his bed ! †

13 I see the ^jewel* best enamelled*
    Will lose* [her] beauty*; yet the gold bides still
    That others touch, and often touching, will
    Where gold; and no man that hath a name,
    By falsehood* and corruption doth it shame. †

First Folio

7/ Adriana

1   His company must do his minions grace,
    Whil'st I at home starve for a merrie looke:
    Hath homelie age th'alluring beauty tooke
    From my poore cheeke? then he hath wasted it.

2   Are my discourses dull?

3   Barren my wit, +

4   If voluble and sharpe discourse be mar'd,
    Unkindnesse blunts it more [then] marble hard.

5   Doe their gay vestments his affections baite?

6   That's not my fault, hee's master of my state.

    What ruines are in me that can be found,
    By him not ruin'd?

7   Then is he the ground

8   Of my defeatures.
                        My decayed faire,

    A sunnie looke of his, x would soone repaire.

9   But, too unruly Deere, he breakes the pale,
    And feeds from home; poore I am but his stale.

10 I know his eye doth homage other-where,
    Or else, what lets it but he would be here?

11 Sister, you know he promis'd me a chaine,
    Would that alone, + a love he would detaine,
    So he would keepe faire quarter with his bed: +
    I see the Jewell best enamaled
    Will loose [his] beautie: x yet the gold bides still
    That others touch, and often touching + will,x
    Where gold + and no man that hath a name,x
    By falshood and corruption doth it shame :

{ctd. over}

14 Since that my beauty* cannot please his eye*,
I'll weep* what's left away, and weeping die.

Since that my beautie cannot please his eie,
Ile weepe_x (what's left away)_x and weeping die.

#'s 8 - 12: MISTAKEN IDENTITY AND LOVE COMPLICATIONS

8/ Adriana   I, I, Antipholus, looke strange and frowne,   2.2.110 - 146

Background: With the reported denial of her (supposed) husband's even knowing her (speech #6 above) coming on top of a (yet another?) ruined lunch, Adrianna, possibly for the first time in her life, has gone to find him and berate him in public about his repeated absences, marital disinterest, and probable philandering.

Style: direct address, mainly to a single character, in a public place with many bystanders

Where: unspecified, presumably a public place or street   **To Whom:** the man she incorrectly believes is her real husband, in fact the startled visiting Antipholus, and for whomever may be in the public space, including her sister Luciana

# of Lines: 45   **Probable Timing: 2.15 minutes**

Modern Text

8/ Adriana

1 Ay*, ay*, Antipholus, look* strange and frown*,
Some other^mistress* hath thy sweet aspects:
I am not Adriana, nor thy wife.

2 The time was once, when thou un°urg'd wouldst vow
That never words were music* to thine ear*,
That never object pleasing in thine eye,
That never touch well welcome to thy hand,
That never meat sweet-savor'd* in thy taste,
Unless* I spake, or look'd, or touch'd, or carv'd to thee.

3 How comes it now, my ^husband* , ^O*, how comes it,
That thou art then estranged from thyself* ?

4 Thyself* I call it, being strange to me,
That, undividable ^incorporate,
Am better [than] thy dear* self's* better part.

5 Ah, do* not tear* away thyself* from me;
For know, my love, as easy*, mayst* thou fall
A drop of water in the breaking gulf* ,
And take unmingled thence that drop again* ,
Without addition or diminishing,
As take from me thyself* and not me too.

First Folio

8/ Adriana

1 I, I, Antipholus, looke strange and frowne,
Some other Mistresse hath thy sweet aspects:
I am not Adriana, nor thy wife.

2 The time was once, when thou un-urg'd wouldst vow,_x
That never words were musicke to thine eare,
That never object pleasing in thine eye,
That never touch well welcome to thy hand,
That never meat sweet-savour'd in thy taste,
Unlesse I spake, or look'd, or touch'd, or carv'd to thee.

3 How comes it now, my Husband, oh^+ how comes it,
That thou art then estranged from thy selfe?

4 Thy selfe I call it, being strange to me:_x
That^+ undividable Incorporate^+
Am better [then] thy deere selfes better part.

5 Ah^+ doe not teare away thy selfe from me;
For know^+ my love:_x as easie maist thou fall
A drop of water in the breaking gulfe,
And take unmingled thence that drop againe^+
Without addition or diminishing,
As take from me thy selfe,_x and not me too.

Once more, the non-embellished lines suggest she is not necessarily the virago she is often encouraged to be in this speech and scene, for though spoken in public, many of the key points are offered quite calmly (apparently), as if she were trying to maintain the socially correct pose of being 'polite' in public, no matter what seething emotional volcano may be raging underneath.

• the key un-embellished phrases include reminding him that earlier in their relationship only things she touched gave him pleasure
"That never object pleasing in thine eye,/That never touch well welcome to thy hand,"

then, asking if she were 'contaminate' by 'Ruffian Lust'
"Wouldst thou not spit at me," & "And from my false hand cut the wedding ring,"

arguing that because of his behaviour she is so contaminated ('doe' being the only long-spelled word in this passage)
"I am possest with an adulterate blot, .../For if we two be one, and thou play false,/I doe digest the poison of thy flesh,/Being strumpeted by thy contagion':"

concluding with
"Come I will fasten on this sleeve of thine:"

arguing that her strength to speak thus comes from him
"married to thy [stronger] state,/Makes me with thy strength to communicate:."

and that all other usurpers (women) will be dealt with, since
"Who all for want of pruning, with intrusion,/Infect thy sap, and live on thy confusion"

6
How dearly* would it touch thee to the quick*,
Shouldst thou but hear* I were licentious*,
And that this body, consecrate to thee,
By ^ruffian ^lust should be contaminate?

7
Wouldst thou not spit at me, and spurn* at me,
And hurl* the name of husband in my face,
And tear* the stain'd skin [off] my ^harlot brow,
And from my false hand cut the wedding-°ring,
And break* it with a deep*-divorcing vow?

8 I know thou canst, and therefore see thou do* it.

9
I am posses'd with an adulterate blot;
My blood* is mingled with the crime of lust:
For if we two be one, and thou play false,
I do* digest the poison of thy flesh,
Being strumpeted by thy contagion. †

10
Keep* then fair* league and truce with thy true bed,
I live [un]stain'd, thou undishonored* .

11
Come, I will fasten on this sleeve of thine:
Thou art an ^elm*, my husband, I a ^vine,
Whose weakeness*, married to thy [stronger] state,
Makes me with thy strength to communicate:
If aught possess* thee from me, it is dross*,
Usurping ^ivy*, ^brier, or idle ^moss*,
Who, all for want of pruning, with intrusion
Infect thy sap, and live on thy confusion.

How deerely would it touch thee to the quicke,
Shouldst thou but heare I were licencious? x
And that this body+ consecrate to thee,
By Ruffian Lust should be contaminate?

7
Wouldst thou not spit at me, and spurne at me,
And hurle the name of husband in my face,
And teare the stain'd skin [of] my Harlot brow,
And from my false hand cut the wedding ring,
And breake it with a deepe-divorcing vow?
I know thou canst, and therefore see thou doe it.

8
I am possest with an adulterate blot,+

9
My bloud is mingled with the crime of lust:
For if we two be one, and thou play false,
I doe digest the poison of thy flesh,
Being strumpeted by thy contagion:
Keepe then faire league and truce with thy true bed,
I live [dis]tain'd, thou undishonoured.

10
Come+ I will fasten on this sleeve of thine:
Thou art an Elme+ my husband, I a Vine: x
Whose weakenesse+ married to thy [stranger] state,
Makes me with thy strength to communicate:
If ought possesse thee from me, it is drosse,
Usurping Ivie, Brier, or idle Mosse,
Who+ all for want of pruning, with intrusion,x
Infect thy sap, and live on thy confusion.

• the surround phrases underscore Adriana's determination to make Antipholus face up to facts and so win him back
": I am not Adriana, nor thy wife ."
"? Thy selfe I call it, being strange to me : "
". Ah doe not teare thy selfe away from me ; / For know my love : "
". Come I will fasten on this sleeve of thine : /Thou art an Elme my husband, I a Vine : "

• when the releases do come, they tend to be emotional (12/37), with occasional clusters that are sometimes emotional ('Ah doe not teare thy selfe away from me'), and tellingly intellectual ('Ruffian Lust'), the argument that while the two of them are strong and wholesome ('an Elme' - Antipholus, and a 'Vine' - Adriana) , all interlopers can be dismissed as 'Usurping Ivie, Brier or idle Mosse'

9/ Antipholus V.   To mee shee speakes, shee moves mee for her theme   2.2.181 - 186

Background: The visiting Antipholus' immediate response to Adrianna's public outpourings, speech #8, immediately above.

Style: probably as an aside, or perhaps just a sotto voce remark to his (visiting) Dromio

Where: as above   **To Whom:** basically to self (and perhaps his own Dromio) and perhaps to the audience

# of Lines: 6   **Probable Timing: 0.25 minutes**

This short speech is amazing in terms of its orthography, with no intellectual capitals and fourteen emotional long spellings in just 6 lines.

• the first line ' . To mee shee speakes, shee moves mee for her theme ;' (a surround phrase with six long spellings and ending via an emotional semicolon) clearly shows the wrong (visiting) Antipholus' amazement

• the following two short one-line sentences (F #2, 0/3 and #3, 0/2) continue the emotional amazement, though the releases calm down a little by F #4 (0/2 in two lines), as if finally he were managing to rein himself in

Modern Text

9/ Antipholus V.

To me* she* speaks*, she* moves me* for her
theme*:

What, was I married to her in my dream* ?

Or sleep* I now and think* I hear* all this?

What error drives our eyes* and ears* amiss* ?.

Until* I know this sure uncertainty*,
I'll entertain* the [offer'd] fallacy*.

First Folio

9/ Antipholus V.

1 To mee shee speakes, shee moves mee for her
theame; +

What, was I married to her in my dreame?

2 Or sleepe I now$_x$, and thinke I heare all this?

3 What error drives our eies and eares amisse?

4 Untill I know this sure uncertaintie,
Ile entertaine the [free'd] fallacie.

10/ {Luciana}   And may it be that you have quite forgot   3.2.1 - 28

Background: The visiting Antipholus and Dromio have returned to Adrianna's residence, allowing others to believe that they are, in fact, those who live there (the local Antipholus and Dromio). Believing him to be her brother-in-law (i.e. the local Antipholus), Luciana, Adriana's sister, has taken the visiting Antipholus aside, asking him to at least give his supposed wife (Adriana) the appearance of being at one with her, even if he is not (thus the theme of the need for keeping up appearances noted in Adriana's speech, #8 above, is repeated here). One note: the First Folio incorrectly assigns this speech to Julianna, a 'ghost' (i.e. non-existent) character.

Style: part of a two-handed scene

Where: somewhere private in Adriana's home   **To Whom:** the visiting Antipholus, believing him to be the true husband of Adrianna

# of Lines: 28   **Probable Timing: 1.30 minutes**

F shows a wondrous transition from an intellectual (book-worm?) start to an emotional (getting involved despite herself) finish. The combination of many unembellished lines at the beginning of the speech, heavy intellectual colons in the middle, and emotional semicolons at the end, as with Adriana in speech #8 above, suggesting a 'polite' start to a highly volatile theme - only here the inexperienced Luciana cannot maintain the veneer of social correctness all the way to the end.

• since she is addressing the 'wrong' Antipholus (believing it to be her brother-in-law), it could be that all of her (to her) innocent non-embellished advice (especially the opening of F #1, F #3, and F #5 plus the last line of the speech) could be taken by him without guilt as direct encouragement from her for him to woo her:

Modern Text

10/ Luciana

1 And may it be that you have quite forgot
A husbands office? +

Shall, Antipholus,
Even in the spring of °love, thy °love-springs rot?

2 Shall love in [building] grow so [ruinous] ?

3 If you did wed my sister for her wealth,
Then for her wealth's ° sake use her with more kindness* :
Or if you like else°where, do* it by stealth,
Muffle your false love with some show of blindness* :

First Folio

10/ {Luciana}

1 And may it be that you have quite forgot
A husbands office? shall+ Antipholus+
Even in the spring of Love, thy Love-springs rot?

2 Shall love in [buildings] grow so [ruinate?]

3 If you did wed my sister for her wealth,
Then for her wealths-sake use her with more kindnesse:
Or if you like else-where+ doe it by stealth,
Muffle your false love with some shew of blindnesse:

this wooing is done verbally in the speech that follows, #11 below, and perhaps physically here during this speech, which might explain her gradual transition from an intellectual start to a total emotional finish, for . . .

• . . . though the introduction to her scolding (F #1-2) is totally intellectual (3/0, with the opening one and a half lines unembellished), the elaboration of how he should conduct himself, ('with kindnesse' and if necessary love elsewhere by 'stealth'), starts out slightly emotional (0/2 in F #3's first five lines, three of which are unembellished), and then her feelings become more free flowing

• the releases start in the last six lines of F#3 (many on the verbs, in advising him to be 'secret false' 2/7) and the short F #4 referring to her sister Adriana, in his, more probably about Luciana herself), is again purely emotional (0/8), as is the final advice (F #6, 0/3), with the last moment heightened with the only two emotional semicolons in the speech (whether because she believes in the advice, or would rather not have him take the advice, is up to each actress to decide)

• certainly her sincerity is not in doubt, as many of her surround phrases attest

" . Let not my sister read it in your eye : /Be not thy tongue thy owne shames Orator : /Looke sweet, speake faire, become disloyaltie : /Apparell vice like vertues harbenger :"

" : what need she be acquainted ?"

" . Then gentle brother get you in againe ; /Comfort my sister, cheere her, call her [wise] ;"

Let not my sister read it in your eye;
Be not thy tongue thy own* shames △orator:
Look* sweet, speak* fair*, become disloyalty*;
Apparel* vice like virtue's harbinger;
Bear* a fair* presence, though your heart be tainted;
Teach sin* the carriage of a holy △saint;
Be secret-°false: what need she be acquainted?
4 What simple thief* brags of his own* [attaint]?
5 'Tis double wrong, to truant with your bed,
And let her read it in thy looks* at board* . †
6 Shame hath a bastard fame, well managed;
Ill deeds [are] doubled with an evil* word . †
7 Alas,* poor* women, make us [but] believe*
(Being compact of credit) that you love us;
Though others have the arm*, show us the sleeve:
We in your motion turn*, and you may move us.
8 Then, gentle brother, get you in again* ;
Comfort my sister, cheer* her, call her [wife]:
'Tis holy sport to be a little vain*,
When the sweet breath of flattery* conquers strife.

Let not my sister read it in your eye: x
Be not thy tongue thy owne shames Orator:
Looke sweet, speake faire, become disloyaltie: x
Apparell vice like vertues harbenger : x
Beare a faire presence, though your heart be tainted, +
Teach sinne the carriage of a holy Saint,
Be secret false: what need she be acquainted?
4 What simple thiefe brags of his owne [attaine]?
5 'Tis double wrong + to truant with your bed,
And let her read it in thy lookes at boord:
Shame hath a bastard fame, well managed, +
Ill deeds [is] doubled with an evill word:
Alas + poore women, make us [not] beleeve +
(Being compact of credit) that you love us, +
Though others have the arme, shew us the sleeve:
We in your motion turne, and you may move us.
6 Then + gentle brother + get you in againe;
Comfort my sister, cheere her, call her [wise] ; +
'Tis holy sport to be a little vaine,
When the sweet breath of flatterie conquers strife.

11/ Antipholus V.   Sweete Mistris, what your name is else I know not;   3.2.29 - 52

Background: An immediate, and obviously highly smitten, response to Luciana's passionate advice shown in speech #11 immediately above. (As part of the chivalric code/approach to courtly love young men were expected, indeed encouraged, to fall in love at first sight - see Protheus in *Two Gentlemen of Verona*; all four young men in *Love's Labours Lost*; and Romeo).

Style: speech as part of a two-handed scene

Where: somewhere private in Adriana's home   **To Whom:** Luciana

# of Lines: 24   **Probable Timing: 1.15 minutes**

Modern Text

11/ Antipholus V.

1   Sweet* ᐃmistress* - what your name is else I know not,
    Nor by what wonder you do hit of mine -
    Less* in your knowledge and your grace you show not
    [Than] our earth's wonder, more [than] earth divine.

2   Teach me, dear* creature, how to think* and speak* :
    Lay open to my earthy*, gross* conceit,
    Smoth'red in errors, feeble, shallow, weak*,
    The folded* meaning of your word's deceit.†

3   Against my soul's* pure truth, why labor* you,
    To make it wander in an unknown* field?

4   Are you a god?†

5   Would you create me new?

6   Transform* me then, and to your pow'r* I'll yield*.

7   But if that I am I, then well I know
    Your weeping sister is no wife of mine,
    Nor to her bed no homage do I owe:
    Far* more, far* more, to you do I decline.†

8   O*, train* me not, sweet ᐃmermaid*, with thy note,
    To drown* me in thy [sister's] flood* of tears* . †

9   Sing, ᐃsiren, for thyself*, and I will dote;
    Spread o'er the silver waves thy golden hairs*,
    And as a [bed] I'll take [them], and there lie,
    And in that glorious supposition think*
    He gains* by death that hath such means* to die:
    Let ᐃlove, being light, be drowned if she sink* !

First Folio

11/ Antipholus V.

1   Sweete Mistris, what your name is else I know not; ₓ
    Nor by what wonder you do hit of mine: ₓ
    Lesse in your knowledge, and your grace you show not,ₓ
    [Then] our earths wonder, more [then] earth divine.

2   Teach me ⁺ deere creature ⁺ how to thinke and speake:
    Lay open to my earthie ⁺ grosse conceit : ₓ
    Smothred in errors, feeble, shallow, weake,
    The foulded meaning of your words deceit:
    Against my soules pure truth, why labour you,
    To make it wander in an unknowne field?

3   Are you a god? would you create me new?

4   Transforme me then, and to your powre Ile yeeld.

5   But if that I am I, then well I know,ₓ
    Your weeping sister is no wife of mine,
    Nor to her bed no homage doe I owe:
    Farre more, farre more, to you doe I decline:
    Oh ⁺ traine me not ⁺ sweet Mermaide, with thy note,
    To drowne me in thy [sister] floud of teares :
    Sing ⁺ Siren ⁺ for thy selfe, and I will dote: ₓ
    Spread ore the silver waves thy golden haires; ₓ
    And as a [bud] Ile take [thee], and there lie: ₓ
    And in that glorious supposition thinke,ₓ
    He gaines by death, that hath such meanes to die:
    Let Love, being light, be drowned if she sinke. ⁺

The onrush of F's final sentence (#5) is one indication of how much Antipholus' passions have been roused by Luciana's mistaken identity advice (speech #10 above). And if this weren't enough, the many surround phrases underscore the fervency of his feelings (the releases an emotional 3/29 overall). Most modern texts create a much more rational finish by splitting F#5 into three grammatically correct units.

• the first two sentences start very strongly, with F #1 (a declaration of wonder) opening with two surround phrases, heightened by being linked with an emotional semicolon

 " . Sweete Mistris, what your name is else I know not ; /Nor by what
               wonder you do hit of mine : "

and F #2 ('Teach me') also starting with two surround phrases,
 " . Teach me deere creature how to thinke and speake : /Lay open
               to my earthie grosse conceit : "

• and the 'love-struckness' continues with two one line sentences, the first (F#3's 'Are you a god?') heightened by being breath-takingly unembellished, and the second (F #4's 'Transforme me') being much more emotional (0/2 in one line)

• within the onrushed last sentence surround phrases again point to his total abandoning of himself to her
 " . Farre more, farre more, to you doe I decline: /. . . :/Sing Siren for
               thy selfe, and I will dote : /Spread ore the silver waves thy
               golden haires : /And as a [bud] Ile take [thee], and there lie : "

• some of the clustered releases point to moments where his passion breaks through even more, as 'Teach me deere creature how to thinke and speake:'; 'Transforme me then, and to your powre Ile yeeld.'; and then the three line extravaganza 'Farre more, farre more, to you doe I decline: /Oh traine me not sweet Mermaide, with thy note,/To drowne me in thy [sister] floud of teares:'

• yet at times the unembellished lines speak to his sense of wonder 'Are you a god? would you create me new?'; his desire for Luciana to understand he is free to woo her legitimately 'But if that I am I, then well I know/Your weeping sister is no wife of mine,'; and his desire to be with her, asking her to spread her hair so that 'And as a bud Ile take thee and there lie:'

12/ Dromio Visitor   .. she's the Kitchin wench, & al grease,   between 3.2.95 – 146

Background: As is the case with his master (the visiting Antipholus) who is supposedly spoken for by a local woman (Adrianna), the visiting Dromio has discovered, to his horror, that Nell, a very large and greasy kitchen wench, believes Dromio belongs to her. (The wordplay on 'Ell' refers to an archaic English unit of measurement approximating the distance of an arm either from wrist to elbow, or fingertip to shoulder: how this came to be about 45 inches is not known but even if the Dutch value of 27 inches were taken, at 1.75 times either width ['an Ell and three quarters']: Nell seems to be quite a spherical lady indeed).

Style: as part of a two handed scene

Where: unspecified, but probably somewhere private in Adriana's home   **To Whom:** his master, the visiting Antipholus

# of Lines: 36   **Probable Timing:** 1.45 minutes

Modern Text

12/ Dromio Visitor

1 {ψ}. . . she's the △kitchin* wench & all* grease, and I know not what use to put her to* but to make a △lamp* of her and run from her by her own* light.   {ψ}

I

2 warrant, her rags* and the △tallow in them, will burn* a Poland △winter: △if she lives till doomsday*, she'll* burn* a week* longer [than] the whole △world.   {ψ}

3 {Her complexion is} swart like my shoe*, but her face nothing like so clean* kept: for why? she sweats*, a man may go* over*shoes* in the grime of it.   {ψ}

4 {Her name is} Nell {ψ}: but her name [and] three quarters, that's an △ell and three quarters, will not measure her from hip to hip.

5 {ψ}{She is} no longer from head to foot [than]from hip* to hip* : she is spherical*, like a globe; I could find out △countries in her.   {ψ}

6 {Ireland stands} in her buttocks* , I found it out by the bogs* .   {ψ}

7 {Scotland} I found {ψ}by the barrenness* , hard in the palm* of the hand.   {ψ}

8 {France} in her forehead*, arm'd and reverted, making war* against her [hair] .   {ψ}

9 {England}, I look'd for the [chalky] △cliffs*, but I could find no whiteness* in them.

10 But I guess* , it stood in her chin, by the salt rheum* that ran* between* France, and it.   {ψ}

11 {Spain*} I saw {ψ}not; but I felt it hot in her breath*.   {ψ}

First Folio

The speech is composed of eleven different sentence parts, created by omitting (or adding one word from) Antipholus' questions. F's orthography lays out a fascinating, and sometimes unexpected, geographical exploration of a rather horrifying event.

- the opening general description of Nell is passionate (7/7, F #1-2) though at the first mention of her he seems to choke back on words, with both 'Kitchin' and 'al' (referring to the grease on her) both being short spellings

- it's also interesting that F #1 contains three extra breath-thoughts (marked ,x), as if Dromio needs the extra breaths simply to recover or get through the description and the idea of running away

- the description of her 'complexion' is highly emotional (F #3, 0/4), while her name and physical size are described factually (2/0, F #4)

- the reference to her apparently less than salubrious body parts, item by item, is highly emotional (F #5-11, 3/17) : though, if you include the capitals starting each new sentence when they refer to a particular country, this section becomes slightly more intellectual (8/17 instead)

- the appalling state of her nose (F #12), and the avoidance of looking at her private parts (F #13), moves him back to a purely intellectual analysis (10/4) - distancing himself from the horror perhaps?

- while the final nightmare that she 'layd claime' to him and that he suspects her of being a witch that could transform him to a working 'Curtull dog' (one with a docked tail) becomes emotional once more (5/15, F #14-15)

12/ Dromio Visitor

1 {ψ} .. she's the Kitchin wench,x & al grease, and I know not what use to put her too,x but to make a Lampe of her,x and run from her by her owne light.   {ψ}

2 [I]

warrant, her ragss and the Tallow in them, will burne a Poland Winter: If she lives till doomesday, she'l burne a weeke longer [then] the whole World.   {ψ}

3 {Her complexion is} swart like my shoo, but her face nothing like so cleane kept: for why? she sweats+ a man may goe o-ver-shoes in the grime of it.   {ψ}

4 {Her name is} Nell {ψ}: but her name [is] three quarters, that's an Ell and three quarters, will not measure from hip to hip.

5 {ψ}{She is} no longer from head to foot, [then] from hippe to hippe: she is sphericall, like a globe:x I could find out Countries in her.   {ψ}

6 {Ireland stands} in her buttockes, I found it out by the bogges.   {ψ}

7 {Scotland} I found {ψ}by the barrennesse, hard in the palme of the hand.   {ψ}

8 {France} in her forhead, arm'd and reverted, making warre against her [heire] .   {ψ}

9 {England}, I look'd for the [chalkie] Cliffes, but I could find no whitenesse in them.

10 But I guesse, it stood in her chin+ by the salt rheume that ranne betweene France, and it.   {ψ}

11 {Spaine} I saw {ψ}not:x but I felt it hot in her breth.   {ψ}

{ctd. over}

12 {America, the Indies, I found} upon her nose, all ore embellished with Rubies, Carbuncles, Saphires, declining their rich Aspect to the hot breath of Spaine,$_x$ who sent whole Armadoes of Carrects to be ballast at her nose. {ψ}

13 {As to Belgia, the Netherlands,} I did not looke so low.

14 To conclude, this drudge or Diviner layd claime to mee, call'd mee Dromio, swore I was assur'd to her, told me what privie markes I had about mee, as the marke of my shoulder, the Mole in my necke, the great Wart on my left arme, that I$^+$ amaz'd$^+$ ranne from her as a witch.

15 And I thinke, if my brest had not beene made of faith, and my heart of steele, she had transform'd me to a Curtull dog, & made me turne i'th wheele.

• that this last is a complete anathema to him seems to be enhanced by F setting the rhyme as if it were still to be spoken as awkward prose, suggesting that Dromio can hardly bring himself to speak the words - a great contrast to the almost cheerfully defiant verse couplet as set by most modern texts

• the few surround phrases point to what weighs most on his mind: ᵞhey are, not in order, ᵞ . Her name is Nell: ᵞ; plus ᵞ : for why ? she sweats a man may goe over-shooes in the grime of it . ᵞ ᵞ : she is sphericall, like a globe : ᵞ , and the awfulness of her breath ᵞ . Spaine I saw not : but I felt it hot in her breth . ᵞ

---

12 {America, the Indies, I found} upon her nose, all o'er embellish'd* with ^rubies, ^carbuncles, ^sapphires, declining their rich ^aspect to the hot breath of Spain* who sent whole armadoes of ^carrects to be ballast at her nose. {ψ}

13 {As to Belgia, the Netherlands,} I did not look* so low.

14 To conclude, this drudge or ^diviner laid* claim* to me* , call'd me* Dromio, swore I was assur'd to her, told me what privy* marks* I had about me* , as the mark* of my shoulder, the ^mole in my neck* , the great ^wart on my left arm* , that I, amaz'd, ran* from her as a witch.

15 And I think* , if my breast* had not been* made of faith, and my heart of steel* , ^She had transform'd me to a ^curtall* dog, & made me turn* i'th wheel* .

#'s 13 - 14: MISTAKEN IDENTITY'S EFFECT ON THE LOCALS

13/ Curtizan   Now out of doubt Antipholus is mad,   4.3.81 - 96

Background: Despite the local Antipholus' suggestion that he would give an expensive chain to the Curtizan to spite Adrianna, he has, in fact, only exchanged it for one of the Curtizan's rings. Indeed, he took her ring well in advance giving her the chain, which, of course, he's never taken possession of as it was given in all good faith to his just-landed identical twin. In the mean time, the Curtizan, believing as everyone else does that the visiting Antipholus is the local Antipholus, has demanded her ring back, which, of course, he has refused since he was not the one who took it. Having just been rejected on every ground and in no uncertain terms by the visiting duo of Antipholus and Dromio, this is her only solo, and naturally bemused, speech in the play.

Style: solo

Where: unspecified, but presumably some public space/street   **To Whom:** direct address to the audience

# of Lines: 16   **Probable Timing: 0.50 minutes**

Modern Text

13/ Curtizan

1 Now out of doubt Antipholus is mad,
   Else would he never so demean* himself* . †

2 A △ring he hath of mine worth forty*△ducats* ,
   And for the same he promis'd me a △chain*:
   Both one and other he denies me now . †

3 The reason that I gather he is mad,
   Besides this present instance of his rage,
   Is a mad tale he told to day at dinner,
   Of his own* doors* being shut against his entrance.

4 Belike his wife, acquainted with his fits,
   On purpose shut the doors* against his way. †

5 My way is now to hie home to his house,
   And tell his wife that, being △lunatic* ,
   He rush'd into my house, and took* perforce
   My △ring away.

6   This course I fittest choose,
   For forty*△ducats* is too much to lose* .

In a money-mad play, and with such a large sum at stake for the Curtizan ('fortie Duckets'), it's surprising so little emotional release is made throughout the speech and is almost matched intellectually (7/9 in sixteen lines). Thus, it would seem she is genuinely disturbed by the potential loss, and, in trying to work out what to do, she has little energy to waste.

• thus, it is the occasional clusters of release that underscore her amazement that he would 'never so demean himselfe'; plus 'Of his owne doores being shut', and the intellectual balance between 'Ring', 'Duckets' and 'Chaine'

• while the non-embellished lines point to where she is working hard to analyse the situation
"Both one and other he denies me now :/The reason that I gather he is mad,/Besides this present instance of his rage,/Is a mad tale he told to day at dinner,"
"My way is now to hie home to his house,/ and tell his wife,"
"He rush'd into my house,"
plus the final
"This course I fittest choose,"

First Folio

13/ Curtizan

1 Now out of doubt Antipholus is mad,
   Else would he never so demeane himselfe,
   A Ring he hath of mine worth fortie Duckets,
   And for the same he promis'd me a Chaine, †
   Both one and other he denies me now:
   The reason that I gather he is mad,
   Besides this present instance of his rage,
   Is a mad tale he told to day at dinner,
   Of his owne doores being shut against his entrance.

2 Belike his wife + acquainted with his fits,
   On purpose shut the doores against his way:
   My way is now to hie home to his house,
   And tell his wife,ₓ that + being Lunaticke,
   He rush'd into my house, and tooke perforce
   My Ring away.

3   This course I fittest choose,
   For fortie Duckets is too much to loose.

14/ Abbesse **And thereof came it, that the man was mad.** between 5.1.68 - 112

Background: In a further complex series of events the visiting duo have taken refuge in the local Priory, where, despite demands from Adriana and sympathetic supporters, including Luciana, the Abbesse refuses to return the men, claiming she will cure them herself, first chastising Adrianna for the very behaviour that the Abbesse herself had just suggested should be used for dealing with the local Antipholus' philandering and non-supportive ways - continuous nagging, at all times, everywhere possible.

Style: public address, directed through one person to all who care to hear
Where: public space outside the Abbey **To Whom:** Adriana, Luciana, the Curtizan, Angelo, the man to whom he owes money, and an unspecified number of 'others'
# of Lines: 31 **Probable Timing: 1.30 minutes**

Modern Text

14/ Abbesse

1   And thereof came it that the man was mad.

2   The venom* clamors of a jealous woman,
    Poisons more deadly [than] a mad dogs* tooth.

3   It seems* his sleeps* were hind'red by thy railing,
    And thereof comes it that his head is light.

4   Thou say'st his meat* was sauc'd* with thy upbraidings:
    Unquiet meals* make ill digestions,
    Thereof the raging fire of fever* bred,
    And what's a ^fever* but a fit of madness*?

5   Thou say'st his sports were hind'red by thy brawls* : ◊

6   Sweet recreation barr'd, what doth ensue
    But moody* and dull melancholy*,
    Kinsman to grim and comfortless* despair*, ◊
    And at her heels* a huge infectious troop*
    Of pale distemperatures, and foes to life?

7   In food, in sport, and life-preserving rest
    To be disturb'd, would mad or man or beast:
    The consequence is then, thy jealous fits
    Hath scar'd thy husband from the use of wits.

8   {ψ};. . . he took* this place for sanctuary,
    And it shall privilege* him from your hands
    Till I have brought him to his wits again* ,
    Or lose* my labor* in assaying it.

9   Be patient, for I will not let him stir*
    'Till I have us'd the approved* means* I have,
    With wholesome* syrups*, drugs*, and holy prayers,
    To make of him a formal* man again* :
    It is a branch and parcel* of mine oath,
    A charitable duty*, of my order,
    Therefore depart, and leave him here* with me.

10 Be quiet and depart, thou shalt not have him.

First Folio

14/ Abbesse

1   And thereof came it, that the man was mad.

2   The venome clamors of a jealous woman,
    Poisons more deadly [then] a mad dogges tooth.

3   It seemes his sleepes were hindred by thy railing,
    And thereof comes it that his head is light.

4   Thou saist his meate was sawc'd with thy upbraidings; [+]
    Unquiet meales make ill digestions,
    Thereof the raging fire of feaver bred,
    And what's a Feaver, but a fit of madnesse?

5   Thou sayest his sports were hindred by thy bralles.

6   Sweet recreation barr'd, what doth ensue
    But moodie and dull melancholly,
    Kinsman to grim and comfortlesse dispaire.

7   And at her heeles a huge infectious troope
    Of pale distemperatures, and foes to life?

8   In food, in sport, and life-preserving rest
    To be disturb'd, would mad or man, [+] or beast:
    The consequence is then, thy jealous fits
    Hath scar'd thy husband from the use of wits.

9   {ψ};. . . he tooke this place for sanctuary,
    And it shall priviledge him from your hands,[x]
    Till I have brought him to his wits againe,
    Or loose my labour in assaying it.

10 Be patient, for I will not let him stirre,[x]
    Till I have us'd the approved meanes I have,
    With wholsome sirrups, drugges, and holy prayers [+]
    To make of him a formall man againe:
    It is a branch and parcell of mine oath,
    A charitable dutie of my order,
    Therefore depart, and leave him heere with me.

11 Be quiet and depart, thou shalt not have him.

In a highly emotional speech (1/29 in thirty-one lines overall), the non-embellished lines show where her mind makes the key discoveries, and the four extra breath-thoughts (marked , x) all add essential heightened details while suggesting extra excitement or purpose.

• interestingly, the speech is framed by opening and closing short sentences, suggesting her opening realisation cuts straight to the point, triggering the rest of the discoveries and explanation, till a final irrevocable decision and order is made

• the opening short sentence is the biggest realisation of all, heightened by being non-embellished and the extra breath thought
    "And thereof came it, x that the man was mad."
while the final short sentence, similarly unembellished, finishes the affair, at least as far as she is concerned

• the second extra breath-thought 'And what's a Feaver, x but a fit of madnesse?' adds depth to her discoveries, while the third and fourth 'And it shall priviledge him from your hands,/Till I have brought him to his wits againe,/Till I have us'd the approved meanes I have,' underline her determination to save him

• in a sea of emotion, the calm of the key unembellished phrases heightens the premise from which all her future actions will stem, yet they don't quite follow a logical order: in the following they are set out as they might be if she were logical (the numbers in brackets show the order in the speech in which they occur): the fact that this logical sequence is not what occurs in the speech might suggest the lady is more scatty than at first appears: thus, not in order, the important phrases seem to be
    ". . In food, in sport, and life-preserving rest/To be disturb'd,
        would mad or man, or beast: /The consequence is then, thy
        jealous fits/Hath scar'd thy husband from the use of wits. " (5)
    "And thereof came it, that the man was mad." (1)
    "And thereof comes it, that his head is light." (2)
    "Sweet recreation barr'd" (3)
leading to
    ". . . of pale distemperatures, and foes to life?' (4)
    "Be quiet and depart, thou shalt not have him." (6)

SPEECHES IN ORDER	TIME	PAGE
TWO GENTLEMEN OF VERONA		
#'s 1 - 3: Young Men In/About Love & the Strange Things They Do		
1/ **Valentine** I Protheus, but that life is alter'd now,	0.50	48
2/ **Protheus** I will. / Even as one heate, another heate expels,	1.10	49
3/ **Protheus** To leave my Julia; shall I be forsworne?	2.00	50
# 4: Interference Of Older Men		
4/ **Duke** Why Phaeton (for thou art Merops sonne)	0.55	52
#'s 5 - 9: Young Women In and About Love		
5/ **Julia** Nay, would I were so angred with the same :	1.15	53
6/ **Julia** Oh, know'st ÿ not, his looks are my soules food?	1.10	54
7/ **Julia** How many women would doe such a message?	0.55	55
8/ **Julia** A vertuous gentlewoman, milde, and beautifull.	1.15	56
9/ **Silvia** Oh Eglamoure, thou art a Gentleman :	1.15	57
#'s 10 - 11: A Servant's Dilemmas		
10/ **Launce** Nay, 'twill bee this howre ere I have done weeping:	1.35	58
11/ **Launce** When a mans servant shall play the Curre with him	1.55	60

SPEECHES BY GENDER	Speech #(s)
SPEECHES FOR WOMEN (5)	
Julia **Traditional & Today:** young woman	#5, #6, #7, #8
Silvia **Traditional & Today:** young woman	#9
SPEECHES FOR EITHER GENDER (3)	
Launce **Traditional:** clown, male, any age **Today:** clown, any gender, any age	#10, #11
Duke **Traditional:** older male **Today:** any gender with adult daughter	#4
SPEECHES FOR MEN (3)	
Valentine **Traditional & Today:** young romantic male	#1
Protheus **Traditional & Today:** young romantic male	#2, #3

TWO GENTLEMEN OF VERONA

#'s 1 - 3: Young Men In and About Love and the Strange Things They Do

1/ Valentine   **I Protheus, but that life is alter'd now,**   2.4.128 - 142

Background: Valentine, a young man of Verona, has embarked on the 'grand tour', as all young men of his generation should; in his case to Milan. Originally, his friend Protheus, in love with Julia, did not join him, and Valentine roundly mocked Protheus for being in love. At his father's insistence, Protheus has joined Valentine in Milan, where Valentine is now singing a completely different tune, for he is now totally (and mutually) in love, with Silvia, the Duke of Milan's daughter.

Style: speech as part of a two handed conversation

Where: somewhere in the Duke of Milan's palace   **To Whom:** his friend Protheus

# of Lines: 15   **Probable Timing: 0.50 minutes**

Modern Text

1/ Valentine

1   Ay*, Protheus, but that life is alter'd now . †

2   I have done penance* for contemning Love,
    Whose high imperious thoughts have punish'd me
    With bitter fasts, with penitential* groans*,
    With nightly tears*, and daily heart*-sore sighs* ,
    For in revenge of my contempt of love,
    Love hath chas'd sleep* from my enthralled eyes,
    And made them watchers of mine own* heart's sorrow.

3   O gentle Protheus, Love's a mighty ⁴lord,
    And hath so humbled me, as I confess *
    There is no woe to his correction,
    Nor to his ᴬservice, no such joy on earth :
    Now no discourse, except it be of love;
    Now can I break* my fast, dine, sup, and sleep* ,
    Upon the very naked name of ⁴love.

First Folio

1/ Valentine

1   I † Protheus, but that life is alter'd now,
    I have done penance for contemning Love,
    Whose high emperious thoughts have punish'd me
    With bitter fasts, with penitentiall grones,
    With nightly teares, and daily hart-sore sighes,
    For in revenge of my contempt of love,
    Love hath chas'd sleepe from my enthralled eyes,
    And made them watchers of mine owne hearts sorrow.

2   O gentle Protheus, Love's a mighty Lord,
    And hath so humbled me, as I confesse
    There is no woe to his correction,
    Nor to his Service, no such joy on earth :
    Now, ₓ no discourse, except it be of love : ˣ
    Now can I breake my fast, dine, sup, and sleepe,
    Upon the very naked name of Love.

Rather than the controlled, almost reflective, short sentence opening of most modern texts, F suggests, via the onrushed fast-link comma at the end of F #1's first line, that the love-struck Valentine is quite disturbed by his new found love experiences, both the painful and the occasional nourishing delight.

• the non-embellished phrases clearly show how and why
  "For in revenge of my contempt of love,"
  "There is no woe to his correction,"
  while the last is doubly weighted by being the only surround line in the speech
  ": Now, no discourse, except it be of love : "

• not surprisingly, Valentine's F #1 confession of 'fasts', 'grones', 'teares' and 'sighes' is highly emotional (2/6)

• however, the definition of humbling 'Love' as a 'mighty Lord' is strongly intellectual (4/1 in the first four lines of F #2, to the first colon)

• though the final summary as to how he can now eat and sleep 'Upon the very naked name of Love' becomes somewhat emotional once more (1/2, the last two lines of F #2)

2/ Protheus   I will. / Even as one heate, another heate expels,   2.4.191 - 214

Background: Protheus has just met the Duke of Milan's daughter Silvia, and, despite Valentine's confession of his and Silvia's mutual love (speech #1 above) and though, before leaving Verona, Protheus and Julia became betrothed, Protheus has fallen head over heels for Silvia too!

Style: solo

Where: somewhere in the Duke of Milan's palace   **To Whom:** direct audience address

# of Lines: 23   **Probable Timing: 1.10 minutes**

Modern Text

2/ Protheus

1 I will.

2 Even as one heat* another heat* expels,
   Or as one nail* by strength drives out another ◊,
   So the remembrance of my former △love
   Is by a newer object quite forgotten . †

4 [Is it] mine [eye], or Valentines praise ,
   Her true perfection, or my false transgression ,
   That makes me reasonless* , to reason thus?

5 She* is faire* , and so is Julia that I love
   (That I did love, for now my love is thaw'd,
   Which like a waxen △image 'gainst a fire
   Bears* no impression of the thing it was.)

6 [Methinks*] my zeal* to Valentine is cold,
   And that I love him not as I was wont :
   O, but I love his △lady too-°too much,
   And that's the reason I love him so little.

7 How shall I dote* on her with more advice,
   That thus without advice begin to love her?

8 'Tis but her picture I have yet beheld,
   And that hath dazzled* my [reason's] light ;
   But when I look* on her perfections,
   There is no reason but I shall be blind* .

9 If I can check* my erring love, I will;
   If not, to compass* her I'll use my skill.

First Folio

2/ Protheus

1 I will.

2 Even as one heate,[x] another heate expels,
   Or as one naile, by strength drives out another .

3 So the remembrance of my former Love
   Is by a newer object quite forgotten,
   [It is] mine [ ], or Valentines praise?[x]
   Her true perfection, or my false transgression?[x]
   That makes me reasonlesse, to reason thus?

4 Shee is faire : [x] and so is Julia that I love,[x]
   (That I did love, for now my love is thaw'd,
   Which like a waxen Image 'gainst a fire
   Beares no impression of the thing it was.)

5 [Me thinks] my zeale to Valentine is cold,
   And that I love him not as I was wont :
   O, but I love his Lady too-too much,
   And that's the reason I love him little.

6 How shall I doate on her with more advice,
   That thus without advice begin to love her?

7 'Tis but her picture I have yet beheld,
   And that hath dazel'd my [reasons] light : [x]
   But when I looke on her perfections,
   There is no reason ,[x] but I shall be blinde.

8 If I can checke my erring love, I will, [+]
   If not, to compasse her Ile use my skill.

While the speech is somewhat emotional overall (6/14), the fact that there are only fourteen emotional releases in twenty-four lines, together with the presence of at least eight non-embellished lines, suggests that Protheus is working very hard to stay calm, trying to make sense of what has just occurred. **However, F's opening sentence structure (much altered by most modern texts) shows that, at times, rationality is difficult to come by.**

• the ungrammatical period establishing F #2 as a separate sentence underscores the enormity of Protheus' realisation that Silvia has driven all thoughts of Julia out of his mind: most modern texts follow the Second Folio and set the 'correct' punctuation (colon or comma), thus removing the emotional need to pause and regroup before continuing: similarly F's again ungrammatical setting (in the eyes of most modern texts) of a fast-link comma at the end of F #3's line two shows just how much Protheus' thoughts are now racing ahead unchecked: once more, most modern texts set the logically correct punctuation (here a period), thus holding him to a much more rational process than originally set

• the one highly emotional surround phrase ' Shee is faire : ' points to the impact the brief meeting with Silvia has had upon him

• it's the calm of the unembellished lines that show how seriously Protheus is trying to come to terms with all the implications of his new 'at-first-sight' love 'Even as one heate . . . /by strength drives out another . ' , so Julia 'Is by a newer object quite forgotten , . . /[Is it] mine . . . /Her true perfection, or my false transgression ?/That makes me . . . , to reason thus?'
then comes the realisation about both Julia 'That I did love, for now my love is thaw'd,' and his former friend Valentine 'And that I love him not as I was wont', because now they both will be rivals for Silvia 'And that's the reason I love him so little.'
finishing with the understanding he is both alone and foolishly in love (having met Silvia for about thirty seconds) 'That thus without advice begin to love her? /'Tis but her picture I have yet beheld,/And that hath dazel'd my reasons light :'

3/ Protheus   **To leave my Julia ; shall I be forsworne ?**   2.6.1 - 43

Background: Despite his attempts at self-control at the end of the previous speech, Protheus cannot stop himself, even though it means going against his loyalty as a friend and his oath as a lover. Here, the first part of the speech (F #1-11), full of wonderful chop logic, deals intellectually with how to resolve the three-fold dilemma. The second part (F #12 on) deals with what rather treacherous action he must take once he has persuaded himself that morally he is allowed do what he wants to do.

Style: solo

Where: somewhere in the Duke of Milan's palace   **To Whom:** direct audience address

                                         # of Lines: 43   **Probable Timing: 2.00 minutes**

Modern Text

3/ Protheus

1 To leave my Julia - shall I be forsworn* ?

2 To love fair* Silvia - shall I be forsworn* ?

3 To wrong my friend, I shall be much forsworn* .

4 And ev'n that ^pow'r* which gave me first my oath
   Provokes me to this three°fold perjury*.

5 Love bad me* swear* , and Love bids me for°swear* . †

6 O sweet-suggesting Love, if thou hast sinn'd*,
   Teach me, thy tempted subject*, to excuse it.

7 At first I did adore a twinkling ^star* ,
   But now I worship a celestial* ^sun* . †

8 Un°heedful* vows* may heedfully be broken,
   And he wants wit that wants resolved will
   To learn* his wit t'exchange the bad for better* . †

9 Fie, fie, unreverend tongue, to call her bad,
   Whose sovereignty so oft thou hast preferr'd*,
   With twenty thousand soul* -confirming oaths* .

10 I cannot leave to love, and yet I do* :
   But there I leave to love where I should love.

11 Julia I lose* , and Valentine I lose* :
   If I keep* them, I needs must lose* my self* ;
   If I lose* them, thus find* I by their loss -
   For Valentine, my self* ; for Julia, Silvia.

12 I to my self* am dearer* [then] a friend,
   For Love is still most precious in itself*
   And Silvia (witness* heaven that made her fair*)
   Shows* Julia but a swarthy Ethiope.

First Folio

3/ Protheus

1 To leave my Julia ; x shall I be forsworne?

2 To love faire Silvia ; x shall I be forsworne?

3 To wrong my friend, I shall be much forsworne.

4 And ev'n that Powre which gave me first my oath
   Provokes me to this three-fold perjure.

5 Love bad mee sweare, and Love bids me for-sweare;
   O sweet-suggesting Love, if thou hast sin'd,
   Teach me x (thy tempted subject) x to excuse it.

6 At first I did adore a twinkling Starre,
   But now I worship a celestiall Sunne :
   Un-heedfull vowes may heedfully be broken,
   And he wants wit, x that wants resolved will, x
   To learne his wit, x t'exchange the bad for better ;
   Fie, fie, unreverend tongue, to call her bad,
   Whose soveraignty so oft thou hast preferd, x
   With twenty thousand soule-confirming oathes.

7 I cannot leave to love ; x and yet I doe :
   But there I leave to love, x where I should love.

8 Julia I loose, and Valentine I loose, +
   If I keepe them, I needs must loose my selfe : x
   If I loose them, thus finde I by their losse,
   For Valentine, my selfe : for Julia, Silvia.

9 I to my selfe am deerer [then] a friend,
   For Love is still most precious in itselfe,
   And Silvia (witnesse heaven that made her faire
   Shewes Julia but a swarthy Ethiope.

F's sentence structure and orthography show how much the speech starts out in full emotional and relatively uncontrolled cry, yet ends up in relative control.

- the emotional dilemma of the opening is amazingly highlighted, starting with three short sentences (F #1-3), each heightened by ending with a long-spelled word, and the first two (F #1-2) even more heightened by being split by emotional semicolons, only set in F

- the surround phrases here and later all point to the same overwhelming problem (these opening surround phrases encompassing the only emotional semicolons in the speech)
  ' . To leave my Julia ; ' plus ' . To love faire Silvia ; ' but that it's not his fault since ' . Love bad mee sweare, and Love bids me for-sweare; '
  which leads to the clear understanding of
  ' . I cannot leave to love ; and yet I doe : /But there I leave to love, where I should love. '
  and that the final prize will be so worthwhile, to substitute ' for Julia, Silvia. ' it justifies his proposed inevitable act of treachery towards Valentine, whom he will place in disfavour with Silvia's father, the Duke, ' : Who (all inrag'd) will banish Valentine : '

- the extra breath-thoughts (marked , x), especially in F #6 and the last three lines of the speech, clearly show Protheus' mind working so much harder than his modern text counterpart in attempting to find any tiny logical justification for his proposed actions

- the biggest release, emotional more than intellectual, comes in F #8 (5 via the proper names/9) as he realises what he will lose if he doesn't act, as well as what he will gain if he does, and this passion continues into F #9's incredibly selfish chop-logic justification of self above all else (4/6)

- then comes the only true intellectual passage in the speech as Protheus finally decides, in theory at least, to act (6/2, F #10-12)

- and, once the decision is reached, so F's text moves much more quickly (especially in F #14-15) as the now resolved questioning of ' should I?' turns to premeditated action: for once at least six pieces of added modern text punctuation (marked + in the F text) are removed, the quick, almost gabled, planning speeds along, suggesting a mind almost running away with itself

13
I will forget that Julia is alive,
Rememb'ring that my △love to her is dead; ◇
And Valentine I'll hold an △enemy*,
Aiming* at Silvia as a sweeter friend.

15
I cannot now prove constant to my self*,
Without some treachery us'd to Valentine.

16
This night he meaneth with a △corded◇ △ladder
To climb◇ celestial* Silvia's chamber-window,
Myself* in counsel* his competitor.

17
Now presently I'll give her father notice
Of their disguising and pretended flight,
Who, all enrag'd*, will banish Valentine;
For Thurio, he intends, shall wed his daughter;
But, Valentine being gone*, I'll quickly* cross*
By some sly* trick* blunt Thurio's dull proceeding.

18
Love, lend me wings, to make my purpose swift,
As thou hast lent me wit to plot this drift.

10
I will forget that Julia is alive,
Remembring that my Love to her is dead.
And Valentine Ile hold an Enemie,
Ayming at Silvia as a sweeter friend.

11

12
I cannot now prove constant to my selfe,
Without some treachery us'd to Valentine.

13
This night he meaneth with a Corded-ladder
To climbe celestiall Silvia's chamber window,
My selfe in counsaile his competitor.

14
Now presently Ile give her father notice
Of their disguising and pretended flight : $_x$
Who $_x$ (all inrag'd) $_x$ will banish Valentine : $_x$
For Thurio $^+$ he intends $^+$ shall wed his daughter, $^+$
But $^+$ Valentine being gon, Ile quickly crosse
By some slie tricke $_x$ blunt Thurio's dull proceeding.

15
Love $^+$ lend me wings, to make my purpose swift $^+$
As thou hast lent me wit, $_x$ to plot this drift.

• yet, despite the emotion the huge moral struggle causes, at key times the unembellished lines are the ones where much of his deeper concerns are faced, and the calm (whether enforced or no) gives some dignity and integrity to a character who often is regarded as a blackguard instead of a young man who, when initially facing a dreadful love quadrangle (of two friends and two women), suggested 'If I can checke my erring love I will'; and now finding that he can't, he goes on to do what he then realised he might have to 'If not, to compasse her Ile use my skill.'

a/ thus in attempting to absolve himself for 'Love's' interference, comes both blame

'Provokes me to this three-fold perjurie.' and plea ' . . . if thou hast sin'd,
/ Teach me (thy tempted subject) to excuse it.'

b/ then comes the 'belief' that above all he must be rational
"And he wants wit, that wants resolved will, . . . t'exchange the bad for better;/ Fie, fie, unreverend tongue, to call her bad,/Whose soveraignty so oft thou hast preferd."

c/ followed by the unavoidable realisation
"I cannot leave to love ; . . ./But there I leave to love, where I should love."

d/ followed first by the plotting
"Now presently Ile give her father notice/Of their disguising and pretended flight."

e/ and then, returning to his excuse and ally 'Love', comes the final plea
"Love lend me wings, to make my purpose swift/As thou hast lent me wit, to plot this drift."

• and it's fascinating to note that at the climax of the plot (F #14) a couple of short spellings ('Valentine being gon' and 'some slie tricke') might suggest the embarrassed twinges of a troubled conscience

4: INTERFERENCE OF OLDER MEN

4/ Duke   Why Phaeton (for thou art Merops sonne)   3.1.153 - 169

Background: Just as Protheus planned, the Duke has uncovered Valentine's plan for eloping with Silvia, including the physical elements of both a letter and a rope ladder. The opening deals with Valentine over-extending himself by reaching for a Duke's daughter - the classical reference to Phaeton is to the young man who, through over-weening ambition and envy, attempted to drive Phoebus' (the sun-God's) chariot alone, and was destroyed by Jupiter once the horses proved unmanageable and threatened both heaven and earth with fiery destruction.

Style: a speech as a two-handed scene

Where: unspecified, somewhere in the Duke's palace   **To Whom:** Valentine

# of Lines: 17   **Probable Timing:** 0.55 minutes

Modern Text

4/ Duke

1
Why, Phaeton (for thou art Merop's son*)
Wilt thou aspire to guide the heavenly △car,
And with thy daring folly burn* the world?

2
Wilt thou reach stars, because they shine on thee?

3
Go,* base △intruder, over °weening △slave,
Bestow thy fawning smiles on equal* mates,
And think* my patience (more [than] thy desert)
Is privilege* for thy departure hence.

4
Thank* me for this, more [than] for all the favors
Which (all too ° much) I have bestowed on thee.

5
But if thou linger in my △territories
Longer [than] swiftest expedition
Will give thee time to leave our royal* △court,
By heaven, my wrath shall far* exceed the love
I ever bore my daughter, or thyself* .

6
Be gone, I will not hear* thy vain* excuse,
But as thou lov'st thy life, make speed from hence. [1]

First Folio

4/ Duke

1
Why⁺ Phaeton (for thou art Merops sonne)
Wilt thou aspire to guide the heavenly Car?ₓ
And with thy daring folly burne the world?

2
Wilt thou reach stars, because they shine on thee?

3
Goe ⁺ base Intruder, over-weening Slave,
Bestow thy fawning smiles on equall mates,
And thinke my patience,ₓ (more [then] thy desert)
Is priviledge for thy departure hence.

4
Thanke me for this, more [then] for all the favors
Which (all too-much) I have bestowed on thee.

5
But if thou linger in my Territories
Longer [then], swiftest expedition
Will give thee time to leave our royall Court,
By heaven, my wrath shall farre exceed the love
I ever bore my daughter, or thy selfe.

6
Be gone, I will not heare thy vaine excuse,
But as thou lov'st thy life, make speed from hence.

Though the sentence structures match, F's orthography reveals an interesting pattern of attempted self-control with occasional emotional flashes breaking through.

• at first, the Duke seems to display self control, with the opening intellectually demeaning classical comparison (F #1, 3/1), followed by the acidly precise unembellished monosyllabic short sentence enquiry 'Wilt thou reach stars, because they shine on thee?'

• then passion begins to break through, with F #3's first line dismissal (2/1 in just the one line), leading to an emotional release from thereon in (2/9 in the remaining twelve lines)

• that the Duke is still attempting to maintain control can be seen in that from now on usually only one word per line shows any release: thus, the two small clusters in the middle of F #5, 'our royall Court' and the opening of F #6 'Be gone, I will not heare thy vaine excuse' are worth exploring for extra loss of control

• that control is difficult to maintain can be seen in that after F #2 there are only three more unembellished lines, about the favors 'Which (all too-much) I have bestowed on thee.', and the need for Valentine to leave the Court as quickly as he can , with the warning not to linger 'Longer than swiftest expedition/Will give thee time to leave . . . But as thou lovs't thy life, make speed from hence.'

---

[1] F2/most modern texts place the Duke's exit here

#'s 5 - 9: YOUNG WOMEN IN AND ABOUT LOVE

5/ Julia   **Nay, would I were so angred with the same :**   1.2.101 - 126

Background: Probably because she didn't want to satisfy the curiosity of her servant/companion Lucetta, Julia has ripped up unread a letter from her chosen sweetheart Protheus. Now Lucetta has left, Julia desperately wants to read what Protheus has written – the complicating factor is that the wind is blowing quite strongly. One note: the first line refers to the just ripped-up letter.

Style: solo

Where: somewhere outdoors, presumably in the garden of Julia's home   **To Whom:** herself, the ripped up letter, and the audience

# of Lines: 26   **Probable Timing: 1.15 minutes**

Modern Text

5/ Julia

1   Nay, would I were so ang'red with the same . †
2   O* hateful* hands, to tear* such loving words ! †
3   Injurious ^wasps* , to feed* on such sweet honey*,
    And kill the ^bees that yield* it, with your stings . †
4   I'll kiss* each several* paper, for amends . †
5   Look , here is writ "kind* Julia" . †
6   Unkind* Julia ,
    As in revenge of thy ingratitude,
    I throw thy name against the bruising* ° stones,
    Trampling contemptuously on thy disdain* .
7   And here is writ, ^"love wounded Protheus" .
8   Poor* wounded name : my bosom* as a bed
    Shall lodge thee till thy wound be throughly heal'd ;
    And thus I search it with a sovereign* kiss* .
9   But twice, or thrice, was "Protheus" written down* :
    Be calm* , good wind* , blow not a word away,
    Till I have found each letter in the ^letter,
    Except mine own name ; ^that, some whirl°wind* bear*
    Unto a ragged, fearful*, hanging ^rock*,
    And throw it thence into the raging ^sea.
10 Lo* , here in one line is his name twice writ ,
    "Poor* forlorn* Protheus, passionate Protheus :
    To the sweet Julia" - that I'll tear* away -
    And yet I will not, sith so prettily
    He couples it to his complaining ^names . †

First Folio

5/ Julia

1   Nay, would I were so angred with the same :
    Oh hatefull hands, to teare such loving words ;
    Injurious Waspes, to feede on such sweet hony,
    And kill the Bees that yeelde it, with your stings ;
    Ile kisse each severall paper, for amends :
    Looke, here is writ, x kinde Julia : unkinde Julia ,
    As in revenge of thy ingratitude,
    I throw thy name against the bruzing-stones,
    Trampling contemptuously on thy disdaine .
2   And here is writ, *Love wounded Protheus* .
3   Poore wounded name : my bosome, x as a bed, x
    Shall lodge thee till thy wound be throughly heal'd ;
    And thus I search it with a soveraigne kisse.
4   But twice, or thrice, was *Protheus* written downe :
    Be calme x (good winde) x blow not a word away,
    Till I have found each letter, x in the Letter,
    Except mine own name: x That, some whirle-winde beare
    Unto a ragged, fearefull, hanging Rocke,
    And throw it thence into the raging Sea.
5   Loe, here in one line is his name twice writ : x
    Poore forlorne Protheus, passionate Protheus :
    To the sweet Julia: x that ile teare away : x
    And yet I will not, sith so prettily
    He couples it, x to his complaining Names ;

The opening onrush (F#1 being split into six by most modern texts) plus the enormous number of surround phrases, thirteen in all, five of which involve the emotional semicolon, are each testimony to the volcanic emotional underpinnings of the speech.

• it's not surprising that overall the releases are far more emotional than intellectual (14/29), though, interestingly, some mental recognition does come into play by the speech's end (5/16 in the thirteen lines of F #13, prior to the really intensive search for all the pieces of the ripped up letter; 9/13 in the thirteen lines of all that occurs thereafter)

• with so much opening emotion, it's not surprising that there are occasional wonderful vocally released clusters, such as
"Oh hatefull hands, to teare such loving words ; /Injurious Waspes, to feede on such sweet hony,"
and, once exploring the ripped up letter
"Looke, here is writ, kinde Julia : unkinde Julia , " therefore
"That, some whirle-winde beare/Unto a ragged, fearefull, hanging Rocke,/ And throw it thence into the raging Sea."

• as noted above, the surround phrases clearly illuminate the different tensions she is undergoing, formed by both logical colons
". Nay, would I were so angred with the same :/Oh hatefull hands, to teare such loving words ; "
" : Ile kisse each severall paper, for amends :/Looke, here is writ, kinde Julia : "
". But twice, or thrice, was *Protheus* written downe : "
"Loe, here in one line is his name twice writ : /*Poore forlorne Protheus, passionate Protheus : To the sweet Julia* : that ile teare away : "
and by, in this case, the more evocatively sensual semicolons
". Poore wounded name : my bosome, as a bed, /Shall lodge thee till thy wound be throughly heal'd ; /And thus I search it with a soveraigne kisse. "

{ctd. over}

11 Thus will I fold them one upon another ;
   Now kiss*, embrace, contend, do* what you will.

"He couples it, to his complaining Names ; /Thus will I fold
them, one upon another ; /Now kisse, embrace, contend,
doe what you will ."

6/ Julia   Oh, know'st ÿ not, his looks are my soules food?   between 2.7.15 - 38

Background: Now that Protheus is in Milan, Julia misses him dreadfully and, determined to find a way to join him there, turns to Lucetta for advice.

Style: a speech as part of a two-handed scene

Where: unspecified, somewhere in or around Julia's home   **To Whom:** Lucetta

# of Lines: 21   **Probable Timing: 1.10 minutes**

Modern Text

6/ Julia
1 O*, know'st [thou] not his looks are my soul's* food?

2 Pity* the dearth that I have pined in,
   By longing for that food so long a time.

3 Didst thou but know the inly touch of △love,
   Thou wouldst as soon* go* kindle fire with snow
   As seek* to quench the fire of △love with words.

4 The more thou dam'st it up, the more it burns* :
   The △current that with gentle murmur* glides,
   Thou know'st, being stopp'd△, impatiently doth rage ;
   But when his fair* course is not hindered,
   He makes sweet music* with th'enamell'd△ stones,
   Giving a gentle kiss* to every sedge
   He over*taketh in his pilgrimage ;◇
   And so by many winding nooks* he strays*
   With willing sport to the wild* △ocean.

5 Then let me go*, and hinder not my course :
   I'll be as patient as a gentle stream*,
   And make a pastime of each weary step,
   Till the last step have brought me to my △love,
   And there I'll rest, as after much turmoil*
   A blessed soul* doth in Elysium .

First Folio

6/ Julia
1 Oh, know'st [ÿ] not,ₓ his looks are my soules food?

2 Pitty the dearth that I have pined in,
   By longing for that food so long a time.

3 Didst thou but know the inly touch of Love,
   Thou wouldst as soone goe kindle fire with snow
   As seeke to quench the fire of Love with words.
   ▩▩▩▩▩▩▩▩

4 The more thou dam'st it up, the more it burnes :
   The Current that with gentle murmure glides⁺
   ₓ(Thou know'st)ₓ being stop'd, impatiently doth rage : ₓ
   But when his faire course is not hindered,
   He makes sweet musicke with th'enameld stones,
   Giving a gentle kisse to every sedge
   He over-taketh in his pilgrimage .

5 And so by many winding nookes he straies
   With willing sport to the wilde Ocean.

6 Then let me goe, and hinder not my course :
   Ile be as patient as a gentle streame,
   And make a pastime of each weary step,
   Till the last step have brought me to my Love,
   And there Ile rest, as after much turmoile
   A blessed soule doth in Elizium.

For a speech with such burning images of love, it's surprising how little release there is (9/12 in twenty-one lines overall). Thus, the small clues (the short opening sentence, the sudden releases of F #3, the two surround phrases and the ungrammatical division between F #4-5) should be fully explored for what they have to offer.

• the opening monosyllabic short sentence really says all that need be said, especially with the added dimension of the extra breath-thought (marked, ₓ) spelling her feelings out even more clearly – and, having admitted to this, the rest of the speech and her subsequent actions are already predetermined

• the surround phrases add more dimension to the depth of her feelings
   " . The more thou dam'st it up, the more it burnes : "
   and the need to act upon them
   " . Then let me goe, and hinder not my course : "

• while the pangs of love are most passionately released in the three lines of F #3 (2/3)

• elsewhere, the occasional non-embellished line (the second of F #2; third and seventh of F #4; the opening of F #5, and the third of F #6) extends the nature image of the peaceful river whose example she'll match in her future actions

• and though at times she is speaking calmly, it seems she needs an ungrammatical break at the end of F #4 before she can finish the image of what will happen once her gentle love meets up with the 'wilde Ocean'

7/ Julia   How many women would doe such a message ?   4.4.90 - 107

Background: Julia has disguised herself as a boy so as to travel unmolested to Milan, where, to her amazement and horror, her beloved and betrothed Protheus is actively wooing Silvia. To get close to him she offers herself as his servant, confident that her disguise as a boy will deceive him into failing to recognise her, as indeed it does. Unconsciously rubbing salt in her wounds, Protheus has ordered her as his new 'boy' to give a ring to Silvia (the giving of the ring being one of the most important parts of the traditional chivalric wooing/betrothal ceremony): to make matters worse, the ring Protheus is planning on giving to Silvia is the very same ring Julia gave Protheus to mark their betrothal when they last saw each other in Verona!

Style: solo

Where: unspecified, somewhere in or near the palace   **To Whom:** direct audience address

# of Lines: 18   **Probable Timing: 0.55 minutes**

Modern Text

7/ Julia

1   How many women would do* such a message ?

2   Alas, poor* Protheus, thou hast entertain'd
     A ᐃfox* to be the ᐃshepherd* of thy ᐃlambs . †
     Alas, poor* fool*, why do* I pity* him
3   That with his very heart despiseth me?

4   Because he loves her, he despiseth me ;
     Because I love him, I must pity* him.

5   This ᐃring I gave him when he parted from me,
     To bind* him to remember my good will ;
     And now am I (unhappy ᐃmessenger)
     To plead for that which I would not obtain*,
     To carry that which I would have refus'd,
     To praise his faith which I would have disprais'd.

6   I am my ᐃmaster's true confirmed ᐃlove;
     But cannot be true servant to my ᐃmaster,
     Unless* I prove false traitor to myself* .

7   Yet will I woo* for him, but yet so coldly
     As, heaven it knows* , I would not have him speed.

First Folio

7/ Julia

1   How many women would doe such a message ?

2   Alas ⁺ poore Protheus, thou hast entertain'd
     A Foxe, ₓ to be the Shepheard of thy Lambs ;
     Alas, poore foole, why doe I pitty him
     That with his very heart despiseth me?

3   Because he loves her, he despiseth me, ⁺
     Because I love him, I must pitty him.

4   This Ring I gave him, ₓ when he parted from me,
     To binde him to remember my good will : ₓ
     And now am I (unhappy Messenger)
     To plead for that, ₓ which I would not obtaine ; ₓ
     To carry that, ₓ which I would have refus'd ; ₓ
     To praise his faith, ₓ which I would have disprais'd.

5   I am my Masters true confirmed Love, ⁺
     But cannot be true servant to my Master,
     Unlesse I prove false traitor to my selfe.

6   Yet will I woe for him, but yet so coldly, ₓ
     As ₓ (heaven it knowes)ₓ I would not have him speed.

The speech is a battle between passion (9/14 overall) and six separate moments of unembellished lines, suggesting that Julia is working very hard to find a balance between the two extremes of release and control.

• the emotional content of the speech is underlined by the opening short sentence; the fact that three of the four pieces of major punctuation are semicolons; and the extra breath-thoughts (marked , ₓ), especially the four in F #4, all of which point to the extra care with which she is exploring and expressing her fears

• the two surround phrases, both of which are heightened by being non-embellished and created by emotional semicolons, point to her dilemma in being asked to work against her own self-interest
     " ; To carry that, which I would have refus'd ; / To praise his faith,
                    which I would have disprais'd . "

• the passion of her love-hate for Protheus gets most release in F #2 (4/7 in just three of the first four lines) only to be counterbalanced by the non-embellished lines that immediately follow, asking herself why should she pity Protheus
     "That with his very heart despiseth me?/Because he loves her, he
                    despiseth me, /Because I love him, . . . "

• and, in this sentence the first semicolon of the speech highlights even further her love hate for Protheus ' ; Alas, poore foole, why doe I pitty him '

• while the final non-embellishment heightens her monosyllabic passionate final wish 'I would not have him speed.'

8/Julia   A vertuous gentlewoman, milde, and beautifull.   4.4.180 - 205

Background: Silvia has granted only one of Protheus' requests, sending him via Julia a picture of herself. With her own awkward self analysis finished, and Silvia's comment before exiting, 'I weepe my self to thinke upon thy words', Julia finally is alone on stage, and, while speaking in praise of Silvia, compares herself as favourably as she can with Silvia's picture.

Style: solo

Where: somewhere in or near the palace in Milan   **To Whom:** self and audience

# of Lines: 26   **Probable Timing: 1.15 minutes**

F's onrushed middle of the speech (F #3-5) suggests a character in the throes of a self-examination far more awkward and urgent than the modern texts show, most of which reset the three sentences as seven.

• the opening short sentence points to her amazement at liking her rival, which might go part way to explain the middle onrush of the speech, for the usual ploy of hating a rival cannot apply here

• the surround phrases highlight both her self-comparison with her rival's portrait
" . Alas, how love can trifle with it selfe : /Here is her Picture : "
" : Her haire is Aburne, mine is perfect Yellow ;"
" : Her eyes are grey as glasse, and so are mine : "
" : I, but her fore-head's low, and mine's as high : "
and, extending the concept of a surround-phrase to a line and a half, to her no-way-out-of-the-dilemma-decision
" . Come, shadow, come, and take this shadow up,/For 'tis thy rivall : "
" . Ile use thee kindly, for thy Mistris sake/That us'd me so : "

• the non-embellished phrases set up the very contained realisations of not only her respect for Silvia
"A vertuous gentlewoman,"
and that hair colour seems to be the only real physical difference between them
"If that be all the difference in his love,"
"I, but her fore-head's low, and mine's as high :"
but also the key question that needs to be answered
"What should it be that he respects in her,"
followed by the sad realisation that
"Thou shalt be worship'd, kiss'd, lov'd, and ador'd/And were there sence
in this . . . /My substance should be statue in thy stead."

• the constant struggle to find a plan of action can be seen in the swings of release from emotion about Silvia (F #1, 0/2), to the intellectual hope Protheus will not succeed in wooing her (F #2, 2/0), to a passionate yet still emotionally tinged examination of her rival (F #3-4, 7/11)

• and, while the inevitability of having to 'take this shadow up' (i.e her rival's picture) is passionate (2/3, F #5), so her decision to not damage the picture, respecting the earlier sympathetic treatment offered her by Silvia, is totally non-emotional (3/0, F #6)

Modern Text

8/Julia

1 A virtuous gentlewoman, mild* and beautiful* .

2 I hope my △master's suit will be but cold,
Since she respects my △mistress' * love so much.

3 Alas, how love can trifle with itself* ! †

4 Here is her △picture : let me see ; I think*
If I had such a △tire* , this face of mine
Were full as lovely as is this of hers ;
And yet the △painter flatter'd her a little,
Unless* I flatter with myself* too much.

5 Her hair* is △auburn* , mine is perfect △yellow :
If that be all the difference in his love,
I'll get me such a color'd △periwig . †

6 Her eyes are grey as glass* , and so are mine ;
Ay*, but her fore△head's low, and mine's as high. †

7 What should it be that he respects in her,
But I can make respective in myself* ,
If this fond Love, were not a blinded god ?

8 Come, shadow, come, and take this shadow up,
For 'tis thy rival* . †

9   O thou senseless* form*,
Thou shalt be worshipp'd*, kiss'd, lov'd, and ador'd ;
And were there sense in his △idolatry,
My substance should be statue in thy stead.

10 I'll use thee kindly, for thy △mistress' * sake
That us'd me so ; or else, by Jove, I vow,
I should have scratch'd out your unseeing eyes,
To make my △master out of love with thee.

First Folio

8/Julia

1 A vertuous gentlewoman, milde,$_x$ and beautifull.

2 I hope my Masters suit will be but cold,
Since she respects my Mistris love so much.

3 Alas, how love can trifle with it selfe :
Here is her Picture : let me see, $^+$ I thinke
If I had such a Tyre, this face of mine
Were full as lovely,$_x$ as is this of hers ;
And yet the Painter flatter'd her a little,
Unlesse I flatter with my selfe too much.

4 Her haire is Aburne, mine is perfect Yellow ; $^+$
If that be all the difference in his love,
Ile get me such a coulour'd Perrywig:
Her eyes are grey as glasse, and so are mine : $_x$
I, but her fore-head's low, and mine's as high :
What should it be that he respects in her,
But I can make respective in my selfe ? $_x$
If this fond Love, were not a blinded god. $^+$

5 Come$^+$ shadow, come, and take this shadow up,
For 'tis thy rivall : O thou sencelesse forme,
Thou shalt be worship'd, kiss'd, lov'd, and ador'd ;
And were there sence in his Idolatry,
My substance should be statue in thy stead.

6 Ile use thee kindly, for thy Mistris sake
That us'd me so : $_x$ or else $^+$ by Jove, I vow,
I should have scratch'd out your unseeing eyes,
To make my Master out of love with thee.

9/ Silvia   **Oh Eglamoure, thou art a Gentleman :**   4.3.11-36

Background: Under the pressure of now doubly unwanted wooing, from the foolish Thurio whom her father is insisting she should marry, and the already betrothed-to-another-woman Protheus, Silvia is determined to leave Milan and journey to Mantua, where she believes her true-love Valentine to be. To achieve this she seeks the aid of the most honourable man she knows, Sir Eglamoure.

Style: speech as part of a two-handed scene   **To Whom:** Sir Eglamoure

Where: unspecified, somewhere in the palace

# of Lines: 26   Probable Timing: 1.15 minutes

Modern Text

9/ Silvia

1 O* Eglamour*, thou art a △gentleman -
Think* not I flatter, for I swear* I do* not -
Valiant, wise, remorse°full, well accomplish'd : ◊
Thou art not ignorant what dear* good will
I bear* unto the banish'd Valentine,
Nor how my father would enforce me marry
Vain* Thurio, whom my very soul* [abhors].

2 Thyself* hast lov'd, and I have heard thee say
No grief* did ever come so near* thy heart,
As when thy △lady and thy true °love died* ,
Upon whose △grave thou vow'dst pure chastity.* . †

3 Sir Eglamour* , I would to Valentine,
To Mantua, where I hear* he makes abode* ;
And for the ways* are dangerous to pass* ,
I do* desire thy worthy company,
Upon whose faith and honor I repose.

4 Urge not my father's anger, Eglamour* ,
But think* upon my grief* , a △lady's* grief* ,
And on the justice of my flying hence,
To keep* me from a most unholy match,
Which heaven and fortune still rewards with plagues.

5 I do* desire thee, even from a heart
As full of sorrows* as the △sea of sands,
To bear* me company, and go* with me,
If not, to hide what I have said to thee,
That I may venture to depart alone.

First Folio

9/ Silvia

1 Oh Eglamoure, thou art a Gentleman : ₓ
Thinke not I flatter ₓ (for I sweare I doe not) ₓ
Valiant, wise, remorse-full, well accomplish'd.
Thou art not ignorant what deere good will
I beare unto the banish'd Valentine : ₓ
Nor how my father would enforce me marry
Vaine Thurio ₓ (whom my very soule [abhor'd] .)

2

3 Thy selfe hast lov'd, and I have heard thee say
No griefe did ever come so neere thy heart,
As when thy Lady, ₓ and thy true-love dide.
Upon whose Grave thou vow'dst pure chastitie :
Sir Eglamoure : ₓ I would to Valentine ⁺
To Mantua, where I heare, ₓ he makes aboad ;
And for the waies are dangerous to passe,
I doe desire thy worthy company,
Upon whose faith and honor, ₓ I repose.

4 Urge not my fathers anger ₓ (Eglamoure) ₓ
But thinke upon my griefe ₓ (a Ladies griefe) ₓ
And on the justice of my flying hence,
To keepe me from a most unholy match,
Which heaven and fortune still rewards with plagues.

5 I doe desire thee, even from a heart
As full of sorrowes, ₓ as the Sea of sands,
To beare me company, and goe with me : ₓ
If not, to hide what I have said to thee,
That I may venture to depart alone.

In its opening sentence structure, F sets up a woman who initially is capable of **making a precise argument, F #1 establishing Eglamoure's good qualities and a separate F #2 reminding him of the basic circumstances which afflict her - circumstances which then seem to become too much for her, for in the onrushed F #3 she jams together his doomed love experience and her own needs. Most modern texts reverse the process, allowing her to start with an onrush (mt. #1 = F #1-2), from which she then recovers (mt. #2-3 = F #3).**

- fascinatingly, whatever struggle she is undergoing, four of the five sentences end with non-embellished lines, as if after each exploration she is able to calm herself before continuing - a sense of necessary well-bred self-control perhaps?

- the quiet of some of the un-embellished phrases point to her belief in Eglamoure's goodness, regarding him as 'Valiant, wise, remorse-full, well accomplish'd', desiring the company of a man 'Upon whose faith and honor, I repose.', trusting him not to betray her if he decides not to help, 'If not, to hide what I have said to thee,/That I may venture to depart alone.'

- other non-embellished lines point to the strength of her moral convictions as regards joining Valentine ('And on the justice of my flying hence,') and avoiding an enforced marriage to Thurio ('Which heaven and fortune still rewards with plagues.')

- two surround phrases also underscore her need for Eglamoure's help - the opening ': Oh Eglamoure, thou art a Gentleman : ' plus the very short and highly unusual ': Sir Eglamoure : '; the latter could almost be a sigh or a momentary loss of thought

- while extending the surround phrase concept to a line and a half, the strength in speaking of her need is self-explanatory (': I would to Valentine/To Mantua, where I heare, he makes aboad ; ')

- naturally the speech is highly emotional (12/27 overall), and, as befits such a bold step by a young woman, there are occasional fascinating bursts of emotional release, such as the praise of Eglamoure ('Thinke not I flatter (for I sweare I doe not)'), loathing for her father's choice of a husband ('Vaine Thurio (whom my very soule abhor'd)), and her own anguish ('But thinke upon my griefe (a Ladies griefe)')

#'s 10 - 11: A SERVANT'S DILEMMAS

10/Launce   Nay, 'twill bee this howre ere I have done weeping: 2.3.1 - 32

Background: This is the first speech for a character who is in the same state as his master Protheus, for Launce has no desire to leave Verona and go to Mantua - nor did his family want him to go, as the following explains.

Style: solo, but the dog Crab is actively mentioned both in this speech and in #12 immediately following; in most productions, a dog (whether real, or a toy, or simply a stiffened collar and leash) accompanies the actor throughout.

Where: unspecified, but somewhere either near his home or close to the point of embarkation   **To Whom:** the audience

    # of Lines: 32   **Probable Timing: 1.35 minutes**

Modern Text

10/Launce

1 Nay, 'twill be* this hour* ere I have done weeping ; all the kind* of the Launces, have this very fault . †

2   I have receiv'd my proportion, like the prodigious △son , and am going with Sir Protheus to the Imperial's* △court . †

3   I think* Crab my dog, be the sourest* natured dog* that lives : △my △mother weeping, my △father wailing , my △sister crying, our △maid howling, our △cat* wringing her hands, and all our house in a great perplexity*, yet did not this cruel*-hearted △cur* shed* one tear* . †

4   He is a stone, a very [pebble stone], and has no more pity* in him [then] a dog* . †

5   A Jew would have wept to have seen* our parting ; why my △grandam having no eyes, look* you, wept herself* blind* at my parting . †

6 Nay, I'll show you the manner of it.

7   This shoe* is my father* ; no, this left shoe* is my father - no, no, this left shoe* is my mother* ; nay, that cannot be* so neither* ; yes, it is so, it is so - it hath the worser sole . †

8   This shoe, with the hole in it, is my mother : and this my father . †

9 a vengeance* on't ! there 'tis . †

10   Now, sir, this staff* is my sister, for, look* you, she is as white as a lilly* and as small as a wand :

11   This hat is Nan, our maid . †

First Folio

10/Launce

1 Nay, 'twill bee this howre ere I have done weeping : x all the kinde of the Launces, have this very fault : I have receiv'd my proportion, like the prodigious Sonne, and am going with Sir Protheus to the Imperialls Court : I thinke Crab my dog, be the sowrest natured dogge that lives : My Mother weeping : x my Father wayling : x my Sister crying : x our Maid howling : x our Catte wringing her hands, and all our house in a great perplexitie, yet did not this cruell-hearted Curre shedde one teare : he is a stone, a very [pibble stone], and has no more pitty in him [then] a dogge : a Jew would have wept to have seene our parting : x why my Grandam having no eyes, looke you, wept her selfe blinde at my parting : x nay, Ile shew you the manner of it.

2   This shooe is my father : x no, this left shooe is my father ; no, no, this left shooe is my mother : x nay, that cannot bee so neyther : x yes ; it is so, it is so; x it hath the worser sole: this shooe ‡ with the hole in it, is my mother : and this my father : a veng'ance on't , + there 'tis : Now + sir, this staffe is my sister : for, looke you, she is as white as a lilly, x and as small as a wand : this hat is Nan + our maid : I am the

---

The onrush of the speech (set as two sentences in F, which most modern texts set as nineteen) together with the heavy punctuation of what modern texts regard as separate sentences plus another eighteen where modern texts usually end each of their new sentences) betokens an incredibly upset hard-working speech – one far different in style to the 'Crab at the Duke's table' speech that follows (# 11 below).

(It is suggested that readers first work through the modern text sentence structure to understand each of the grammatical points being made before exploring F's onrush.)

* the enormous number of surround phrases thus created (nearly forty) build to an interesting pattern, from just eight in the thirteen and half lines of F #1, the set-up to the story, to an enormous thirty-one in the nineteen lines of F #2, the story itself

* that the recounting of the story seems to have great impact on Launce can be seen in the fact all seven emotional semicolons are found just in F #2

* the speech starts out quite passionately, (12/9 in the first seven lines, up to and including 'our Maid howling', mid mt. #3)

* but it seems the mention of all the tears being shed 'My Mother weeping : my Father/wayling : my Sister crying : our Maid howling;' creates some emotional response in Launce, for the rest of F #1 becomes quite emotional (4/11 in seven lines)

* and he becomes much more emotional once he starts telling the story, even as he tries to establish which shoe should represent his mother and which his father (0/6 the first five lines of F #2, up to 'there 'tis', end mt. #8)

dogge : ₓ no, the dogge is himselfe, and I am the dogge: ₓ
oh,⁺ the dogge is me, and I am my selfe: ₓ I; ₓ so, so: now
come I to my Father; ⁺ Father, your blessing : now
should not the shooe speake a word for weeping : ₓ
now should I kisse my Father; well, hee weepes on :
Now come I to my Mother: Oh that she could speake
now, ₓ like a [would]-woman : ⁺ well, I kisse her : ₓ why⁺
there 'tis; heere's my mothers breath up and downe :
Now come I to my sister; marke the moane she makes:
now the dogge all this while sheds not a teare : ₓ nor
speakes a word: ₓ but see how I lay the dust with my
teares.

• a tiny moment of intellect creeps in as he tries to set up other physical objects to represent the others present at the farewell (4/10 in the four lines up to 'and I am my selfe :' almost at the end of mt. #12)

• in reference to asking his father for a blessing and he becomes totally factual (2/0 in just one line, mt. #13)

• and the mention of weeping once more sets him off emotionally (5/11 in the six lines from 'now should not the shooe' to approaching his final family member 'Now come I to my sister;', start of mt. #18

• while the finale, comparing his silent 'dogge' shedding 'not a teare' with all that has gone on before, becomes totally emotional once more (0/6 in the last three lines of the speech)

                                        I am the
12 dog* - no, the dog* is himself*, and I am the dog* -
    ᐃO!*, the dog* is me, and I am myself*; ay*, so, so. †
13   Now
    come I to my ᐃfather : "Father, your blessing". †
14   Now
    should not the shoe* speak* a word for weeping;
    now should I kiss* my ᐃfather; well, he* weeps* on. †
15 Now come I to my ᐃmother. †
16   O* that she could speak*
    now like a [wood] ∘ woman! †
17   Well, I kiss* her; why,
    there 'tis; here's* my mothers breath up and down* . †
18 Now come I to my sister; mark the moan* she makes. †
19 Now the dog* all this while sheds not a tear*, nor
    speaks* a word; but see how I lay the dust with my
    tears* .

11/Launce   When a mans servant shall play the Curre with him   4.4.1 - 39

Background: Now in Milan, Launce was supposed to present Silvia a presumably pedigree dog dog from Protheus, which was stolen from him on the way, so he tried to substitute his mongrel Crab, with disastrous results, as the following explains. As mentioned in the background to speech #10 above it's very useful to have something onstage to represent the dog (or have a very good sense of where the invisible dog might be). One extra point - as a result of this utter catastrophe Protheus tells Launce 'Go get thee hence, and finde my dog againe;/Or nere returne againe into my sight.', after which Launce is not seen in the play again.

Style: solo

Where: unspecified, somewhere either near the palace, or close to Protheus' lodgings   **To Whom:** direct audience (and dog) address

# of Lines: 37   **Probable Timing:** 1.55 minutes

Modern Text

11/ Launce

1   When a man's servant shall play the △cur* with
him, look* you, it goes hard : one that I brought up of
a puppy ; one that I sav'd from drowning, when three or
four* of his blind* brothers and sisters went to it .   I have

2   taught him ,even as one would say precisely, "Thus I
would teach a dog. "†

3   I was sent to deliver him as a pre-
sent to Mistress Silvia, from my △master ; and I came no
sooner into the dining* -chamber but he steps me to her
△trencher and steals* her △capon's ° leg . †   O, 'tis a foul*

4 thing, when a △cur cannot keep* himself* in all companies ! †

5   I would have (as one should say) one that take
upon him to be a dog indeed* , to be, as it were, a dog at
all things .

6   If I had not had more wit [than] he, to take a fault
upon me that he did, I think* verily he* had been* hang'd
for't ; sure as I live he had suffer'd for't . †   You shall judge :

7   He*

8 △he* thrusts me himself* into the company of three or
four* gentleman°like ° dogs, under the Duke's table . . †   He*

9 had not been* there (bless* the mark*) a pissing ° while,
but all the chamber smelt him . †

10   "Out with the dog", says* one . †

   "What cur is that ?" says* another . †

First Folio

11/ Launce

1   When a mans servant shall play the Curre with
him x(looke you) x it goes hard : one that I brought up of
a puppy : x one that I sav'd from drowning, when three or
foure of his blinde brothers and sisters went to it : I have
taught him x (even as one would say precisely, thus I
would teach a dog) x I was sent to deliver him, x as a present to Mistris Silvia, from my Master ; and I came no
sooner into the dyning-chamber, x but he steps me to her
Trencher, x and steales her Capons-leg : O, 'tis a foule
thing, when a Cur cannot keepe himselfe in all companies : I would have (as one should say) one that take upon him to be a dog indeede, to be, as it were, a dog at all
things .

2   If I had not had more wit [then] he, to take a fault
upon me that he did, I thinke verily hee had bin hang'd
for't : x sure as I live he had suffer'd for't : you shall judge :
Hee thrusts me himselfe into the company of three or
foure gentleman-like-dogs, under the Dukes table : hee
had not bin there (blesse the marke) a pissing while, but
all the chamber smelt him : out with the dog x(saies one) x
what cur is that + x(saies another) x whip him out x (saies the

---

The onrush of this speech (F's three sentences, which most modern texts set as twenty-three) betokens a highly concerned situation – yet one much different in style to the 'farewell' speech, #10 above. Here there is far less major punctuation and release, suggesting that the just whipped Launce is at times resigned to what has occurred (or that it almost hurts to talk).

(It is suggested that readers first work through the modern text sentence structure to understand each of the grammatical points being made before exploring F's onrush .)

• the few surround phrases (seven versus the nearly forty of the previous speech) point to his affection for Crab

   ": one that I brought up of a puppy : "

   ": sure as I live he had suffer'd for't : you shall judge : "

   "I having bin acquainted with the smell before, knew it was Crab ; and goes me to the fellow that whips the dogges : friend (quoth I) you meane to whip the dog : "

   ": he makes me no more adoe, but whips me out of the chamber : "

as well as to Crab's ingratitude and lack of social graces

   ": thou think'st not of this now : nay, I remember the tricke you serv'd me, when I tooke my leave of Madam Silvia : did not I bid thee still marke me, and doe as I do ; "

• while, unlike the previous speech, several non-embellished lines give calm reinforcement to all that has befallen (as if it doesn't give rise to too much emotional release - perhaps its happened before and Launce expects it will happen again, and the lack of energy involved would be only natural for a man who has just been whipped), first explaining the background

   "I have/taught him (even as one would say precisely, thus I would teach a dog) I was sent to deliver him,"

   "If I had not had more wit then he, to take a fault/upon me that he did, I thinke verily hee had bin hang'd for't : sure as I live he had suffer'd for't : "

and then setting up what has just ensued

   "I having bin acquainted with the smell before, knew it was Crab;"

                "Whip him out," says* the

11   third . †

12   "Hang him up", says* the Duke .

13   I, having been* ac-
quainted with the smell before, knew it was Crab, and
goes me to the fellow that whips the dogs* : "Friend,"
quoth I, "you mean* to whip the dog"?†
            "Ay, * marry do* I"

14   quoth he . †

15   "You do* him the more wrong," quoth I, "'twas
I did the thing you wot of" . †

16   He makes me no more ado* ,
but whips me out of the chamber .

17   How many △masters
would do* this for his △servant ?

18   Nay, I'll be sworn* , I have
sat in the stocks * , for puddings he hath stol'n* , otherwise
he had been* executed ; I have stood on the △pillory for
△geese he hath kill'd*, otherwise he had suffer'd for't . †
          Thou

19   think'st not of this now . †

20   Nay, I remember the trick* you
serv'd me, when I took* my leave of Madam Silvia . †

21   Did
not I bid thee still mark* me, and do* as I do . †

22   When did'st
thou see me heave up my leg, and make water against a
△gentlewoman's farthingale ?

23   Did'st thou ever see me do*
such a trick* ?"

"'twas I did the thing you wot of"
going on to explain
"otherwise he had bin executed' and/or 'otherwise he had
  sufferd for't : "
finally leading to his regular berating of Crab for his ingratitude
  "thou think'st not of this now"
and finishing with
  "when did'st thou see me heave up my leg, and make water.."

• when released the energy is naturally somewhat more
emotional than intellectual(19/28), with F #1 starting slowly but
emotionally (1/3 in the first four lines set up of Crab), followed by
a much more passionate explanation of Crab's stealing Mistris
Silvia's 'Capons-leg' (7/6 in the eight lines ending sentence #1)

• F #2 again starts out slowly (0/1 in the first three lines, again
setting up that Crab had performed another heinous act), but
moves to emotion-tinged passion as Launce explains Crab's
unfortunate act of incontinence (3/6 in the remaining five and a
half lines of F #2)

• however, F #3 is a surprising mix of approximately five
unembellished lines, as described above, and emotion tinged
passion once again (8/13 in the other eleven lines)

3

third)ₓ hang him up ₓ(saies the Duke.)ₓ
               I⁺ having bin ac-
quainted with the smell before, knew it was Crab ; ₓ and
goes me to the fellow that whips the dogges : friend
(quoth I)ₓ you meane to whip the dog : ₓ I⁺ marry doe I
ₓ(quoth he)ₓ you doe him the more wrong ₓ(quoth I) ₓ 'twas
I did the thing you wot of : he makes me no more adoe,
but whips me out of the chamber : how many Masters
would doe this for his Servant ? nay, ile be sworne ⁺ I have
sat in the stockes, for puddings he hath stolne, otherwise
he had bin executed : ₓ I have stood on the Pillorie for
Geese he hath kil'd, otherwise he had sufferd for't : thou
think'st not of this now : nay, I remember the tricke you
serv'd me, when I tooke my leave of Madam Silvia : did
not I bid thee still marke me, and doe as I do ; when did'st
thou see me heave up my leg, and make water against a
Gentlewomans farthingale ? did'st thou ever see me doe
such a tricke?

THE TAMING OF THE SHREW

SPEECHES IN ORDER	TIME	PAGE
# 1: The Set Up to the Play Within The Play		
1/ **Lord or Servant** Oh Noble Lord, bethinke thee of thy birth,	1.55	63
#'s 2 - 3: The Problem Facing the Suitors Wanting to Marry Bianca		
2/ **Baptista** Gentlemen, importune me no farther,	0.55	65
3/ **Gremio** You may go to the divels dam .	0.30	66
#'s 4 - 5: Lucentio's Arrival and Falling in Love		
4/ **Lucentio** Tranio, since for the great desire I had	1.15	67
5/ **Lucentio** Oh Tranio, till I found it to be true,	0.55	68
#'s 6 - 9: Petruchio, The Answer to Hortensio's and Gemios's Prayers		
6/ **Petruchio** Signior Hortensio, thus it stands with me,	0.50	69
7/ **Petruchio** But will {I} woo this Wilde-cat ?	0.50	70
8/ **Petruchio** Now by the world, it is a lustie Wench,	0.50	71
9/ **Petruchio** Father, 'tis thus, your selfe and all the world	1.15	72
#'s 10 - 11: The Winning of Bianca		
10/ **Gremio** First, as you know, my house within the City	0.55	73
11/ **Bianca** Now let mee see if I can conster it.	0.20	74
#'s 12 - 14: Petruchio's Machiavellian Testosterone Behaviour		
12/ **Gremio** A bridegroome say you ?	1.15	74
13/ **Petruchio** O Kate content thee, prethee be not angry.	0.50	76
14/ **Petruchio** Thus have I politickely begun my reigne,	1.15	77
# 15: Kate's Stunning Triumph Over All, Including Petruchio		
15/ **Kate** Fie, fie, unknit that thretaning unkinde brow,	2.10	78

SPEECHES BY GENDER

		Speech #(s)
SPEECHES FOR WOMEN (2)		
Bianca	**Traditional & Today:** young woman, younger sister to Kate	#11
Kate	**Traditional & Today:** young woman	#15
SPEECHES FOR EITHER GENDER (2)		
Lord or Servant	**Traditional:** male, any age **Today:** any gender, any age	#1
Baptista	**Traditional:** older male, parent to two daughters of marriageable age	#2
	Today: with the age proviso, any gender	
SPEECHES FOR MEN (11)		
Lucentio	**Traditional & Today:** young lover	#4, #5
Petruchio	**Traditional & Today:** young male	#6, #7, #8, #9, #13, #14
Gremio	**Traditional & Today:** an older male, listed as a 'Pantelowne', viz. the	#3, #10, #12
	Commed'ia figure known a 'lustful and avaricious old man'	

THE TAMING OF THE SHREW

1: THE SET-UP TO THE PLAY WITHIN THE PLAY

1/ Lord or Servant   **Oh Noble Lord, bethinke thee of thy birth,**   Induction 2. 25 -67

Background: Conducted to the Lord's home, and changed and bathed while asleep, the tinker Christopher Sly has awoken, promptly denies he is anything other than a tinker, and calls for his old Ale-house friends. This constructed speech is the attempt to set the joke up that Sly really is a Lord and has all the wonderful diversions mentioned at his finger-tips, all his to command. One note: as this is a constructed speech, combining three characters into one, the first part (the opening 11 F sentences) taken from the Lord, the remainder from the two Servants who work Sly over, it could be played by any age and any gender.

Style: as part of a two-handed scene (perhaps with other servants watching)

Where: in the Lord's home   **To Whom:** the tinker, Christopher Sly

# of Lines: 38   **Probable Timing: 1.55 minutes**

Modern Text

1/ Lord or Servant

1 O*△noble △lord, bethink* thee of thy birth,
   Call home thy ancient thoughts from banishment,
   And banish hence these abject lowly* dreames* . †

2 Look* how thy servants do attend on thee,
   Each in his office ready* at thy beck* .

3 Wilt thou have △music*?

      Hark,* Apollo plays*,

      [Musick]

4 And twenty,* caged △nightingales do sing.

5 Or wilt thou sleep* ?

6   We'll* have thee to a △couch,
   Softer and sweeter [than] the lustful* bed
   On purpose trimm'd* up for Semiramis.

7 Say thou wilt walk* ; we will* bestrow the ground.

8 Or wilt thou ride ?

9   Thy horses shall* be trapp'd*,
   Their harness* studded all with △gold and △pearl*.

10 Dost thou love hawking ?

11   Thou hast hawks* will soar*

12   Or wilt thou hunt ?

13 Thy hounds shall make the △welkin answer them
   And fetch shrill echoes* from the hollow earth.

14{ψ} Say thou wilt course, thy gray△hounds are as swift
   As breathed △stags : ay*, fleeter [than] the △roe.

First Folio

1/ Lord or Servant

1 Oh Noble Lord, bethinke thee of thy birth,
   Call home thy ancient thoughts from banishment,
   And banish hence these abject lowlie dreames :
   Looke how thy servants do attend on thee,
   Each in his office readie at thy becke.

2 Wilt thou have Musicke ?

3   Harke + Apollo plaies,

      [Musick]

   And twentie caged Nightingales do sing.

4 Or wilt thou sleepe ?

5   Wee'l have thee to a Couch,
   Softer and sweeter [then] the lustfull bed
   On purpose trim'd up for Semiramis.

6 Say thou wilt walke : we wil bestrow the ground.

7 Or wilt thou ride ?

8   Thy horses shal be trap'd,
   Their harnesse studded all with Gold and Pearle.

9 Dost thou love hawking ?

10   Thou hast hawkes will soare
   Above the morning Larke.

11   Or wilt thou hunt,
   Thy hounds shall make the Welkin answer them
   And fetch shrill ecchoes from the hollow earth.

12{ψ} Say thou wilt course, thy gray-hounds are as swift
   As breathed Stags : I + fleeter [then] the Roe.

As described above, seven consecutive speeches have been joined as one.

- the second of two surround phrases ' . Thou art a Lord, and nothing but a Lord . ' underscores the repeated attempts to dupe the Tinker into believing what he is most definitely not

- while the very early non-embellished phrases (quiet so as not to disturb him too much as he recovers from his drunken sleep?) stress the reality which he should forget 'Call home thy ancient thoughts from banishment,/ And banish hence these abject lowlie . . . ' ending with the long-spelled word 'dreames'

- of the seventeen sentences, seven are short, all offering Sly various delicious temptations of the traditional trappings of a Lord, 'Musicke' (F #2-3); 'sleepe' (F #4); 'walking on ground' 'we wil bestrow', presumably with rose petals (F #6); riding (F #7); and 'hawking' (F#9-10), two of which are non-embellished (F #7 and #9)

- the other non-embellished lines point to a slightly naughtier temptation, racy paintings, viz. starting innocently enough with the opening of F #13, 'Dost thou love pictures?' only to go on to explain that what is being offered are candid portraits of Venus ('Cytherea') and lo, the latter 'And how she was beguiled . . . '

- not surprisingly, the speech is expressed in somewhat emotionally tinged passion (24/33 in thirty-eight lines overall), with the only fully intellectual moment the commencement of hunting (3/0 in the two lines of F #12), and the only fully emotional extended moment the final reference to the 'teares' that 'ore-run' the face of Sly's supposed 'Ladie'-wife (0/4 in the four lines of F #17)

- thus, rather than sentence by sentence, the occasional clustered releases underscore both the tempted delights being offered and the fun of those that are offering them, such as the opening 'Oh Noble Lord, bethinke thee . . . '; the temptation of F #2-3's 'Wilt thou have Musicke? Harke, Apollo plaies, '; the fulsome description of the horses

{ctd. over}

15{ψ} Dost thou love pictures? †
       We will* fetch thee straight*
Adonis painted by a running brook*,
And Cytherea* all in sedges hid,
Which seem* to move and wanton with her breath
Even as the waving sedges play with ¹ wind* .

16 We'll* show thee Io, as she was a ᴬmaid,
And how she was beguiled and surpris'd*,
As lively* painted, as the deed* was done.

17{ψ} Or Daphne roaming* through a thorny* wood,
Scratching her legs that one shall* swear* she bleeds,
And at that sight shall* sad Apollo weep*,
S o workmanly* the blood and tears* are drawn* .

18 Thou art a ᴬlord, and nothing but a ᴬlord .

19 Thou hast a ᴬlady far* more ᴬbeautiful* ,
[Than] any woman in this waining age.

20{ψ} And till* the tears* that she hath shed for thee
Like envious floods* o'er-run her lovely face,
She was the fairest creature in the world,
And yet she* is inferior* to none .

13{ψ} Dost thou love pictures? we wil fetch thee strait
Adonis painted by a running brooke,
And Citherea all in sedges hid,
Which seeme to move and wanton with her breath,ₓ
Even as the waving sedges play with winde.

14 Wee'l shew thee Io, as she was a Maid,
And how she was beguiled and surpriz'd,
As livelie painted, as the deede was done.

15{ψ} Or Daphne roming through a thornie wood,
Scratching her legs,ₓ that one shal sweare she bleeds,
And at that sight shal sad Apollo weepe,
So workmanlie the blood and teares are drawne.

16 Thou art a Lord, and nothing but a Lord :
Thou hast a Ladie farre more Beautifull,
[Then] any woman in this waining age.

17{ψ} And til the teares that she hath shed for thee,ₓ
Like envious flouds ore-run her lovely face,
She was the fairest creature in the world,
And yet shee is inferiour to none .

---

and hawks Sly supposedly owns, F #8's 'Their harnesse studded all with Gold and Pearle.'; plus 'Thou hast hawkes will soare/Above the morning Larke.', F #10

• unusually, there are a large number of short spellings, especially at key moments of temptation: Officers being 'readie' (F #1); Apollo 'plaies' and 'twentie' Nightingales sing (F #3); they 'wil' bestrow the ground, presumably with rose petals (F #6); his horses 'shal be trap'd' lavishly (F #8); they 'wil' fetch him 'strait' naughty pictures including Venus ('Citherea', F #13), Io 'livelie' painted (F #14), and Daphne 'roming' a 'thornie' wood in a very 'workmanlie' fashion (F #15)!

---

¹ though most modern texts agree with Ff and set this as 'with 'wind'; one excellent gloss = 'wi'th'wind'

#'s 2 - 3: THE PROBLEM FACING THE SUITORS WANTING TO MARRY BIANCA

2/ Baptista   Gentlemen, importune me no farther,   1.1.48 - 54 and 92 - 104

Background: His first speech in the play, which sets up the difficulties facing the two local suitors for his youngest daughter Bianca - because, as all the locals know, the older, Kate, also known as Katherina, is such a scold that no man would willingly go near her.

Style: part of a three-handed scene, with others watching

Where: unspecified, but presumably a public place/street in Padua   **To Whom:** the old suitor Gremio, listed as a 'Pantelowne' (a Commed'ia type figure at his first entry), and the younger Hortentio, in front of both of his daughters Kate ('Katherina') and Bianca, with, unknown to all of them, the hidden Lucentio and Tranio watching what's going on

# of Lines: 17   **Probable Timing: 0.55 minutes**

Modern Text

2/ Baptista

1 Gentlemen, importune me no farther,
   For how I firmly am resolv'd you know :
   That is, not to bestow my youngest* daughter
   Before I have a husband for the elder . †

2 If either of you both love Katherina,
   Because I know you well, and love you well,
   Leave shall you have to court her at your pleasure.

3 And for I know {Bianca} taketh most delight
   In △music* , △instruments, and △poetry,
   Schoolmasters* will I keep* within my house,
   Fit to instruct her youth.

4   If you, Hortentio,
   Or, △Signior Gremio, you, know any such,
   Prefer* them hither ; for to cunning men
   I will be very kind,* and liberal*
   To mine own* children in good bringing up,
   And so farewell . †

5   Katherina, you may stay,
   For I have more to commune with Bianca.

First Folio

2/ Baptista

1 Gentlemen, importune me no farther,
   For how I firmly am resolv'd you know :
   That is, not to bestow my yongest daughter,'x
   Before I have a husband for the elder :
   If either of you both love Katherina,
   Because I know you well, and love you well,
   Leave shall you have to court her at your pleasure.

2 And for I know {Bianca} taketh most delight
   In Musicke, Instruments, and Poetry,
   Schoolemasters will I keepe within my house,
   Fit to instruct her youth.

3   If you + Hortensio,
   Or + signior Gremio + you + know any such,
   Preferre them hither : x for to cunning men,'x
   I will be very kinde + and liberall,'x
   To mine owne children,'x in good bringing up,
   And so farewell : Katherina + you may stay,
   For I have more to commune with Bianca.

What is so startling about the speech is the totally unembellished seven line opening sentence (save for the proper name Katherina), suggesting that for some reason Baptista, is taking great efforts to remain calm (an attempt to avoid public embarrassment perhaps? or perhaps so as not to be overheard by Katherina?).

• this apparent need to stay calm is seen in the continuation of the speech, for the ever money-conscious Baptista seems to pulse back and forth between intellect, in the first two lines of F #2 (4/1) talking of Bianca's supposed joys in things artistic; and emotion, when talking about spending money on 'Schoolmasters' (the last two lines of F #2, 0/2)

• and this switching back and forth continues through F #3, where the direct appeal to Bianca's two rival suitors (2/0 in the first line and a half) turns again to emotion with reference to spending money (kinde and liberall) on his own children (0/4 in the next three lines) and back to intellectual as he says farewell to all on stage, wishing to separate himself from his 'shrew' daughter, Katherina

• even the two intellectual passages in F #3 could be regarded as non-embellished (for all four capitalised words are proper names): if so, Baptista's struggle to maintain his sense of dignity becomes even more marked

3/ Gremio   **You may go to the divels dam**   between 1.1.105-145

Background: Gremio's response to speech #2 above, and to Hortensio: this is his first major speech of the play.

Style: as part of a two handed scene

Where: unspecified, but presumably a public place/street in Padua   **To Whom:** to his younger Bianca-wooing rival, Hortensio

# of Lines: 8   **Probable Timing:** 0.30 minutes

Modern Text

3/ Gremio

1   You may go to the devil's* dam {.}

2   {ψ}   Think'st thou, Hortensio, though her father be very* rich, any man is so very* a fool* to be married to hell?

3   I cannot tell ; but I had as lief take her dowry* with this condition : ᐃto be whipt at the high* cross* every* morning.

4   I {will give } him the best horse in Padua to begin his wooing* that would tho-roughly woo* her, wed her, and bed her, and rid* the house of her!

First Folio

3/ Gremio

1   You may go to the divels dam {.}

2   {ψ}   Think'st thou [+] Hortensio, though her father be verie rich, any man is so verie a foole to be married to hell?

3   I cannot tell :ₓ but I had as lief take her dowrie with this condition ;[+] To be whipt at the hie crosse everie morning.

4   I {will give } him the best horse in Padua to begin his wooing that would tho-roughly woe her, wed her, and bed her, and ridde the house of her. [+]

Again, a very careful speech, with the opening non-embellished short sentence suggesting the cursing out of Kate is not yelled but kept very quiet (in case she might hear and respond?).

• the three surround phrases comprising F #3 point to the depth of Gremio's loathing (and fear?) of Kate, especially with the only (emotional) semicolon of the speech

• interestingly, in F #3 the short spelling of what modern texts set as 'woo' is equated to that of grief, 'woe', suggesting it is almost choked back as something too distasteful to be spoken aloud - yet the other verb associated with Kate, the more desirable 'ridde', is given extra weight

• and there are a lot of other short spellings ('verie', 'dowrie', 'hie', 'everie', 'woing' as well as woe') - perhaps reinforcing the idea of distaste (or trying to prevent Kate from overhearing)

#'s 4 - 5: LUCENTIO'S ARRIVAL AND FALLING IN LOVE

4/ Lucentio   **Tranio, since for the great desire I had**   1.1.1 - 24

Background: His first speech in the play sets up exactly who and what he is.

Style: as part of a two-handed scene

Where: unspecified, but presumably a public place/street in Padua   **To Whom:** his man-servant Tranio

# of Lines: 24   **Probable Timing: 1.15 minutes**

Modern Text

4/ Lucentio

1
Tranio, since for the great desire I had
To see fair* Padua, nursery* of ᐃarts,
I am arriv'd for fruitful* Lombardy*,
The pleasant garden of great Italy,
And by my father's love and leave am arm'd
With his good will and thy good company, ◇

My trusty* servant, well approv'd in all,
Here* let us breath, and haply institute
A course of ᐃlearning and ingenious studies.

2
Pisa, renowned for grave ᐃcitizens,
Gave me my being and my father first
A ᐃmerchant of great ᐃtraffic* through the world,
[Vincentio,] come of the Bentivolii* ;
Vincentio's son* , brought up in Florence,
It shall become to serve all hopes conceiv'd,
To deck* his fortune with his virtuous deeds* . †

3
And therefore, Tranio, for the time I study*∗,
Virtue and that part of ᐃphilosophy*
Will I apply*∗, that treats of happiness*
By virtue specially to be achiev'd* .

4
Tell me thy mind* , for I have Pisa left
And am to Padua come, as he that leaves
A shallow plash, to plunge him in the deep*,
And with society*₂ seeks* to quench his thirst.

First Folio

4/ Lucentio

1
Tranio, since for the great desire I had
To see faire Padua, nurserie of Arts,
I am arriv'd for fruitfull Lumbardie,
The pleasant garden of great Italy,
And by my fathers love and leave am arm'd
With his good will,ₓ and thy good companie.

2
My trustie servant ⁺ well approv'd in all,
Heere let us breath, and haply institute
A course of Learning,ₓ and ingenious studies.

3
Pisa ⁺ renowned for grave Citizens ⁺
Gave me my being,ₓ and my father first
A Merchant of great Trafficke through the world :ₓ
[Vincentio's] come of the Bentivoly,⁺
Vincentio's sonne, brought up in Florence,
It shall become to serve all hopes conceiv'd ⁺
To decke his fortune with his vertuous deedes :
And therefore ⁺ Tranio, for the time I studie,
Vertue and that part of Philosophie
Will I applie, that treats of happinesse,ₓ
By vertue specially to be atchiev'd.

4
Tell me thy minde, for I have Pisa left,ₓ
And am to Padua come, as he that leaves
A shallow plash, to plunge him in the deepe,
And with sacietie seekes to quench his thirst.

This opening speech is often played as one of great braggadocio, as might befit the audience grabbing first lines of the play within the play. Yet, the mix of non-embellished lines, three extra breath-thoughts at key times, virtual lack of logical punctuation (just two colons), and overall intellectual weight over emotion (18/10), all support the idea of Lucentio being a young man on his first trip away from home, and none too sure of himself.

• the unembellished lines point to his youth and need for guidance from others "And by my fathers love and leave am arm'd/With his good will and thy good companie." along with "My trustie servant well approv'd in all,"
plus his initial determination to be a good student to study 'Vertue' and 'Philosophie', so as to get the rewards 'By vertue specially to be atchiev'd'

• dealing with their arrival in Padua, the speech opens intellectually (5/2 in F #1's first four lines), followed by a non-embellished reference to his father to finish the sentence (scared of him perhaps? – which would certainly explain his and Tranio's behaviour towards the real Vincentio later in the play)

• F #2 approaches the subject of learning quite gingerly (1/1 in three lines)

• the praise of his own family and city background is highly (proudly?) intellectual (8/2 in the first five lines of F #3), while the next two lines, hoping to be a credit to his father, become monetarily emotional (0/2)

• in F #3's final four lines, the hopes for the rewards of study move from intellect (2/0 to the first two lines), through emotion (the penultimate line), to neutrality (the last line) – perhaps he is not a particularly good student (certainly he is not particularly smart in the ways of the world as later actions in the play clearly show)

• but it seems he manages to recover his spirits, for the final sentence, where he essentially puts himself in Tranio's hands, becomes passionate (2/3, F #4)

---

² though some commentators suggest Ff's 'sacietie' may be a pun on 'satiety' through 'society', most modern texts = 'satiety'

5/ Lucentio   **Oh Tranio, till I found it to be true,**   1.1.148 – 158 (with inserts from 1.1.167 – 170 & 1.1.174 – 176)

Background: Lucentio, as many young men in the Shakespeare comedies, has fallen in love at first sight, unfortunately with Bianca, who, as seen above, is being fought over by the two local wooers. As to the classical references,

1/ Agenor's daughter was Europa, whose beauty so moved Jupiter (Jove) that he changed himself into a bull on whose back she crossed the sea to Crete whereupon he resumed his true shape and successfully wooed her

2/ the Queen of Carthage was Dido, Anna her sister and confidant

Style: as part of a two-handed scene

Where: unspecified, but presumably a public place/street in Padua   **To Whom:** Tranio

       # of Lines: 18   **Probable Timing: 0.55 minutes**

Modern Text

5/ Lucentio

1
O* Tranio, till I found it to be true,
I never thought it possible or likely* .

2
But see, while idly* I stood looking on,
I found the effect of ᴬlove in idleness* ,

{insert 1}
{I saw sweet beauty* in her face,
Such as the daughter of Agenor had,
That made great Jove to humble him to her hand,
When with his knees he kiss'd the Cretan strand* . }

{insert 2} 3
{Tranio, I saw her coral* lips to move,
And with her breath she did perfume the air* .

4
Sacred and sweet was all I saw in her} {.}
And now in plainness* do confess* to thee,
That art to me as secret and as dear*
As Anna to the Queen* of Carthage was :
Tranio, I burn*, I pine, I perish, Tranio,
If I achieve* not this young* modest girl* . †

5
Counsel* me, Tranio, for I know thou canst :
Assist me, Tranio, for I know thou wilt.

First Folio

5/ Lucentio

1
Oh Tranio, till I found it to be true,
I never thought it possible or likely.

2
But see, while idely I stood looking on,
I found the effect of Love in idlenesse,

{insert 1}
{I saw sweet beautie in her face,
Such as the daughter of Agenor had,
That made great Jove to humble him to her hand,
When with his knees he kist the Cretan strond. }

{insert 2} 3
{Tranio, I saw her corrall lips to move,
And with her breath she did perfume the ayre,

Sacred and sweet was all I saw in her} {.}
And now in plainnesse do confesse to thee, ⁺
That art to me as secret and as deere
As Anna to the Queene of Carthage was :
Tranio ⁺ I burne, I pine, I perish ⁺ Tranio,
If I atchieve not this yong modest gyrle :
Counsaile me ⁺ Tranio, for I know thou canst :
Assist me ⁺ Tranio, for I know thou wilt.

Bianca's impact on Lucentio is beautifully underscored by the slow start building to an enormous release by the finish.

• what struck him most is spoken quietly without any embellishment, ' . . . till I found it to be true,/I never thought it possible or likely ./But see, while idely I stood looking on,' which leads to 'Sacred and sweet was all I saw in her'

• while his need for Tranio's help is highlighted by the only two surround phrases of the speech that end the speech, ' : Counsaile me Tranio, for I know thou canst : / Assist me Tranio, for I know thou wilt.' - the plea made even stronger by a faster release without the extra modern commas (shown in the F text by the ⁺)

• after Lucentio's somewhat 'gob-smacked' first two words ('Oh Tranio'), the rest of F #1 is breath-takingly quiet, while F #2 becomes carefully factual in the classical references to her (4/1 in the six lines), as if trying not disturb the vision perhaps?

• but, once he describes her physical attributes, so passion bursts through (0/5 in F #3's first five lines), while his fervent last five lines expressing 'I burne, I pine, I perish' becomes intellectually passionate (8/4)

The Taming of the Shrew / 69

#'s 6 - 9: PETRUCHIO, THE ANSWER TO HORTENSIO'S AND GREMIO'S PRAYERS

6/ Petruchio   Signior Hortensio, thus it stands with me,   between 1.2.53 - 76

Background: This is Petruchio's first major speech, and as such is self-explanatory; as to the classical references

1/ Florentius is a figure appearing in several stories, including *The Wife of Bath's Tale* by Chaucer, a knight who marries an ugly old woman to save his life; in some
stories the knight was named Florent or Florentius

2/ Sybil is a reference to the prophetess in Ovid who was awarded by Apollo ' as many years of life as there were grains in a handful of sand she picked up ' [3]

3/ Xanthippe, wife of the celebrated philosopher Socrates, 'remarkable for her shrewish disposition, for which her name has become proverbial' [4]

Style: direct address as part of a three handed scene

Where: outside Hortentio's home   **To Whom:** his friend Hortensio in front of his own servant, Grumio

# of Lines: 15   **Probable Timing: 0.50 minutes**

Modern Text	First Folio
6/ Petruchio	**6/ Petruchio**
1 Signior Hortensio, thus it stands with me :	1 Signior Hortensio, thus it stands with me, [+]
Antonio, my father is deceas'd,	Antonio [+] my father is deceast,
And I have thrust myself* into this maze,	And I have thrust my selfe into this maze,
Happily to wive and thrive as best I may . [†]	Happily to wive and thrive, [x] as best I may :
Therefore, if thou know	therefore, if thou know [+]
2 One rich enough to be Petruchio's wife	One rich enough to be Petruchio's wife : [+]
(As wealth is burthen of my wooing* dance),	(As wealth is burthen of my woing dance) [x]
Be she as foul* as was Florentius' [△]love,	Be she as foule as was Florentius Love,
As old as Sibyl*, and as curst and shrewd*	As old as Sibell, and as curst and shrow'd
As Socrates' Xantippe*, or a worse,	As Socrates Zentippe, or a worse : [+]
She moves me not, or not removes, at least,	She moves me not, or not removes, [+] at least [+]
Affections edge in me, ◇ were she [ ] as rough	Affections edge in me.
As are the swelling Adriatic* seas, ◇	2 Were she [is] as rough
I come to wive it wealthily in Padua ;	As are the swelling Adriaticke seas.
If wealthily, then happily in Padua.	3 I come to wive it wealthily in Padua : [x]
	If wealthily, then happily in Padua.

Fascinatingly for such a needy speech, F's predominantly intellectual orthography (12/4 overall) suggests that Petruchio is very serious.

• the few surround phrases show Petruchio making his need totally clear
" : therefore, if thou know/One rich enough to be Petruchio's wife : "
leading to
" I come to wive it wealthily in Padua : /If wealthily, then happily in Padua. "
heightened by the fact that these last two surround phrases form a separate sentence (F #3), which makes so much more of both his need and the expressing of it: most modern texts fold the lines into the earlier material

• in addition, the ungrammatical F #2 suggests just how much he is prepared to put up with to 'wive it wealthily', the dreadful syntax pointing to the need for a complete break before he can voice the appalling possibility: most modern texts correct the grammar by folding F #2 into the previous material, thus spoiling the potential horrified moment

• the unembellished lines point to how much he is prepared to put up with because '(As wealth is burthen of my woing dance)' it won't matter how many bad qualities she may possess, for 'she moves me not, or not removes at least/Affections edge in me.' – the statement perhaps made more powerful thanks to the extra speed of thought and delivery without the modern added commas (marked in the F text by the [+])

---

[3] *Shakespeare's Ovid.* Arthur Golding, ed. W.H.D.Rowse, page 278, as quoted in The Arden *The Taming of the Shrew*, fn to line 69, pp 187-8

[4] *Dictionary of Classics & Mythology*; an apprentice training/vanity press publication based on the works of Lampiere. (London: Asprey & Co. Ltd. undated - late nineteenth century)

7/ Petruchio   **But will {I} woo this Wilde-cat ?**   1.2.197 - 210

Background: Hortentio has introduced Petruchio to Bianca-wooing-rival Gremio, whose doubt that Petruchio will woo 'this Wilde-cat' gives rise to the following.

Style: address primarily to two people as part of a four handed scene

Where: outside Hortentio's home   **To Whom:** initially to the would-be-Bianca-wooer Gremio, and then expands the speech to include both his friend Hortentio and his own servant, Grumio

# of Lines: 15   Probable Timing: 0.50 minutes

Modern Text

7/ Petruchio

1   But will {I} woo this ᐃwild*ᵒcat ?

2   Why came I hither but to that intent ?

3   Think* you, a little din* can daunt mine ears* ?

4   Have I not in my time heard ᐃlions roar* ?

5   Have I not heard the sea, puff'd up with winds* ,
    Rage like an angry ᐃboar* chafed with sweat ?

6   Have I not heard great ᐃordnance in the field,
    And heavens ᐃartillery* thunder in the skies ?

7   Have I not in a pitched battle* heard

    Loud 'larums, neighing steeds, & trumpets' clang*?

8   And do you tell me of a woman's tongue,
    That gives not half* so great a blow to hear*
    As will* a ᐃchest*ᵒnut* in a ᐃfarmer's fire.

9   Tush, tush, fear* boys* with bugs {} for {I fear*} none.

First Folio

7/ Petruchio

1   But will {I} woo this Wilde-cat ?

2   Why came I hither,ₓ but to that intent ?

3   Thinke you, a little dinne can daunt mine eares ?

4   Have I not in my time heard Lions rore ?

5   Have I not heard the sea, puft up with windes,
    Rage like an angry Boare,ₓ chafed with sweat ?

6   Have I not heard great Ordnance in the field ? ₓ
    And heavens Artillerie thunder in the skies ?

7   Have I not in a pitched battell heard

    Loud larums, neighing steeds, & trumpets clangue ?

8   And do you tell me of a womans tongue ? ₓ
    That gives not halfe so great a blow to heare,ₓ
    As wil a Chesse-nut in a Farmers fire.

9   Tush, tush, feare boyes with bugs {,} {→} }
    For {I feare} none.

With the speech displaying no colons, and the fact that five of the nine sentences are short, it would seem that rather, than a statement of already absorbed philosophy, **Petruchio is discovering/improvising as he goes.**

• orthographically, the speech falls into two halves; a slow building intellectual and emotional start (5/4 in the first eight lines, F #1-6), and then a highly emotional finale (2/8 in the last six and a half lines, F #7-9)

• given the slow build of the opening, the sudden intense emotional release of F #3's 'Thinke you, a little dinne can daunt mine eares?' seems splendidly braggadocio, while it may be Petruchio is trying to persuade himself as well as others of his bravery with the intellectual concentration of F #6's 'Have I not heard great Ordnance in the field ? /And heavens Artillerie thunder in the skies?', especially with the F only question-mark at the end of the first line, since the Elizabethan question mark also functions as an exclamation point

• similarly, the final release of F #8's 'Tush, tush, feare boyes with bugs,/For I feare none.' has a splendid flourishing ring to it

• also, it could be that Petruchio is attempting to calm himself down, or convince others of his calm, with the two unembellished lines: F #2's 'Why came I hither, but to that intent?' (especially with the extra breath-thought, marked ,ₓ) and F #8's opening line 'And do you tell me of a womans tongue?', again with the F only question mark/exclamation point

8/ Petruchio   **Now by the world, it is a lustie Wench,**   between 2.1.160 - 181

Background: All the wooers have now been introduced to and accepted by Baptista, two as themselves viz. Petruchio to woo Kate, and Gremio to woo Bianca, and three in various disguises, all intending to woo Bianca, viz. Tranio disguised as Lucentio; Lucentio disguised as Cambio a schoolteacher; and Hortentio, who has decided to go under-cover as a music teacher (calling himself Litio) so as to have private access to Bianca (just as the real Lucentio has done). The disguised Hortentio has just come back from attempting to teach music to Kate, who hit him so forcibly with the lute that 'through the instrument my pate made way'. All eyes are now on Petruchio to see how he will react and what he will do.

Style: the first three lines to a large group, the remainder as a solo
Where: at Baptista's home   **To Whom:** initially Baptista, Gremio, the injured Hortentio, and Tranio pretending to be Lucentio, then self and direct audience address

# of Lines: 16   **Probable Timing: 0.50 minutes**

Modern Text

8/ Petruchio

1 Now by the world, it is a lusty* ᐃwench!†

2 I love her ten times more [than] e'er I did . †

3 O*, how I long to have some chat with her.
   ▪▪▪▪▪▪▪▪▪▪▪▪▪▪▪▪▪

4 {I'll} woo her with some spirit when she comes . †

5 Say that she rail*, why then I'll tell her plain*
   She sings as sweetly as a ᐃnightingale* ;
   Say that she frown*, I'll say she looks* as clear*
   As morning ᐃroses newly wash'd with dew;
   Say she be mute, and will not speak* a word,
   Then I'll commend her volubility,
   And say she uttereth piercing eloquence;
   If she do bid me pack*, I'll give her thanks*,
   As though she bid me stay by her a week*;
   If she deny* to wed, I'll crave the day
   When I shall ask* the banes, and when be married.

6 But here* she comes, and now, Petruchio, speak* .

First Folio

8/ Petruchio

1 Now by the world, it is a lustie Wench,
   I love her ten times more [then] ere I did,
   Oh⁺ how I long to have some chat with her.

2 {Ile} woo her with some spirit when she comes,
   Say that she raile, why then Ile tell her plaine,ₓ
   She sings as sweetly as a Nightinghale : ₓ
   Say that she frowne, Ile say she lookes as cleere
   As morning Roses newly washt with dew : ₓ
   Say she be mute, and will not speake a word,
   Then Ile commend her volubility,
   And say she uttereth piercing eloquence : ₓ
   If she do bid me packe, Ile give her thankes,
   As though she bid me stay by her a weeke : ₓ
   If she denie to wed, Ile crave the day
   When I shall aske the banes, and when be married.

3 But heere she comes, and now ⁺ Petruchio ⁺ speake.

With their first five sentences, most modern texts offer a far more rational Petruchio than F's original two onrushed sentences show. That in F he displays nowhere near as much self-control as he did in speech #7 above can be seen in the overall pattern of releases in the speech **(4/12)**.

• in the onrushed F #1, although the images in the monosyllabic non-embellished line 'I love her ten times more than ere I did' followed by the equally monosyllabic phrase 'how I long to have some chat with her' seem splendidly brave, the style hardly matches the substance – raising the questions just who this is for? and how brave is he really feeling?

• within the onrushed F #2, the non-embellished lines show that Petruchio's wasting no energy as he discovers a possible plan,
   "Ile woo her with some spirit when she comes,"
   realising opposites may work, for example
      "Say she be mute . . . /Then Ile commend her volubility,/And say she uttereth
         piercing eloquence" and
      "If she denie to wed, Ile crave the day . . . and when be married."
the discoveries perhaps forcing him to a state of apparent calmness

• the release in the final one line sentence (1/2, F #3) speaks volumes as to his whole state, especially given his inability to continue his previous onrush (through apprehension perhaps)

9/ Petruchio — Father, 'tis thus, your selfe and all the world

Background: After the first wooing where Petruchio has admitted being moved by Kate's beauty, and probably impressed by the fact that she scores more points than he in their verbal battle, presumably in part to satisfy the men to whom he had earlier boasted of certain victory, and in part to keep confounding and confusing Kate, he gives the greedy-for-news-of-success-men a totally false description of what took place between the two of them, in front of Kate who is there with him!, ending with the amazing announcement, and total surprise to her, that they 'will be married a sonday'.

Style: at least a five-handed scene, with a general address towards one person to impress him and quiet others

Where: in or about Baptista's home **To Whom:** Baptista, with Gremio, Tranio disguised as Lucentio, and Kate, all in attendance

between 2.1290 - 324

# of Lines: 25 **Probable Timing: 1.15 minutes**

Modern Text

9/ Petruchio

1 Father, 'tis thus : yourself* and all the world
That talk'd of her, have talk'd amiss* of her . †

2 If she be curst, it is for policy*,
For she's* not froward, but modest as the ᐃdove;
She* is not hot, but temperate as the morn*;
For patience she* will prove a second Grissel*,
And Roman* Lucrece for her chastity*;
And to conclude, we have 'greed so well together
That upon ᐃSunday* is the wedding ° day. †

3 I tell you 'tis incredible to believe*
How much she loves me . †

4   O*, the kindest Kate,
She* hung about my neck*, and kiss* on kiss*
She* vied* so fast, protesting oath on oath,
That in a twink* she won me to her love.

5 O* , you are novices! 'tis a world to see
How tame*, when men and women are alone,
A meacock* wretch can make the curstest shrew . †

6 Give me thy hand, Kate, I will unto Venice
To buy apparel* 'gainst the wedding day. †

7 Provide the feast, father, and bid the guests,
I will be sure my Katherine shall be fine.

8 Father, and wife, and gentlemen adieu . †

9 I will to Venice, ᐃSunday* comes apace . †

10 We will have rings and things, and fine array ;
And kiss* me Kate, we will be married a' ᐃSunday* .

First Folio

9/ Petruchio

1 Father, 'tis thus, + your selfe and all the world
That talk'd of her, have talk'd amisse of her :
If she be curst, it is for pollicie,
For shee's not froward, but modest as the Dove, +
Shee is not hot, but temperate as the morne, +
For patience shee will prove a second Grissell,
And Romane Lucrece for her chastitie :ₓ
And to conclude, we have greed so well together,ₓ
'That upon sonday is the wedding day.

2 I tell you 'tis incredible to beleeve
How much she loves me : oh + the kindest Kate,
Shee hung about my necke, and kisse on kisse
Shee vi'd so fast, protesting oath on oath,
That in a twinke she won me to her love.

3 Oh + you are novices, + 'tis a world to see
How tame + when men and women are alone,
A meacocke wretch can make the curstest shrew :
Give me thy hand + Kate, I will unto Venice
To buy apparell 'gainst the wedding day ;
Provide the feast + father, and bid the guests,
I will be sure my Katherine shall be fine.

4 Father, and wife, and gentlemen adieu,
I will to Venice, sonday comes apace,
We will have rings,ₓ and things, and fine array, +
And kisse me Kate, we will be married a sonday.

With ten sentences offered by most modern texts compared to F's onrushed four, plus the fact that five of F's six capitalised words are real names and therefore might be discounted - suggesting the speech is almost totally emotional (1/23 overall) - F offers a less controlled Petruchio than modern texts show.

• the onrush of F #1 suggests Petruchio is very determined to persuade the listeners of Kate's (supposed) simply pretending to be a shrew just for 'pollicie'; that (F #2 allows him to dwell more and build more on the (untrue) details of 'how much she loves me'

• the onrush of F #3 suggests something else, as the one sentence starts with the dismissal of the others as 'novices' (mt. #5), then suddenly turns to a farewell to Kate (mt. #6), followed by another swift change of focus to ignoring her and addressing her father and the other men (mt. #7) – the suddenness of the switches from one totally unrelated topic to another are perhaps an indication that Petruchio can no longer control the situation (Kate getting ornery or uncontrollable perhaps)

• yet, within the emotion there are surprisingly calm non-embellished lines
"And to conclude, we have greed so well together."
". . . you are novices, 'tis a world to see/How tame when men and women are alone,"
"Provide the feast father, and bid the guests,"
"Father and wife, and gentlemen adieu/. . ./We will have rings, and things, and fine array,"
where an actor/reader would normally expect to have more boasting and flourish – perhaps Petruchio is either exhausted or stunned by what has taken place

• the few capitals (only six overall) are clustered either towards the end of the F #1 (lines four through seven) in his description of Kate as (supposedly) gentle, and the repetition in F #3 and #4 of his going to Venice to prepare for the wedding

#'s 10 - 11: THE WINNING OF BIANCA

10/ Gremio   **First, as you know, my house within the City**   2.1.346 - 362

Background: At last Gremio makes his formal move in the wooing - dealing with Bianca's father as a matter of commerce, rather than dealing directly with her as a matter of love. Essentially Baptista has turned the whole thing into a bidding process for a commodity, having assured Gremio and the supposed Lucentio (Tranio in disguise) that whoever can offer the most in worldly goods shall have Bianca ('he . . ./that can assure my daughter greatest dower./Shall have my Biancas love.'). The following is Gremio's first offer (which turns out to be nowhere near enough, and whether Tranio's responses as Lucentio make Gremio aware of this is up to each production to decide).

Style: direct address to one person as part of a three handed scene
Where: in or about Baptista's home   **To Whom:** Baptista in front of Tranio disguised as Lucentio
# of Lines: 17   **Probable Timing: 0.55 minutes**

Modern Text

10/ Gremio

1
First, as you know, my house within the ᴬcity
Is richly furnished with plate and gold,
Basins* and ewers to lave her dainty hands ;
My hangings all of ᴬTyrian* tapestry ;
In ᴬivory coffers* I have stuff'd* my crowns* ;
In ᴬcypress₊ chests my arras counterpoints,
Costly apparel*, tents, and ᴬcanopies,
Fine ᴬlinen, Turkey cushions boss'd* with pearl*,
[Valance] of Venice gold in needlework* :
Pewter and brass*, and all things that belongs
To house or house-keeping . †
                    Then at my farm*

2
I have a hundred milch-kine to the [pail],
Six* ˢscore fat ᴬoxen standing in my stalls,
And all things answerable to this portion.

3
Myself* am strook* in years*, I must confess* ,
And if I die tomorrow, this is hers,
If whil'st I live she will be only* mine.

First Folio

10/ Gremio

1
First, as you know, my house within the City
Is richly furnished with plate and gold,
Basons and ewers to lave her dainty hands :ₓ
My hangings all of tirian tapestry :ₓ
In Ivory cofers I have stuft my crownes :ₓ
In Cypres chests my arras counterpoints,
Costly apparell, tents, and Canopies,
Fine Linnen, Turky cushions bost with pearle,
[Vallens] ⁵ of Venice gold,ₓ in needle worke :
Pewter and brasse, and all things that belongs
To house or house-keeping : then at my farme
I have a hundred milch-kine to the [pail],
Sixe-score fat Oxen standing in my stalls,
And all things answerable to this portion.

2
My selfe am strooke in yeeres⁺ I must confesse,
And if I die to morrow⁺ this is hers,
If whil'st I live she will be onely mine.

• Gremio's opening salvo in the bidding war starts out very quietly (1/0 in the first four lines), with the initial listing of his worldly goods all unembellished
"Is richly furnished with plate and gold,/Basons and ewers to lave her dainty hands :/My hangings all of tirian tapestry :"
as if he were nervous and/or taking great care to get the words out

• with the last of the unembellished lines also being the first of the (only) two consecutive surround phrases in the speech 'My hangings all of tirian tapestry :/In Ivory cofers I have stuft my crownes : ', it would seem that Gremio is beginning to find his verbal feet

• for the next six and a half lines, dealing with all his city wealth (from 'In Ivory cofers' through to 'or house-keeping'), he becomes both intellectually and emotionally passionate (6/7)

• while the speech finishes almost totally emotionally (1/7 in the last three and a half lines of F # 1 plus all of F #2)

• interestingly within this emotion, as the description of his extra country wealth begins so he starts out in calm unembellished self-control once again (I have a hundred milch-kine to the pale), finishing the same way when hinting at even more matching wealth ('And all things answerable to this portion.')

• rather ingenuously (or nauseatingly, dependent upon your point of view), the final 'bribe' is also unembellished: 'And if I die to morrow this is hers' (the middle line of F #2)

---

⁵ Ff = 'Vallens', for clarity most modern texts spell it as 'Valance' (i.e. fringes on the bed canopy)

11/ Bianca Now let mee see if I can conster it. 3.1.41 -45

Background: Seeming to thoroughly enjoy all the rival attention, especially here between the two (disguised) suitors, Bianca responds to Lucentio's speech dismissing him with no chance to elaborate further so she can talk (flirt?) with the disguised Hortentio.

Style: three-handed scene

Where: in or about Baptista's home   **To Whom:** Lucentio, disguised as Cambio, at the same time attempting to prevent the disguised Hortentio from overhearing

# of Lines: 4   **Probable Timing: 0.20 minutes**

First Folio

11/ Bianca

1 Now let mee see if I can conster it.

        Hic [ibas] sim-

2 *ois,* I know you not, *bic est [sigeria] tellus,* I trust you not,
   bic [staterat] priami; take heede he heare us not, *regia* presume not, *Celsa senis,* despaire not.

- in a very straightforward speech, the cautionary release in the penultimate line 'take heede he heare us not' and in the final line's encouraging 'despaire not' are well worthy of exploration

Modern Text

11/ Bianca

1 Now let me* see if I can conster it: ◊   " △*Hic [ibat] sim-
   ois",* I know you not, *"bic est [Sigeia] tellus",* I trust you not,
   "△*Hic [steterat] △Priami"*, take heed* he hear* us not, *"regia"*
   presume not, " △*celsa senis",* despair* not.

#'s 12 - 14: PETRUCHIO'S MACHIAVELLIAN TESTOSTERONE BEHAVIOUR   between 3.2.152 - 183

12/ Gremio   A bridegroome say you ?

Background: Since Tranio and Lucentio were busily planning strategy, neither witnessed the wedding ceremony for Kate and Petruchio, which, as Gremio tells the disguised Tranio in great detail, was hardly conventional.

Style: initially verse, and then, in the First Folio at least, prose, as part of a possible three-hander, though the real Lucentio might have left the stage as Gremio entered

Where: somewhere close to where the wedding took place, either the Church or Baptista's home   **To Whom:** the disguised Tranio, still believing him to be Lucentio, with perhaps the real Lucentio also present

# of Lines: 24   **Probable Timing: 1.15 minutes**

First Folio

12/ Gremio

1 A bridegroome⁺ say you ? '

2 Why⁺ hee's a devill, a devill, a very fiend.

3 Ile tell you ⁺ sir Lucentio ;ₓ when the Priest
   Should aske if Katherine should be his wife,
   I, by goggs woones⁺ quoth he, and swore so loud,
   That all amaz'd the Priest let fall the booke,
   And as he stoop'd againe to take it up,
   This mad-brain'd bridegroome tooke him such a cuffe,ₓ
   That downe fell Priest and booke, and booke and Priest,
   Now take them up ⁺ quoth he, if any list.

Modern Text

12/ Gremio

1 A bridegroom*, say you ? '

2 Why, he's* a devil*, a devil*, a very fiend.

3 I'll tell you, △Sir Lucentio : when the △priest
   Should ask* if Katherine should be his wife,
   "Ay*, by gogs* wouns*, *" quoth he, and swore so loud,
   That all amaz'd the Priest let fall the book*,
   And as he stoop'd again* to take it up,
   This mad-brain'd bridegroom* took* him such a cuff*

4 That down* fell Priest and book*, and book* and △priest.†
   "Now take them up," quoth he, "if any list*.

- the opening two short sentences, in themselves an indication of the uncommon moment about to be described, start emotionally (0/4)

The shaded text shows where, as on several other occasions, F1 allows Gremio to slip from the polite formality of verse to somewhat more street smart and earthy prose as the better of him. Most modern texts follow F2 and set the passage as verse, thus removing this potential character trait. They spoil the moment even further by taking F's onrushed F #4, which suggests Gremio just cannot stop the prose description from pouring out of him, and creating a much more rational recollection by splitting it into no fewer than seven sentences.

4 {The wench} trembled and shooke:ₓ for why, he stamp'd and swore,ₓ as if the Vicar meant to cozen him :but after many ceremonies done, hee calls for wine, a health⁺ quoth he, as if he had beene aboord,⁺ carowsing to his Mates af-ter a storme, quaft off the Muscadell, and threw the sops all in the Sextons face :having no other reason,ₓ but that his beard grew thinne and hungerly, and seem'd to aske him sops as hee was drinking :This done, hee tooke the Bride about the necke, and kist her lips with such a cla-morous smacke, that at the parting all the Church did eccho :and I seeing this, came thence for very shame, and after mee I know the rout is comming, such a mad mar-ryage never was before : harke, harke, I heare the min-strels play.

• that the story affects Gremio emotionally (whether amazement or amusement is up to each reader to decide) can be seen in the surround phrase that opens F #3 ('Ile tell you, sir Lucentio; ') ending as it does with the only emotional semicolon in the speech

• and, after F #3's intellectual two line opening (3/1), the recollection becomes highly emotional (3/9 in the remaining six lines of F #3; 7/21 in the thirteen and a half prose lines of F #4)

• thus, within the emotional sea, the occasional cluster release shows Gremio illustrating or commenting upon certain moments burned into his brain such as: 'hee's a devill, a devill'; by 'goggs woones' (i.e. 'God's wounds'); 'This mad-brain'd bridegroome tooke him such a cuffe, /That downe fell Priest and booke; and booke and Priest,'; 'as if he had beene aboord, carowsing to his Mates after a storme'; 'hee tooke the Bride about the necke;'

• the art of story-telling doesn't seem to escape him either, for the end of F #3 finishes with an incredibly calm 'Now take them up, quoth he, if any list', and if not the art of story-telling, then this particular incident (Petruchio's knocking the Priest and bible to the floor) seems to have struck Gremio almost dumb

5 {The wench} trembled and shook* ; for why, he stamp'd
   and swore
   As if the △vicar meant to cozen him . †
6 But after many ceremonies done,
   He calls for wine . †
7   "A health !" quoth he, as if
   He had been* aboard*, carousing* to his △mates
   After a storm*, quaff'd△ off the △'muscadel*,
   And threw the sops all in the △sexton's face :
   Having no other reason
   But that his beard grew thin* and hungerly,
   And seem'd to ask* him sops as he* was drinking . †
8 This done, he* took* the Bride about the neck*,
   And kiss'd her lips with such a clamorous smack* . †
   That at the parting all the △church did echo* . †
9 And I seeing this, came thence for very shame,
   And after me* I know the rout is coming* . †
10 Such a mad marriage* never was before . †
11 Hark* , hark* , I hear* the minstrels play.

13/ Petruchio   O Kate content thee, prethee be not angry .   between 3.2.215 -235

Background: Having destroyed two highly bourgeois conventional traits of any mercantile wedding through his impossible attire and behaviour, Petruchio now uses a mercantile analysis to describe Kate as his possession, which in many ways parallels the way Bianca was auctioned off to the highest bidder. Whether this is genuine boorish behaviour or a deliberate attempt in part to show Kate just how appalling the society she is already at odds with is and in part to keep everyone off balance is up to each production to decide. What triggers the speech is Kate's public insistence that, though Petruchio has stated they must leave straight away and not wait for the wedding feast, she has commanded that the Gentlemen go 'forward to the bridall dinner', telling her father for all to hear that Petruchio 'shall stay my leisure'.

Style: public address to the assembled company at large

Where: as above   **To Whom:** initially Kate and then to Baptista, Bianca, the disguised Tranio, Gremio, Grumio, Biondello, perhaps Lucentio and Hortentio, plus however many guests the acting company can afford

# of Lines: 15   **Probable Timing: 0.50 minutes**

Modern Text

13/ Petruchio

1 O Kate, content thee, prithee be not angry.

2 They shall go* forward, Kate, at thy command. †

3 Obey the ^bride, you that attend on her.

4 Go* to the feast, revel* and domineer* ,
   Carouse* full measure to her maiden °head,
   Be mad* and merry, or go* hang your selves ;
   But for my bonny Kate, she must with me . †

5 Nay, look* not big, nor stamp* , nor stare, nor fret,
   I will be master of what is mine own* . †

6 She* is my goods, my chattels, she is my house,
   My household "stuff* , my field, my barn* ,
   My horse, my ox* , my ass* , my any thing :
   And here* she stands, touch her who ever dare,
   I'll bring mine action on the proudest he
   That stops my way in Padua .

First Folio

13/ Petruchio

1 O Kate + content thee, prethee be not angry .

2 They shall goe forward + Kate + at thy command,
   Obey the Bride + you that attend on her.

3 Goe to the feast, revell and domineere,
   Carowse full measure to her maiden-head,
   Be madde and merry, or goe hang your selves : x
   But for my bonny Kate, she must with me :
   Nay, looke not big, nor stampe, nor stare, nor fret,
   I will be master of what is mine owne,
   Shee is my goods, my chattels, she is my house,
   My houshold-stuffe, my field, my barne,
   My horse, my oxe, my asse, my any thing, +
   And heere she stands, touch her who ever dare,
   Ile bring mine action on the proudest he
   That stops my way in Padua :

F's sentence structure suggests a deceptively calm and rational opening (F #1-2 matched with mt.'s #1-2), which is then blown apart by one long final F #3 onrush, the impact of which most modern texts reduce by splitting F #3 into three.

• the deceptively calm opening is matched by an apparent intellectual calm (3/1), coupled with two small unembellished phrases addressed to Kate that also seem to suggest a (as it turns out unwarranted) calm: 'content thee, prethee be not angry.'

• and once the onrush comes, it comes with an enormously full emotional release (2/15 in the twelve lines of F #3)

• it is fascinating that the long-spelled words do not come in clusters in this case, but rather seem to fall as one per phrase, as if his argument were emotionally important to him – perhaps an attack on the very bourgeois beliefs of all present that allowed Kate's sister Bianca to be auctioned off to the highest bidder

• thus the one double release ('revell and domineere,') coming as it does at the start of F #3, may be deceptive, serving only to grab the listeners' attention to 'yet another Petruchio harangue' before moving into something rather more serious

• the colon ending the speech suggests that Petruchio hasn't really finished, but rather is still energised awaiting and any challenge that may come his way as a result of what he has just said

14/ Petruchio   **Thus have I politickely begun my reigne,**   4.1.118 - 211

Background: Having reached home in Verona, Petruchio's startling ways continue. Faced with a rabble of incompetent servants, he has destroyed the meal provided for himself and Kate, thus ensuring she goes to bed without any nourishment - which is all part of his plan, as he now explains.

Style: solo

Where: unspecified, somewhere in Petruchio's home   **To Whom:** direct audience address, ending with a challenge

# of Lines: 24   **Probable Timing: 1.15 minutes**

Modern Text

14/ Petruchio

1
Thus have I politickly* begun my reign*,
And 'tis my hope to end successfully* . †

2
My △falcon* now is sharp* and passing empty*,
And till she stoop*, she must not be full-°gorg'd,
For then she never lookes* upon her lure.

3
Another way I have to man my △haggard,
To make her come, and know her △keeper's call,
That is, to watch her, as we watch these △kites
That baite*, and beat*, and will not be obedient . †

4
She eat* no meat* to day, nor none shall eat* ; ◇
Last night she slept not, nor to night she shall not ;
As with the meat* , some undeserved fault
I'll find* about the making of the bed,
And here* I'll fling the pillow, there the bolster* , †
This way the △coverlet, another way the sheets . †

5
Ay*, and amid this hurly* I intend
That all is done in reverend care of her,
And in conclusion, she shall* watch all night,
And if she chance to nod I'll rail* and brawl*
And with the clamor keepe* her still* awake . †

6
This is a way to kill* a △wife with kindness*
And thus I'll curb* her mad and headstrong humor . †

7
He that knows* better how to tame a shrew,
Now let him speak* ; 'tis charity to shew.

First Folio

14/ Petruchio

1
Thus have I politickely begun my reigne,
And 'tis my hope to end successfully : [x]
My Faulcon now is sharpe, and passing emptie,
And til she stoope, she must not be full gorg'd,
For then she never lookes upon her lure.

2
Another way I have to man my Haggard,
To make her come, and know her Keepers call, [x]
That is, to watch her, as we watch these Kites, [x]
That baite, and beate, and will not be obedient :
She eate no meate to day, nor none shall eate.

3
Last night she slept not, nor to night she shall not : [x]
As with the meate, some undeserved fault
Ile finde about the making of the bed,
And heere Ile fling the pillow, there the boulster,
This way the Coverlet, another way the sheets :
I, and amid this hurlie I intend, [x]
That all is done in reverend care of her,
And in conclusion, she shal watch all night,
And if she chance to nod, Ile raile and brawle, [x]
And with the clamor keepe her stil awake :
This is a way to kil a Wife with kindnesse,
And thus Ile curbe her mad and headstrong humor :
He that knowes better how to tame a shrew,
Now let him speake, † 'tis charity to shew.

F's onrushed three sentences suggest a man discovering what might work, not a character explaining what he already knows is going to be successful. Not only do most modern texts reset the speech as seven sentences, thus rendering Petruchio far more rational than F suggests, they also transfer the triumphant, sentence-ending 'She eate no meate to day, nor none shall eate.' (end of F #2) to start a new idea (mt. #4), reducing the 'I've done it' of the original to a mere first stepping stone in a further litany of deprivation.

• while the speech overall is tremendously emotional (5/23 overall), reinforcing the idea of a Petruchio not in complete self-control, two unembellished lines in F #3 show a totally different spirit underlying the supposed public madman
"I, and amid this hurlie I intend, /That all is done in reverend care of her," leading into the equally unembellished
"And in conclusion, she shall watch all night,/And if she chance to nod,"
it might just suggest that his imposed lack of sleep is not being done maliciously, but is instead a key element in his plan, especially since the earlier unembellished line opening F #3 ('Last night she slept not, nor to night she shall not:') also refers to sleep deprivation, itself heightened by being both monosyllabic and a surround phrase

• F #1 opens highly emotionally (1/7), perhaps a suggestion that his success (by depriving Kate of any substantial food) may have taken him by surprise

• after the intellectual image (3/0 in the first three lines of F #2) of comparing his handling of Kate as to how he would a very special hawk (i.e. the 'Haggard', defined by the O.E.D as 'a wild female hawk caught in her adult plumage'; and as Ann Thompson notes in her Arden version of the play 'the purpose of training a falcon is not to break the bird's spirit'), the remainder of the speech becomes almost completely emotional (2/16 in the remaining sixteen lines)

15: KATE'S STUNNING TRIUMPH OVER ALL, INCLUDING PETRUCHIO

15/ Kate   Fie, fie, unknit that thretning unkinde brow,   5.2.136 - 179

Background: After an encounter with Vincentio, Lucentio's father, on the journey from Verona to Padua, Petruchio has at last got Kate to realise she can get her point across not by being an offensive harridan or shrew, but simply by defining the world as she sees it and then speaking her mind from a clear understanding and definitive personal philosophy, and that so doing can be a wonderfully fun experience. Indeed her word games with Vincentio are far more rich and witty than Petruchio's - especially if Vincentio does sometimes fuss like an old woman (Act Four Scene 5). She puts this into practice here, not necessarily as an act of submission but as an act of joyous retribution, getting her own back on all those who have scorned her to date - including Petruchio, for the extra Folio only period in the middle of line thirteen (separating sentences F #4-5), as shown here, allows her to spell out just how much a man (Petruchio amongst others) is expected and going to have to do to fulfill his side of the marriage contract. The one phrase at the end of the speech, 'if the please', has given great offense to many women over the ages, for it seems so male oriented. Yet a simple reworking of the thought that her 'hand is readie', the 'please' referring to only if she adjudges his behaviour to be worthy of her hand, thus allowing the phrase to mean 'if he pleases <u>me</u>' strengthens the notion of her stating that a contract between equal partners is the only base of true male-female relationship, and that, if necessary, a woman should fight (but not as a man) to get her rights.

Style: initially towards two people, gradually bringing in all the others listening, especially Petruchio
Where: wherever the wedding 'Banket' is taking place   **To Whom:** initially her sister Bianca and the Widow, then Petruchio, and so for the benefit of all others present
# of Lines: 44   **Probable Timing: 2.10 minutes**

Modern Text

15/ Kate

1 Fie, fie, unknit that threat'ning* unkind* brow,
  And dart not scornful* glances from those eyes*,
  To wound thy ᐃlord, thy ᐃking, thy ᐃgovernor* .

2 It blots thy beauty*, as frosts do* bite the ᐃmeads,
  Confounds thy fame, as whirlwinds* shake fair* buds* ,
  And in no sence is meet* or amiable.

3 A woman mov'd, is like a fountain* troubled,
  Muddy*, ill seeming, thick*, bereft of beauty*,
  And while it is so, none so dry or thirsty*
  Will deign* to sip, or touch one drop of it.

4 Thy husband is thy ᐃlord, thy life, thy keeper,
  Thy head, thy sovereign* ; ᐃone that cares for thee,
  And for thy maintenance; ◇ᐃcommits his body

First Folio

15/ Kate

1 Fie, fie, unknit that thretaning unkinde brow,
  And dart not scornefull glances from those eies,
  To wound thy Lord, thy King, thy Governour.

2 It blots thy beautie, as frosts doe bite the Meads,
  Confounds thy fame, as whirlewinds shake faire budds,
  And in no sence is meete or amiable.

3 A woman mov'd, is like a fountaine troubled,
  Muddie, ill seeming, thicke, bereft of beautie,
  And while it is so, none so dry or thirstie
  Will daigne to sip, or touch one drop of it.

4 Thy husband is thy Lord, thy life, thy keeper,
  Thy head, thy soveraigne :ₓ One that cares for thee,
  And for thy maintenance.

I do not believe this needs to be handled as a submission speech: it can be interpreted as an argument that a **wonderful male-female partnership is possible, provided both parties understand the rules of the game and treat each other well.**

• thus among a large number of unembellished lines, the one ending F #9 seems to be the most important, suggesting that one can win by finding one's true strength instead of ' … seeming to be most, which indeed we least are'; thus, she has at last realised why she suffered so many rejections earlier in the play - as the only emotionally (semicoloned) formed strongly released surround phrase shows '; But now I see our Launces are but strawes : '

• the other surround phrases in the speech point to the pivotal key in Kate's argument, a husband must perform his duty well, in that first he is
  ": One that cares for thee,/And for thy maintenance."
which she elaborates via a vital F only period [9]
  ". Commits his body/To painfull labour, both by sea and land : "
then, and only then, can a woman agree with the traditional view that
  ". Thy husband is thy Lord, thy life, thy keeper,/Thy head, thy soveraigne : "
because he then will have <u>earned</u> the soubriquets

• within the overall emotional release (11/37) throughout the forty-five line speech, there are many key unembellished lines, perhaps suggesting not only has she been doing a lot of thinking, she is taking great care to ensure that

6 in many ways, the F #4 period, rarely set in modern texts, is the key to the new understanding Kate has of her relationship with Petruchio: in the just completed F #4 she spelled out the traditional view of the male in the relationsh and in the new F #5 she spells out, presumably as much for Petruchio's benefit as anyone else's, just exactly how much a husband has to endure to secure the regard and dues laid out in F #4: the fact that the modern text merges both sentences blurs Kate's expression of her clear understanding of the rules of the game, and reduces the F #5 to a mere continuance of the praise of the F #4

Commits his body
To painfull labour, both by sea and land :ₓ
To watch the night in stormes, the day in cold,
Whil'st thou ly'st warme at home, secure and safe,
And craves no other tribute at thy hands,ₓ
But love, faire lookes, and true obedience ;ₓ
Too little payment for so great a debt.

5

Such dutie as the subject owes the Prince,
Even such a woman oweth to her husband :ₓ
And when she is froward, peevish, sullen, sowre,
And not obedient to his honest will,
What is she but a foule contending Rebell,
And gracelesse Traitor to her loving Lord?

6

I am asham'd that women are so simple,ₓ
To offer warre, where they should kneele for peace :ₓ
Or seeke for rule, supremacie, and sway,
When they are bound to serve, love, and obay.

7

Why are our bodies soft, and weake, and smooth,
Unapt to toyle and trouble in the world,
But that our soft conditions, and our harts,
Should well agree with our externall parts?

8

Come, come, you froward and unable wormes,
My minde hath bin as bigge as one of yours,
My heart as great, my reason haplie more,
To bandie word for word,ₓ and frowne for frowne ;
But now I see our Launces are but strawes :ₓ
Our strength as weake, our weakenesse past compare,
That seeming to be most,ₓ which we indeed least are.

9

Then vale your stomackes, for it is no boote,
And place your hands below your husbands foote :ₓ
In token of which dutie, if he please,
My hand is readie, may it do him ease.

10

---

everyone will understand her complex argument

• referring to her own previous shrewish actions as well as the rather dismissive behaviour Bianca and the Widow have shown towards their new husbands during the earlier part of the evening's celebration, Kate compares women who behave so to a 'a fountaine troubled'
"And while it is so, none so dry or thirstie/Will daigne to sip, or touch one drop of it."

• she then goes on to argue that yes, while men will expect
"And craves no other tribute at thy hands, /But love, faire lookes, and true obedience ;/Too little payment for so great a debt"
the wife is not expected to be submissively supportive, and will only be blamed if the husband behaves decently yet the wife shows herself
"And not obedient to his honest will"
thus stressing the fact taht the only thing that could possibly justify a woman accepting the traditional concept of a wife's 'dutie' as that of a 'subject' to a 'Prince', is if the husband shows an 'honest will': in such (rare?) circumstances, as Kate suggested earlier, 'Even such a woman oweth to her husband'

• as seen in the surround phrases, Kate has already found her strength as a woman, probably completed in the teasing of Vincentio described in the background above: her power lies in her mind, (not in being a destructive shrew or pseudo-man), hence there is no weakness in her admission
"I am asham'd that women are so simple,"
for, as she explains to the women she is scolding,
"My heart as great, my reason haplie more,/To bandie word for word"
but there's no need, provided a husband 'please', and is 'honest': so
"In token of which dutie, if he please,/My hand is readie, may it do him ease."

• in scolding the women, Kate opens passionately (3/3, F #1), then becomes emotional as she strips them of their 'beautie' and 'fame' (1/4, F #2) and compares them to a 'fountaine troubled' (0/3, F #4)

• in defining the traditional view of the husband, Kate becomes slightly factual (2/1, F #4), and then totally emotional as she spells out all he has to do, 'commits his body' to earn a wife's 'love' and 'duty' (0/7, F #5)

• following her intellectual and emotional equating of a wife's duty to that of a subject if the husband is honest (4/4, F #6), Kate is for the remainder of the speech (F #7-10) both carefully expressive (seven and a half unembellished lines) and highly (even giddily? joyously?) emotional (1/15 in the other eleven and a half line) as she finally voices her own foolishness and her realisation of how to be an equal partner (without having to resort to fighting men on their terms)

• thus it's fascinating to see a sudden flurry of short spellings as she explains herself and her view of an ideal relationship: 'bin', 'haplie' and 'bandie' in F #6; 'dutie' and 'readie' in the last two lines of the speech

---

To painful* labor*, both by sea and land ;
To watch the night in storms* , the day in cold,
Whilst thou li'st* warm* at home, secure and safe,
And craves no other tribute at thy hands
But love, fair* looks* , and true obedience -
Too little payment for so great a debt.

5

Such duty,* as the subject owes the prince,
Even such a woman oweth to her husband ;
And when she is froward, peevish, sullen, sour* ,
And not obedient to his honest will,
What is she but a foul contending ᐃrebel*,
And graceless* ᐃtraitor to her loving ᐃlord ?

6

I am asham'd that women are so simple
To offer war* where they should kneel* for peace,
Or seek* for rule, supremacy*, and sway,
When they are bound to serve, love, and obey.

7

Why are our bodies soft, and weak*, and smooth,
Unapt to toil* and trouble in the world,
But that our soft conditions, and our hearts*,
Should well agree with our external* parts ?

8

Come, come, you froward and unable worms*! †
My mind* hath been* as big* as one of yours,

9

My heart as great, my reason haply* more,
To bandy* word for word and frown* for frown* ;
But now I see our ᐃlances* are but straws* ,
Our strength as weak*, our weakness* past compare,
That seeming to be most which we indeed least are.

10

Then vale your stomachs* , for it is no boot* ,
And place your hands below your husbands foot* ,
In token of which duty,* if he please,
My hand is ready*, may it do him ease.

LOVE'S LABOUR'S LOST

SPEECHES IN ORDER	TIME	PAGE
# 1: Ferdinand's Achademe		
1/ **Ferdinand** Let Fame, that all hunt after in their lives,	1.10	81
#'s 2 - 4: Breaking the Oath #1: Young Men Falling In Love		
2/ **Boyet** If my observation (which very seldome lies) . . .	1.00	82
3/ **Berowne** O, and I forsooth in love,	1.40	83
4/ **Berowne** The King he is hunting the Deare,	1.00	84
#'s 5 - 7: Breaking The Oath #2: Recriminations and Absolution		
5/ **King** Come sir, you blush: as his, your case is such,	1.00	86
6/ **Berowne** Now step I forth to whip hypocrisie.	1.40	87
7/ **Berowne** O 'tis more then neede.	2.50	89
#'s 8 - 11: Young Women in Love		
8/ **Queene** Good L. Boyet, my beauty though but mean,	1.10	91
9/ **Maria/1. Lady** I know {Longavill}; at a marriage feast,	0.40	92
10/ **Katherine/2. Lady** The yong Dumaine, a well accomplisht youth,	0.30	92
11/ **Rosaline** Another of these Students at that time,	0.45	93
#'s 12 - 14: Unmercifull Teasing of the Oath Breakers		
12/ **Queene** And will they so? the Gallants shall be taskt:	1.30	94
13/ **Rosaline** We are wise girles to mocke our Lovers so.	0.40	95
14/ **Berowne** Thus poure the stars down plagues for perjury.	1.15	96
#'s 15 - 16: Entertainment		
15/ **Braggart** I doe affect the very ground (which is base)	0.55	97
16/ **Braggart** Sir, it is the Kings most sweet pleasure . . .	1.00	98
# 17: Reality Intrudes		
17/ **Queene** A time me thinkes too short,	1.15	99

SPEECHES BY GENDER

		Speech #(s)
SPEECHES FOR WOMEN (7)		
Queene	**Traditional & Today:** young woman of marriageable age	#8, #12, #17
Maria/{1. Lady}	**Traditional & Today:** young woman of marriageable age	#9
Katherine/{2. Lady}	**Traditional & Today:** young woman of marriageable age	#10
Rosaline	**Traditional & Today:** young woman of marriageable age, from the text slightly more experienced than the others	#11, #13
SPEECHES FOR EITHER GENDER (0)		
SPEECHES FOR MEN (10)		
Ferdinand/King	**Traditional & Today:** young man of marriageable age	#1, #5
Boyet	**Traditional:** older male acting as both chaperone and possibly match-maker: the character is described by one of the young women as 'Cupids Grandfather'	#2
	Today: could be played by any gender and probably any age, though someone older than the eight young people falling in love is usually preferred	
Berowne	**Traditional & Today:** young man of marriageable age	3, #4, #6, #7, #14
Braggart	**Traditional:** older man, to separate him as much possible from the young woman with whom he has fallen in love	#15, #16
	Today: usually the same, but can be played younger if the 'foreigness' is followed through to allow for the same distancing as described above	

LOVE'S LABOUR'S LOST

1: FERDINAND'S ACHADEME

1/ Ferdinand   Let Fame, that all hunt after in their lives,   1.1.1 - 23

Background: As the first speech of the play, it explains both circumstances and character.

Style: as an opener to a four-handed scene

Where: unspecified, somewhere in or close to Ferdinand's palace   **To Whom:** Longavile and Dumaine, out and out supporters, and, as it turns out, the somewhat doubtful Berowne

# of Lines: 23   **Probable Timing: 1.10 minutes**

Modern Text	First Folio
1/ Ferdinand	**1/ Ferdinand**
1 Let △fame, that all hunt after in their lives,	1 Let ⁺Fame, that all hunt after in their lives,
Live regist'red upon our brazen △tombs*,	Live registred upon our brazen Tombes,
And then grace us in the disgrace of death ;	And then grace us in the disgrace of death : ₓ
When spite* of cormorant devouring Time,	{W}hen spight of cormorant devouring Time,
Th'endeavor* of this present breath may buy	Th'endeavour of this present breath may buy : ₓ
That honor* which shall bate his scythe's keen* edge,	That honour which shall bate his sythes keene edge,
And make us heirs* of all eternity.*₊	And make us heyres of all eternitie.
2 Therefore, brave △conquerors* - for so you are,	2 Therefore ⁺ brave Conquerours, for so you are,
That war* against your own* affections	That warre against our owne affections, ₓ
And the huge △army* of the worlds desires - ◇	And the huge Armie of the worlds desires.ₓ
Our late edict shall strongly stand in force :	3 Our late edict shall strongly stand in force, ⁺
Navarre* shall be the wonder of the world; ◇	Navar shall be the wonder of the world.
Our △court shall be a little △academe* ,	4 Our Court shall be a little Achademe,
Still and contemplative in living △art.	Still and contemplative in living Art.
3 You three, Berowne, Dumaine, and Longaville,*,	5 You three, Berowne, Dumaine, and Longavill,
Have sworn* for three years'* term* to live with me :	Have sworne for three yeeres terme,ₓ to live with me :
My fellow △scholars*, and to keep* those statutes	My fellow Schollers, and to keepe thost statutes, ₓ
That are recorded in this schedule.* here* .	That are recorded in this scedule heere.
4 Your oaths* are pass'd, and now subscribe your names,	6 Your oathes are past, and now subscribe your names : ₓ
That his own* hand may strike his honor* down* ,	That his owne hand may strike his honour downe,
That violates the smallest branch herein . ⁺	That violates the smallest branch heerein :
5 If you are arm'd to do*, as sworn* to do,	If you are arm'd to doe, as sworne to do,
Subscribe to your deep* [oath]* , and keep* it too.	Subscribe to your deepe [oathes], and keepe it to.

F's orthography reveals a King who, despite his circumspect opening, cannot contain his excitement about what he and his three friends are about to do.

• the three unembellished lines point to Ferdinand's deep-held longings and beliefs that they should not seek fame but (F #1 line three) let it

"And then grace us in the disgrace of death : ", because
"Our late edict shall strongly stand in force,/Navar shall be the wonder of the world."

• and the single surround phrase points to the importance of what they have done and are about to do
" . Your oathes are past, and now subscribe your names : "

• Ferdinand begins quite carefully, the opening maxim starting intellectually (4/1 in the first five lines of F #1)

• the totally ungrammatical colon at the end of line five suggests that Ferdinand believes he is about to say something truly important for himself and those with him (that they will be 'heyres of all eternitie') and needs to gather himself before speaking - not surprisingly, it's at this point that emotions flood him (0/3 in the last two lines of F #1)

• but Ferdinand manfully recovers self-control, as he names the four of them 'Conquerours' of their 'owne affections' and the 'worlds desires' (F#2, 2/1), though he needs an extra breath-thought (marked , ₓ) to do so; this is followed by F #3's unembellished (dramatically quiet?) importance of 'Navar' becoming the 'wonder of the world', while the thought that his three companions will help form the 'Achademe' is almost totally intellectual once more (6/1, F #4 and the first line of F #5)

• and then the emotional floodgates swing wide open, calling upon them to now sign the 'scedule' as they have earlier 'sworne to do' (1/16 in the last eight lines of the speech)

#'s 2-4: BREAKING THE OATH #1: YOUNG MEN FALLING IN LOVE

2/ Boyet   **If my observation (which very seldome lies) . . .**   between 2.1.228-249

Background: Even though there has only been one short meeting between the Princesse and Ferdinand, Boyet's keen eye has already discerned that Navar (Ferdinand) is already completely smitten. The rhyming couplets suggest Boyet's exuberance, either at the discovery and/or simply in the delight of speaking his findings, stylishly improvising the embellishment of the content as he goes.

Style: a tour-de-force aria-type speech as part of an at least five-handed scene

Where: somewhere close to, but beyond, the palace grounds   **To Whom:** essentially, the Princess of France, in front of and for the entertainment of her three Lady companions, plus perhaps any Lords and/or servants with the French party

# of Lines: 20   **Probable Timing: 1.00 minutes**

Modern Text

2/ Boyet

1 If my observation (which very seldom* lies),
By the hearts still rhetoric*, disclosed with eyes,
Deceive me not now, Navarre* is infected {.}
——————————
With that which we ᐃlovers entitle "affected'" .

2 Why, all his behaviors* [did] make their retire
To the court of his eye, peeping thorough desire: ◊
His heart* like an ᐃagot with your print impressed,
Proud with his form*, in his eye* pride expressed; ◊
His tongue all impatient to speak* and not see,
Did stumble with haste in his eye*"sight to be ;
All senses to that sense did make their repair*,
To feel* only* looking on fairest of fair*:
[Methought] all his senses were lock'd in his eye,
As ᐃjewels in ᐃcrystal* for some ᐃprince to buy, ◊
Who tend'ring their own worth from [where] they
                                    were glass'd, ◊
Did point [you] to buy them along as you pass'd,
His face's own* margent did cote* such amazes
That all eyes saw his eyes* enchanted with gazes.

3 I'll give you Aquitaine and all that is his,
And you give him for my sake, but one loving ᐃkiss* .

First Folio

2/ Boyet

1 If my observation (which very seldome lies +
By the hearts still rhetoricke, disclosed with eyes)
Deceive me not now, Navar is infected {.}
With that which we Lovers intitle affected.

2 Why+ all his behaviours [doe] make their retire,ₓ
To the court of his eye, peeping thorough desire.
His hart like an Agot with your print impressed,
Proud with his forme, in his eie pride expressed.
His tongue all impatient to speake and not see,
Did stumble with haste in his eie-sight to be, +
All sences to that sence did make their repaire,
To feele onely looking on fairest of faire :
[Me thought] all his sences were lockt in his eye,
As Jewels in Christall for some Prince to buy.
Who tendring their own worth from [whence] they
                                    were glast,
Did point [out] to buy them along as you past.

6 His faces owne margent did coate such amazes,ₓ
That all eyes saw his eies inchanted with gazes.

7 Ile give you Aquitaine,ₓ and all that is his,
And you give him for my sake, but one loving Kisse.

Though Boyet and this speech are often played with great flamboyance, F's sentence structure and orthography suggest that, though the 'aria' quality of the speech is self-evident, there may be a deeper purpose (and character) lurking underneath.

• in F, Boyet takes a five sentence build (F #2-6) to set out all the evidence of Ferdinand ('Navar') being head over heels in love, suggesting that no matter how exuberant Boyet may be, he is still capable of shrewd and rational judgement as well as ensuring, as a good diplomat must, that other people understand what he has to say

• in the sea of rhyming couplets, themselves a verbal sign of personal intensity, (more likely exhilaration in this case), the few unembellished lines point to Boyet's recognising Ferdinand's besottedness through what lay in his eyes
    "To the court of his eye, peeping thorough desire."
even Ferdinand's tongue
    "Did stumble with haste in his eie-sight to be,"
thus Ferdinand's eyes
    "Who tendring their own worth from whence they were glast,/Did point [you]
    .   to buy them along as you past."

• as Boyet informs all the women that 'Navar is infected', he starts passionately (2/2, F #1), then becomes momentarily emotional when realising 'all his behaviours' scream of being in love (0/2, F #2), and returning to passion when beginning the more detailed analysis starting with Navar's 'hart' (1/1, F #3)

• though starting emotionally as he moves from Navar's eyes to 'All sences', (0/5 in the first four lines of F #4), Boyet finishes intellectually for the only time in the speech (3/1, the last two lines of F #4), and then comes the realisation inherent in the unembellished and thus quietly spoken F #5 that Navar's eyes plead for the Princess to 'buy' them, and thus Navar too

• from this realisation springs emotion (0/2, F #6) ending with a rather passionate, naughty-but-fun, kissing suggested finale (2/1, F #7)

3/ Berowne   O, and I forsooth in love,   3.1.174-205

Background: Berowne has written and dispatched a love poem to Rosaline, thus breaking his oath - which is bad enough in itself. What's even worse, and what he is teased for unmercifully later in the play, is that Rosaline being dark-haired and -eyed (lines refer to a 'velvet brow' and 'two pitch bals stucke in her face for eyes'), the woman for whom he is breaking his oath, fails miserably in conforming to the Elizabethan ideal of female beauty: one of blonde hair, blues eyes, and a complexion of peaches and cream.   The final blow is that she seems to be sensually experienced, hence the reference to 'one that will do the deede/Though Argus were her Eunuch and her garde' - the reference to Argus (he of the 1,000 eyes) suggesting Rosaline could do whatever she wished no matter how closely she were watched.

Style: solo

Where: unspecified outdoors, perhaps in the gardens of or the woods beyond the palace   **To Whom:** direct audience address

          # of Lines: 33   **Probable Timing: 1.40 minutes**

Modern Text

3/ Berowne

1 O, and I, forsooth, in love .
          I, that have been* love's whip,

2 A very* ᴬbeadle to a humorous sigh: ◊
   A critic*, ᴬnay, a night-watch ᴬconstable,
   A domineering pedant o'er the ᴬboy,
   [Than] whom no ᴬmortal* so magnificent!

3 This wimpled, whining*, purblind* wayward* ᴬboy,
   This Senior* Junio[r], giant* dwarf*, ᴬ[Dan] Cupid,
   Regent of ᴬlove-rhymes*, ᴬlord of folded arms*,
   Th'anointed* sovereign* of sighs* and groans*,
   Liege* of all loiterers* and malecontents*,
   Dread ᴬprince of ᴬplackets*, ᴬking of ᴬcodpieces* ◊
   Sole ᴬimperator and great general
   Of trotting ᴬparitors* (O my little heart!)

4 And I to be a ᴬcorporal* of his field,
   And wear* his colors* like a ᴬtumblers hoop*!

5 What?

6   I love, I sue, I seek* a wife -
   A woman, that is like a German* [ᴬclock*],
   Still a-°repairing, ever out of frame,
   And never going aright, being a ᴬwatch:
   But being watch'd, that it may still go* right!

7 Nay, to be perjur'd*, which is worst of all;
   And among three, to love the worst of all,
   A whitely¹* wanton, with a velvet brow, ◊

First Folio

3/ Berowne

1 O, and I + forsooth + in love,
          I + that have beene loves whip? ₓ

2 A verie Beadle to a humerous sigh: A Criticke,
   Nay, a night-watch Constable.

3 A domineering pedant ore the Boy,
   [Then] whom no mortall so magnificent. +

4 This wimpled, whyning, purblinde waiward Boy,
   This signior [Junios] + gyant dwarfe, [don] Cupid,
   Regent of Love-rimes, Lord of folded armes,
   Th'annointed soveraigne of sighes and groanes : ₓ
   Liedge of all loyterers and malecontents : ₓ
   Dread Prince of Placcats, King of Codpeeces.

5 Sole Emperator and great generall
   Of trotting Parrators (O my little heart.) +

6 And I to be a Corporall of his field,
   And weare his colours like a Tumblers hoope. +

7 What?

8   I love, I sue, I seeke a wife.
   A woman + that is like a Germane [Cloake],
   Still a repairing: ₓ ever out of frame,
   And never going a right, being a Watch :
   But being watcht, that it may still goe right. +

9 Nay, to be perjurde, which is worst of all : ₓ
   And among three, to love the worst of all,
   A whitly wanton, with a velvet brow.

          {ctd. over}

There are two very different openings to the speech. As the shaded text shows, F starts with two lines of minute hesitations (7/6 syllables), as if Berowne cannot quite find the words to express himself (a very unusual moment for the normally voluble young man), followed by the blurt of a much longer line (13 or 14 syllables), and then another short one - all of which support the idea of a young man in love despite himself. However, most modern texts follow Q1 and pair the opening six lines, one with two, three with four, and five with six, replacing hesitations and blurt with an overall rush.

- as befits such a disturbing sequence there is enormous release (27/329 in thirty-two lines), however the unembellished (presumably quietly spoken) lines point to his dilemma

     "What? I love, I sue . . ."
   followed by
     "Nay, to be perjurde, which is the worst of all:/And among three to love the worst of all,/A whitly wanton, with a velvet brow."
     "And I to sigh for her, to watch for her,/To pray for her, go to: it is a plague"
     "Well, I will love, write, sigh, pray, shue, grone,"

- in F, the orthography of Berowne's opening three sentences of self-destructive analysis (including the surround phrase describing himself as at one time being '. A Criticke,/ Nay a night-watch Constable. ' over love) points to the struggle within, ranging from emotion through intellect, to passion, (0/1, F #1 ; 4/1, F #2 ; 1/1, F #3): modern texts diminish this internal struggle by jamming F #2-3 together

- and his two sentence anti-Cupid diatribe also displays this internal dichotomy, with the separate lists of descriptions, including the surround phrase 'Liedge of all loyterers and malecontents', being very passionate (9/13 in just six lines of F #4), while the overall summary of Cupid as 'Sole Emperator and great generall' becomes intellectual (3/1, F #5)

- and once more, the restructuring of the modern texts robs Berowne of this important transition point; for, as F moves from a passionate analysis to an intellectual summation a period is set: most modern texts set a comma, as shown,

---

¹ most modern texts follow F3-4 and set 'whitely', Qq/Ff = 'whitly'; one good modern gloss = 'witty'

(continuation of Berowne speech #3)

Modern Text (continued)

With two pitch-°balls* stuck* in her face for eyes;◊
Ay*, and, by heaven, one that will do* the deed*
Though Argus were her △eunuch and her guard*.

8 And I to sigh for her, to watch for her,
  To pray for her, go to!†

9   It is a plague
  That Cupid will impose for my neglect
  Of his almighty dreadful* little might.

10 Well, I will love, write, sigh, pray, sue*, [and] groan*:
   Some men must love my △lady, and some Joan.

First Folio (continued)

10 With two pitch bals stucke in her face for eyes.

11 I, and,+ by heaven, one that will doe the deede,x
   Though Argus were her Eunuch and her garde.

12 And I to sigh for her, to watch for her,
   To pray for her, go to: it is a plague
   That Cupid will impose for my neglect,x
   Of his almighty dreadfull little might.

13 Well, I will love, write, sigh, pray, shue, [ ]grone, +
   Some men must love my Lady, and some Jone.

Commentary

• suggesting that the information simply continues as one generalised sentence

• and then, punctuated by the careful non-embellished lines described above, Berowne veers once more between

a/ emotion, with the realisation that he, a one-time 'Criticke' of love, must now become a 'Corporall of his field' (F #6, 2/4), and with the less than flattering physical descriptions of his love Rosaline (2/4, F #10-11)

b/ passion, with the realisation that he actually seeks 'a wife' in a woman who will be, according to the surround phrases' : ever out of frame,/And never going a right, being a Watch: /But being watcht, that it may still goe right.' (3/3, F #8), and the belief that this love is Cupid's revenge on him (the last two lines of F #12)

c/ finishing with a final flash of intellect, as he gives in to the inevitable (the last line of the speech, 2/0)

4/ Berowne   The King he is hunting the Deare,   4.3.1 - 20

Background: Though later in the play and thus the day, this is essentially a continuation of the mood of Beowne's horror-struck speech #3 above. What is interesting is that, unlike the previous speech, this switches to more immediate prose after the first two lines - perhaps suggesting that Berowne cannot be as graceful about his dilemma as he was in the earlier speech. (These first two lines refer to the fact that supposedly Ferdinand, the King, is hunting, though he appears onstage equally in love in a few moments as the 'one with a paper').

Style: solo

Where: unspecified outdoors, perhaps in the gardens of or the woods beyond the palace, an area where there is one tree in which Berowne hides at the end of the speech

To Whom: direct audience address

# of Lines: 19   **Probable Timing: 1.00 minutes**

Modern Text

4/ Berowne

1 The King he is hunting the △deer*: I am coursing myself*.

2 They have pitch'd a △toil*: I am toiling* in a pitch - pitch that defiles - defile! a foul* word.†

3   Well, "set thee down* sorrow!" for so they say the fool* said, and so say I, and I the fool* : △well proved, wit!†

4   By the Lord, this

5   It kills* sheep; it kills* me*, I a sheep*: △well proved again* a my side!†

6   I will not love;

7 if I do, hang me; i'faith* I will not.
        O but her eye - by
this light, but for her eye, I would not love her; yes, for her two eyes.

First Folio

4/ Berowne

1 The King he is hunting the Deare, + I am coursing my selfe.

2 They have pitcht a Toyle, + I am toyling in a pytch, pitch that defiles;x defile, + a foule word: Well, set thee downe sorrow;+ for so they say the foole said, and so say I, and I the foole: Well proved+ wit.+
        By the Lord + this

3 Love is as mad as Ajax, it kils sheepe,+ it kils mee, I a sheepe: Well proved againe a my side.+

4   I will not love; :
        if I do+ hang me: x   yfaith I will not.

5   O but her eye: x   by
this light, but for her eye, I would not love her; yes, for her two eyes.

Commentary

To open, F and Q set two short, possibly verse, lines, as if the enormity of the situation makes it difficult for Berowne to start talking - only the second time in the F version of the play that he is so dumb-struck. Most modern texts not only render the opening as normal, by folding the opening back into the speech, but set the whole as one continuous passage of prose, instead of allowing F and Q's verse opening to fall back into prose as the enormity hits.

• the enormity of Berowne's struggle can also be seen in the wild mood swings - the passionate opening of hunting, 'coursing my selfe' (2/2, F #1); followed immediately by the emotional recognition that he is defiling himself (1/4, the first one and a half lines of F #2, up to 'a foule word'); proving himself to be a fool several times over is passionate (6/7, the remainder of F #2 through F #4); then, the unembellished adoration of 'her eye' (F #5); returning to passion as he realises the depth of his love and therefore his 'mallicholie' (2/9, F #6-7); at last comes some intellect, still tinged with emotion, as he riffs on the word 'sweet' (F #8, 7/4); finishing with almost no energy; as if the previous

8 Well, I do* nothing in the world but lie*, and lie* in my throat*.

9 By heaven, I do* love, and it hath taught me* to ᴬrhyme*, and to be [melancholy]; and here is part of my ᴬrhyme*, and here* my [melancholy].

   Well, she

10 hath one a'my ᴬsonnets already : the ᴬclown* bore it, the ᴬfool* sent it, and the ᴬlady hath it : sweet ᴬclown*, sweeter ᴬfool*, sweetest ᴬlady! †

11 By the world, I would not care a pin, if the other three were in.

12 Here comes one with a paper, God give him grace to groan*!

---

6 Well, I doe nothing in the world but lye, and lye in my throate.

7 By heaven † I doe love, and it hath taught mee to Rime, and to be [mallicholie] :ₓ and here is part of my Rime, and heere my [mallicholie].

   Well, she

8 hath one a'my Sonnets already, † the Clowne bore it, the Foole sent it, and the Lady hath it : sweet Clowne, sweeter Foole, sweetest Lady. †

9 By the world, I would not care a pin, if the other three were in.

10 Here comes one with a paper, God give him grace to grone. †

---

part of the speech has been too much for him (F #9-10. 1/0)

• that this speech is much more disturbing than #3 above can also be seen in the first appearance of semicolons (four); the large number of possible surround phrases (eleven); and the fact that not only are there two totally unembellished sentences (the monosyllabic F #5, once more dealing with the power of 'eyes' to enchant; and the monosyllabic F #9 wishing that his three friends were similarly entrapped), but two more short sentences are also unembellished, save for one word each (the almost monosyllabic F #4, vowing he will not love and the final F #10, hoping the newcomer to the scene is one of his colleagues who will prove to be in love too)

• while the unembellished lines underscore his wishes, most of the surround phrases point to what disturbs him : 'Well, set thee downe sorrow: for so they say the foole said, and so say I, and I the foole : Well proved wit . ' ; plus 'I will not love : if I do hang me : yfaith I will not . ' plus ' ; yes, for her two eyes . ' plus ' : and here is part of my Rime, and heere my [mallicholie] . '

#'s 5- 7: Breaking The Oath #2: Recriminations and Absolution

5/ King Come sir, you blush : as his, your case is such,

4.3.129 - 148

Background: Having seen Longavile hypocritically berate Dumaine for exactly the same offence Longavile has committed, (trying to contact a woman and thus breaking his oath), the King, equally hypocritically, steps forward and berates both of them, and bids them think how appallingly they would be treated if Berowne only knew . . .which of course he does (see speech #6 immediately following).

Style: rebuke, as part of a three-handed scene

Where: unspecified: presumably, anywhere in the palace grounds or woods which offers bushes or trees in which the first three perjured lovers can hide to spy on the others

To Whom: Dumaine and Longavile

# of Lines: 20   Probable Timing: 1.00 minutes

Modern Text

5/ King

1   Come, sir, you blush ; as his your case is such ;
  You chide at him, offending twice as much.

2   You do* not love Maria?

3   Longaville*
  Did never ^sonnet for her sake compile,
  Nor never lay his wreathed arms* athwart
  His loving bosom* to keep* down* his heart.

4   I have been* closely shrouded* in this bush
  And mark'd you both, and for you both did blush.

5   I heard your guilty ^rhymes*, observ'd your fashion,
  Saw sighs* reek* from you, noted well your passion.

6   "Ay* me", says* one, † "O Jove", the other cries; ◊
  [One] her hairs* were ^gold, ^crystal* the other's eyes.

7   You would for ^paradise break* ^faith and troth,

8   And Jove for your ^love would infringe an oath.

9   What will Berowne say when that he shall hear*
  ²Faith ³ infringed, which such zeal* did swear* ?

10   How will he scorn*! how will he spend his wit!

11   How will he triumph, leap,* and laugh at it!

12   For all the wealth that ever I did see,
  I would not have him know so much by me.

First Folio

5/ King

1   Come + sir, you blush : x   as his, x your case is such, +
  You chide at him, offending twice as much.

2   You doe not love Maria?

3   Longavile, +
  Did never Sonnet for her sake compile; x
  Nor never lay his wreathed armes athwart
  His loving bosome, x to keepe downe his heart.

4   I have beene closely shrowded in this bush, x
  And markt you both, and for you both did blush.

5   I heard your guilty Rimes, observ'd your fashion : x
  Saw sighes reeke from you, noted well your passion.

6   Aye me, sayes one!

7   O Jove, the other cries!

8   [On] her haires were Gold, Christall the others eyes.

9   You would for Paradise breake Faith and troth,

10   And Jove for your Love would infringe an oath.

11   What will Berowne say when that he shall heare
  Faith infringed + which such zeale did sweare. +

12   How will he scorne ? + how will he spend his wit ? +

13   How will he triumph, leape, and laugh at it ? +

14   For all the wealth that ever I did see,
  I would not have him know so much by me.

That six of the fourteen sentences are short and that five of them come when Ferdinand (the King) is either berating Longavile and Dumaine or worrying what Berowne will say, suggests how little he is able to mask his feelings.

• Ferdinand becomes momentarily much more factual as he repeats back to them phrases from their love-sick poems 97/3, (F #7-10), but then very emotional as he fears Berowne's learning of their behaviour (1/5, F #11-13), finishing with a very self-contained (concerned) unembellished finale (F #14)

• the extreme quiet of the unembellished rebukes show what Ferdinand wishes them to believe has disturbed him (whether good hypocritical play-acting or genuine is up to each reader to decide)
"Come sir, you blush: as his, your case is such,/You chide at him, offending twice as much.'

"…closely shrowded in this bush, /And markt you both, and for you both did blush.' & "noted well your passion"
for Ferdinand has hidden
though from what almost immediately follows, his unembellished fear of Berowne
"For all the wealth that ever I did see,/I would not have him know so much by me."
is genuine, and, as it turns out, highly justified

• the few surround phrases suggest where Ferdinand's indignancy (whether play acting or genuine) might just get the better of him, from the opening monosyllabic '. Come sir, you blush :', through to the (semicolon) emotionally created '. Longavile,/Did never Sonnet for her sake compile ;' to the final denunciation of both of them '. I heard your guilty Rimes, observ'd your fashion : /Saw sighes reeke from you, noted well your passion .'

• the speech starts neutrally as Ferdinand faces down Longavile (F #1), then moves into a little intellect and emotional release as he begins to detail Longavile's equally culpable love (2/1, F #2 and the first line and a half of F #3), then becomes emotional as he rips them both apart (0/9, from the last two lines of F #3 through to F #6)

---

² to create a line of pentameter, some modern texts add 'A' here

³ Qq/Ff set a metrically short line (8 or 9 syllables): some modern texts add 'so' to create pentameter metrically for the moment

... a fit of short-sighted righteous indignation that he is incapable of speaking metrically for the moment

6/ Berowne   Now step I forth to whip hypocrisie.   between 4.3.149 - 186

Background: Having seen the King hypocritically berate Longavile and Dumaine for exactly the same offence the king is guilty of, (trying to contact a woman and thus breaking his oath), and having heard the King suggest how appallingly they would be mocked if Berowne only knew, Berowne, who of course does know, steps forward (equally hypocritically) to berate all three of them.

Style: rebuke, as part of a four-handed scene

Where: unspecified: presumably, anywhere in the palace grounds or woods which offers bushes or trees in which the first three perjured lovers can hide to spy on the others

To Whom: the King, Dumaine and Longavile

# of Lines: 34   Probable Timing: 1.40 minutes

Modern Text

6/ Berowne

1 Now step I forth to whip hypocrisy*.

2 Ah, good my △liege*, I pray thee pardon me!

3 Good heart, △what grace hast thou thus to reprove

4 'These worms*' for loving, that art most in love?

5 Your eyes do* make no [coaches;] in your tears*; ◇
   There is no certain △princess* that appears*; ◇
   You'll not be perjur'd, 'tis a hateful* thing;
   Tush, none but △minstrels like of △sonneting*!

6 But are you not asham'd?

7   Nay, are you not,
   All three of you, to be thus much o'ershot?

9 You found his [△mote], the King your [△mote] did see:
   But I a △beam* do* find* in each of three.

9 O, what a △scene of fool'ry have I seen,* ◇
   Of sighs*, of groans*, of sorrow, and of teen*! †

10 O me, with what strict patience have I sat,
   To see a △king transformed to a △gnat!

11 To see great Hercules whipping a △gig*,
   And profound Salomon [to tune] a △jig*, ◇
   And Nestor play at push-pin with the boys*,
   And △critic* Timon* laugh at idle toys*!

12 Where lies thy grief*, ◇ O, tell me, good Dumaine?
   And gentle Longaville*, where lies thy pain*?

13 And where my △liege's*?

14   All about the breast*!

A [△caudle] ho*!

First Folio

6/ Berowne

1 Now step I forth to whip hypocrisie.

2 Ah + good my Liedge, I pray thee pardon me. +

3 Good heart, What grace hast thou thus to reprove

4 These wormes for loving, that art most in love?

5 Your eyes doe make no [couches] + in your teares.

6 There is no certaine Princesse that appeares.

7 You'll not be perjur'd, 'tis a hatefull thing: x
   Tush, none but Minstrels like of Sonnetting. +

8 But are you not asham'd? nay, are you not +
   All three of you, to be thus much ore shot?

9 You found his [Moth], the King your [Moth] did see:
   But I a Beame doe finde in each of three.

10 O + what a Scene of fool'ry have I seene.

11 Of sighes, of grones, of sorrow, and of teene : +
   O me, with what strict patience have I sat.
   To see a King transformed to a Gnat? +

12 To see great Hercules whipping a Gigge,
   And profound Salomon [tuning] a Jygge?

13 And Nestor play at push-pin with the boyes,
   And Critticke Tymon laugh at idle toyes. +

14 Where lies thy griefe?

15   O + tell me + good Dumaine ; +
   And gentle Longavill, where lies thy paine?

16 And where my Liedges? all about the brest : +
   A [Candle] hoa? + {→}

{ctd.over}

F's orthography shows two sides of Berowne: first, his ability to **play a very good game of quiet overall rebuke (followed with high energy releases as details of his three friends' indiscretions are humiliatingly piled one on top of another), and then his panic once he realises his own letter to Rosaline is about to be revealed.**

• each time Berowne wishes to establish an area he is about to attack, he opens with calm unembellished lines, first (F #1)
   "Now step I forth to whip hypocrisie."
then, having dealt with Ferdinand, he focuses on all three of them
   "But are you not asham'd ? nay, are you not /All three of you, to be thus much ore shot?"
plus
   "O me, with what strict patience have I sat,"
and then (hypocritically) starts to declare his own innocence
   "I {am} betrayed {by} you. /I that am honest,"
   "I am betrayed by keeping company/With men, like men of inconstancie. /When shall you see me write a thing in rime ? "

• and the short one line sentences jab his barbs home even more (F #1; #2; #5; #6; #10; #14; #17; #20; #21)

• and if that weren't enough, the surround phrases play their part, many of them heightened by being monosyllabic
   ". You'll not be perjur'd, 'tis a hatefull thing : /Tush, none but Minstrels like of Sonnetting. /But are you not asham'd ? "
   ". You found his Moth, the King your Moth did see : /But I a Beame doe finde in each of three. "
   ". Of sighes, of grones, of sorrow, and of teene : "
   ". O tell me good Dumaine ; /And gentle Longavill, where lies thy paine ? /And where my Liedges ? all about the brest : /A [Candle] hoa? "
   ". When shall you see me write a thing in rime ? /Or grone for Joane?"

• after the deceptively calm non-embellished F #1 comes a somewhat emotionally tinged passionate attack on Ferdinand (5/9, F #2-7); and, after a similar deceptively quiet non-embellished F #8, the renewed attack on all of them starts passionately (5/6, F #9 to the first line of F #11) but becomes highly factual as he describes their transformation (6/2 the remainder of F #11 plus F #12)

15   I {am} betrayed {by} you : ◊
     I that am honest, I that hold it sin*
     To break* the vow I am engaged in.

16   I am betrayed by keeping company
     With men like [you], men of inconstancy*.
     When shall you see me write a thing in rhyme*, ◊
     Or groan* for Joan*, or spend a minutes time,

17   In pruning me*? †

18   When shall you hear* that I
     Will praise a hand, a foot, a face, an eye,
     A gait*, a state, a brow, a breast*, a [waist],
     A leg*, a limb* - ◊⁴

19   I post from ⁴love; good ⁴lover, let me go.

---

17   I {am} betrayed {by} you.

18   I that am honest, I that hold it sinne
     To breake the vow I am ingaged in .

19   I am betrayed by keeping company
     With men, like [ ] men of inconstancie.

20   When shall you see me write a thing in rime?

21   Or grone for Joane?   or spend a minutes time,
     In pruning⁵ mee, when shall you heare that I will praise a
     hand, a foot, a face, an eye: a gate, a state, a brow, a brest,
     a [waste], a legge, a limme.

22   I post from Love, good Lover⁺ let me go.

• the further ridicule and dismissal (F #13-16) becomes passionate (7/8), while the (false) declaration of his own innocence becomes very calm (0/2 in the five and a half lines, F #17-20)

• however, as Jaquenetta and Costard appear in the distance with the letter that will prove Berowne as guilty as the rest of them so emotion springs forth (1/5, F #21), heightened by the fact that F shows Berowne crumbling into prose from the previous verse of the speech - suggesting that the shock of seeing them really knocks him off-stride (most modern texts spoil this moment by resetting F #21 as verse, as the shaded text shows)

• it could be that, after this momentary glitch, Berowne recovers his composure, for though short, as if he has little to say, F #22 as set is both purely intellectual (2/0) and appears to be in verse

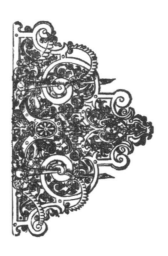

⁴ though Qq/Ff set this as prose, most modern texts turn it into verse as shown: however, it could be that Berowne can see Jaquenetta and Costard about to enter, and, given the distinctiveness of the Elizabethan letter, Berowne might recognise his letter and be so thrown as to lose verse for a moment

⁵ most modern texts set Qq/Ff's 'pruning'; commentators offer the gloss 'preening'

7/ Berowne   O 'tis more then neede.   4.3.287 - 362

Background: Mercifully, Berowne's hypocrisy has been exposed when, at the schoolmaster Holofernes' urging, Jaquenetta and Costard bring Berowne's poem to Rosaline (delivered to Jaquenetta in error) to the King. After recriminations which almost lead to fisticuffs, the other young oath-breakers beg Berowne to use all his wits and debating skills to get them out of this mess so they can woo the Frenchwomen with a clear conscience.

Style: the climax of a wonderfully poetic (but nevertheless chop-) logic, as part of a four-handed scene

Where: unspecified: presumably, anywhere in the palace grounds or woods which offers bushes or trees in which the first three perjured lovers can hide to spy on the others

To Whom: the King, Dumaine, and Longavile

# of Lines: 55   Probable Timing: 2.50 minutes

Modern Text

7/ Berowne

1 O, 'tis more [than] need* .

2 Have at you then affections men-°at-°arms* .
   Consider what you first did swear* unto:
   To fast, to study, and to see no woman -
   Flat treason [°gainst] the ᐃkingly state of youth.

3 Say, ᐃcan you fast? †
                 Your stomachs* are too young,
   And abstinence engenders maladies.

4 O, we have made a ᐃvow to study,* ᐃlords,
   And in that vow we have forsworn* our ᐃbooks* . †

5 For when would you , my ᐃliege* , or you, or you,
   In leaden contemplation have found out
   Such fiery ᐃnumbers as the prompting eyes
   Of beauty's* tutors have enrich'd you with? †

6 Other slow ᐃarts entirely keep* the brain* ,
   And therefore, finding barren* practicers* ,
   Scarce show a harvest of their heavy toyl* ; ◊
   But ᐃlove first learned in a ᐃlady's* eyes,
   Lives not alone immured* in the brain* ,
   But with the motion of all elements,
   Courses as swift as thought in every power,
   And gives to every power a double power,
   Above their functions and their offices.

7 It adds* a precious seeing to the eye:
   A ᐃlover's eyes will gaze an °eagle blind* .

8 A ᐃlover's ear* will hear* the lowest sound, ◊
   When the suspicious head of theft is stopp'd.

First Folio

7/ Berowne

1 O⁺ 'tis more [then] neede .

2 Have at you then affections men at armes,
   Consider what you first did sweare unto:
   To fast, to study, and to see no woman : ₓ
   Flat treason against the Kingly state of youth.

3 Say, Can you fast? your stomacks are too young: ₓ
   And abstinence ingenders maladies.

4 O⁺ we have made a Vow to studie, Lords,
   And in that vow we have forsworne our Bookes :
   For when would you (ₓmy Leege) ₓ or you, or you?ₓ
   In leaden contemplation have found out
   Such fiery Numbers as the prompting eyes,ₓ
   Of beauties tutors have inrich'd you with :
   Other slow Arts intirely keepe the braine : ₓ
   And therefore + finding barraine practizers,
   Scarce shew a harvest of their heavy toyle .

5 But Love first learned in a Ladies eyes,
   Lives not alone emured in the braine : ₓ
   But with the motion of all elements,
   Courses as swift as thought in every power,
   And gives to every power a double power,
   Above their functions and their offices.

6 It adds a precious seeing to the eye:
   A Lovers eyes will gaze an Eagle blinde.

7 A Lovers eare will heare the lowest sound.

8 When the suspicious head of theft is stopt.

{ctd. over}

In a speech full of Berowne's very complex, and, ultimately, chop-logic reasoning, F's orthography shows three very interesting patterns: **sometimes there is tremendous unembellished restraint; and sometimes key thoughts are heightened as surround phrases; and sometimes there are moments of concentrated release.** Also, **the sentence structure, as discussed at the end of the commentary, shows just how difficult a task this attempting to legitimately break their oaths proves to be.**

• the surround phrases drive home the (occasionally chop-) logic by which he wants to prove that they will not break their oaths as scholars if they spend time with women: for, while they have sworn
     " . To fast, to study, and to see no woman : "
the question is
     " . Say, Can you fast ? your stomacks are too young : /And abstinence ingenders maladies. "
after all
     " : Other slow Arts intirely keepe the braine : " but Love
     " . It adds a precious seeing to the eye : " therefore
     " . Then fooles you were these women to forsweare : "
thus by all that's holy
     " : Or for Loves sake, a word that loves all men . /Or for Mens sake,
         the author of these Women : /Or Womens sake, by whom we men
         are Men . "
it would be a sin not to be with women
     " : It is religion to be thus forsworne . /For Charity it selfe fulfills the
         Law : /And who can sever love from Charity."

• the unembellished phrases seem to suggest that Berowne is concentrating very hard to make his points, as with the opening surround phrases already seen, 'To fast, to study, and to see no woman:' plus 'And abstinence ingenders maladies:', or when he thinks he might have discovered a loophole in what they have done (swearing to have nothing to do with women for three years!)
     "For when would you . . . or you, or you? /In leaden contemplation
         have found out/Such . . . as the prompting eyes, /Of beauties
             tutors have inrich'd you with : "
or when trying to establish that 'Love first learned in a Ladies eyes' in fact is much better than book study can ever be; because it
     "But with the motion of all elements, /Courses as swift as thought in
         every power, /And gives to every power a double power, /Above their
             functions and their offices . "

9 Loves feeling is more soft and sensible, ₓ
[Then] are the tender hornes of Cockled Snayles.

10 Loves tongue proves dainty, ₓ Bachus grosse in taste,
For Valour, is not Love a Hercules? ₓ
Still climing trees in the Hesporides. +

11 Subtill as Sphinx, as sweet and musicall, ₓ
As bright Apollo's Lute, strung with his haire.

12 And when Love speakes, the voyce of all the Gods, ₓ
Make heaven drowsie with the harmonie.

13 Never durst Poet touch a pen to write, ₓ
Untill his Inke were tempred with Loves sighes :
O then his lines would ravish savage eares, ₓ
And plant in Tyrants milde humilitie.

14 From women's eyes this doctrine I derive.

15 They sparcle still the right promethean fire, +
They are the Bookes, the Arts, the Achademes,
That shew, containe, and nourish all the world.

16 Else none at all in ought proves excellent.

17 Then fooles you were these women to forsweare : ₓ
Or keeping what is sworne, you will prove fooles,
For Wisedomes sake, a word that all men love :
Or for Loves sake, a word that loves all men.

18 Or for Mens sake, the [author] of these Women : ₓ
Or Womens sake, by whom we men are Men.

19 [Let's] once loose our oathes to finde our selves,
Or else we loose our selves, ₓ to keepe our oathes :
It is religion to be thus forsworne.

20 For Charity it selfe fulfills the Law : ₓ
And who can sever love from Charity. +

---

10 Love's feeling is more soft and sensible
[Than] are the tender horns* of ^cockled ^snails* .

11 Love's tongue proves dainty Bacchus* ^gross* in taste,
For ^valor* , is not Love a Hercules,
Still climbing* trees in the Hesperides? †

12 Subtile* as Sphinx, as sweet and musical*
As bright Apollo's ^lute, strung with his hair* .

13 And when Love speaks* , the voice* of all the ^gods
Make heaven drowsy* with the harmony*.

14 Never durst ^poet touch a pen to write
Until* his △ink* were temp'red with Love's sighs* :
O then his lines would ravish savage ears*
And plant in ^tyrants mild* humility*.

15 From women's eyes this doctrine I derive; ◇
They sparkle* still the right △Promethean fire;
They are the ^books* , the ^arts, the ^academes ,*
That show, contain, and nourish all the world, ◇
Else none at all in ought proves excellent.

16 Then fools* you were these women to forswear* ,
Or keeping what is sworn* , you will prove fools* . †

17 For ^wisdom's* sake, a word that all men love :
Or for ^love's sake, a word that loves all men, ◇
Or for ^men's sake, the [authors] of these ^women,
Or ^women's sake, by whom we men are ^men, ◇
[Let us] once lose* our oaths* to find* our selves,
Or else we lose* our selves to keep* our oaths* . †

19 It is religion to be thus forsworn* : ◇
For ^charity itself* fulfills the ^law,
And who can sever love from ^charity ?

• sometime the unembellishment might suggest that the is drawn into, perhaps even lost within, the beauty of his own imagery:
"Loves feeling is more soft and sensible"
"Loves tongue proves dainty,"
"Make heaven drowsie with the harmonie,"
or in the subtlety of his own argument
"From women's eyes this doctrine I derive./They sparcle still the right promethean fire,"
"Else none at all in ought proves excellent."

• the speech begins with a few sparks of occasional intellect and emotion (2/4 in the first seven lines of F #1-3), though these are found amidst an opening sea of non-embellished lines - suggesting Berowne is concentrating very hard and has little time for energetic release as he embarks on his momentous task

• as the 'Vow' is first mentioned and explored (the first six lines of F #4) so Berowne's passion begins to rise (5/3), but is quickly swallowed up with an emotional release as he finds a way to discard 'Other slow Arts' in favour of 'Ladies eyes' (2/7, the last three lines of F #4, and the first two of F #5)

• and, after a non-embellished elaboration of 'Love so learned', as Berowne both envisages the different senses (seeing, hearing and feeling) love can so wonderfully enhance and celebrates Love's qualities and its effects on the 'Poet', so his passions start to roll (19/19 in the seventeen lines F #6-13)

• but as Berowne describes how he has discovered this from 'womens eyes', the hush of the embellished lines hold him somewhat in check (3/3 in the five lines of F #14-16)

• and now the triumphant celebration of the way out of their dilemma triggers his passions to the fullest (15/13 in the final eleven lines, F #17-22)

• that this has been a struggle can be seen in F's sentence structure when compared to modern texts:

a/ first with the onrushes at the beginning of the questioning (F #3) tuned into two more rational sentences by most modern texts; exploring the stupidity of their 'Vow' (F #4) badly reworked into two and half modern sentences: the importance of setting 'Love as a separate topic ' (F#5) spoiled by being set as a continuance of mt. #6;

b/ and the enthusiastic if not always grammatical seven smallish sentence overly careful point by point final proof that 'womens eyes' will allow them to 'loose their oathes' (F #14-22) spoiled by modern texts reshaping the whole into four easier, longer sentences of grammatical correctness: (F #14-16 = mt. #15; half of F #17 = mt. #16; the remainder of F #17, #18 and the first line of F #19-20 = mt. #17) and F #19-20 = mt. #19)

Love's Labor's Lost / 91

#'s 8- 11: YOUNG WOMEN IN LOVE

8/Queene   Good L. Boyet, my beauty though but mean,   2.1.13 - 34

Background: Because of the men's oath, the women cannot enter the palace grounds of Navar 'on pain of losing their tongue' (!). The women, especially the Princesse, are mightily displeased from the moment they arrive, which of course affects the remainder of the male-female relationships throughout the rest of the play. In this, her first speech of the play, following an extravagant speech in her praise from Boyet, her chief counsellor cum chaperone (whose hidden agenda may well be to marry her off to Navar's King Ferdinand), the Princesse charges Boyet in no uncertain terms to summon Navar so that they can get down to settling the business of land and money still outstanding between his father and hers, just as soon as possible.

Style: one on one address as part of at least a five handed scene

Where: unspecified, presumably outdoors somewhere near the palace   **To Whom:** directed toward counsellor/chaperone Boyet in front of her three Lady companions plus (possibly) some accompanying gentlemen and servants

# of Lines: 22   Probable Timing: 1.10 minutes

Modern Text

8/ Princess

1 Good [Lord] Boyet, my beauty though but mean,
   Needs not the painted flourish of your praise :
   Beauty is bought by judgment* of the eye,
   Not utt'red by base sale of chapmen's tongues . †

2 I am less* proud to hear* you tell my worth
   [Than] you much willing to be counted wise
   In spending your wit in the praise of mine.

3 But now to task* the tasker : good Boyet,
   You are not ignorant all-telling fame
   Doth noise* abroad Navarre* hath made a vow,
   Till painful* study* shall out°wear* three years*
   No woman may approach his silent △court ;
   Therefore to's seemeth it a needful* course,
   Before we enter his forbidden gates,
   To know his pleasure; and in that behalf* ,
   Bold of your worthiness* , we single you
   As our best°°moving fair° solicitor . †

4 Tell him, the daughter of the King of France,
   On serious business* craving quick* dispatch,
   Importunes personal* conference with his △Grace.

5 Haste, signify* so much, while we attend,
   Like humble -°visag'd suitors* , his high will.

First Folio

8/ Queene

1 Good [L.] Boyet, my beauty though but mean,
   Needs not the painted flourish of your praise :
   Beauty is bought by judgement of the eye,
   Not uttred by base sale of chapmens tongues :
   I am lesse proud to heare you tell my worth,ₓ
   [Then] you much willing to be counted wise,ₓ
   In spending your wit in the praise of mine.

2 But now to taske the tasker, + good Boyet,
Princesse ⁶ You are not ignorant all-telling fame
   Doth noyse abroad Navar hath made a vow,
   Till painefull studie shall out-weare three yeares,ₓ
   No woman may approach his silent Court : ₓ
   Therefore to's seemeth it a needfull course,
   Before we enter his forbidden gates,
   To know his pleasure, + and in that behalfe +
   Bold of your worthinesse, we single you,ₓ
   As our best moving faire soliciter :
   Tell him, the daughter of the King of France,
   On serious businesse craving quicke dispatch,
   Importunes personall conference with his grace.

   Haste, signifie so much + while we attend,
   Like humble visag'd suters + his high will.

Despite the annoyance of Boyet's flattery and the apparent snub from the Court of Navar, in this speech the Princesse/Queene does not even resort to large-scale excesses (there aren't even any surround phrases in what follows). Instead, the sting of her rebukes, orders, and pointed comments are found in the non-embellished lines.

• thus it's interesting that most of these calm lines are focused on Boyet
   "my beauty though but mean, /Needs not the painted flourish of your praise :"
   "Beauty is . . . /Not uttred by base sale of chapmens tongues:"
   "Than you much willing to be counted wise, /In spending your wit in the praise of mine."

then, dealing with Navar's refusal to allow the ladies admission to his palace
   "Before we enter his forbidden gates, /To know his pleasure,"
   and then back to dealing with Boyet once more
   "Haste, signifie so much while we attend, /Like humble visag'd suters his high will."

• thus the opening dealing with Boyet is amazingly calm (just 1/3 in the seven lines of F #1, four of which are unembellished), but releases begin to appear as she turns to deal with the Navar situation

• first, there is a rare show of emotionally tinged passion as she (sarcastically?) lists the reason for women not being allowed to even 'approach his silent Court' (3/6 in the first six lines of F #2) ; but, after a non-embellished line and a half, this changes first to pure emotion as she selects Boyet (0/3), and then to passion once more as she describes what she wants him to do (the last three lines of F #2)

• and, having selected and briefed Boyet, so she finishes with an apparently quite easy non-embellished dismissal of him (F #3)

⁶ though Q1/F1 describe her as the Princesse in the entry, both set her prefix for the opening speech as Queene (F1 or the first 8 lines only, suggesting she might be using more authority than usual in her reply/rebuke) : thereafter Q1/F1 refer to her as Princesse throughout; F1 is alone in changing the prefix midway though the speech

9/ Maria/1. Lady	I know {Longavill}; at a marriage feast,	2.1.40 - 51
10/ Katherine/2. Lady	The yong Dumaine, a well accomplisht youth,	2.1.56 - 63
11/ Rosaline	Another of these Students at that time,	2.1.64 - 76

Background: While awaiting Boyet's return as charged in speech #8 above, the Princess has innocently asked 'Who are the Votaries … that are vow fellowes' with Ferdinand only to be greeted by three successive admissions from her closest companions that each one of them is most definitely attracted to one specific man making up the 'achademe'. Each speech is the first in the play for that particular Lady.

Style: probable four handed scene, just for the women

Where: unspecified, presumably outdoors somewhere near the palace   **To Whom:** the Princesse and her two fellow travellers, possibly with the gentlemen and servants in attendance excluded from the essentially highly personal women's confessions

speech #9, # of Lines: 12	**Probable Timing: 0.40 minutes**	
speech #10, # of Lines: 8	**Probable Timing: 0.30 minutes**	
speech #11, # of Lines: 13	**Probable Timing: 0.45 minutes**	

Modern Text

9/ Maria as 1. Lady

1 I know {Longaville*₃}; at a marriage ° feast,
    Between* [Lord] Perigort and the beauteous heir*
    Of Jacques Falconbridge, solemniz'd ◊
    In Normandy*, saw I this Longaville*,
    A man of sovereign* parts, [peerless] esteem'd;
    Well fitted in ᐃarts, glorious in ᐃarms*;
    Nothing becomes him ill that he would well.

2 The only* soil* of his fair* virtue's gloss*,
    If virtues gloss* will stain* with any soil*,
    Is a sharp wit match'd with too blunt a ᐃwill*;
    Whose edge hath power to cut, whose will still wills
    It should none spare that come within his power.

10/ Katherine as 2. Lady

1 The young* Dumaine, a well accomplish'd youth,
    Of all the ᐃvirtue love, for ᐃvirtue loved;
    Most power to do* most harm* , least knowing ill ;
    For he hath wit to make an ill shape good,
    And shape to win grace though [he] had no wit.

2 I saw him at the Duke [Alanson's] once,
    And much too little of that good I saw
    Is my report to his great worthiness* .

First Folio

9/ 1. Lady

1 I know {Longavill}; at a marriage feast,
    Betweene [L.] Perigort and the beautious heire
    Of Jacques Fauconbridge ⁺ solemnized.

2 In Normandie ⁺ saw I this Longavill,
    A man of soveraigne parts ⁺ [he is] esteem'd :
    Well fitted in Arts, glorious in Armes : ₓ
    Nothing becomes him ill that he would well.

3 The onely soyle of his faire vertues glosse,
    If vertues glosse will staine with any soile,
    Is a sharp wit match'd with too blunt a Will : ₓ
    Whose edge hath power to cut ⁺ whose will will wills, ₓ
    It should none spare that come within his power.

10/ 2. Lady

1 The yong Dumaine, a well accomplisht youth,
    Of all the Vertue love, for Vertue loved : ₓ
    Most power to doe most harme, least knowing ill : ₓ
    For he hath wit to make an ill shape good,
    And shape to win grace though [she] had no wit.

2 I saw him at the Duke [Alansoes] once,
    And much too little of that good I saw,ₓ
    Is my report to his great worthinesse.

9/ Maria as 1. Lady

- Maria starts out quite factually (7/1, F #1 plus the first line of F #2), though the emotional semicolon establishing her opening as a surround phrase, " . I know Longavill ; ' sets up the tone to come

- for, after two passionate lines full of praise for Longavile, again involving a second surround phrase ' : Well fitted in Arts, glorious in Armes : ' (2/2, lines two and three of F #2), and an unembellished line of self-control still full of praise, 'Nothing becomes him ill that he would well.' - attempting to establish self control perhaps, but the struggle is not necessarily successful, for …

- … emotion gushes forth for just two lines (0/7, the start of F #3) from which the re-establishes self-control, first intellectually (line three, 1/0), and finally with two unembellished yet equally praise-full lines
    "Whose edge hath power to cut whose will still wills, /It should none spare that come within his power."

10/ Katherine as 2. Lady

- while Kate also starts factually (3/0 the first two lines of F #1), she only has three emotional releases - two in the only surround phrase of the speech that immediately follows, as she attests to the attractions of Dumaine's innocence
    ' : Most power to doe most harme, least knowing ill : '

- instead of emotion, the quiet confession of the unembellished lines speaks to why she is drawn to him
    "For he hath wit to make an ill shape good,/And shape to win grace
      though [he] had no wit." and
    "I saw him at … once,/And much too little of that good I saw,"

Modern Text

11/ Rosaline

1
Another of these △students at that time
Was there with him, [if] I have heard a truth.

2
Berowne they call him, but a merrier man,
Within the limit of becoming* mirth,
I never spent an hour's* talk* withall* .

3
His eye begets occasion for his wit,
For every object that the one doth catch,
The other turns* to a mirth-moving jest.

4
Which his fair* tongue, conceit's expositor,
Delivers in such apt and gracious words
That aged ears* play truant* at his tales,
And younger* hearings are quite ravished, ◊
So sweet and voluble is his discourse.

First Folio

11/ Rosaline

1
Another of these Students at that time,x
Was there with him, [as] I have heard a truth.

2
Berowne they call him, but a merrier man,
Within the limit of becomming mirth,
I never spent an houres talke withall.

3
His eye begets occasion for his wit,
For every object that the one doth catch,
The other turnes to a mirth-moving jest.

4
Which his faire tongue (xconceits expositor)x
Delivers in such apt and gracious words,x
That aged eares play treuant at his tales,
And yonger hearings are quite ravished.

5
So sweet and voluble is his discourse.

- though Rosaline has far fewer releases (seven in thirteen lines) than either Maria (twenty in twelve lines) or Kate (ten in eight lines), the others at least start out with some intellectual control (Maria 10/10, Kate 5/5), whereas Rosaline is almost totally emotional (1/6), nearly all of which appears at the end of F #2

- instead, there is a complete casualness (or high degree of self-control) in the speech, for her interest in Berowne is spoken in almost non-embellished terms throughout, and without any surround phrases: the only lines with any release are the first in F #1; the two-line tremendously emotional ending of F #2, 'Within the limit of becomming mirth,/I never spent an houres talke withall.' (0/4), a praise-full assessment of Berowne; and lines one and three of F #4

- what betrays her apparent nonchalance is the totally ungrammatical period ending F #4 that allows a final one line unembellished sentence summing up his key attraction 'So sweet and voluble is his discourse.': that this is a separate appallingly syntactically incorrect sentence speaks volumes as to what is going on underneath the seemingly calm exterior: no modern texts set this sentence as such, instead folding it into the general paean of praise in their mt. #4, thus losing this all important marker of not quite controlled desire

#'s 12 - 14: UNMERCIFUL TEASING OF THE OATH BREAKERS

12/ Queene   **And will they so ? the Gallants shall be taskt :**   between 5.2.126 - 156

Background: Persuaded by Berowne's wonderful chop-logic (speech #7 above) the four young men have abandoned the 'achademe's' restrictions on being with women, essentially breaking their oaths, no matter how cleverly Berowne has justified it. Boyet has overheard their plans to disguise themselves as Russians before coming to woo the four French women via a Masque, and has described to the Ladies in great detail what he saw and heard.   As a consequence, the Princesse (not yet Queen) now plans just how the men are to be teased and punished for their oath-breaking. One note: the two sentences marked {ψ} are taken from interjections originally spoken by Rosaline and Boyet.

Style: as part of a five handed scene

Where: wherever the French Ladies private encampment is   **To Whom:** the three young Frenchwomen and Boyet

# of Lines: 29   **Probable Timing:** 1.30 minutes

Modern Text

12/ Queene

1 And will they so ? †

2 The ᐃgallants shall be task'd :
For, ᐃladies, we will every one be mask'd,
And not a man of them shall have the grace,
Despite* of suit*, to see a ᐃlady's* face.

3 Hold, Rosaline, this ᐃfavor* thou shalt wear*,
And then the King will court thee for his ᐃdear* . †

4 Hold, take thou this, my sweet, and give me thine,
So shall Berowne take me for Rosaline.

5 And change [you] ᐃfavors* too, so shall your ᐃloves
Woo contrary, deceiv'd by these removes.

6 The effect of my intent is to cross* theirs* :
They do* it but in [mockery] merriment,
And mock* for mock* is only* my intent.

7 Their several* counsels they unbosom* shall
To ᐃloves mistook* , and so be mock'd* withal* †
Upon the next occasion that we meet*,
With ᐃvisages display'd, to talk* and greet* .

8 {ψ} {φW}e {shall not} dance, if they desire us too't!

9 No, to the death we will not move a foot,
Nor to their penn'd* speech render we no grace,
But while 'tis spoke each turn* away [her] face.

10 {ψT}hat contempt will kill the [speaker's] heart,
And quite divorce his memory from his part.

11 Therefore I do* it, and I make no doubt
The rest will [ne're] come in, if he be out.

First Folio

12/ Queene

1 And will they so ? the Gallants shall be taskt :
For⁺ Ladies;ₓ we will every one be maskt,
And not a man of them shall have the grace⁺
Despight of sute, to see a Ladies face.

2 Hold⁺ Rosaline, this Favour thou shalt weare,
And then the King will court thee for his Deare :
Hold, take thou this⁺ my sweet, and give me thine,
So shall Berowne take me for Rosaline.

3 And change [your] Favours too, so shall your Loves
Woo contrary, deceiv'd by these removes.

4 The effect of my intent is to crosse theirs :
They doe it but in [mocking] merriment,
And mocke for mocke is onely my intent.

5 Their severall counsels they unbosome shall,ₓ
To Loves mistooke, and so be mockt withall.

6 Upon the next occasion that we meete,
With Visages displayd⁺ to talke and greete.

7 {ψ} {φW}e {shall not} dance, if they desire us too't?

8 No, to the death we will not move a foot,
Nor to their pen'd speech render we no grace : ₓ
But while 'tis spoke,⁺ each turne away [his] face.

9 {ψ} {φT}hat contempt will kill the [keepers] heart,
And quite divorce his memory from his part.

10 Therefore I doe it, and I make no doubt,ₓ
The rest will [ere] come in, if he be out.

Later in the play, the basis for the Princesse/Queene's attack on Navar is for breaking his oath – suggesting tremendous intellectual integrity. Here F's orthographical structure supports this, for she moves from a sharply intellectual start (indignation perhaps?), through (for her) an unusual burst of emotion, into a virtually determinedly non-embellished ending.

• the Princesse/Queene responds to the news of the young men's oath-breaking approach highly intellectually (3/0, F #1), which continues into the exchanging of favours to be worn by the women so as to fool the men (11/4, F #2-3), but her emotions burst forth unheralded once she explains what her intentions are (2/11, F #4-6)

• then, in the latter part of the speech, she seems to recover all sense of self, for the large passage of unembellished lines point to a quiet (unshakeable) determined explanation of how they all must behave to achieve her goal (just 0/4 in the final twelve lines of the speech, F #7-12)
  "We shall not dance, if they desire us too't?/No, to the death we will not move a foot,/Nor to their pen'd speech render we no grace:/ . . . / that contempt will kill the [keepers] heart,/And quite divorce his memory from his part./ . . . / and I make no doubt, /The rest will [ere] come in, if he be out./ . . . /So shall we stay mocking entended game,/ And they well mockt, depart away with shame."

• the surround phrases already show her concerns, from the opening emotional (semicoloned)
  " . And will they so ? the Gallants shall be taskt : /For Ladies ; "
to the determined statement that
  " . The effect of my intent is to crosse theirs ; "
explaining both how, and why
  " : But while 'tis spoke, each turne away [her] face. "
  " : Theres no such sport, as sport by sport orethrowne: /To make theirs ours, and ours none but our owne . "

12 There's no such sport as sport by sport o'erthrown*,
    To make theirs ours, and ours none but our own*;◊
    So shall we stay, mocking intended game,
    And they, well mock'd, depart away with shame.

11 Theres no such sport, as sport by sport orethrowne:x
    To make theirs ours, and ours none but our owne.
12 So shall we stay+ mocking entended game,
    And they+ well mockt, depart away with shame.

13/ Rosaline   We are wise girles to mocke our Lovers so.   5.2.58 - 68

Background: The women seem to take the fact of the men having broken their oaths seriously, and, though they have been sent both poetry and gifts, are still determined to punish them as oath-breakers. Here Rosaline explains what she would like to do to Berowne. Two notes: the word 'pertaunt', line ten, has given rise to much discussion and alternative readings [7]: and the first line, marked {ψ}, is taken from an earlier speech by the Princess.

Style: as part of a five handed scene
Where: wherever the French Ladies private encampment is   **To Whom:** the three young Frenchwomen and Boyet
# of Lines: 11   **Probable Timing: 0.40 minutes**

Modern Text

13/ Rosaline
1 {ψ} We are wise girls* to mock* our Δlovers so.
2   They are worse fools* to purchase mocking so.
3   That same Berowne I'll torture ere I go*.
4   O that I knew he were but in by th'week*! †
5   How I would make him fawn*, and beg*, and seek*,
       And wait the season, and observe the times,
       And spend his prodigal* wits in bootless* rhymes*,◊
       And shape his service wholly to my device,8
       And make him proud to make me proud that jests!
6   So [pair-°taunt] like would I o'er'sway his state
       That he should* be my fool* and I his fate.

First Folio

13/ Rosaline
1 {ψ} We are wise girles to mocke our Lovers so.
2   They are worse fooles to purchase mocking so.
3   That same Berowne ile torture ere I goe.
4   O that I knew he were but in by th'weeke,
       How I would make him fawne, and begge, and seeke,
5   And wait the season, and observe the times,
       And spend his prodigall wits in booteles rimes.
       And shape his service wholly to my device,
       And make him proud to make me proud that jests.+
6   So [pertaunt] like would I o'resway his state,x
       That he shold be my foole,x and I his fate.

As with speech #11 above, F's ungrammatical structure undermines Rosaline's apparent ease.

• not only does the speech start rather more emotionally than intellectually (2/4, F #1-3), the fact that is starts with three short sentences shows just how much Rosaline is revealing herself, quickly moving from idea to idea without unnecessary elaboration

• though most modern texts set a rational single line sentence (mt. #4) expressing the hope that Berowne is trapped (the contemporary meaning of 'in by the weeke'), F's onrushed ungrammatical fast-link connection (via a comma) to what follows clearly shows a somewhat enthusiastic and uncontrolled Rosaline on an imaginative roll

• and the emotional listing of what Rosaline would like to put Berowne through (F #4, 1/6) also ends ungrammatically (according to modern texts) with a period: yet intellectually F's period is splendid, for it allows her a moment before going on via a new sentence to sum up, and this new sentence is orthographically enhanced by being completely unembellished, as if the thought almost takes her breath away

---

7 'the quarto's 'perttaunt-like' was long regarded as unintelligible and probably corrupt. Theobald read 'pedant-like', Hanmer 'portent-like', Capell 'pageant-like'; Dover Wilson (1923) read 'planet-like': in 1945, Percy Simpson offered a justification of the phrase on the grounds that 'paire-taunt' is the winning hand in an obsolete card game of 'Post and Pair', which presumably implies Rosaline will be able to beat whatever winning cards Berowne thinks he can play in their relationship

8 to provide a matching rhyme for the following line ('jests'), some modern texts follow F2-4's setting of 'hests', a far cry from Qq/F1's 'device'

14/ Berowne   **Thus poure the stars down plagues for perjury.**   5.2.394 - 418

Background: Even the men's attempts to deny any knowledge of the Russian fiasco blows up as the women mock and challenge the men to confess they were the Russians. Rosaline has the bit between her teeth as she triumphantly defeats their every evasion, and in the following Berowne attempts to placate her both by confessing and promising his future wooing will be nowhere near as flamboyant in manner or language. One note: line 23, Rosaline's comment, marked ⟨ψ⟩, has been adapted and given to Berowne so that he catches himself using a foreign language ('sans' = unnecessary flamboyance) rather than she.

Style: supposedly one on one in front of a large group

Where: close to wherever the French Ladies' private encampment is   **To Whom:** directly to his love Rosaline, in front of his three fellow oath-breakers, her three friends, and Boyet

# of Lines: 25   Probable Timing: 1.15 minutes

Modern Text

14/ Berowne

1 Thus pour* the stars down plagues for perjury.
   Can any face of brass* hold longer out?
2 Here* stand I, ᐃlady,* dart thy skill at me,
   Bruise me with scorn*, confound me with a flout, ◇
   Thrust thy sharp* wit quite through my ignorance, ◇
   Cut me to pieces* with thy keen* conceit;
   And I will wish thee never more to dance,
   Nor never more in Russian habit wait*.
3 O, never will I trust to speeches penn'd*,
   Nor to the motion of a ᐃschool°boys,* tongue, ◇
   Nor never come in vizard to my friend,
   Nor woo in rhyme*, like a blind °harper's song* ,
   Taffeta phrases, silken terms* precise,
   Three-pil'd ᐃhyperboles, spruce affection,
   Figures pedantical* - these summer flies,
   Have blown* me full of maggot ostentation.
4 I do forswear* them, and I here* protest,
   By this white ᐃglove (how white the hand, God knows!) †
   Henceforth my wooing* mind* shall be express'd
   In russet yeas and honest kersey* noes.
5 And to begin, ᐃwench, so God help* me law!
   My love to thee is sound, sans crack* or flaw.
6 ⟨ψSans, "sans", {you'll} pray {me}.
                                    Yet I have a trick*
7 Of the old rage. †
            Bear* with me, I am sick* ; ◇
8 I'll leave it by degrees.

First Folio

14/ Berowne

1 Thus poure the stars down plagues for perjury.
2 Can any face of brasse hold longer out?
3 Heere stand I, Ladie dart thy skill at me,
   Bruise me with scorne, confound me with a flout.
4 Thrust thy sharpe wit quite through my ignorance.
5 Cut me to peeces with thy keene conceit : ₓ
   And I will wish thee never more to dance,
   Nor never more in Russian habit waite.
6 O! ₓ never will I trust to speeches pen'd,
   Nor to the motion of a Schoole-boies tongue.
7 Nor never come in vizard to my friend,
   Nor woo in rime + like a blind-harpers songue,
   Taffata phrases, silken tearmes precise,
   Three-pil'd Hyperboles, spruce affection ; ₓ
   Figures pedanticall, these summer flies,
   Have blowne me full of maggot ostentation.
8 I do forsweare them, and I heere protest,
   By this white Glove (how white the hand+ God knows+)
   Henceforth my woing minde shall be exprest
   In russet yeas, ₓ and honest kersie noes.
9 And to begin + Wench, so God helpe me law, +
   My love to thee is sound, sans cracke or flaw.
10 ⟨ψSans, sans, {you'll} pray {me}.
11   Yet I have a tricke
   Of the old rage : beare with me, I am sicke.
12 Ile leave it by degrees : +

There is a tendency for the speech to be played as if Berowne were still being glib. Yet F's sentence structure and orthography suggest that, while he may still be attempting to joke his way out of trouble, he may not be finding it quite so easy as most modern texts suggest.

- three of the first four sentences are short, suggesting he cannot immediately access his customary elaborate word spinning abilities

- also the first surround phrase opening F #5 ˊ . Cut me to peeces with thy keene conceit : ˊ could suggest the invitation has more bite to it than might at first be expected

- and in finishing, once he realises he has fallen into the trap of word-play yet again, the last threes sentences are short, perhaps suggesting that there is some sincerity to the apology, especially considering sentences F #11-12 are also formed by surround phrases ˊ . Yet I have a tricke/Of the old rage : beare with me, I am sicke . /Ile leave it by degrees : ˊ

- it also seems that Berowne is taking great care to advance his argument detailed step by step, far more so than his modern counterpart, for, in first inviting Rosaline to mock him, and in decrying his former behaviour, whereas most modern texts set just two sentences (mt. #3-4), F allows him five sentences to make the same points (F #3-7)

- the speech opening himself to attack starts quite emotionally (2/8 in the eight lines of F #1-5)

- Berowne's start to denying any future similar foolish behaviour becomes passionate (5/6, F #6 and the first four lines of F #7), but he turns again to emotion as he forswears any further elaborate language (0/4 in the last two lines of F #7 and the first line of F #8)

- and in starting his new linguistic form he becomes passionate once again (4/4 in the last three lines of F #8 plus F #9), only to waver between the (deliberate?) calm of non-embellishment (F #10 and #12) and emotion (0/3, F #11) once the short sentences begin

- the colon ending the speech suggests that Berowne interrupts himself as he sees the reactions of his fellow oath-breakers to his speech

#'s 15- 16: Entertainment

15/ Braggart   I doe affect the very ground (which is base)   1.2.167 -185

Background: Don Armado (the Braggart) is kept at the court for his entertainment value - described by Ferdinand as 'A man in all the worlds new fashion planted/that hath a mint of phrases in his braine:/One, who the musicke of his owne vaine tongue,/Doth ravish like enchanting harmonie'; for, as a Spaniard, he mangles or overelaborates or creates malapropisms in nearly every speech. He too is supposed to abstain from contact with women. Unfortunately, he has fallen for Jaquenetta, doubly unfortunate in that, however impoverished, he is supposedly of noble birth and she a simple country girl who cannot read. The following is his first solo address to the audience just after she has exited with her true beau, Costard the Clowne.

Style: solo

Where: unspecified, within the palace grounds   **To Whom:** direct audience address

                    # of Lines: 18   **Probable Timing: 0.55 minutes**

Modern Text

15/ Braggart

1 I do* affect the very ground (which is base)
where her shoe* (which is baser) guided by her foot*
(which is basest) doth tread.
              I shall be forsworn (which
is a great argument of falsehood*) if I love.
                            And how can
that be true love, which is falsely* attempted?
                    Love is a fa-
miliar ; Love is a △devil* ; ◊ there is no evil* △angel* but
Love. †

5 Yet [was Sampson] so tempted, and he had an excellent strength ; △yet was Salomon so seduce†, and he* had
a very good wit*.

6 Cupid's △butt*-°shaft is too hard for Hercules' △club*, and therefore too much odds* for a Spaniard's △rapier. †

7 The first and second cause will not serve
my turn* ; the △passado he* respects not, the △duello he
regards not: his disgrace is to be called △boy, but his
glory* is to subdue men.

8   Adieu₄, △valor* , rust, △rapier, be*
still, △drum, for your manager is in love ; yea, he* loveth.

9 Assist me, some extemporal* god of △°rhyme*, for I am sure
I shall turn *△sonnet.

10   Devise, △wit, write, △pen, for I am for
whole volumes in folio.

First Folio

15/ Braggart

1 I doe affect the very ground (which is base)
where her shooe (which is baser) guided by her foote
(which is basest) doth tread.
                    I shall be forsworn (which
is a great argument of falshood) if I love.

3   And how can
that be true love, which is falsly attempted?

4   Love is a Divell.

5 miliar, + Love is a Divell.
              There is no evill Angell but
Love, yet [Sampson was] so tempted, and he had an excellent strength :, x   Yet was Salomon so seduced, and hee had
a very good witte.

6   Cupids Butshaft is too hard for Hercules Clubbe, and therefore too much ods for a Spa-
niards Rapier: The first and second cause will not serve
my turne : x   the Passado hee regards not, the Duello he
regards not; + his disgrace is to be called Boy, but his
glorie is to subdue men.

7   Adue + Valour, rust + Rapier, bee
still + Drum, for your manager is in love ; yea + hee loveth.

8 Assist me + some extemporall god of Rime, for I am sure
I shall turne Sonnet.

9   Devise + Wit, write + Pen, for I am for
whole volumes in folio.

F's orthography reveals clearly defined stages of an older man finding a way to break his oath so as to woo a young woman.

- the speech starts very carefully, only slightly emotional as Armado confesses his total adoration of Jaquenetta (0/2, F #1), and then completely unembellished as he uncovers the double dilemma of being dishonourable and how that might affect 'true love' (F #2-3): thus it's interesting to note the words 'falshood' and 'falsly' are both set in their withheld (short-spelling) form

- and then, as with Berowne earlier (speech #3 above), as he determines to define 'Love', so the releases start coming thick and fast

- with the the first definitions, 'Love' as a 'Divell' and references to how men of strength (Sampson) and intelligence (Solomon) were felled by it, so Armado becomes highly passionate (7/5 in just the three and a half lines of F #4-5)

- the wonderful realisation/excuse that if even Hercules cannot withstand 'Love' how can he, becomes an exercise in mental self deception (9/3 in the six lines of F #6): and this passage is well served by F's onrush allowing the thoughts to flow: most modern texts spoil this by splitting the sentence in two, with mt. #6 offering the chop-logic excuse that if Hercules cannot withstand love how can he, and mt. #7 dealing with how each of his military defences will be useless in protecting him from 'Love'

- in his moment of self-redefinition, with the farewell to arms, the admittance of being in love' and the appeal for help from a new source (the 'god of Rime'), Armado becomes passionate (5/5, F #7-8) – though 'Adue' and 'Rime' are short spelled

- and in the final self-encouragement to become a poet, Armado becomes intellectual once more (2/0, F #9)

16/ Braggart   **Sir, it is the Kings most sweet pleasure and affection**   between 5.1.87 - 116

Background: With the failure of the Russian Masque, the four young men have charged Armado to prepare an entertainment for the French visitors. He, in turn, has come to ask the locals, especially the schoolmaster/pedant Holofernes for help: hence the following-

Style: as part of four handed scene

Where: unspecified, but presumably either near Holofernes' home/school, or close to where he and Nathaniel have just dined 'at the fathers of a certaine Pupill of mine'

To Whom: Holofernes, the curate Sir Nathaniel, and Constable Dull

# of Lines: 20   Probable Timing: 1.00 minutes

Modern Text

16/ Braggart

1 Sir, it is the King's most sweet pleasure and affection, to congratulate the Princess* at her ^pavilion in
the posteriors of this day, which the rude multitude call
the afternoon*.

2 {ψ} The King is a noble ^gentleman, and my familiar; I do* assure ye, very good friend {.}

3   For I
must tell thee it will please his Grace (by the world)
sometime to lean* upon my poor* shoulder, and with
his royal* finger, thus, dally* with my excrement, with my
mustachio; but sweet heart, let that pass*.

4   By the world,
I recount no fable : some certain* special* honors* it
pleaseth his greatness* to impart to Armado, a ^soldier*,
a man of travel*, that hath seen* the world; but let that
pass* . †

5   The very all of all is - but, sweet heart, I do implore
secrecy*- that the King would have me* present the
Princess* (sweet chuck*) with some delightful* ostentation, or show, or pageant, or antic*, or fire-^work* . †

6 Now, understanding that the ^curate and your sweet self
are good at such eruptions, and sudden* breaking out of
mirth* (as it were), I have acquainted you withal*, to
the end to crave your assistance.

First Folio

16/ Braggart

1 Sir, it is the Kings most sweet pleasure and affection, to congratulate the Princesse at her Pavilion, + in
the posteriors of this day, which the rude multitude call
the afternoone.

2 {ψ} The King is a noble Gentleman, and my familiar, I doe assure ye+ very good friend {.}

3   For I
must tell thee it will please his Grace (by the world)
sometime to leane upon my poore shoulder, and with
his royall finger + thus + dallie with my excrement, with my
mustachio: x but sweet heart + let that passe.

4   By the world +
I recount no fable, + some certaine speciall honours it
pleaseth his greatnesse to impart to Armado + a Souldier,
a man of travell, that hath seene the world: x but let that
passe; the very all of all is: x but + sweet heart, I do implore
secrecie, that the King would have mee present the
Princesse (sweet chucke) with some delightfull ostentation, or show, or pageant, or anticke, or fire-worke:
Now, understanding that the Curate and your sweet self
are good at such eruptions, and sodaine breaking out of
myrth (as it were) + I have acquainted you withall, to
the end to crave your assistance.

The language conveys Armado's palpable excitement, so, not surprisingly, the speech is much more emotional than intellectual (13/23 overall).

• the one moment of capitalised release ('the Princesse at her Pavilion') seems to allow the actor alliterative fun with Armado's love of language and florid self-expression

• and at times it seems that even he is aware that his mouth is running away with him, for the surround phrases show him reigning in his enthusiasm ': but sweet heart, let that passe .' : followed by ': but let that passe ; the very all of all is : '

• yet at least he starts out with some semblance of controlled passion (5/3, F #1-2) as he lays in the preamble as to why he has approached the two supposed learned men known to be good at 'eruptions'

• but, as the conversation veers off topic as to how he, Armado, is regarded (or would like to be regarded) by royalty, he becomes highly emotional (6/17, F #3 and F #4's first eight lines - to the final colon)

• thus the few clusters of emotional release point to where his revery (of his – supposed? – relations with the King) seems to be getting the better of him: 'sometime to leane upon my poore shoulder'; 'some certaine speciall honours'; 'a Souldier, a man of travell that hath seene the world'

• however, finally getting back to the point at hand and asking for their assistance, Armado brings himself back to a modicum of self-control (2/3, the last four lines of the speech)

17: REALITY INTRUDES

17/ Queene   **A time me thinkes too short,**   5.2.788 - 812

Background: As the joviality surrounding the presentation of 'The Nine Worthies' peaks, a figure dressed in black arrives to announce the death of the Princesse's father the King of France. As Boyet and she realise, now Queene rather than Princesse, she and her train must leave immediately. Both Navar (awkwardly) and Berowne (much more succinctly) try to express their true feelings so as to get some indication in return from the four French women as to how they regard the men who have professed their love. The following is the Princesse/Queene's no holds barred response to Navar's (finally) plain-speaking request, 'Now at the latest minute of the houre/Grant us your loves.'

Style: one on one, probably with six others overhearing

Where: somewhere near either the palace or the French Ladies' encampment, amidst the detritus left behind by the players   **To Whom:** Ferdinand of Navar, in front of the three other would-be couples, Berowne-Rosaline, Longavile-Maria, Dumaine-Katherine

# of Lines: 25   **Probable Timing: 1.15 minutes**

Modern Text

17/ Queene

1 A time [methinks*] too short
   To make a world-without-end bargain* in . †

2 No, no, my △lord, your Grace is perjur'd much,
   Full of dear* guiltines* , and therefore this:
   If for my △love (as there is no such cause)
   You will do aught, this shall you do for me:◊
   Your oath* I will not trust, but go with speed
   To some forlorn* and naked △hermitage,
   Remote from all the pleasures of the world;
   There stay until* the twelve △celestial* △signs
   Have brought about their annual* reckoning.

3 If this austere insociable life,
   Change not your offer made in heat* of blood;
   If frosts and fasts, hard lodging, and thin weeds
   Nip not the gaudy* blossoms* of your △love
   But that it bear* this trial* , and last love ;
   Then at the expiration of the year*
   Come challenge me, challenge me by these deserts,
   And by this △virgin palm* now kissing thine,
   I will be thine; and till that instant shut
   My woeful* self* up in a mourning house,
   Raining the tears* of lamentation
   For the remembrance of my △father's death.

4 If this thou do deny*, let our hands part,
   Neither intitled in the other's heart*.

First Folio

17/ Queene

1 A time [me thinkes] too short,ₓ
   To make a world-without-end bargaine in;
   No, no + my Lord, your Grace is perjur'd much,
   Full of deare guiltinesse, and therefore this:
   If for my Love (as there is no such cause)
   You will do ought, this shall you do for me.

2 Your oth I will not trust: ₓ but go with speed
   To some forlorne and naked Hermitage,
   Remote from all the pleasures of the world: ₓ
   There stay,ₓ untill the twelve Celestiall Signes
   Have brought about their annuall reckoning.

3 If this austere insociable life,
   Change not your offer made in heate of blood: ₓ
   If frosts,ₓ and fasts, hard lodging, and thin weeds
   Nip not the gaudie blossomes of your Love, ₓ
   But that it beare this triall, and last love: ₓ
   Then at the expiration of the yeare,
   Come challenge me, challenge me by these deserts,
   And by this Virgin palme, ₓ now kissing thine,
   I will be thine: ₓ and till that instant shut
   My wofull selfe up in a mourning house,
   Raining the teares of lamentation.
   For the remembrance of my Fathers death.

4 If this thou do denie, let our hands part,
   Neither intitled in the others hart.

With so much having just occurred, the announcement of the death of her father, her resultant accession as Queene of France, and Ferdinand's last minute proposal, it's not surprising that F shows the speech as a struggle between self-control via trying to remain calm (five and a half unembellished lines) and emotion.

• with the overall emotional imbalance (9/18) , at no time does she succeed in retaining intellectual control: the closest she comes is the passionate denunciation of Ferdinand for being 'perjur'd much' (2/2) - though the ensuing adjective seems to suggest that she not only understands but might actually approve of his love ('deare guiltinesse') - and the subsequent emotionally tinged passionate challenge that the go into retreat for twelve months (4/5 to the end of F #2)

• the unembellished lines (not in order) show her mind at its clearest
   "You will do ought, this shall you do for me."
   "If this austere insociable life,/Change not your offer . . ."
   "Come challenge me, challenge me by these deserts,"
   "If this thou do denie, let our hands part,/Neither intitled in the others hart."
   and especially the unembellished monosyllabic surround phrase : Your oth I will not trust:ₓ

• F #3's three extra breath-thoughts (marked , ₓ) all point to key moments where the Princesse/Queene needs an extra thought for clarification or breath for self-control as she anticipates the pain she will have to endure over the next twelve months

• rejecting the timing of and time-line inherent in Ferdinand's proposal, F #1's first two lines start emotionally, heightened by line two ending with a semicolon (0/2); then comes F #12's mix of unembellished lines and passion as discussed above

• her determined elaboration in F #3 that this is the only way to win her is emotional once again (3/9)

• and it is a tribute to her sense of self that the speech ends completely unembellished (0/0, F #4), though the short spelling of 'denie' and 'hart' suggest she is struggling hard to hold herself in check (restraining from tears perhaps)

MIDSUMMER NIGHT'S DREAM

SPEECHES IN ORDER	TIME	PAGE	SPEECHES BY GENDER	Speech #(s)
#'s 1 - 5: The World of Theseus			**SPEECHES FOR WOMEN (16)**	
1/ **Egeus** Full of vexation, come I, with complaint	1.15	102	**Hermia** Traditional & Today: young woman of small stature & marriageable age	#13, #14, #15, #16
2/ **Theseus** What say you Hermia? be advis'd faire Maide,	1.45	103		
3/ **Theseus** More strange then true.	1.00	105	**Helena** Traditional & Today: tall young woman of marriageable age	#17, #18, #19, #20, #21, #22, #23
4/ **Theseus** Come now, what maskes, what dances shall we . . .	1.15	106		
5/ **Egeus** A play there is, my Lord, some ten words long,	1.00	108	**Fairie** Traditional & Today: (usually) woman of any age	#27
#'s 6 - 9: Lysander In Love			**Titania/Queene** Traditional: young woman or child Today: (sometimes) woman of any age	#30, #31, #36, #37
6/ **Lysander** I am my Lord, as well deriv'd as he,	0.40	109		
7/ **Lysander** How now my love? Why is your cheek so pale?	1.30	110		
8/ **Lysander** Transparent Helena, nature her shewes art,	0.45	111		
9/ **Lysander** She sees not Hermia: Hermia sleepe thou there,	0.35	112	**SPEECHES FOR EITHER GENDER (12)**	
#'s 10 - 12: Demetrius In Love			**Egeus** Traditional: male, with teenage daughter Today: any gender	#1, #5
10/ **Demetrius** You doe impeach your modesty too much,	0.20	112	**Pucke/Robin** Traditional: young man or child Today: often any gender but, because of the mistakes made throughout the play, usually still young	#28, #29, #34, #35, #47, #48
11/ **Demetrius** O Helen, goddesse, nimph, perfect, divine,	0.30	113	**Quince** Traditional: male of any age Today: any age, and, if his given name 'Peter' is changed to 'Petra' or 'Mistress', any gender	#39, #40
12/ **Demetrius** My Lord, faire Helen told me of their stealth,	0.55	114	**Snout {Wall}** Traditional & Today: character actor of any age	#41
#'s 13 - 16: Hermia In Love			**Snug {Lyon}** Traditional & Today: character actor of any age	#42
13/ **Hermia** My good Lysander,/I sweare to thee, by Cupids. . . .	0.40	115		
14/ **Hermia** Lysander; finde you out a bed,	0.35	116		
15/ **Hermia** Helpe me Lysander, helpe me; do thy best	0.40	117		
16/ **Hermia** Puppet? why so? I, that way goes the game.	0.35	118	**SPEECHES FOR MEN (20)**	
#'s 17 - 23: Helena In Love			**Theseus** Traditional & Today: male of some authority	#2, #3, #4
17/ **Helena** Cal you me faire? that faire againe unsay,	0.45	119	**Lysander** Traditional & Today: young man of marriageable age	#6, #7, #8, #9
18/ **Helena** How happy some, ore othersome can be?	1.15	120	**Demetrius** Traditional & Today: young man of marriageable age	#10, #11, #12
19/ **Helena** You draw me, you hard-hearted Adamant;	0.40	121	**Bottome/Clowne** Traditional: usually a man of an early middle-age on up Today: man of any age	#24, #25, #26, #38, #43, #44, #45
20/ **Helena** Your vertue is my priviledge:	0.40	122	**Oberon** Traditional: usually a man of an early middle-age on up, capable of playing the Fairy King	#32, #33
21/ **Helena** O I am out of breath, in this fond chace,	0.50	123	Today: man of any age capable of playing the Fairy King	
22/ **Helena** O spight! O hell! I see you are all bent	0.55	124	**Flute {Thisby}** Traditional & Today: young man that has 'a beard comming'	#46
23/ **Helena** Loe, she is one of this confederacy,	1.30	125		
#'s 24 - 26: The Mechanicals Prepare Their Play				
24/ **Bottome** A Lover that kills himselfe most gallantly for love?	0.40	126		
25/ **Bottome** Let mee play the Lyon too, I will roare that I	0.30	127		
26/ **Bottome** Masters, you ought to consider with your selves, to	0.45	128		

#'s 27 - 29: The World of the Lower Fairies

27/	**Fairie**	**Whether wander I?**	0.45	129
28/	**Robin**	Thou speak'st aright; /I am that merrie wanderer . . .	0.55	130
29/	**Pucke**	My Fairie Lord, this must be done with haste,	0.35	131

#'s 30 - 34: The Fairy Quarrel

30/	**Queene**	These are the forgeries of jealousie,	1.50	131
31/	**Queene**	Set your heart at rest,/The Fairy land buyes not . . .	0.55	133
32/	**Oberon**	My gentle Pucke come hither; thou remembrest	1.55	134
33/	**Oberon**	I know a banke where the wilde time blowes,	0.35	135
34/	**Pucke**	**Through the Forrest have I gone,**	0.55	136

#'s 35 - 37: Titania In Love

35/	**Pucke**	My Mistris with a monster is in love,	1.30	137
36/	**Titania**	What Angell wakes me from my flowry bed?	0.20	138
37/	**Titania**	Out of this wood, do not desire to goe,	1.10	138

#'s 38 - 46: The Mechanicals and the Playing of the Play

38/	{Bottome as} **Clowne**	When my cue comes, call me, and I will answer.	0.55	140
39/	{Quince as} **Prologue**	If we offend, it is with our good will.	0.35	141
40/	{Quince as} **Prologue**	Gentles, perchance you wonder at this show,	1.15	142
41/	{Snout as} **Wall:**	In this same Interlude, it doth befall,	0.35	143
42/	{Snug as} **Lyon:**	You Ladies, you (whose gentle harts do feare	0.30	143
43/	{Bottome as} **Piramus:**	O grim lookt night, ô night with hue so blacke,	0.40	144
44/	{Bottome as} **Piramus:**	Sweet Moone, I thank thee for thy	0.40	145
45/	{Bottome as} **Piramus**	O wherefore Nature, did'st thou Lions frame ?	0.40	146
46/	{Flute as} **Thisby**	Asleepe my Love ?	0.50	147

#'s 47 - 48: The End

47/	**Pucke**	**Now the hungry Lyons rores,**	1.00	148
48/	**Robin**	**If we shadowes have offended,**	0.50	149

MIDSUMMER NIGHT'S DREAM

#'s 1 - 5: The World of Theseus

1/Egeus   **Full of vexation, come I, with complaint**   1.1.22 - 45

Background: Alone with his shortly to be wedded love Hippolita, the amorous Theseus is interrupted by the domestic problems of one his subjects. As such, this, the first speech for Egeus, father of the, to him, disobedient Hermia, is self-explanatory.

Style: speech of appeal for help directed to one person in front of a listening larger group who are also involved

Where: somewhere in Theseus' palace   **To Whom:** Duke Theseus, in front of two young male wooers (the chosen Demetrius and the unwelcome Lysander), Egeus' daughter Hermia, and Hippolita, and perhaps with court officials also in attendance, though none are indicated in the original stage directions.

# of Lines: 25   **Probable Timing: 1.15 minutes**

Modern Text

1/Egeus

1 Full of vexation come I, with complaint
   Against my child* , my daughter Hermia.

2 Stand forth, Demetrius . [1]

3   My ᴬnoble ᴬlord,
   This man hath my consent to marry* her.

4 Stand forth, Lysander .

5   And, my gracious Duke,

6 This man [2] hath bewitch'd the bosom* of my child* . †
   Thou, thou, Lysander, thou hast given her rhymes*,
   And interchang'd love ° tokens with my child* ;
   Thou hast by ᴬmoon ᴼlight at her window sung
   With faining voice verses of faining love,
   And stol'n* the impression of her fantasy*
   With bracelets of thy hair* , rings, gawds*, conceits,
   Knacks* , trifles, ᴬnose°gays*, sweetmeats - messengers
   Of strong prevailment in unhardened* youth . †

7 With cunning hast thou filch'd my daughter's heart,
   Turn'd her obedience (which is due to me)
   To stubborn* harshness* .

First Folio

1/Egeus

1 Full of vexation, ₓ come I, with complaint
   Against my childe, my daughter Hermia.

STAND FORTHₓ DEMETRIUS

2 My Noble Lord,
   This man hath my consent to marrie her.

STAND FORTH ⁺ LYSANDER

3 And⁺ my gracious Duke,
   This man hath bewitch'd the bosome of my childe :
   Thou, thou ⁺ Lysander, thou hast given her rimes,
   And interchang'd love-tokens with my childe :   x
   Thou hast by Moone-light at her window sung,ₓ
   With faining voice, ₓ verses of faining love,
   And stolne the impression of her fantasie,ₓ
   With bracelets of thy haire, rings, gawdes, conceits,
   Knackes, trifles, Nose-gaies, sweet meats (ₓmessengers
   Of strong prevailment in unhardened youth) ₓ
   With cunning hast thou filch'd my daughters heart,
   Turn'd her obedience (which is due to me)
   To stubborne harshnesse.

There seems to be a tug of war between Egeus' description of the circumstances and his reaction to them, which are established either intellectually or by non-embellished phrases, and the emotional handling of the individual details of what he presumes or knows of Lysander's means of wooing his daughter.

• the non-embellished lines suggest attempts at self control, not only in setting up the facts
   "Full of vexation, come I, with complaint"
   "This man hath my consent to marrie her."
and what he wishes done if Hermia refuses to marry Demetrius
   "As she is mine, I may dispose of her;"
   "Immediately provided in that case."
but also in both summing and then assessing the result (not the details) of Lysander's dubious wooing methods
   " . . . at her window sung/With faining voice, verses of faining love,/And stolne the impression of her fantasie,"
   "(messengers/Of strong prevailment in unhardened youth)/With cunning hast thou filch'd my daughters heart,/Turn'd her obedience (which is due to me)"

• thus, the speech opens and closes intellectually enough (3/1, F #1-2, 6/2, F #4), but the long onrushed Lysander-accusatory sentence is quite emotional (4/8, F #3), and the three extra breath-thoughts (marked , ₓ two in F #3, and the third before the last line of the speech) also suggest that at times Egeus needs to take an extra breath before he can voice what needs to be said

• yet in both there are exceptions, supporting the idea and detailing the moments of the character's inner struggle, for even in the emotionally onrushed F #3 (made much more rational by most modern texts which split the sentence into three) there are five lines of unembellished description and summation, as noted above

---

[1] as shown opposite, the source texts (both F and Q) print this as a stage direction; many modern texts print this (and the exact same direction for Lysander two lines later) as a spoken command from Egeus

[2] some modern texts follow F2 and omit the word 'man', thus reducing the line to ten syllables

8

And, my gracious Duke,
Be it so she will not here* before your Grace
Consent to marry* with Demetrius,
I beg the ancient privilege* of Athens:
As she is mine, I may dispose of her;
Which shall be either to this △gentleman,
Or to her death, according to our △law
Immediately provided in that case.

4

And⁺ my gracious Duke,
Be it so she will not heere before your Grace,ₓ
Consent to marrie with Demetrius,
I beg the ancient priviledge of Athens; ⁺
As she is mine, I may dispose of her;
Which shall be either to this Gentleman,
Or to her death, according to our Law,ₓ
Immediately provided in that case.

• and, despite the intellect of F #4, the double semicoloned surround phrase
"; As she is mine, I may dispose of her ; "
shows that, for whatever reason, the demand has an enormous emotional impact on Egeus (though, as noted above, the phrase is non-embellished, underscoring the emotional-intellectual struggle even more)

2/ Theseus   What say you Hermia? be advis'd faire Maide,   between 1.1.46 - 90

Background: A grouping together of Theseus' reasoning in trying to provide some rational solution to the very awkward problem presented him, especially since Hermia has stated publicly she will never 'yeeld my virgin patent up' to her father's choice as husband for her, Demetrius.

Style: a reasoning speech directed to one person in front of a listening larger group who are also involved

Where: somewhere in Theseus' palace   **To Whom:** Hermia, in front of two young male wooers (the, to her, unwelcome Demetrius and her chosen Lysander), her father Egeus, and Hippolita, and perhaps with court officials also in attendance, though none are indicated in the original stage directions.

# of Lines: 36   Probable Timing: 1.45 minutes

Modern Text

2/ Theseus

1   What say you, Hermia? †
        Be advis'd fair* △maid* ,

2

3   To you your △father should be as a △god;
    One that compos'd your beauties; yea, and one
    To whom you are but as a form* in wax,*
    By him imprinted, and within his power,
    To leave the figure, or disfigure it. †

4   Demetrius is a worthy △gentleman {,}

{ψ} {ψ} and in himself* {so is Lysander}; ◊
    But in this kind* , wanting your fathers voice,* ◊
    The other must be held the worthier.

5   {Y}our eyes* must with {your father's} judgment look* .

6   {Thus you must} know

{ψ} The worst that may befall {you} in this case,
    If {you} refuse to wed Demetrius.

7   Either to die* the death, or to abjure
    For ever the society of men.

First Folio

2/ Theseus

1   What say you⁺ Hermia? be advis'd faire Maide,
    To you your Father should be as a God;
    One that compos'd your beauties; yea⁺ and one
    To whom you are but as a forme in waxe⁺
    By him imprinted:ₓ and within his power,
    To leave the figure, or disfigure it:
    Demetrius is a worthy Gentleman{,}

{ψ} {ψ} and in himselfe {so is Lysander}.

2   But in this kinde, wanting your fathers voyce.

3   The other must be held the worthier.

4   {Y}our eies must with {your father's} judgment looke.

5   {Thus you must} know

{ψ} The worst that may befall {you} in this case,
    If {you} refuse to wed Demetrius.

6   Either to dye the death, or to abjure
    For ever the society of men.

{ctd. over}

F's orthography reveals an authority figure who, while taking great care to spell out the details of what he may have to impose on Hermia, shows some personal strains as he does.

• the logical non-embellished surround phrase
"; and within his power, /To leave the figure, or disfigure it : "
as well as the large number of other non-embellished lines
"The other must be held the worthier."
"{Thus you must} know/The worst that may befall {you} in this case,/If {you} refuse to wed Demetrius."
" or to abjure/For ever the society of men."
"Therefore ... question your desires,/Know of your youth, examine well your blood,"
"To live a barren sister all your life/ . . . /Thrice blessed they that master so their blood,/To undergo such maiden pilgrimage,"
"Take time to pause"
"The sealing day betwixt my love and me, /For everlasting bond of fellowship:"
"For disobedience to your fathers will,"
"For aie, austerity, and single life."
suggest a Theseus well in careful intellectual control of the situation

• yet there are certain orthographical glitches that suggest a well of humanity bubbling underneath

a/ F #1 indicating that although control may be shown later in the speech it certainly is difficult to establish (this difficulty often gutted

104 / The Speeches

7

Therefore + faire Hermia + question your desires,
Know of your youth, examine well your blood,
Whether (if you yeeld not to your fathers choice)
You can endure the liverie of a Nunne,
For aye to be in shady Cloister mew'd,
To live a barren sister all your life,
Chanting faint hymnes to the cold fruitlesse Moone,
Thrice blessed they that master so their blood,+
To undergo such maiden pilgrimage,+
But earthlier happie is the Rose distill'd,
[Then] that which withering on the virgin thorne,ₓ
Growes, lives, and dies, in single blessednesse .

8

Take time to pause, and by the next new Moon+
The sealing day betwixt my love and me,ₓ
For everlasting bond of fellowship:ₓ
Upon that day either prepare to dye,ₓ
For disobedience to your fathers will,
Or else to wed Demetrius+ as hee would,
Or on Dianaes Altar to protest
For aie,ₓ austerity,ₓ and single life.

by most modern texts that split F #1 into three sentences and two lines of a fourth)

b/ there is the early emotionally (semicolon created) surround phrase
" ; One that compos'd your beauties ;"
underlining Theseus' understanding of the traditional/patriarchal father-child relationship and (perhaps) his appreciation of Hermia's 'beauties'

c/ there is the very strange series of one line sentences (F #2-4) emphasising, according to the patriarchal view, how she should follow her father's wishes (the three are usually set as one sentence in most modern texts and in Q)

d/ there are the five extra breaths towards the end of the speech (the penultimate line of F #7 and on, marked , ₓ) in at least four of them where Theseus seems to be taking extra care to explain to Hermia what might happen

• despite the onrush, Theseus manages to stay in control - for in establishing her supposed duty to her father, the speech opens intellectually (7/4, F #1)

• then, in the spelling out of what might happen to her, Theseus becomes somewhat emotional (5/14, in the twenty lines F #2-7)

• while the final challenge to Hermia to make up her mind by 'the next new Moon' is a mixture of unembellished lines (four and a half in eight) and intellect (4/1, F #8)

8

Therefore, fair* Hermia, question your desires,
Know of your youth, examine well your blood,
Whether (if you yield* not to your father's choice)
You can endure the livery* of a ᐃnun*,
For aye to be in shady ᐃcloister mew'd,
To live a barren sister all your life,
Chanting faint hymns* to the cold fruitless *ᐃmoon* .

9

Thrice blessed they that master so their blood,
To undergo such maiden pilgrimage;
But earthlier happy* is the ᐃrose distill'd*ₓ,
[Than] that which withering on the virgin thorn*
Grows*, lives, and dies, in single blessedness* .

10

Take time to pause, and by the next new ᐃmoon -
The sealing day betwixt my love and me
For everlasting bond of fellowship -
Upon that day either prepare to die*
For disobedience to your father's will,
Or else to wed Demetrius, as he* would,
Or on Diana's* ᐃaltar to protest
For aye* austerity and single life.

3/ Theseus   **More strange then true.**   5.1.2–22

Background: Their marriage having taken place, at last, Theseus and Hippolita are waiting for the two other just-married couples (Helena and Demetrius, Hermia and Lysander) and the provider of the evening's entertainment to join them. They are discussing the story told to them by the other two couples of their night's adventures.

Style: speech as part of a two handed scene

Where: somewhere in the palace where a post-supper pre-wedding bed entertainment is to be offered   **To Whom:** his new bride Hippolita

# of Lines: 20   **Probable Timing: 1.00 minutes**

Modern Text

3/ Theseus

1 More strange [than] true.
        I never may believe*
2 These antic* fables, nor these ᐃfairy toys* . †
3 Lovers and madmen have such seething brains* ,
4 Such shaping fantasies* , that apprehend
   Moreᶟ [than] cool* reason ever comprehends.
5 The ᐃlunatic* , the ᐃlover, and the ᐃpoet
   Are of imagination all compact.
6 One sees more devils* [than] vast* hell can hold;
   That is the madman.
7   The ᐃlover, all as frantic* ,
   Sees Helen's beauty in a brow of Egypt*.

8 The ᐃpoet's eye, in a fine frenzy rolling,
   Doth glance from heaven to earth, from earth to heaven;‡
   And as imagination bodies forth
   The forms of things unknown* , the ᐃpoet's pen
   Turns* them to shapes, and gives to aery* nothing
   A local* habitation, and a name.
9 Such tricks hath strong imagination,
   That if it would but apprehend some joy,
   It comprehends some bringer of that joy.
10 Or in the night, imagining some fear* ,
   How easy* , is a bush suppos'd a ᐃbear* !

First Folio

3/ Theseus

1 More strange [then] true.
        I never may beleeve
2 These anticke fables, nor these Fairy toyes,
   Lovers and mad men have such seething braines,
   Such shaping phantasies, that apprehend more
   [Then] coole reason ever comprehends.
3 The Lunaticke, the Lover, and the Poet,ₓ
   Are of imagination all compact.
4 One sees more divels [then] vaste hell can hold;
   That is the mad man.
5   The Lover, all as franticke,
   Sees Helens beauty in a brow of Egipt.

6 The Poets eye⁺ in a fine frenzy rolling, doth glance
   From heaven to earth, from earth to heaven.
7 And as imagination bodies forth the forms of things
   Unknowne;ₓ the Poets pen turnes them to shapes,
   And gives to aire nothing,ₓ a locall habitation,
   And a name.
8   Such tricks hath strong imagination, ⁴
   That if it would but apprehend some joy,
   It comprehends some bringer of that joy.
9 Or in the night, imagining some feare,
   How easie is a bush suppos'd a Beare?⁺

While Theseus still shows some swaths of self-control, the speech is nowhere near as logical as elsewhere in the play (see the speech #2 above for example) – indeed, footnote #4, referring to the shadowed texts, points to just how much F suggests that here **Theseus is lost in his own imagination and is attempting to reach an understanding.**

• the philosophical assessment seems to force Theseus to a very quiet and controlled exploration, as all the non-embellished phrases seem to suggest, starting with the short sentence
        "More strange [then] true."
moving into
        "Such shaping phantasies"
        "From heaven to earth, from earth to heaven./And as imagination
        bodies forth the forms of things"
realising that
        "Such tricks hath strong imagination,/That if it would but
        apprehend some joy,/It comprehends some bringer of that
        joy."

• as he expresses his skepticism, the speech opens emotionally (1/5, F #1-2) and closes equally emotionally as he tries to justify the skepticism (2/6, F #7-8),

• and, while the central section contains the intellectual exploration (7/3, F #3-6), he may not be as controlled as most modern texts would indicate, for, as footnote #4 explains, his struggle to understand comes at the cost of a very irregular line structure in F #6, and extends into the emotional F #7, suggesting that the exploration is more than somewhat taxing

• which is confirmed by the two emotional semicolons in F #4 and F #7

---

³ as shown opposite, F sets 'more' at the end of the previous line, the irregularity (9/11 syllables) suggesting Theseus' is beginning-to-get-excited: modern texts remove the excitement by setting normal poetry

⁴ save for Q1's placing of 'And as' at the end of a line instead of starting a new one, the F setting follows Q1 exactly: the irregular passage (13/8 - 10/14/10/12 or 13/12 or 13 syllables) shows Theseus struggling to express himself in matters we have never heard him attempt to talk of before in a brand new situation where, for the first time in the play, Hippolita has initiated the conversation: the modern texts' poetical restructuring (11/10 - 12/10/10/10 or 11/10/9 or 10) smoothes away both awkwardness and excitement, creating somewhat bland posturing where half-formed new concepts originally existed

4/ Theseus   **Come now, what maskes, what dances shall we have**   between 5.1.32 -40

Background: The questioning and discussion of potential entertainments.

Style: a group address

Where: somewhere in the palace where a post-supper pre-wedding bed entertainment is to be offered   **To Whom:** Hippolita, Helena and Demetrius, Hermia and Lysander, whoever is in charge of the evening's entertainment (the quarto suggests Philostrate, the First Folio Egeus), and any court retainers present

# of Lines: 26   **Probable Timing: 1.15 minutes**

Modern Text

4/ Theseus

1 Come now ; what masques *, what dances shall
          we have *,

   To wear * away this long age of three hours *
   Between our after-°supper, and bed-time?

2 Where is our usuall * manager of mirth?

3 What ᐃrevels are in hand?

4   Is there no play *?

5 To ease the anguish of a torturing hour *?

   {ψ}, what abridgment * have {we} for this evening?

6 What masque *? ◊ what music *?

7   How shall we beguile

8 The lazy⸝ time, if not with some delight?

Reads List "The battle * with the Centaurs ,to be sung
          By an Athenian ᐃeunuch to the ᐃharp * . "

9 We'll none of that : ◊ that have I told my ᐃlove *,
   In glory of my kinsman Hercules.

10 **List** "The riot of the tipsy *, Bacchanals *,
   Tearing the Thracian singer, in their rage *?"

11 That is an old device, and it was play'd.
   When I from Thebes came last a ᐃconqueror.

12 **List** "The thrice three Muses, mourning for the death
   Of ᐃlearning, late deceas'd in beggary *. "

13 That is some ᐃsatire, keen * and critical *,
   Not sorting with a nuptial * ceremony *.

First Folio

4/ Theseus

1 Come now, [+] what maskes, what dances shall
          we have,

   To weare away this long age of three houres,[x]
   Between our after supper, and bed-time?

2 Where is our usuall manager of mirth?

3 What Revels are in hand?

4   Is there no play,

5 To ease the anguish of a torturing houre?

   {ψ}, what abridgement have {we} for this evening?

6 What maske?

7   What musicke?

8   How shall we beguile
   The lazie time, if not with some delight?

9 **Reads List** The battell with the Centaurs [+] to be sung
          By an Athenian Eunuch,[x] to the Harpe.

10 Wee'l none of that.

11   That have I told my Love [+]
   In glory of my kinsman Hercules.

12 **List** The riot of the tipsie Bacchanals,
   Tearing the Thracian singer, in their rage.

13 That is an old device, and it was plaid
   When I from Thebes came last a Conqueror.

14 **List** The thrice three Muses, mourning for the death
   of learning, late deceast in beggerie.

15 That is some Satire [+] keene and criticall,
   Not sorting with a nuptiall ceremonie.

There is often confusion about who actually reads the list, for while the quarto suggests it is Theseus, as shown here, the First Folio suggests Theseus only comments after each entertainment is mentioned.

• that whichever entertainment chosen may have an awkward time with interruptions from the noble audience, as indeed happens with Pyramus and Thisby, might be seen in the fact that in this twenty-six line speech only two lines are unembellished, first the short (perhaps an almost petulant) F #8, 'How shall we beguile/The lazie time, if not with some delight?', second the similar short (almost bemused perhaps) comment on the Mechanicals' offering 'That is hot ice, and wondrous strange snow.' (F #19)

• the single surround phrase ' ; very tragicall mirth. ' points to why Theseus decides Pyramus and Thisby should be the evening's entertainment

• the opening enquiry as to entertainment is all emotional (1/8, the first eight and a half lines, F #1-7)

• following the unembellished F #8 comes the passionate dismissal of the 'battell with the Centaurs' (4/3, F #9-10),

• the explanation as to why and the dismissal of the 'riot of the tipsie Bacchanals' becomes totally factual (6/0, F #11-13)

• and the rejection of the Three Muses' as a 'Satire, keene and criticall' becomes passionate once more (3/2, F #14-15)

• the reading of the title and puffery of the mechanicals' 'tedious breefe Scene' is passionate (F #16, 3/2) with the piece's appeal perhaps stemming from the long-spelled 'breefe', and the final surround phrase ' ; very tragicall mirth. '

• in ending the speech, F (as Q2) sets emotional prose (F #17-20, 0/4) which might suggest that Theseus is handling matters quiet casually, which would throw Philostrate/Egeus' somewhat more formal reply (at least initially, see speech #5 below) into stark contrast : most modern texts restructure the shaded passage into more regular verse, thus wiping out the potential contrast

14 **List** "A tedious brief* Scene of young* Pyramus,*⁵
And his love Thisby; very tragical* mirth. "

15 Merry and tragical*?
16 Tedious and brief*?
17 That is hot ice and wondrous strange snow.
18 How shall wee find* the concord of this discord?

---

16 **List** *A tedious breefe Scene of yong Piramus,ₓ*
And his love Thisby; very tragicall mirth.

17 Merry and tragicall?
18 Tedious,ₓ and briefe? That
19 is,ₓ hot ice,ₓ and wondrous strange snow. How shall wee
20 finde the concord of this discord?

• F #18-19's three extra breath-thoughts (marked ,ₓ) could suggest that Theseus' interest is piqued by the rather foolish description "Tedious,ₓ and briefe?' and so is moved into making his own wittily foolish comparison, 'That is,ₓ hot ice,ₓ and wondrous strange snow.'

---

⁵ most modern texts refer to the play and characters as 'Pyramus and Thisby': the predominant F1 spellings are 'Piramus' (throughout) and 'Thisbie' (twice as often as 'Thisby')

5/ Egeus[6]   **A play there is, my Lord, some ten words long,**   between 5.1.61-81

Background: The response to Theseus' questioning: as such it is self-explanatory.

Style: a group address, directed primarily towards the Duke

Where: somewhere in the palace where a post-supper pre-wedding bed entertainment is to be offered   **To Whom:** Theseus, including also Hippolita, Helena and Demetrius, Hermia and Lysander, and any court retainers present

# of Lines: 20   **Probable Timing: 1.00 minutes**

F suggests that Egeus has great difficulty in keeping his composure, for while he may seem to start it in relative control, his inability to keep to a regular line structure (see footnote # 7 below) anticipates the emotional swamping that finally overtakes him.

• setting up the basic facts of the play, the speech starts out passionately (5/4, F #1-3) - at least on the surface, for the two emotional semicolons and extra breath-thoughts (marked ₓ) suggest something is about to burst forth

• which it does, for the rest of the speech (details and denial of suitability), is highly emotional (2/14, the twelve lines F #4-7)

• with F setting his description of the rehearsal as two sentences (F #3-4) instead of most modern texts one (mt. #2) it might be that Egeus is trying to maintain some element of self-control — which he fails to do, as the irregular line structure only too clearly shows

• if the irregular lines (shaded, F #3-4) weren't a sufficient indicator of Egeus' disapproval/enjoyment of the Mechanicals' play 'Piramus and Thisby' the surround phrases explain why: first the emotional (semicoloned)
" ; But by ten words, my Lord it is too long : /Which makes it tedious . "
which, as Egeus goes on to explain
" And tragicall my noble Lord it is : for Piramus/Therein doth kill himselfe . /Which when I saw/Rehearst, I must confesse, made mine eyes water : /But more merrie teares, the passion of loud laughter/ Never shed . "
leading to yet another emotional response
" . I have heard/It over, and it is nothing, nothing in the world ;"
though yet again Egeus might be attempting to establish some self-control, since the lines are unembellished

Modern Text

5/ Egeus

1
A play there is, my △lord, some ten words long,
Which is as brief* as I have known* a play;
But by ten words, my Lord, it is too long,
Which makes it tedious;* ◊ for in all the play
There is not one word apt, one ◊player fitted.

2
And tragical*, my noble △lord, it is;
For Pyramus *therein doth kill himself*; ◊
Which when I saw rehears'd, I must confess*,
Made mine eyes water* ; but more merry* ,tears*
The passion of loud laughter never shed.

3
{Ψ} They that do play it {are}
Hard handed men that work* in Athens here*,
Which never labor'd* in their minds* till now;
And now have toiled* their unbreathed memories
With this same play, against your nuptial* .

4
{Ψ} My noble △lord, it is not for you.
                              I have heard

5
It over, and it is nothing, nothing in the world;
Unless* you can find* sport in their intents,
Extremely* stretch'd, and conn'd* with cruel* pain* ,
To do* you service.

First Folio

5/ Egeus

1
A play there is, my Lord, some ten words long,
Which is as breefe,ₓ as I have knowne a play;
But by ten words, my Lord, it is too long;ₓ
Which makes it tedious.
                    For in all the play.ₓ
There is not one word apt, one Player fitted.

2
There is not one word apt, one Player fitted.

3
And tragicall⁺ my noble Lord⁺ it is:ₓ for Piramus
Therein doth kill himselfe.   Which when I saw

4
Rehearst, I must confesse, made mine eyes water :ₓ
But more merrie teares,ₓ the passion of loud laughter
Never shed.

5 {Ψ} They that do play it {are}
Hard handed men,ₓ that worke in Athens heere,
Which never labour'd in their mindes till now;
And now have toyled their unbreathed memories
With this same play, against your nuptiall.

6 {Ψ} My noble Lord, it is not for you.
                              I have heard

7
It over, and it is nothing, nothing in the world;
Unless you can finde sport in their intents,
Extremely strecht, and cond with cruell paine,
To doe you service.

---

[6] Q1 shows two distinct characters, Egeus the father of Hermia: and Philostrate, a court official, the manager of entertainments to Theseus. By the time of the First Folio, although (page 1, line 12, Applause First Folio Edition) Philostrate is still addressed by name in the first scene, his speaking part has been reduced to just this one speech). His other lines have been redistributed in two ways: to Egeus, and to whoever reads the list of entertainments to pass away the first part of the marriage night (speech #4 above). It is safe to assume that the additional text used in preparing F1 had a speaking part removed because of company size and/or economy, but the problem still remains, whether to maintain both characters (as in Q1) or to reassign everything, including the single F1 Philostrate speech. Some modern texts follow Q1; others follow F1, and assign Philostrate's remaining Act Five speech to Egeus.

[7] as shown alongside, the F1/Qq layout (14/10/11/12/3) allows Egeus/Philostrate a wonderful lack of self-control, especially on the opening line, as he describes the aesthetic horrors of the piece: the modern restructuring to regular poetry (10/10/10/10/) completely destroys this

#'s 6 - 9: LYSANDER IN LOVE

6/ Lysander   **I am my Lord, as well deriv'd as he,**   1.1.99 - 110

Background: Egeus has chosen Demetrius (a 'Lordship') as husband for his daughter, Hermia, even though Demetrius has been involved with the other young Athenian woman in the play, Helena. However, Lysander and Hermia are in love. This, Lysander's first major speech in the play, is self-explanatory.

Style: public statement

Where: somewhere in Theseus' palace   **To Whom:** Duke Theseus, in front of the rival Demetrius; Hermia's father, Egeus; Hermia; and Hippolita; perhaps with court officials also in attendance, though none are indicated in the original stage directions.

# of Lines: 12   **Probable Timing: 0.40 minutes**

Modern Text	First Folio
6/ Lysander	**6/ Lysander**
1 I am, my Lord, as well deriv'd as he, As well possess'd; my love is more [than] his; My fortunes every way as fairly* rank'd* (If not with vantage) as Demetrius; And (which is more [than] all these boasts can be) I am belov'd of beauteous Hermia.	1 I am⁺ my Lord, as well deriv'd as he, As well possest:ₓ my love is more [then] his:ₓ My fortunes every way as fairely ranck'd (If not with vantage) as Demetrius:ₓ And (which is more [then] all these boasts can be) I am belov'd of beauteous Hermia.
2 Why should not I then prosecute my right?	2 Why should not I then prosecute my right?
3 Demetrius, I'll avouch it to his head, Made love to Nedar's daughter, Helena, And won her soul*; and she, sweet Lady*, dotes, Devoutly dotes, dotes in ᵈIdolatry, Upon this spotted and inconstant man.	3 Demetrius, Ile avouch it to his head, Made love to Nedars daughter, Helena, And won her soule:ₓ and she (ₓsweet Ladie)ₓ dotes, Devoutly dotes, dotes in Idolatry, Upon this spotted and inconstant man.

Though Lysander is often portrayed as a brash young man, here F seems to that suggest he is being very careful in justifying his actions – possibly aware of both the seriousness of the situation and the need for decorum in front of the Duke.

- as a whole, the speech is highly factual and self-contained (8/2 overall), with no fewer than four logical colons, with the one surround phrase clearly pointing to his belief that he is behaving fairly, ': my love is more than his : ', doubly heightened by being both monosyllabic and unembellished

- this is supported by F #2, the only short sentence, again unembellished,
    "Why should not I then prosecute my right?'

- and even his exposition of Demetrius' unfaithfulness is summarised with great care, via the final unembellished statement that Helena
    "dotes/Devoutly dotes . . . /Upon this spotted and inconstant man."

7 / Lysander   **How now my love? Why is your cheek so pale?**   between 1.1.128 - 168

Background: Having delivered the deadline by which Hermia must decide her future (speech # 2 above), Theseus, whether deliberately or not, has managed to leave the two lovers alone. The following is Lysander's growth from despair to plan. Overall the speech is made up of six smaller units, formed by omitting Hermia's responses.

Style: part of a two-handed scene

Where: somewhere in Theseus' palace where confrontation with her father has just ended   **To Whom:** his beloved Hermia

# of Lines: 30   **Probable Timing: 1.30 minutes**

Modern Text

7 / Lysander

1   How now, my love? † why is your cheek so pale?

2   How chance the ^roses there do fade so fast?

3   [Ay me!] for ought that ever I could read*,
Could ever hear* by tale or history*,
The course of true love never did run smooth ;
But either it was different in blood - ◊
Or else misgraffed in respect of years* - ◊
Or else it stood upon the choice of [friends] .

4   Or if there were a sympathy* in choice,
War*, death, or sickness,* did lay siege to it,
Making it [momentary*] as a sound,*
Swift as a shadow, short as any dream*,
Brief* as the lightning in the collied night,
That (in a spleen*) unfolds both heaven and earth ;
And ere a man hath power to say, "Behold !",
The jaws* of darkness* do devour* it up:
So quick* bright things come to confusion.

5 {ψ}   {T}herefore hear* me Hermia,
I have a ^widow* ^aunt, a dowager,
Of great revenue*, and she hath no child* . †

6   From Athens is her house [remote] seven leagues,
And she respects me, as her only* son* . † 8

7   There, gentle Hermia, may I marry*, thee,
And to that place the sharp* Athenian ^law
Cannot pursue us.

8   If thou lovest* me, then
Steal* forth thy fathers house tomorrow night:

First Folio

7 / Lysander

1   How now + my love?

2   Why is your cheek so pale?

3   How chance the Roses there do fade so fast?

4   [] For ought that ever I could reade,
Could ever heare by tale or historie,
The course of true love never did run smooth, +
But either it was different in blood. x

5   Or else misgraffed,x in respect of yeares. . x

6   Or else it stood upon the choise of [merit] .

7   Or if there were a simpathie in choise,
Warre, death, or sicknesse, did lay siege to it ; x
Making it [momentarie]x as a sound: x
Swift as a shadow, short as any dreame,
Briefe as the lightning in the collied night,
That (in a spleene) unfolds both heaven and earth;
And ere a man hath power to say, behold, +
The jawes of darknesse do devoure it up:
So quicke bright things come to confusion.

8 {ψ}   {T}herefore heare me Hermia,
I have a Widdow Aunt, a dowager,
Of great revennew, and she hath no childe,
From Athens is her house [remov'd] seven leagues,
And she respects me, as her onely sonne:
There + gentle Hermia, may I marrie thee,
And to that place,x the sharpe Athenian Law
Cannot pursue us.

9   If thou lov'st me, then
Steale forth thy fathers house to morrow night:

Though Lysander again starts out quite carefully (1/3 in the first nine lines), eventually his inner feelings get the better of him (9/20 in the last twenty).

- the opening assessment that testimony from the past (a fine Elizabethan rhetorical technique for trying to gather support for one's theories or proposed actions) will be of no help to them in their situation is almost completely unembellished, perhaps suggesting a great depth of self examination (or no energy at all)
"How now + my love?/Why is your cheek so pale?"
"Could ever heare by tale or historie,/The course of true love never did run smooth,/But either it was different in blood."
"Or else it stood upon the choise of merit./Or if there were a simpathie in choise,"

- the final realisation that love loses out either to a marriage of convenience between an older man and younger woman (F # 6) or to inter-family agreements (F # 6) are far stronger as separate sentences than as presented by most modern texts that join the two sentences together

- and it is from this discovery/realisation that the passions start to flow – first a totally emotional suggestion that, if there is true love, it is doomed to a very short existence (0/9, F #7)

- the surround phrases underscore his wonderful adolescent angst, the unembellished and partially emotional (opening with a semicolon)
" ; Making it momentarie, as a sound : "
followed by the final devastating
" ; So quicke bright things come to confusion . "

- out of which comes the only answer available to them, the extremely bold and passionate plan to run away (7/7, F #8) – and as footnote #8 explains, this seems more a grab-bag of ideas than an already worked out logical progression, in turn suggesting that the idea may have only just come to him

- and it's quite lovely that the final sentence putting together 'If thou lov'st me' with the running away, and opening and closing with unembellished phrases (nervous as to the outcome perhaps) , should become emotional once more (2/4)

---

8 some modern editions reverse the F1/Qq order of these two lines: the source text shows Lysander skittering between two topics, the modern texts turn his scattiness into a logical progression

And in the wood, a league without the towne,ₓ
(Where I did meete thee once with Helena,
To do observance [for] a morne of May)⁺
There will I stay for thee.

8/ Lysander: **Transparent Helena, nature her shewes art,**
9/ Lysander: **She sees not Hermia :   Hermia sleepe thou there,**

Background: Oberon, king of the fairies, taking pity on the abandoned Helena, believes he has ordered Puck to enchant Demetrius' eyes so that he will fall in love with her when he wakes. Unfortunately, he didn't realise that two Athenian men were in the woods that night and told Puck he would recognise the man by the 'Athenian garments he hath on', so, Puck correctly zaps a man wearing Athenian garments, falls immediately in love with her. In speech #8, he thus begins to woo her as ardently as he possibly can. Speech #9 is a follow-up to the previous speech - with Helena having run away, Lysander quickly abandons his once-loved Hermia and vows he will be a chivalric figure for Helena and become 'her Knight'.

Style: speech #8 a two handed scene;   speech #9 solo
Where: somewhere in the wood

To Whom: speech #8 to Helena, who then runs off in dismay
speech #9 audience/self address

between 2.2.103 - 122
2.2.135- 144

speech #8, # of Lines: 14	**Probable Timing: 0.45 minutes**
speech #9, # of Lines: 10	**Probable Timing: 0.35 minutes**

Modern Text

8/ Lysander

1 Transparent Helena, nature [shows* her art],
   That through thy bosom* makes me see thy heart.

2 Content with Hermia?

3   No; I do repent
   The tedious minutes I with her have spent.

4 Not Hermia, but Helena [ ] I love. †

5 Who will not change a △raven for a △dove?

6 The will of man is by his reason sway'd;
   And reason says* you are the worthier △maid* .

7 Things growing are not ripe until* their season,
   So, I being young*, till now ripe not to reason;
   And touching now the point of [human]* skill,
   Reason becomes the △marshal* to my will,
   And leads* me to your eyes, where I o'erlook*
   Loves stories written in Love's richest book* .

First Folio

8/ Lysander

1 Transparent Helena, nature [her shewes art]⁻
   That through thy bosome makes me see thy heart.
   ‑‑‑‑‑‑‑‑‑‑‑

2 Content with Hermia?

3   No,⁺ I do repent
   The tedious minutes I with her have spent.

4 Not Hermia, but Helena [now] I love;
   Who will not change a Raven for a Dove?

5 The will of man is by his reason sway'd;ₓ
   And reason saies you are the worthier Maide.

6 Things growing are not ripe untill their season;ₓ
   So⁺ I being yong, till now ripe not to reason,⁺
   And touching now the point of [humane] skill,
   Reason becomes the Marshall to my will,
   And leades me to your eyes, where I orelooke
   Loves stories,ₓ written in Loves richest booke.

F's orthography clearly shows that Lysander's struggles to put some logic in the emotional turmoil of his new found/magically induced adoration, for the speech veers rapidly between emotion, intellect and, a single moment of unembellished self-control, all within just fourteen lines of heightened rhyming couplets.

• the first sight of Helena awakes his (initially tongue stumbling) emotions (1/2, F #1), which prompts him to move into a mix of intellect (F #2 and #4, 5/0) and non-embellishment (F #3) as he puts Hermia quite out of his mind

• and then the chop-logic finale (an illogical bending of words and/or ideas to prove something that cannot actually be proven) turns highly emotional (3/7, F #5-6)

• the final long-spelling rhyming couplet ('orelooke', 'booke') underscores that he finally believes the chop-logic illogicality he has offered to prove that though once betrothed to Hermia (when 'yong'), now he is mature ('ripe to reason'), he is free to put Hermia aside so as to woo Helena

• the underlying struggle between emotion and intellect can be seen in the surround phrases, for the on-the-surface intellectual F #4 rejection of Hermia is comprised of two surround phrases created by the emotional semicolon, while the two surround phrases of F #5's emotional ending statement of Helena's worth are created by a logical colon

Modern Text

9/ Lysander

1 She sees not Hermia. [†]
  Hermia, sleep* thou there,
2 And never mayst* thou come Lysander near*! [†]

3 For as a surfeit of the sweetest things
  The deepest loathing to the stomach* brings,
  Or as the heresies that men do leave
  Are hated most of those [they] did deceive :
  So thou, my surfeit, and my heresy*,
  Of all be hated, but the most of me! [†]

4 And, all my powers, address* your love and might
  To honor* Helen and to be her ᵃknight.

First Folio

9/ Lysander

1 She sees not Hermia : Hermia [+] sleepe thou there,
  And never maist thou come Lysander neere ;
  For as a surfeit of the sweetest things

3 The deepest loathing to the stomacke brings : ₓ
  Or as the heresies that men do leave, ₓ
  Are hated most of those [that] did deceive :
  So thou, my surfeit, and my heresie,
  Of all be hated ; ₓ but the most of me ;
  And [+] all my powers [+] addresse your love and might ₓ
  To honour Helen ₓ and to be her Knight.

Often played as a loud and knowing rejection from the start, F's one sentence , (as opposed to most modern texts' four), orthography, and surprisingly long swathe of unembellished lines suggests a very different, much less callous approach.

• while the words seem quite hateful, excusable only because they are magic induced, the fact of
  a/ six pieces of major punctuation in ten lines, half are emotional semicolons
  b/ more than half of the ten lines are unembellished (lines three, and five to eight, and the first four words of line nine)
  c/ the speech again being in rhyming couplets suggests that they are not uttered carelessly or without a great deal of personal struggle

• the passion of the opening two lines (3/2) and especially the last line and half could well indicate that Lysander has in fact changed to a more exuberant form of speech, as behooves the 'Knight' he claims he will now be so as to 'honour' Helen, the claim enhanced by the wonderful extra breath-thought (marked , ₓ) in the last line

---

#'s 10 - 12: DEMETRIUS IN LOVE

10/ Demetrius You doe impeach your modesty too much, 2.1.214 - 219

Background: Inspired by Lysander's urgings, (see speech #7 above) Hermia and Lysander have fled Athens. Helena, determined to win Demetrius back again (see speech # 18 below) tells Demetrius of their flight and he enters the woods to reclaim his beloved Hermia and punish Lysander. Helena, unbidden, has dogged his every step, despite his warnings that he doesn't want her around. This is part of his remonstrations with her.

Style: part of a two-handed scene **To Whom:** Helena
Where: somewhere in the woods

# of Lines: 6 **Probable Timing: 0.20 minutes**

Modern Text

10/ Demetrius

1 You do* impeach your modesty too much,
  To leave the ᵃcity* and commit yourself*
  Into the hands of one that loves you not ;
  To trust the opportunity of night,
  And the ill counsel* of a desert place,
  With the rich worth of your virginity.

First Folio

10/ Demetrius

1 You doe impeach your modesty too much,
  To leave the Citty, ₓ and commit your selfe
  Into the hands of one that loves you not, [+]
  To trust the opportunity of night,
  And the ill counsell of a desert place,
  With the rich worth of your virginity.

Given the circumstances, it is not surprising that this is essentially an emotional speech. What is interesting is that it is still fairly contained, just 1/4 in six lines, as if he was exhibiting a fair degree of self-control.

• however, unlike the modern setting, with no major punctuation in the speech the self-control cannot be said to be at all logical

• and the extra breath in the second line (marked , ₓ), dealing with the possible problem that Helena's 'modesty' may be compromised by having entrusted herself to him, suggests that this self-control doesn't necessarily come all that easily

11/ Demetrius   O Helen, goddesse, nimph, perfect, divine,   3.2.137 - 144

Background: In an effort to undo the damage caused by Puck's mistake in zapping Lysander with the love charm instead of Demetrius (see background to speech # 8 above) Oberon now enchants Demetrius, who indeed awakens, and as Helena is the first person he sees, he too falls head over heels in love with her, adding his ardent wooing to that of Lysander. Thus Oberon has compounded the original error, for, as Puck points out, 'Then will two at once wooe one/That must needs be sport alone'.

Style: ardent wooing speech as part of a three-handed scene   **To Whom:** Helena, in front of the soon-to-be annoyed Lysander

Where: somewhere in the woods

# of Lines: 8   **Probable Timing: 0.30 minutes**

Modern Text

11/ Demetrius

1 O Helen, goddess*, nymph*, perfect, divine!†

2 To what, my love, shall I compare thine eyne?†

3 Crystal* is muddy.†

4   O, how ripe in show

    Thy lips, those kissing cherries, tempting grow!

5 That pure congealed white, high Taurus snow,

    Fann'd*△ with the △eastern* wind*, turns* to a crow

    When thou hold'st up thy hand.

          O, let me kiss*

6 This [△pureness]* of pure white, this seal* of bliss*!

First Folio

11/ Demetrius

1 O Helen, goddesse, nimph, perfect, divine,

    To what⁺ my love, shall I compare thine eyne!

2 Christall is muddy, O⁺ how ripe in show,ᵪ

    Thy lips, those kissing cherries, tempting grow!

3 That pure congealed white, high Taurus snow,

    Fan'd with the Easterne winde, turnes to a crow,ᵣₓ

    When thou holdst up thy hand.

             O⁺ let me kisse

4 This [Princesse] of pure white, this seale of blisse.⁺

With the most unusual and rare F setting of two exclamation marks (ending F #1 and #2); the two extra breath-thoughts (marked ‚ₓ in F #2-3; 1/1, F #1; 1/1, F #2; 2/3, F #3; 1/4, F #4), it seems that when Demetrius finally lets loose, he really lets loose.

• as a side-bar, whereas Lysander might be a chest-fixated man ('That through thy bosome makes my see thy heart', speech #8 above) Demetrius seems more fixated on the mouth, as the only unembellished line might suggest

    "Thy lips, those kissing cherries, tempting grow!"

• once more, logic does not seem Demetrius' strong suit, for, as with speech #10 above, there is no major punctuation here either

12/ Demetrius   My Lord, faire Helen told me of their stealth, [9]   4.1.160 - 176

Background: To Egeus' horror, the royal hunting party have discovered side by side Demetrius with Helena and Lysander with Hermia. Triggered by an anguished plea from Egeus that the full impact of the law be visited upon Lysander, they are called upon to explain themselves. This is Demetrius' response.

Style: direct address involving two people as part of a larger scene

Where: somewhere in the woods   **To Whom:** Duke Theseus, also Helena, and probably the others immediately involved in his discovery, notably Hermia, Lysander and Egeus; also present is Hippolita, and perhaps members of Theseus' retinue

# of Lines: 17   **Probable Timing: 0.55 minutes**

Modern Text

12/ Demetrius

1 My Lord, fair* Helen told me of their stealth,
   Of this their purpose hither, to this wood,
   And I in fury* hither followed them,
   Fair* Helena in fancy [following] me.

2 But, my good Lord, I wot not by what power
   (But by some power it is), my love to Hermia
   (Melted as the snow) seems to me now
   As the remembrance of an idle gaud* [10]
   Which in my childhood* I did dote* upon ;
   And all the faith, the virtue of my heart,
   The object and the pleasure of [my] eye,
   Is only* Helena.

3   To her, my Lord,
   Was I betrothed* ere I [saw] Hermia ;
   But like a sickness* did I loathe* this food ;
   But, as in health, come to my natural* taste,
   Now [I do*] wish it, love it, long for it,
   And will for evermore be true to it.

First Folio

12/ Demetrius

1 My Lord, faire Helen told me of their stealth,
   Of this their purpose hither, to this wood,
   And I in furie hither followed them,
   Faire Helena,ₓ in fancy [followed] me.

2 But⁺ my good Lord, I wot not by what power,ₓ
   (But by some power it is) ⁺ my love
   To Hermia (melted as the snow)
   Seems to me now as the remembrance of an idle gaude,
   Which in my childhood I did doat upon : ₓ
   And all the faith, the vertue of my heart,
   The object and the pleasure of [mine] eye,
   Is onely Helena.

3   To her, my Lord,
   Was I betroth'd,ₓ ere I [see] Helena, ⁺
   But like a sickenesse did I loath this food, ⁺
   But ⁺ as in health, come to my naturall taste,
   Now [doe I] wish it, love it, long for it,
   And will for evermore be true to it.

Commentary (center column):

• the speech starts out passionately (F # 13/2), though fascinatingly the two long spellings both are in praise of 'faire' Helen/Helena

• the discovery of true love explanation starts out factually (2/0 the first three lines of F #2), both capitals referring to names or titles, then becomes emotional (1/4 the remainder of F #2)

• and F #3's self-blame summary follows a similar pattern (2/0 the first line and a half, 0/3 to finish)

• while the unembellished explanation that Helena
"… told me of their stealth,/Of this their purpose hither, to this wood,/And I in furie hither followed them'
may be expected as a circumspect acknowledgement both of the status of the Duke and of the bombshell he is about to drop on Egeus

• however, the similarly unembellished, essentially quiet, statement of his love (allowing for the capitalised names and titles) is not
"But my good Lord, I wot not by what power, /(But by some power it is) my love/To Hermia (melted as the snow)/ …/And all the faith, the vertue of my heart,/The object and the pleasure of mine eye,"
"To her, my Lord, /Was I betroth'd, ere I [see] Hermia, "
"…. I wish it, love it, long for it,/And will for evermore be true to it."

---

[9] much critical anguish has been expressed over this speech, stemming from the fact that, for Demetrius to be still in love with Helena, as he was forced to be when enchanted, the spell must not have been removed from his eyes as it was from Lysander's: indeed, Puck's 'dis-enchanting' comment is 'Ile applie to your eie gentle lover, remedy', that is 'lover' singular, NOT plural: however, Demetrius' rarely used early quarto comment to Helena 'I do not, NOT I cannot love you' can resolve this current speech's awkwardness: unfortunately, most modern texts follow the First Folio and have Demetrius say earlier 'I do not, NOR I cannot love you' - a much nastier and more awkward comment once this scene is taken into account

[10] the F1/Qq lineation is wonderfully revealing: following an emotional (though highly ungrammatical) period, the two slightly short lines (8 or 9/8 or 9 syllables) give Demetrius two halting attempts to explain before rushing into a fourteen syllable admission: the modern restructuring (11 - 13/9/10) totally destroys the psychology of the build from hesitancy to explosion that was originally given him

#'s 13 - 16: HERMIA IN LOVE

13/ Hermia   **My good Lysander,/I sweare to thee, by Cupids strongest bow,**   1.1.168 - 178

Background: This is Hermia's enthusiastic response to Lysander's urgings that they run away from Athens   (speech #7 above).

Style: part of a two-handed scene, essentially self-explanatory

Where: somewhere in Theseus' palace where the confrontation has just ended   **To Whom:** her beloved Lysander

# of Lines: 11   **Probable Timing: 0.40 minutes**

Modern Text

13/ Hermia

1 My good Lysander,
   I swear* to thee, by Cupids strongest bow,
   By his best arrow with the golden head,
   By the simplicity* of Venus' Doves,
   By that which knitteth souls* and prospers [loves],
   And by that fire which burn'd the Carthage [△]queen* ,
   When the false Troyan under sail* was seen* ,
   By all the vows* that ever men have broke,
   (In number more [than] ever women spoke)
   In that same place thou hast appointed me
   To-morrow truly will I meet* with thee.

First Folio

13/ Hermia

1 My good Lysander,
   I sweare to thee, by Cupids strongest bow,
   By his best arrow with the golden head,
   By the simplicitie of Venus Doves,
   By that which knitteth soules,_x and prospers [love],
   And by that fire which burn'd the Carthage Queene,
   When the false Troyan under saile was seene,
   By all the vowes that ever men have broke,
   (In number more [then] ever women spoke)
   In that same place thou hast appointed me,_{xx}
   To morrow truly will I meete with thee.

- given the circumstances, the onrushed single line sentence is only to be expected, as is the fact that Hermia starts out strongly intellectually (7/3 in the first five and a half lines), calling upon classical allusions for support (a traditional Elizabethan rhetorical device) and providing most of the capitals

- what may be surprising is that before her agreement comes a three line attack on deceitful men ('false Troyan' etc.), the first two of which start out emotionally (0/4) and then, quite fascinatingly, comes an unembellished line, also concentrating on all men's deceptions 'In number more [then] ever women spoke' (is this one of her greatest fears? and does this affect her in the 'two men pursuing Helena sequence' later in the play?)

- and the big step of agreeing to run away remains unembellished though, given what has just been said, the calm may be more than just an awareness of the enormity of what they are about to do
   "In that same place thou hast appointed me/To morrow truly . . ."

14/ Hermia   Lysander ; finde you out a bed,   between 2.2.39 - 61

Background: On their way to his Aunt's and having lost his way in the woods, Lysander has suggested to Hermia that they stop for the night, and (possibly innocently) has assumed that they were going to cuddle together. However attractive the suggestion may be, the following is Hermia's somewhat awkward reputation-saving response.

Style: part of a two-handed scene

Where: somewhere in the woods   **To Whom:** her beloved Lysander

# of Lines: 10   **Probable Timing:** 0.35 minutes

Modern Text

14/ Hermia

1 Lysander { }; find* you out a bed ;
   For I upon this bank* will rest my head.

2 Nay, good Lysander ; for my sake, my dear* ,
   Lie further off yet, do* not lie so near* .

3 {ψ} Gentle friend, for love and courtesy*,
   Lie further off, in human* modesty ;
   Such separation as may well be said
   Becomes a virtuous bachelor* and a maid* ,
   So far* be distant ; and good night, sweet friend. †

4 Thy love ne'er alter, till thy sweet life end.

First Folio

14/ Hermia

1 Lysander { }; finde you out a bed, +
   For I upon this banke will rest my head. +

2 Nay+ good Lysander, + for my sake+ my deere +
   Lie further off yet, doe not lie so neere.

3 {ψ} Gentle friend, for love and courtesie +
   Lie further off, in humane modesty, +
   Such separation,ₓ as may well be said,
   Becomes a vertuous batchelour,ₓ and a maide,
   So farre be distant, + and good night+ sweet friend ;
   Thy love nere alter+ till thy sweet life end.

Though often played as a model of virginal propriety, F's orthography suggests that Hermia may be as much affected by Lysander's closeness as he is by hers.

• the opening and closing semicolons, both creating surround phrases, suggest a strong emotional content, especially with the very rare for F and Q one word phrase opening the speech ('Lysander;')

• at several points the text moves far faster than the punctuation added by modern texts (marked +) allows, again suggesting an occasional urgency in her release (notably the first line of F #2 and the last two lines of the speech)

• the last line of the speech is onrushed (a final plea for understanding and no more temptation perhaps), unlike the modern texts, which set a separate sentence (mt. #4) and split it in two

• not surprisingly, the speech is highly emotional (1/8 overall)

15/ Hermia   **Helpe me Lysander, helpe me ; do thy best**   2.2.145 - 156

Background: Not knowing that the now enchanted/love potion zapped Lysander has deliberately left her to embark on his new chivalric and knightly quest to woo Helena.

Hermia awakes from a bad dream, as she eventually discovers, alone.

Style: though in fact solo, initially to a supposedly present partner

Where: in the woods   **To Whom:** the absent Lysander

       # of Lines: 12   **Probable Timing: 0.40 minutes**

Modern Text

15/ Hermia

1   Help* me, Lysander, help* me! do thy best
     To pluck* this crawling serpent from my breast*!

2   Ay* me, for pity*! what a dream* was here!

3   Lysander, look* how I do quake with fear* . †

4   Me°thought a serpent eat* my heart away,
     And [you] sat smiling at his cruel* prey.

5   Lysander ! what remov'd*?
              Lysander !, ⁴lord !

6   What, out of hearing gone?
              No sound, no word?

7   Alack* , where are you? †

- 8   Speak* , and if you hear* ;

9   Speak* , of all loves ! †
           I [swoon] almost with fear* .

10

11 No ? then I well perceive you are not nigh* :
     Either death, or you, I'll find* immediately .

First Folio

15/ Hermia

1   Helpe me ⁺ Lysander, helpe me ; ⁺ do thy best
     To plucke this crawling serpent from my brest . ⁺

2   Aye me, for pitty ; ⁺ what a dreame was here? ⁺

3   Lysander ⁺ looke ,ₓ how I do quake with feare :
     Me-thought a serpent eate my heart away,
     And [yet] sat smiling at his cruell prey.

4   Lysander , ⁺ what remoov'd ?

5   Lysander , ⁺ Lord , ⁺

6   What, out of hearing ,ₓ gone?
           No sound, no word?

7   Alacke ⁺ where are you? speake ⁺ and if you heare : ₓ
     Speake ⁺ of all loves ; I [sound] almost with feare.

8   No, ⁺ then I well perceive you are not nye , ⁺
     Either death ⁺ or you ⁺ Ile finde immediately .

The onrush of F #3 and F #7 allows Hermia a much more understandable, faster release and/or dismissal of her fear than most modern texts (which split the text into two and three sentences, respectively).

- that six of the seven surround phrases are formed in part by emotional semicolons goes a long way to underscore how emotional she really is

     " . Helpe me Lysander, helpe me ; do thy best/To plucke this crawling serpent from my brest . /Aye me, for pitty ; what a dreame was here ? "

     " : Speake of all loves ; I [sound] almost with feare . "

as does her logical (colon created surround phrase) self-assessment

     " . Lysander looke, how I do quake with feare : "

- while the non-embellished phrases speak to her fear of being left alone

     " . What, out of hearing, gone? No sound, no word?"

with the quiet being either non-energised fear, or, more in the heroine-type genre, a deliberately self-enforced calm

- not surprisingly, the speech is emotional throughout (2/18 overall)

16/ Hermia   **Puppet? why so? I, that way goes the game .**   3.2.289 - 298

Background: Thanks to both the zapped/love-potioned men wooing Helena (since she was the first thing each saw on awaking), the accusations and counter-accusations of the now highly dysfunctional quartet has reached its height, with the once twice-beloved and now doubly-scorned Hermia having had her small stature mocked. With Helena being so much the taller, it is to her that Hermia directs her fury - (remember Helena's later comment that Hermia, 'was a vixen when she went to schoole').

Style: as part of a four-handed love-potion induced quarrel
Where: somewhere in the woods   **To Whom:** directed towards Helena, for both Lysander's & Demetrius' response
# of Lines: 10   **Probable Timing: 0.35 minutes**

Modern Text

16/ Hermia

1 "Puppet?" †
2   Why so?
3   Ay*, that way goes the game.
4 Now I perceive that she hath made compare
   Between* our statures : she hath urg'd her height,
   And with her personage, her tall personage,
   Her height, forsooth, she hath prevail'd with him.
5 And are you grown* so high in his esteem*,
   Because I am so dwarfish and so low?
6 How low am I, thou painted ᐃmay'pole?
                            Speak*!
7 How low am I?
8   I am not yet so low
9 But that my nails* can reach unto thine eyes.

First Folio

16/ Hermia

1   Puppet? why so?
2   I, that way goes the game .
3 Now I perceive that she hath made compare
   Betweene our statures, + she hath urg'd her height,
   And with her personage, her tall personage,
   Her height $_x$(forsooth)$_x$ she hath prevail'd with him.
4 And are you growne so high in his esteeme,
   Because I am so dwarfish,$_x$ and so low?
5 How low am I, thou painted May-pole?
6   Speake, +
7 How low am I?
                I am not yet so low,$_x$
        But that my nailes can reach unto thine eyes.

What is startling in this speech is that so much of the expected fury is kept bottled up. Surprisingly, five of the ten lines are unembellished, with the first half of the speech almost totally self-contained (0/1 in the first five lines, F #1-3), with a still quite careful release coming only later (1/4, F #4-5)

• it would seem that this may be a speech of working matters out, and is inward directed an rather than out and out attack – the attack will come only later

• the unembellished phrases could well delineate the various moments of Hermia's discoveries

"Puppet? why so?/I, that way goes the game./Now I perceive that she hath made compare"

". . . she hath urg'd her height,/And with her personage, her tall personage,/Her height (forsooth) she hath prevail'd with him."

"Because I am so dwarfish, and so low?/How low am I,"

"How low am I?/I am not yet so low,"

#'s 17 - 23: Helena In Love

17/ Helena   Cal you me faire? that faire againe unsay,   1.1.181 - 193

Background: This is Helena's first sequence in the play, triggered by Hermia's greeting 'God speede faire Helena, whither away?'.   With the knowledge that her one-time boyfriend Demetrius has abandoned her to pursue Hermia, even though Hermia loves and is loved by Lysander, the speech is self-explanatory.

Style: essentially a woman to woman address, as part of a three-handed scene

Where: somewhere in Theseus' palace, where the confrontation with Egeus has just ended   **To Whom:** Hermia, with Lysander in attendance

# of Lines: 13   **Probable Timing: 0.45 minutes**

There is a great difference between the sentence structures of the two texts, for while the modern texts set a somewhat rational well balanced eight sentence argument, the two sentence F structure suggests a much more uncontrolled release, at least until the end.

- quite remarkably, the huge onrushed F #1 splits in two orthographically, a very emotional (overwrought? melodramatic?) start (2/15 in the first five and a half lines), and a finish only occasionally intellectual or emotional (3/3 in the final seven and a half)

- the split occurs once Helena comes up with the idea that, if only she could imitate Hermia's behaviour, she might yet win back Demetrius, for at this moment nearly all the earlier emotion disappears

- thus, while the much calmer second part of F #1 might be directed towards Hermia and Demetrius, it may also be inner directed (perhaps a dream of what could/might be, if only . . .)

Modern Text

17/ Helena

1 Cal₍ you me fair*?₊ †

2   That fair* again* unsay . †

3 Demetrius loves [your] fair*. †

4   O happy₍ fair*'!

5 Your eyes are lodestars* , and your tongues sweet air*
   More tuneable [than] ᴬlark* to shepherd's* ear*
   When wheat* is green* , when hawthorn* buds appear* . †

6 Sickness* is catching ; O, were favor so,
   [Yours would] I catch, fair* Hermia, ere I go ;
   My ear* should catch your voice, my eye, your eye,
   My tongue should catch your tongue's sweet melody*₊ †

7 Were the world mine, Demetrius being bated,
   The rest I'll give to be to you translated.

8 O, teach me how you look* , and with what art
   You sway the motion of Demetrius' heart*.

First Folio

17/ Helena

1 Cal you me faire? that faire againe unsay,
   Demetrius loves[you] faire: O happie faire!
   Your eyes are loadstarres, and your tongues sweet ayre
   More tuneable [then] Larke to shepheards eare,ₓ
   When wheate is greene, when hauthorne buds appeare,
   Sicknesse is catching : O⁺ were favor so,
   [Your words] I catch, faire Hermia ⁺ ere I go, ⁺
   My eare should catch your voice, my eye, your eye,
   My tongue should catch your tongues sweet melodie,
   Were the world mine, Demetrius being bated,
   The rest Ile give to be to you translated.

2 O⁺ teach me how you looke, and with what art
   You sway the motion of Demetrius hart.

18/ Helena   How happy some, ore othersome can be?   1.1.226 - 251

Background: On top of everything else Helena has just learned that Hermia, her closest friend, is planning to flee Athens with her true beloved Lysander, to 'seeke new friends', thus leaving Helena totally alone. In the following, one of the finest pieces of female chop-logic in Shakespeare, Helena finally decides on what could be a very risky, masochistic, and eventually possibly unsuccessful, approach to getting Demetrius back.

Style: solo

Where: somewhere in Theseus' palace where the confrontation with Egeus has just ended   **To Whom:** direct audience address

# of Lines: 26   **Probable Timing:** 1.15 minutes

Modern Text

18/ Helena

1 How happy some, o'er other some can be?

2 Through Athens I am thought as fair* as she.

3 But what of that?

4   Demetrius thinks* not so;
He will not know, what all, but he [do] know ;
And as he* errs*, doting on Hermia's eyes,
So I, admiring of his qualities . †

5 Things base and [vile]*, holding no quantity,
Love can transpose to form* and dignity . †

6 Love looks* not with the eyes but with the mind*,
And therefore is wing'd Cupid painted blind* .

7 Nor hath ^Love's mind* of any judgment* taste;
Wings and no eyes, figure, unheedy haste, †
And therefore is Love said to be a child*,
Because in choice he is [so oft] beguil'd . †

8 As waggish boys* in game themselves forswear* ,
So the boy Love is perjur'd every where ; ◊
For ere Demetrius look'd on Hermia's eyne,
He hail'd down* oaths* that he was only* mine ; ◊
And when this ^hail* some heat from Hermia felt,
So he dissolv'd, and show'rs* of oaths* did melt . †

9 I will go* tell him of fair* Hermia's flight;
Then to the wood will he, tomorrow night
Pursue her; and for [this] intelligence
If I have thanks*, it is a dear* expense . †

11 But herein* mean* I to enrich my pain* ,
To have his sight thither and back* again* .

First Folio

18/ Helena

1 How happy some, ore othersome can be?

2 Through Athens I am thought as faire as she.

3 But what of that?

4   Demetrius thinkes not so; ×
He will not know, what all, but he [doth] know, +
And as hee erres, doting on Hermias eyes; +
So I, admiring of his qualities :
Things base and [vilde], holding no quantity,
Love can transpose to forme and dignity,
Love lookes not with the eyes, but with the minde,
And therefore is wing'd Cupid painted blinde.

5 Nor hath loves minde of any judgement taste : ×
Wings and no eyes, figure, unheedy haste.

6 And therefore is Love said to be a childe,
Because in choise he is [often] beguil'd,
As waggish boyes in game themselves forsweare ; ×
So the boy Love is perjur'd every where.

7 For ere Demetrius lookt on Hermias eyne,
He hail'd downe oathes that he was onely mine.

8 And when this Haile some heat from Hermia felt,
So he dissolv'd, and showres of oathes did melt,
I will goe tell him of faire Hermias flight: ×
Then to the wood will he, to morrow night
Pursue her; and for [his] intelligence,×
If I have thankes, it is a deere expence :
But heerein meane I to enrich my paine,
To have his sight thither,× and backe againe.

After the matching opening three sentences, the two texts diverge quite markedly. Most modern texts present Helena's chop-logic (an illogical bending of words and/or ideas to prove something that cannot actually be proven) in a quite rational sentence structure, while F's onrushed and grammatically incorrect (F #4, #6, and #8) suggest a sentence structure as peculiar and confused as the logic expressed therein.

• not surprisingly the speech is strongly emotional (10/26), the only passion naturally being released in the five lines dealing with Demetrius' abandoning her for Hermia, and her own response (5/6, F#7 and opening F #8)

• F's opening three short sentences, the first unembellished, and the third both monosyllabic and unembellished, suggest just how low in energy and spirit Helena is at the start of the speech (1/1)

• the two surround phrases in the opening of F #2, ' . Demetrius thinkes not so : ' and ' ; So I, admiring of his qualities : ', pinpoint from where her troubles stem

• and the later surround phrases point to her attack both on the unfairness of 'Love',
" . Nor hath loves minde of any judgement taste : "
as well as on deceiving 'waggish boyes'
" ; So the boy Love is perjur'd every where . "

• so, it's not surprising that, though perhaps ungrammatical, the creation of Helena's separate sentences of F #6 (the comment on how easily love can be deceived, especially by 'waggish boyes') and the short F #7 (how Demetrius was once hers alone) speaks volumes as to the vehemence of her feelings

• and so it may not be surprising that, unlike the rational setting of most modern texts, Helena's decision to tell Demetrius of Hermia's flight (line three onward in F #8) springs out of a fast-link comma, linking the decision to the preceding derisive assessment of how Demetrius became ensnared by Hermia's 'heat', suggesting an almost irrational subconscious desire of Helena's to hurt or punish him

• and though the only possible course of action (telling him of 'faire Hermia's flight') almost takes her breath away with the unembellished surround phrase realisation/plan
" . Then to the wood will he, to morrow night/Pursue her ; "
the emotional semicolon leads to an emotional understanding that this will not really help her (since Demetrius will be in chase of Hermia, not her)
" ; and for [t]his intelligence,/If I have thankes, it is a deere expence : "
but the emotional resolution of the last three lines (0/7) speaks volumes as to her seemingly irrational determination to win out no matter what

19/ Helena   **You draw me, you hard-hearted Adamant ;**

Background: Having followed Demetrius into the wood as he searches for both Hermia and Lysander, it looks as if Helena's plan may not be working too well, for Demetrius'
speech that triggers the following speech starts with 'I love thee not, therefore pursue me not,' and finishes with 'Hence, get thee gone, and follow me no more.'

Style: as part of a two-handed scene

Where: somewhere in the woods   **To Whom:** Demetrius

between 2.1.195 - 210

# of Lines: 12   **Probable Timing: 0.40 minutes**

Modern Text

19/ Helena

1   You draw me, you hard-hearted ᐃadamant ;
    But yet you draw not ᐃiron, for my heart
    Is true as steel* .

2   Leave you your power to draw,
    And I shall have no power to follow you.
    ▬▬▬▬▬▬▬▬▬▬▬▬

3   I am your spaniel* ; and, Demetrius,
    The more you beat me, I will fawn* on you.

4   Use me but as your spaniel* ; spurn* me, strike me,
    Neglect me, lose me; only* give me leave,
    Unworthy as I am, to follow you.

5   What worser place can I beg in your love
    (And yet a place of high respect with me)
    [Than] to be used as you [use] your dog* .

First Folio

19/ Helena

1   You draw me, you hard-hearted Adamant ;
    But yet you draw not Iron, for my heart
    Is true as steele.

2   Leave you your power to draw,
    And I shall have no power to follow you.
    ▬▬▬▬▬▬▬▬▬▬▬▬

3   I am your spaniell, + and + Demetrius,
    The more you beat me, I will fawne on you.

4   Use me but as your spaniell; spurne me, strike me,
    Neglect me, lose me; onely give me leave +
    x (Unworthy as I am)x to follow you.

5   What worser place can I beg in your love,x
    (And yet a place of high respect with me)
    [Then] to be used as you [doe] your dogge.

It seems Helena may have heeded her own words from the second part of
speech #17 and here tries to imitate Hermia in speech and action, for here
her style shows little of the excesses of speech #18 or the first five and a half
lines of speech #17.

• while the opening manages to stay intellectual (F #1, 2/1), the rest of the speech
becomes moderately emotional (1/7 in the nine and half lines F #2-5)

• however, the five surround phrases caused by the emotional semicolons suggest that
there is much going on underneath the apparently calm surface (all of F #1 and F #4)

• the unembellished lines reinforce what her previous speeches have already shown,
his power to attract and her own sense of fundamental unworthiness
    "Leave you your power to draw,/And I shall have no power to follow you."
    "What worser place can I beg in your love, /(And yet a place of high respect with
    me)"

20/ Helena   Your vertue is my privilege :   between 2.1.220 - 234

Background: Despite her previous attempts (speech # 19 above) Demetrius still doesn't want her around, and has (speech # 10 above) suggested quite strongly that her virginity may be at risk if she stays alone in the wood. The following is her (wonderfully ingenuous? or knowing?) reply.

Style: as part of a two-handed scene
Where: somewhere in the woods   **To Whom:** Demetrius   **# of Lines: 12**   **Probable Timing: 0.40 minutes**

Modern Text	First Folio
20/ Helena	**20/ Helena**
1 Your virtue is my privilege* . †	1 Your vertue is my priviledge : for that
2 For that	It is not night when I doe see your face.
It is not night when I do* see your face, ◊	
Therefore I think* I am not in the night,	2 Therefore I thinke I am not in the night,
Nor doth this wood lack* worlds of company,	Nor doth this wood lacke worlds of company,
For you in my respect are all the world.	For you in my respect are all the world.
3 Then how can it be said I am alone,	3 Then how can it be said I am alone,
When all the world is here* to look* on me?	When all the world is heere to looke on me?
4 Run* when you will ; the story shall be chang'd:	4 Runne when you will, + the story shall be chang'd:
Apollo flies, and Daphne holds the chase;	Apollo flies, and Daphne holds the chase;
The ᐃdove pursues the ᐃgriffin ; the mild* ᐃhind*	The Dove pursues the Griffin, + the milde Hinde
Makes speed to catch the ᐃtiger* - ◊ᐃbootless* speed* ,	Makes speed to catch the Tyger.
When cowardice pursues and valor* flies.	Bootlesse speede,
	5 When cowardise pursues,x and valour flies.

• in the midst of the opening emotion (0/6 the first seven lines, F #1-3), the calm quiet of the unembellished
"For you in my respect are all the world./ Then how can it be said I am alone,"
speaks volumes as to her hopes and desires

• the surround phrases start out logically, ' . Your vertue is my priviledge : for that/It is not night when I doe see your face . ' and ' . Runne when you will, the story shall be chang'd . '

• but as her imagination runs away with her, so the surround phrases turn emotional - ' . Apollo flies, and Daphne holds the chase ; /The Dove pursues the Griffin, the milde Hinde/Makes speed to catch the Tyger . '

• this, coupled with the image's intellectual start (4/0, F #4's line two and the first half of line three) turning to tremendous emotion (1/6, the last two and half lines of the speech), suggests that Helena might be reverting back to her old flamboyance (whether joyfully or painfully is up to each actress to decide)

21/ Helena   **O I am out of breath, in this fond chace,**   2.2.88 - 102

Background: Though Demetrius ran away from her as threatened, the still very game Helena pursued him and caught up with him, only to be almost immediately abandoned again, his last words warning 'Stay on thy perill, I alone will goe'. The following is her response, and discovery.

Style: solo, until F #7/mt. #8

Where: somewhere in the woods   **To Whom:** direct audience address, and then the sleeping/potion zapped Lysander

# of Lines: 15   **Probable Timing:** 0.50 minutes

Modern Text	First Folio
21/ Helena	**21/ Helena**
1 O, I am out of breath, in this fond chase! †	1 O⁺ I am out of breath, in this fond chace,
2 The more my prayer, the lesser is my grace. †	The more my prayer, the lesser is my grace,
3 Happy is Hermia, whereso'er* she lies,	Happy is Hermia, wheresoere she lies; ₓ
For she hath blessed and attractive eyes.	For she hath blessed and attractive eyes.
4 How came her eyes so bright?	2 How came her eyes so bright?
5 Not with salt tears*; ◊	3 Not with salt teares.
If so, my eyes are oft'ner wash'd [than] hers.	4 If so, my eyes are oftner washt [then] hers.
6 No, no, I am as ugly as a ᴬbear*;	5 No, no, I am as ugly as a Beare;
For beasts that meet* me run* away for fear*. †	For beasts that meete me,ₓ runne away for feare,
7 Therefore no marvel* though Demetrius	Therefore no marvaile, ⁺ though Demetrius
Do*, as a monster, fly* my presence thus.	Doe⁺ as a monster, flie my presence thus.
8 What wicked and dissembling glass* of mine	6 What wicked and dissembling glasse of mine,ₓ
Made me compare with Hermia's sphery eyne! †	Made me compare with Hermias sphery eyne?⁺
9 But who is here?	7 But who is here?
10 Lysander ! on the ground? †	8 Lysander⁺ on the ground;
11 Dead*, or asleep*?	Deade⁺ or asleepe?
12 I see no blood, no wound . †	9 I see no bloud, no wound,
13 Lysander, if you live, good sir, awake.	Lysander, if you live, good sir⁺ awake.

It seems that the opening words are very true and she really is out of breath, in that save for the single proper name 'Hermia', the first four and half lines (F #1-2) show no release and, thus unembellished, offer a very quiet opening (probably more exhausted and despairing than calm).

• but as Helena slowly recovers and begins to focus yet again on her own inadequacies as compared to Hermia, the depths of feeling in this unflattering comparison can be seen in that the three sentences of F #2-4 are all short, one (#2) unembellished and monosyllabic, and a second (#4) unembellished

• and in the comparison her emotions are released once more (0/9, F #3-6)

• while the discovery of Lysander forces her back to some semblance of restrained self-control (0/2, F #7-9)

• even in the supposedly controlled moments, the semicolons show that emotions still bubble underneath, first about Hermia's beauty ", For she hath blessed and attractive eyes . " and then in the apparently calm discovery of Lysander ". Lysander on the ground ; /Deade or asleepe ? "

22/ Helena   O spight! O hell! I see you are all bent   3.2.145 - 161

Background: Since both the zapped/love-potioned Lysander and Demetrius are wooing her so extravagantly, and even though Demetrius is saying everything she has longed to hear (calling her 'goddesse, nimph, perfect, divine'), Helena highly doubts their sincerity - as she tells them in no uncertain terms.

Style: as part of a three-handed scene

Where: somewhere in the woods   **To Whom:** to the love potion zapped Lysander and Demetrius

# of Lines: 17   **Probable Timing:** 0.55 minutes

Modern Text

22/ Helena

1 O spite*!
2   O hell!
3   I see you [all are] bent
   To set against me, for your merriment. †
4 If you were civil* and knew courtesy*,
   You would not do* me thus much injury.
5 Can you not hate me, as I know you do*,
   But you must join* in souls* to mock* me too*?
6 If you [were] men, as men you are in show,
   You would not use a gentle ᵃlady so;
   To vow, and swear*, and superpraise my parts,
   When I am sure you hate me with your hearts.
7 You both are ᵃrivals, and love Hermia;
   And now both ᵃrivals, to mock* Helena.
8 A trim exploit, a manly enterprise*
   To conjure tears* up in a poor* maid's eyes
   With your derision! †
9   None of noble sort
   Would so offend a ᵃvirgin, and extort
   A poor* soul's* patience, all to make you sport.

First Folio

22/ Helena

1 O spight!
2   O hell!
3   I see you [are all] bent
   To set against me, for your merriment :
   If you were civill,ₓ and knew curtesie,
   You would not doe me thus much injury.
4 Can you not hate me, as I know you doe,
   But you must joyne in soules to mocke me to?
5 If you [are] men, as men you are in show,
   You would not use a gentle Lady so;
   To vow, and sweare, and superpraise my parts,
   When I am sure you hate me with your hearts.
6 You both are Rivals, and love Hermia;
   And now both Rivals ⁺ to mocke Helena.
7 A trim exploit, a manly enterprize,
   To conjure teares up in a poore maids eyes,ₓ
   With your derision; none of noble sort,ₓ
   Would so offend a Virgin, and extort
   A poore soules patience, all to make you sport.

Here there seems to be a fine struggle between control and emotion, emphasised by the most unusual setting of, for F, two extraordinarily rare exclamation marks (at the end of F #1 & #2), and the fact that the speech starts with two very short sentences.

• right from the start, the clash between the exclamation points of F #1-2 (indicating unusually excessive release) and the attempted control shown in the two and a half unembellished lines in the opening four lines of F #1-3 shows the extremes she is undergoing (the demands of social politeness and personal need clashing perhaps)

• the two onrushed sentences (F #3 and F #7) also show where the rational character created by modern texts (which split both F sentences in two) cracks a little in her hurt accusation of the men not being 'civill' (F #3) and not being of 'noble sort' (F #7)

• the three semicolons (F #5, #6, #7) all relate to moments of her belief in their mistreatment of her
   "You would not use a gentle Lady so;"
plus the surround phrases
   " . You both are Rivals, and love Hermia ; /And now both Rivals to mocke Helena . "
with the final summation
   " ; none of noble sort/Would so offend a Virgin, . . . "

• despite the struggles, the speech opens under a fair degree of control (0/2 in the first four lines, F #1-3), then becomes much more emotional (0/4, F #4) as she accuses them of mocking her

• then, though mental discipline momentarily takes over as her stripping them down intensifies (5/2, F #5-6), it cannot last, and her emotions come to the fore once more in the final, onrushed, F #7 (1/5)

23/ Helena   **Loe, she is one of this confederacy,**   3.2.192 - 219

Background: Hermia, having found, as-she-thinks, her friends, chides her lover Lysander for leaving her alone, and refuses to believe his statement that not only does he now love Helena and not her, and that it was 'The hate I beare thee, made me leave thee so'. Helena immediately jumps to the wrong conclusion, believing Hermia to be in on a joke at her expense.

Style: a one to one woman speech, as part of a four-handed scene

Where: somewhere in the woods   **To Whom:** the puzzled Hermia, in front of the love potion zapped Lysander and Demetrius

# of Lines: 28   **Probable Timing: 1.30 minutes**

Modern Text

23/ Helena

1 Loe* ! she is one of this confederacy . †

2 Now I perceive, they have conjoin'd* all three
   To fashion this false sport in spite* of me.

3 Injurious Hermia, most ungrateful* maid ! †

4 Have you conspir'd, have you with these contriv'd
   To bait* me with this foul* derision?

5 Is all the counsell* that we two have shar'd,
   The sisters vows*, the hours* that we have spent,
   When we* have chid the hasty footed time
   For parting us - O, is all ¹¹ forgot?

6 All schooldays* friendship, child°hood innocence?

7 We, Hermia, like two ▵artificial* gods,
   Have with our needles, created both one flower,
   Both on one sampler, sitting on one cushion,
   Both warbling of one song, both in one key ,
   As if our hands, our sides, voices, and minds*
   Had been* incorporate.

8   So we grew together,
   Like to a double cherry, seeming parted,
   But yet [an] union in partition,
   Two lovely berries moulded* on one stem ;
   So with two seeming bodies, but one heart,
   Two of the first, [like] coats in ▵heraldry,
   Due but to one, and crowned with one crest.

9 And will you rent our ancient love asunder,
   To join* with men in scorning your poor* friend?

10 It is not friendly, 'tis not maidenly.

First Folio

23/ Helena

1 Loe, + she is one of this confederacy,
   Now I perceive + they have conjoyn'd all three
   To fashion this false sport in spight of me.

2 Injurious Hermia, most ungratefull maid,
   Have you conspir'd, have you with these contriv'd
   To baite me, ₓ with this foule derision?

3 Is all the counsell that we two have shar'd,
   The sisters vowes, the houres that we have spent,
   When wee have chid the hasty footed time,ₓ
   For parting us ; ₓ O, is all forgot?

4 All schooledaies friendship, child-hood innocence?

5 We + Hermia, like two Artificiall gods,
   Have with our needles, created both one flower,
   Both on one sampler, sitting on one cushion,
   Both warbling of one song, both in one key ; ₓ
   As if our hands, our sides, voices, and mindes
   Had beene incorporate.

6   So we grew together,
   Like to a double cherry, seeming parted,
   But yet [a] union in partition,
   Two lovely berries molded on one stem. +
   So with two seeming bodies, but one heart,
   Two of the first + [life] coats in Heraldry,
   Due but to one + and crowned with one crest.

7 And will you rent our ancient love asunder,
   To joyne with men in scorning your poore friend?

8 It is not friendly, 'tis not maidenly.

{ctd. over}

F's faster opening (F #1 = mt. #1-2, F #2 = mt. #3-4), suggests a Helena swiftly putting ideas together, rather than one already on the warpath.

- there seems to be quite an emotional need for her friend's support, for the two semicoloned surround phrases focus in on what Helena believes they used to mean to each other
  " ; O is all forgot ? " and
  " ; As if our hands, our sides, voices and mindes/Had beene incorporate . "

- what is fascinating about her initial reprimand (F #2-3) is that, while emotional (1/7), within her very carefully chosen argument one word per line becomes singled out, as though it was striking an emotional chord in either herself or Hermia (save for line two of F #3 which is doubly marked soand F #2 line two in which there is no long-spelling)

- the recollection of what the two women did as 'two Artificiall gods' is handled very quietly, for after F F5's first line, nine and a half of the next twelve lines are unembellished: whether this a personal calm brought about by memories of happier (and not lonely) times, or a deliberate ploy to ensnare Hermia is up to each actress to decide

- by the finish of the extended unembellished passage the images flow fast, for in F #6's last two lines, while the extra punctuation added by most modern texts (marked + in the F text) suggest a hard working Helena, F's speed suggests rather that she is on a fine roll

- and the final unembellished line in the speech(F #8)
  "It is not friendly, 'tis not maidenly."
  heightened by being a short sentence, offers her a moment of control before the emotional outburst of the last chiding sentence (0/3, F #9)

---

¹¹ F1/Qq show no extra word, some modern texts add 'quite' (to preserve the pentameter)

11 Our sex*, as well as I, may chide you for it,
   Though I alone do* feel* the injury*.

9 Our sexe⁺ as well as I, may chide you for it,
   Though I alone doe feele the injurie*.

#'s 24 - 26: THE MECHANICALS PREPARE THEIR PLAY

24/ Bottome   A Lover that kills himselfe most gallantly for love?   1.2.24 - 41

Background: The producer of the play 'Pyramus and Thisbie', Quince, is a carpenter, and whether he is used to theatrics, and whether he wrote the play himself, is up to each production to decide. In the following, Bottome (the most theatrically experienced of the group) provides his initial response to both Quince and his fellow actors about being offered the lead, a romantic rather than a swashbuckling role. One note: the first line, marked {ψ}, is taken from Quince's earlier explanation of the role.

Style: group address as part of a six-handed scene

Where: unspecified, but somewhere in Athens   **To Whom:** Quince, Flute, Starveling, Snug, and Snout   **# of Lines:** 11   **Probable Timing:** 0.40 minutes

Modern Text	First Folio

F's orthography suggests Bottome's love of the theatre knows no bounds.

- the surround phrases underscore Bottome's passionate belief as to how theatre should work from a performer's viewpoint, as the whole of F #2 and F #7 clearly show

- the short sentences (F #1, #3, and #6) also focus totally on the theatre, the first three on himself, the latter on more practical matters

- after a careful musing of what he is asked to play (F #1, 1/0), emotions begin to flow as he envisages perfomance ideas (0/7, F #2-3)

- in performing before them (F #4), he starts out intellectually (2/1 in the first two lines) but finishes, as many an experienced amateur performer will, somewhat more emotionally (2/3 in the last line and a half)

- within the midst of F #4's 'performance' comes a most wickedly wonderful 'performer's moment' of deliberate quiet, viz. 'and shivering shockes shall break the locks of prison gates'

- one note about F #4: F/Qq all present Bottome's 'raging rocks' extravaganza (shaded) passage as prose, most modern texts lay it out according to its rhyming pattern: one reading of the source text could be that Bottome is not completely comfortable with (perhaps is even inventing) the doggerel, certainly it is not presented as accomplished and polished speech - even though the modern restructuring presents the material as 'pure' verse which it presumes Bottome can handle with ease

- then, post performance, comes a moment of relative 'calm' (1/0, F #6-7), though whether real or theatrical is up to each actor to explore, with the summary being emotional once more (1/2, F #7)

First Folio

24/ Bottome

1 {ψ}A Lover⁺ that kills himselfe most [gallantly] for love {?}

2 That will aske some teares in the true perfor-ming of it: if I do it, let the audience looke to their eies: I will condole in some measure.

3 To the rest⁺ yet, ₓ my chiefe humour is for a tyrant.

4 I could play Ercles rarely, or a part to teare a Cat in, to make all split the raging Rocks; ₓ and shivering shocks shall break the locks of prison gates, ⁺ and Phibbus carre shall shine from farre, and make and marre the foolish Fates.

5 This was lofty. ⁺

6 Now name the rest of the Players. ⁺

7 This is Ercles vaine, a tyrants vaine: ₓ a lover is more condo-ling.

Modern Text

24/ Bottome

1 {ψ}A ᐃlover, that kills himself* most [gallant] for love {?}

2 That will ask* some tears* in the true perfor-ming of it. ⁺

3 If I do it, let the audience look* to their eyes*. ⁺

4 I will move* storms*; I will condole in some measure.

5 To the rest - yet my chief* humor* is for a tyrant.

6 I could play Ercles rarely, or a part to tear* a ᐃcat in, to make all split. ⁺

7 "The raging ᐃrocks
   And shivering shocks
   Shall break the locks
   Of prison gates;
   And ᐃ'phibbus' car*
   Shall shinevfrom far* ,
   And make and mar*
   The foolish Fates. "

8 This was lofty !

9 Now name the rest of the ᐃplayers.   This

10 is Ercles' vein*, a tyrant's vein*; a lover is more condo-ling.

25/ Bottome   **Let mee play the Lyon too, I will roare that I . . .**   between 1.2.70 - 84

Background: The following is Bottome's immediate would-be role-enhancement response once Snug expresses the tiniest concern ('Have you the Lions' part written? pray you if it be, give it me, for I am slow of studie') followed by Quince's reassurance that the part is 'nothing but roaring'.

Style: group address as part of a six-handed scene

Where: unspecified, but somewhere in Athens   **To Whom:** Quince, Flute, Starveling, Snug, and Snout

# of Lines: 9   **Probable Timing: 0.30 minutes**

Modern Text

25/ Bottome

1 Let me* play the △lion* too .†

    I will roar*, that I

2 will do* any mans heart good to hear* me .

                              I will roar*,

3 that I will make the Duke say, "Let him roar* again*; let him roar* again* . "

4 I grant* you, friends, if [ ] you should fright the △ladies out of their △wits*, they would have no more discretion but to hang us; but I will ag-gravate my voice* so that I will roar* you as gently as any sucking △dove; I will roar* [you] and 'twere any △nightin-gale.

First Folio

25/ Bottome

1 Let mee play the Lyon too, I will roare+ that I will doe any mans heart good to heare me.

2   I will roare, that I will make the Duke say, Let him roare againe, + let him roare againe.

3 I graunt you+ friends, if [that] you should fright the Ladies out of their Wittes, they would have no more discretion but to hang us : x but I will ag-gravate my voyce so, x that I will roare you as gently as any sucking Dove; I will roare [ ] and 'twere any Nightin-gale.

- as seen in the previous speech, #24 above, Bottome seems to have a splendid, often emotional, imagination as to his performing abilities, as the only surround phrase, ending this speech, attests ". ; I will roare and 'twere any Nightingale . " the semicolon reinforcing the emotion of the moment

- his desire to 'play the Lyon too' is enthusiastically emotional (3/10 in just the three plus lines, F #1-2)

- yet, when challenged, he is still able to add some intellect to the self-justification mix, (4/5, F #3) re-assuring his colleagues he will not 'fright the Ladies out of their Wittes'

26/ Bottome   **Masters, you ought to consider with your selves, to**   between 3.1.29 - 46

Background: Following the casting meeting and now assembling in the woods to rehearse so that they are not 'dog'd with company' nor their 'devices known', Bottome and the others have had time to inspect the script, and have come up with a problem.

Style: group address as part of a six-handed scene

Where: somewhere in the woods near the Fairies' haunts   **To Whom:** Quince, Flute, Starveling, Snug, & Snout

# of Lines: 14   **Probable Timing: 0.45 minutes**

Once more, Bottome's mind and emotions come into play as the company still tries to come to terms with how to avoid getting into trouble with the Duke when presenting the 'Lyon' . . .

- . . . at least at the beginning (3/2, F #1)

- but then, as the problem is fully spelled out (F #2) and an answer begins to present itself (the first three lines of F #3), so his emotions have full sway (2/12 in just five lines)

- and though his intellect comes to the fore for a moment as the performer's imagination takes over once more (2/1, the last two and a half lines of F #3), his emotions are soon in full cry as he nears the conclusion of the performance he envisages for the performer of the Lyon (1/3, F #4)

- once again, the performers 'quiet moment' strikes as he suggests that the Lyon finishes with an unembellished surround phrase '. No, I am no such thing, I am a man as other men are ; ' – without the extra heavy punctuation (an exclamation mark and two semicolons) offered by most modern texts

Modern Text

26/ Bottome

1 Masters, you ought to consider with yourselves, to bring in (God shield us !) a ᐃlion* among ᐃladies, is a most dreadful* thing; ◇ for there is not a more fearful* wild*- fowl* [than] your ᐃlion* living; and we* ought to look* [to't].

2 {ψY}ou must name his name, and half* his face must be seen* though the ᐃlion's* neck*, and he himself* must speak* through, saying thus, or to the same defect: "Ladies", or " ᐃFair* Ladies, I would wish you", or "I would request you", or "I would entreat you, not to fear*, not to tremble: my life for yours*.

3   If you think* I come hither as a ᐃlion*, it were pity* of my life.

4   No ! I am no such

thing ; I am a man as other men are"; and there indeed let him name his name, and tell [them] plainly he* is Snug the joiner*.

First Folio

26/ Bottome

1 Masters, you ought to consider with your selves, to bring in (God shield us⁺) a Lyon among Ladies, is a most dreadfull thing.

2   For there is not a more fearefull wilde foule [then] your Lyon living; ₓ and wee ought to looke [to it].

3 {ψY}ou must name his name, and halfe his face must be seene though the Lyons necke, and he himselfe must speake through, saying thus, or to the same defect; ⁺ Ladies, or faire Ladies, I would wish you, or I would request you, or I would entreat you, not to feare, not to tremble: my life for yours.

4   If you thinke I come hither as a Lyon, it were pitty of my life.

5   No, ⁺ I am no such thing, ⁺ I am a man as other men are; and there indeed let him name his name, and tell [him] plainly hee is Snug the joyner.

#'s 27 - 29: THE WORLD OF THE LOWER FAIRIES

27/ Fairie   Whether wander I?   2.1.2 -17

Background: One of Titania's fairies (the character's first speech in the play), responding to Pucke's challenge. One note: the first line is a re-working of Pucke's enquiry.

Style: part of a two-handed scene, written partly in magic (hence the bolded text) [12]

Where: somewhere in the woods   To Whom: Oberon's prime helper, Pucke

# of Lines: 13   Probable Timing: 0.45 minutes

Modern Text

27/ Fairie

1   [Whither] wander I?

2   Over hill, over dale,
     [Thorough] bush, [thorough] brier,
     Over park*, over pale,
     [Thorough] flood, [thorough] fire,
     I do wander every* where,
     Swifter then [the] ᐃmoon's sphere ;
     And I serve the Fairy Queen*,
     To dew her orbs upon the green.

3   The ᐃcowslips tall her pensioners be* ,
     In their gold coats* spots you see :
     Those be ᐃrubies, ᐃfairy* favors,
     In those freckles, live their savors. †

4   I must go seek* some dew drops here* ,
     And hang a pearl* in every cowslips ear* . †

5   Farewell, thou ᐃlob of spirits; I'll be gone*. †

6   Our Queen* and all her ᐃelves come here* anon.

First Folio

27/ Fairie

1   [Whether] wander I?

2   Over hil, over dale, [through] bush, [through] briar,
     Over parke, over pale, [through] flood, [through] fire,
     I do wander everie where, swifter then [ÿ] Moons sphere ;
     And I serve the Fairy Queene, to dew her orbs upon the green.

3   The Cowslips tall,ₓ her pensioners bee,
     In their gold coats,ₓ spots you see, ⁺
     Those be Rubies, Fairie favors,
     In those freckles, live their savors,
     I must go seeke some dew drops heere,
     And hang a pearle in every cowslips eare.

4   Farewell⁺ thou Lob of spirits; ⁺Ile be gon,
     Our Queene and all her Elves come heere anon.

F1/Qq print the shaded text in four lines as shown. While the modern text version is certainly neater and creates the conventional image of a pretty and delicate creature, the alterations could mask. . . .

   a/ how the Fairie is behaving at the top of the scene (so rushed as to be unable to control or match Robin/Pucke's magic greeting)

   b/ the moment of its moving momentarily into a more ritual/magical form of utterance (which follows this rushed passage) - before

   c/ dropping the magical patterns in the realisation of having to go back to work

• the speech starts out with apparent calm, with a very short non-embellished F #1, followed by little or no release (the first two rhyming lines of F #2, 0/1)

• then, as the conversation refers to (brags?) of both her/his speed and describes the secrets of the 'Cowslips tall' intellect, takes over (6/2 in the last two lines of F #2 and the first four of F #3)

• with the onrush fast-link via the comma as s/he becomes fully emotional (0/4 the last two lines of F #3), it might be that s/he has suddenly remembered what s/he still has to do and is in somewhat of a tizzy, rather than offering the more rational explanation suggested by the modern texts' new sentence mt. #4

• while the farewell and notification that the Queene (Titania) is about to arrive is both factual and emotional (3/3, F #4)

---

[12] for details, see Appendix 3

[13] F1/Q2 = 'through', Q1 and most modern texts = 'thorough' (both spellings yielded either pronunciation for the Elizabethan: if the longer 'thorough' is used, as in most modern texts, the pattern of magic is maintained (see Appendix 3); if the short sound - 'through' - is used, as in F, then the effect is more rushed (see the opening note in the commentary above)

28/ Robin   **Thou speak'st aright ; /I am that merrie wanderer of the night :**   2.1.42 - 58

Background: The Fairie now thinks she recognises Pucke. Thus Pucke, as his kindlier alter ego Robin, responds to the Fairie's enquiring 'Either I mistake your shape and making quite . . . .'.

Style: part of a two-handed scene

Where: somewhere in the woods   **To Whom:** one of Titania's fairies

# of Lines: 17   **Probable Timing: 0.55 minutes**

Robin/Pucke is often played with a generalised unfocused energy. Here, F's 'ungrammatical' structure pin-points much more accurately where Robin/Pucke is having even more fun than usual.

- some modern texts join the opening to the previous line to form a single split verse line: however, the line so created would only be eight syllables long: Q1/Q2 join it to Robin/Pucke's following line thus creating an exuberant 14 or 15 syllable reply: as set in F, Pucke gives himself a splendid moment's pause before his acknowledgment – the pause offering a deceptive opening calm (1/0) for the first two lines of emphatic unembellished surround phrases and the third line

- after that, as might be suspected with the onrush of F #1, the speech becomes splendidly (celebratory?) emotional (2/15 in thirteen lines, the remainder of F #1 through to F #3)

- the ungrammatical F #3, rejoicing in the 'whole quire's' reaction to what he set up in F #2 (the 'wisest Aunt' falling off him to the floor thinking he was a stool), allows Robin/Pucke much more of a story-telling finale than the modern texts that fold the two sentences together (mt. #3)

- only in the final (trouble-anticipating) F #4 does intellect match emotion (2/2)

Modern Text

28/ Robin

1 Thou speak'st aright ;
   I am that merry△ wanderer of the night . †

2 I jest to Oberon and make him smile
   When I a fat and bean*-fed horse beguile,
   Neighing in likeness* of a [filly] foal*;
   And sometime lurk* I in a △gossip's bowl*
   In very likeness* of a roasted crab,
   And when she drinks*, against her lips I bob,
   And on her withered dewlop pour* the △ale.

3 The wisest △aunt, telling the saddest tale,
   Sometime for three-foot stool* mistaketh me;
   Then slip I from her bum, down* topples she,
   And ''tailor''* cries, and falls* into a cough*; ◇
   And then the whole quire hold their hips and laugh*,
   And waxen in their mirth, and neeze, and swear*,
   A merrier hour* was never wasted there.

4 But room*, △fairy! here* comes Oberon.

First Folio

28/ Robin

1 Thou speak'st aright;
   I am that merrie wanderer of the night :
   I jest to Oberon, + and make him smile,x
   When I a fat and beane-fed horse beguile,
   Neighing in likenesse of a [silly] foale, +
   And sometime lurke I in a Gossips bole,
   In very likenesse of a roasted crab: x
   And when she drinkes, against her lips I bob,
   And on her withered dewlop poure the Ale.

2 The wisest Aunt + telling the saddest tale,
   Sometime for three-foot stoole,x mistaketh me, +
   Then slip I from her bum, downe topples she,
   And tailour cries, and fals into a coffe.

3 And then the whole quire hold their hips,x and loffe,
   And waxen in their mirth, and neeze, and sweare,
   A merrier houre was never wasted there.

4 But roome + Fairy,fx heere comes Oberon.

29/ Pucke   **My Fairie Lord, this must be done with haste,**   3.2.378 - 388

Background: With all the damage control Pucke has been commanded to achieve to bring all the lovers back together so that Oberon can undo the various spells, he is concerned that it may not be completed before the (to him) dangerous time just before dawn.

Style: as part of a two-handed scene

Where: somewhere in the woods   **To Whom:** Oberon   **# of Lines:** 10   **Probable Timing:** 0.35 minutes

Modern Text

29/ Pucke

1 My ᐃfairy* ᐃlord, this must be done with haste,
For [Night's ᐃ° swift] ᐃdragons cut the ᐃclouds full full fast,
And yonder shines Aurora's harbinger,
At whose approach, ᐃghosts wand'ring here and there,
Troop* home to ᐃchurch°yards. †
                                    Damned spirits all,

2 That in cross°ways* and floods* have buriall* ,
Already* to their wormy* beds are gone. †

3 For fear* lest* day should look* their shames upon,
They willfully* themselves [exiled] from light,
And must for aye consort with black*°brow'd ᐃNight.

First Folio

29/ Pucke

1 My Fairie Lord, this must be done with haste,
For [night-swift] Dragons cut the Clouds full fast,
And yonder shines Auroras harbinger; x
At whose approach + Ghosts wandring here and there,
Troope home to Church-yards; damned spirits all,
That in crosse-waies and flouds have buriall,
Alreadie to their wormie beds are gone;
For feare least day should looke their shames upon,
They wilfully themselves [exile] from light,
And must for aye consort with blacke browd night.

F's single sentence onrush underscores Pucke's concerns much more than the more rational three sentence setting of most modern texts.

• for such a spontaneous and emotional character, the opening is startlingly factual (5/0 the first three lines)

• and, even though the surround phrase ", At whose approach Ghosts wandring here and there, /Troope home to Church-yards. ; " is created by two emotional semicolons, he still manages to maintain control (2/1)

• and then, with his mind spinning more details of the 'Ghosts' as 'damned spirits all', emotion breaks through unchecked (0/8 in the last five and a half lines of the speech)

#'s 30 - 34: THE FAIRY QUARREL

30/ Queene   **These are the forgeries of jealousie,**   2.1.81 - 117

Background: Oberon has attacked Titania's reputation, more than hinting at her previous relationship with Theseus. The following is her reply.

Style: one on one address in front of an unspecified number of others

Where: somewhere in the woods   **To Whom:** Oberon, in front of both their trains including the Fairie and Pucke who were talking earlier   **# of Lines:** 37   **Probable Timing:** 1.50 minutes

Modern Text

30/ Queene

1 These are the forgeries of jealousy*;
And never since the middle ᐃsummer's spring,
Met we on hill*, in dale, forest* , or mead,
By paved fountain* or by rushy* brook* ,
Or in the beached margent of the sea,
To dance our ringlets to the whistling ᐃwind*
But with thy brawls* thou hast disturb'd our sport.

First Folio

30/ Queene

1 These are the forgeries of jealousie, +
And never since the middle Summers spring +
Met we on hil, in dale, forrest, or mead,
By paved fountaine, x or by rushie brooke,
Or in the beached margent of the sea,
To dance our ringlets to the whistling Winde,
But with thy braules thou hast disturb'd our sport.

That it is very difficult for Titania to maintain composure can be seen in the vast swings between the three stages of emotion, passion, and facts.

• after a very quiet three line opening dismissing Oberon's accusations and establishing how long his actions have disturbed her and her train, as she begins to cite details of where and what he has interrupted, and the initial result of that interruption ('Contagious fogges'), so she becomes emotional (3/7), while the flooding that has occurred because of the 'fogges' seems to be strongly fixed in her mind (4/1, the last two and half lines of F #2)

{ctd. over}

2
Therefore the Windes, piping to us in vaine,
As in revenge, have suck'd up from the sea
Contagious fogges::   Which⁺ falling in the Land,
Hath everie [petty] River made so proud,ₓ
That they have over-borne their Continents.

3
The Oxe hath therefore stretch'd his yoake in vaine,
The Ploughman lost his sweat, and the greene Corne
Hath rotted,ₓ ere his youth attain'd a beard:
The fold stands empty in the drowned field,
And Crowes are fatted with the murrion flocke,⁺
The nine mens Morris is fill'd up with mud,
And the queint Mazes in the wanton greene,
For lacke of tread⁺ are undistinguishable.

4
The humane mortals want their winter [heere],⁺
No night is now with hymne or caroll blest;
Therefore the Moone (the governesse of floods)⁺
Pale in her anger, washes all the aire;ₓ
That Rheumaticke diseases doe abound.

5
And [through] this distemperature, we see
The seasons alter;⁺ [hoared] headed frosts
Fall in the fresh lap of the crimson Rose,
And on old Hyems [chinne] and Icie crowne,ₓ
An odorous Chaplet of sweet Sommer buds
Is as in mockry⁺ set.

6
            The Spring, the Sommer,
The childing Autumne, angry Winter⁺ change
Their wonted Liveries,⁺ and the mazed world,
By their increase, now knowes not which is which ;
And this same progeny of evills,ₓ
Comes from our debate, from our dissention,⁺
We are their parents and originall.

2
• in describing the results of the flooding, especially its effect on the surrounding countryside, she becomes passionate (6/9, F #3), while the effect on the humans (no night with hymne or caroll blest' and 'Rheumaticke diseases) is described very emotionally (2/9 in just the five lines F #4)

• however, the worst result of all (the altering of the seasons) is once more inescapably burned in her mind and handled intellectually (10/5 F #5 and the first three and a half lines of F #6)

3
• finally, Titania's acceptance of her responsibility in creating this appalling turn of events and (by finishing with 'we are their parents and originall') demanding Oberon do the same, is handled as a mixture of one unembellished line and emotion (0/2, the last three lines of the speech)

4
• and it's interesting to see that at this very moment, while F sets a two line irregularity (9/11 syllables), that suggests the moment is very difficult for Titania, most modern texts remove this clue by resetting the shaded text as two normal lines, as shown

4
• in the midst of the struggle, the unembellished lines seem to suggest certain incidents and memories have to be handled very carefully (otherwise they might upset her too much, perhaps?), from the opening 'These are the forgeries of jealousie,' and listing of special places she and her Fairies can no longer dance in without being disturbed
"Met we on hil, in dale, . . . /Or in the beached margent of the sea."
to what the 'Windes, piping to us in vaine' have done
"As in revenge, have suck'd up from the sea,"
so, as a result
"The fold stands empty in the drowned field,"
"And through this distemperature, we see/The seasons alter;
hoared headed frosts/Fall in the lap of . . ."
all of which
"Comes from our debate, from our dissention,"

5

6
• one final note to intensify the actor's understanding of the imagery - one of the two surround phrases, created in part by the emotional semicolon, points to Shakespeare's own hatred of illness,
" ; That Rheumaticke diseases doe abound ."
while the other deals with the Elizabethan fear of disorder in nature
" . And through this distemperature, we see/The seasons alter ; "

2
Therefore the △winds*, piping to us in vain*,
As in revenge, have suck'd up from the sea
Contagious △fogs* ; △which, falling in the △land,
Hath every* [pelting] △river made so proud
That they have over∘borne their △continents.

3
The △ox* hath therefore stretch'd his yoke* in vain*,
The △ploughman lost his sweat, and the green* △corn*
Hath rotted ere his youth attain'd a beard. †
The fold stands empty in the drowned field,
And △crows* are fatted with the murrion flock*;
The nine men's △morris is fill'd* up with mud,
And the quaint Mazes in the wanton green*,
For lack* of tread, are undistinguishable.

4
The human* mortals want their winter [cheer]* ;
No night is now with hymn* or carol* blest. †

7
Therefore the △moon* (the governess* of floods),
Pale in her anger, washes all the △air*,
That △rheumatic* diseases do* abound.

8
And [thorough] this distemperature, we see
The seasons alter : [hoary*]-∘ headed frosts
Fall in the fresh lap of the crimson △rose,
And on old Hiems* [thin]* and △icy* crown*
An odorous △chaplet of sweet △summer buds
Is as in mockery*, set; ◊ the △spring, the △summer*,
The childing △autumn*, angry △winter, change
Their wonted △liveries; and the mazed world,
By their increase, now knows* not which is which. †

9
And this same progeny of evils* comes
From our debate, from our dissension ;
We are their parents and original* .

31/ Queene   **Set your heart at rest,/The Fairy land buyes not the childe of me,**   2.1.121 -137

Background: In response to the deeply felt chaos expressed in her previous speech (#30 above), Oberon offers a truce if only she will surrender to him the Indian Boy (the root of their more than year-long quarrel) to be his 'Henchman', a bargain that she emphatically refuses.

Style: one on one address in front of an unspecified number of others
Where: somewhere in the woods   **To Whom:** Oberon, in front of both their trains including the Fairie and Pucke who were talking earlier
# of Lines: 17   **Probable Timing: 0.55 minutes**

Modern Text	First Folio
31/ Queene	**31/ Queene**
1 Set your heart at rest **;** The ^fairy land buys* not the child* of me . †	1 Set your heart at rest, + The Fairy land buyes not the childe of me, His mother was a Votresse of my Order, And in the spiced Indian aire, by night + Full often hath she gossipt by my side, And sat with me on Neptunes yellow sands, Marking th'embarked traders on the flood, + When we have laught to see the sailes conceive,ₓ
2 His mother was a ^vot'ress * of my ^order, And in the spiced Indian air*, by night, Full often hath she gossip'd by my side, And sat with me on Neptune's yellow sands, Marking th'embarked traders on the flood **;** When we have laugh'd to see the sails* conceive And grow big-°bellied with the wanton wind* **;** Which she, with pretty and with swimming [gait], Following (her womb* then rich with my young* squire) Would imitate, and sail* upon the ^land To fetch me trifles, and return* again* , As from a voyage, rich with merchandise* .	And grow big bellied with the wanton winde: ₓ Which she + with pretty and with swimming [gate], Following (her wombe then rich with my yong squire) Would imitate, and saile upon the Land,ₓ To fetch me trifles, and returne againe, As from a voyage, rich with merchandize.
3 But she, being mortal* , of that boy did die, And for her sake [do* I] rear* up her boy **;** And for her sake I will not part with him.	2 But she + being mortall, of that boy did die, And for her sake [I doe] reare up her boy, + And for her sake I will not part with him.

Though still deeply emotionally affected, here Titania offers far less logic and intellect than in comparison to the previous chaos speech.

• the fact that Titania's opening emotion is matched by her intellect (5/6 in F #1's first nine lines), especially when balanced against the final emotion of the speech, is great proof of how much she needs to have all present (Oberon especially) understand the factual base of her refusal

• yet F #1's onrush, with the introduction of the all important explanation of who the Boy's mother was springing forth via a non-grammatical fast-link comma after the first two lines, gives the clue to her still unbalanced state

• as the good times of her Votresse's pregnancy are so lovingly described, emotion takes over (1/5 in the last five lines of F #1)

• the description of her death is equally emotional (0/3 in the first two lines of F #2)

• and the refusal to hand over the boy is icily calm in its monosyllabic unembellished finality 'And for her sake I will not part with him.', matching the equally icy opening 'Set your heart at rest,'

32/ Oberon   **My gentle Pucke come hither; thou remembrest**   between 2.1.148 - 185

Background: Following Titania's coruscating and embarrassing public attack on him, Oberon plans his revenge.

Style: as part of a two-handed scene

Where: somewhere in the woods, just after the contretemps with Titania   **To Whom:** Pucke

# of Lines: 37   **Probable Timing: 1.55 minutes**

Modern Text

32/ Oberon

1 My gentle Puck*, come hither. †
    Thou rememb'rest †

2 Since once I sat upon a promontory,
And heard a ᴬmer°maid* on a ᴬdolphin's back*
Uttering such dulcet and harmonious breath
That the rude sea grew civil* at her song,
And certain* stars* shot madly from their ᴬspheres* ,
To hear* the ᴬsea-maids music* ?

3 That very time I saw (but thou couldst not)
Flying between* the cold ᴬmoon* and the earth,
Cupid all arm'd . †

4   A certain* aim* he took*
At a fair* ᴬvestal* throned by the ᴬwest,
And loos'd his love-shaft smartly from his bow,
As it should pierce a hundred thousand hearts ;
But I might see young Cupid's fiery shaft
Quench'd in the chaste beams* of the wat'ry ᴬmoon* ,
And the imperial* ᴬvot'ress* passed on,
In maiden meditation, fancy free. †

5 Yet mark'd I where the bolt of Cupid fell.

6 It fell upon a little western* flower ,
Before, milk* ° white; now purple with love's wound,
And maidens call it, ᴬlove-°in-°idlenesse* .

7 Fetch me that flow'r* ; the herb* I showed* thee once . †

8 The juice* of it on sleeping eye°lids laid
Will make or man or woman madly dote
Upon the next live creature that it sees.

9 Fetch me this herb* , and be thou here* again*
Ere the ᴬleviathan can swim a league.

First Folio

32/ Oberon

1 My gentle Pucke + come hither; thou remembrest
Since once I sat upon a promontory,
And heard a Meare-maide on a Dolphins backe,ₓ
Uttering such dulcet and harmonious breath,ₓ
That the rude sea grew civill at her song,
And certaine starres shot madly from their Spheares,
To heare the Sea-maids musicke. +

2 That very time I saw (but thou couldst not)
Flying betweene the cold Moone and the earth,
Cupid all arm'd; a certaine aime he tooke
At a faire Vestall, throned by the West,
And loos'd his love-shaft smartly from his bow,
As it should pierce a hundred thousand hearts,
But I might see young Cupids fiery shaft
Quencht in the chaste beames of the watry Moone; ₓ
And the imperiall Votresse passed on,
In maiden meditation, fancy free.

3 Yet markt I where the bolt of Cupid fell.

4 It fell upon a little westerne flower; ₓ
Before, milke-white; now purple with loves wound,
And maidens call it, Love in idlenesse.

5 Fetch me that flower; the hearb I shew'd thee once,
The juyce of it, on sleeping eye-lids laid,
Will make or man or woman madly dote
Upon the next live creature that it sees.

6 Fetch me this hearbe, and be thou heere againe,ₓ
Ere the Leviathan can swim a league.

F's opening onrush (#1-2) suggests that Oberon is not as much in control as most modern texts (which split both F sentences in two) would have him.

• yet the non-embellished moments show his, at times, enormous concentration, first as to the time when
"thou remembrest/Since once I sat upon a promontory"
then, the special qualities of the 'Meare-maide'
"Uttering such dulcet and harmonious breath,'
and how powerfully Cupid
". . . loos'd his love-shaft smartly from his bow/As it should pierce a hundred thousand hearts,"
but the 'imperiall Votresse' (thought to be a reference to Queen Elizabeth)
" . . .passed on/In maiden meditation, fancy free."
so that the flower
"now purple with loves wound,"
gained such power that it
"Will make or man or woman madly dote/Upon the next live creature that it sees."
and it is with the essence of this most powerful charm that he will control Titania
"And drop the liquor of it in her eyes:"

• that Oberon is emotionally involved in the moment can be seen in that five of the six pieces of major punctuation are semicolons, three of them focusing on the all-important 'little westerne flower' without which his magic cannot take effect

• the five surround phrases created by the emotional punctuation are also testimony to the depth of his current emotional state: unusually, three follow consecutively, all focusing on the flower,
". It fell upon a little westerne flower; /Before, milke-white; now purple with loves wound,/And maidens call it, Love in idlenesse. / Fetch me that flower ; "

• in setting up the circumstances Oberon is passionate (3/4 in F #1's first three lines), and then emotional in remembering how the 'Meare-maid' calmed the sea with her song (F #1's final three lines): as he describes Cupid preparing himself Oberon's intellect starts to come back (7/11, F #2), but is still subsumed in his emotions as he describes the whereabouts and state of this now powerful flower (2/5, F #3-5)

First Folio

10

Having once this juyce,
Ile watch Titania, when she is asleepe,
And drop the liquor of it in her eyes:_x
The next thing [when] she waking lookes upon,_x
(Be it on Lyon, Beare, or Wolfe, or Bull,
On medling Monkey, or on busie Ape)+
Shee shall pursue it,_x with the soule of love.

11

And ere I take this charme [off from] her sight,_x
(As I can take it with another hearbe)+
Ile make her render up her Page to me.

7

Having once this juyce,
Ile watch Titania, when she is asleepe,
And drop the liquor of it in her eyes:_x
The next thing [when] she waking lookes upon,_x
(Be it on Lyon, Beare, or Wolfe, or Bull,
On medling Monkey, or on busie Ape)+
Shee shall pursue it,_x with the soule of love.

8

And ere I take this charme [off from] her sight,_x
(As I can take it with another hearbe)+
Ile make her render up her Page to me.

Modern Text

Having once this juice* ,
I'll watch Titania, when she is asleep* ,
And drop the liquor of it in her eyes;
The next thing [then] she waking looks* upon
(Be it on △lion* △bear* , or △wolf* , or △bull,
On medling* △monkey, or on busy* △ape),
She* shall pursue it with the soul* of love.

And ere I take this charm* [from off] her sight
(As I can take it with another herb*),
I'll make her render up her △page to me.

- though in commanding Puck to fetch the flower and the lead-up to dropping 'the liquor of it in her eyes' Oberon is highly emotional (2/6 in F #6 and the first three lines of F #7), his fantasising what animal the enchanted Titania might become ensnared by becomes strongly intellectual (6/3 in F #7's lines five and six), while the final dreaming of her humiliation and his releasing her turns emotional once more (1/4, the final four lines of the speech)

- interestingly, as Oberon begins to envisage what will happen once he has the flower, so F introduces six extra breath-thoughts (marked ,_x), almost as if he has to take extra care to prevent his thoughts from running away with him

---

33/ Oberon   I know a banke where the wilde time blowes,   2.1.248 - 258

Background: Pucke has delivered him the flower the juice of which Oberon needs to create the love-charm, and now Oberon anticipates what is to come.

Style: as part of a two-handed scene   **To Whom:** Pucke

Where: somewhere in the woods

# of Lines: 10   **Probable Timing: 0.35 minutes**

Modern Text

33/ Oberon

1 I know a bank* where the wild* thyme* blows* ,
Where △oxslips and the nodding △violet grows* ,
Quite over-[canopied] with luscious woodbine,
With sweet musk* roses, and with △eglantine;
There sleeps* Titania* sometime of the night,
Lull'd_* in these flowers with dances and delight;
And there the snake throws* her enamell'd_* skin* ,
Weed wide enough to rap a △fairy in; ◇
And with the juice* of this I'll streak* her eyes,
And make her full of hatefull fantasies.

First Folio

33/ Oberon

1 I know a banke where the wilde time blowes,
Where Oxslips and the nodding Violet growes,
Quite over-[cannoped] with luscious woodbine,
With sweet muske roses, and with Eglantine;
There sleepes Tytania,_x sometime of the night,
Lul'd in these flowers,_x with dances and delight:_x
And there the snake throwes her enammel'd skinne,
Weed wide enough to rap a Fairy in.

2 And with the juyce of this Ile streake her eyes,_x
And make her full of hatefull fantasies.

F's orthography clearly points to where Oberon speaks more than mere romance, for while the speech is wildly emotional overall (4/12 in just ten lines), two F settings point to darker moments.

- though most modern texts set the speech as just one sentence, the final two line F #2 highlights far more Oberon's desire to 'make her full of hatefull fantasies'

- thus, in a sea of emotion, the carefully unembellished one and a half lines contained within the (admittedly extended) two-line surround phrase
" ;There sleepes Tytania, sometime of the night,/Lul'd in these flowers, with dances and delight : "
point to a very careful and purposeful understanding of how the 'Lul'd' Tytania may be targeted

34/ Pucke   **Through the Forrest have I gone,**   2.2.66 - 83

Background: Having seen sad Helena abandoned by Demetrius, Oberon has told Pucke to use some of the juice of the flower to enchant Demetrius to fall (back) in love with her, telling him to find a man with 'Athenian garments'. As the following starts, Pucke is attempting to do just that, and when he does (line five) he's not to know he's stumbled across Lysander and not Demetrius.

Style: solo, and then one on one to a sleeping character, written mainly in the pattern of magic (the bolded text) [14]

Where: somewhere in the woods   **To Whom:** direct audience address, and then the sleeping Lysander

# of Lines: 18   **Probable Timing: 0.55 minutes**

Modern Text

34/ Pucke

1   **Through the △forest* have I gone,**
    But Athenian [found] I none,
    [On] whose eyes I might approve
    This flower's force in stirring love.

2   **Night and silence - △Who is here*?**

3   **Weeds* of Athens he doth wear*:**
    This is he, my master said
    Despised the Athenian maid* ;
    And here* the maiden, sleeping sound,
    On the dank* and dirty* ground .

4   **Pretty soul*, she durst not lie***
    Near* this lack*-love, this kill-courtesy*.

5   **Churl*, upon thy eyes I throw**
    All the power this charm* doth owe*. [†]

6   **When thou wak'st, let love forbid**
    Sleep* his seat* on thy eyelid.

7   **So awake when I am gone,**
    For I must now to Oberon.

First Folio

34/ Pucke

1   **Through the Forrest have I gone,**
    But Athenian [finde] I none,
    [One] whose eyes I might approve
    This flowers force in stirring love.

    Night and silence : + who is heere?

    Weedes of Athens he doth weare :
    This is he x(my master said)x
    Despised the Athenian maide : x
    And heere the maiden + sleeping sound,
    On the danke and durty ground .

4   Pretty soule, she durst not lye
    Neere this lacke-love, this kill-curtesie.

5   Churle, upon thy eyes I throw
    All the power this charme doth owe :
    When thou wak'st, let love forbid
    Sleepe his seate on thy eye-lid.

6   So awake when I am gone : x
    For I must now to Oberon.

Pucke/Robin's magic/ritual pattern (set in bold type) momentarily slips when he sees the human female (the slippage shown in normal font). This change in speaking style when faced with women is a pattern that is repeated several times later. The magic also slips later as he realises he must leave the humans (especially the woman?) to return to Oberon.

• that his energy might be somewhat dissipated can be seen in that, while the opening two lines about going through the whole 'Forrest' are passionate (2/2), the next two, finding no-one to 'zap', are unembellished

• indeed, the unembellished lines spell out when and where he really has to concentrate
    "On[e] whose eyes I might approve/This flowers force in stirring love./Night and silence."
    "This is he (my master said)" & "upon thy eyes I throw/All the power"
    "When thou wak'st, let love forbid"
    as well as his thralldom to Oberon's will
    "For I must now to Oberon."

• the short sentence discovery of Lysander and Hermia (F #2, 0/1) leads to one more passion released three line segment (3/2) as he believes (mistakenly) that he has found the man Oberon has told him to enchant

• and then emotion floods in as first he closely examines Hermia and then zaps Lysander (0/8 in the nine lines ending F #3 through to F #5)

• the recalling of Oberon returns Pucke to a factual state (1/0)

14   see Appendix 3

#'s 35 - 37: TITANIA IN LOVE

35/ Pucke   **My Mistris with a monster is in love,**   3.2.6 - 34

Background: Pucke reports back to Oberon how, as the following explains in great detail, Oberon's charm has worked so well that, on waking, Titania has fallen in love with an 'Asse'.

Style: as part of a two-handed scene   **To Whom:** Oberon

Where: somewhere in the woods, possibly near Oberon's headquarters

# of Lines: 29   **Probable Timing:** 1.30 minutes

Modern Text		First Folio

35/ Pucke

1 My △mistress* with a monster is in love . †

2 Neer* to her close and consecrated bower,
While she was in her dull and sleeping hour* ,
A crew of patches, rude △mechanicals
That work* for bread upon Athenian stalls*,
Were met together to rehearse a △play
Intended for great Theseus nuptial* day . †

3 The shallowest thick-°skin of that barren sort,
Who Pyramus* presented, in their sport,
Forsook* his △scene, and ent'red in a brake ;
When I did him at this advantage take,
An △ass's* nole I fixed on his head.

4 Anon his Thisby* must be answered,
And forth my △mimic* comes . †

5   When they him spy*,
As △wild*° geese that the creeping △fowler eye,
Or [russet] -pated choughs* , many in sort
(Rising and cawing at the gun's report),
Sever themselves, and madly sweep* the sky* ,
So, at his sight, away his fellows* fly* ;
And at our stamp* , here o'er and o'er one falls* ;
He murther cries, and help* from Athens calls. *

6 Their sense thus weak* , lost with their fears thus strong,
Made senseless* things begin to do them wrong, ◇
For briars and thorns* at their apparel* snatch* ,
Some sleeves, some hats, from yielders* all things catch. †

7 I led them on in this distracted fear* ,
And left sweet* Pyramus* translated there;
When in that moment (so it came to pass*) ,
Titania* wak'd , and straightway lov'd an △ass. * .

35/ Pucke

1 My Mistris with a monster is in love,
Neere to her close and consecrated bower,
While she was in her dull and sleeping bower,
A crew of patches, rude Mechanicals,
That worke for bread upon Athenian stals,
Were met together to rehearse a Play, ₓ
Intended for great Theseus nuptiall day :
The shallowest thick-skin of that barren sort,
Who Piramus presented, in their sport,
Forsooke his Scene, and entred in a brake, †
When I did him at this advantage take,
An Asses nole I fixed on his head.

2 Anon his Thisbie must be answered,
And forth my Mimmick comes: when they him spie,
As Wilde-geese, ₓ that the creeping Fowler eye,
Or [russed] -pated choughes, many in sort
(Rising and cawing at the guns report) †
Sever themselves, and madly sweepe the skye : ₓ
So⁺ at his sight, away his fellowes flye, †
And at our stampe, here ore and ore one fals;
He murther cries, and helpe from Athens cals.

3 Their sense thus weake, lost with their fears thus strong,
Made senselesse things begin to do them wrong.

4 For briars and thornes at their apparell snatch, ⁺
Some sleeves, some hats, from yeelders all things catch,
I led them on in this distracted feare,
And left sweete Piramus translated there : ₓ
When in that moment (so it came to passe) †
Tytania waked, and straightway lov'd an Asse.

The opening and conclusion of F's speech are very different from most modern texts, which set a far more 'correct' reporting of what, within the play at least, is Pucke's greatest triumph to date.

• the onrush of F #1 and F #2 suggests a Pucke much more excitable than his modern counterpart: most modern texts split F #1 into three, and F #2 into two

• thus the fast-link connection of the first line to what follows via a simple comma shows a Pucke that hasn't got time to follow logical niceties (and might well suggest a Pucke who still cannot believe he's managed to pull off what he has)

• similarly the fast-link connection of 'The shallowest thick-skin' (Bottome – mt. #3) to the previous general description of the 'rude Mechanicals' (mt. #2) via a colon suggests that Pucke wants to get rid of the introductory details as quickly as possible to get to meatier matters

• and F's conjoining mt. #4 (the transfixed Bottome's re-appearance) to mt. #5 (how the Mechanicals fled in all directions like frightened 'Wilde-geese') via another fast-link colon suggests that Pucke still hasn't reached the apex of the story

• for it would seem that the F only two line sentence explaining that in the Mechanical's fear 'senselesse things begin to do them wrong' (F #3), while perhaps syntactically incorrect in being separated from the next two lines that follow (set grammatically correctly by most modern texts as mt. #6), is all an excited Pucke needs to set up the most fun part of what he witnessed, the ungrammatical F #4 summary

• the speech starts with the telling of the introductory facts up to the moment the Mechanicals see Bottome with the 'Asses nole fixed on his head' slightly outweighing Pucke's emotional reaction to them (12/7 in the twelve lines of F #1 and first three lines of F #2)

• and then Pucke's emotions take over as the glorious details are recounted one by one (4/16 in the remaining fourteen lines of the speech)

| 36/ Titania | What Angell wakes me from my flowry bed? | between 3.1.129 - 141 |
| 37/ Titania | Out of this wood, do not desire to goe, | between 3.1.152 - 174 |

Background: In speech #36 the love potion zapped Titania is awoken by the singing of the just transformed-into-an-Asse Bottome, and the full force of Oberon's magic potion hits straightaway. In speech #37, despite Titania's obvious charms, Bottome has expressed the desire to 'get out of this wood', something Titania will not allow.

Style: as part of a two-handed scene

Where: Titania's bower   **To Whom:** the just transformed-into-an-Asse Bottome

	speech #36, # of Lines: 6	Probable Timing: 0.20 minutes
	speech #37, # of Lines: 22	Probable Timing: 1.10 minutes

Modern Text

First Folio

36/ Titania

36/ [15] Queene as Titania

1 What Angel* wakes me from my flow'ry bed?

1 What Angell wakes me from my flowry bed?

2 I pray thee, gentle mortal*, sing again* .[†]
Mine ear* is much enamored of thy note;
And I do* love thee; therefore go* with me. .[†]

2 I pray thee⁺ gentle mortall, sing againe,
Mine eare is much enamored of thy note;
On the first view to say, to sweare⁺ I love thee.

3 So is mine eye enthralled to thy shape ; ◊
And thy fair* virtue's force (perforce) doth move me [†]
On the first view to say, to swear*, I love thee.

3 So is mine eye enthralled to thy shape,

4 And thy faire vertues force (perforce) doth move me.

37/ Titania

37/ Titania

1 Out of this wood do not desire to go*;
Thou shalt remain* here, whether thou wilt or no.

1 Out of this wood,_x do not desire to goe, ⁺
Thou shalt remaine here, whether thou wilt or no.

2 I am a spirit of no common rate;
The [△]summer still doth tend upon my state ;
And I do* love thee; therefore go* with me. .[†]

2 I am a spirit of no common rate:_x
The Summer still doth tend upon my state, ⁺
And I doe love thee; therefore goe with me,

3 I'll give thee [△]fairies to attend on thee;
And they shall fetch thee [△]jewels from the deep*,
And sing, while thou on pressed flowers dost sleep* . .[†]

Ile give thee Fairies to attend on thee;
And they shall fetch thee Jewels from the deepe,
And sing, while thou on pressed flowers dost sleepe:

4 And I will purge thy mortal* grossness* so,
That thou shalt like an aery* spirit go.

And I will purge thy mortall grossenesse so,
That thou shalt like an airie spirit go.

5 Pease°blossom*! Cobweb! Moth! Mustard°seed*!

3 Pease-blossome,⁺ Cobweb,⁺ Moth,⁺ Mustard-seede⁺!

6 Be kind* and courteous* to this [△]gentleman,
Hop in his walks* and gambol* in his eyes;
Feed* him with [△]apricocks, and [△]dewberries,

4 Be kinde and curteous to this Gentleman,
Hop in his walkes,_x and gamble in his eies, ⁺
Feede him with Apricocks, and Dewberries,

- after F #1's passionate opening (F #1, 1/1) the speech becomes emotional (0/5), with F's four sentences suggesting that the bewitched Titania is working even harder than her modern counterpart to keep everything together

- as F's peculiar placing of the penultimate line 'So is mine eye enthralled to thy shape.' is both a short sentence and unembellished, it would seem that the magic has caused her to become highly aware of the physical side of the mortal world!

- F's peculiar setting of the last two lines is usually reversed by most modern texts which follow Q1, though if she is truly shaken up the disoriented F/Q2 reading could stand

- the surround phrases seem to reinforce her physical awareness, first as noted in the previous speech
" . I am a spirit of no common rate : "
especially the second, created by the emotional semicolons
" ; therefore goe with me,/Ile give thee Fairies to attend on thee ; "

- the onrushed F #2 suggests that the bribery comes out in one long gush, much more understandable than the rather calculating stepping stones the modern texts have created by splitting F #2 in three

- not surprisingly, the speech starts out emotionally (2/8, F #1.2), which, after the calling in of her retinue (F #3), continues momentarily for the first two lines of instruction opening F #4 (1/3)

- the proposed feeding of him, the next three lines, becomes quite intellectual (6/3) as she spells out exactly what food (aphrodisiacs perhaps?) she wants (6/3), while the two-line order to prepare torches for the bedroom becomes somewhat emotional (1/2)

- however, the thought of 'To have my love to bed, and to arise' drives her into a momentary unembellished reverie, though whether quite calm or her

---

LSALT
¹⁵ this is the first time that the prefix has referred to her as Titania rather than Queene: (apart from making her fall in love with the first thing seen, how else has the potion affected her personality and behaviour?)

With purple △grapes, green* △figs, and △mulberries;
The honey*, °bags steal* from the humble-° △bees,
And for night-tapers crop their waxen thighs* ,
And light them at the fiery* °△ glow-worm's* eyes,
To have my love to bed, and to arise;
And pluck* the wings from painted △butterflies,
To fan the △moon*°beams* from his sleeping eyes*.

7 Nod to him, △elves, and do* him courtesies*.

breath being taken by the image is up to each actress to decide

• from which she recovers quickly, for the last two (sybaritic) lines of F
#4 and F #5's final short line order become passionate (3/4)

With purple Grapes, greene Figs, and Mulberries; +
The honie-bags steale from the humble Bees,
And for night-tapers crop their waxen thighes,
And light them at the fierie-Glow-wormes eyes,
To have my love to bed, and to arise: x
And plucke the wings from painted Butterflies,
To fan the Moone-beames from his sleeping eies.

5 Nod to him + Elves, and doe him curtesies.

#'s 38 - 46: THE MECHANICALS AND THE PLAYING OF THE PLAY

38/ {Bottome as} **Clowne**   **When my cue comes, call me, and I will answer.**   4.1.200 - 219

Background: Though the spell on him has been removed and he is back to his human play-rehearsal self, Bottome still has some memories of what happened when he was an 'Asse' - though it appears he's not going to voice them.

Style: solo

Where: somewhere in the woods   **To Whom:** direct audience address

# of Lines: 18   **Probable Timing:** 0.55 minutes

Modern Text

38/ {Bottome as} **Clowne**

1 When my cue comes, call me, and I will answer.
2 My next is, "Most faire Pyramus*."
3 Hey ho !
  Peter Quince!
4 Flute the bellows*-mender!
5 Snout the tinker!   Starve-
6 ling!
7 Gods my life, ◊ stol'n* hence, and left me asleep*!† I
9 have had a most rare vision.
10 I [have] had a dream*, past the wit of man, to say, what dream* it was.
11 Man is but an ᐃass*, if he go* about ['t]expound this dream*.
12 Methought I was - there is no man can tell what.
13 Me•thought I was, and me•thought I had - ◊ but man is but a patch'd fool*, if he will offer to say what me•thought I had.
14 The eye of man hath not heard, the ear* of man hath not seen, man's hand is not able to taste, his tongue to conceive, nor his heart to report, what my dream* was.
15 I will get Peter Quince to write a ballet[16] of this dream*.†
  It shall be called
16 "Bottom's* Dream*", because it hath no bottom*; and I will sing it in the latter end of a play, before the Duke.

First Folio

38/ {Bottome as} **Clowne**

1 When my cue comes, call me, and I will answer.
2 My next is, most faire Piramus.
3 Hey ho+ Peter Quince?+
4 Flute the bellowes-mender?+
5 Snout the tinker?+   Starve-
6 ling?+   Gods my life!x
7 Stolne hence, and left me asleepe: I
8 have had a most rare vision. I [ ] had a dreame, past the wit
9 of man, to say, what dreame it was.   Man is but an Asse,
10 if he goe about [to expound] this dreame.   Me-thought I
11 was, there is no man can tell what.   Me-thought I was,
12 and me-thought I had.   But man is but a patch'd foole,
13 if he will offer to say,x what me-thought I had.   The eye of
14 man hath not heard, the eare of man hath not seen, mans hand is not able to taste, his tongue to conceive, nor his heart to report, what my dreame was.
  I will get Peter Quince to write a ballet of this dreame, because it hath no bottome; and I will sing it in the latter end of a play, before the Duke.

The highly unusual proliferation of very short sentences is a sure sign that Bottome is unable to deflect what he has undergone with his usual long and complex thoughts.

• in addition, the very small scale releases scattered throughout the speech suggest that Bottome is still lost in his world of (Fairy) wonders

• the factual/intellectual releases are almost completely restricted to the 'real' world of his friends (F #2-6, 7/2); while the mix of intellectual and emotional passion focuses on the forthcoming performance (5/4, F #14) . . .

• . . . the recollection of his 'rare vision' is almost completely emotional (1/9, F #7-13)

• after the quiet awaking (F #1), the majority of the other unembellished lines relate to what he has just experienced "I have had a most rare vision." and, with the exception of the one word 'foole' "Me-thought I was, there is no man can tell what. Me-thought I was, and me-thought I had. But man is but a patch'd foole, if he will offer to say, what me-thought I had."

• however, with the exception of the word Duke, the last line of F #14 and all of F's final #15, which put forward the possibility of his singing in the forthcoming play are also unembellished (the dream of possible success almost taking his breath away perhaps?)

---

[16] F1/Qq = 'ballet', F4 and some modern texts = 'ballad'

17

Per-

adventure, to make it the more gracious, I shall sing it
at her death .

15

Per-

adventure, to make it the more gracious, I shall sing it
at her death .

- the surround phrases underscore the most important
moment within each of the three worlds, first his being
abandoned by his friends coupled with a syntactically incorrect
linking to what happened thereafter 'Stolne hence and left me
asleepe : I have had a most rare vision . ', and then the hopes
of theatrical success (perhaps leading to his becoming one of
the Duke's favoured actors) ' ; and I will sing it in the latter
end of a play, before the Duke . '

39/ {Quince as} **Prologue:**   **If we offend, it is with our good will.**   5.1.108 - 117
40/ {Quince as} **Prologue:**   **Gentles, perchance you wonder at this show,**   5.1.127 - 151

Background: Despite Philostrate/Egeus' objections (speech #5 above). 'Pyramus and Thisbe' has been 'preferred' as the wedding evening's celebrations. Speech #39 is Quince's first presentation about the company and their purpose - and he makes an absolute hash of it as all the royal/aristocratic party note once he leaves the stage. Amazingly, he immediately returns and, in speech #40, makes a splendidly coherent introduction to both the cast of characters and the action of the play

Style: public addresses, to a large group

Where: somewhere in the palace where a post-supper pre-wedding bed entertainment is to be offered   **To Whom:** at least the seven royals/aristocrats plus court members, in front of at least the five members of his company

speech #39, # of Lines: 10   **Probable Timing: 0.35 minutes**
speech #40, # of Lines: 25   **Probable Timing: 1.15 minutes**

Modern Text

39/ {Quince as} **Prologue**

1   If we offend, it is with our good will .
2   That you should think* , we come not to offend,
      But with good will .
3   To show our simple skill,
      That is the true beginning of our end .
4   Consider then, we come but in despite* .
5   We do not come, as minding to content you ,
      Our true intent is.
          All for your delight
6   We are not here* .
7   That you should here repent you,
      The Actors are at hand; and by their show,
      You shall know all, that you are like to know.

First Folio

39/ {Quince as} **Prologue**

1   If we offend, it is with our good will.
2   That you should thinke, we come not to offend,
      But with good will.
3   To shew our simple skill,
      That is the true beginning of our end.
4   Consider then, we come but in despight.
5   We do not come, as minding to content you,
      Our true intent is.
          All for your delight,x
6   We are not heere.
7   That you should here repent you,
      The Actors are at hand; and by their show,
      You shall know all, that you are like to know.

Apart from the appalling punctuation so wonderfully indicative of Quince's nervousness that most modern texts set as is, the speech is startling in that it is virually unembellished (just 1/2 scattered throughout the ten lines).

- the shortness of the illogical middle sentences, F #2-6, underscores Quince's inability to keep any coherent thought together

- the last moment seems to be one of despair as Quince passes on the responsibility of any success to the shoulders of his actors, via an emotionally (semicolon) created, unembellished, monosyllabic surround phrase '; and by their show,/You shall know all, that you are like to know."

Modern Text

40) {Quince as} **Prologue**

1 Gentles, perchance you wonder at this show;
But wonder on till truth make all things plain* .

2 This man is Pyramus*, if you would know;
This beauteous ^lady, Thisby is certain* .

3 This man, with lime* and rough-cast, doth present
Wall, that vile ^Wall, which did these lovers sunder ;
And through ^Wall's chink, poor souls*, they are content
To whisper .

4   At the which let no man wonder .

5 This man, with ^lantern*, dog, and bush of thorn*,
Presenteth ^Moon*shine ; ◊for if you will know,*
By moon*shine did these ^lovers think* no scorn*
To meet at Ninus' tomb*, there, there, to woo* . †

6 This [grisly*] beast, which Lion* hight by name
The trusty Thisby, coming* first by night,
Did scare* away, or rather did affright ;
And as she fled, her mantle she did fall,
Which Lion* vile with bloody mouth did stain* .

7 Anon comes Pyramus*, sweet youth and tall,
And finds* his [trusty] Thisby's* ^mantle slain*;
Whereat, with blade, with bloody blameful* blade,
He bravely broach'd his boiling bloody* breast;
And Thisby, tarrying in ^mulberry shade,
His dagger drew, and died .

8   For all the rest,
Let Lion*, Moon*shine, Wall, and ^lovers twain*
At large discourse, while here they do* remain* .

While the speech opens in the same quiet vein as the disastrous #39 above (F #1, 0/1), as he delves into what are for him magical details of the play so F shows his energy (and courage?) growing to a triumphant concluding finish.

• as the 'leading' actors are introduced, via two emotionally created surround phrases (F #2)
" . This man is Piramus, if you would know ; /This beauteous Lady, Thisby is certaine ."
so the intellect starts to grow (3/1)

• the introduction of, to the company at least, the wondrous device of 'Wall' (F #4) seems very important with

a/ the first sentence being emotional (0/2)
b/ F #3's final line, explaining the 'chink', presented as a surround phrase
c/ F #4, advising against 'wonder', being both short and unembellished
": And through walls chink (poor soules) they are content /To whisper ."

• and then, with the introduction of 'moone-shine and 'Lyon' (F #5-6), Quince's emotion takes over, (5/9) with the final special effect once again presented as an (emotional) surround phrase
"; Which Lyon vile with bloody mouth did staine ."

• but, with the return of Pyramus and Thisby, so his intellect matches his emotions (F #7, 5/4)

• while the almost "ta-da!" rousing summary re-introducing the support actors (F #8, 5/4) starts intellectually (5/2 in the first line and a half) and finishes emotionally (0/2 in the last line)

First Folio

40) {Quince as} **Prologue**

1 Gentles, perchance you wonder at this show, +
But wonder on, x till truth make all things plaine .

2 This man is Piramus, if you would know;
This beauteous Lady, Thisby is certaine .

3 This man, with lyme and rough-cast, doth present
Wall, that vile wall, which did these lovers sunder : x
And through walls chink, x(poor soules)x they are content
To whisper .

4   At the which,x let no man wonder .

5 This man, with Lanthorne, dog, and bush of thorne,
Presenteth moone-shine.

6   For if you will know,
By moone-shine did these Lovers thinke no scorne
To meet at Ninus toombe, there, there + to wooe :
This [grizy] beast,x (which Lyon hight by name)x
The trusty Thisby, comming first by night,
Did scarre away, or rather did affright ,+
And as she fled, her mantle she did fall; x
Which Lyon vile with bloody mouth did staine.

7 Anon comes Piramus, sweet youth and tall,
And findes his [ ] Thisbies Mantle slaine;
Whereat, with blade, with bloody blamefull blade,
He bravely broacht his boiling bloudy breast; +
And Thisby, tarrying in Mulberry shade,
His dagger drew, and died.

8   For all the rest,
Let Lyon, Moone-shine, Wall, and Lovers twaine,x
At large discourse, while here they doe remaine.

41/ ⟨Snout as⟩ **Wall**   **In this same Interlude, it doth befall,**   5.1.155 - 164

Background: His single speech within 'Pyramus and Thisbe'.

Style: public address, to a large group

Where: somewhere in the palace where a post-supper pre-wedding bed entertainment is to be offered   **To Whom:** at least the seven royals/aristocrats, in front of at least the five members of his company and whatever court members there may be present

# of Lines: 10   **Probable Timing: 0.35 minutes**

Modern Text

41/ ⟨Snout as⟩ **Wall**

1   In this same ᐃenterlude* it doth befall
    That I, one Snout* by name, present a wall ;
    And such a wall, as I would have you thinke* ,
    That had in it a crannied hole or chink* ,
    Through which the ᐃlovers, Pyramus* and Thisby* ,
    Did whisper often, very secretly .

2   This loam* , this rough-cast, and this stone doth show
    That I am that same ᐃwall; the truth is so ; ◊
    And this the cranny is, right and sinister,
    Through which the fearfull* ᐃlovers are to whisper .

First Folio

41/ ⟨Snout as⟩ **Wall**

1   In this same Interlude,x it doth befall,x
    That I, one Snowt x (by name)x present a wall : x
    And such a wall, as I would have you thinke,
    That had in it a crannied hole or chinke : x
    Through which the Lovers, Piramus and Thisbie +
    Did whisper often, very secretly .

2   This loame, this rough-cast, and this stone doth shew,x
    That I am that same Wall; the truth is so .

3   And this the cranny is, right and sinister,
    Through which the fearefull Lovers are to whisper .

- F's extra breaths (marked , x), especially the two in the first line, points to Snout starting out somewhat nervously, especially with the overspelling of his own name as 'Snowt'

- this nervousness seems to be supported by the fact that F #1 switches back and forth between facts (2/0 in the first two lines and again in the last two lines) and emotion (0/2 in F #1's middle two lines)

- as opposed to the single sentence of most modern texts (mt. #2), the presenting of the last four lines as two sentences (F #2-3) suggests, that whether nervous or no, in ending Snout is taking more pains to point out the special effects associated with his costume (F #2) and the clever device of his fingers presenting 'the cranny' (F #3) than his modern counterpart

---

42/ ⟨Snug as⟩ **Lyon**   **You Ladies, you, whose gentle harts do feare**   5.1.219 - 226

Background: His single speech within 'Pyramus and Thisbe'. Snug is a character who speaks virtually nothing in the rest of the play (and when he does it's always in prose), and who admits he's 'slow of learning'. He finally comes into his own when performing as the Lion in the play Pyramus and Thisbe before the three royal and aristocratic couples. Originally given no text, just extempore roaring, the rhythmic unblemished tidiness of the speech suggests that here Snug surpasses everyone's expectations as a performer, perhaps even his own.

Style: public address, to a large group

Where: somewhere in the palace where a post-supper pre-wedding bed entertainment is to be offered   **To Whom:** at least the seven royals/aristocrats, in front of at least the five members of his company and whatever court members there may be present

# of Lines: 8   **Probable Timing: 0.30 minutes**

Modern Text

42/ ⟨Snug as⟩ **Lyon**

1   You, ᐃladies, you, whose gentle hearts* do fear*
    The smallest monstrous mouse that creeps* on floor* ,
    May now, perchance, both quake and tremble here* ,
    When ᐃlion rough in wildest rage doth roar* .

First Folio

42/ ⟨Snug as⟩ **Lyon**

1   You + Ladies, you x (whose gentle harts do feare
    The smallest monstrous mouse that creepes on floore)x
    May now + perchance, both quake and tremble heere,
    When Lion rough in wildest rage doth roare.

- F's Snug presents story and self quite speedily, especially when the extra commas added by most modern texts (marked + in the F text) are discounted

- the extra spellings, most noticeably at the end of each line of F #1 as he introduces the 'Lyon' (2/5), underscore both Snug's emotions and the simple story-telling of the speech: however, F #2's

{ctd. over}

2   Then know that I, [as] Snug the joiner* am
A lion fell, nor else no lions dam,
For, if I should, as lion, come in strife
Into this place, 'twere pity* [on] my life.

presentation of self becomes much more factual (controlled?) (5/2) and the whole finishes via an F only colon in a triumphant elegant two-line flourish

2   Then know that I, [one] Snug the Joyner am
A Lion fell, nor else no Lions dam :$_x$
For + if I should + as Lion + come in strife
Into this place, 'twere pittie [of] my life.

43/ {Bottome as} **Piramus**   **O grim lookt night, ô night with hue so blacke,**   5.1.170 - 181

Background: His opening speech as Pyramus.

Style: public address, to a large group

Where: somewhere in the palace where a post-supper pre-wedding bed entertainment is to be offered   **To Whom:** at least the seven royals/aristocrats, in front of at least the five members of his company and whatever court members there may be present

# of Lines: 12   **Probable Timing: 0.40 minutes**

Modern Text

43/ {Bottome as} **Piramus**

1 O grim-look'd night! †
2   ^O night with hue so black*! †
3 O night, which ever art when day is not ! †
4 O night, ^O night! alack*, alack*, alack* ,
    I fear* my Thisby's* promise is forgot !
5 And thou, ^O wall, ^O sweet, [^O] lovely wall,
    That stands between* her father's ground and mine!
    Thou wall, ^O wall, ^O sweet and lovely wall,
    Show me thy chink*, to blink* through with mine eyne* !
6 Thanks* courteous wall ; ◊Jove shield thee well for this!
7 But what see I?
8   No Thisby* do* I see .
9 O wicked wall, through whom I see no bliss* ! †
10 Curs'd be thy stones for thus deceiving me* !

First Folio

43/ {Bottome as} **Piramus**

1 O grim lookt night, + ô night with hue so blacke, +
    O night, which ever art, when day is not :$_x$ +
    O night, ô night, + alacke, alacke, alacke,
    I feare my Thisbies promise is forgot. +
2 And thou + ô wall, [thou sweet+ [and] lovely wall,
    That stands betweene her fathers ground and mine, +
    Thou wall, ô wall, ô sweet and lovely wall,
    Shew me thy chinke, to blinke through with mine eine . +
3 Thankes courteous wall.
4   Jove shield thee well for this. +
5 But what see I?
6   No Thisbie doe I see .
7 O wicked wall, through whom I see no blisse .
8 Curst be thy stones for thus deceiving mee . +

- save for the mention of Thisbie (short-spelled each time, as if he treasures her name, perhaps?), the speech is totally emotional (2/13)

- yet it need not be as flamboyant as most modern texts suggest, for their nine exclamation marks are not to be found in F or Q (unlike speech #44 below)

- this is especially so in the first four lines where most modern texts have added five of the nine, creating much more bombast than was originally set

- another indication that might suggest Bottome 'flows' more, and is not so deliberate at the start of his performance, is F #1's onrush, a clue removed by most modern texts which split F #1 into four

- while there is earlier verbal repetition and alliteration ('O night', 'alacke' and 'o wall'), the moment he really begins to enjoy himself might be found in the (overly?) clever within line rhyme in F #2's last line ('chinke' and 'blinke')

44/ {Bottome as} **Piramus: Sweet Moone, I thank thee for thy sunny beames,** 5.1.272 - 287 **45/ O wherefore Nature, did'st thou Lions frame?** 5.1.291 - 306

Background: Further speeches as Pyramus.

Style: public address, to a large group

Where: somewhere in the palace where a post-supper pre-wedding bed entertainment is to be offered **To Whom:** at least the seven royals/aristocrats, in front of at least the five members of his company and whatever court members there may be present

Probable Timing: 0.40 minutes	speech #44, # of Lines: 12
Probable Timing: 0.40 minutes	speech #45, # of Lines: 11

Modern Text

44/ {Bottome as} **Piramus**

1 Sweet Moon*, I thank thee for thy sunny beams*;
   I thank* thee Moon*, for shining now so bright ;
   For by thy gracious, golden, glittering [gleams]17 ,
   I trust to [take] of truest [Thisby*] sight.

2 But stay ! +

3   O spite*!

4 But mark*, poor* ^knight,
   What dreadful dole is here* !

5 Eyes do you see?

6 How can it be?

7 O dainty ^duck*! O dear*!

8 Thy mantle good,
   What stain'd with blood?

9 Approach* [ye] Furies fell !

10 O Fates! come, come,
   Cut thread* and thrum,
   Quail* , crush, conclude, and quell !

First Folio

44/ {Bottome as} **Piramus**

1 Sweet Moone, I thank thee for thy sunny beames, +
   I thanke thee Moone, for shining now so bright : x
   For by thy gracious, golden, glittering [beames],
   I trust to [taste] of truest [Thisbies] sight.

2 But stay : + O spight! but marke, poore Knight,
   What dreadfull dole is heere? +

3 Eyes do you see! x
        How can it be! x

4 O dainty Ducke : + O Deere!

5

6 Thy mantle good; x what staind with blood! x

7 Approch [you] Furies fell : +
   O Fates! come, come : x Cut thred and thrum,
   Quaile, crush, conclude, and quell . +

Quince offered earlier to write a passage with lines alternating in syllable length of 'eight and six', and this is how F1/Qq print it for speeches #44-6. Despite this, most modern texts rework the (shaded) section according to its rhyme scheme and the extra line breaks so caused create an entirely different rhythm for the speaker from that the source text suggests, often creating a pattern that a current audience laughs at, rather than as originally set where an audience would often be both moved by and laugh with the characters at one and the same time.

• unlike the previous speech, here the six exclamation marks (extraordinarily unusual in an Elizabethan/Jacobean text) suggest that Bottome is giving full rein to Pyramus' passionate release

• and the surround phrases seem to underscore the special moments of bombast, as with '. But stay : O spight!'; '. O dainty Ducke : O Deere!'; '. Approch you Furies fell : /O Fates! come, come :'

• in direct contrast, Bottome's penchant for underplaying certain dramatic moments (see speeches #24-26 above) is seen here at the most theatrical of moments, the spying of Thisby's blood-stained mantle, with the unembellished and short sentences F #3, #4, and #6 – whether an 'acting' trick or no, it certainly marks the character's most personal of moments

• thus the happy opening of the speech starts emotionally (1/4 in the first two lines), then becomes quietly passionate (1/1 in the last two lines of F #1): the discovery of the mantle is a mixture of passion (4/4) and unembellished lines F #2-6, while the final act of defiance is splendidly intellectual (3/1, F #7)

---

17 F1/Qq = 'beames', most modern texts = 'gleams' (to preserve the alliterative quality of the line - though, of course, in not keeping to it, Bottome may have momentarily forgotten the correct word): also, what is quite peculiar, here the modern texts alter the word to create alliteration, but in the very next line they go back to Qq and destroy Ff's alliteration of 'trust/taste/truest'

{ctd. over}

First Folio

45/ {Bottome as} **Piramus**

1
O + wherefore + Nature, did'st thou Lions frame?
Since Lion vilde hath heere deflour'd my deere : x
Which is:+ no, no, which was the fairest Dame
That liv'd, that lov'd, that lik'd, that look'd with cheere.

2
Come teares, confound: x Out + sword, and wound
The pap of Piramus: x
I, that left pap, where heart doth hop;
Thus dye I, thus, thus, thus.

3
Now am I dead, now am I fled,+ my soule is in the sky,
Tongue+ lose thy light, Moone+ take thy flight,
Now dye, dye, dye, dye, dye.

Modern Text

45/ {Bottome as} **Piramus**

1
O, wherefore, Nature, did'st thou ⁴lions frame?
Since ⁴lion [vile*] hath here* deflowr'd* my dear* ;
Which is - no, no - which was the fairest ⁴dame
That liv'd, that lov'd, that lik'd, that look'd with cheer* .

2
Come tears* , confound,
Out, sword, and wound
The pap of Piramus*;
Ay*, that left pap,
Where heart doth hop . †
Thus die* I, thus, thus, thus . †

4
Now am I dead,
Now am I fled; my soul* is in the sky . †

5
Tongue, lose thy light,
Moon* , take thy flight,
Now die* , die* , die* , die* , die* .

• with Pyramus' attack on 'Nature' for creating 'Lions', Bottome starts out passionately (4/4, F #1); he becomes slightly more controlled as he draws his sword (2/1, the first two lines of F #2); and then turns almost totally emotional in the self-stabbing and farewell (1/8, the last four lines of the speech)

• the tendency toward dramatic quiet (noted in speeches #2-6 and #44) can still be seen here in the unembellished monosyllabic dramatic moments of where to stab, 'I, that left pap, where heart doth hop' and death 'Now am I dead, now am I fled,'

• as in speech #44, the surround phrases seem to mark the moments of bombast, ': Which is : ' and the whole of F #2, though, since in this speech there are no exclamation marks, the scale of release may not now be so great as before .

• ' . . save for the ' ; Thus dye I, thus, thus, thus . ', as he begins to stab himself: this is heightened even more by being both monosyllabic and ungrammatically linked to the previous thoughts (preceded as it is by the emotional semicolon) instead of being set as a separate sentence as it is in most modern texts (mt. #3)

• the onrushed F #3 provides Bottome a much finer free-flowing finale than most modern texts which split the sentence in two

46/ {Flute as} **Thisby**   **Asleepe my Love?**   5.1.324 - 347

Background: His last speech as Thisbe.

Style: public address, to a large group

Where: somewhere in the palace where a post-supper pre-wedding bed entertainment is to be offered   **To Whom:** at least the seven royals/aristocrats, in front of at least the five members of his company and whatever court members there may be present

Probable Timing: 0.50 minutes   **# of Lines: 16**

Modern Text

46/ {Flute as} **Thisby**

1 Asleep*, my △love?
2   What, dead, my △dove?
3 O Pyramus* arise !†
4 Speak*, △speak*!
5   Quite dumb*?:
6 Dead, dead?   A tomb*
7 Must cover thy sweet eyes.
8 These △lily* △lips,
   This cherry nose,
   These yellow △cowslip cheeks*,
   Are gone, are gone ! †
9 Lovers, make moan*;
   His eyes were green* as △leeks* .
10 O △Sisters △Three,
   Come, come to me ,*
   With hands as pale as △milk*;
   Lay them in gore,
   Since you have shore
   With shears* his thread* of silk* .
11 Tongue, not a word ! †
12 Come, trusty sword :
   Come, blade, my breast* imbrue !† 18
13 And farewell*, friends,
   Thus Thisby* ends;
   Adieu, adieu, adieu .

First Folio

46/ {Flute as} **Thisby**

1 Asleepe + my Love?
2   What, dead + my Dove?
3 O Piramus arise :
   Speake, Speake . +
4   Quite dumbe?
5   Dead, dead?
6   A tombe
   Must cover thy sweet eyes.
7 These Lilly Lips, this cherry nose,
   These yellow Cowslip cheekes+
   Are gone, are gone : Lovers+ make mone : x
   His eyes were greene as Leekes .
8 O sisters three, come, come to mee,
   With hands as pale as Milke,+
   Lay them in gore, since you have shore
   With sheeres,x his thred of silke .
9 Tongue+ not a word : + Come+ trusty sword :
   Come+ blade, my brest imbrue : +
   And farewell+ friends, thus Thisbie ends;
   Adieu, adieu, adieu .

As noted in speech #44, F/Q's original line structure offers a rhythm pattern likely to earn a sympathetic response from both onstage and offstage audiences, a pattern much different than the more obvious rhyming structure set by most modern texts.

• that the speech can be played as a wonderful aria can be seen in
  a/ the short sentences opening the speech (F #1-6), which provide an enormous series of quick acting switches
  b/ the fact that so many of the long-spelled words come at the end of phrases and/or lines seems to be great encouragement to let loose verbally, especially in the four sentences occupying line three (end of F #3 through to F #6), and sentences F #7-8

• the innocent opening of the speech is intellectual (F #1-2 and the first line of F #3)

• the realisation that something is wrong and discovering that Pyramus is dead becomes emotional (0/4, the last line of F #3 through to F #6)

• the farewell to Pyramus (beloved?) features becomes passionate (5/5, F #7)

• the appeal for the fates to come and take 'her' is emotional once more (1/4, F #8)

• while the stabbing and farewell is a fine mix of intellect (F #9, 2/0, lines one and three) and calm unembellishment (lines two and four), all heightened by the fact that the sentence is completely made up of surround phrases

• as with Pyramus/Bottome's speech #44, the surround phrases point to where bombast might be heard, as already noted for F #9, and the plea of F #3 ('. O Piramus arise :/Speake, Speake .) and with the appeal to the audience ': Lovers make mone : ')

• and there may even be a 'touch of the Bottome's', with the two direct references to death being unembellished, F #5's 'Dead, dead?' and F #8's 'Lay them in gore, since you have shore', as is the moment of stabbing 'Come blade, my breast imbrue; and the farewell 'Adieu, adieu, :' (dramatic underplaying once more perhaps?)

---

18 most modern texts add a stage direction that Flute/Thisby stabs him/herself

#'s 47 - 48: THE END

47/ Pucke   Now the hungry Lyons rores,   5.1.371 - 390

Background: With the three newly married couples at last away to their beds, and the Mechanicals having left the palace, Pucke appears, setting the final scene and explaining why he is here - and for the first time speaks magic throughout without any breaks (hence the bolded text).

Style: solo, in the pattern of magic [19]

Where: wherever in the palace the post-supper pre-wedding bed entertainment has played   **To Whom:** direct audience address

# of Lines: 20   **Probable Timing: 1.00 minutes**

Modern Text

47/ {Robin as} **Pucke**

1
Now the hungry △[lion]* roars*],
And the △wolf* [behowls] the △moon ;
Whilst* the heavy ploughman snores,
All with weary task* foredone .

2
Now the wasted brands do* glow,
Whilst the screech*-owl*, [screeching*] loud,
Puts the wretch that lies in woe
In remembrance of a shroud* .

3
Now it is the time of night
That the graves, all gaping wide*,
Every one lets forth his sprite* ,
In the △church-way paths to glide .

4
And we △fairies, that do run*
By the triple Hecat's* team*
From the presence of the △sun* ,
Following darkness* like a dream ,
Now are frolic* . †
            Not a △mouse
Shall disturb* this hallowed house .

5

6
I am sent with broom* before,
To sweep the dust behind* the door* .

First Folio

47/ {Robin as} **Pucke**

1
Now the hungry [Lyons rores],
And the Wolfe [beholds] the Moone :ₓ
Whilest the heavy ploughman snores,
All with weary taske fore-done .

2
Now the wasted brands doe glow,
Whil'st the scritch-owle, [scritching] loud,
Puts the wretch that lies in woe,ₓ
In remembrance of a shrowd .

3
Now it is the time of night,ₓ
That the graves, all gaping wide,
Every one lets forth his spright,
In the Church-way paths to glide .

4
And we Fairies, that do runne,ₓ
By the triple Hecates teame,ₓ
From the presence of the Sunne,
Following darkenesse like a dreame,
Now are frollicke ; not a Mouse
Shall disturbe this hallowed house .

5
I am sent with broome before,
To sweep the dust behinde the doore .

Once more the speech is spoken as the potentially more mischievous side of himself, the one known as Pucke.

• the one surround phrase, created as it is in part by the emotional semicolon, underscores the purpose of the Fairies' visit to the palace
" ; not a Mouse/Shall disturbe this hallowed house . "

• the speech starts passionately (3/4, F # 1), but as his mind moves towards 'the wretch' fearing the 'shrowd', so emotions begin to arise (0/3, F #2)

• and the one extended moment of calm, dealing with the time of night when each grave 'lets forth his spright' (0/1, the four lines of F #3), reflects his earlier fears of the 'damned spirits all', as expressed in an entirely different way speech #29 above

• however, realising his strength in numbers - 'we Fairies' - allows time for 'frollicke', so his emotions come into play once more (4/8, F #4)

• the final couplet-enhanced statement of what his part in preparing the blessing is to be is completely emotional (0/3, F #5)

48/ Robin   **If we shadowes have offended,**   5.1.423 - 438

Background: With the blessing of three newly married couples complete the Fairies have departed, leaving Pucke, as his kindlier alter ego Robin, to finish the play.

Style: solo, written in part in the pattern of magic (the bolded text) [20]

Where: wherever in the palace the post-supper pre-wedding bed entertainment has played   **To Whom:** direct audience address

# of Lines: 16   **Probable Timing: 0.50 minutes**

Modern Text	First Folio
48/ Robin	**48/ Robin**
1 If we shadows* have offended, Think* but this, and all is mended, That you have but slumbered here* While these visions did appear* .	1 If we shadowes have offended, Thinke but this x (and all is mended)x That you have but slumbred heere,x While these visions did appeare .
2 And this weak* and idle theme* , No more yielding* but a dream* , Gentles, do* not reprehend.	2 And this weake and idle theame, No more yeelding but a dreame, Gentles, doe not reprehend.
3 If you pardon, we will mend.	3 If you pardon, we will mend.
4 And, as I am an honest Puck* , If we have unearned luck* Now to scape the △ serpent's tongue, We will make amends ere long : Else the Puck* a liar* call.	4 And + as I am an honest Pucke. If we have unearned lucke,x Now to scape the Serpents tongue, We will make amends ere long : Else the Pucke a lyar call.
5 So, good night unto you all.	5 So + good night unto you all .
6 ' Give me your hands, if we be friends, And Robin shall restore amends .	6 Give me your hands, if we be friends, And Robin shall restore amends .

F's othography underscores the importance for the actor of Robin to seek for good future actor-audience relationships.

- the two unembellished short sentences point to how calmly the actor is attempting to deal with the audience (whether out of necessity, seduction or fear is up to each actor to decide), assuring them
 "If you pardon, we will mend."
 and the wish for the audience's well-being
 "So good night unto you all."

- and the other two unembellished lines reinforce the relationship further - F #4's 'We will make amends ere long'; and the opening of F #6, 'Give me your hands, if we be friends,'

- the opening attempt to apologise for any offence that might have been offered to the audience is highly emotional (0/9 in the seven lines of F #1-2)

- however, following F #3's unembellished request for pardon, the extra assurance (also unembellished) that 'We will make amends ere long' is found in the middle of a passionate five line F #4 (3/4)

- which leads to very careful final farewell-appeal (1/0, F #5-6)

---

[20] see Appendix 3

[21] as he refers to his 'honesty', so the magic pattern of the speech slips for a moment

[22] the pattern of the magic/ritual (see Appendix 3) is dispensed with for the final couplet

THE MERCHANT OF VENICE

SPEECHES IN ORDER	TIME	PAGE
#'s 1 - 3: The Friends of and Character of Anthonio		
1/ **Solanio** — Your minde is tossing on the Ocean,	1.40	152
2/ **Anthonio** — Marke you this Bassanio,	0.40	154
3/ **Anthonio** — But little: I am arm'd and well prepar'd.	0.55	155
#'s 4 - 6: Bassanio In Love		
4/ **Bassanio** — Tis not unknowne to you Anthonio	0.45	156
5/ **Bassanio** — In my schoole dayes, when I had lost one shaft	0.45	156
6/ **Bassanio** — In Belmont is a Lady richly left,	0.50	157
#'s 7 - 9: Portia's Dilemma: The Foolish Suitors		
7/ **Portia** — What warmth is there in {my} affection. . . .	2.35	158
8/ **Morochus** — Let's see once more this saying grav'd in gold.	1.40	161
9/ **Arragon** — I am enjoynd by oath to observe three things;	2.35	163
#'s 10 - 15: Love Eventually Triumphs		
10/ **Portia** — I pray you tarrie, pause a day or two	1.10	165
11/ **Portia** — Away then, I am lockt in one of them,	1.10	167
12/ **Bassanio** — What finde I here? /Faire Portias counterfeit.	1.45	168
13/ **Portia** — You see [my] Lord Bassanio where [I] stand,	1.15	170
14/ **Lorenzo** — How sweet the moone-light sleepes . . .	0.50	171
15/ **Lorenzo** — The reason is, your spirits are attentive:	1.00	172
#'s 16 - 17: Those Refusing to Stay with Shylocke		
16/ **Clowne** — Certainely, my conscience will serve me to run	1.30	173
17/ **Jessica** — I am sorry thou wilt leave my Father so,	0.50	175
#'s 18 - 21: The Character of Shylocke		
18/ **Shylocke** — Anthonio is a good man. My meaning in saying	1.00	176
19/ **Jew** — How like a fawning publican he lookes.	0.40	177
20/ **Shylocke** — Signior Anthonio, many a time and oft	1.10	178
21/ **Shylocke** — What's{a man's flesh} good for?	1.00	180
# 22: Anthonio's Dilemma		
22/ **Jew** — Jaylor, looke to him, tell not me of mercy,	0.50	182

SPEECHES BY GENDER

		Speech #(s)
SPEECHES FOR WOMEN (7)		
Portia	Traditional & Today: young woman of marriageable age	#7, #10, #11, #13, #25, #26
Jessica	Traditional & Today: young Jewish woman of marriageable age	#17
SPEECHES FOR EITHER GENDER (2)		
Solanio	Traditional: male, any age Today: any gender, any age, probably close in age to Anthonio	#1
Duke	Traditional: older male Today: any gender, possessing great authority	#23
SPEECHES FOR MEN (17)		
Anthonio	Traditional & Today: man of early middle age, older than Bassanio	#2, #3
Bassanio	Traditional & Today: young man of marriageable age	#4, #5, #6, #12
Morochus	Traditional: a brash man of colour Today: as above, the key to his failure and deserved mockery is his testosterone driven behaviour rather than his race	#8
Arragon	Traditional & Today: older man, of academic bent	#9
Lorenzo	Traditional & Today: young-(early ?) middle age man	#14, #15
Clowne	Traditional & Today: male of any age (with father still alive)	#16
Shylocke/Jew	Traditional: initially a comedic figure, often with a red wig, the character has become, probably incorrectly, a figure of wronged dignity Today: older Jewish male, with a daughter of marriageable age	#18, #19, #20, #21, #22, #24

#'s 23 - 26: The Trial			
23/ Duke	Make roome, and let him stand before our face.	1.00	183
24/ Jew	I have possest your grace of what I purpose,	1.30	184
25/ Portia	The quality of mercy is not strain'd,	1.10	185
26/ Portia	Tarry a little, there is something else,	0.55	187

THE MERCHANT OF VENICE

#'s 1- 3: THE FRIENDS AND CHARACTER OF ANTHONIO

1/ Solanio   **Your minde is tossing on the Ocean,**   1.1.8 - 41

Background: The merchant Anthonio has admitted to his friends 'I know not why I am so sad', and the following is an attempt by one of his friends to cheer/console him. One
note: this speech is a combination of lines from both Solanio and his fellow merchant Salarino - the shifts being marked 'ψ'.

Style: part of a three-handed scene

Where: unspecified   **To Whom:** Anthonio, in front of Salarino, a fellow merchant

# of Lines: 33   **Probable Timing :1.40 minutes**

Modern Text

1/ Solanio

1
Your mind* is tossing on the △ocean,
There where your △argosies with portly sail*
Like △signiors and rich △burghers* on the flood,
Or as it were the △pageants of the sea,
Do over*peer* the petty* △traffickers*
That curtsy* to them, do them reverence,
As they fly* by them with their woven wings.

2ψ Believe* me, sir, had I such venture forth,
The better part of my affections, would
Be with my hopes abroad.

3   I should be still

Plucking the grass* to know where sits the wind*,
Peering in △maps for ports and piers* and roads* ;
And every object that might make me fear*
Misfortune to my ventures, out of doubt
Would make me sad.

4ψ   My wind* cooling my broth
Would blow me to an △ague, when I thought
What harm* a wind* too great might do* at sea.

5 I should not see the sandy* hour*-glass* run*
But I should think* of shallows and of flats,
And see my wealthy Andrew [dock'd] in sand,
Vailing her high top lower then her ribs
To kiss* her burial*.†

        Should I go* to △church

6
And see the holy edifice of stone,
And not bethink* me straight of dangerous rocks,

First Folio

1/ Solanio

1
Your minde is tossing on the Ocean,
There where your Argosies with portly saile
Like Signiors and rich Burgers on the flood,
Or as it were the Pageants of the sea,
Do over-peere the pettie Traffiquers
That curtsie to them, do them reverence +
As they flye by them with their woven wings.

2ψ Beleeve me + sir, had I such venture forth,
The better part of my affections, would
Be with my hopes abroad.

3   I should be still

Plucking the grasse to know where sits the winde,
Peering in Maps for ports,x and peers,x and rodes : x
And every object that might make me feare
Misfortune to my ventures, out of doubt
Would make me sad.

4ψ   My winde cooling my broth,x
Would blow me to an Ague, when I thought
What harme a winde too great might doe at sea.

5 I should not see the sandie houre-glasse runne,x
But I should thinke of shallows,x and of flats,
And see my wealthy Andrew [docks] in sand,
Vailing her high top lower then her ribs
To kisse her buriall; should I goe to Church
And see the holy edifice of stone,
And not bethinke me straight of dangerous rocks,
Which touching but my gentle Vessels side

This is a combination of speeches by two characters, Solanio and Salarino. There is little structural difference between the F and modern settings, with just the longer F #5 being split into two by most modern texts. However, F's orthography suggests some interesting shifts in the attempt to cheer Anthonio up.

• F #1 is the only sentence in which there are more capital letters than longer spellings (6/5), suggesting that Solanio is quite passionately taken with the images he is creating – rather interestingly so since they reflect a belief in a class system even amongst ships! and especially so since most of the capitals are in the first four lines establishing the hierarchy, with the emotional spellings coming after as he envisages the respect the better sort of ship commands

• after this, emotion dominates (6/22 in twenty-six lines), which suggests Solanio becomes less intellectually and more personally involved as he explores the fine details of potential financial loss

• and the outpouring seems to be spontaneous rather than specific, for there are only two pieces of major punctuation in the speech, and no surround phrases

• the five extra breath-thoughts in F #3-5 (marked,x) suggest that, in focusing in on small details not so singled out by his modern counterpart, Solanio is working much harder than might be necessary – whether to joke Anthonio out of his sadness, or whether because he is caught up in the lurid descriptions is up to each actor to explore: and the orthographic details both in F #4, the preamble to, and the onrushed F #5, the shipwreck sentence (split in two by most modern texts), reinforce this idea, for it is here that the images seem to bite home most with the greatest fears being emotionally highlighted (1/10 F #4 plus the first four and half lines of F #5, seven lines in all)

• seven of the ten releases are found in three clusters, two following hard on one another (ending sentence #4 and starting sentence #5) viz. 'What harme a winde too great might doe at sea' (0/2) and 'the sandie houre-glasse runne' (0/3), while the third summarises the horror of a run-aground ship turning topsy-turvy, 'To kisse her buriall' (0/2)

Which touching but my gentle ^vessel's side
Would scatter all her spices on the stream* ,
Enrobe the roaring* waters with my silks* ,
And in a word, but even now worth this,
And now worth nothing?
             Shall I have the thought
To think* on this, and shall I lack* the thought
That such a thing bechanc'd* would make me sad?

7

But tell not me ;   I know Antonio*
Is sad to think* upon his merchandise* .

8

• and this image is even further enhanced by the speech's one emotive semicolon which after ending the image of the ship being overturned, leads to the equally frightful prospect of a ship destroying itself and its cargo on the rocks

• this latter part of the speech becomes much less emotional (2/4 in seven lines, as opposed to 1/10 in the previous seven), though whether this is a calm for Anthonio's sake - or a more personal quietness because of the images explored is again up to each actor to decide

• but as the speech ends so the energy picks up (1/5 in the last four and a half lines, F #6-7), as if the somewhat chop-logic conclusion that Anthonio-must-be-sad-because I-would-be-under-such-circumstances is delivered with somewhat of a flourish (triumphantly perhaps? or perhaps in an attempt to mask a sudden lack of conviction that he has in fact cheered Anthonio up with all the proffered images of doom and gloom)

Would scatter all her spices on the streame,
Enrobe the roring waters with my silkes,
And in a word, but even now worth this,
And now worth nothing. +
             Shall I have the thought
To thinke on this, and shall I lacke the thought
That such a thing bechaunc'd would make me sad?

6

But tell not me, + I know Anthonio
Is sad to thinke upon his merchandize .

7

2/ Anthonio   **Marke you this Bassanio,**

Background: Not having the money to loan Bassanio immediately to hand, Anthonio has given him free rein to borrow from whomever he can. Unwittingly, Bassanio has contacted Shylocke, a man with whom Anthonio shares a reciprocal loathing and contempt. Much of this is based on the fact that Shylocke charges interest for the money that he lends, a condition Anthonio abhors. The following springs from the attempt Shylocke has just made to justify charging interest by quoting a supposed parallel from the bible, that of Jacob, Laban, and the sheep.

Style: as part of a three-handed scene

Where: unspecified   **To Whom:** Bassanio, perhaps as an aside or perhaps for Shylocke to hear

# of Lines: 12   between 1.3.97 – 102 and 1.3.132 - 137   **Probable Timing: 0.40 minutes**

Modern Text	First Folio
2/ Anthonio	**2/ Anthonio**
1 Mark* you this, Bassanio, The devil* can cite Scripture for his purpose . †	1 Marke you this + Bassanio, The divell can cite Scripture for his purpose,
2 An evil* soul* producing holy witness* Is like a villain* with a smiling cheek*, A goodly apple rotten at the heart.	An evill soule producing holy witnesse, Is like a villaine with a smiling cheeke, A goodly apple rotten at the heart.
3 O, what a goodly outside falsehood hath.	2 O + what a goodly outside falsehood hath.
4 If thou wilt lend this money, lend it not As to thy friends, for when did friendship take A breed* of barren* metal* of his friend?	3 If thou wilt lend this money, lend it not As to thy friends, for when did friendship take A breede of barraine mettall of his friend?
5 But lend it rather to thine enemy*, Who if he break*, thou mayst* with better face Exact the [penalty].	4 But lend it rather to thine enemie, Who if he breake, thou maist with better face Exact the [penalties] .

The extra spellings of the F text reveals it to be a very personally emotional speech, though the opening F clues are more than somewhat gutted by the tidiness of the modern resetting, especially creating a second sentence at the end of F #1's second line.

• the larger of the two explosions comes at the start of the speech, where not only is the onrushed F #1 (split in two by modern texts) but most of the speech's emotional release is found in the first four lines (0/7), all of it concentrating on Anthonio's view of Shylocke as something inherently wicked ('divell', 'evill soule', 'villaine')

• however, in expressing his own hatred of pretence ('what a goodly outside falsehood hath') and that Shylocke shouldn't believe he is lending money 'to thy friends', it does seem that Anthonio has managed to calm himself, for by the last line of F #1, through F #2 and the opening of F #3, all excesses have disappeared, but this is only temporary for …

• … another explosion is released (0/3 in one line) when Anthonio describes friendship as never stooping to usury, 'A breede of barraine mettall', (which was destroying contemporary English landed families at the time the play was written)

• and then apparent public self control returns to end the speech (0/1, F #4)

3/ Anthonio   But little : I am arm'd and well prepar'd.   4.1.264 - 281

Background: Shylocke has not been dissuaded to abandon what seems to be legally his, the pound of his own flesh that Anthonio owes him. Thus Anthonio has been asked if he has anything to say before the execution of the terms of the bond, which would inevitably cause Anthonio's death, be carried out.

Style: one on one, with occasional playing for the much larger group also present

Where: the room/court where the hearing to gratify Shylocke's bond is being held   **To Whom:** primarily Bassanio, in front of the Duke, Gratiano, Shylocke, the legal team appearing to defend Anthonio (the unrecognised and disguised Portia and Nerrissa), court officials, and possibly friends and supporters of both parties

# of Lines: 18   Probable Timing: 0.55 minutes

Modern Text

3/ Anthonio

1 But little ; I am arm'd and well prepar'd.

2 Give me your hand, Bassanio, fare you well.

3 Grieve* not that I am fall'n* to this for you ;
   For herein* fortune shows* herself* more kind*
   Then is her custom* .

          It is still her use

4 To let the wretched man out⁰live his wealth,
   To view with hollow eye and wrinkled brow
   An age of poverty; ◊ from which ling'ring penance
   Of such misery* doth she cut me off. †

5 Commend me to your honorable* △wife,
   Tell her the process* of Antonio's* end,
   Say how I lov'd you, speak* me fair* in death;
   And when the tale is told, bid her be judge
   Whether Bassanio had not once a △love. †

6 Repent [but] you that you shall loose your friend,
   And he repents not that he pays* your debt; †
   For if the Jew do cut but deep* enough,
   I'll pay it instantly with all my heart.

First Folio

3/ Anthonio

1 But little : ₓ I am arm'd and well prepar'd.

2 Give me your hand ⁺ Bassanio, fare you well.

3 Greeve not that I am falne to this for you : ₓ
   For heerein fortune shewes her selfe more kinde
   Then is her custome.

          It is still her use

4 To let the wretched man out-live his wealth,
   To view with hollow eye,ₓ and wrinkled brow
   An age of poverty.

          From which lingring penance
5 Of such miserie,ₓ doth she cut me off:
   Commend me to your honourable Wife,
   Tell her the processe of Anthonio's end: ₓ
   Say how I lov'd you ; ₓ speake me faire in death: ₓ
   And when the tale is told, bid her be judge,
   Whether Bassanio had not once a Love :

6 Repent [not] you that you shall loose your friend,
   And he repents not that he payes your debt.
   For if the Jew do cut but deepe enough,
   Ile pay it instantly,ₓ with all my heart.

While the modern texts maintain Anthonio's dignity throughout, F shows key moments when his personal feelings momentarily break through.

*   the first moment of referring to death, no matter how obliquely (at the end of F #3) suddenly shows emotion for the first time in the speech (five long spelled words out of twelve in one and a half lines), and a further reference to death, at the start of F #5 is completely ungrammatical, and rarely followed by any modern text

*   three of the five surround phrases occur as Anthonio finally begins to speak, no matter how obliquely, of his love for Bassanio
    " . Greeve not that I am falne to this for you : "
    " . : Say how I lov'd you ; speake me faire in death : "
    yet, when attempting to console Bassanio, Anthonio manages to return to some (enforced?) dignified unembellished calm (the opening three lines to the speech – save for the naming of his beloved 'Bassanio' ; the whole of F #3; and the opening two lines of F #4)

*   it is by the end of the speech, where F #5 and #6 have been markedly reshaped by most modern texts, that the F Anthonio's control seems to slip
    a/ there is the totally ungrammatical period ending F #4, suggesting how desperately he needs a pause to establish self-control before he opens F #5 with an appearance of unembellished calm, which then jumps into passion (2/2) as he refers to what would forever be a rift between Anthonio and his hopes, Bassanio's new 'honourable Wife'
    b/ there is F #5's ungrammatical onrush, with its five pieces of heavy punctuation in as many lines, suggesting that his mind is working much harder than his modern counterpart who maintains a much more grammatical, rational structure throughout
    c/ and when he finally gets enough courage to make a public statement of his love for Bassanio, 'Whether Bassanio had not once a Love', it is so determinedly factual (2/0), yet he then plunges on ungrammatically via a colon (embarrassment for both of them, perhaps? or determination to prove how much he loves Bassanio) into the 'repent not' images, whereas modern texts create their tidy new sentence #6, reducing the impact of the blurt

*   the value of F starting the new sentence (#6) when it does is that it emphasises the last line's wonderfully unembellished dignified wit in the face of death, 'Ile pay it instantly, with all my heart' (an attempt to recover from embarrassment again perhaps?)

#'s 4- 6: BASSANIO IN LOVE

4/ Bassanio	'Tis not unknowne to you Anthonio	1.1.122 - 134
5/ Bassanio	In my schoole dayes, when I had lost one shaft	1.1.140 - 152
6/ Bassanio	In Belmont is a Lady richly left,	1.1.161 - 176

Background: All three speeches are Bassanio's responses to Anthonio's requests for information: #4 is a response to Anthonio's 'tell me now, what Lady is the same/To whom you swore a secret Pilgrimage': #5 is a response to Anthonio's assurance 'My purse, my person, my extreamest meanes/Lye all unlock'd to your occasions': speech #6 is his final revelation of all the details of the lady in question, Portia, in response to Anthonio's rather naked plea 'therefore speake'.

Style: all three speeches as part of a two-handed scene

Where: unspecified   **To Whom:** Anthonio, to whom Bassanio is already financially indebted

	speech #4, # of Lines: 13	**Probable Timing: 0.45 minutes**
	speech #5, # of Lines: 13	**Probable Timing: 0.45 minutes**
	speech #6, # of Lines: 16	**Probable Timing: 0.50 minutes**

First Folio

4/ Bassanio

1 'Tis not unknowne to you [+] Anthonio [+]
How much I have disabled mine estate,
By something shewing a more swelling port
Then my faint meanes would grant continuance [:]
Nor do I now make mone to be abridg'd
From such a noble rate, but my cheefe care
Is to come fairely off from the great debts
Wherein my time something too prodigall
Hath left me gag'd: to you [+] Anthonio [+]
I owe the most in money, and in love,
And from your love I have a warrantie
To unburthen all my plots and purposes,[x]
How to get cleere of all the debts I owe.

Modern Text

4/ Bassanio

1 'Tis not unknown[*] to you, Antonio[*] ,
How much I have disabled mine estate,
By something showing a more swelling port
Then my faint means[*] would grant continuance. [†]
Nor do I now make moan[*] to be abridg'd
From such a noble rate, but my chief[*] care
Is to come fairly[*] off from the great debts
Wherein my time something too prodigal[*]
Hath left me gag'd. [†]

3   To you, Antonio,[*]
I owe the most in money, and in love,
And from your love I have a warranty[*]
To unburthen all my plots and purposes
How to get clear[*] of all the debts I owe.

Whereas in speech #5 immediately following, modern texts match F's seemingly grammatical structure, here F/Q's obvious clue of one long onrushed sentence showing Bassanio cannot speak logically and is finding the start very awkward has been totally removed by the modern texts splitting F's one sentence into three.

• and though it seems as if, in the preamble to asking Antonio for more money, Bassanio is being very careful and circumspect, it is not just the onrush that suggests he has having difficulty . . .

• . . . apart from the twice used name 'Anthonio' there are no capital letters, suggesting that mental control is hardly a keynote of the speech

• and, surprisingly, there are relatively very few long-spelled words, especially when compared to the following speech (0/8 compared to 1/15, both in thirteen lines), and they are scattered throughout the speech, underscoring that he wants Antonio to know he is now taking responsibility for his past and future behaviours - 'not unknowne to you'; 'my faint meanes'; 'my cheefe care/Is to come fairely off; 'too prodigall'; 'get cleere of all the debts I owe'

• one sidebar: the additional modern commas (marked [†]), surrounding 'Anthonio' at the top of modern text sentences #1 and #3, slow Bassanio's speedier Q/F flow

First Folio

5/ Bassanio

1 In my schoole dayes, when I had lost one shaft [+]
I shot his fellow of the selfesame flight

Though matching the modern texts in structure, which might make it seem that Bassanio is now in control of himself, there are still clues in F to suggest that the appeal is not quite as easy as it might appear.

Modern Text

5/ Bassanio

1 In my school[*] days[*], when I had lost one shaft,
I shot his fellow of the self[~]same flight

Modern Text (continued)

The self*-°same way with more advised watch
To find* the other forth, and by adventuring both
I oft found both.

2   I urge this child*-°hood*°proof*,
    Because what follows* is pure innocence.

3   I owe you much, and like a willful* youth,
    That which I owe is lost, but if you please
    To shoot* another arrow that self* way
    Which you did shoot the first, I do not doubt,
    As I will watch the aim*, ᐃor to find* both,
    Or bring your latter hazard back* again*,
    And thankfully rest debtor for the first.

Modern Text

6/ Bassanio

1 In Belmont is a ᐃlady richly left,
   And she is fair* and, fairer then that word,
   Of wondrous virtues. †
                    Sometimes from her eyes
   I did receive faire speechless* messages. †

3 Her name is Portia, nothing undervalu'd*
   To Cato's daughter, Brutus' Portia. †

4 Nor is the wide world ignorant of her worth,
   For the four* winds* blow in from every coast
   Renowned sutors*, and her sunny locks
   Hang on her temples like a golden fleece,
   Which makes her seat of Belmont [Colchis'] strond,
   And many Jasons come in quest of her.

5 O my Antonio*, had I but the means*
   To hold a rival* place with one of them,
   I have a mind* presages me such thrift
   That I should questionless* be fortunate!

First Folio (continued)

The selfesame way,x with more advised watch
To finde the other forth, and by adventuring both,:
I oft found both.

2   I urge this child-hoode proofe,
    Because what followes is pure innocence.

3   I owe you much, and like a wilfull youth,
    That which I owe is lost:x   but if you please
    To shoote another arrow that selfe way
    Which you did shoot the first, I do not doubt,
    As I will watch the ayme:x   Or to finde both,
    Or bring your latter hazard backe againe,
    And thankfully rest debter for the first.

First Folio

6/ Bassanio

1 In Belmont is a Lady richly left,
   And she is faire,x and+ fairer then that word,
   Of wondrous vertues, sometimes from her eyes
   I did receive faire speechlesse messages:
   Her name is Portia, nothing undervallewd
   To Cato's daughter, Brutus Portia,
   Nor is the wide world ignorant of her worth,
   For the foure windes blow in from every coast
   Renowned sutors, and her sunny locks
   Hang on her temples like a golden fleece,
   Which makes her seat of Belmont [Cholchos] strond
   And many Jasons come in quest of her.

2 O my Anthonio, had I but the meanes
   To hold a rivall place with one of them,
   I have a minde presages me such thrift,x
   That I should questionlesse be fortunate. +

Commentary (previous speech)

- as with the previous speech, just one capital letter ('Or') suggests that intellectual control is hardly foremost here (1/15 in thirteen lines)

- no fewer than fifteen longer spelled words are scattered throughout the thirteen lines of the speech, sometimes in emphatic small clusters ('schoole-dayes', 'child-hoode proofe', 'backe againe') suggesting extra expressive energy as the point in question is advanced

- the two extra F breath-thoughts (marked x) towards the end of sentence #1 suggest he is taking great care to explain in minute detail what he is hoping to do

- similarly, when he finally nears his request for more money, the two F only colons of sentence #3 (': but if you please', and ': Or to finde both,') advance the stepping stones of his plan far more emphatically than the commas that replace them in most modern texts

Commentary (First Folio)

Again, modern texts suggest far more self control than F establishes, this time by splitting F's onrushed opening sentence into four.

- with ten capitals overall, it seems that Bassanio finally establishes some form of mental discipline for himself: however, with four of them occurring in just two lines (as he first describes Portia) plus only one piece of major punctuation in the piece, it seems it is the images of Portia (and ensuing classical ones of the quest) that are guiding him, rather than a sustained act of logical presentation of information

- while there are ten long-spelled words, they tend to come in three clusters (the 'faire speechlesse messages' he received from her; rival suitors coming from everywhere on the 'foure windes', and the final F #2 indirect plea for more money), suggesting a struggle as to when the mind is in control and when the emotions

- thus in the opening line his mind works (2/0), then for the next three his emotions (0/3): then, as he mentions Portia's name his mind takes over again (4/1) but just for two lines: then there is a period of relative calm (just 2 long spelled words in four lines) followed by a final flourish of three capitals in the last two classical analogy lines of the sentence - all this is encompassed in F #1, the overly-long sentence suggesting a see-saw battle within him, a totally different opening to that offered by modern texts

- with its four long spelled words, F #2 reverts once more to something of the emotional blur of the previous speech

#'s 7-9: PORTIA'S DILEMMA: THE FOOLISH SUITORS

7/ Portia   **What warmth is there in {my} affection towards any of these Princely suters**   between 1.2.33 - 99

Background: By terms of her father's will, Portia has no say in whom she will marry - whoever chooses the correct (lead) casket of the three on display will be her husband, whether she likes him or no. As Bassanio accurately described it (speech #6 above) being very rich and very beautiful, she is besieged with a myriad of suitors, and, as she describes in the following, the most recent crop of would-be husbands have been particularly trying.

Style: part of a two-handed scene

Where: unspecified, but presumably somewhere in her private chambers in Belmont   **To Whom:** her companion Nerrissa

# of Lines: 51   **Probable Timing: 2.35 minutes**

{created by removing the occasional question and/or comment from Nerrissa and modifying a phrase or word accordingly}

The difficulty for most actresses playing Portia lies in the modern texts altering both the phrasing and sentence structure originally offered by F and the quartos. The original texts offer far fewer sentences and often less punctuation when her mind is on an improvisational discovery roll (see the "+" markings in F sentences #6, #10, and #12 below). They also offer a great vivacity in the orthographic setting of her language and thus her verbal dexterity and delight. Sometimes capitals are in great evidence as she discovers or analyses some new idea or situation, and sometimes there are a plethora of long spellings as her own personal feelings bubble to the surface. The extra sentences and heavier punctuation offered by the modern texts usually create a much more prosaic Portia than the young woman growing up and mentally dancing with delight as presented in the original texts. And nowhere is this contrast in more evidence than in the following, where F's twelve sentences are reshaped into twenty-seven by most modern texts.

• the best way of analyzing the following is to go appalling suitor by appalling suitor, noting the speaking patterns F offers: in brackets, following each character's name, the number(s) of the F sentences will be shown and then the number(s) of the modern sentences used to express the same text

• the opening (F #1-2/mt. #1-2)
an apparently very laconic start, with just one capital and one long spelling in the opening two sentences

• the Neapolitane Prince (F #3/mt. #3-4)
and then the personal feelings (exasperation? amusement?) begin to break through (2/8), until the only colon of this passage, when all of a sudden a fine intellectual summary finishes the horse-lover off once and for all (2/1)

Modern Text

7/ Portia

1   What warmth
ψ is there in {my} affection towards any of these
princely suters that are already come? ψ

2   I will describe them ; and according to my description level* at my affection.

3   ψ The [Neapolitan]* Prince
{is} a colt indeed*, for he doth nothing but
talk* of his horse, and he* makes it a great appropria-
tion to his own* good parts that he can shoe* himself* . †

4   I am much [afeard] my ^lady* his mother play'd*
false with a ^smith* . ψ

5   The County* [Palatine]
ψ doth nothing but frown* , as who should
say, "And you will not have me, choose" . †

6   He hears*
merry* tales and smiles not . †

7   I fear* he* will prove the
weeping ^philosopher* when he grows* old, being so
full of un^mannerly sadness* in his youth.

8   I had rather [ ] be marri-
ed to a death's-°head with a bone in his mouth then
to either of these . †

9   God defend me from these two.

First Folio

7/ Portia

1   What warmth
ψ is there in {my} affection towards any of these
Princely suters that are already come? ψ

2   I will describe them, + and according to my description levell at my affection.

3   ψ [The Neopolitane] Prince
{is} a colt indeede, for he doth nothing but
talke of his horse, and hee makes it a great appropria-
tion to his owne good parts that he can shoo him himselfe :   I am much [afraid] my Ladie his mother plaid
false with a Smyth. ψ

4   The Countie [Palentine]
ψ doth nothing but frowne x(as who should
say, and you will not have me, choose : he heares
merrie tales and smiles not, I feare hee will prove the
weeping Phylosopher when he growes old, being so
full of un-mannerly sadnesse in his youth.)x

5   I had rather to be marri-
ed to a deaths head with a bone in his mouth,x then
to either of these :   God defend me from these two.

[Folio text — 6–9]

6 God made the {French Lord, Mounsier Le [Boune]} , and therefore let him passe for a man, in truth[+] I know it is a sinne to be a mocker, but he,[+] why[+] he hath a horse better then the [Neopolitans], a better bad habite of frowning then the Count [Palentine],[+] he is every man in no man, if a Trassell sing, he fals straight a capring, he will fence with his own shadow . If I should

7 marry him, I should marry twentie husbands : if hee would despise me, I would forgive him, for if he love me to madnesse, I [should] never requite him . ᴪ

8 I say nothing to [Fauconbridge], the yong Baron of England, for hee understands not me, nor I him : he hath neither Latine, French, nor Italian, and you will come into the Court & sweare that I have a poore pennie-worth in the English : hee is a proper mans picture, but alas[+] who can converse with a dumbe show? how odly he is suited : I thinke he bought his doublet in Italie, his round hose in France, his bonnet in Germanie, and his behaviour every where . ᴪ

9 The [other] Lord his neighbour hath a neighbourly charitie in him, for he borrowed a boxe of the eare of the Englishman, and swore he would pay him againe when hee was able : I thinke the Frenchman became his suritie,[x] and seald under for another.

[Commentary]

• the Countie Palentine (F #4/mt. #5-7)
the mental dismissal is maintained for the start in assessing the second irritation (2/1 up to the only colon in this passage): and then her personal feelings break through once more (1/6 to finish the sentence)

• a pause to assess both (F #5/mt. #8-9)
once more the ease and laconic response seen at the top of the speech returns, with no embellishment of any sort before the colon and just one capital letter after (so perhaps these are easier to dismiss than those who follow)

• the French Lord, Monsiuer Le Boune (F #6-7/mt. #10-15)
here Portia's mind goes into overdrive, for five of the first eight words are capitalised, and the remainder of sentence #6 moves more quickly than the modern texts allow (+) but with much intellectual and personal gusto (4/4) : it also marks the beginning of a series of longer sentences (with the exception of #7) about each of the remaining suitors (perhaps suggesting it is more difficult to shake these particular men from her mind): it's only by the second summary sentence (F #7) does some form of calming result, for up to the colon there are no embellishments, and just two long spellings after

• Fauconbridge, the yong Baron of England (F #8/mt. #16-20)
the passionate mental and personal quality of the assessment continues as she dismisses the Englishman for both his lack of language skills and dress sense, with not only capitals slightly outweighing the long spellings (10/8) but also a couple of strong spin-off colons leading to extra developments in this, the longest sentence (ideas running away with her?) in the speech

• the other Lord his neighbour [1] (F #9/mt. #21-22)
and now her feelings take over once again (3/7), as if the Scot's barbaric testosterone driven behavior was especially repugnant to her

• the Duke of Saxonies Nephew (F #10-12/mt. #23-26)
this character creates more shifts within her than any other
a/ the introduction is highly mental, four capitals in the first ten words to identify him not by name (perhaps she can't bear to mention it) but by relationships
b/ this is followed by a highly concentrated personal response (0/6 in less than two lines) with less punctuation than set by modern texts (marked [†])
c/ then, for virtually the first time come, nearly three non-embellished lines as she regains (forces?) calm, accompanied by one of the few surround passages in the speech

{ctd. over}

[Modern text — 10–22]

10 God made {the French Lord, Monsieur* Le [Bon]} , and therefore let him pass* for a man .[†]

11 In truth, I know it is a sin* to be a mocker, but he! why, he hath a horse better then the [Neapolitan's], a better bad habit* of frowning then the Count [Palatine] ; he is every man in no man .[†]

12 If a [°throstle] sing, he falls* straight a -°cap'ring .[†]

13 He will fence with his own shadow .

14 If I should

15 marry him, I should marry twenty* husbands .[†]

16 would despise me, I would forgive him, for if he love me to madness*, I [shall] never requite him . ᴪ

    If I*[†]   If he*

17 I say nothing to [Falconbridge], the young* Baron of England, for he* understands not me, nor I him .[†]

18 He hath neither Latin*, French, nor Italian, and you will come into the △court & swear* that I have a poor* penny*△worth in the English .   He* is a

19 proper man's picture, but alas, who can converse with a dumb* show? [†]

20 How oddly* he is suited !* [†]   I think* he bought

21 his doublet in Italy*, his round hose in France, his bonnet in Germany*, and his behavior* every where . ᴪ

22 {The [Scottish] Lord his neighbor*} hath a neighborly* charity*, in him, for he borrowed a box* of the ear* of the Englishman, and swore he would pay him again* when he* was able .[†]
    I think* the Frenchman became his surety*, and seal'd under for another.

[1] Qq and most modern texts = 'Scottish', FF = 'other' : commentators explain that since James VI of Scotland had become King of England (as James I) by the time F was published, the word 'other' was tactfully substituted for the original 'Scottish' so as to avoid giving offence

23 {I} like { } the young* German*, the Duke of Saxony's* ᐃnephew*very vildly* in the morning, when he* is sober, and most vildly* in the afternoon*, when he* is drunk* . †

24 When he is best, he is a little worse then a man, and when he is worst he is little better then a beast. †

25 And the worst fall that ever fell, I hope I shall make shift to go* without him.

26 Therefore for fear* of the worst, I pray thee set a deep* glass* of [Rhenish] °wine on the contrary ᐃcasket, for if the devil* be within, and that temptation without, I know he will choose it.

27 I will do* [anything], Nerrissa, ere I will be married to a spunge.

10 {I} like { } the yong Germaine, the Duke of Saxonies Nephew{v}ery vildely in the morning,+ when hee is sober, and most vildely in the afternoone+ when hee is drunke: when he is best, he is a little worse then a man, and when he is worst he is little better then a beast: and the worst fall that ever fell, I hope I shall make shift to goe without him.

11 Therefore for feare of the worst, I pray thee set a deepe glasse of [Reinish]-wine on the contrary Casket, for if the divell be within, and that temptation without, I know he will choose it.

12 I will doe [any thing]+ Nerrissa+ ere I will be married to a spunge.

": when he is best, he is a little worse then a man, and when he is worst he is little better then a beast : "

d/ the close-to-the-wind-in-almost-cheating-on-her-father's-intentions planning session (the penultimate F #11, 2/5) once more creates a surge of strong thoughts and even stronger emotion within her

e/ F's final resolution (sentence #12, 1/1) is much more definitive than the modern equivalent - by the simple fact that it is delivered as one uninterrupted unpunctuated thought: most modern texts spoil the drive by adding two grammatical commas before and after 'Nerrissa'

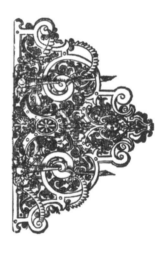

8/ Morochus   **Let's see once more this saying grav'd in gold .**   (the latter part of a larger speech)   between 2.7.36 – 77

Background: Faced with a choice of the three caskets, Morochus, falling into the trap all Elizabethan children were warned against (mistaking appearances for essence and reality), finally chooses the gold. One note: the bolded text in F #8 denotes the possibility of a 'magical' metrical pattern (one where the heartbeat is reversed). [2]

Style: self and public address to a larger group
Where: the casket room   **To Whom:** self and the caskets in front of Portia and Nerrissa and members of their respective trains, and occasionally to the group at large or even individuals therein

# of Lines: 33   Probable Timing: 1.40 minutes

Modern Text

8/ Morochus

1 Let's see once more this saying grav'd in gold: ◊
   "Who chooseth me shall gain* what many men desire". †

2 Why, that's the △lady, all the world desires her . †

3 From the four* corners of the earth they come
   To kiss* this shrine, this mortal* breathing △saint.

4 The Hyrcanian* deserts and the [vasty] * wilds*
   Of wide Arabia are as throughfares now
   For △princes to come view fáire Portia.

5 The watery* △kingdom* , whose ambitious head
   Spets in the face of heaven, is no bar*
   To stop the foreign* spirits, but they come
   As o'er a brook* to see fair* Portia.

6 They have in England
   A coin* that bears* the figure of an △angel*
   Stamp'd in gold, but that's insculp'd upon;
   But here an △angel* in a golden bed
   Lies all within.
                    Deliver me the key . †

7

8 Here do* I choose, and thrive I as I may ! †

9 O hell! what have we here? †

10 A carrion △Death, within whose empty* eye
    There is a written scroll*! †

11   I'll read* the writing.

First Folio

8/ Morochus

1 Let's see once more this saying grav'd in gold.

2 Who chooseth me shall gaine what many men desire:
   Why+ that's the Lady, all the world desires her:
   From the foure corners of the earth they come
   To kisse this shrine, this mortall breathing Saint.

3 The Hircanion deserts,ₓ and the [vaste] wildes
   Of wide Arabia are as throughfares now
   For Princes to come view faire Portia.

4 The waterie Kingdome, whose ambitious head
   Spets in the face of heaven, is no barre
   To stop the forraine spirits, but they come
   As ore a brooke to see faire Portia.

5 They have in England
   A coyne that beares the figure of an Angell
   Stampt in gold, but that's insculpt upon: ₓ
   But here an Angell in a golden bed
   Lies all within.

6   Deliver me the key:

7 Here doe I choose, and thrive I as I may . +
   O hell! what have we here, a carrion death,
   Within whose emptie eye there is a written scroule;
   Ile reade the writing.

                                        {ctd. over}

As with many smaller one or two scene characters, F allows for both **speed of mind and more controlled moments of debate and self-examination. As with most modern restructurings the two elements are often reduced to a single grammatical exactness – as here, where F's nine sentences are expanded to seventeen by many modern editors. But, when the F sentence structure is coupled with the original orthography, a far more complex character is available than the modern texts present.**

• the surround phrases that open his re-examination of the gold casket (sentence #2) lay out how easily he can be seduced by appearances ". Who chooseth me shall gaine what many men desire : / Why that's the Lady, all the world desires her : "

• sometimes the mind of the F Morochus moves far more speedily and irrevocably than that of his modern counterpart (F #2 versus mt. #2–#3; F #6 versus mt. #7–#8; F #7 versus mt. #9–#11; F #8 versus mt. #12–#15; F #9 versus mt. #16–#17)

• yet at other times there are elements of great unembellished self control, even at key moments,
   "Let's see once more this saying grav'd in gold . "
   "Deliver me the key : " & "and thrive I as I may . "
more surprisingly, control is exhibited when things go wrong, as with
   "O hell ! what have we here, a carrion death,"
and when he (presumably) reads the opening of the scroll
   "All that glisters is not gold, Often have you heard that told ;/Many a man
             his life hath sold/But my outside to behold "

and very surprisingly on parting
   "I have too griev'd a heart/To take a tedious leave : "
which suggests that there may be someone interesting underneath his testosterone drenched earlier self

---

12
"All that glisters is not gold,
Often have you heard that told;
Many a man his life hath sold
But my outside to behold. †

13
Gilded* [tombs] ˉdo* worms* infold . †

14
Had you been * as wise as bold,
Young* in limbs, in judgment* old,

15
Your answer* had not been * inscroll'd* . †

15
[Fare you well], your suit* is cold . "

16
Cold indeed*, and labor* lost :
Then farewell heat*, and welcome frost! †

17
Portia, adieu*, I have too griev'd a heart
To take a tedious leave; thus losers* part.

• there are quick shifts between firm image creation (F #3, 4/2) and personal release (F #4, 2/5)

• as he edges closer to a decision (F #5), mind and feelings become passionately interlinked (3/4)

• his emotional nervousness is apparent with three semicolons in quick succession as he reaches for the scroll and starts reading his fate, (F #7 to the opening of F #8); one extra note here - the modern rewrite of F #7 (shaded modern text #9-#11) puts the pause as Morochus takes hold of the scull; as originally set the pause comes at the end of the sentence, as he unrolls and takes a first look at the scroll

• following the remarkable absolute self-control of the introductory four lines of the scroll there is a sudden explosion of personal feelings in F #8's final five lines of the scroll, which finally contains the bad news, and the first two and a half lines of his response (0/12)

All that glisters is not gold,
Often have you heard that told; :
Many a man his life hath sold
But my outside to behold;
Guilded [timber] doe wormes infold:

8 [3]
Had you beene as wise as bold,
Yong in limbs, in judgement old,
Your answere had not beene inscrold,
[Fareyouwell], your suite is cold,

9
Cold indeede, and labour lost , +
Then farewell heate, and welcome frost :
Portia + adew, I have too griev'd a heart
To take a tedious leave: ₓ thus loosers part.

3 the major part of the scroll is written in the ritual/magical 7 syllable/reversed heartbeat utterance pattern, see Appendix 3

9/ Arragon   **I am enjoynd by oath to observe three things ;**   (one note: the speech is somewhat reduced)

Background: As with Morochus (speech #8 above), faced with a choice of the three caskets, Arragon, falls into the trap all Elizabethan children were warned against (mistaking appearances for essence and reality), and after much analysis chooses the silver. One note: the bolded text ending the speech (from F #15 on) denotes the possibility of a 'magical' metrical pattern (one where the heartbeat is reversed). [4]

Style: self and public address to a larger group

Where: the casket room   **To Whom:** self and the caskets in front of Portia and Nerrissa and members of their respective trains, and occasionally to the group at large or even individuals therein

between 2.9.9 - 78

# of Lines: 51   **Probable Timing: 2.35 minutes**

Modern Text

9/ Arragon

1 I am enjoin'd* by oath to observe three things :
First, never to unfold to any one
Which casket 'twas I chose; next, if I fail*
Of the right casket, never in my life
To woo* a maid* in way of marriage ; lastly,
If I do* fail* in fortune of my choice*,
Immediately to leave you, and be gone.

2 And so have I addres'd me . †

3   Fortune now
To my heart's hope! †

4   Gold, silver, and base lead.

5 "Who chooseth me must give and hazard all he hath ."

6 You shall look* fairer ere I give or hazard.

7 What says* the golden chest ? †

8   Ha, let me see:

   "Who chooseth me, shall gain* what many men desire.." †

9 What many men desire ! †

10   That many may be meant
By the fool* multitude that choose by show {.}

11 I will not choose what many men desire,
Because I will not jump* with common spirits,
And rank* me with the barbarous multitudes.

First Folio

9/ Arragon

1 I am enjoynd by oath to observe three things ; +
First, never to unfold to any one
Which casket 'twas I chose; next, if I faile
Of the right casket, never in my life
To wooe a maide in way of marriage : x
Lastly, [5] if I doe faile in fortune of my choyse,
Immediately to leave you, and be gone.

2 And so have I addresst me, fortune now
To my hearts hope : gold, silver, and base lead.

3 Who chooseth me must give and hazard all he hath.

4 You shall looke fairer ere I give or hazard.

5 What saies the golden chest, ha, let me see:
Who chooseth me, shall gaine what many men desire :
What many men desire, that many may be meant
By the foole multitude that choose by show{.}

6 I will not choose what many men desire,
Because I will not jumpe with common spirits,
And ranke me with the barbarous multitudes.

{ctd. over}

The F orthography suggests that the character can maintain a great deal of self control, at least until the scroll reveals the futility of his choice (just 1/19 in F's first fourteen sentences, thirty-five lines in all); tremendous control when compared with Morochus in speech #8 above (14/21 in nineteen lines). However, the speedier F sentence structure, together with its occasional non-grammatical links, suggests much more may be bubbling beneath the surface. Unfortunately, and as usual, many modern texts after the thinking process, in this case doubling the F sentence structure from seventeen to thirty-four.

• as Arragon begins to review the oath (F #1) there are two highly unusual semicolons in the first three lines (which could suggest anything from amusement or scorn through to genuine concern) followed by a quarter of all the extra spellings in the first thirty-five lines of the speech (five of nineteen in just three and a half lines) as he finishes his review

• then, though unembellished, the very quick F #2 connection of three different thoughts (split into three rational sentences, #2-4 in most modern texts), especially the last surround phrase re-assessment of the caskets, suggests a somewhat less than academic self-control

• then, quite calmly, he quickly dismisses the lead casket (0/1, F #3-#4, matched by mt's #5-#6)

• and then the gold chest is not quite as easily dismissed as the lead, but far more rapidly than the modern texts allow (F #6-#7 - two sentences as opposed to mt's five, #7-11)

---

[4] see Appendix 3

[5] forgetting that 'marriage' could be pronounced as four syllables, some modern texts add 'Lastly' to the previous line, thus creating two almost normal lines (11/10 syllables): the Qq/Ff settings (9/12) allow for a minute pause (9 syllables) before the lengthier line begins here (12 syllables), perhaps reflecting Arragon's incredulity or apprehension that such an event could occur

7
Why then to thee, + thou Silver treasure house,
Tell me once more, what title thou doost beare; +
Who chooseth me shall get as much as he deserves :
And well said too; for who shall goe about
To cosen Fortune, and be honourable
Without the stampe of merit {.}

8
Who chooseth me shall get as much as he deserves.

9
I will assume desert; give me a key for this,
And instantly unlocke my fortunes here.

10
What's here, + the portrait of a blinking idiot
Presenting me a scedule, I will reade it:
How much unlike art thou to Portia? +

11
How much unlike my hopes and my deservings? +

12
Who chooseth me, shall have as much as he deserves. +

13
Did I deserve no more then a fooles head,
Is that my prize, are my deserts no better? +

14
What is here? 6

15
The fier seaven times tried this,
Seaven times tried that judgement is,
That did never choose amis,
Some there be that shadowes kisse :
Such have but a shadowes blisse :
There be fooles alive + Iwis +
Silver'd o're, and so was this :
Take what wife you will to bed,
I will ever be your head :
So be gone, you are sped.

• as he turns to the silver casket, his eventual choice (F #7), the (enforced?) calmness begins to dissipate: two more semicolons appear, which, together with the colon, create the two all deceiving yet important to him surround phrases
"; Who chooseth me shall get as much as he deserves : / And well said too; "
with a quarter of the long spellings released in just four and a half lines (2/5)

• his repeating aloud F #8's assessment of the silver casket's engraving is enhanced by being both short and unembellished

• and, as he chooses (F #9), one more emotional semicolon makes itself felt (pride? nerves?): again the choice is quicker than the mt's two sentences # 15-16 suggest

• yet despite the first signs that he has chosen wrong (F's seven sentences #8-#14, seven and a half lines in all), he manages to re-establish an amazing semblance of calm (whether natural or forced, the latter more likely in that three of the five sentences are short), for five and a half lines are unembellished, the few releases(0/2) referring to the 'scedule' ('I will reade it') and his own unexpected reward ('Did I deserve no more than a fooles head')

• but once Arragon begins to read the scroll, two things occur that are not shared by the modern texts

• the scroll is read as one long sentence of on-rolling pronouncement (F #15) as if he cannot stop himself, as opposed to mt's five sentences (#26 - #29)

• and, though Arragon seems to be trying to maintain his dignity nevertheless, two bursts of personal reactions come flooding through
a/ 0/8 in the introductory opening six lines of the scroll
b/ then calm is again enforced as his future is spelled out in the scroll's last unembellished four lines
c/ and then, once more, the personal feelings break through as he makes his farewell, trying to show his mental acumen by phrasing his farewell so as to match if not better, the 'magic' style of the scroll (0/7 in six lines F #16-17), a direct contrast to Morochus' much more dignified final farewell in speech #8 above

---

12
Why then to thee, thou △silver treasure house,
Tell me once more, what title thou dost* bear*:
"Who chooseth me shall get as much as he deserves."†

13
And well said too; for who shall go* about
To cozen* △fortune, and be honorable*
Without the stamp* of merit {.}

14
"Who chooseth me shall get as much as he deserves".

15
I will assume desert.†

16
Give me a key for this,
And instantly unlock* my fortunes here.

17
What's here? the portrait of a blinking idiot
Presenting me a schedule*.! †

18
I will read* it. •

19
How much unlike art thou to Portia?

20
How much unlike my hopes and my deservings!

21
"Who chooseth me, shall have as much as he deserves"!

22
Did I deserve no more then a fool's* head?†

23
Is that my prize? †

24
Are my deserts no better?

25
What is here?

26
"The fire* seven* times tried this:
Seven* times tried that judgment* is,
That did never choose amiss .†

27
Some there be that shadows* kiss*,
Such have but a shadow's* bliss* .†

28
There be fools* alive, △Iwis,
Silver'd o'er, and so was this .†

29
Take what wife you will to bed,
I will ever be your head .

30
So be gone, you are sped."

SDM 6 most modern texts add a stage direction that he reads aloud the scroll or 'scedule': as with Morochus the bulk of the message is written in the magic/ritual pattern: see Appendix 3

31 Still more fool* I shall appear*
    By the time I linger here . †
32 With one fool's* head I came to woo,
    But I go* away with two .
33 Sweet adieu* . †
        I'll keep* my oath,
34 Patiently to bear* my wroth* .

16 Still more foole I shall appeare
    By the time I linger here ,
    With one fooles head I came to woo,
    But I goe away with two .
17 Sweet adue, Ile keepe my oath,
    Patiently to beare my wroath .

#'s 10- 15: LOVE EVENTUALLY TRIUMPHS

10/ Portia   I pray you tarrie, pause a day or two   3.2.1- 24

Background: This is the first face-to-face speech and scene between the mutually smitten Portia and Bassanio. As her rather awkward attempt to prevent him from making a casket choice just yet (for if he makes the wrong choice, by terms of her father's will he must never see Portia again), it is self-explanatory.

Style: one on one, in front of a small group
Where: near or in the casket-room   **To Whom:** Bassanio, in front of Gratiano and Nerrissa, perhaps some of Portia's household, including musicians
# of Lines: 24   **Probable Timing: 1.10 minutes**

Modern Text	First Folio

First Folio

10/ Portia
1   I pray you tarrie, pause a day or two
    Before you hazard, for in choosing wrong
    I loose your companie ; therefore forbeare a while,
    There's something tels me (but it is not love)
    I would not loose you, and you know your selfe,
    Hate counsailes not in such a qualitie ;
    But least you should not understand me well,
    And yet a maiden hath no tongue, but thought,
    I would detaine you here some month or two
    Before you venture for me.
2   I could teach you
    How to choose right, but then I am forsworne,

{ctd. over}

The modern text's ten sentences present a Portia much more in control than the 4 sentence Folio (matched exactly by the quarto). Also, F's setting of three semicolons as opposed to just two colons (two of the three coming in the extended first sentence) suggests that Portia's F inner volcano is much more difficult to control than that of her modern counterpart.

• amazingly, yet not surprisingly given the circumstances, there are only three capital letters in the whole speech, hardly a sign of mind over matter

• the fact that the F #1 is split into three by the modern texts, and F #2 into four again suggests that, compared to her modern counterpart, Portia's feelings are running away with her verbally as well as emotionally

• this is even more so in the onrushed F #2 which suggests her decision to still abide by her father's will, for she never will be 'forsworne' spills out of her: most modern texts split the decision into three sentences, implying far more rationality than the original Portia seems to be capable of at such a time

Modern Text

10/ Portia
1   I pray you tarry,*, pause a day or two
    Before you hazard, for in choosing wrong
    I lose* your company,* ; therefore forbear* a while †.
2   There's something tells* me (but it is not love)
    I would not lose* you, and you know yourself*,
    Hate counsels* not in such a quality*. . †
3   But lest* you should not understand me well -
    And yet a maiden hath no tongue, but thought -
    I would detain* you here some month or two
    Before you venture for me.
4   I could teach you
    How to choose right, but then I am forsworn* . †

5
So will I never be, so may you miss* me,
But if you do*, you'll* make me wish a sin*,
That I had been* forsworn*. †

6
        Beshrow your eyes,
They have o'er*°look'd me and divided* me :
One half* of me is yours, the other half* yours -
Mine own*, I would say ; but [if] mine, then yours,
And so all yours. †

7
        O, these naughty* times
Puts bars between* the owners and their rights! †

8
And so though yours, not yours. †

9
            Prove it so,

10
Let △fortune go* to hell for it, not I.
I speak* too long, but 'tis to peize⁷ the time,
To [eche] it, and to draw it out in length.
To stay you from election.

7 modern glosses include 'poise' and 'piece'

• the Freudian slip, in part emotionally formed (by the semicolon)/surround phrase ' : but [if] mine then yours/And so all yours ; ' is a complete give away

• and yet there are attempts at self control, with the above phrase and at least three unembellished others, all of which are very important to her desires,

"I pray you tarrie, pause a day or two/Before you hazard, for in choosing wrong"

"But least you should not understand me well,/And yet a maiden hath no tongue, but thought,"

"but 'tis to peize the time,/To [ich] it, and to draw it out in length,/To stay you from election"

which, containing neither long-spelling nor capitals, suggest a tremendous vulnerability, and therefore at these moments she is speaking in an essentially unadorned, straight from the heart – something very important in an essentially emotional speech (3/20)

So will I never be, so may you misse me,
But if you doe, youle make me wish a sinne,
That I had beene forsworne : Beshrow your eyes,
They have ore-lookt me and devided me, ⁺
One halfe of me is yours, the other halfe yours, ⁺
Mine owne⁺ I would say : ₓ but [of] mine ⁺ then yours,
And so all yours ; O⁺ these naughtie times
Puts bars betweene the owners and their rights.
And so though yours, not yours ₓ (prove it so)ₓ
Let Fortune goe to hell for it, not I.
I speake too long, but 'tis to peize the time,
To [ich] it, and to draw it out in length,
To stay you from election.

3

4

11/ Portia   Away then, I am lockt in one of them,   3.2.40 - 62

Background: Despite wanting to stay with her, Bassanio claims he is on the 'racke', and must to his 'fortune and the caskets'. The following is Portia's response.

Style: initially one on one, in front of a small group, and then to other members of the group

Where: near or in the casket-room   **To Whom:** Bassanio, with the larger group including Gratiano and Nerrissa, some of Portia's household, and musicians

# of Lines: 23   **Probable Timing: 1.10 minutes**

Modern Text

11/ Portia

1 Away then !†

  I am lock'd in one of them ;

2 If you do* love me, you will find* me out.

3 Nerrissa* and the rest, stand all aloof* .†

4 Let music* sound while he doth make his choice ;

  Then if he lose* he makes a ^swan°like end,

  Fading in music* .

5   That the comparison

  May stand more proper, my eye shall be the stream*

  And war'ry death-bed for him .†

6   He may win,

  And what is music* [then] ?

7   [Then] music* is

  Even as the flourish, when true subjects bow*

  To a new crowned ^monarch ; ^such it is,

  As are those dulcet sounds in break* of day,

  That creep* into the dreaming bride°groom's* ear* ,

  And summon him to marriage.

                              Now he goes

8 With no less* presence, but with much more love*,

  Then young* Alcides, when he did redeem*

  The virgin* tribute paid* by howling Troy

  To the ^sea-monster. †

9   I stand for sacrifice ;

  The rest aloof* are the Dardanian wives,

  With bleared visages, come forth to view

  The issue of th'exploit. †

First Folio

11/ Portia

1 Away then, + I am lockt in one of them, +

  If you doe love me, you will finde me out. +

2 Nerryssa and the rest, stand all aloofe, +

  Let musicke sound while he doth make his choise, +

  Then if he loose he makes a Swan-like end,

  Fading in musique.

3   That the comparison

  May stand more proper, my eye shall be the streame

  And watrie death-bed for him : he may win,

  And what is musique [than] ?

4   [Than] musique is

  Even as the flourish, when true subjects bowe

  To a new crowned Monarch : x Such it is,

  As are those dulcet sounds in breake of day,

  That creepe into the dreaming bride-groomes eare,

  And summon him to marriage.   Now he goes

5 With no lesse presence, but with much more love +

  Then yong Alcides, when he did redeeme

  The virgine tribute, x paied by howling Troy

  To the Sea-monster : I stand for sacrifice, +

  The rest aloofe are the Dardanian wives : x

  With bleared visages + come forth to view

  The issue of th'exploit : Goe + Hercules,

{ctd. over}

F's five sentences suggest that Portia is much more immediate in connecting and releasing her innermost thoughts than her ten sentence modern equivalent. F's speech falls into two parts, an emotional opening (3/10 the thirteen and a half lines, F #1-4) and a forced control finish (6/4 in the nine and a half onrushed lines of F #5).

• unlike speech #10, here Portia is eventually able to bring her somewhat unruly thoughts under control, for though the final F sentence starts from the passion of equal capitals and spellings as she watches Bassanio approach the caskets (3/3 up to the first colon); then, with more capitals than spellings (3/1), she shows her ability to use her considerable mental discipline to draw strength from comparing herself to Dido, the classical heroine of Greece (up to the third colon) – though this doesn't come without a struggle, for the comparison is expressed via two surround phrases; but this seems to work, for after 'Goe Hercules the last two lines are free of any embellishment, as if she is finally under control, no matter how vulnerable

• that this final struggle doesn't come easily is undermined by most modern texts, which split the onrushed F #5 into three

• similarly, F sentences #1-2 move quickly as she begins to face the possibility she may lose Bassanio, a speed most modern texts reduce by splitting each of these F sentences into two

• that she is not under such complete control at the top of the speech as the modern texts suggest is beautifully illustrated by the four tiny F commas at the middle and end of F #1 line one and at the end of the first two lines of F #2, which link somewhat distinct thoughts together far more quickly than the relentlessly logical heavier punctuation (an exclamation mark, a period, and two semicolons) that the modern texts set

• F's longer spelled words emphasize action throughout ('doe love', 'finde', 'loose', 'bowe' 'creepe', 'redeeme', 'Goe') while, amongst other emotional releases, there is a fixed need for 'musique x 3/musicke', as well as the wonderfully hopeful 'bride-groomes eare'

• F #3's surround phrase ' : he may win,/And what is musique then ?' seems to anticipate her later F #4 'bride-groome' hope, while F #5's surround phrases highlights her understanding of her desperate situation
' : I stand for sacrifice, /The rest aloofe are the Dardanian wives :
/With bleared visages come forth to view/The issue of th'exploit : '

10

Go*, Hercules,
Live thou, I live ; with much much, 8 more dismay
I view the fight [than] thou that mak'st the fray.

Live thou, I live + with [ ] much + more dismay
I view the fight,x [then] thou that mak'st the fray.

12/ Bassanio   **What finde I here? /Faire Portias counterfeit.**   3.2.114 - 148

Background: Having chosen the (correct) lead casket, Bassanio discovers a clue to his reward and fate. One note: the bolded text (F #6-7) denotes the possibility of a 'magical' metrical pattern (one where the heartbeat is reversed). 9

Style: essentially solo (though any part of the larger group may be included at any time) until the final ten lines

Where: the casket room   **To Whom:** self, Portia's portrait, the message within the leaden casket, and, eventually, Portia herself, in front of Portia and Nerrissa and members of their respective trains

# of Lines: 35   Probable Timing: 1.45 minutes

Modern Text

12/ Bassanio

1 What find* I here?

2 Fair* Portia's counterfeit!

3 What demi*△god
   Hath come so near* creation?†

4 Move these eyes*?†
   Or whether, riding on the balls* of mine,
   Seem* they in motion?

5 Here are sever'd lips,
   Parted with sugar* breath; so sweet a bar*
   Should sunder such sweet friends. †

6 Here in her hairs*
   The △painter plays* the △spider; and hath woven
   A golden mesh t'entrap the hearts of men
   Faster then gnats in cobwebs. †

7 But her eyes* -
   How could he see to do* them?†

First Folio

12/ Bassanio

1 What finde I here?

2 Faire Portias counterfeit. +

3 Hath come so neere creation? move these eies?
   Or whether+ riding on the bals of mine+
   Seeme they in motion?

   What demie God

4 Here are sever'd lips, + so sweet a barre
   Parted with suger breath, +
   Should sunder such sweet friends: here in her haires
   The Painter plaies the Spider; and hath woven
   A golden mesh t'intrap the hearts of men
   Faster then gnats in cobwebs: but her eies,
   How could he see to doe them? having made one,

Once more F's structure allows the character moments of great rationality, and then on-rolling moments as his thoughts almost run away with him. In this case, the onrush occurs as the F Bassanio examines Portia's picture – the key to the fact that he has chosen correctly (**F's two sentences #3-#4, which modern texts expand to seven sentences, #3-#9). There is also a strange modern rewrite at the end of the speech which will be discussed below.**

• in this speech there are three times as many long spelled words as capitals (9/27), and when the capitals do occur they are often found alongside the long spellings, as if the personal releases lead him to explore and revel even more in the images at hand (the early discoveries in sentences #2, #3, and the opening of #4, viz. 'Faire Portias'; 'What demie God'; 'The Painter plaies the Spider'; and once the victorious scroll has been read, 'Faire Lady'; twice)

• the few bursts of passion relate to F #2's discovery of Portia's portrait and the start of F #3's ensuing surround phrase praise of it (2/3); her further praise between the first two colons of F #4 (2/2); and F #8's first line of appeal for confirmation(2/2)

• there are other moments when the releases are purely personal/emotional – from the moment of talking about her eyes (mid F #4, 1/9), the reading of the scroll (F #6-#7,1/5), and his final appeal for Portia to confirm that he has indeed won her (F #9, 1/3)

---

8 F = 'much', setting a nine syllable line, Q = 'much much', maintaining pentameter: the shorter F setting suggests Portia is so nervous that she cannot even speak 'proper' verse at this moment
9 see Appendix 3

[Me thinkes] it should have power to steale both his
And leave it selfe unfurnisht : Yet looke how farre
The substance of my praise doth wrong this shadow
In underprising it, so farre this shadow
Doth limpe behinde the substance.   Here's the scroule,

5
The continent, and summarie of my fortune.

6
You that choose not by the view,[+]
Chance as faire, and choose as true :
Since this fortune fals to you,
Be content, and seeke no new.

7
If you be well pleasd with this,
And hold your fortune for your blisse,
Turne you where your Lady is,
And claime her with a loving kisse.

8
A gentle scroule: Faire Lady, by your leave,
I come by note[+] to give, and to receive,
Like one of two contending in a prize[+]
That thinks he hath done well in peoples eies : x
Hearing applause and universall shout,
Giddie in spirit, still gazing in a doubt
Whether those peales of praise be his or no.

9
So[+] thrice faire Lady[+] stand I[+] even so,
As doubtfull whether what I see be true,
Untill confirm'd, sign'd, ratified by you.

• and there are moments where he simply stays calm, though probably more benumbed by events than an actual exercise of will, such as the extended (and notice how he compresses spellings of some words)
"move these eies ?/Or whether riding on the bals of mine/ . . . Here are sever'd lips/ Parted with suger breath,"
and once the scroll confirms his victory, the equally lengthy
"by your leave,/I come by note to give, and to receive./Like one of two contending in a prize /That thinks he hath done well in peoples eies:'
and, as with other suitors, a moment of enforced calm as he begins to face the scroll

"The continent, and summarie of my fortune."

• and, quite naturally, the reading of the 'scroule' is emotional (1/5, F #6-7), with one lovely unembellished line
"If you be well pleasd with this,"

• F's sentences #8-#9 are rewritten by most modern texts (#13-#15) . . . .

• . . . the original F #8 is much more ungrammatical than the modern texts' revamping: but it's only natural that Bassanio should run three different, yet connected, thoughts together as one onrush – he's been dreaming about this moment for more than two years, and has won

• the original final three line sentence (F #9) makes much more of Bassanio's appeal to Portia for confirmation of his good fortune than the modern texts' simply folding it into the end of the previous sentence (mt #15)

• and, most unusually for a modern rewrite, mt's longer #15 offers much less dramatic action than F originally set - there is no longer any direct appeal, merely a statement of bewilderment

• and it's a much more speedy appeal, for modern texts have added three grammatically correct (but rhetorically unnecessary) commas to F #9's first line, thus inordinately slowing the start of F's appeal

---

8
              Having made one,
[Methinks] * it should have power to steal* both his
And leave itself* unfurnish'd . †

9
              Yet look* how far*
The substance of my praise doth wrong this shadow
In underprizing* it, so far* this shadow
Doth limp* behind* the substance.
                              Here's the scroll* ,

10
The continent, and summary* of my fortune .

11
    "You that choose not by the view,
    Chance as fair* , and choose as true :
    Since this fortune falls* to you,
    Be content, and seek* no new.

12
    If you be well pleas'd with this,
    And hold your fortune for your bliss* ,
    Turn* you where your ^lady is,
    And claim* her with a loving kiss* ."

13
A gentle scroll* . †

14
              Faire ^lady, by your leave,
I come by note, to give, and to receive . †

15
Like one of two contending in a prize,
That thinks he hath done well in people's eyes* ,
Hearing applause and universal* shout,
Giddy* in spirit, still gazing in a doubt
Whether those peals* of praise be his or no, ◊
So, thrice-°fair* ^lady, stand I, even so,
As doubtful* whether what I see be true,
Until* confirm'd, sign'd, ratified by you.

13/ Portia You see [me] Lord [Bassanio] where I stand,

3.2.149 - 174

Background: To their mutual delight, Bassanio has chosen the correct casket, and, despite the lead casket's message that Portia is his for the taking, he publicly refuses to assume anything 'Untill confirm'd, sign'd, ratified by you.'. The following is both her response and her warning as expressed quite clearly in the last four lines.

Style: one on one address in front of a larger group

Where: the casket-room   **To Whom:** Bassanio, with the larger group including Gratiano and Nerrissa, some of Portia's household, and musicians

# of Lines: 26   **Probable Timing: 1.15 minutes**

Modern Text

13/ Portia

1 You see [me], Lord [Bassanio], where I stand,
  Such as I am.†

2   Though for myself* alone
  I would not be ambitious in my wish
  To wish myself* much better, yet for you,
  I would be trebled twenty times myself*
  A thousand times more fair*, ten thousand times more rich,
  'That only* to stand high in your account,
  I might in virtues, beauties, livings, friends,
  Exceed account.†

3   But the full sum of me
  Is sum of [something] ; which, to term* in gross* ,
  Is an unlesson'd* girl*, unschool'd, unpractic'd* ,
  Happy in this, she is not yet so old
  But she may learn* ; happier [than] this,
  She* is not bred so dull but she can learn* ;
  Happiest of all, is that her gentle spirit
  Commits [itself*] to yours to be directed,
  As from her ᴬlord, her ᴬgovernor*, her ᴬking.

4 Myself*, and what is mine, to you and yours
  Is now converted.

5   But now I was the Lord
  Of this fair* mansion, master of my servants,
  Queen* o'er myself*; and even now, but now,
  This house, these servants, and this same myself*
  Are yours - my [ᴬlord's!] - I give them with this ring,
  Which when you part from, lose*, or give away,
  Let it presage the ruin* of your love,
  And be my vantage to exclaim* on you.

First Folio

13/ Portia

1 You see [my] ⁺ Lord [Bassanio] ⁺ where I stand,
  Such as I am; though for my selfe alone
  I would not be ambitious in my wish,ₓ
  To wish my selfe much better, yet for you,
  I would be trebled twenty times my selfe,
  A thousand times more faire, ten thousand times
  More rich, that onely to stand high in your account
  I might in vertues, beauties, livings, friends,
  Exceed account: but the full summe of me
  Is sum of [nothing]:ₓ which ⁺ to terme in grosse,
  Is an unlessoned girle, unschool'd, unpractiz'd,
  Happy in this, she is not yet so old
  But she may learne: happier [then] this,
  Shee is not bred so dull but she can learne;
  Happiest of all, is that her gentle spirit
  Commits [it selfe] to yours to be directed,
  As from her Lord, her Governour, her King.

2 My selfe, and what is mine, to you and yours
  Is now converted.

3   But now I was the Lord
  Of this faire mansion, master of my servants,
  Queene ore my selfe:: and even now, but now,
  This house, these servants, and this same my selfe
  Are yours, my [Lord], ⁺ I give them with this ring,
  Which when you part from, loose, or give away,
  Let it presage the ruine of your love,
  And be my vantage to exclaime on you.

As with speech #11, Portia is eventually able to gain some measure of self control, with the final two sentences of each text matching in content. That the F Portia has more difficulty at the start is structurally supported by F's opening onrushed sentence (split into three by most modern texts), which is only natural, considering she has finally and legitimately – despite all the struggling temptations voiced in speech #10 - been won by the man of her choice.

• quite naturally, emotion over intellect is the speech's keynote, with three times as many long spelled words (22) as capitals (just 7), and of the seven capitals, six concentrate either on Bassanio directly ('Lord Bassanio' and 'Lord') or her feelings towards him as she willingly gives herself to 'her Lord, her Governour, her King.'

• sadly, the modern texts' reworking of the shaded lines seems to diminish Portia's love, for whereas in F the overlong 12 syllable line is the second of the pair, so emphasizing her desire to be of more worth for Bassanio's sake, the modern reversal just emphasizes the stated desire for more (probably un-needed) wealth

• the struggle to establish control inherent in the onroll of F #1's onrush is enhanced by the two semicolons underscoring both her stated lack of ambition for herself and her joy that she feels can grow under Bassanio's influence, with the three surround phrases summing up her feelings quite splendidly, especially the two formed in part by the emotional semicolon, notably the opening vulnerability
  " . You see [me] Lord [Bassanio] where I stand,/Such as I am ; "
  " : but the full summe of me/Is sum of nothing : "
  (and the actress has a wondrous choice between sum 'of nothing' as F suggests, or 'of something' as the quarto and most modern texts offer)
  " : happier then this,/Shee is not bred so dull but she can learne ; "

• F #1's first line and a half stays factual (2/0) for the only time in the speech, then she becomes emotional (0/5) for the five and half line more-wealthy-wish-for-you; and after the unembellished 'capper' I might in vertues, beauties, livings, friends/Exceed account:', her five and a half line self-definition is even more emotional (0/8), then finishing F #1 with a final three line passionate flourish (starting with 'Happiest of all', 3/2)

• and while F #2-3 are still emotional (2/7 in nine lines), proportionately they are less so than F #1 (5/15 in seventeen lines), while the excess spelling in the last three lines ('loose' for 'lose', 'ruine' and 'exclaime') clearly illustrates her belief in her own values despite giving herself willingly to Bassanio, especially her sense of right and wrong, and as such foreshadows the end of the play

14/ Lorenzo How sweet the moone-light sleepes upon this banke, 5.1.54 - 68

15/ Lorenzo The reason is, your spirits are attentive : 5.1.70 - 88

Background: Looking after Portia's home in Belmont, having been told that both Portia and Nerrissa, and Bassanio and Gratiano with the saved Anthonio, will be returning soon independently of each other, the now married Lorenzo and Jessica (Shylocke's daughter) are enjoying a final moment of togetherness before the hustle of the returning groups envelops them. These two successive speeches are Lorenzo's longest in the play; #14 is self explanatory, while #15 is triggered by Jessica's remark, offered as music is heard from offstage. 'I am never merry when I heare sweet musique.'

Style: each are part of a two-handed scene

Where: outdoors, perhaps a terrace or garden, part of Portia's palace

To Whom: each to Jessica

speech #14, # of Lines: 15 **Probable Timing: 0.50 minutes**

speech #15, # of Lines: 19 **Probable Timing: 1.00 minutes**

Modern Text

14/ Lorenzo

1 How sweet the moon*°light sleeps* upon this bank*!†
   Here* will we sit, and let the sounds of music*
   Creep* in our ears*. †

2 Soft stillness*. and the night
   Become the touches* of sweet harmony*. .†

3 Sit Jessica . †

4 Look* how the floor* of heaven
   Is thick* inlaid* with patens* of bright gold. †

5 There's not the smallest orb* which thou behold'st
   But in his motion like an △angel* sings,
   Still quiring to the young-°ey'd* △cherubins;
   Such harmony* is in immortall* souls*. ,
   But whilst this muddy vesture of decay
   Doth grossly* close [it in], we cannot hear* it . †

6 Come ho*, and wake Diana with a hymn* ,
   With sweetest touches* pierce* your △mistress'* ear* ,
   And draw her home with music*.

First Folio

14/ Lorenzo

1 How sweet the moone-light sleepes upon this banke,
   Heere will we sit, and let the sounds of musicke
   Creepe in our eares soft stilnes,ₓ and the night
   Become the tutches of sweet harmonie :
   Sit Jessica, looke how the floore of heaven
   Is thicke inlayed with pattens of bright gold,
   There's not the smallest orbe which thou beholdst
   But in his motion like an Angell sings,
   Still quiring to the young eyed Cherubins;
   Such harmonie is in immortall soules,
   But whilst this muddy vesture of decay
   Doth grosly close [in it], we cannot heare it :
   Come hoe, and wake Diana with a hymne,
   With sweetest tutches pearce your Mistresse eare,
   And draw her home with musicke.

With its one sentence, F seems to suggest that Lorenzo never stops talking (whether he is enchanted by the music, the night, and his beloved, or is merely a talkative bore is up to each actor to explore). The modern texts split the speech into six grammatically correct sentences, perhaps emphasising the potential for boredom above all else.

· this is very much a speech of personal belief rather than an intellectual thesis (only 4 capitals as opposed to 24 long spellings in just 15 lines)

• his enthusiasm seems to come in two emotional bursts, the first focusing on the 'moone-light' and 'the floore of heaven' (1/12 in the first six lines), and the instructions for the musicians to play so as to please and awaken mythical Diana and speed Portia's return home (1/7 the last three lines)

• apart from the proper name 'Jessica', the other three capitals seem to suggest a love of things mystical and mythical, viz. 'Angell'; 'Cherubins'; and the allusion to the classical goddess of chastity and the hunt, 'Diana', also a name for the moon

• there is only one phrase in the speech where there is no embellishment, and it deals with the rather darker side of the human condition,

   "But whilst this muddy vesture of decay/Doth grosly close [it in],"

Modern Text

15/ Lorenzo

1 The reason is, your spirits are attentive;
For do* but note a wild* and wanton herd*
Or race of youthful and unhandled colts,
Fetching mad bounds, bellowing and neighing loud,
Which is the hot condition of their blood,
If they but hear* perchance a trumpet sound,
Or any air* of music* touch their ears*,
You shall perceive them make a mutual* stand,
Their savage eyes turn'd to a modest gaze,
By the sweet power of music* ; therefore the △poet
Did feign△ that Orpheus drew trees, stones, and floods; ◊
Since nought so stockish, hard, and full of rage,
But music* for time doth change his nature . †

2 The man that hath no music* in himself*,
Nor is not moved with concord of sweet sounds,
Is fit for treasons, stratagems, and spoils* ;
The motions of his spirit are dull as night,
And his affections dark* as [Erebus],
Let no such man be trusted. †

3 Mark* the music* .

First Folio

15/ Lorenzo

1 The reason is, your spirits are attentive: x
For doe but note a wilde and wanton heard
Or race of youthful and unhandled colts,
Fetching mad bounds, bellowing and neighing loud,
Which is the hot condition of their bloud,
If they but heare perchance a trumpet sound,
Or any ayre of musicke touch their eares,
You shall perceive them make a mutuall stand,
Their savage eyes turn'd to a modest gaze,
By the sweet power of musicke: x   therefore the Poet
Did faine that Orpheus drew trees, stones, and floods.

2 Since naught so stockish, hard, and full of rage,
But musicke for time doth change his nature,
The man that hath no musicke in himselfe,
Nor is not moved with concord of sweet sounds,
Is fit for treasons, stratagems, and spoyles,
The motions of his spirit are dull as night,
And his affections darke as [Erobus]
Let no such man be trusted: marke the musicke .

Though the modern texts almost maintain F's sentence pattern, the seemingly minor and highly grammatical restructuring of the end of sentence #1 suppresses Lorenzo's inarticulate wonder at the power of music, and replaces it with normal rationality.

• this speech, though still highly personal, is somewhat less passionate than speech #14 above (here 3/18 in eighteen lines, compared to the earlier 4/24 in fifteen)

• this could be partially because here Lorenzo's love of music seems to generate moments of total calm and/or non-embellished concentration as he explains its powers , from the opening surround phrase
" . The reason is, your spirits are attentive : "
'attentive' meaning 'concentrated', going on to explain music's appeal to nearly everyone
"Since naught so stockish, hard, and full of rage,"
"Or race of youthful and unhandled colts, /Fetching mad bounds,
    bellowing and neighing loud,"
and that anyone not so moved is not to be trusted
"Nor is not moved with concord of sweet sounds,/Is fit for treasons,
    stratagems . . . "

• even so, there is only one really emotional outburst as he describes how the 'rough and unhandled colts' can be charmed by music (0/7, six and a half lines from the fifth line 'Which is the hot condition of their bloud,'); and from this springs the one intellectual (capitalised) cluster, embracing once more the classical/mythical with the surround phrase ' : therefore the Poet/Did faine that Orpheus drew trees, stones, and floods . ', with the power of his lute (2/1)

• the final phrase, surround as it also is, reinforces his all-encompassing pre-occupation ' : marke the musicke . '

#'s 16-17: THOSE REFUSING TO STAY WITH SHYLOCKE

16/ Clowne   Certainely, my conscience will serve me to run   2.2.1-32

Background: The first speech for Launcelet Gobbo, the servant to Shylocke – someone, as some commentators suggest, interested in the sensual things of life [10] : as such it is self-explanatory.

Style: solo

Where: unspecified, somewhere in a public place   **To Whom:** direct audience address   **Probable Timing: 1.30 minutes**

# of Lines: 27

Modern Text

16/ Clowne

1 Certainly*, my conscience will serve me to run from this Jew my ^master* . †

2 The fiend is at mine elbow and tempts me, saying to me, "[Gobbo], Launcelet [Gobbo], good Launcelot," or "good [Gobbo]," or "good Launcelot [Gobbo], use your legs, take the start, run away*" . †

3 My conscience says*, "No; take heed* honest Launcelot, take heed, honest [Gobbo]," or as afore'said, "honest Launcelot [Gobbo], do* not run*, scorn running with thy heels*" . †

4 Well, the most couragi-ous* fiend bids me pack*. †

5 "*Fia!*" says* the fiend ; "away!" says* the fiend; "[fore*] the heavens, rouse up a brave mind*," says* the fiend, "and run" . †

6 Well, my conscience, hanging about the neck* of my heart, says* very* wisely to me, "My honest friend Launcelot, being an honest man's son*" - or rather an honest woman's son*, for indeed* my ^father did something smack, something grow to*, he had a kind* of taste - well*, my conscience says*, "Lancelet, [budge] not" . †

7 "[Budge]," says* the fiend . †

8 "[Budge] not', says* my conscience. †

First Folio

16/ Clowne

1 Certainely,ₓ my conscience will serve me to run from this Jew my Maister : the fiend is at mine elbow,ₓ and tempts me, saying to me, [[Jobbe]] ⁺ Launcelet [Jobbe], good Launcelet, or good [Jobbe], or good Launcelet [Jobbe], use your legs, take the start, run awaie : my conscience saies ⁺ no ; take heede honest Launcelet, take heed⁺ honest [Jobbe], or as afore-said⁺ honest Launcelet [Jobbe], doe not runne, scorne running with thy heeles ; well, the most coragi-ous fiend bids me packe, *fia*⁺ saies the fiend, away⁺ saies the fiend, ⁺ [for] the heavens⁺ rouse up a brave minde⁺ saies the fiend, and run ; well, my conscience⁺ hanging about the necke of my heart, saies verie wisely to me : ₓ my honest friend Launcelet, being an honest mans sonne, or rather an honest womans sonne, for indeede my Father did something smack, something grow too ; ₓ he had a kinde of taste : ₓ wel, my conscience saies⁺ Lancelet⁺ [bouge] not, [bouge] ⁺ not saies my conscience.

The two texts couldn't be more different, with F's one onrushed sentence, encompassing more emotional semicolons (seven) than the more rational idea building colons (five), being reworked as a more rational thirteen sentence speech. However, while F's speed should be explored in rehearsal and maintained in performance, this is one of those occasions where the modern text should be first examined sentence by sentence just to see what stepping stones the F sentence jam together in his (frantic) speed (after all, he is contemplating breaking the law in leaving his indentured master and he is talking to fiends and angels!).

• the enormity of his situation seems to be marked by the fact that, apart from the first word 'Certainely', there are no further long spellings until the sixth line, i.e., the speech starts very quietly

• of the thirty long spellings fourteen (save for 'Maister') come in just four clusters, 'doe not runne, scorne running with thy heeles'; (who God blesse the marke) is a kinde of divell'; 'is the divell himselfe'; and, 'I will runne fiend, my heeles are at your commandement, I will runne'

• that the Clowne's personal emotional response rather than pure intellectual analysis is the keynote to the start of the speech can be seen in that, apart from the opening 'Jew my Maister' and the later 'Father', the only capital letters in the equivalent of what the modern texts set as the speech's first ten sentences (eighteen lines in all) are references to Launcelet's own name

{ctd. over}

---

[10] As Mahood points out (Mahood, M M. ed., *The Merchant of Venice*, The New Cambridge Shakespeare, Cambridge: Cambridge University Press. 1987), 'Lancelot' is the name ascribed to the medieval Romance hero, and the name usually set by most modern texts, even though it only appears once in Q2. However, the Q1/Q2/F 'Launcelet' means 'little knife', which has at least three implications; one referring to his cutting witticisms; another to his size - either fat (if played by Kemp, the clown of the company) or thin; the third to his expressed desire for sexual involvement with 'fifteen wives, a leven widdowes and nine maides', which he acknowledges is 'a simple comming in for one man'

9 "Conscience," say I, "you counsel* well". †

10 "Fiend," say I, "you counsel* well". †

11 To be rul'd by my conscience, I should stay with the Jew my ᵈmaster*, who (God bless* the mark*) is a kinde of de-vil* ; and to run away from the Jew, I should be ruled by the fiend, who, saving your reverence, is the devil* him-self* . †

12 Certainly* the Jew is the very* devil* incarnation, and in my conscience, my conscience is [but] a kind* of hard conscience, to offer to counsel* me to stay with the Jew. †

13 The fiend gives the more friendly counsel* : I will run* , fiend; my heels* are at your commandment* , I will run* .

• the surround phrases deal not only with the opening problem and final resolution of the situation,
": my conscience saies no ; "
": the fiend gives the more friendly counsaile : "
there is also a lovely moment highlighted as he touches upon his father's sexual appetite
"; he had a kinde of taste ; "

• modern texts add no fewer than nineteen extra pieces of punctuation (†) not to be found in F, which has the unfortunate effect of slowing down the more frenetic of the Clowne's deliberations: for example, in the following three line passage, modern texts add eight extra commas
"wel, my conscience saies 'Lancelet † bouge not, bouge † saies the fiend, bouge not sates my conscience, conscience † say I † you counsaile well, fiend † say I † you counsaile well."
(try reading the passage first observing all the †'s as pauses or new thoughts - the modern version - and then without, by going back to how F set the text)

conscience † say I † you counsaile well, fiend † say I † you counsaile well, to be rul'd by my conscience † I should stay with the Jew my Maister, (ₓwho † God blesse the marke) is a kinde of divell ; and to run away from the Jew † I should be ruled by the fiend, who † saving your reverence † is the divell himselfe : certainely the Jew is the verie divell incarnation, and in my conscience, my conscience is a kinde of hard conscience, to offer to counsaile me to stay with the Jew ; the fiend gives the more friendly counsaile : I will runne † fiend, † my heeles are at your commandement, I will runne.

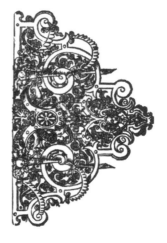

17/ Jessica   **I am sorry thou wilt leave my Father so,**   between 2.3.1 - 21

Background: This is the first speech in the play for Shylocke's daughter: as such it is self-explanatory.

Style: as part of a two-handed scene

Where: somewhere in Shylocke's home   **To Whom:** Launcelet, who is leaving Shylocke's employment to become a member of Bassanio's entourage

# of Lines: 15   **Probable Timing: 0.50 minutes**

Modern Text

17/ Jessica

1   I am sorry thou wilt leave my ᐃfather so . †

2   Our house is hell, and thou, a merry⁎ devil⁎ ,
    Did'st rob it of some taste of tediousness⁎ . †

3   But fare⁎ thee well, there is ducat for thee,
    And, Lancelot, soon⁎ at supper shalt thou see
    Lorenzo, who is thy new ᐃmaster's⁎ guest . †

4   Give him this ᐃletter, do⁎ it secretly,
    And so farewell⁎ . †

5   I would not have my ᐃfather
    See me [in] talk⁎ with thee.

6   Alack⁎, what heinous sin⁎ is it in me
    To be ashamed to be my Fathers child⁎! †

7   But though I am a daughter to his blood,
    I am not to his manners . †

8   O Lorenzo,
    If thou keep⁎ promise, I shall end this strife,
    Become a Christian and thy loving wife.

First Folio

17/ Jessica

1   I am sorry thou wilt leave my Father so,
    Our house is hell, and thou ‡ a merrie divell ⁺
    Did'st rob it of some taste of tediousnesse;
    But far thee well, there is ducat for thee,
    And ⁺ Lancelet, soone at supper shalt thou see
    Lorenzo, who is thy new Maisters guest,
    Give him this Letter, doe it secretly,
    And so farwell: I would not have my Father
    See me [ ] talke with thee.

2   Alacke, what hainous sinne is it in me
    To be ashamed to be my Fathers childe,
    But though I am a daughter to his blood,
    I am not to his manners: O Lorenzo,
    If thou keepe promise ⁺ I shall end this strife,
    Become a Christian, ₓ and thy loving wife.

The modern texts create for their Jessica a very precise rational eight sentence farewell, while F's Jessica has a two sentence speech full of ungrammatical links, redolent both of urgency and fear of discovery.

• that Jessica is rushed is clearly seen in the first long F sentence (which modern texts split into five rational separate statements) where the end of lines 1 and 6 are joined to the next simply by onrolling quick-link commas, whereas modern texts have replaced them with periods: this device is also seen at the end of line two of F sentence #2, and in all three cases the F setting suggests an immediacy not maintained by the modern texts

• the single surround phrase in the speech explains just why the F Jessica is so rushed

" . : I would not have my Father/See me talke with thee . "

• though there are the same number of capitals as long spellings (9/9), each come in clusters: there seems to be a three way struggle within her: sometimes her emotions get the better of her, as with the first two lines of F sentence #2, dealing with her disloyalty to her father (0/3); sometimes she can establish personal self control with no embellishment, as she does with the decision to reject her father in the next line and a half, and the passion of both head and heart sometimes are given sway, as with the plotting to get a message to Lorenzo, in the last five lines of sentence #1 (5/5)

#'s 18 - 21: THE CHARACTER OF SHYLOCKE

18/ Shylocke   Anthonio is a good man. My meaning in saying he is a   between 1.3.12 - 39

Background: This is Shylocke's first major speech in his opening sequence in the play, as Bassanio is negotiating for his much needed loan.

Style: as part of a two-handed scene

Where: unspecified, in some public space - possibly the Rialto   **To Whom:** Bassanio

# of Lines: 20   **Probable Timing:** 1.00 minutes

Modern Text

18/ Shylocke

1 Antonio* is a good man.

2 My meaning in saying he is a good man, is to have you understand me that he is sufficient .†

3 Yet his means* are in supposition : he hath an ᐃargo-sy,* bound to Tripolis, another to the Indies; I understand moreover upon the [Ryalto], he hath a third at Mexico, a fourth for England, and other ventures he* hath squand'red abroad .†

4 But ships are but boords*, sailors* but men ; there be land rats and water rats, water thieves* and land thieves*, I mean* ᐃpirates* , and then there is the peril* of waters, winds* , and rocks. †

5 The man is notwithstanding sufficient. †

6 Three thousand ducats : I think* I may take his bond.

7 {A}nd that I may be assured, I will bethink* me .†

8 May I speak* with Antonio*?

9 {I will not} smell pork*, {I will not} eat* of the habitation which your ᐃprophet the Nazarite conjur'd* the devil* into.†

10 I will buy with you, sell with you, talk* with you, walk* with you, and so following; but I will not eat* with you, drink* with you, nor pray with you .

First Folio

18/ Shylocke

1 Anthonio is a good man.

2 My meaning in saying he is a good man, is to have you understand me that he is suffi{ci}-ent ; yet his meanes are in supposition : he hath an Argo-sie bound to Tripolis, another to the Indies, † I understand moreover upon the [Ryalta], he hath a third at Mexi-co, a fourth for England, and other ventures hee hath squandred abroad, but ships are but boords, Saylers but men, † there be land rats,ₓ and water rats, water theeves ₓ and land theeves,¹¹ and then there is the perrill of waters, windes, and rocks: the man is notwith-standing sufficient, three thousand ducats, † I thinke I may take his bond.

3 {A}nd that I may be assured, I will bethinke mee, may I speake with Anthonio?

4 {I will not} smell porke, {I will not} eate of the habitation which your Prophet the Nazarite conjured the divell into: I will buy with you, sell with you, talke with you, walke with you, and so following : ₓ but I will not eate with you, drinke with you, nor pray with you.

Prior to this speech, the opening twelve lines of F (and the quarto) could be read as either verse or prose (though most modern texts set the passage as prose). Bassanio has questioned Shylocke's possible maligning of Anthonio's reputation - and if the scene opened in verse, by this point **whatever forced verse of polite elegance the scene might have started with would disappear.**

• F's long sentence #2 allows Shylocke to easily, almost casually, assess and dismiss Anthonio's financial situation: by splitting the sentence into five, most modern texts make it a much more determined and calculated exploration

• that he knows Anthonio has very deep financial pockets might lie in the three unembellished phrases
  "Anthonio is a good man "
  "My meaning in saying he is a good man, is to have you understand me that he is sufficient,
  "the man is notwithstanding sufficient, three thousand ducats,"
  which in turn suggests the rest is flim-flam to earn more loan points

• the majority of both spelling and capitals lies mainly in two places :

• the first comes in two contrasting sweeps in F #2, where in listing Anthonio's assets Shylocke's careful intellectual analyzing capitals come to the fore (F #2's first six lines, 6/2), to be immediately followed by a much more emotional statement of the risks involved (2/7, the rmainder of F #2) plus F #3's request to speak to Anthonio (1/3)

• and emotions continue in F #4 as he refuses to break bread with the Christians (2/7), emphasised by the firmness of the long surround lines that finish the sentence, ' : I will buy with you, sell with you, talke with you, walke with you, and so following : but I will not eate with you, drinke with you, nor pray with you . ', themselves heightened by being monosyllabic save the one word 'following'

ʷ ¹¹ traditionally actors have made two words of Ff's 'Pyrats', pronouncing it as 'Py-rats' so as to pun on the earlier images of the 'land' and 'water' rats: one commentator furthers this by offering 'pier rats' for the original word

11 What news* on the [Ryalto] ? †
12   Who is he comes here?

5 What newes on the [Ryalta], who is he comes here?

19/ Jew   **How like a fawning publican he lookes.**   1.3.41 - 52

Background: Anthonio has now joined the loan-seeking Bassanio and Shylocke. While he and Bassanio talk, Shylocke reveals his innermost feelings about Anthonio, with whom Shylocke is locked in a mutually loathing relationship.

Style: aside

Where: unspecified, in some public space - possibly the Rialto   **To Whom:** direct audience address

# of Lines: 12   **Probable Timing: 0.40 minutes**

Modern Text

19/ Jew

1 How like a fawning publican he looks*!

2 I hate him for he is a Christian;
But more, for that in low simplicity*
He lends out money gratis, and brings down*
The rate of usance here with us in Venice.

3 If I can catch him once upon the hip,
I will feed* fat the ancient grudge I bear* him.

4 He hates our sacred △nation, and he rails*
Even there where △merchants most do* congregate
On me, my bargains* , and my [well-won*]thrift,
Which he calls* interest* . †
            Cursed be my △tribe*

5 If I forgive him.

First Folio

19/ Jew

1 How like a fawning publican he lookes. †

2 I hate him for he is a Christian : x
But more, for that in low simplicitie
He lends out money gratis, and brings downe
The rate of usance here with us in Venice.

3 If I can catch him once upon the hip,
I will feede fat the ancient grudge I beare him.

4 He hates our sacred Nation, and he railes
Even there where Merchants most doe congregate
On me, my bargaines, and my [well-worne] thrift,
Which he cals interest : Cursed be my Trybe
If I forgive him.

The underlying orthography of the F text beautifully expands the statement of hatred clearly visible in the modern texts.

• F clearly shows that, while Shylocke is in relative control of himself at the start of the speech (just six embellishments in seven lines in the opening three sentences, 2/4), as the second part of the speech starts at F #4, there is a sudden explosive release of ten embellishments (4/6) in just four and a half lines as Shylocke narrows in on Anthonio's presumed hatred of things Hebraic

• it's fascinating where the emotional (long-spelled) words are found, for nearly all of them are spoken at the end of a phrase or line, as if the words were being forced out of his mouth: the same can also be found for the first two of six capitals

• the two surround phrases
" . I hate him for he is a Christian ." and " . : Cursed be my Trybe/If I forgive him ." make Shylocke's focus and future actions absolutely unequivocally clear

• the fact that this last phrase ends the speech as somewhat of a blurt ending in F #4 adds great power to the curse: however, the inevitability of this powerful statement is rather gutted when set as a deliberate (even rational) new sentence by most modern texts

20/ Shylocke **Signior Anthonio, many a time and oft** 1.3.106 - 129

Background: The following is triggered by Anthonio's asking 'Well Shylocke, shall we be beholding to you?', a seemingly innocent question. However, immediately prior to the question Anthonio has revealed his true feelings about Shylocke 'The divell can cite scripture for his purpose,/An evill soule . . .', (speech #2 above) in a remark meant either as an aside or deliberately for Shylocke to overhear.

Style: part of a three-handed scene

Where: unspecified, in some public space - possibly the Rialto   **To Whom:** Anthonio

# of Lines: 23   **Probable Timing: 1.10 minutes**

Modern Text	First Folio

20/ Shylocke

1 Signior Antonio*, many a time and oft
   In the Rialto* you have rated me
   About my moneys* and my usances. †

2 Still have I born* it with a patient shrug
   (For suff'rance is the badge of all our ^tribe) .

3 You call me misbeliever*, cut-throat* dog,
   And [spit*] upon my Jewish gaberdine,
   And all for use of that which is mine own* .

4 Well then, it now appears* you need* my help* . †

5 Go* to then, you come to me, and you say,
   "Shylock*, we would have moneys*", you say so -
   You, that did void* your rheum* upon my beard,
   And foot* me as you spurn* a stranger cur*
   Over your threshold; moneys* is your suit* .

6 What should I say to you?
                               Should I not say,

7 "Hath a dog money?
               Is it possible

8 A cur* [can] lend three thousand ducats?" †
                         Or

9 Shall I bend low, and in a bond°man's key,
   With bated breath, and whisp'ring humbleness* ,

   Say this:
   "Fair* sir, you [spat*] on me on Wednesday last,

First Folio

20/ Shylocke

1 Signior Anthonio, many a time and oft
   In the Ryalto you have rated me
   About my monies and my usances :
   Still have I borne it with a patient shrug,
   (For suffrance is the badge of all our Tribe.)

2 You call me misbeleever, cut-throate[12] dog,
   And [spet] upon my Jewish gaberdine,
   And all for use of that which is mine owne.

3 Well then, it now appeares you neede my helpe :
   Goe to then, you come to me, and you say,
   Shylock, we would have moneys, you say so :
   You ⁺ that did voide your rume upon my beard,
   And foote me as you spurne a stranger curre
   Over your threshold, ⁺ moneyes is your suite.

4 What should I say to you?
                               Should I not say,

5 Hath a dog money?
               Is it possible

6 A curre should lend three thousand ducats? ⁺ or
   Shall I bend low, and in a bond-mans key, ⁺
   With bated breath, and whispring humblenesse,
   Say this :   Faire sir, you [spet] on me on Wednesday last; x

---

While critics suggest the Elizabethan Shylocke was meant to be regarded both as a figure of fun and a villain, there is a modern (and a naturally humanist) political correctness tendency to recast Shylocke as a dignified and sympathetic victim. The modern sentence restructuring of this speech often contributes to this revision, for whereas the modern explanation seems quite reasonable, the seething ripples underneath the F text is a constant reminder of Shylocke's disturbed anger and loathing.

• at first it seems as if Shylocke is maintaining self-control: the first F sentence is only slightly passionately released (3/2 in five lines): then this is undercut by a more emotional second F sentence (1/4 in just three lines)

• then in F #3 emotional hell breaks loose with no fewer than twelve long spellings in just six lines

• even more dangerous is the sudden sense of control in the very short and unembellished sentences #4 (which is also monosyllabic) and #5

• and the danger seems to carry through into F's onrushed sentence #6 (split into two by most modern texts) with its opening surround phrase and icy calm broken by just two potentially very self-demeaning sarcastic long spelled words ('curre' and 'humblenesse'): then in the speech's last four lines Shylocke suddenly explodes via the overly-long shaded line (twelve syllables as shown, reset as a normal line plus pause by most modern texts) followed by four heavy pieces of punctuation in three lines (as opposed to only three in the previous nineteen)

this cluster has a double effect
• first, it's as if his mind is suddenly bursting, overflowing, with a series of powerful thoughts too strong to reign in — especially when two of the four are emotional semicolons
• second, the thoughts themselves are shown as five most unusual successive surround phrases ending the speech, as such all revealing the depth of his anger and hate,

---

[12] some modern texts insert a comma here to create two insults, 'cut-throate' and 'dog' from the single Qq/Ff phrase 'cut-throate dog'

You spurn'd me such a day, another time
You call'd* me dog; and for these courtesies*
I'll lend you thus much moneys*. "

" : Faire sir, you spet on me on Wednesday last ; / You spurn'd me such a
day ; another time/You cald me dog : and for these curtesies/Ile lend
you thus much moneyes . "

You spurn'd me such a day; ₓ   another time
You cald me dog: ₓ and for these curtesies
Ile lend you thus much moneyes .

21/ Shylocke   What's {a man's flesh} good for?   3.1.53 - 73

Background: Jessica has eloped with her Christian lover Lorenzo, taking a considerable portion of money and jewelry with her. As a consequence, Shylocke has been running round the streets with 'all the boyes in Venice follow him,/Crying his stones, his daughter, and his ducats.'. The lovers were aided in their elopement by two of Anthonio's friends, who now, having teased Shylocke in the public street about the elopement, make the mistake of also teasing him about how he may lose more money since Anthonio cannot repay his bond on the due date. Shylocke's response makes them fear for Anthonio's life, and thus Salerio asks/comments 'thou wilt not take his flesh, what's that good for?'. Hence the following, the first line - marked ψ- an adaptation of Salerio's question.

Style: as part of a three-handed scene
Where: unspecified, in some public space   **To Whom:** the merchants Salerio and Solanio

# of Lines: 20   **Probable Timing: 1.00 minutes**

Modern Text

21/ Shylocke

1   (ψ) What's {a man's flesh} good for?

2   To bait* fish withal* - if it will feed* nothing else, it will feed, my revenge . †

3   He hath disgrac'd me, and hind'red me half* a million, laugh'd at my losses; mock'd at my gains*, scorn'd my △nation, thwarted my bargains* cool'd* my friends, heat'd* mine enemies; and what's [his] reason?

4   I am a Jew* . †

5   Hath not a Jew eyes? †

6   Hath not a Jew hands, organs, [dimensions*], senses, affections, passions; fed with the same food*, hurt with the same weapons, subject to the same diseases, healed by the same means*, warm'd* and cool'd* by the same △winter and △summer* as a Christian is. †

7   If you prick* us, do* we not bleed*? †

8   If you tickle us, do* we not laugh? †

9   If you poison us, do* we not die? †

10 And if you wrong us, shall we not revenge? †

11 If we are like you in the rest, we will resemble you in that.

First Folio

21/ Shylocke

1   (ψ) What's {a man's flesh} good for?

2   To baite fish withall, if it will feede nothing else, it will feede my revenge ; he hath disgrac'd me, and hindred me halfe a million, laught at my losses, mockt at my gaines, scorned my Nation, thwarted my bargaines, cooled my friends, heated mine enemies , and what's [the] reason?

3   I am a Jewe : Hath not a Jew eyes? hath not a Jew hands, organs, [dementions], sences, affections, passions,+ fed with the same foode, hurt with the same weapons, subject to the same diseases, healed by the same meanes, warmed and cooled by the same Winter and Sommmer as a Christian is : if you pricke us + doe we not bleede? if you tickle us, doe we not laugh? if you poison us + doe we not die? and if you wrong us + shall we not revenge? if we are like you in the rest, we will resemble you in that.

Nowhere is the contrast between Shylocke as victim and Shylocke as a dangerous man to be found more than in the modern text handling of this speech. The sprawling mixed intellectual and emotive six sentence F text (five sentence quarto) with its enormous onrush as Shylocke reaches the famous and critical self-definition stage of 'I am a Jew' could not be more different than the clear, controlled, dignified statement the modern texts have created by turning the original setting into at least sixteen logical sentences.

• a deceptive unembellished icy calm opens F #1

• then F #2's 'it will feede my revenge;' suddenly plunges into emotional release (1/8 in just five lines), heightened by the emotional semicolon following 'my revenge' and the single capital letter highlighting the all important concept to him of 'my Nation'

• F #3's 'I am a Jewe' is fascinating in two ways, for it is one huge onrushed release (totally changed by most modern texts which split F #3 into an enormously logical eight sentences) and it markedly changes energies three times

• the demand of the precise intellectual 'jews-and-christians-are-the-same argument is intensified by opening with two surround phrases
'. I am a Jewe : Hath not a Jew eyes ? '
the passionate drive of which (7/5 in six lines) continues down to the second colon

• then the next two lines, starting with 'if you pricke us', burst into full emotional release (0/5), the whole being expresed via three consecutive surround phrases ': if you pricke us doe we not bleede? if you tickle us, doe we not laugh? if you poison us doe we not die?'

12   If a Jew wrong a Christian, what is his humility .†
13 Revenge?
14   If a Christian wrong a Jew, what should his suf-ferance be by Christian example .†   Why, revenge?   The vil-
15 lainy* you teach me, I will execute, and it shall go* hard
16 but I will better the instruction.

4   If a Jew wrong a Christian, what is his humility, revenge?
5   If a Christian wrong a Jew, what should his suf-ferance be by Christian example, why[+] revenge?   The vil-
6 lanie you teach me [+] I will execute, and it shall goe hard but I will better the instruction.

• and the sentence finishes with absolute (presumably enforced) unembellished calm as the dreadful " . . . .? and if you wrong us shall we not revenge ? if we are like you in the rest, we will resemble you in that . " is uttered, highlighted by being set as two more surround phrases

• then, rather frighteningly, in F #4 and #5 Shylocke's intellectual control is re-established once more (5/0 in just two lines) – a fine indication of a dangerously determined assessment as he describes what he has learned to do thanks to 'Christian example'

• by F #6 Shylocke returns to an almost completely controlled non-embellished neutrality (0/1) – (like a cobra biding his time to strike?): also, with the non-setting of two added modern commas ([+]) the potential danger in the quicker uttered threats of 'revenge' at the end of F #5 and 'I will execue' in F #6 become much more purposeful

22: ANTHONIO'S DILEMMA

22/ Jew   **Jaylor, looke to him, tell not me of mercy,**   between 3.3.1 -18

Background: This is the first appearance of Shylocke since his avowal to his friend Tuball that as regards Anthonio 'I will have the heart of him if he forfeit', and, presumably, his first sight of Anthonio at large since Anthonio's imprisonment for debt. As such, the following is self explanatory.

Style: as part of a four handed scene

Where: unspecified, somewhere in the public view   **To Whom:** a Jaylor accompanying Anthonio, and Anthonio himself who is accompanied by his friend Solanio

# of Lines: 16   **Probable Timing: 0.50 minutes**

Modern Text

22/ [Shylocke as] **Shylocke**

1   Jailer*, look* to him, tell not me of mercy . †

2   This is the fool* that [lent] out money gratis.

3   Jaylor*, look* to him.

4   I'll have my bond, speak* not against my bond,
   I have sworn* an oath that I will have my bond. †

5   Thou call'dst me dog before thou hadst a cause,
   But since I am a dog, beware my fangs* . †

6   The Duke shall grant me justice . †

7   I do wonder,
   Thou naughty ᐞjailer*, that thou art so fond
   To come abroad with him at his request.

8   I'll have my bond; I will not hear* thee speak* . †

9   I'll have my bond, and therefore speak* no more.

10   I'll not be made a soft and dull-°ey'd fool*
   To shake the head, relent, and sigh, and yield*
   To Christian intercessors. †

11   Follow not,
   I'll have my bond.

First Folio

22/ [Shylocke as] **Jew**

1   Jaylor, looke to him, tell not me of mercy,
   This is the foole that [lends] out money gratis.

2   Jaylor, looke to him.

3   Ile have my bond, speake not against my bond,
   I have sworne an oath that I will have my bond:
   Thou call'dst me dog before thou hadst a cause,
   But since I am a dog, beware my phangs,
   The Duke shall grant me justice, I do wonder +
   Thou naughty Jaylor, that thou art so fond
   To come abroad with him at his request.

4   Ile have my bond, + I will not heare thee speake,
   Ile have my bond, and therefore speake no more.

5   Ile not be made a soft and dull ey'd foole,ₓ
   To shake the head, relent, and sigh, and yeeld
   To Christian intercessors : follow not,
   Ile have no speaking, I will have my bond.

When last seen with the taunting Christians and Tuball the Q/F prefix was the personal 'Shy.'. Now, in public, the Q/F prefix names him 'Jew', a prefix he keeps until the first signs of defeat in the trial scene. Q2 and most modern texts use 'Shy.' throughout and thus lose the transition in public persona. **This is of even more concern when coupled with the modern text determination to show Shylocke still capable of dignified debate, which here leads them to expand F's onrushed five sentences into eleven short self-controlled rational statements - somewhat surprising when F's orthography shows the speech as emotional rather than intellectual (3/14 overall).**

• throughout F, there is a greater spontaneous flow and immediacy: the frequent quick-link comma connections (reset as periods by most modern texts for mt. #5, #6 and #8, and then with more periods replacing the F colons mt. #4 and #10) suggest a mind working far more quickly than its modern counterpart

• yet, startlingly, within this onrush and the sudden bursts of emotion, the previously seen non-embellished and controlled Shylocke moments (speeches #18-21) are even more magnified here, with such supposedly emotive phrases as
   "Ile have my bond" – no fewer than three separate times!
   "Thou call'dst me dog before thou hadst a cause, /But since I am a dog"
   "The Duke shall grant me justice,"
   "I do wonder . . . that thou art so fond /To come abroad with him at his request."
   "follow not, . . . I will have my bond"
all being uttered with no embellishment whatsoever, suggesting a very dangerous calm, especially given the circumstances

• within this calm there are occasional small powerful bursts of emotion, such as 'Jaylor, looke to him' twice, and 'I will not heare thee speake', but apart from these and the reference to his own 'phangs' and Anthonio as a 'foole' the sense of vocal control, even while the flow of the speech almost runs away with him, is quite remarkable

#'s 23 - 26: THE TRIAL

23/ Duke **Make roome, and let him stand before our face.** 4.1.16 - 34

Background: This is the first and only scene for the Duke of Venice, who, having expressed his private sympathies for and directly to Anthonio, now addresses Shylocke publicly as soon as the latter enters for the hearing of his suite. As such it is self-explanatory.

Style: public address, aimed specifically at one man

Where: wherever the trial/hearing is taking place, presumably in a court or the Duke's official chambers **To Whom:** Shylocke, in front of at least Anthonio, Bassanio and Gratiano, together with any other judges ('Magnificoes' as the First Folio suggests), court officials, and perhaps supporters of both Anthonio and Shylocke

# of Lines: 19 **Probable Timing: 1.00 minutes**

Modern Text

23/ Duke

1 Make room*, and let him stand before our face. 13

2 Shylock*, the world thinks*, and I think* so too*,
   That thou but leadest this fashion of thy malice*
   To the last hour* of act, and then 'tis thought
   Thou'lt show thy mercy and remorse more strange
   Than is thy strange apparant cruelty;
   And where thou now [exacts*] the penalty,
   Which is a pound of this poore* Δmerchant's flesh,
   Thou wilt not onely* loose14 the forfeiture,
   But touch'd with [human*] gentleness* and love,
   Forgive a moi'ty* of the principal*,
   Glancing an eye of pity* on his losses*,
   That have of late so huddled* on his back* ,
   Enow to press* a royal* Δmerchant down* ,
   And pluck* commiseration of his state
   From brassy* bosoms* and rough hearts of [flint],
   From stubborn* Turks* and Tartars never train'd
   To offices of tender curtesy*. †

3 We all expect a gentle answer, Jew!

First Folio

23/ Duke

1 Make roome, and let him stand before our face.

2 Shylocke + the world thinkes, and I thinke so to +
   That thou but leadest this fashion of thy mallice
   To the 'last houre of act, and then 'tis thought
   Thou'lt shew thy mercy and remorse more strange,x
   Than is thy strange apparant cruelty;
   And where thou now [exact'st] the penalty,
   Which is a pound of this poore Merchants flesh,
   Thou wilt not onely loose the forfeiture,
   But touch'd with [humane] gentlenesse and love : x
   Forgive a moytie of the principall,
   Glancing an eye of pitty on his losses +
   That have of late so hudled on his backe,
   Enow to presse a royall Merchant downe; x
   And plucke commiseration of his state
   From brassie bosomes,x and rough hearts of [flints],
   From stubborne Turkes and Tarters never traind
   To offices of tender curtesie,
   We all expect a gentle answer + Jew?+

Once more the F orthography underscores the personal concerns and humanity beneath the apparent dignity usually and automatically ascribed to the status of a character known as a 'Duke'

• the task is not as easy for the Duke as it may first appear, and the speech is far more personally emotional (twenty-three long spellings) than intellectual (just four capitals and only three pieces of major punctuation)

• that the Duke is affected can be seen in that two of the three pieces of heavy punctuation are emotional semicolons, one following the suggestion that Shylocke's act could be seen as 'strange apparent cruelty; and the other acknowledging that Anthonio is faced with enough horrors sufficient 'to presse a royall Merchant downe;'

• the long second sentence is a constant struggle between control and personal emotion

a/ the first two and a half lines are emotional (0/5) as he describes Shylocke's current behavior

b/ then there are two and a half lines of non-embellished self-control as the Duke appeals to Shylocke's mercy

c/ then comes a highly emotional explosion (4/17 in 11 lines) as he expresses the hope/command (couched in the terms of generalities) that Shylocke should release Anthonio from the bond

d/ and finally the apparent calm of F's last two lines are undermined by the comma linking them, suggesting that the final uninterrupted "We all expect a gentle answer Jew?" (as opposed to the modern comma preceding 'Jew') comes out somewhat unexpectedly and uncontrolled (exasperated perhaps at Shylocke's current non-response): unfortunately most modern texts set the last line as a much more controlled separate sentence, mt. #3

---

13 most modern texts suggest Shylocke does as requested

14 F and some modern texts = 'loose', F4/other modern texts = 'lose'

13 most modern texts = 'loose', F4/other modern texts = 'lose'

24/ Jew   I have possest your grace of what I purpose,   4.1.35 - 62

Background: This is Shylocke's immediate response to the Duke's public address (speech # 23 above), triggered by the final line 'We all expect a gentle answer Jew?'

Style: public address

Where: wherever the trial/hearing is taking place, presumably in a court or the Duke's official chambers   **To Whom:** ostensibly the Duke, and at least Anthonio, Bassanio and Gratiano, together with any other judges ('Magnificoes') as the First Folio suggests, court officials, and perhaps supporters of both Anthonio and Shylocke

# of Lines: 28   **Probable Timing: 1.30 minutes**

In what starts out as a formal oratorical reply to a personal challenge in the public court, it is not surprising that the modern texts supports F's debate-like sentence structure point for point. But the moment Shylocke shows signs of losing total formality as he moves into exceedingly coarse imagery (sentence #7 in both texts), the modern text does not follow F's somewhat erratic structure, but instead revamps sentences #7 and #8 to maintain formality where the earlier text shows something very different is taking place.

• in the first seven F sentences Shylocke maintains intellectual control even with the very strong predictions and images that he uses (10/5 in sixteen lines)

• however, by the somewhat ungrammatical start to F #8, as he begins to answer the oratorical questions he raised earlier in the speech, his intellect is almost completely subsumed by the personal/emotional long spellings suddenly released (3/12 in twelve lines) - as if the situation or admiration of his own cleverness is getting the better of him

• thus the non-embellished containment of F's final short sentence ('Are you answered?') is chilling in its self control after all the previous excess

• this chilly pattern is also present in the earlier part of the speech, nearly always when he is essentially challenging (whether directly or passive-aggressively) the Duke viz.

"I have possest your grace of what I purpose,/ . . ./To have the due and forfeit of my bond. / If you denie it, let the danger light"
"What, are you answer'd yet?" and "now for your answer:"
"So can I give no reason, nor I will not,/More then a lodg'd hate"

• and this arrogant (in terms of social status) self-asserting series of challenges to the Duke is reinforced with the three surround phrases making up all of F #4. viz.
"Ile not answer that : / But say it is my humor; Is it answered?"

Modern Text

24/ Jew

1
I have possess'd* your ^Grace of what I purpose,
And by our holy Sabbath have I sworn*
To have the due and forfeit of my bond.

2
If you deny* it, let the danger light
Upon your ^charter and your ^city's* ^freedom*! †

3
You'll* ask* me why I rather choose to have
A weight of carrion flesh, [than] to receive
Three thousand ^ducats?

4
I'll not answer that;
But say it is my humor, ^is it answered?

5
What if my house be troubled with a ^rat,
And I be pleas'd to give ten thousand ^ducats*
To have it ban'd?*

6
What, are you answer'd yet?

7
Some men there are love not a gaping ^pig* ;
Some that are mad, if they behold a ^cat;
And others, when the bag^pipe sings i'th nose,
Cannot contain* their ^urine: for affection, ◊
[Mistress] of passion, sways* it to the mood*
Of what it likes or loathes*. †

8
Now for your answer:
As there is no firm* reason to be rendr'd
Why he cannot abide a gaping ^pig* ;
Why he, a harmless* necessary* ^cat;
Why he, a woollen bag^pipe, but of force
Must yield* to such inevitable shame
As to offend himself* being offended;

First Folio

24/ Jew

1
I have possest your grace of what I purpose,
And by our holy Sabbath have I sworne
To have the due and forfeit of my bond.

2
If you denie it, let the danger light
Upon your Charter,ₓ and your Cities freedome. +

3
You'll aske me why I rather choose to have
A weight of carrion flesh,ₓ [then] to receive
Three thousand Ducats?

4
Ile not answer that : ₓ
But say it is my humor; ₓ Is it answered?

5
What if my house be troubled with a Rat,
And I be pleas'd to give ten thousand Ducates
To have it bain'd?

6
What, are you answer'd yet?

7
Some men there are love not a gaping Pigge: ₓ
Some that are mad, if they behold a Cat: ₓ
And others, when the bag-pipe sings i'th nose,
Cannot containe their Urine+ for affection.
[Masters] of passion + swayes it to the moode
Of what it likes or loaths, now for your answer:

8
As there is no firme reason to be rendred
Why he cannot abide a gaping Pigge?ₓ
Why he+ a harmlesse necessarie Cat?ₓ
Why he+ a woollen bag-pipe: ₓ but of force
Must yeeld to such inevitable shame,ₓ
As to offend himselfe being offended: ₓ

So can I give no reason, nor I will not,
More [then] a lodg'd hate, and a certaine loathing
I beare Anthonio, that I follow thus
A loosing suite against him?
                              Are you answered?

9

25/ Portia   The quality of mercy is not strain'd,   4.1.184 - 205 /

Background: Disguised as a lawyer, Portia has offered Shylocke the saving feminine grace of 'mercy'. He has replied that all he stands for is the masculine absolute of 'justice'.
The following is her response to his rejection of her statement 'Then must the Jew be mercifull.' with the stark comment 'On what compulsion must I? Tell me that.'.
Whether her famous reply is a pre-planned speech, as it so often has been performed, or a series of new thoughts and discoveries marking her growing up in the world, is up to each actress and production to decide.

Style: public address, aimed specifically at one man

Where: wherever the trial/hearing is taking place, presumably in a court or the Duke's official chambers   **To Whom:** Shylocke, in front of at least Anthonio, Bassanio and Gratiano, Nerrissa, together with any other judges ('Magnificoes' as the First Folio suggests), court officials, and perhaps supporters of both Anthonio and Shylocke

# of Lines: 22   **Probable Timing: 1.10 minutes**

Modern Text

25/ Portia

1 The quality of mercy is not strain'd,
   It droppeth as the gentle rain* from heaven
   Upon the place beneath.
                        It is twice blest: †
2 It blesseth him that gives and him that takes. †
3 'Tis mightiest in the mightiest, it becomes
   The throned ᐃmonarch better then his ᐃcrown* .
4 His ᐃsceptre shows* the force of temporal* power,
   The attribute to awe and ᐃmajesty*,
   Wherein doth sit the dread and fear* of ᐃkings;
   But mercy is above this sceptred sway,
   It is enthroned in the hearts of ᐃkings,
   It is an attribute to God himself* ;
   And earthly power doth then show likest God's
   When mercy* seasons ᐃjustice.

First Folio

25/ Portia

1 The quality of mercy is not strain'd,
   It droppeth as the gentle raine from heaven
   Upon the place beneath.
                        It is twice blest, +
2 It blesseth him that gives, ₓ and him that takes,
   'Tis mightiest in the mightiest, it becomes
   The throned Monarch better then his Crowne.
3 His Scepter shewes the force of temporall power,
   The attribute to awe and Majestie,
   Wherein doth sit the dread and feare of Kings: ₓ
   But mercy is above this sceptred sway,
   It is enthroned in the hearts of Kings,
   It is an attribute to God himselfe;
   And earthly power doth then shew likest Gods
   When mercie seasons Justice.

{ctd. over}

The two occasions the F text offers onrushed sentences, which most modern texts split in two, centre on expanding the idea of mercy - first as belonging to the mighty (F #2) and - being inextricably bound up with the fundamental of (all? certainly Christian) religion, 'prayer' (F #4). This might suggest that the speech is not so oratorically cut and dried as modern texts suggest (and the sentence structure of the quarto text shows even less control).

• the onrushed F #2 (split into two by most modern texts) might suggest Portia is moved by the discovery or expression of the initial idea of the first two lines, how mercy is 'twice blest': similarly, the onrush of F #4 (again split in two by most modern texts0, might suggest she is working harder than her modern counterpart to get Shylock to understand how Christians are taught to 'render . . . mercie'

• unlike most of her earlier speeches, here, in the role of lawyer, capitals outstrip longer spelled words almost two to one (14 to 8) 2 with the climax of the intellectual argument coming at the end of F #3 and the start of #4

• and rather than being broken up by the embellishments of personal emotion, there are several important unembellished moments, testifying to the importance of maintaining self-control, especially in the opening argument (whether this is from nerves at having to play the role of the male lawyer, the

5
Therefore, Jew,
Though △justice be thy plea, consider this,
That in the course of △justice, none of us
Should see salvation. †

6
    We do pray for mercy*,
And that same prayer doth teach us all to render
The deeds of mercy*.   I have spoke thus much

7
To mitigate* the justice of thy plea,
Which if thou follow, this strict [court] of Venice
Must needs* give sentence 'gainst the △merchant there.

4
Therefore⁺ Jew,
Though Justice be thy plea, consider this,
That in the course of Justice, none of us
Should see salvation: we do pray for mercie,
And that same prayer,$_x$ doth teach us all to render
The deeds of mercie.   I have spoke thus much

5
To mittigate the justice of thy plea:$_x$
Which if thou follow, this strict [course] of Venice
Must needes give sentence 'gainst the Merchant there.

---

unexpected ferocity of Shylocke's response, or the seriousness of the matter at hand is up to each actress to explore)
"The quality of mercy is not strain'd,"

"It is twice blest,/It blesseth him that gives, and him that takes,/'Tis mightiest in the mightiest,"
and the argument's further development
"But mercy is above this sceptred sway,"
"none of us/Should see salvation : we do pray for mercie/And that same prayer, doth teach us all to render/The deeds of mercie ."

• while the single surround phrase opening the final sentence ' . I have spoke thus much/To mitigate the justice of thy plea : ' could well indicate just how hard she has worked to try, in her eyes, to save Shylocke

• the one emotional semicolon towards the end of F #3 could well serve to show how personally important balance is to her in her own life, viz.
" ; And earthly power doth then shew likest Gods/When mercie seasons Justice ."

26/ Portia   **Tarry a little, there is something else,**   between 4.1.305 - 332

Background: With Anthonio having made his farewells and bared his breast for Shylocke's knife, at the very last minute Portia offers a completely legal saving of Anthonio's life. Again, whether her famous argument was discovered before she came to court and therefore pre-planned, as it so often has been presented, or is a wonderful series of brilliant on-stage discoveries, is up to each actress and production to decide. However, for this commentator, if it is a pre-discovered, pre-planned argument it seems very cruel to offer it so late in the proceedings.

Style: public address, aimed specifically at one man

Where: wherever the trial/hearing is taking place, presumably in a court or the Duke's official chambers   **To Whom:** Shylocke, in front of at least Anthonio, Bassanio and Gratiano, Nerrissa, together with any other judges ('Magnificoes' as the First Folio suggests), court officials, and perhaps supporters of both Anthonio and Shylocke

# of Lines: 17   **Probable Timing: 0.55 minutes**

Modern Text

26/ Portia

1 Tarry a little, there is something else . †

2 This bond doth give thee here° no jot of blood°,
The words expressly* are "a pound of flesh. " †
[Take then] thy bond, take thou thy pound of flesh,
But in the cutting it, if thou dost shed
One drop of Christian blood°, thy lands and goods
Are by the △laws* of Venice confiscate
Unto the state of Venice.
⁓⁓⁓⁓⁓⁓⁓

3 Therefore prepare thee to cut off the flesh . †

4 Shed thou no blood*, nor cut thou less* nor more
But just a pound of flesh. †

5   If thou tak'st more
Or less* then a just pound, be it [but] so much
As makes it light or heavy in the substance,
Or the division* of the twentieth part
Of one poor* scruple, nay, if the scale do* turn*
Of one poore° scruple, nay° if the scale doe turne
But in the estimation of a hair*,
Thou diest, and all thy goods are confiscate.

First Folio

26/ Portia

1 Tarry a little, there is something else,
This bond doth give thee heere no jot of bloud,
The words expresly are a pound of flesh:
[Then take] thy bond, take thou thy pound of flesh,
But in the cutting it, if thou dost shed
One drop of Christian bloud, thy lands and goods
Are by the Lawes of Venice confiscate
Unto the state of Venice.
⁓⁓⁓⁓⁓⁓⁓

2 Therefore prepare thee to cut off the flesh,
Shed thou no bloud, nor cut thou lesse nor more
But just a pound of flesh: if thou tak'st more
Or lesse then a just pound, be it [ ]so much
As makes it light or heavy in the substance,
Or the devision of the twentieth part
Of one poore scruple, nay⁺ if the scale doe turne
But in the estimation of a hayre,
Thou diest, and all thy goods are confiscate.

Having found the loophole to save Anthonio's life, despite the fascinating moments of control, the two sentence structure of F's Portia is far more spontaneous than the usual modern five sentence rewrite

• unlike speech #25, emotional words far outweigh capitals (11 to 4)

• and all four capitals are compressed into just three lines at the end of F #1, as she reads the law which will block Shylocke

• unlike the five step progression of the modern text, the F speech splits neatly into just two parts – F #1's statement of the law and then F #2's incitement to Shylocke to carry out his intent but limited by the rigid restrictions of that law: the difference between the two texts seems to be, that while F's Portia is much more personally involved in the moment as herself, the modern Portia seems to be upholding and maintaining the facade of the male lawyer

• the intrusion of the F Portia's personal responses seems to be supported by F's fast-link commas at the end of the first line of each of the two F sentences: while ungrammatical F's speedy onrush is very understandable emotionally, most modern texts replace both commas with 'correct' periods

• alongside the seemingly more personal responses there are moments of still calm with no embellishment, usually at the moment of her spelling out precisely what might occur if Shylocke is careless in continuing with his quest (save for the word 'devision' below)
   "The words expresly are a pound of flesh:/[Then take] thy bond, take thou
      thy pound of flesh,/But in the cutting it, if thou dost shed"
   "Therefore prepare thee to cut off the flesh"
   "be it so much/As makes it light or heavy in the substance,/Or the devision
      of the twentieth part"
   "Thou diest, and all thy goods are confiscate ."

• the two key emotional clusters underscore first her discovery or pronouncement of the legal loophole by which Shylocke will be thwarted, 'This bond doth give thee heere no jot of bloud' (0/2), and then her pointing to how carefully his weighing of Anthonio's flesh must be, for if he takes too much even by 'Of one poore scruple, nay if the scale doe turne/But in the estimation of a hayre,' (0/4), he will forfeit his life as well as his goods

MUCH ADO ABOUT NOTHING

SPEECHES IN ORDER	TIME	PAGE
#'s 1 - 4: Beatrice		
1/ Beatrice — There is a kind of merry war betwixt Signior	1.00	189
2/ Beatrice — Lord, I could not endure a husband with a	1.10	191
3/ Beatrice — The fault will be in the musicke cosin, if you	0.35	192
4/ Beatrice — {You will} not tell me who told you so, nor …	0.45	193
#'s 5 - 7: Benedicke		
5/ Benedicke — I doe much wonder, that one man seeing	1.30	194
6/ Benedicke — I noted not {the daughter of signior Leonato}, but	0.55	196
7/ Benedicke — O she misusde me past the indurance of a block:	1.30	197
#'s 8 - 10: The Tricking Of Beatrice & Benedicke Into Love Once Again		
8/ Benedicke — This can be no tricke, the conference was sadly ….	1.15	198
9/ Hero — Good Margaret runne thee to the parlour,	1.15	200
10/ Hero {*} — Doth not the {Benedicke}/Deserve as full a bed	1.55	201
#'s 11 - 13: Don John's Dastardly Devices		
11/ Don John — I wonder that thou (being as thou saist thou art,	0.55	203
12/ 'Bastard' — My Lord and brother, God save you./If ….	1.30	204
13/ Claudio — Father, by your leave, /Will you with free and ….	1.30	206
#'s 14 - 17: Serious Differences Between One-Time Friends		
14/ Beatrice — Is not {Claudio} approved in the height a villaine,	0.55	208
15/ Benedicke — Shall I speake a word in your eare?	0.45	209
16/ Prince — Ile tell thee how Beatrice prais'd thy wit …	0.50	210
17/ Leonato — Tush, tush, man, never fleere and jest at me,	1.00	211
#'s 18 - 19: The Watch		
18/ Dogberry — Come hither neighbour Sea-coale, God hath …	2.00	212
19/ Dogberry/Kemp — Gods my life, where's the Sexton?	0.50	214

SPEECHES BY GENDER

		Speech #(s)
SPEECHES FOR WOMEN (7)		
Beatrice	**Traditional & Today:** young or very early middle-aged woman: - see also 'Background' to speech #1	#1, #2, #3, #4, #14
Hero	**Traditional & Today:** Leonato's young daughter, of marriageable age	#9, #10
SPEECHES FOR EITHER GENDER (0)		
SPEECHES FOR MEN (12)		
Benedicke	**Traditional & Today:** young or early middle-aged man: - see also 'Background' to speech #1	#5, #6, #7, #8, #15
Don John/Bastard	**Traditional & Today:** young or younger middle aged man	#11, #12
Claudio	**Traditional & Today:** a young man, hoping to be married	#13
Don Pedro/Prince	**Traditional:** male of some authority, often close in age to Leonato **Today:** adult male of any age	#16
Leonato	**Traditional & Today:** older man of some authority, with a daughter of marriageable age	#17
Dogberry/Kemp	**Traditional:** the clown figure, middle aged man **Today:** a clown type figure of any age, usually male	#18, #19

MUCH ADO ABOUT NOTHING

's 1 - 4: BEATRICE

1/ Beatrice   **There is a kind of merry war betwixt Signior Benedick, & {my selfe} :**   between 1.1.61 - 90

Background: Commentators suggest that initially Beatrice and Benedicke were considered secondary comedy leads to the much younger romantic complications between her cousin Hero and his military colleague Claudio, leading to justifiably older and often more unusual casting than is usually current: here she indulges in one of her many put-downs, this time in front of not only her immediate family but a young soldier-Messenger who has just announced the imminent arrival of the military led by the Prince, Don Pedro, and Benedicke, in search of rest and relaxation: N.B. the first sentence has been reassigned from a short speech by her uncle Leonato

Style: teasing address to a group of intimates, plus one unexpected messenger   **To Whom:** Leonato, Hero and a Messenger, with

Where: at the house of her uncle Leonato (the 'Governour of Messina'), though indoors or outdoors is unspecified

perhaps others of the household including her uncle Anthonio

# of Lines: 19   **Probable Timing: 1.00 minutes**

Modern Text

1/ Beatrice

1   There is
a kind of merry war betwixt Signior Benedick, & {myself} ;
{we} never meet but there's a skirmish of wit between
{us}.

2   {And}, alas, he gets nothing by that. †

3   In our last con-
flict four* of his five wits went halting off, and now is
the whole man govern'd with one ; so that if he * have
wit enough to keep * himself* warm*, let him bear* it
for a difference between* himself* and his horse, ◊for it
is all the wealth that he hath left to be known* a reasonable creature .

4   Who is his companion now? ◊ he hath
every month a new sworn* brother .

5   He wears* his faith but as the
fashion of his hat : it ever changes with [the] next block.

6   But

7   Is there no young
squarer now, that will make a voyage with him to the
devil*?

8   {*} Lord, {Benedick} will hang upon him like a disease ;
he is sooner caught [than] the pestilence, and the taker
runs presently mad.

First Folio

1/ Beatrice

1   There is a
kind of merry war betwixt Signior Benedick, & {my selfe} ; x
{we} never meet, x but there's a skirmish of wit between
{us}.

2   {And}, alas, he gets nothing by that.   In our last con-

3   flict, x foure of his five wits went halting off, and now is
the whole man govern'd with one : x so that if hee have
wit enough to keepe himselfe warme, let him beare it
for a difference betweene himselfe and his horse ; x For it
is all the wealth that he hath left, x to be knowne a reasonable creature .

4   Who is his companion now?   He hath

5   every month a new sworne brother .

6   He weares his faith but as
the fashion of his hat : + it ever changes with [ỹ] next block.

7   But

8   Is there no young
squarer now, that will make a voyage with him to the
divell?

9   {*} Lord, {Benedick} will hang upon him like a disease : x
he is sooner caught [then] the pestilence, and the taker
runs presently mad.

Beatrice seems blessed with the ability to take things quite easily, only letting loose when the occasion demands. Thus this speech is a fascinating mix of large chunks of unembellished lines coupled with a sudden burst of energetic release.

- the few surround phrases point directly to the basis of her anti-Benedicke stance, especially the whole of F #1 and #9

    " . There is a kind of merry war betwixt Signior Benedicke, & {my
    selfe} : {we} never meet, but there's a skirmish of wit
    between{us} . "

    "Lord, {Benedick} will hang upon him like a disease : he is sooner
    caught than the pestilence, and the taker runs presently mad. "
interspersed with the acerbic comment as to his one remaining wit
(out of the usual five)

    " . : For it is all the wealth that he hath left, to be knowne a
    reasonable creature . "

- and in the sea of unembellished lines, most point to her easy dismissal of Benedicke the 'disease', some already seen in the surround phrases noted above

    "{we} never meet, but there's a skirmish of wit between{us}. And
    alas, he gets nothing by that."
especially his lack of constancy, which she compares to a hat, for

    "it ever changes with {the} next block."
and the inability to get rid of him

    "he is sooner caught [then] the pestilence, and the taker runs
    presently mad. . . It will cost him a thousand pound ere he be
    cur'd."

- Beatrice opens in total unembellished control (0/0, F #1-2), only to slip into a wonderful emotional release as to Benedicke's (lack of) wit (1/8, F #3)

{ctd. over}

9   God help* {any man,} if he*
have caught the [Benedick], it will cost him a thousand
pound ere [a'] be cur'd.

10   God helpe {any man,} if hee
have caught the [Benedict], it will cost him a thousand
pound ere he be cur'd.

• then for most of the remainder of the speech she returns to the
easy calm waters of the opening (just 2/5 in the remaining ten lines),
with only the final summary showing any further ripples in the calm
of her put downs (1/2, F #10)

2/ Beatrice   Lord, I could not endure a husband with a beard   between 2.1.29-65

Background: The family are gossiping prior to the Mask to celebrate Don Pedro's arrival: Beatrice now aims her wit at the idea of husbands, triggered in part by the teasing of both uncles, Leonato and Anthonio, that she will never 'get thee a husband, if thou be so shrewd of thy tongue.'

Style: teasing address to a group of intimates

Where: at the house of her uncle Leonato wherever the Mask is about to begin (indoors or outdoors is unspecified)   **To Whom:** Leonato, Hero, her uncle Anthonio with perhaps others of the household

# of Lines: 21   Probable Timing: 1.10 minutes

Modern Text

2/ Beatrice

1 Lord, I could not endure a husband with a beard on his face, I had rather lie in the woollen !
{As for}a husband that hath no beard? {w}hat should I do* with him? dress* him in my apparel* and make him my waiting gentlewoman? †

2 He

3 that hath a beard is more [than] a youth, and he that hath no beard is less* [than] a man; and he* that is more then a youth is not for me*, and he that is less* [than] a man, I am not for him; therefore I will even take sixpence* in earnest of the [△bear-ward], and lead* his △apes {to the gates of} hell.

4 And there will the △devil* meet* me* like an old △cuckold with horns* on his head, and say, "Get you to heaven, Beatrice, get you to heaven, here's* no place for you maids. "†

5 So deliver I up my △apes, and way to [Saint] Peter. †

6 For the heavens, he* shows* me* where the △bachelors* sit, and there live we* as merry as the day is long.

7 {*} {I will never be} fitted with a husband
{*} till God make men of some other metal* [than] earth. †

8 Would it not grieve a woman to be over-master'd with a piece* of valiant dust? to make [an] account of her life to a clod of wayward* marl*? †

9 No, uncle, I'll none. †

10 Adam's sons* are my brethren, and truly I hold it a sin* to match in my kinred.

First Folio

2/ Beatrice

1 Lord, I could not endure a husband with a beard on his face, I had rather lie in the woollen. †

2 {As for}a husband that hath no beard? {w}hat should I doe with him? dresse him in my apparell, x and make him my waiting gentlewoman? he that hath a beard, is more [then] a youth: x and he that hath no beard, x is lesse [then] a man; and hee that is more [then] a youth, x is not for mee; and he that is lesse [then] a man, I am not for him; therefore I will even take sixpence in earnest of the [Berrord], and leade his Apes {to the gates of} hell.

3 And there will the Devill meete mee like an old Cuckold with homes on his head, and say, get you to heaven + Beatrice, get you to heaven, heere's no place for you maids, so deliver I up my Apes, and way to [S.] Peter: for the heavens, hee shewes mee where the Batchellers sit, and there live wee as merry as the day is long.

4 {I will never be} fitted with a husband {*} till God make men of some other mettall [then] earth, would it not grieve a woman to be over-mastred with a peece of valiant dust? to make [ ] account of her life to a clod of waiward marle? no+ unckle, ile none: Adams sonnes are my brethren, and truly I hold it a sinne to match in my kinred.

Unlike the first speech, save for the opening phrase there are very few phrases where Beatrice does not show some form of vocal release (mainly emotional, 11/27 overall) – it seems the party has got to her a little, anticipation of the forthcoming festivities perhaps (or even a drink or two) has begun to loosen her tongue.

• after the almost thesis like quality of the shortish opening sentence (0/1), the onrushed F 2-4 show what a fine roll she is on, highlighting her ability to spin out a complex seemingly never-ending stream of thoughts building one on top of another (most modern texts make her work much harder, and therefore her wit a little heavier, by turning F's three sentences into nine)

• the superb relentlessness of F #2, dismissing both mature and young men alike, is underscored by all seven and half lines being completely formed by eight surround phrases – the hardest working sentence of the speech, and the fun of this is obviously emotional (2/9)

• allowing herself to relish the thoughts of abandoning all her man-'Apes' in hell leads to the only intellectual release in the speech and even this is almost matched by emotional delight (6/4, the first four lines of F #3), while her dreams of being 'merry as the day is long' with the 'Batchellers' in heaven becomes emotional once more (1/5, the last two lines of F #3)

• interestingly in the finale, though her refusal to be fitted with a husband seems to start out in full and easy control (1/1 in the first three lines of F #4, to the first question-mark), the refusal becomes much more emotional by the finish (1/5 in the last three lines), no matter how witty the images may seem to be

3/ Beatrice   The fault will be in the musicke cosin, if you   2.1.69 - 80

Background: There is a mutual attraction between Hero, Leonato's only child, and a protégé of Don Pedro, the young nobleman, Count Claudio: Leonato has learnt that the Prince intends to speak on Claudio's behalf to Hero at the ensuing Mask: Beatrice now aims her wit at the whole process of 'wooing, wedding, & repenting'

Style: teasing address to her younger cousin in front of a group of intimates

Where: at the house of her uncle Leonato wherever the Mask is about to begin (indoors or outdoors is unspecified)   **To Whom:**   Hero, in front of Leonato, Anthonio and perhaps others of the household

# of Lines: 10   **Probable Timing: 0.35 minutes**

Modern Text

3/ Beatrice

1 The fault will be in the music* , cousin*, if you be not woo'd* in good time .†

2   If the Prince be* too important tell him there is measure in every thing, & so dance out the answer* .†

3   For hear* me Hero : wooing, wedding, & repenting, is as a Scotch* jig*, a measure, and a cinque-pace ; the first suit* is hot and hasty, like a Scotch† jig*, and full as fantastical* ; the wedding, mannerly*-modest, as a measure, full of state & ancientry* ; and then comes repentance, and with his bad legs falls into the cinque-pace faster and faster, till he [sink] into his grave.

First Folio

3/ Beatrice

1 The fault will be in the musicke+ cosin, if you be not woed in good time : if the Prince bee too important, x tell him there is measure in every thing, & so dance out the answere, for heare me Hero, + wooing, wedding, & repenting, is as a Scotch {ji}gge, a measure, and a cinque-pace : x the first suite is hot and hasty+ like a Scotch† jigge (and full as fantasticall) + the wedding + manerly modest, (,as a measure)x full of state & aunchentry, + and then comes repentance, and with his bad legs falls into the cinque-pace faster and faster, till he [sinkes] into his grave.

As with the previous speech, the onrush of this speech, part and parcel of the same scene, seems to suggest whatever devilment sparked Beatrice then is still in force here. The modern texts which set the speech as three sentences seem to make her far heavier and much more pedantic than originally set.

• once more the opening thesis is stated quite easily (0/1, the first line and a half)

• then the set-up of wooing being akin to dancing demands both her intellect and emotion (3/4, the four lines between the two colons)

• and then the conclusion is free flowing, both faster than the modern texts when their three extra pieces of punctuation – marked + in the F text – are removed, and splendidly emotional (1/5, the last five lines)

4/ Beatrice   **{You will} not tell me who told you so, {*}nor tell me who you are ?**   between 2.1.125 - 150

Background: At the dance part of the Masque, Benedicke thinks his mask has disguised him sufficiently so as to insult Beatrice directly to her face and escape with impunity: Beatrice of course knows he is, and, cleverly, instead of unmasking him, demeans and belittles Benedicke to the 'stranger' with whom she is dancing

Style: as part of a two-handed scene

Where: wherever the Mask is taking place (whether indoors or outdoors is unspecified)   **To Whom:** the disguised Benedicke

# of Lines: 14   **Probable Timing: 0.45 minutes**

Modern Text	First Folio
4/ Beatrice	**4/ Beatrice**
1 {You will} not tell me who told you so{,*} nor tell me who you are?	1 {You will} not tell me who told you so{,*} nor tell me who you are?
2 That I was disdainful*, and that I had my good wit out of the "△Hundred △Merry △Tale"'s - well, this was Signior Benedick* that said so.	2 That I was disdainfull, and that I had my good wit out of the hundred merry tales : x well, this was Signior Benedicke that said so.
3 . . . {H}e is the Prince's jester*, a very dull fool*; only* his gift is in devising impossible slanders . †	3 . . . {He} is the Princes jeaster, a very dull foole, + onely his gift is, x in devising impossible slanders, none
4 None but △libertines delight in him, and the commendation is not in his wit*, but in his villainy*, for he* both [pleases] men and angers them, and then they laugh at him and beat him . †	but Libertines delight in him, and the commendation is not in his witte, but in his villanie, for hee both [pleaseth] men and angers them, and then they laugh at him, x and beat him : I am sure he is in the Fleet, + I would he had boorded me.
5 I am sure he is in the △fleet ; I would he had boarded* me.	
6 {T}ell him what{I} say	4 {T}ell him what{I} say
{and} he'll* but break* a comparison or two on me, which peradventure, not marked, or not laughed at, strikes him into melancholy*, and then there's a △partridge wing saved, for the fool* will eat* no supper that night.	{and} hee'l but breake a comparison or two on me, which peradventure ⟨not markt, or not laugh'd at⟩x strikes him into mellancholly, and then there's a Partridge wing saved, for the foole will eate no supper that night.

Once more F's orthography and sentence structure clearly display the patterns by which Beatrice so easily guides her barbs to the most tender portions of any target that has offended her.

- the speech opens with an unembellished, monosyllabic (and deceptive) calm (F #1, 0/0)

- and even the summation of Benedicke's put-down stays fairly controlled (F#2. 2/1)

- and then all sorts of release are let loose as she embarks on a much stronger and onrushed put-down of Benedicke than he ever ascribed to her (F #3, 3/7) : and since he later describes her attack as 'a whole army shooting at me' it would seem F #3's onrush is very important to both characters and the play – so it seems a shame that most modern texts split the sentence into three

- and if this extended put down weren't enough, the final additional character assassination is also emotional (1/5, F #4)

- despite her splendid victory, the surround phrases might suggest that underneath the wit she is somewhat stung

" . That I was disdainfull, and that I had my good wit out of the hundred merry tales : well, this was Signior Benedicke that said so . "

" : I am sure he is in the Fleet, I would he had boorded me . "

#'s 5 - 7: BENEDICKE

5/ Benedicke   I doe much wonder, that one man seeing   2.3.7- 36

Background: As noted in speech #1, commentators suggest that initially Beatrice and Benedicke were considered secondary comedy leads to the much younger romantic complications between her cousin Hero and his military colleague Claudio, leading to justifiably older and often more unusual casting than is usually current: here, alone in the garden, Benedicke initially ruminates on Claudio's imminent abandoning of the blessed state of bachelordom, which leads him to ask certain, quickly dismissed, questions of himself.

Style: solo

Where: the gardens at Leonato's   **To Whom:** self, and direct audience address

# of Lines: 27   Probable Timing: 1.30 minutes

Modern Text

5/ Benedicke

1   I do* much wonder that one man, seeing
how much another man is a fool* when he dedicates his
behaviors* to love, will, after he hath laugh'd at such
shallow follies in others, become the argument of his
own* scorn*, by falling in love - & such a man is Claudio . †

2   I have known when there was no music* with him but
the drum and the fife, and now had he* rather hear* the
tabor and the pipe ;   I have known* when he would have
walk'd ten mile afoot to see a good armor, and now will
he lie ten nights awake carving the fashion of a new doublet *;   he was wont to speak* plain* & to the purpose (like
an honest man & a soldier*), and now is he turn'd orthography - his words are a very fantastical* banquet, just so
many strange dishes . †

3   May I be so converted & see with
these eyes?

4   I cannot tell ;   I think* not . †

5   I will not be*
sworn* but love may transform* me to an oyster, but I'll
take my oath on it, till he have made me an oyster of me, he
shall never make me such a fool* . †

6   One woman is fair*, yet
ous, yet I am well ; but till all graces be in one woman
one woman shall not come in my grace . †

First Folio

5/ Benedicke

1   I doe much wonder, $_x$ that one man$^+$ seeing
how much another man is a foole, $_x$ when he dedicates his
behaviours to love, will$^+$ after hee hath laught at such
shallow follies in others, become the argument of his
owne scorne, by falling in love, & such a man is Claudio,
I have known when there was no musicke with him but
the drum and the fife, and now had hee rather heare the
taber and the pipe : $_x$ I have knowne when he would have
walkt ten mile afoot, $_x$ to see a good armor, and now will
he lie ten nights awake carving the fashion of a new dub-
let : $_x$ he was wont to speake plaine, $_x$ & to the purpose (like
an honest man & a souldier)$^+$ and now is he tur{n}'d orthography, his words are a very fantasticall banquet, just so
many strange dishes : may I be so converted, $_x$ & see with
these eyes?

2   I cannot tell, $^+$ I thinke not : I will not bee
sworne, $_x$ but love may transforme me to an oyster, but Ile
take my oath on it, till he have made an oyster of me, he
shall never make me such a foole : one woman is faire, yet
I am well : another is wise, yet I am well ; $_x$ another vertuous, yet I am well : $_x$ but till all graces be in one woman, $_x$
one woman shall not come in my grace: rich shee shall

Often played throughout simply as an ongoing self-amused speech of relaxation, F's onrush and orthography suggest that **while the opening may fall into this pattern, and the thought of himself becoming similarly changed (F #2) may start this way, his dreams of an 'ideal' woman have far more bite than he might initially care to admit.**

• now alone, and in a sea of release, the occasional unembellished lines point to what is disturbing him:

a/ first as to his loss of a companion with whom he can do the
     manly things, such as walking

     "ten mile afoot, to see a good armor"
     for instead Claudio now

     " will lie ten nights awake carving the fashion of a new dublet:"
     because

     "now is he turn'd orthography, his words are . . just so many
     strange dishes"

b/ then, via a surround phrase, concern about his own future

     " : may I be so converted, & see with these eyes ? I cannot tell"

• and when the unembellished lines are found within surround
phrases it seems as if the self-searching is reaching new depths,
especially as to love - for it seems if love does 'transforme me to an
oyster' he will do his best to guarantee himself a splendid multi-faceted
partner

     " : another is wise, yet I am well : another vertuous, yet I am well :
     but till all graces be in one woman, one woman shall not come in
     my grace : . . : wise, or lle none : vertuous, or lle never cheapen
     her : "

• the speech starts out dismissing Claudio, and, with the exception of
his name, is completely emotional (F #1, 1/14)

7

    Rich she* shall
be, that's certain*; wise, or I'll none; virtuous, or I'll never cheapen her; fair*, or I'll never look* on her; mild*,
or come not near* me; ^noble, or not [I] for an ^angel*;
of good discourse, an excellent ^musician*, and her hair*
shall* be of what color* it please God. †

    Hah! the Prince and

8 Monsieur Love. †

9   I will hide me in the ^arbor.

• the assertion that he shall never be made 'such a foole' is also emotional (0/6, the first four lines of F #2), while after the unembellished start to assessing women for their different qualities ('another is wise . . .') the usual attributes of 'rich', 'wise', 'vertuous', 'faire' and 'milde' are voiced emotionally, the extras, and the fact of being interrupted by the Prince and Claudio trigger his only intellectual release in the speech (8/4, the last four lines of the speech)

be, that's certaine ₓ wise, or Ile none ₓ vertuous, or Ile never cheapen her ₓ faire, or Ile never looke on her ₓ milde,
or come not neere me ₓ Noble, or not [ ] for an Angell : ₓ
of good discourse : ₓ an excellent Musitian, and her haire
shal be of what colour it please God, hah! the Prince and
Monsieur Love, I will hide me in the Arbor.

6/ Benedicke   I noted {*} not {the daughter of signior Leonato } , but I lookt on her .   between 1.1.164 - 203

Background: Prior to the personal explorations of speech #5 above Benedicke has been his usual somewhat crusty public self in response to Claudio's obvious attraction to and questioning about Hero

Style: as part of a two-handed scene

Where: at Leonato's where Don Pedro's party first arrived, though indoors or outdoors is unspecified   **To Whom:** the smitten Claudio

# of Lines: 18   **Probable Timing: 0.55 minutes**

Modern Text

6/ Benedicke

1   I noted {*} not {the daughter of signior Leonato} ,
    but I look'd on her.

┄┄┄┄┄┄┄┄┄┄┄┄┄┄┄

2   Do* you question me, as an honest man should
    do*, for my simple true judgment*? or would you have
    me speak* after my custom*, as being a professed tyrant
    to their sex*?

┄┄┄┄┄┄┄┄┄┄┄┄┄┄┄

3   {*} Ifaith* me thinks she's* too low for a high
    praise, too brown* for a fair* praise, and too little for a
    great praise ; only* this commendation I can afford* her,
    that were she* other [than]she is, she were unhandsome,
    and being no other, but as she is, I do* not like her.

┄┄┄┄┄┄┄┄┄┄┄┄┄┄┄

4   There's her cousin*, and she were not possess'd*
    with a fury*, exceeds* her as much in beauty* as the first
    of May* doth the last of December . †

5   But I hope you have
    no intent to turn* husband, have you?

6   In faith, hath not the world one
    man but he will wear* his cap with suspicion *? †

7   Shall I ne-
    ver see a batchelor* of three score again*? †

8   Go* to, i'faith* ,
    and thou wilt needs* thrust thy neck* into a yoke, wear*
    the print of it, and sigh away △Sundays*. †

9   Look*, △Don Pedro

    is returned to seek* you.

First Folio

6/ Benedicke

1   I noted {*} not {the daughter of signior Leonato} ,
    but I lookt on her.

┄┄┄┄┄┄┄┄┄┄┄┄┄┄┄

2   Doe you question me+ as an honest man should
    doe, for my simple true judgement? or would you have
    me speake after my custome, as being a professed tyrant
    to their sexe?

┄┄┄┄┄┄┄┄┄┄┄┄┄┄┄

3   {*} Yfaith me thinks shee's too low for a hie
    praise, too browne for a faire praise, and too little for a
    great praise, + onely this commendation I can afford her,
    that were shee other [then] she is, she were unhandsome,
    and being no other, but as she is, I doe not like her.

┄┄┄┄┄┄┄┄┄┄┄┄┄┄┄

4   There's her cosin, and she were not possest
    with a furie, exceeds her as much in beautie, ₓ as the first
    of Maie doth the last of December : but I hope you have
    no intent to turne husband, have you?

5   In faith + hath not the world one
    man but he will weare his cap with suspition ? shall I ne-
    ver see a batcheller of three score againe? goe to + yfaith,
    and thou wilt needes thrust thy necke into a yoke, weare
    the print of it, and sigh away sundaies: looke, don Pedro
    is returned to seeke you.

F's orthography and sentence structure suggest vis-a-vis Beatrice Benedicke makes an interesting Freudian slip.

• the speech starts out so casually (0/1, F #1) it's almost as if Benedicke might not be paying much attention

• and then even before he realises Claudio may be serious about Hero the emotional releases associated with his (Benedicke's) being a 'professed tyrant' towards women start to flow (0/14 in the eight lines F #2-3)

• very interestingly his unasked for praise of Beatrice's beauty as 'the first of Maie' is offered fairly straightforwardly (2/1, the first two lines of F #4) as if the facts were sufficient to speak for themselves – though it's interesting that the one long spelled word 'exceedes' adds extra weigh to his assessment of Beatrice's beautie

• the end of F #3, the hope that Claudio 'has no intent to turn husband' is usually set as a separate sentence by most modern texts, but this is a shame, for F's ungrammatical fast-link setting via the colon suggests Benedicke is nowhere near as controlled as most modern texts would have him – and in fact the surround phrase question may be his attempt to make a quick face-saving recovery from his Freudian slip over his out-of-place praising of Beatrice's 'beautie' – a slip perhaps heightened by the short spellings that suddenly appear associated with Beatrice, 'cosin', 'possest', 'furie', beautie', and 'Maie'

• and whether 'recovery' or no, the remainder of the speech is handled emotionally throughout (1/12 the last line of F #4 and all of F #5, six lines in all)

7/ Benedicke   O she misusde me past the indurance of a block :   between 2.1.239 - 275

Background: Knowing well the intercine warfare between Beatrice and Benedicke, his friends tease him about her whenever they can: the following, during or just after the Masque, is triggered by Don Pedro's 'the Lady Beatrice hath a quarrell to you': it's also triggered in part by the stinging comments she zinged at him in speech #4 above

Style: as part of a two-handed scene

Where: wherever the Mask is taking/has taken place (indoors or out)   **To Whom:** the prince, Don Pedro

# of Lines: 31   **Probable Timing: 1.30 minutes**

Modern Text

7/ Benedicke

1 O, she misus'd* me past the endurance of a block ; an oak* but with one green* leaf* on it would have an-swered her . †

2   My very visor began to assume life, and scold with her . †

3   She* told me*, not thinking I had been* my self*, that I was the Prince's △jester ; [ ] that I was duller [than] a great thaw, huddling* jest upon jest, with such im-possible conveyance* upon me that I stood like a man at a mark*, with a whole army shooting at me . †

4   She* speaks* poniards*, and every word stabs* . †

5   If her breath were as terrible as [her] terminations, there were no living near* her, she would infect to the north star* . †

6   I would not marry her, though she were endow'd* with all that Adam had left him before he transgress'd . †

7   She would have made Hercules have turn'd spit, yea, and have cleft his club to make the fire too . †

8   Come, talk* not of her ; you shall find* her the infernal* Ate in good apparel* .

9   I would to God some scholar* would conjure her, for certainly*, while she is here*, a man may live as quiet in hell as in a sanctuary, and people sin* upon purpose, because they would go* thither ; so indeed all disquiet, horror, and perturbation follows* her.

10 {*}   Look* here* she comes.

11 Will your Grace command me* any service to the world's end?

First Folio

7/ Benedicke

1 O⁺ she misusde me past the indurance of a block : x an oake but with one greene leafe on it, x would have an-swered her : my very visor began to assume life, and scold with her : shee told mee, not thinking I had beene my selfe, that I was the Princes Jester, [and] that I was duller [then] a great thaw, hudling jest upon jest, with such im-possible conveiance upon me, x that I stood like a man at a marke, with a whole army shooting at me : shee speakes poynyards, and every word stabbes : if her breath were as terrible as terminations, there were no living neere her, she would infect to the north starre : I would not marry her, though she were indowd with all that Adam had left him before he transgrest, she would have made Hercules have turnd spit, yea, and have cleft his club to make the fire too : come, talke not of her, ⁺ you shall finde her the infernall Ate in good apparell.

2   I would to God some scholler would conjure her, for certainely⁺ while she is heere, a man may live as quiet in hell, x as in a sanctuary ; and people sinne upon purpose, because they would goe thither, ⁺ so indeed all disquiet, horror, and perturbation followes her.

3   {*}   Looke heere she comes.

4 Will your Grace command mee any service to the worlds end?

As with the previous speech, but in very different circumstances, F's orthography and sentence structure suggest vis-à-vis Beatrice Benedicke makes an interesting Freudian slip yet again.

• the opening onrush of F #1 shows a Benedicke much more disturbed than as shown by most modern texts: their splitting of F #1 into eight sentences simply creates a much more petulant character than the deeply disturbed one originally set

• given the circumstances it's not surprising the speech starts out so emotionally (2/15 the first ten and a half lines of total protestation)

• but in the next three and a half lines comes another intellectual (2/0) Freudian slip (see the previous speech) – for where on earth does the subject of marriage come from

• and again, as with the previous speech, an ungrammatical fast-link colon allows Benedicke a supposedly final dismissal ('come, talke not of her' – though of course he does for another fifteen lines) – a dismissal most modern texts set as a normal progression via a new sentence (mt. #8) instead of a (perhaps) none too subtle hasty attempt at digression

• the emotion continues through his wished for attempts to rid himself of her, whether by 'some scholler' or a 'command' from Don Pedro (2/9, the seven lines of F #3-4)

• however, the attempt to get Don Pedro to agree to any of his outlandish escape suggestions (9/6, F #5-6) becomes intellectually driven

• F #1's surround phrases all focus on Benedicke's worst moments of dealing with and/or his less than charitable opinions of Beatrice
   " . O she misuse me past the indurance of a block : an oake but with one greene leafe on it, would have answered her : my very visor began to assume life, and scold with her : "
   " : shee speakes poynyards, and every word stabbes : "
   " : come, talke not of her, you shall finde her the infernall Ate in good apparell . "

{ctd. over}

Modern Text

12 I will go* on the slightest errand* now to the Antipodes* that you can devise to send me on ; I will fetch you a toothpicker now from the furthest inch of Asia, bring you the length of Prester John's foot, fetch you a hair* off the great Cham's beard, do* you any embassage to the Pigmies, rather [than] hold* three words' conference with this △harpy . †

13 You have no employment for me?

14 O God, sir, here's* a dish I love not, I cannot indure [my] Lady △Tongue.

• while those of F #5, nearly the whole sentence, deal with the extra extraordinary tasks he will undergo so as to avoid further contact with her

"I will goe on the slightest arrand now to the Antypodes that you can devise to send me on : I will fetch you a tooth-picker now from the furthest inch of Asia : bring you the length of Prester Johns foot : fetch you a hayre off the great Chams beard :"

• after such an enormous set of releases throughout the speech, the final unembellished line (one of the very few in the speech) seems so sad in its calm desperate surround phrase realisation there is going to be no friendly help in escaping 'this harpy', 'this Lady tongue', finishing with the sinking realisation that

": you have no employment for me ?"

First Folio

12 I will goe* on the slightest arrand now to the Antypodes that you can devise to send me on ; x I will fetch you a tooth-picker now from the furthest inch of Asia ; bring you the length of Prester Johns foot ; x fetch you a hayre off the great Chams beard ; doe you any embassage to the Pigmies, rather [then] hould three words conference, + with this Harpy : you have no employment for me ?

13

14 O God + sir, heeres a dish I love not, I cannot indure this Lady tongue.

#'s 8 - 10: THE TRICKING OF BEATRICE AND BENEDICKE INTO LOVE ONCE AGAIN

8/ Benedicke   **This can be no tricke, the conference was sadly borne**   2.3.220 - 246

Background: To while away the time till their marriage, Hero and Claudio, together with Leonato, Margaret & Ursula (two of Hero's women), all with the encouragement and leadership of Don Pedro, have resolved to undertake 'one of Hercules labors' even though 'it cost . . . ten nights watchings' and get Benedicke and Beatrice to fall in love (again it would seem to be, at least on Beatrice's part): by allowing Benedicke to overhear their supposedly private conversation the men have succeeded mightily, as the following two speeches show: this comes immediately after the men have left him

Style: solo

Where: the gardens at Leonato's   **To Whom:** self, and direct audience address

# of Lines: 24   **Probable Timing:** 1.15 minutes

Modern Text

8/ Benedicke

1 This can be no trick*: the conference was sadly born*; they have the truth of this from Hero ; they seem* to pity* the △lady . †

2 It seems* her affections have [their] full bent .

3 Love me? why, it must be required . †

4 I hear* how I am censur'd ; they say I will bear* myself* proudly, if I perceive the love come from her ; they say too, that she will rather die than give any sign* of affection . †

First Folio

8/ Benedicke

1 This can be no tricke, + the conference was sadly borne, + they have the truth of this from Hero, + they seeme to pittie the Lady : it seemes her affections have [the] full bent : love me? why+ it must be requited : I heare how I am censur'd, + they say I will beare my selfe proudly, if I perceive the love come from her : x they say too, that she will rather die than give any signe of affection : I did ne-

---

Once more the opening rush, split into eight by most modern texts, and patches of unembellished lines, show a Benedicke far more concerned, and much more in personally surprising discovery mode than most modern texts (and traditional performances) suggest.

• the surround phrases point to which tempting ideas thrown his way have had most impact

": it seemes her affections have the full bent : love me ? why it must be required :"

": they say too, that she will rather die than give any signe of affection :"

": they say the Lady is faire, 'tis a truth, I can beare them witnesse :"

and the final triumphant highly emotional (1/4) conclusion

": by this day, shee's a faire Lady, I doe spie some markes of love in her :"

4   I did ne-
ver think* to marry . †

5   I must not seem* proud ; happy are they that hear* their detractions, and can put them to mending . †

6   They say the △lady is fair* ; 'tis a truth, I can bear* them witness* ; and virtuous* ; 'tis so, I cannot re-prove* it ; and wise, but for loving me ; by my troth, it is no addition to her wit*, nor no great argument of her folly, for I will* be horribly in love with her . †

7   I may chance have some odd* quirks* and remnants of wit* broken on me*, because I have rail'd so long against marriage ; but doth not the appetite alter? †

8   A man loves the meat in his youth that he cannot endure in his age.

9   Shall quips and sentences and these paper bullets of the brain* awe a man from the career* of his humor*?

10   No, the world must be peopled.

11   When I said I would die a bachelor*, I did not think I should live till I were married* . †

12   Here comes Beatrice . †

13   By this day, she's a fair* △lady . †

14   I do* spy* some marks* of love in her.

---

ver thinke to marry, I must not seeme proud, + happy are they that heare their detractions, and can put them to mending : they say the Lady is faire, + 'tis a truth, I can beare them witnesse : x and vertuous, + tis so, I cannot re-proove it, + and wise, but for loving me, + by my troth + it is no additon to her witte, nor no great argument of her folly ; x for I wilbe horribly in love with her, I may chance have some odde quirkes and remnants of witte broken on mee, because I have rail'd so long against marriage : x but doth not the appetite alter? a man loves the meat in his youth, x that he cannot indure in his age.   Shall quips and sentences, x and these paper bullets of the braine awe a man from the careere of his humour?   No, the world must be peopled.   When I said I would die a batcheler, I did not think I should live till I were maried, here comes Beatrice : by this day, shee's a faire Lady, I doe spie some markes of love in her.

2

3

4

• the unembellished lines point to where the self-examination seems to have full bent, first as to Beatrice herself
"they have the truth of this from Hero"
"love me? why it must be requited"
"they say the Lady is . . . vertuous . . . and wise, but for loving me,"
" : I wil be horribly in love with her,"
(this latter heightened be being the only phrase in the speech preceded by an emotional semi-colon), then as to he might handle the 'remnants of witte broken on mee'
"because I have rail'd so long against marriage: but doth not the appetite alter? a man loves the meat in his youth, that he cannot indure in his age."

• while the ensuing short non-embellished sentence, points to the wonderful chop-logic by which Benedicke manages to persuade himself he can, after all his anti-marriage diatribes, wed
"No, the world must be peopled."

• not surprisingly the speech starts out almost totally emotionally (1/21, the first thirteen lines, to the only semi-colon), and after the unembellished resolution 'for I wil be horribly in love with her', and the totally emotional (0/4) realisation of the 'odde quirks' that might be broken against him, the sentence finishes without release

• F #2's build to withstanding such 'paper bullets' is also emotional (0/3), and while the chop-logic assertion (F #3) is again unembellished; the final resolution and realisation Beatrice is about to join him finishes triumphantly (2/5) – though the ungrammatical connection of her arrival to his affirmation (via a fast-link comma) suggests he may not be as much in control as most modern texts would suggest, which usually set his noticing her as three separate sentences

9/ Hero	Good Margaret runne thee to the parlour,	between 3.1.1 - 33
10/ Hero {*}	Doth not the {Benedicke}/Deserve as full as fortunate a bed,	between 3.1.44 - 86

Background: And now the women begin their part of the plot: as such, each speech is self-explanatory, with #9 setting up how they are going to do it, and #10 the 'attack' on Beatrice, with Hero pulling her apart for her pride and carping   N.B. speech #10's first sentence has been reassigned from Ursula

Style: #9 is a three-handed scene, #10 two-handed scenes for the benefit of a known-to-be-hiding third character

Where: the gardens at Leonato's   **To Whom:** #9 to Margaret in front of Ursula, and then to to Ursula; #10 to Ursula for the benefit of the hidden Beatrice

speech #9, # of Lines: 26   Probable Timing: 1.15 minutes
speech #10, # of Lines: 37   Probable Timing: 1.55 minutes

Though the last two sentences almost match, the onrush of F # 1and #2 suggest much more excitement for Hero as the speech opens (as befits a young woman about to trick her cousin into re-falling in love) than the modern texts which by splitting F #1 into five and F #2 into four create a series of much more rational instructions and comments.

• while setting up the factual details of the scam for Margaret to follow may of necessity be intellectual there still seems a fair amount of emotion involved (7/8, F #1's first eight and a half lines to the only colon in the sentence) - anticipation perhaps?, especially since the capitals disappear after the first five lines

• following the colon, offers a much more careful and calm elaboration as to how Beatrice will behave ('there will she hide her,/To listen our purpose', 1/2 the last four and half lines)

• that Margaret and Ursula are not yet ready to move (finding this elaboration perhaps enjoyable or even somewhat startling) might be seen in the ungrammatical fast-link comma by which Hero moves on into the sentence - ending instruction 'this is thy office' which starts halfway through the penultimate line: most modern texts remove this possibility by setting the instruction as a separate sentence (mt. #5)

• the instructions to Ursula are equally intellectual with even more emotional involvement (8/12, F #2)

• and then excitement takes over, both as to how she intends to operate (the first), and the instruction to let the tempting start (the second)
" : of this matter,/Is little Cupids crafty arrow made,/That onely wounds by heare-say : now begin . "

• that 'now begin' continues F's sentence (#2) rather, than as most modern texts set it, starting a new one (mt. #10) suggest, Hero is more excited than her modern text counterpart

• and the excitement seems to be emotional, for after the passion of spotting where and how Beatrice is trying to hide, the (exciting) suggestion that they go near her is totally non-intellectual (0/5, F #3)

Modern Text

9/ Hero

1
Good Margaret, run* thee to the parlor*,
There shalt thou find* my Cousin* Beatrice
Proposing with the Prince and Claudio . †
Whisper her ear*, and tell her I and Ursula,
Walk* in the ^orchard, and our whole discourse
Is all of her . †

2
Say that thou overheardst us,
And bid her steal* into the pleached bower,
Where honey*suckles ripened by the sun*,
Forbid the sun* to enter, like favorites* ,
Made proud by ^princes, that advance their pride
Against that power that bred it . †

4
There will she hide her,
To listen our [propose] . †

5
This is thy office ;
Bear* thee well in it, and leave us alone.

6
Now, Ursula, when Beatrice doth come,
As we do trace this alley up and down*
Our talk* must only* be of Benedick* . †

7
When I do* name him, let it be thy part
To praise him more [than] ever man did merit . †

8
My talk* to thee must be how Benedick* .
Is sick* in love with Beatrice . †

9
Of this matter
Is little Cupids crafty arrow made,
That only* wounds by hearsay . †

10
Now begin,
For look* where Beatrice like a ^lapwing runs
Close by the ground, to hear* our conference.

First Folio

9/ Hero

1
Good Margaret+ runne thee to the parlour,
There shalt thou finde my Cosin Beatrice,x
Proposing with the Prince and Claudio,
Whisper her eare, and tell her I and Ursula,
Walke in the Orchard, and our whole discourse
Is all of her, say that thou over-heardst us,
And bid her steale into the pleached bower,
Where hony-suckles ripened by the sunne,
Forbid the sunne to enter: x like favourites,
Made proud by Princes, that advance their pride,x
Against that power that bred it, there will she hide her,
To listen our [purpose], this is thy office, +
Beare thee well in it, and leave us alone.

2
Now+ Ursula, when Beatrice doth come,
As we do trace this alley up and downe,
Our talke must onely be of Benedicke,
When I doe name him, let it be thy part,x
To praise him more [then] ever man did merit,
My talke to thee must be how Benedicke
Is sicke in love with Beatrice: of this matter,x
Is little Cupids crafty arrow made,
That onely wounds by heare-say: now begin,
For looke where Beatrice like a Lapwing runs
Close by the ground, to heare our conference.

Modern Text

11 Then go we near* her, that her ear* lose* nothing
Of the false sweet* bait* that we lay for it {.}

10/ Hero

1 {*} Doth not the {Benedick}
Deserve as full as fortunate a bed
As ever Beatrice shall couch upon?

2 O God of love!

3 I know he doth deserve
As much as may be yielded* to a man;
But Nature never fram'd a woman's heart
Of prouder* stuff* [than] that of Beatrice . †

4 Disdain* and △scorn* ride sparkling in her eyes,
Misprising* what they look* on, and her wit
Values itself* so highly that to her
All matter else seems* weak* . †   She cannot love,

5 Nor take no shape nor project of affection,
She* is so self*-endeared.

6   I never yet saw man,
How wise, how noble, young*, how rarely featur'd,◊
But she would spell him backward. †
                          If fair*-fac'd,

7 She would swear* the gentleman should be her sister ;
If black*, why, Nature, drawing of an antic* ,
Made a foul* blot ; if tall, a lance* ill-headed,
If low, an agot very vildly* cut ;
If speaking, why, a vane blown* with all winds* :
If silent, [why], a block* moved with none.

8 So turns* she every man the wrong side out,
And never gives to △truth and △virtue that
Which simpleness* and merit purchaseth.

9 {} Sure, sure, such carping is not commendable.

The onrush of F #3 (establishing while Benedicke may be deserving of love Beatrice cannot give because she is 'so selfe indeared'); the onrush of F #8 (what on earth can be done) and the ungrammatical period between F #4-5 all point to spur of the moment improvisation and glitches rather than the more meticulous handling of the Beatrice-tease by the modern texts which split F #3 and #8 into three sentences apiece, and 'correct' the period to a more grammatically accurate (but less fun-in-the-moment) comma.

• at the start of the tease, there is a lovely tension between self-control (4/0) including several unembellished lines in the first five and a half lines opening the speech, F #1-2, and the first two and half lines of F #3) and the extra breath-thoughts presumably needed to establish that self control (marked , x) to ensure that excitement or the giggles don't run away with her

• but once Beatrice's faults are brought into play, so intellect disappears and for the remainder of F #3, for whatever reason (revenge? mischief? delight? sheer enjoyment?) Hero becomes highly emotional (2/9 in six and a half lines)

• and after F #4's unembellished (self-control once more ?) praise of Benedicke, matching exactly the opening of F #3, so emotion takes over as she then minutely details the way Beatrice will pull apart every man she meets (F #5, 1/9)

• F #6's summation of Beatrice's behaviour 'So turnes she every man . . .' becomes passionate for a moment (2/2) and F #7's final summation of Beatrice herself (such carping is not commendable') is once more (playfully?) calm and unembellished

---

3 Then go we neare her+ that her eare loose nothing,x
Of the false sweete baite that we lay for it :

First Folio

10/ Hero

1 {*} Doth not the {Benedicke}
Deserve as full as fortunate a bed,x
As ever Beatrice shall couch upon?

2 O God of love!

3   I know he doth deserve,x
As much as may be yeelded to a man : x
But Nature never fram'd a womans heart,x
Of prowder stuffe [then] that of Beatrice :
Disdaine and Scorne ride sparkling in her eyes,
Mis-prizing what they looke on, and her wit
Values it selfe so highly, x that to her
All matter else seemes weake : she cannot love,
Nor take no shape nor project of affection,
Shee is so selfe indeared.

4   I never yet saw man,
How wise, how noble, yong, how rarely featur'd.

5 But she would spell him backward : if faire fac'd,x
She would sweare the gentleman should be her sister : x
If blacke, why+ Nature+ drawing of an anticke,
Made a foule blot : x if tall, a launce ill headed : x
If low, an agot very vildlie cut : x
If speaking, why+ a vane blowne with all windes :
If silent, [then] + a blocke moved with none.

6 So turnes she every man the wrong side out,
And never gives to Truth and Vertue, x that
Which simplenesse and merit purchaseth.

7 {} Sure, sure, such carping is not commendable.

{ctd. over}

10 But who dare tell her so? †

12   If I should speak*,
    She would mock* me into air*, O, she would laugh me
    Out of myself*, press* me to death with wit . †

13 Therefore let Benedick*, like covered fire,
    Consume away in sighs*, waste inwardly*,;
    It were a better death [than] die with mocks*,
    Which is as bad as die with tickling.
    ~~~~~~~~~~~~~~~

14 No, rather I will go* to Benedick*,
    And counsel* him to fight against his passion,
    And truly I'll devise some honest slanders
    To strain* my cousin* with . †

15   One doth not know
    How much an ill word may empoison* liking.

• but by the time of F #8's supposed decision to let Benedicke 'Consume away in sighes', emotion is in full sway once more (2/8), while Hero's envisaged supposedly noble act to 'goe to Benedicke,/And counsaile him to fight against his passion' is handled (mock?) calmly yet again, (1/2 in the four lines of F #9)

• the first unembellished lines (with the exception of 'yeelded') are in praise of Benedicke (a lovely play-acting 'poor fellow' approach, perhaps)
"I know he doth deserve,/As much as may be yeelded to a man:"
followed by the lead up to Beatrice's bad behaviour
"I never yet saw man,/How wise, how noble, yong, how rarely featur'd."
this description enhanced by ending with this most ungrammatical of periods - a period replaced by a comma in most modern texts thus removing the potential play-acting of Hero finding the image too much/too painful for her, perhaps, with the unembellished lines then continuing via the (horrified?)
"But she would spell him backward!"
and then she turns to the condemnation of Beatrice, with the short sentence "Sure, sure, such carping is not commendable." and "who dare tell her so?" but rather to help Benedicke 'fight against his passion Hero will
"And truly Ile devise some honest slanders,/ . . .one doth not know/How much an ill word may impoison liking."

• the seven surround phrases, found only in F #5 and unusually comprising all of F #5, all concentrate on the way Beatrice will dismiss any man

---

8 But who dare tell her so? if I should speake,
   She would mocke me into ayre, O[+] she would laugh me
   Out of my selfe, presse me to death with wit,
   Therefore let Benedicke[+] like covered fire,
   Consume away in sighes, waste inwardly: [x]
   It were a better death, [x] [ ]to die with mockes,
   Which is as bad as die with tickling.
   ~~~~~~~~~~~~~~~

9 No, rather I will goe to Benedicke,
   And counsaile him to fight against his passion,
   And truly Ile devise some honest slanders, [x]
   To straine my cosin with, one doth not know, [x]
   How much an ill word may impoison liking.

#'s 11 - 13: DON JOHN'S DASTARDLY DEVICES

11/ Don John   I wonder that thou (being as thou saist thou art,   between 1.3.10 - 37

Background: Don John had led an insurrection against his eventually victorious brother, Don Pedro: in the following he justifies his malevolence and current status as a prisoner

Style: as part of a two handed scene

Where: unspecified, but presumably in quarters assigned to him at Leonato's home   **To Whom:** his man, Conrade

# of Lines: 17   Probable Timing: 0.55 minutes

Modern Text

11/ Don John

1 I wonder that thou (being, as thou say'st* thou art, born* under Saturn*) goest about to apply a moral* medicine to a mortifying mischief* . †   I cannot hide what I

2 am : I must be* sad when I have cause, and smile at no man's jests;   eat when I have stomach*, and wait for no man's leisure ; sleep* when I am drowsy*, and tend on no man's business* ; laugh when I am merry, and claw no man in his humor.

3 I had rather be a canker in a hedge, [than] a rose in {my *brother's}* grace, and it better fits my blood* to be disdain'd of all [than] to fashion a carriage to rob love from any . †   In

4 this (though I cannot be said to be a flattering honest man) it must not be denied but I am a plain*-dealing villain* . †   I

5 am trusted with a muzzle* , and enfranchis'd* with a clog, therefore I have decreed not to sing in my cage. †

6 If I had my mouth, I would bite ; if I had my liberty, I would do my liking. †

7 In the mean* time let me be that I am, and seek* not to alter me.

First Folio

11/ Don John

1 I wonder that thou (being + as thou saist thou art, borne under Saturne) goest about to apply a morall medicine, x to a mortifying mischiefe : I cannot hide what I am : I must bee sad when I have cause, and smile at no mans jests, + eat when I have stomacke, and wait for no mans leisure : x sleepe when I am drowsie, and tend on no mans businesse, + laugh when I am merry, and claw no man in his humor.

2 I had rather be a canker in a hedge, [then] a rose in {my Brother's} grace, and it better fits my bloud to be disdain'd of all, x [then] to fashion a carriage to rob love from any : in this (though I cannot be said to be a flattering honest man) it must not be denied but I am a plaine dealing villaine, I am trusted with a mussell, and enfranchisde with a clog, therefore I have decreed, x not to sing in my cage : x if I had my mouth, I would bite : x if I had my liberty, I would do my liking : in the meane time, x let me be that I am, and seeke not to alter me.

That F's Don John's self-definition is very dangerous can be seen **in both the onrush (two F sentences compared to most modern texts' seven), and the bursts of emotional releases combined with many unembellished lines.**

• in the put down of Conrade F #1 starts emotionally (1/4 in the first two and a half lines) then the first unembellished phrase is followed by more emotion as John describes how he 'must be' in his various behaviours (0/4, the last four and a half lines)

• then in describing how he wishes to be perceived in society he becomes very quiet (1/1 the first four lines of F #2), while the two lines describing himself as 'plaine dealing villaine' releases the emotions once more (0/4) before finishing quietly (0/2 the last two and a half lines)

• the surround phrases spell the character out very precisely
" : I cannot hide what I am : " and the final
" : if I had my mouth, I would bite : if I had my liberty, I would do my liking : in the meane time, let me be that I am, and seeke not to alter me . "
made all the more remarkable in that the first three are also unembellished – a very precise self-definition indeed. with the warning of " : if I had my mouth, I would bite : ", made even more dangerous by being monosyllabic too

• and the occasional non-surround unembellished lines point to even more prickly anti-social qualities, including
"and claw no man in his humor."
"I had rather be a canker in a hedge,"
"in this (though I cannot be said to be a flattering honest man)"
"therefore I have decreed, not to sing in my cage:"
made more dangerous in their icy calm

12/ •Bastard•   My Lord and brother, God save you . / {*} If your leisure serv'd,   between 3.2.178-135

Background: To get back at all his perceived enemies, Don John is attempting to block the proposed marriage of Claudio and Hero: his first attempt failed, but one of his men, Borachio - the name suggesting one who loves his drink - has come up with a plan that has far more chance of succeeding (letting Claudio see a woman whom he believes to be Hero, actually Borachio's girl-friend Margaret, one of Hero's attendants, in a highly compromising sexual situation the night before the marriage): Don John begins to put his part of the plan in action: one note, for greater continuity sentences F #4-5 have been reversed from their original setting

Style: as part of a three-handed scene

Where: unspecified, but presumably somewhere in Leonato's home   **To Whom:** Don Pedro and Claudio

# of Lines: 28   **Probable Timing: 1.30 minutes**

Don John's patterns follow those of a very skilful manipulator, the shifts between intellect and passion, as well as the personal habits of calm accompanied by sudden bursts of emotion as seen in the previous speech all show a man shifting tactics and secretly rejoicing when his barbs seem to strike home.

• thus the opening greeting is handled quite factually (2/0, F #1) with only a hint of emotion released as the request to talk with Don Pedro is made (0/1, F #2)

• then skillfully bringing Claudio into the conversation (to ensure he doesn't leave) so passion is released (2/3, F #3) followed by a burst of emotion in the (supposedly) do-gooding camaraderie self-effacement (0/8 in the onrushed F #4)

• having caught the attention of Claudio and Pedro with the appalling surround-phrase prognostication as to Claudio's marriage ' : surely sute ill spent, and labour ill-bestowed ' , so John now goes quiet as he promises to prove 'the Lady is disloyall' (2/4, the five lines F #5-7)

• then comes the (deliberately?) passionate short F #8 naming Claudio's beloved and betrothed Hero as 'every mans Hero' (2/2 in just one line)

• and it looks as if the poisoned words might have taken, for as John expands on the theme of 'disloyall' so he shows more of his personal pattern of emotional burst (0/3, F #9's first two and a half lines) then an unembellished surround phrase proffering the tainted proof (see the introduction above) ' : wonder not till further warrant : ' , followed by a further mix of unembellished and emotional lines to finish the sentence (0/4), once more ending with another damming surround phrase ' : But it would better fit your honour to change your minde . ' (0/4 the last three and a half lines of F #9)

Modern Text

12/ {Don John as} **'Bastard•**

1 My ^lord and brother, God save you !

2 {*} If your leisure serv'd,   I would speak* with you .

3 Yet Count Claudio may hear*,   for what I would speak* of concerns* him.

4{ You may think* I love you not ; let that appear* hereafter, and aim* better at me by that I now will manifest . †

5 For my brother, I think*, he holds you well, and in dearness* of heart hath hope* to effect your ensuing marriage - surely suit* ill spent and labor* ill-bestow'd* .

6 Means* your ^lordship to be married to-morrow ?

[to Don Pedro]

7 You know he does, {yet} I know not that, when he knows* what I know .

8 I came hither to tell you, and circumstances short'ned, (for she hath been* too long a-talking of), the ^lady is disloyal* .

9 Even she - Leonato's* Hero, your Hero, every man's Hero.

10 The word {disloyal*}is too good to paint out her wickedness* . †

11 I could say she were worse ; think* you of a worse title, and I will fit her to it . †

12 Wonder not till further warrant . †

First Folio

12/ {Don John as} **'Bastard•**

1 My Lord and brother, God save you. +

2 I would speake with you,   {*} If your leisure serv'd,

3 Yet Count Claudio may heare,   for what I would speake of, x concernes him.

4{ You may thinke I love you not, + let that appeare hereafter, and ayme better at me by that I now will manifest, for my brother (I thinke, he holds you well, and in dearenesse of heart)x hath hope to effect your ensuing marriage : x surely sute ill spent ,and labour ill-bestowed.

5 Meanes your Lordship to be married to morrow ?

[to Don Pedro]

6 You know he does, {yet} I know not that+ when he knowes what I know.

7 I came hither to tell you, and circumstances shortned, (for she hath beene too long a talking of)+ the Lady is disloyall.

8 Even shee, Leonatoes Hero, your Hero, every mans Hero.

9 The word {disloyall} is too good to paint out her wickednesse, I could say she were worse,+ thinke you of a worse title, and I will fit her to it: wonder not till further warrant : goe but with mee tonight, you shal see her cham-

ber window entred, even the night before her wedding day, if you love her, then⁺ to morrow wed her:ₓ But it would better fit your honour to change your minde.

10 If you dare not trust that you see, confesse not that you know: if you will follow mee, I will shew you enough, and when you have seene more, & heard more, proceed accordingly.

11 I will disparage her no farther, till you are my witnesses, beare it coldly but till [ ]night, and let the issue shew it selfe.

12 O plague right well prevented! so will you say, when you have seene the sequele.

• and the speech ends in emotional mode (whether twisting the knife or secretly enjoying the manipulation is up to each actor to decide), (0/8, the last eight lines of the speech, F #10-12)

• as noted above, it seems Don John realises his poison has begun its work after F #8, and certainly it is only now that ice-cold unembellished lines are inserted to add their damage, including

"I could say she were worse,"
"tonight, you shal see her chamber window entred, even the night before her wedding day, if you love her, then to morrow wed her:"
"I will shew you enough, ... proceed accordingly."
"I will disparage her no farther . . . let the issue shew it selfe."
"O plague right well prevented! so will you say, ..."

• in F #12 the combination of the rare exclamation mark followed by a lower-case letter suggests there may be more to the remark then just a generalised statement on Claudio's and Pedro's behalf: F's setting offers the possibility it may slip out of John unchecked as a note of personal triumph at probably having prevented the wedding – a release from which he quickly has to recover with the ungrammatical continuation of 'so you will say . . . '

---

13   Go* but with me* to-night, you shall see her chamber-window ent'red, even the night before her wedding-day .†

14   If you love her then, to-morrow wed her; ⁴but it would better fit your honor* to change your mind* .

15   If you dare not trust that you see, confess* not that you know. †

16   If you will follow me* , I will show you enough, and when you have seen* more, & heard more, proceed accordingly.

12   I will disparage her no farther till you are my witnesses .†

17   Bear* it coldly but till [mid]night, and let the issue show itself*.

18   O plague right well prevented! †

19   So will you say, when you have seen* the sequel* .

13/ Claudio   {*} **Father, by your leave, /Will you with free and unconstrained soule**   between 4.1.23 - 61

Background: Thanks to the insinuations of Don John (speech #12 above) and the successful execution of Borachio's plan, both Claudio and Don Pedro have no other choice to believe Hero has been visibly unfaithful the night before her marriage: the following is Claudio's public repudiation of her in front of all assembled for the wedding

Style: public address, via one man to a larger assembled group

Where: unspecified in or outside Leonato's home, wherever the wedding was due to be solemnized   **To Whom:** Leonato, in front of Hero, Anthonio, Beatrice and Benedicke, Don Pedro, Don John, perhaps Borachio and Conrade, presumably some members of the household including Margaret and Ursula, and the Frier

# of Lines: 28   Probable Timing: 1.30 minutes

First Folio

13/ Claudio

1
{*} Father, by your leave,
Will you with free and unconstrained soule
Give me this maid[+] your daughter?

2
And what have I to give you back, x whose worth
May counterpoise this rich and precious gift?

3
{*} Leonato, take her backe againe,
Give not this rotten Orenge to your friend,
Shee's but the signe and semblance of her honour :
Behold how like a maid she blushes heere!

4
O[+] what authoritie and shew of truth
Can cunning sinne cover it selfe withall!

5
Comes not that bloud, x as modest evidence, x
To witnesse simple Vertue? would you not sweare[+]
All you that see her, that she were a maide,
By these exterior shewes?

6
But she is none :
She knowes the heat of a luxurious bed : x
Her blush is guiltinesse, not modestie.

7
I know what you would say : if I have knowne her,
You will say, she did imbrace me as a husband,
And so extenuate the forehand sinne : No[+] Leonato,
I never tempted her with word too large,
But as a brother to his sister, shewed
Bashful sinceritie and comely love.

Modern Text

13/ Claudio

1
{*} Father, by your leave,
Will you with free and unconstrained soul*
Give me this maid, your daughter?

x
And what have I to give you back whose worth
May counterpoise this rich and precious gift?

3
{*} Leonato, take her back* again* . †
Give not this rotten △orange* to your friend,
She's* but the sign* and semblance of her honor* . †
Behold how like a maid she blushes here* !

5
O, what authority* and show of truth
Can cunning sin* cover itself* withal* !

7
Comes not that blood* as modest evidence
To witness* simple △Virtue? †
Would you not swear* ,
All you that see her, that she were a maid* ,
By these exterior shows* ?

9
But she is none :
She knows* the heat of a luxurious bed :
Her blush is guiltiness* , not modesty* .

10
I know what you would say . †

11
If I have known* her,
You will say, she did embrace* me as a husband,
And so extenuate the 'forehand sin* . †

12
No, Leonato,
I never tempted her with word too large,
But as a brother to his sister, show'd
Bashful sincerity* and comely love.

This is a most difficult speech for a young actor, for if played with flat out emotion there is a great danger of him becoming a whining wimp, a prig and a fool - see especially the discussion of F #1-2, and #6-7 below. With its mix of careful (even, surprisingly, loving) unembellished lines being sometimes swamped by sudden bursts of emotion, F goes a great way to show the hurt and struggle within Claudio as he undertakes a seemingly repugnant act all based on Don John's trumped-up proof – Hero's earlier joking comment 'How much an ill word may empoison liking' (speech #10) here proven beyond all doubt.

• many unembellished lines point to the difficulties Claudio is undergoing, indeed with the exception of the one word 'soule' Claudio opens extraordinarily quietly and carefully (0/1, the first four and half lines, F #1-2)
"Father, by your leave, /Will you with free and unconstrained soule/Give me this maid your daughter? / And what have I to give you back, whose worth/May counterpoise this rich and precious gift?"
and continues to carefully advance his argument with F #7's monosyllabic opening surround phrase
" . I know what you would say : ", continuing with
"I never tempted her with word too large, /But as a brother to his sister, shewed/Bashful sincerite and comely love."

• after the deceptively calm opening of F #1-2 comes a sustained emotional outburst as Claudio gives her back again to her father (1/7, F #3); he describes the bewildered Hero's modest demeanor at first as 'cunning sinne' (0/3, F #4) and then moving to decry her 'exterior shewes' as a 'maide' (0/5, F #5)

• that F #5 is even more difficult than the words and emotions suggest can be seen in the two extra breath-thoughts in the first line (marked, x) - perhaps suggesting he is caught between belief and disbelief himself

• then comes the extraordinarily quiet denunciation of Hero for knowing 'the heat of a luxurious bed' (F #6, made up of three surround phrases, yet only 0/2) – and it's essential to play this quietly if Claudio is to maintain any sense of worth or dignity for the rest of the play – followed by the

13 {She seemed} to me as Dian* in her orb*,
    As chaste as is the bud* ere it be blown*;
    But {she is} more intemperate in {her} blood
    Than Venus, or those pamp'red animals*
    That rage in savage sensuality*.

passionate denial that he was the fellow- dissolute (2/2 the first three lines
of F #7), again followed by a must-be-played-quietly-to maintain-dignity
unembellished three line expression of modesty to end the sentence

• finally the emotions come through once more, accompanied by classical
references - perhaps an attempt to ease the pain by finding an applicable
analogy from traditional mythology – (3/5, F #8)

8   {She seemed} to me as Diane in her Orbe,
    As chaste as is the budde ere it be blowne :ₓ
    But {she is} more intemperate in {her} blood,ₓ
    Than Venus, or those pampred animalls,ₓ
    That rage in savage sensualitie.

#'s 14 - 17: Serious Differences Between One-Time Friends

14/ Beatrice   Is {Claudio} not approved in the height a villaine,   between 4.1.300 - 323

Background: After the wedding fiasco and saving argument from the Frier, all have left the stage save Beatrice and Benedicke: following her amazing 'Kill Claudio' response to Benedicke's suggestion he would do anything to prove his love for her, Benedicke asks her 'Is Claudio thine enemie?': this is her reply

Style: as part of a two-handed scene

Where: unspecified in or outside Leonato's home, wherever the wedding was due to be solemnized   **To Whom:** Benedicke

# of Lines: 17   Probable Timing: 0.55 minutes

Modern Text

14/ Beatrice

1 Is {Claudio} not approv'd in the height a villain*, that hath slander'd, scorn'd, dishonor'd* my kinswoman?
          ◇

2 that I were a man! †

3   What, bear* her in hand until* they come to take hands, and then with public* accusation uncover'd* slander, unmitigated* rancor* - ◇ O God, that I were a man!

4   I would eat his heart in the market-place.

5 Talk* with a man out at a window! a proper* saying.

6 Sweet Hero, she is wrong'd, she* is slander;d, she is undone.

7 Princes and Counties! †

8   Surely* a ᐃprincely testi-monie*, a goodly |count|, Count Comfect, a sweet Gallant surely* . †

9   O that I were a man for his sake! or that I had any friend would be a man for my sake!

10   But manhood is mel-ted into |courtesies|, valor* into compliment, and men are only* turn'd into tongue, and trim ones too. †

11   He is now as valiant as Hercules that only tells a lie, and swears* it . †

12 I cannot be a man with wishing, therefore* I will die a wo-man with grieving.

First Folio

14/ Beatrice

1 Is {Claudio} not approved in the height a villaine, that hath slandered, scorned, dishonoured my kinswoman?
          O

2 that I were a man! what, beare her in hand untill they come to take hands, and then with publike accusation uncovered slander, unmitigated rancour?
          O God⁺ that I were a man!

4   I would eat his heart in the market-place.

5 Talke with a man out at a window, ⁺ a proper saying.

6 Sweet Hero, she is wrong'd, shee is slandered, she is undone.

7 Princes and Counties! surelie a Princely testi-monie, a goodly |] Count, Comfect, a sweet Gallant sure-lie, O that I were a man for his sake! or that I had any friend would be a man for my sake!

8   But manhood is mel-ted into cursies, valour into complement, and men are onelie turned into tongue, and trim ones too: he is now as valiant as Hercules, ₓ that onely tells a lie, and sweares it : I cannot be a man with wishing, therfore I will die a wo-man with grieving.

As with Claudio immediately above, this is a most difficult speech for an actress, for if played with flat out emotion there is a great danger of her becoming an emotional screaming virago - see especially the discussion of F #1-2, and #6-7 below. With its mix of careful initial emotion (not surprising given the circumstances) and then the incredible move first into intellect and then calm unembellished lines to finish, F highlights the greatness of Beatrice's mind, heart and spirit.

• fascinatingly, Beatrice's repeated 'O God that I were a man!' may not be mere hyperbole, but a deep seated wish, underscored as the phrases are by being monosyllabic, unembellished and each finishing with, for F, the very rare exclamation mark: and if any more proof were needed, the second statement is preceded by 'O God', with the whole set as a short sentence

• the emotional opening (1/6, F #1-2) leads to an unfinished thought in both texts, F marking the inability to continue even more strongly than most modern texts by setting a new sentence thereafter (F #3)

• Beatrice's struggle to regain self-control can be seen in that though there are hardly any releases in the next three lines (1/1, F #3-5), each sentence is very short – a far cry from the bulk of her earlier speeches (#1-4 above)

• once the key passionate sentence defending Hero is made (F #6, 1/1), Beatrice's ferocious intellect takes over, for there is not a single emotional release throughout F #7 (7/0) with the short spellings of the build ('testimonie' and 'surelie' twice) suggesting the strength of her belief beautifully underscored by three more (rare) exclamation marks

• interestingly, the despite the power of the exclamation marks, the indirect (none-too-suble?) hint for Benedicke's help that ends F #7, ': or that I had any friend would be a man for my sake !' is made very carefully, being both unembellished and a surround phrase

• and then it seems her energy gives way, for the despairing final almost unembellished surround phrases ': he is now as valiant as Hercules, that only tells a lie, and sweares it : I cannot be a man with wishing, therfore I will die a woman with grieving .' are part of a very non-released sentence (1/2, the five lines of F #8)

15/ Benedicke   Shall I speake a word in your eare ?   between 5.1.143 - 193

Background: Moved both by his love for Beatrice and her passionate defense of Hero, Benedicke has decided not only to part company with the Prince and thus Claudio, but to challenge Claudio to a duel; hence the following, in which he first offers the challenge; the remainder of the speech is self-explanatory, save for the comment of Pedro and Claudio having 'kill'd a sweet and innocent Ladie' - Hero is not dead, though the family must publicly behave as if she is

Style: as part of a three-handed scene

Where: unspecified, presumably in a public place   **To Whom:** Claudio, and then Don Pedro

# of Lines: 14   **Probable Timing: 0.45 minutes**

Modern Text

15/ Benedicke

1   Shall I speak* a word in your ear*?

2   You are a villain* .†

3   I jest not, I will make it good
    how you dare, with what you dare, and when you dare .†

4   Do me right, or I will protest your cowardice . †
                                    You have

5   kill'd a sweet* △lady*, and her death shall fall heavie* on
    you . †

6   Let me hear* from you.

7   Fare you well, △boy, you know my mind* . †
                                    I will

8   leave you now to your gossip*-like humor . †
                                    You break*

9   jests as braggards do their blades, which, God be thank'd,
    hurt not . †

10   My Lord, for your many* courtesies I thank
    you . †

11 I must discontinue your company* . †
                                    Your brother

12 the △bastard is fled from Messina . †
                                    You have among you,

13 kill'd a sweet and innocent △lady* . †

14   For my Lord Lack*-
    beard there, he and I shall meet* , and till then peace be
    with him.

First Folio

15/ Benedicke

1   Shall I speake a word in your eare ?

2   You are a villaine, I jest not, I will make it good
    how you dare, with what you dare, and when you dare :
    do me right, or I will protest your cowardise : you have
    kill'd a sweete Ladie, and her death shall fall heavie on
    you, let me heare from you.

3   Fare you well, Boy, you know my minde, I will
    leave you now to your gossep-like humor, you breake
    jests as braggards do their blades, which⁺ God be thank-
    ed⁺ hurt not : my Lord, for your manie courtesies I thank
    you, I must discontinue your companie, your brother
    the Bastard is fled from Messina : you have among you,
    kill'd a sweet and innocent Ladie : for my Lord Lacke-
    beard there, he and I shall meete, and till then peace be
    with him.

Given the circumstances, here there are very few passages of sustained emotion - very surprising when compared to his previous high release speeches (#5-8 above).

- the opening short emotional sentence is the first hint as to how difficult this challenge to a one-time friend and subsequent withdrawal from his patron's service and protection is going to be (0/2)

- and then the subsequent onrush of F #2's challenge and especially F #3's ungrammatical mixture of reinforcing the challenge, discontinuing Don Pedro's 'companie', giving the news of Don John's flight, and his own withdrawal reinforces the difficulty: unfortunately the modern texts reworking F #2 as five sentences and #3 as eight allows the modern Benedicke a much more dignified series of self-controlled and elegant statements – a far cry from the original setting

- Benedicke's internal struggle is beautifully suggested by the fact though F #2 is onrushed, there is, for him, very little release therein (1/3 in four and a half lines)

- similarly though F #3 opens passionately (2/3 in the first three lines plus), the withdrawal from Don Pedro's company, news of his brother's flight, and simple statement that they are responsible for Hero's death, all are handled without passion (3/0 the next four lines) – though the intellectual control is joined by emotion for the final belittling reminder of the challenge to Claudio (2/2, the last two lines)

- the two surround phrases point to how serious Benedicke now is
    " : do me right, or I will protest your cowardise : "
    " : you have among you, kill'd a sweet and innocent Ladie : "
    both of which are further heightened by being unembellished icily-calm

- and the one remaining section of unembellished lines showing this is not time for casual excess, for Benedicke has this to say about Claudio's being a 'villaine'
    "I jest not, I will make it good how you dare, with what you dare, and
        when you dare:"
    the monosyllables of the challenge heightened by being followed with the
    first surround phrase set above

16/ Prince   Ile tell thee how Beatrice prais'd thy wit the other day: 5.1.159 - 184

Background: Stung by Benedicke's rebuke of both he and Claudio, speech #15 immediately above, Don Pedro attempts to sting him in return (perhaps to deflect attention from Claudio to himself) by telling Benedicke the 'real' truth how Beatrice feels about him

Style: as part of a three-handed scene

Where: unspecified, presumably in a public place   **To Whom:** Benedicke, in front of Claudio

# of Lines: 16   **Probable Timing:** 0.50 minutes

First Folio

16/ Prince

1 Ile tell thee how Beatrice prais'd thy wit the o-
ther day: I said thou hadst a fine wit: true⁺ [saies] she, a fine
little one: no⁺ said I, a great wit: right⁺ saies shee, a great
grosse one: nay⁺ said I, a good wit: just⁺ said she, it hurts
no body: nay⁺ said I, the gentleman is wise: certain⁺ said
she, a wise gentleman: nay⁺ said I, he hath the tongues: that
I beleeve⁺ said shee, for hee forswore on tuesday morning, a
thing to me on munday night, which he forswore on tuesday morning:
there's a double tongue, there's two tongues: thus did
she an howre together trans-shape thy particular vertues, yet at last she concluded with a sigh, thou wast the
proprest man in Italie,

       and if shee
did not hate {you} deadlie, shee would love {you} dearely, .

2 But when shall we set the savage Bulls hornes
on the sensible Benedicks head?

3{*}   Yea⁺ and text under-neath, heere
dwells Benedicke the married man.

For a man who mainly uses commas throughout the play, and whose interests following the brief civil war with his brother are R & R (relaxation and recreation) this speech is utterly startling – indeed there are very few in Shakespeare where the relentlessness of no fewer than twelve colons in one sentence are to be found. When these are added to the onrush of F #1 (split into no fewer than fourteen component sentences in most modern texts) it seems that Don Pedro is fully committed to living up to his obligations as a prince, protecting his ward Claudio and verbally ruthlessly destroying anyone foolish enough to challenge his reputation.

• that the opening of F #1 is comprised of ten surround phrases with very little embellishment (1/2 in the first six lines) shows just how serious and deathly calm Don Pedro can be when he has to - especially when once the verbal pummeling of Benedicke has finished the colons completely disappear

• with so little excess in the opening it's quite fascinating that Don Pedro's quoting Beatrice about Benedicke's breaking of his word to her ('that I beleeve said shee, for hee swore a thing to me on munday night, which he forswore on tuesday morning:') is so emotional (0/4) in such a short space – but since the act of being foresworne is a complete anathema to the honourable Elizabethan such a sudden release is understandable sociologically, morally, personally - for Don Pedro has shown an on-stage interest in Beatrice - and theatrically

• following this uncharacteristic release, uncharacteristic for this speech at least, Don Pedro reasserts some degree of control, (1/3 in the last five lines of F #1)

• surprisingly for such an onrushed opening, the final two sentences match in both texts with intellect slightly dominating the ironic question (2/1, F #2) and a deceptively quiet unembellished moment (the first part of F #3) before the final passionate skilful picador-like stab of 'heere dwells Benedicke the married man.', (1/1, the last half of F #3)

Modern Text

16/ Prince

1 I'll tell thee how Beatrice prais'd thy wit the o-
ther day . †

2   I said thou hadst a fine wit . †

3   "True," [said] she, "a fine
little one" . †

4   "No," said I, "a great wit" . †

5   "Right," says* she* , "a great
gross* one" . †

6   "Nay," said I, "a good wit" . †

7   "Just," said she, "it hurts
no body" . †

8   "Nay," said I, "the gentleman is wise" . †

9   "Certain," said
she, "a wise gentleman" . †

10   "Nay," said I, "he hath the tongues" . †

11 "That I believe* , said she* , "for he* swore a thing to me on
ᐃMonday* night, which he forswore on ᐃTuesday morning . †

12 There's a double tongue, there's two tongues . "†

13   Thus did
she an hour* together trans-shape thy particular virtues, yet at last she concluded with a sigh, thou wast the
proper'st man in Italy* . †

14   And if she*
did not hate {you} deadly*, she* would love {you} dearly* .

15 But when shall we set the savage ᐃbull's horns
on the sensible Benedick's head?

16{*}   Yea, and text underneath, "ᐃHere*
dwells Benedick* the married man" .

17/ Leonato   **Tush, tush, man, never fleere and jest at me,**   between 5.1.58 - 79

Background: Even though Hero is not dead, Leonato and the family must act as if she were: having accidentally encountered Claudio and Don Pedro in the street, Leonato's anger gets the better of him, especially when insulted by Claudio who in response to Leonato's comment 'Nay, never lay thy hand upon thy sword,/I feare thee not' offers the rather demeaning reply 'Marry beshrew my hand/If it should give your age such cause of feare./Infaith my hand meant nothing to my sword.'

Style: part of a four-handed scene

Where: unspecified, presumably in a public place   **To Whom:** to Claudio, in front of Don Pedro and Anthonio

# of Lines: 19   Probable Timing: 1.00 minutes

Modern Text

17/ Leonato

1 Tush, tush, man, never fleer* and jest at me ;
   I speak* not like a dotard nor a fool*,
   As under privilege* of age to brag*
   What I have done being young*, or what would do*
   Were I not old . †

2   Know, Claudio, to thy head,
   Thou hast so wrong'd [mine] innocent child* and me
   That I am forc'd to lay my reverence by,
   And with grey hairs* and bruise of many days*,
   Do* challenge thee to trial* of a man . †

3 I say thou hast belied mine innocent child*!

4 Thy slander hath gone through and through her heart
   And she lies buried with her ancestors -
   O, in a tomb* where never scandal* slept,
   Save this of hers, fram'd by thy villainy*,!

5 I'll prove it on {your} body, if {you} dare,
   Despite* {your} nice fence and {your} active practice,
   {Your} May* of youth and bloom* of lustihood.
   ▨▨▨▨▨▨▨▨▨▨▨▨▨▨▨▨▨▨▨▨▨▨▨▨

6   {*}   Thou hast kill'd* my child . †

7 If thou kill'st* me, boy, thou shalt kill a man.

First Folio

17/ Leonato

1 Tush, tush, man, never fleere and jest at me, +
   I speake not like a dotard,x nor a foole,
   As under privilege of age to bragge,x
   What I have done being yong, or what would doe,x
   Were I not old, know+ Claudio + to thy head,
   Thou hast so wrong'd [my] innocent childe and me,x
   That I am forc'd to lay my reverence by,
   And with grey haires and bruise of many daies,
   Doe challenge thee to triall of a man, +
   I say thou hast belied mine innocent childe. +

2 Thy slander hath gone through and through her heart,x
   And she lies buried with her ancestors : x
   O+ in a tombe where never scandall slept,
   Save this of hers, fram'd by thy villanie. +

3 Ile prove it on {your} body+ if {you} dare,
   Despight {your} nice fence, and {your} active practise,
   {Your} Maie of youth, and bloome of lustihood.
   ▨▨▨▨▨▨▨▨▨▨▨▨▨▨▨▨▨▨▨▨▨▨▨▨

4   {*}   Thou hast kild my child,
   If thou kilst me, boy, thou shalt kill a man.

As with Beatrice (#14), Benedicke (#15) and Claudio (#13), when faced with a very disturbing emotional situation, rather than ranting off in all directions F shows the character, here the wronged Hero's father Leonato, struggling between bursts of passion and attempts, via the unembellished lines, at self-control.

● the unembellished lines speak as to from where Leonato's words and would-be actions stem: initially
   " . . . I am forc'd to lay my reverence by,"
followed by the very long extended passage, much of F #2-4,
   "Thy slander hath gone through and through her heart,/And she lies buried with her ancestors : . . . , fram'd by thy villanie. / Ile prove it on {your} body if {you} dare, . . . /Thou hast kild my child,/If thou kilst me, boy, thou shalt kill a man."

● thus the opening scornful scolding of Claudio starts emotionally (0/3, the first three lines): then Leonato seems to recover as he formally condemns Claudio for wronging 'my innocent childe and me' (1/2 the next four lines), but this does not last and he reverts to emotion as the formal challenge is made (0/4 the last three lines of F #1)

● and while F #2's opening two lines spelling out exactly what Claudio's 'slander' has done are unembellished, the notion of the 'scandall' it has brought to Leonato's family becomes emotional once more (0/2 the last two lines of F #2)

● the repetition of the invitation to fight (F #3-4) starts and finishes with great unembellished self-control, though the dismissal of Claudio's youthful strength becomes a mix of passion (1/2, the last two lines of F #3) and attempted control via short spellings 'villanie', 'Maie', 'kild' and 'kilst'

#'s 18 - 19: THE WATCH

18/ Dogberry   Come hither neighbour Sea-coale, God hath . . .   between 3.3.13 - 82

Background: The first appearance for the local constabulary, lead by Dogberry who is one of the finest manglers of the English language ever created: here he first chooses who will be the special member to 'beare . . . the lanthorne', and then instructs the members of the watch as to their duties for that evening

Style: public address to at least three people

Where: unspecified, but either public street or the watch-house   **To Whom:** at least three members of the watch, possibly more if the production can afford it

# of Lines: 40   **Probable Timing: 2.00 minutes**

First Folio

18/ Dogberry

1   Come hither+ neighbour Sea-coale, God hath blest you with a good name : to be a wel-favoured man,x is the gift of Fortune, but to write and reade,x comes by Nature.

2   Well, for your favour+ sir, why+ give God thankes, & make no boast of it, and for your writing and reading+ let that appeare when there is no need of such vanity, you are thought heere to be the most senslesse and fit man for the Constable of the watch :x   therefore beare you the lan-thorne: this is your charge: You shall comprehend all vagrom men, + you are to bid any man stand+ in the Prin-ces name.

3   {*}   {*} If a will not stand,
{*} then take no note of him, but let him go, and presently call the rest of the Watch together, and thanke God you are ridde of a knave.

4   You are to call at all the Alehouses, and bid [them] that are drunke get them to bed: {*} If they will not? why then, + let them alone till they are sober.

{*}

5   If you meet a theefe, you may suspect him, by vertue of your office, to be no true man : and for such kinde of men, the lesse you meddle or make with them, why+ the more is for your honesty.

- as seen in the following speech, Dogberry rarely is factual or intellectual, thus the opening here is somewhat suspicious – (4/2, F #1) – perhaps suggesting a good deal of flattery is going on, especially when the extra breath-thoughts (marked , x) come into play serving to split up and thus intensify the praise of Sea-coale even more

- certainly the emotion that joins the intellect for the first five and a half lines of F #2 (2/7) suggests that Dogberry is working even harder to get Sea-coale to accept

- and the ungrammatical fast-link connection via the comma of 'you are thought heere . . .' suggests Dogberry is riding roughshod over grammatical niceties to rush Sea-coale so he cannot refuse (most modern texts replace the comma with period, and set this as a new sentence mt. # 5 thus removing any chance of such a possibility)

- and once Sea-coale has accepted, or rather, not refused, so the pressure seems to be off, for all of a sudden passion and then intellect comes into play, with a great deal of quiet cautioning too

- the charge to bid men 'stand in the Princes name' is intellectual (2/0) though the caution to be exercised if they refuse is very quietly handled via the unembellished opening line and a half of F #3, followed by a passionate if some what chop-logic resolution of self-congratulation to be 'ridde of such a knave' (2/2 the last line and a half of F #3)

- the charge to deal with drunks is similarly intellectual (F #4) with the last phrase of what to do if they won't obey once again cautiously unembellished

- however , unlike the previous warnings, the advice of how to deal with a 'theefe' causes Dogberry emotional concerns both initially (0/3, F #5, with once again the final phrase of chop-

---

Modern Text

18/ Dogberry

1   Come hither, neighbor* Seacole*.†
2   God hath blest you with a good name.. †
3   To be a well*-favor'd* man is the gift of ^fortune, but to write and read* comes by ^nature.
4   Well, for your favor*, sir, why, give God thanks*, & make no boast of it, and for your writing and reading, let that appear* when there is no need of such vanity.†   You are
5   thought here* to be the most senseless* and fit man for the ^constable of the watch; therefore bear* you the lan-thorn*. †
6   This is your charge: ^you shall comprehend all vagrom men; you are to bid any man stand, in the Prin-ce's name.
7   {*}   {*} If'a will not stand,
{*} then take no note of him, but let him go, and presently call the rest of the ^watch together, and thank* God you are rid* of a knave.
8   You
are to call at all the ^alehouses, and bid [those] that are drunk* get them to bed.†
{*}
9   {*} If they will not,
why then let them alone till they are sober.
10   If you meet a thief*, you may suspect him, by virtue of your office, to be no true man; and for such kind* of men, the less* you meddle or make with them, why, the more is for your honesty.

6{*} {You need} {*} not lay hands on him, {for} Truly {while}by your office you may, {*} I think they that touch pitch will be defil'd : the most peaceable way for you, if you doe take a theefe, is, to let him shew him-selfe what he is, and steale out of your company.

7{*} If you heare a child crie in the night+ you must call to the nurse_x and bid her still it. {*}

8{*} If the nurse be asleepe and will not heare {*, } why then depart in peace, and let the childe wake her with crying, for the ewe that will not heare her Lambe when it baes, will never answere a calfe when he bleates.

9 This is the end of the charge : you constable+ are to present the Princes owne person, if you meete the Prince in the night, you may staie him.

10 Five shillings to one on't+ with anie man that knowes the Statues, he may staie him, + marrie+ not with-out the prince be willing, for indeed the watch ought to offend no man, and it is an offence to stay a man against his will .

---

logic praise-worthy caution being unembellished), and especially in the final summation (F #6, 1/5) as he advises the Watch how to avoid being 'defil'd' by letting him 'steale out of your company'

• and for some reason the whole advice of how to handle a 'child crie in the night' and its nurse so 'asleepe and will not heare' is totally emotional (0/8, F #7-8) - perhaps offering the rather stretched metaphor of 'ewe', 'Lambe', 'calfe' gives him great pleasure in showing off his wit

• the ending of the charge (F #9) is passionate (2/2), not surprisingly since he reminds that they represent 'the Princes owne person': so is the opening bet of F #10 - up to the malapropism of 'Statue's for the more usual 'statutes' (2/1)

• however, once more caution comes into play when discussing the possible arrest of the prince himself (with the lovely nonsensical caveat 'not without the prince be willing'), for the final three lines of the speech are completely unembellished – a very rare happening in any Shakespeare play

• to offset the moments of caution, there are the occasional times when certain moments of officialdom seem to be intensified in that they are offered via surround phrases - as to Sea-coale

" : therefore beare you the lanthorne : "
and the readying of all the Watch with
" : this is your charge : "
the way of dealing with non-complying drunks
: If they will not ? why then, let them alone till they are sober . "
and the final
" . This the end of the charge : "
but these moments are few and far between

11{*} {You need} {*} not lay hands on him, {for} truly {while}by your office you may, {*} I think they that touch pitch will be defil'd . †

12 The most peaceable way for you, if you do* take a thief*, is, to let him show him-self* what he is, and steal* out of your company.

13{*} If you hear* a child cry* in the night, you must call to the nurse and bid her still it. {*}

14{*} If the nurse be asleep* and will not hear* {*, } why then depart in peace, and let the child* wake her with crying, for the ewe that will not hear* her △lamb* when it baes, will never answer* a calf* when he bleats* .

15 This is the end of the charge : you constable, are to present the Prince's own* person . †

16 If you meet* the Prince in the night, you may stay* him.

17 Five shillings to one on't, with any* man that knows* the △statutes, he may stay* him ; marry*, not with-out the △Prince be willing, for indeed the watch ought to offend no man, and it is an offense to stay a man against his will .

---

1 Q/F2/most modern texts = 'statutes', F1 = 'Statues' (a lovely malapropism)

19/ Kemp   **Gods my life, where's the Sexton ? let him write**   between 4.2.70 - 87

Background: Having arrested Don John's men Conrade and Borachio, and put them on one of the most maladroit trial scenes Shakespeare ever wrote, the two 'malefactors' have finally lost their patience, especially Conrade, and called Dogberry (here given the prefix of 'Kemp', the name of the original actor) an 'Asse': this is his horrified response

Style: public address to a large and confused group
Where: wherever the hearing for Conrade and Borachio took place   **To Whom:** the group at large, including the watch, plus Conrade and Borachio, and various individuals therein

# of Lines: 15   Probable Timing: 0.50   minutes

Given the insults just thrown his way it's not surprising that very little of the relative calm of Dogberry's previous speech is to be found here, yet there does seem to be a definite struggle throughout to put a cap on the hurt feelings, though the moments of forced calm of the occasional unembellished lines rarely last for long.

• what is surprising is the intellectual cluster that opens this speech, perhaps suggesting that he regards the barbs as doubly insulting, against himself personally and as the 'Princes Officer' who, according to the previous speech, presents 'the Princes owne person'

• that he is deeply affected by the insult can be seen that though the short F #2 is unembellished till the very last word, the emotional flood-gates open (0/5 in the first line of F #3) with the rare exclamation mark concluded ,
" O that hee were heere to write mee downe an asse ! "

• and then just for a moment either dignity (or real personal hurt) takes over, for there follows the unembellished double surround phrases (save for the hurtful 'asse', the final word in each phrase)
" ! but masters remember that I am an asse: though it be not
written down, yet forget not ÿ I am an asse"
but this doesn't last, for he breaks into a passionate attack on 'thou villaine' (1/2 in just two lines)

• the struggle for self-control is seen yet again as the self-definition begins
"I am a wise fellow, and which is more, an officer, "
but once more this unembellished control cannot last, and the detailing of his especial qualities ('a houshoulder'; 'as pretty a peece of flesh'; and has 'two gownes') quickly moves him into strong emotion (2/6 in the next five lines), though once more he manages to control himself with the finale of self praise being stated via the unembellished 'and every thing handsome about him'

• and though the final surround phrase order also maintains calm ' : bring him away : ' (a self-conscious attempt to restore some form of order perhaps) this calm is destroyed by the passionate outburst for the last surround phrase of the speech
' : O that I had been writ downe an asse ! "
even further emphasised by the rare F exclamation mark

Modern Text

19/ Kemp

1 Gods my life, where's the △sexton? †
2   Let him write
down* the Prince's △officer △coxcomb* . †
3   Come, bind* them . †
~~~~~~~~~~
4 Thou naughty varlet !
5 Dost thou not suspect my place? †
6   Dost thou not
suspect my years*?.
7   O that he* were here* to write me*
down* an ass* ! †
8   But, masters, remember that I am an ass* ;
though it be not written down, yet forget not [that] I am an
ass* . †
9   No, thou villain*, [thou] art full of piety as shall be prov'd
upon thee by good witness* . †
10   I am a wise fellow, and
which is more, an officer, and which is more, a houshol-
der*, and which is more, as pretty a piece* of flesh as any [is]
in Messina, and one that knows* the △law, go* to, & a rich
fellow enough, go* to, and a fellow that hath had losses,
and one that hath two gowns* , and every thing handsome about him. †
11   Bring him away . †
12   O that I had been writ
down* an ass* !

First Folio

19/ Kemp

1 Gods my life, where's the Sexton? let him write
downe the Princes Officer Coxcombe :come, binde them
thou naughty varlet. +
~~~~~~~~~~
2 Dost thou not suspect my place? dost thou not
suspect my yeeres?
3   O that hee were heere to write mee
downe an asse ! but⁺ masters, remember that I am an asse;
though it be not written down, yet forget not [ÿ] I am an
asse:No⁺thou villaine, [ÿ] art full of piety as shall be prov'd
upon thee by good witnesse, I am a wise fellow, and
which is more, an officer, and which is more, a houshoulder, and which is more, as pretty a peece of flesh as any‖in
Messina, and one that knowes the Law, goe to, & a rich
fellow enough, goe to, and a fellow that hath had losses,
and one that hath two gownes, and every thing handsome about him : bring him away : O that I had been writ
downe an asse!

THE MERRY WIVES OF WINDSOR

SPEECHES IN ORDER	TIME	PAGE
#'s 1 - 6: Falstaffe Sets Up His Targets		
1/ **Falstaffe** My honest Lads, I will tell you what I am about.	1.15	216
2/ **Mistris Page** What, have {I} scap'd Love-letters in the . . .	1.15	218
3/ **Mistris Page** {Did you ever heare the like?}	1.00	220
4/ **Pistoll** Sir John affects thy wife.	0.40	221
5/ **Nym** And this is true : I like not the humor of lying :	0.30	222
6/ **Mistris Quickly** Why, Sir ; {mistrisse Ford's} a good-creature ;	1.55	223
#'s 7 - 8: Ford's Interference		
7/ **Falstaffe** Want no Mistresse Ford (Master Broome) . . .	0.55	225
8/ **Ford** What a damn'd Epicurian-Rascall is this?	1.15	226
#'s 9 - 12: The Wooing of Mistris Ford		
9/ **Falstaffe** Have I caught thee, my heavenly Jewell?	0.55	228
10/ **Falstaffe** Have I liv'd to be carried in a Basket like a . . .	0.45	229
11/ **Falstaffe** Nay, you shall heare (Master Broome) what I	1.40	230
12/ **Ford** Hum: ha? Is this a vision? Is this a dreame?	0.45	232
#'s 13 - 14: Falstaffe's Final Downfall		
13/ **Falstaffe** The Windsor-bell hath stroke twelve:	1.00	233
14/ **Mistris Quickly** About, about : /Search Windsor Castle (Elves)	1.10	234
#'s 15 - 18: A Key Sub-Plot, The Wooing of Anne Page		
15/ **Evans** There is also another device in my praine,	0.40	235
16/ **Slender** I will marry her (Sir) at your request; but . . .	0.25	236
17/ **Evans** 'Plesse my soule : how full of Collors I am,	0.35	237
18/ **Host** Peace, I say, Gallia and Gaule, French & Welch,	0.45	238
19/ **Slender** Whoa hoe, hoe, Father Page.	0.45	239

SPEECHES BY GENDER

		Speech #(s)
SPEECHES FOR WOMEN (4)		
Mistris Page	**Traditional & Today:** married woman, with young daughter of just marriageable age	#2, #3
Mistris Quickly	**Traditional & Today:** a gossipy woman of middle to advancing years, still attractive to Pistoll	#6, #14
SPEECHES FOR EITHER GENDER (1)		
Host	**Traditional:** male, any age **Today:** any gender, any age	#18
SPEECHES FOR MEN (14)		
Falstaffe	**Traditional & Today:** older and very corpulent man	#1, #7, #9, #10, #11, #13
Pistoll	**Traditional & Today:** man of indeterminate age	#4
Nym	**Traditional & Today:** man of indeterminate age	#5
Ford	**Traditional & Today:** male, usually middle age and upward	#8, #12
Evans	**Traditional & Today:** older character male	#15, #17
Slender	**Traditional & Today:** younger character man of marriageable age, not particularly bright	#16, #19

THE MERRY WIVES OF WINDSOR

#'s 1 - 6: FALSTAFFE SETS UP HIS TARGETS

1/ Falstaffe   **My honest Lads, I will tell you what I am about .**   between 1.3.39 - 74

Background: Falstaffe has come to Windsor, presumably in the hopes of repairing his non-existent fortunes (he's just managed to reduce expenses by getting his one-time crony/servant, Bardolfe, employment with the Host of the Inn in which Falstaffe is currently residing.

Style: as part of a four-handed scene

Where: Falstaffe's room(s) in the Inn   **To Whom:** his remaining crony/servants Nym and Pistoll, and Robin his page

# of Lines: 24   **Probable Timing: 1.15 minutes**

The gigantic number of surround phrases (at least twenty-five) underscore the fact that this very early speech is probably the height of Falstaffe's dreams anywhere in the play. Additionally, F's onrush suggests unleashed – though by re-setting F's five sentences as **seventeen** most modern texts establish a far more **factual** and much **less romantic character than** originally set.

- the speech starts almost hushed (F #1, 1/0), its shortness suggesting that Falstaffe may be struggling to keep himself in check, which he cannot do for long . . .

- . . . for the first four and a half lines of F #2 are not just highly emotional (1/8), they are exceedingly important for Falstaffe's plans, for they are formed by nothing but eight surround phrases

- but as he dreams on Mistris Ford and the 'rule of her husbands Purse' so his intellect takes over (5/1, the last two and a half lines of F #2, plus F #3)

- as he voices the idea of the letter he has written both to her and to Mistris Page so limited emotions are released (just 1/3 in the four and a half lines of F #4), especially when he recalls how Mistris Page 'examind my parts' , a recollection triggered by the first of only two semicolons in the speech

- and the beginning of F #5, which extends the image to when she did 'course o're my exteriors' , starts out unembellished as if he is so involved that he doesn't wish to break the mood by letting too much out at once

- but this calm does not last for as Falstaffe dreams on the riches both may bring him an intellectual frenzy takes over (17/4 in the last six and a half lines), supported by another burst of nine surround phrases which finish the sentence

---

Modern Text

1/Falstaffe

1   My honest ᐱlads, I will tell you what I am about .

{hears **Pistol's whispered aside** "Two yards, and more"}

2   No quips now Pistol * ! †

3   (Indeed* I am in the [waist] two yards about ; but I am now about no waste : I am a-bout thrift) . †

4   Briefly* - I do* mean* to make love to Ford's wife . †

5   I spy* entertainment in her . †

6   She* discourses, she* carves, she gives the leer* of invitation . †

7   I can construe the action of her familiar style*, & the hardest voice of her behavior*, to be ᐱEnglish'd rightly, is, "I am Sir John Falstaff's *" .

8   Now, the report goes she has all the rule of her husband's ᐱpurse . †

9   [She] hath a [legion] of ᐱangels . †

10   I have writ me here a letter to her ; & here ano-ther to Page's wife, who even now gave me* good eyes too, examin'd my parts with most judicious iliads* ; some-times the beam* of her view, gilded* my foot* , some-times my portly belly .

11   O, she did so course o'er my exteriors with such a greedy intention, that the appetite of her eye did seem* to scorch me up like a burning-glass ! †

12   Here's another letter to her . †

13   She bears* the ᐱpurse too ; ᐱshe is a ᐱregion in Guiana, all gold, and bounty* . †

First Folio

1/ Falstaffe

1   My honest Lads, I will tell you what I am about .

{hears **Pistoll's whispered aside** "Two yards, and more"}

2   No quips now Pistoll : (Indeede I am in the [waste] two yards about : ₓ but I am now about no waste : I am a-bout thrift) briefely : ₓ I doe meane to make love to Fords wife : I spie entertainment in her : shee discourses : ₓshee carves : ₓ she gives the leere of invitation : I can construe the action of her familier stile, & the hardest voice of her behaviour (to be english'd rightly) is, I am Sir John Falstafs .

3   Now, the report goes ₓ she has all the rule of her husbands Purse : [he] hath a [legend] of Angels .

4   I have writ me here a letter to her : ₓ & here ano-ther to Pages wife, who even now gave mee good eyes too; ₓ examind my parts with most judicious illiads: ₓ sometimes the beame of her view, guilded my foote : ₓ sometimes my portly belly .

5   O⁺ she did so course o're my exteriors with such a greedy intention, that the appetite of her eye, ₓ did seeme to scorch me up like a burning-glasse : here's another letter to her : She beares the Purse too : ₓ She is a Region in Guiana : ₓ all gold, and bountie : I will be Cheaters to

them both, and they shall be Exchequers to mee : they shall be my East and West Indies, and I will trade to them both : Goe, beare thou this Letter to Mistris Page ; and thou this to Mistris Ford : we will thrive $_x$(Lads)$_x$ we will thrive .

- the final semicolon enhances the sending of the letters, for it marks the wooing of both women quite splendidly

  " : Goe, beare thou this Letter to Mistris Page ; and thou this to Mistris Ford : "

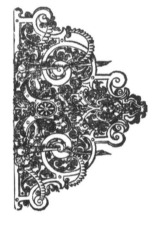

14   I will be Cheaters to them both, and they shall be ᵃexchequers to me* . †   They

15 shall be my East and West Indies, and I will trade to them both. †

16   Go*, bear* thou this Letter to Mistress* Page ; and thou this to Mistress* Ford . †   We will thrive, ᵃlads, we

17 will thrive .

2/ Mistris Page   What, have {I} scap'd Love-letters in the . . .   2.1.1 - 32

Background: As the first speech suggests, though Falstaffe has met Mistris Page only briefly he nevertheless has sent her a love-letter, in which she seems quite interested, at least until she finds out who it's from.

Style: solo

Where: unspecified, presumably a public place in the town of Windsor   **To Whom:** direct audience address

# of Lines: 25   **Probable Timing: 1.15 minutes**

Modern Text

2/ Mistris Page

1 What, have [I] scap'd ^love-letters in the
holi°day*-time ° of my beauty, and am I now a subject
for them? †

2   Let me see.

3 Ask* me no reason why I love you, for though Love use Reason for his precisian, he* admits him not for his ^counsellor* . †

3 You are not young*, no more am I;   go* to then, there's
sympathy*. *
          †

3   You are merry, so am I;   ha, ha! then there's
more sympathy*. †

3   You love sack*, and so do I; would you
desire better sympathy*. ?

4 Let it suffice thee, Mistress* Page - at the least if the Love
of ^soldier* can suffice - that I love thee. †

3   I will not say, pity*
me* - tis not a ^soldier*-like phrase - but I say, love me. ‡

3 By me,
        Thine own* true ^knight,
        By day or night,
        Or any kind* of light,
        With all his might
        For thee to fight.
                        John Falstaff* "

5 What a Herod of Jewry* is this!

6   O wicked, wicked world! †

7   One

8 that is well-nigh* worn* to pieces* with age to show
himself* a young* gallant!

First Folio

2/ Mistris Page

1 What, have [ ] scap'd Love-letters in the
holly-day-time of my beauty, and am I now a subject
for them? let me see? x

2 Aske me no reason why I love you, for though Love use Reason for his precisian, bee admits bim not for his Counsailour:
you are not yong, no more am I x, goe to then, there's simpathie :
you are merry, so am I x, ba, ba, +'ben there's more simpathie :
you love sacke, and so do I : x would you desire better
simpathie ?

3 Let it suffice thee x (Mistris Page)x at the least if the Love of
Souldier can suffice, that I love thee : I will not say+ pitty mee,
tis not a Souldier-like pbrase ; but I say, love me :

   By me, thine owne true Knight, by day or night: x
   Or any kinde of light, with all his might,x
   For thee to fight.

4   John Falstaffe .

5 What a Herod of Jurie is this? +

6 One that is well-nye worne to peeces with age
   To show himselfe a yong Gallant? +

                                    O wicked, wicked world :

• putting the contents of the letter aside, the few unembellished lines chart Mistris Pages' journey from anticipation to angry disbelief: first as to the so far anonymous love-letter

"and am I now a subject for them? let me see?"

and then the discovery it came from Falstaffe

" ? O wicked, wicked world : "

followed by the monosyllabic heightened

" : what should I say to him ?"

with the speech-ending resolution that drives the rest of the play

" : how shall I be reveng'd on him ? for reveng'd I will be ? as sure as his guts are made of puddings . "

the last three quotes further intensified by all being formed by surround phrases

• before the final disappointment, that the onrushed letter itself builds into something very important for her can be seen in the last six 'simpathie'-building phrases of F #2, all of which are surround phrases, as are the middle three 'not pity but love' phrases of F #3

• quite naturally, the 'Love-letters' opening of the speech starts off carefully (F #1, 1/1 with the ending unembellished;) equally understandably, the 'simpathie' part of the letter releases some passion (3/4 in the five lines of F #2); and the love portion, plus the appalling revelation who the letter is from releases the greatest passion of all (8/7 in the six lines of F #3-4)

• that the identity of the sender of the letter rather than its contents is deeply disturbing to Mistris Page can be seen in the following: Q's text is totally different and set as prose throughout: most modern texts set the shaded F text, but without the verse/prose balance, arguing that F's verse is both far too irregular and that the last two lines degenerate into prose anyway: perhaps, but with its peculiar verse structure [1], the F setting allows Mistris Page to maintain, but with exceeding difficulty, a formal quality to her passion and thus avoid an unnecessary fish-wife like screech

---

[1] F's verse lines reading as 15/11/12/11/12/14/13/14/11/12/15 syllables

What an unwaied

Behaviour hath this Flemish drunkard pickt (with
'The Devills name⁺) out of my conversation, that he dares
In this manner assay me? why, hee hath not beene thrice
In my Company : what should I say to him?

                I was then

7

8 Frugall of my mirth : ₓ(heaven forgive mee:), why⁺ Ile
Exhibit a Bill in the Parliament for the putting downe
of men :   how shall I be reveng'd on him? for reveng'd I
will be?⁺ as sure as his guts are made of puddings .

• in addition, the rapid switches in the onrushed post letter build shows her enormous struggles to regain self-control

• she starts the post discovery release intellectually (2/0 in the seven word F #5), and, following a brief unembellished moment, becomes very strongly emotional if only momentarily (1/4 the last two lines of F #6)

• her examination of her earlier behaviour towards Falstaffe becomes passionate (4/5, F #7 and the first line of F #8), but finally she gains intellectual control, first with the (possible) joke about a Bill for the 'putting downe of men' (3/1), and then the unembellished ice-calm resolve to be 'reveng'd'

What an unweigh'd∗ behavior∗
hath this Flemish drunkard pick'd (with the ᐃdevil's∗ name!)
out of my conversation, that he dares in this manner
assay me? †

10 Why, he∗ hath not been∗ thrice in my
ᐃcompany! †

11 What should I say to him?

12   I was then ᐃfrugal∗
of my mirth . †

13 Heaven forgive me∗! †

14   Why, I'll
ᐃexhibit a ᐃbill in the ᐃparliament for the putting down∗
of men . †

15 How shall I be reveng'd on him? for reveng'd I
will be! as sure as his guts are made of puddings .

3/ Mistris Page   {Did you ever heare the like? }   2.1.68-93

Background: Joined by her closest friend, Mistris Ford, Mistris Page discovers to her amazement, and presumably growing righteous anger, that Falstaffe has sent them exactly the same letters, despite the fact that both are married. One note: the opening sentence, marked {ψ}, was originally assigned to Mistris Ford.

Style: as part of a two-handed scene

Where: unspecified, presumably a public place in the town of Windsor   **To Whom:** Mistris Ford

# of Lines: 19   **Probable Timing: 1.00 minutes**

Modern Text	First Folio
3/ Mistris Page	**3/ Mistris Page**
1 hear* the like?	1 {ψ} {Did you ever
{ψ} {Did you ever	heare the like?}
2 Letter for letter ; but that the name of	2 Letter for letter ; but that the name of
Page and Ford differs!†	Page and Ford differs : to thy great comfort in this my-
3 To thy great comfort in this my-	stery of ill opinions, heere's the twyn-brother of thy Let-
stery of ill opinions, here's* the twin*-brother of thy ᐃlet-	ter : ₓ but let thine inherit first, for I protest mine never
ter ; but let thine inherit first, for I protest mine never	shall : I warrant he hath a thousand of these Letters, writ
shall . †	with blancke-space for different names (sure+ more+) : ₓand
4 I warrant he hath a thousand of these ᐃletters, writ	these are of the second edition : hee will print them+ out
with blank* ° space for different names (sure, more!) ; and	of doubt : ₓ for he cares not what hee puts into the presse,
these are of the second edition . †	when he would put us two : I had rather be a Giantesse,
5 He* will print them, out	and lye under Mount Pelion : Well ; ₓ I will find you twen-
of doubt; for he cares not what he* puts into the press* ,	tie lascivious Turtles ere one chaste man . {ψ}
when he would put us two . †	3 What doth
6 I had rather be a ᐃgiantess* ,	he thinke of us? {ψ}
and lie* under Mount Pelion . †	4 It makes me almost rea-
7 Well - I will find you twen-	die to wrangle with mine owne honesty : Ile entertaine
ty* lascivious ᐃturtles ere one chaste man . {ψ}	my selfe like one that I am not acquainted withall : ₓ for
8 What doth	sure unlesse hee know some straine in mee, that I know
he think* of us? {ψ}	not my selfe, hee would never have boorded me in this
9 It makes me almost rea-	furie .
dy* to wrangle with mine own* honesty . †	5 Boording, call {I} it?
10 I'll entertain*	6 Ile bee sure to keepe
myself* like one that I am not acquainted withall* ; for	him above decke .
sure unless* he* know some strain* in me* that I know	7 {ψ} If hee come under my hatches,
not myself*, he* would never have boarded* me in this	Ile never to Sea againe .
fury* .	
11 "Boarding*," call {I} it?	
12 I'll be* sure to keep*	
him above deck* .	
13 {ψ} If he* come under my hatches,	
I'll never to ᐃsea again* .	

First Folio

The speech starts as confusingly as the previous one ended, with its onrushed start finally settling down into a slightly more composed finish.

- she opens with a (startled?) very short sentence (0/1, F #1), while the onrushed F #2 shows no consistency whatsoever, as both the switches in style and the surround phrases clearly show

- F #2's emotionally (semicolon) created surround phrases underscore Mistris Page's rightful indignation

  " Letter for letter; but that the name of Page and Ford differs :"

  " : Well ; I will find you twenty lascivious Turtles ere one chaste man . "

  while the more controlled (colon) surround phrases of F #2 add extra weight to her self-deprecating ridicule of Falstaffe

  " : and these are of the second edition : hee will print them out of doubt : for he cares not what hee puts into the presse, when he would put us two : I had rather be a Giantesse, and lye under Mount Pelion :"

- in terms of style, while she starts out F #2 intellectually (2/0, the first surround-phrases line), she then becomes passionate in both denying any interest in taking the invitation up, and in beginning to comprehend his 'thousand of these Letters' method of operation (2/3, the next four and a half lines); this in turn becomes emotional as she elaborates even more on 'the second edition' nature of his wooing (0/3 the next two and a half lines), but she finishes more intellectually than emotionally with a two line absolute refusal ('I had rather . . . lye under Mount Pelion') and sentence ending surround phrase maxim (4/2)

- but this momentary intellectual control does not last, for the rest of the speech becomes almost totally emotional (1/17 in the remaining nine lines comprising F #3-7)

- whether this final emotion is all high powered indignation or eventually turns into something more light hearted is up to each actress to decide, though the shortness of the last three sentences (F #5-7) are certainly different in content from the onrushed F #4, the speech ending with a much earthier sense of humour directed towards herself

4/ Pistoll Sir John affects thy wife .

5/ Nym And this is true : I like not the humor of lying :

between 2.1.111 - 125

2.1.127 - 135

Background: Having refused to deliver the love-letters to Mistresses Page and Ford (not out of morality but from indignation that such a menial task would be beneath them) Pistoll and Nym have been fired by Falstaffe . In revenge, each informs the respective husbands of Falstaffe's amorous (or should that be financial?) intentions.

Style: each as a two-handed scene

Where: unspecified, presumably a public place in the town of Windsor **To Whom:** Pistoll is talking to Master Ford, who is only too ready to believe him: Nym to Master Page, who most definitely is not

speech #4, # of Lines: 12 **Probable Timing: 0.40 minutes**

speech #5, # of Lines: 8 **Probable Timing: 0.30 minutes**

Modern Text

4/ Pistoll

1 Sir John affects thy wife .

2 He woos* both high and low, both rich & poor,
Both young* and old, one with another , Ford . †

3 He loves the ᐃgalliᵒmaufry* , Ford . †

4 Perpend.

5 {He loves thy wife,}

With liver, burning hot . †

6 Prevent; or go* thou
Like Sir Acteon he, with Ring-wood at thy heels* -
O, odious is the name !

7 The horn* I say . †

8 Farewell . †

9 Take heed, have open eye, for thieves* do* foot by night .

10 Take heed, ere summer* comes or ᐃcuckoo-birds do sing .

11 Away, ᐃSir Corporal* Nym*. †

12 Believe* it, Page, he speaks* sense .

First Folio

4/ Pistoll

1 Sir John affects thy wife .

2 He wooes both high and low, both rich & poor,
both yong and old, one with another ₓ(Ford)ₓ, he loves the
Gally-mawfry ₓ (Ford)ₓ perpend.

3 {He loves thy wife, }

4 With liver, burning hot : prevent : ₓ
Or goe thou like Sir Acteon he, with
Ring-wood at thy heeles : ₓ O, odious is the name . ⁺

5 The horne I say : Farewell:
Take heed, have open eye, for theeves doe foot by night .

6 Take heed, ere sommer comesₓ or Cuckoo-birds do sing .

Away⁺ sir Corporall Nim: →
Beleeve it ₓ (Page)ₓ he speakes sence .

F sets the shaded text as prose, with Pistoll not using verse until after F #2 – which might well suggest, realising Ford has taken the bait, he can move into an **even more powerful speaking mode: most modern texts remove the possibility of this transition by setting the whole speech as verse.**

• not surprisingly, the speech is passionate throughout (11/12 overall) – the only factual section being the opening short sentence warning (1/0, F #1), the only emotional section being F #4's warning to Ford about possibly becoming a cuckold (1/3)

• the short sentences (F #1 and #5) lay in the key points which drive Ford to distraction for the rest of the play

• the surround phrases making up the whole of F #3, #4, and #6 add extra dimension as to how Falstaffe loves (F #3), the warning of becoming a cuckold (F #4), and the final assertion to Page that he should believe what Pistoll is telling him

• the two shorter lines of F #6 (6-7/7 syllables) allow for a splendid final flourish to the exit

Modern Text

5 / Nym

1   And this is true ;   I like not the humor of lying . †

2   He* hath wronged me* in some humors. †

3   I should have borne the humor'd* ᴬletter to her; but I have a sword, and it shall bite upon my necessity* . ᵗ †

4   ᴬHe loves your wife : ᴬthere's the short and the long . †

5   My name is Corporal* Nym*; I speak* , and I avouch ; 'tis true ; my name is Nym*, and Falstaff* loves your wife . †

6   Adieu . †

7   I love not the hu-mor* of bread and cheese [and there's the humor of it] . †

8   Adieu.

First Folio

5 / Nym

1   And this is true : ₓ   I like not the humor of lying : hee hath wronged mee in some humors : I should have borne the humour'd Letter to her : ₓ   but I have a sword : ₓ and it shall bite upon my necessitie : he loves your wife;⁺ There's the short and the long : My name is Corporall Nim :ₓ I speake, and I avouch ; 'tis true :ₓ my name is Nim :ₓ and Falstaffe loves your wife : adieu, I love not the hu-mour of bread and cheese [ ] : adieu.

Unlike his very rational modern counterpart who passes his information on via **eight grammatically correct sentences, the fact that Nym is more than somewhat disturbed can be seen both in F's text, set as one onrushed sentence, and being completely composed of fifteen surround phrases.**

• in addition to the probability of simple revenge, most of the unembellished lines point to a possible deeper-seated reason for Nym's betrayal of Falstaffe, as with the opening

" . And this is true : I like not the humor of lying : "

followed by the simple statement of how he intends to live

" . ; but I have a sword : and it shall bite upon my necessitie:"

with the emotional (semicoloned lead into) repetition of

" ; 'tis true : "

all heightened by being set as surround phrases

• not surprisingly the speech is passionate throughout (7/7)

6/ Mistris Quickly   Why, Sir ; {mistresse Ford's} a good-creature ; Lord, Lord,   between 2.2.55 -104

Background: As planned, the two 'wronged' wives have begun their revenge-plot against Falstaffe, having enlisted Dr. Caius' housekeeper, Mistris Quickly (described by Parson Evans as his 'Nurse; or his dry-Nurse; or his Cooke; or his Laundry; his Washer, and his Ringer'), to entice Falstaffe to a secret rendez-vous.

Style: as part of a three-handed scene   **To Whom:** Falstaffe, in front of Pistoll

Where: Falstaffe's rooms   **# of Lines: 38**   **Probable Timing: 1.55 minutes**

Modern Text

6/ Mistris Quickly

1 Why, Sir ; { △Mistress* Ford's} a good-△creature . †

2   your Worship's a wanton ! †

                      Well - heaven forgive you,

3 and all of us, I pray ———— .

════════════════════════════════

4 Marry, this is the short, and the long of it : you have brought her into such a △canaries, as 'tis wonderful* . †

5   The best △courtier of them all (when the △court lay at Windsor) could never have brought her to such a △canary*; yet there has been* △knights, and △lords, and △gentlemen, with their △coaches; I warrant you, △coach after △coach, letter after letter, gift after gift; smelling so sweetly, all △musk*, and so [rustling] I warrant you, in silke and gold*, and in such alligant terms*, and in such wine and sugar of the best, and the fairest, that would have won* any woman's heart;   and I warrant you, they could never get an eye-wink* of her . †

            I had myself* twenty* △angels given me this morning, but I defy* all △angels (in any such sort, as they say) but in the way of honesty*;   and I warrant you, they could never get her so much as sip* on a cup with the proudest* of them all, and yet there has been* △earls*: nay (which is more) △pensioners*, but I warrant you all is one with her.

════════════════════════════════

6

7 Marry, she hath receiv'd your △letter - for the which she thanks* you a thousand times - and she gives you to notify*, that her husband will be absence from his house between* ten and eleven.

First Folio

6/ Mistris Quickly

1 Why, Sir; {mistresse Ford's} a good-creature ; Lord, Lord, your Worship's a wanton : well : _x_ heaven forgive you, and all of us, I pray ———— .

2 Marry+ this is the short, and the long of it : you have brought her into such a Canaries, as 'tis wonderfull : the best Courtier of them all (when the Court lay at Windsor) could never have brought her to such a Canarie : _x_ yet there has beene Knights, and Lords, and Gentlemen, with their Coaches;   I warrant you+ Coach after Coach, letter after letter, gift after gift, + smelling so sweetly ; _x_ all Muske, and so [rushling], I warrant you, in silke and golde, and in such alligant termes, and in such wine and suger of the best, and the fairest, that would have wonne any womans heart : _x_ and I warrant you, they could never get an eye-winke of her : I had my selfe twentie Angels given me this morning, but I defie all Angels (in any such sort, as they say) but in the way of honesty : _x_ and I warrant you, they could never get her so much as sippe on a cup with the prowdest of them all, and yet there has beene Earles : nay,_xx_ (which is more) Pentioners; but I warrant you all is one with her.

3 Marry, she hath receiv'd your Letter : _x_ for the which she thankes you a thousand times; _x_ and she gives you to notifie,_x_ that her husband will be absence from his house, _x_ betweene ten and eleven.

Commentary (left column footnotes)

Despite the apparently deliberate factual opening (16/3 in the first nine and a half lines), the clues of the twenty-two surround phrases, the seven semicolons, and the fifteen rational stepping-stone sentences of the modern texts) all point to the emotion and excitement bubbling underneath.

• throughout the play it's the rare occasion when Mistris Quickly can keep to the point, and after the opening nine and a half lines of factual information about 'mistresse Ford' and the fact that Falstaffe has 'brought her into such Canaries', and the (romantic but not truthful) idea that there have been aristocrats in chase of her, 'Coach after Coach', ...

• . . . she suddenly becomes emotional as she elaborates on the (fictional) idea of the aristocrats' scented letters, silk gifts, 'wine and suger' (1/8 the next five lines), which then becomes passion as she claims (imagines?) herself to have been given gifts to act as an aristocratic go-between

• as she gets back to the matter at hand, Falstaffe's letter to Mistris Ford and her response notifying him that her husband will be away from home (F #3 and the first two and a half lines of F #4), so emotion gives way to passion (3/4), though the sidebar about Mistris Ford's 'fampold life' with her 'jealousie-man' husband becomes emotional again (0/2)

{ctd. over}

4   I, forsooth:$_x$ and then you may come and see the picture,$_x$ (she sayes)$_x$ that you wot of: Master Ford her husband will be from home: alas, the sweet woman leades an ill life with him: hee's a very jealousie-man; she leads a very frampold life with him,$_x$ (good hart.)$_x$

5   I have another messenger to your worship: Mistresse Page hath her heartie commendations to you to:$_x$ and let mee tell you in your eare, shee's as fartuous a civill modest wife, and one (I tell you) that will not misse you morning nor evening prayer, as any is in Windsor, who ere bee the other:$_x$ and shee bade me tell your worship, that her husband is seldome from home, but she hopes there will come a time.

6   I never knew a woman to doate upon a man; surely I thinke you have charmes, la:$_x$ yes in truth.

• and while the information about Mistresse Page also being interested starts out factually (2/0, the first two lines of F #5), so the whole speech veers off into emotionalism for the somewhat away from the point elaboration of Mistresse Page's good points (1/11 the remainder of the speech)

• the fact that all of F #1 (the linking of the 'good' Mistris Ford and the 'wanton' Sir John), the start of F #3 (the first real indication that his letter has been received), and all of F #4 (the timing of his meeting Mistris Ford, poor woman), and F #6 (Mistresse Page's doting on him) are totally created by surround phrases suggests that Mistris Quickly is pushing the information therein very hard

---

8   Ay*, forsooth; and then you may come and see the picture, she says*, that you wot of.†

9   Master Ford her husband will be from home.†

10   Alas, the sweet woman leads* an ill life with him.†

11   He's* a very jealousy.° man.† She leads

12   a very frampold life with him,*.

13   I have another messenger to your worship.†

14   Mistress* Page hath her hearty* commendations to you too*; and let me* tell you in your ear*, she's* as fartuous a civill modest* wife, and one (I tell you) that will not miss* you morning nor evening prayer, as any is in Windsor, whoe'er* be* the other; and she* bade me tell your worship, that her husband is seldom* from home, but she hopes there will come a time.

15   I never knew a woman to dote* upon a man; surely I think* you have charms*, la; yes in truth.

#'s 7 - 8: FORD'S INTERFERENCE

7/ Falstaffe   **Want no Mistresse Ford (Master Broome) . . .**   between 2.2.260 - 286

Background: Believing Pistoll (speech #4 above) that Falstaffe will attempt to woo his wife, Ford has come to Falstaffe's rooms (disguised as one Master Brooke [2]) to encourage him in the act, presumably to expose him publicly for what he is, and perhaps his wife too. Since Falstaffe is now being offered money to achieve what he already intends to do, and, as he believes, already has an open invitation from Mistris Ford to woo her, the following is joyously self-explanatory.

Style: as part of a two-handed scene

Where: Falstaffe's rooms   **To Whom:** Ford, disguised as Master Brooke

# of Lines: 18   **Probable Timing: 0.55 minutes**

Modern Text

1 Want no Mistress* Ford, Master [Brook], you shall want none.†

2 I shall be with her (I may tell you) by her own* appointment; even as you came in to me, her assi-stant or go*-between* parted from me.†   I say I shall be
with her between* ten and eleven; for at that time the jealous°rascally° knave her husband will be forth.†

4 ᴪ} (Poor* ᴬcuckoldly
knave) ᴪ}.†

5   They say

6 Yet I wrong him to call him poor*.†

the jealous wittolly° knave hath masses of money, for the which his wife seems* to me well-favor'd*.†
                    I will use
her as the key of the ᴬcuckoldly °rogue's ᴬcoffer, ᴪ}

ᴪ} mechanical* ° salt-butter rogue !†
8   I will*
stare him out of his wits; I will awe°him with my cud-gel*; it shall hang like a ᴬmeteor o'er the ᴬcuckold's horns.†

9 Master [Brook], thou shalt know I will predominate o-ver the peasant*, and thou shalt lie* with his wife.

1

What with three sentences (instead of most modern texts' twelve), the first of two onrushed modern sentences equaling ten modern sentences, and at least thirteen surround phrases, it seems Falstaffe's delusional enthusiasm knows no bounds.

• there are hardly any unembellished phrases, so to find within the first three lines the quiet of 'even as you came in to me, her assistant . . parted from me' could suggest that Falstaffe can hardly believe his luck, especially when coupled with the intervening phrase describing Mistris Ford's assistant as doubly long-spelled 'goe-betweene'

• the line and a half brag starting the speech is intellectual (4/2) and, even though the capitals involved all refer to names, the speech needn't have started this way so the idea of an opening flourish still stands

• the next four and a half lines boasting of being with her 'by her owne appointment' 'betweene ten and eleven' when 'her husband will be forth' is out and out emotional (0/4)

• starting with 'poore Cuckoldly knave', dwelling on Ford's 'masses of money' and using Mistris Ford as 'the key' to the 'Coffer', right through to the triumphant belief 'I will predominate over the pezant' releases

---

First Folio

Want no Mistresse Ford,ₓ(Master [Broome]),ₓ you shall want none : I shall be with her (I may tell you) by her owne appointment, † even as you came in to me, her assi-stant,ₓ or goe-betweene,ₓ parted from me : I say I shall be with her betweene ten and eleven : ₓ for at that time the jealious-rascally-knave her husband will be forth:

ᴪ} (poore Cuckoldly
knave) ᴪ}: yet I wrong him to call him poore : They say the jealous wittolly-knave hath masses of money, for the which his wife seemes to me well-favour'd: I will use her as the key of the Cuckoldly-rogues Coffer, ᴪ}

ᴪ} mechanicall-salt-butter rogue; I wil stare him out of his wits: I will awe-him with my cud-gell : ₓ it shall hang like a Meteor ore the Cuckolds horns : Master Broome, thou shalt know, † I will predominate o-ver the pezant, and thou shalt lye with his wife.

{ctd. over}

---

2 the F1 altering of Ford's disguised persona from Q1's 'Brooke' to 'Broome' requires some explanation, for there had been a huge fall-out from the first printing of the *First Part Of King Henry The Fourth*, which could be described as a hang-over from the Cobham-Oldcastle-Falstaffe affair. In that play, the character now known as Falstaffe was originally named Oldcastle, which quickly got Shakespeare into a lot of political trouble. Indeed, in the Epilogue to *The Second Part of Henry the Fourth* Shakespeare apologises. Referring to a future play - presumably *The Life of Henry the Fift*, in which, paradoxically the Oldcastle/Falstaffe figure dies offstage without ever making an appearance - Shakespeare writes

"Falstaffe shall dye of a sweat, unlesse he already be kill'd with your hard Opinions:/For Old-Castle dyed a Martyr, and this is not the man."

The problem was, that though historically there was an Oldcastle at the time of Henry IV (nowhere near the Vice figure Shakespeare portrays), his powerful descendants included members of the Cobham (Brooke) family, the 7th Lord of whom had held the post of Lord Chamberlain to Queen Elizabeth. The 8th Lord protested, and the name 'Oldcastle' was hastily changed to one reminiscent of the cowardly figure already seen in The first Part of Henry the Sixt, Sir John Falstaffe. So expeditious was the change that the frontispiece of Q1 1598, printed so hard on the heels of the first printing, known as Q0, contains the proclamation 'with the humorous conceits of Sir John Falstaffe'.

Trouble didn't end with *The First Part of King Henry the Fourth*; the affair seems to have spilled over into the Q1 version of *The Merry Wives of Windsor* too. Whether a deliberate dig or no, Shakespeare allows the character Master Ford to adopt for his disguise (as the would-be wooer of his own wife) the name of 'Brooke,' which was in fact the Cobham family name. Prudently, F1 alters 'Brooke' to 'Broome', thus avoiding further political fall-out.

Come
to me soone at night: Ford's a knave, and I will aggra-vate his stile:_x thou _x(Master [Broome])_x shalt know him for knave, and Cuckold.

Come to me soone at night.

2

Falstaffe's passions to the full (8/10 in the remaining eight and a half lines of F #1)

• the totally surround phrase created F #2, promising to tell all that evening, becomes intellectual (4/2), again returning to the style of the boast opening the speech

3

• and the final monosyllabic short sentence, repeating the promise of telling all that evening, becomes emotional (0/1). Falstaffe envisioning a-plenty perhaps

---

First Folio

8/ Ford

1

What a damn'd Epicurian-Rascall is this? my heart is ready to cracke with impatience : who saies this is improvident jealousie? my wife hath sent to him, the howre is fixt, the match is made : would any man have thought this? see the hell of having a false woman : my bed shall be abus'd, my Coffers ransack'd, my reputati-on gnawne at, and I shall not onely receive this villanous wrong, but stand under the adoption of abhominable termes, and by him that does mee this wrong : Termes, + names : + Amaimon sounds well :_x Lucifer, well :_x Barbason, well :_x yet they are Divels additions, the names of fiends :_x But Cuckold, + Wittoll, + Cuckold?+ the Divell himselfe hath not such a name.

10

to me soon* at night . †

11

Ford's a knave, and I will aggra-vate his style*; thou, Master [Brooke], shalt know him for knave, and ^cuckold.

12

Come to me soon* at night .

8/ Ford   **What a damn'd Epicurian-Rascall is this?**   2.2.287 - 314

Background: The following is Ford's immediate shocked response to Falstaffe's genuinely believed brag of having an imminent appointment with Mistris Ford, speech #7 above. Unaware of his wife's plot with Mistris Page to lure Falstaffe to the house so as to punish him, Ford can only believe his wife is at the very least considering an affair.

Style: solo

Where: Falstaffe's rooms   **To Whom:** self, and direct audience address

# of Lines: 25   **Probable Timing:** 1.15 minutes

Modern Text

Given the circumstances, F's opening onrush (compared to the nine sentences most modern texts take to set the same material) is hardly surprising. What is surprising are the sudden patches of intellectual bleakness when Ford envisages what the outcome may be unless he can prevent the apparent love-tryst.

• after the first-phrase passionate denunciation of Falstaffe as a 'damn'd Epicurian-Rascall' (2/1), it seems that for at least the next four lines establishing why his is not 'improvident jealousie', Ford can maintain some form of self-control (0/2) - though the speech to date being composed of six surround phrases shows just how difficult this is

• but once he begins to envisage what will result, 'bed', 'Coffers', 'reputation' all ruined and himself called 'abhominable termes', so the emotions grow (1/5 in the next four lines), and the 'termes', even worse than those ascribed to various devils, turn him to a highly intellectual set of releases (10/4, the remaining three and a half lines of F #1), even more marked by being totally made up of seven surround phrases

• though F #2's opening two surround phrase dismissal of Page as an 'Asse' because 'hee will trust his wife' (emphasised by the emotional semicolon) is highly passionate (3/4 in less than two lines), Ford quickly switches to an intellectual assessment of why he will not trust 'my wife with her selfe'

8/ Ford

1

What a damn'd ○ Epicurian ^rascall* is this! †

2

My †

heart is ready to crack* with impatience . †

3

Who says* this

is improvident jealousy* ? †

4

My wife hath sent to him, the

hour* is fix'd, the match is made . †

5

Would any man have

thought this? †

6

See the hell of having a false woman ! †

7

My

bed shall be abus'd, my ^coffers ransack'd, my reputati-on gnawn* at, and I shall not only* receive this villainous* wrong, but stand under the adoption of abhominable* termes*, and by him that does me* this wrong . †

Terms*!

names . ! †

Amaimon sounds well; Lucifer, well; Barbason, well; yet they are ^devils* additions, the names of fiends; ^but Cuckold! Wittol*! - Cuckold! the ^devil* himself hath not such a name.

2 Page is an Asse, a secure Asse; hee will trust his wife, hee will not be jealous : I will rather trust a Fleming with my butter, Parson Hugh the Welsh-man with my Cheese, an Irish-man with my Aqua-vitae-bottle, or a Theefe to walke my ambling gelding, [then] my wife with her selfe.

3 Then she plots, then shee ruminates, then shee devises:x and what they thinke in their hearts they may effect;x they will breake their hearts but they will effect.

4 [Heaven] bee prais'd for my jealousie : eleven o'clocke the howre, I will prevent this, detect my wife, bee reveng'd on Falstaffe, and laugh at Page.

5 I will about it,+ better three houres too soone,x [then] a my-nute too late : fie, fie, fie:+ Cuckold, Cuckold, Cuckold.+

• the explanation as to why, the three surround phrase F #3, becomes purely emotional once more (0/4), emphasised by the emotional semicolon separating ' : and what they thinke in their hearts they may effect ; they will breake their hearts but they will effect .'

• the resolution, the monosyllabic, unembellished 'I will prevent this, detect my wife' is surrounded by a sea of emotion (2/7, F #4 and the opening line and a half of F #5, four lines in all)

• but then his mind switches to what people will say, and the emotion disappears into the short spelled repartition of 'fie, fie, fie', and the intellectually burning exit cry of 'Cuckold, Cuckold, Cuckold'

10 Page is an △ass*, a secure △ass*; he* will trust his wife, he* will not be jealous . †

11 I will rather trust a Fleming with my butter, Parson Hugh the Welsh man with my △cheese, an Irish·man with my △aqua-vitae ° bottle, or a △thief* to walk* my ambling gelding; [than] my wife with herself*.

12 Then she plots, then she* ruminates, then she* devises; and what they think* in their hearts they may effect, they will break* their hearts but they will effect.

13 [God] be* prais'd for my jealousy*,! † Eleven o'clock* the hour*.†

14 I will prevent this, detect my wife, be* reveng'd on Falstaff*, and laugh at Page. †

15 I will about it ; better three hours* too soon* [than] a mi-nute* too late.†

16 Fie, fie, fie ! cuckold, cuckold, cuckold !

#'s 9 - 12: THE WOOING OF MISTRIS FORD

9/ Falstaffe   **Have I caught thee, my heavenly Jewell?**   between 3.3.43 -74

Background: Not knowing of the Ladies' secret agenda to entice him into a laundry basket and dump him into the river Thames, and thus believing he is there to court an interested Mistris Ford, Falstaffe begins his wooing blandishments, couched in flattering hyperbole (with modern texts' regarding the opening line as one taken from a contemporary song). One note: the speech has been created by removing most of Mistris Ford's responses.

Style: as part of a two-handed scene
Where: Fords' home   **To Whom:** Mistris Ford   **# of Lines:** 18   **Probable Timing:** 0.55 minutes

Modern Text

9/ Falstaffe

1   "Have I caught thee, my heavenly △jewell*?"

2   Why,†
     This is the
  now let me die, for I have liv'd long enough.†

3   period of my ambition.†

4   O this blessed*hour*!

5   Mistress* Ford, I cannot cog, I cannot prate, [Mistress] Ford.†

6   Now shall I sin in my wish: I would thy △husband were dead.†

7   I'll speak* it before the best △lord, I would make thee my △lady.

8   I see how thine eye would emulate the △diamond.†

9   Thou
hast the right arch'd° beauty of the brow that becomes the △ship-tyre*, the △tire*-valiant, or any △tire of Venetian admittance.

10   Thou wouldst make
an absolute △courtier, and the firm* fixture of thy foot* would give an excellent motion to thy [gait] in a semi-circled △farthingale.

11   Come, I
cannot cog and say thou art this and that, like a ° many* of these lisping°hawthorn*° buds, that come like women in men's apparel*, and smell like Bucklers°bury in sim-ple time - I cannot, but I love thee, none but thee; and thou deserv'st it.

First Folio

9/ Falstaffe

1   Have I caught thee, my heavenly Jewell?

2   Why+
  now let me die, for I have liv'd long enough: This is the period of my ambition: O this blessed houre.+

3   Mistris Ford, I cannot cog, I cannot prate (x[Mist.] Ford)x now shall I sin in my wish; + I would thy Husband were dead, Ile speake it before the best Lord, I would make thee my Lady.

4   I see how thine eye would emulate the Diamond: Thou hast the right arched-beauty of the brow,x that becomes the Ship-tyre, the Tyre-valiant, or any Tire of Venetian admittance.

5   Thou wouldst make
an absolute Courtier; and the firme fixture of thy foote,x would give an excellent motion to thy[gate],x in a semi-circled Farthingale.

6   Come, I
cannot cog,x and say thou art this and that, like a-manie of these lisping-hauthorne buds, that come like women in mens apparrell, and smell like Bucklers-berry in sim-ple time : x I cannot, but I love thee, none but thee; and thou deserv'st it.

Given Falstaffe's earlier enthusiasm (speeches #1 and #7 above) this speech is surprisingly restrained - whether because he is a skilful wooer allowing in the early stages his images to do his work, or whether he is so out of practice he doesn't quite know how to go about it is up to each actor to decide.

• here the few surround phrases (somewhat surprising both for character and play) underscore his wooing tactics, as in all of F #2 ('now let me die'); the opening of F #4 (likening her eye as a 'Diamond'); and the end of F #6 - see the final • below

• there is a splendid quiet opening to the wooing, with only one released word breaking into the unembellished short F #1 and start of F #2, though it may be that Falstaffe considers that one word, the doubly emphasised 'Jewell' coupled with the descriptive 'heavenly' might be more than enough to start the softening up process

• and then, as he moves into high-attack onrushed mode (F's remaining four and a bit sentences, reset as nine in most modern texts), surprisingly the wooing becomes much more intellectual than emotional - even in wishing 'thy Husband were dead' and when praising her brow 'that would do grace to any form of 'Tyre', i.e. head-dress (14/4, the ending of F #2 and all of F #3-4, eight lines in all)

• but as the wooing becomes more overall praising (she would make 'an absolute Courtier') and intimately physical-specific ('thy foote'), so Falstaffe becomes at one and the same time more controlled yet passionate, which is continued into the protestation that he 'cannot cog' (F #5) and the opening three and a half lines of F #6, just 3/4 in six and half lines)

• while the final two surround phrases unembellished declaration of love seems to be a wonderfully tricky piece of magnificent understatement, though Falstaffe does seem to lose his way at the last moment, for the excellent first phrases ': . . but I love thee, none but thee :' is more than somewhat undercut by the final self-aggrandizing '; and thou deserv'st it .'

10/ Falstaffe   Have I liv'd to be carried in a Basket like a barrow of butchers Offal   3.5.4 -18

Background: Falstaffe has not succeeded in seducing Mistris Ford, but she and Mistris Page do succeed in getting him to climb voluntarily into a laundry basket full of stinking clothes and then having their men stagger with it to the river and empty him into it – though their plan is almost scuppered by the unexpected arrival of Master Ford and friends before the basket leaves the home. Thus Falstaffe doesn't realise he's been punished by the women for daring to woo them, but rather believes they have in fact saved him from the wrath of a vengeful husband. The following deals with the river-dumping incident.

Style: solo

Where: Falstaffe's rooms   **To Whom:** direct audience address   **# of Lines:** 13   **Probable Timing:** 0.45 minutes

Modern Text	First Folio

10/ Falstaffe

10/ Falstaffe

1   Have I liv'd to be carried in a ᐃbasket like a barrow of butcher's ᐃoffal*! and to be thrown* in the Thames?

Well*.

2   [and] I be serv'd such another trick*, I'll have my brains* ta'en out and butter'd, and give them to a dog* for a ᐃnew-year's gift.

3   The rogues slighted me into the river with as little remorse, as they would have drown'd* a blind* bitch's* ᐃpuppies, fifteen* i'th litter; and you may know by my size, that I have a kind* of alacrity in sinking; [and] the bottom* were as deep* as hell, I should* down.

4   I had been* drown'd, but that the shore was shelvy and shallow - a death that I abhor*; for the water swells* a man; and what a thing should I have been*, when I had been* swell'd*!

5   I should have been* [a] ᐃmountain* of ᐃmummy*.

10/ Falstaffe

1   Have I liv'd to be carried in a Basket like a barrow of butchers Offall?+ and to be throwne in the Thames?

Wel,

2   [if] I be serv'd such another tricke, Ile have my braines 'tane out and butter'd, and give them to a dogge for a New-yeares gift.

3   The rogues slighted me into the river with as little remorse, as they would have drown'de a blinde bitches Puppies, fifteene i'th litter: x and you may know by my size, that I have a kinde of alacrity in sinking: x [if] the bottome were as deepe as hell, I shold down.

4   I had beene drown'd, but that the shore was shelvy and shallow: x a death that I abhorre: x for the water swelles a man; and what a thing should I have beene, when I had beene swel'd? +

5   I should have beene [ ] Mountaine of Mummie.

First Folio

Unusually both Folio and modern structures match, and, without F's usual onrush, Falstaffe seems to be in a much more contained mood, though whether he is relaxed as he talks to the audience as friends, or amazed at what has just occurred (or simply suffering from a chill) is up to each actor to decide.

• he opens quite passionately (3/2, the two lines of F #1) as he summarizes in surround phrases the double indignity of 'Have I liv'd to be carried in a Basket like a barrow of butchers Offall? and to be throwne in the Thames ?'

• and quite naturally the vow never to 'be serv'd such another tricke' becomes emotional (1/4, F #2)

• equally naturally remembering how he was 'slighted into the river', Falstaffe becomes very quiet, the recollection tinged with only a moment of passion (1/1, in the first three lines of F #3)

• and then the self-deprecating elaboration of how he has 'a kinde of alacrity in sinking' and he could drown even if 'the shore was shelvy and shallow', and what a sight he would be if he 'had beene swel'd', becomes emotional (0/7 in the remainder F #3 and F #4, six lines in all) - possibly Falstaffe's innate sense of story-teller's delight in direct audience address seen in Henry Four Parts One and Two has come to the fore once more, the whole underscored by being composed of six surround phrases

• and the short passionate F #5 (2/2) provides a wonderful flourish to the story

11/ Falstaffe   Nay, you shall heare (Master Broome) what I   from between 4.5.88 - 112

Background: Not realising Brooke and Ford are one and the same, Falstaffe describes in great detail how he managed to escape when Ford and his friends made their search for him. One note: to allow for a full explanation of the indignities Falstaffe suffered, mt. #2-#3 (and the equivalent ending of F #1) have been inserted from slightly earlier in the scene.

Style: as part of a two-handed scene
Where: Falstaffe's rooms   **To Whom:** Ford, disguised as Brooke
# of Lines: 33   **Probable Timing: 1.40 minutes**

Modern Text

11/ Falstaffe

1 Nay, you shall hear*, Master [Brook], what I have suffer'd* to bring this woman to evil* for your good .†

2 {One [Mistress] Page, gives intelligence of Fords approach*; and in her invention, and Fords wives distraction, they convey'd me into a buck*-basket} .†

3 {Ramm'd* me* in with foul* ᐃshirts and ᐃsmocks* , ᐃsocks, foul* ᐃstockings, greasy* ᐃnapkins, that, Master [Brook], there was the rankest compound of villainous* smell, that ever offended no-stril* .}

4 Being thus cramm'd* in the ᐃbasket, a couple of Ford's knaves, his ᐃhinds*, were call'd* forth by their ᐃmistress* to carry me* in the name of foul* ᐃclothes* to Datchet ° lane .†

5 They took* me on their shoulders; met the jealous knave their ᐃmaster in the door*, who ask'd them once or twice what they had in their ᐃbasket.

6 I quak'd for fear*, least the ᐃlunatic* ᐃknave would have search'd it ; but ᐃfate (ordaining he should be a ᶜcuckold) held his hand.†

7 Well, on went he*, for a search, and away went I for foul* ᐃclothes* .†

8 But
mark* the sequel*, Master [Brook] .†

9 I suffered the pangs of three several* deaths: ᐃfirst, an intolerable* fright, to be detected [by] a jealous* rotten ᐃbell-wether*; ◊ and ᐃnext, to be compass'd like a good ᐃbilbo in the circumference of a ᐃpeck*, hilt to point, heel* to head; ◊ and then to be stopp'd*, in like a strong distillation with stinking ᐃclothes* that fretted in their own* grease .†

Though most actors seem to regard either being crammed into a 'bucke-basket' or being 'throwne into the Thames' as the worst of three things Falstaffe claims he has 'sufferd' on Ford's behalf, F's orthography suggests that this may not in fact be so.

• the somewhat onrushed F #1 releases Falstaffe's passions as he gets straight down to how he first 'sufferd' in being hidden in the 'bucke-basket', (13/8 in just eight lines), much of the horror stemming from the memory of the 'foule Shirts and Smockes, Socks, foule Stockings, greasie Napkins', the focal point to be found in the consecutive surround phrases

" ; one Mist. Page gives intelligence of Fords approch : and in her invention, and Fords wives distraction, they convey'd me into a bucke-basket : "

• the recounting of what he 'sufferd' next (almost being discovered) starts equally passionately (6/4 in the first three lines of F #2), but as the moment of discovery draws nigh so the story-telling becomes very quiet, with the final three (surround-phrase) lines showing surprisingly little release as Mistris Ford's men

" : they tooke me on their shoulders : met the jealous knave their Master in the doore ; who ask'd them once or twice what they had in their Basket ? "

(0/1, 1/1, 0/0 per phrase), the story-telling calmness somewhat undermined by the emotional semicolon linking the second and third surround phrase (a hushed recounting perhaps)

• after dwelling on his 'feare' of the 'Lunatique Knave' (i.e. Ford), his recalling of being saved by 'Fate' intervening becomes intellectual (4/2 in the first two and a half lines of F #3), but in asking the disguised Ford to 'marke the sequell' Falstaffe's emotions are quickly released (3/6 the next three lines), and, in starting to recount the 'three severall deaths' he underwent, he brings some intellect to bear on the emotion (5/4, the last three and a half lines of F #3), at least for the first two of these lines

• the third death, the 'stinking Cloathes' yet again, really seems to be upsetting him, for not only is it reintroduced by what most modern texts regard as an ungrammatical F #4, the whole sentence is highly emotional (2/6), marked by two extra breath-thoughts (shown as ₓₓ), and finishes via four surround phrases, three of which are created in part by two emotional semicolons

---

First Folio

11/ Falstaffe

1 Nay, you shall heare ₓ(Master [Broome])ₓ what I have sufferd,ₓ to bring this woman to evill, for your good: {one [Mist.] Page, gives intelligence of Fords approch: ₓ and in her invention, and Fords wives distraction, they convey'd me into a bucke-basket:}{ram'd mee in with foule Shirts and Smockes, Socks, foule Stockings, greasie Napkins, that ₓ(Master [Broome])ₓ there was the rankest compound of villanous smell, that ever offended no-stril.}

2 Being thus cram'd in the Basket, a couple of Fords knaves, his Hindes, were cald forth by their Mistris,ₓ to carry mee in the name of foule Cloathes to Datchet-lane: they tooke me on their shoulders: ₓ met the jealous knave their Master in the doore; ₓ who ask'd them once or twice what they had in their Basket? ₓ

3 I quak'd for feare⁺ least the Lunatique Knave would have search'd it: ₓ but Fate (ordaining he should be a Cuckold) held his hand: well, on went hee, for a search, and away went I for foule Cloathes: But marke the sequell (Master [Broome]) I suffered the pangs of three severall deaths: First, an intollerable fright, to be detected [with] a jealous rotten Bell-weather: ₓ Next⁺ to be compass'd like a good Bilbo in the circumference of a Pecke, hilt to point, heele to head.

4 And then to be stopt like a strong distillation with stinking Cloathes,ₓ that fretted in their owne grease:

thinke of that, a man of my Kidney; thinke of that, that am as subject to heate as butter; a man of continuall dissolution,ₓ and thaw: it was a miracle to scape suffocation.

5   And in the height of this Bath (when I was more [then] halfe stew'd in grease (ₓlike a Dutch-dish)ₓ to be throwne into the Thames, and coold, glowing-hot, in that [serge]⁺ like a Horse-shoo; thinke of that;ₓ hissing hot;ₓ thinke of that ₓ(Master [Broome] •)ₓ

10   Think* of that - a man of my Kidney. †
11   Thinke of that -
     that am as subject to heat* as butter; a man of conti-
     nual* dissolution and thaw . †
12   It was a miracle to scape
     suffocation.
13   And in the height of this ᵈbath (when I
     was more [than] half* stew'd in grease, like a Dutch-
     dish) to be thrown* into the Thames, and
     cool'd, glowing ° hot, in that [surge], like a ᵈhorse⁰
     shoe*; think** of that - hissing hot - think* of that, Master
     [Brook].

" : thinke of that, a man of my Kidney ; thinke of that, that am as subject to heate as butter ; a man of continuall dissolution, and thaw : it was a miracle to scape suffocation . "

the semicoloned surround phrase presumably pointing to what he 'sufferd' most, the 'heate'

• and passion returns as the final indignity of being 'throwne into the Thames' is revealed (6/5), though again the surround phrases that end F #5 and the emotional semicolons seem to point to the horror of the heat being the worst part of his memories

" ; thinke of that ; hissing hot : thinke of that (Master Broome .) "

12/ Ford   **Hum : ha? Is this a vision? Is this a dreame?**   3.5.138 - 152

Background: The disguised Ford's (hopeful?) question 'My suite then is desperate: You'll undertake her no more?' has triggered Falstaffe into making a defiant and triumphant claim to the contrary, based on the fact that Falstaffe genuinely believes he has been invited back by Mistris Ford that very morning to finish his as yet uncompleted wooing (not realising that she and Mistris Page are setting him up a second time). Unaware of his wife's plot with Mistris Page to lure Falstaffe to the house in order to punish him yet again, Ford is now even more convinced his wife is planning to have an affair.

Style: solo

Where: Falstaffe's rooms   **To Whom:** self, and direct audience address

# of Lines: 13   **Probable Timing: 0.45 minutes**

Modern Text

12/ Ford

1 Hum ! ha?

2   Is this a vision?

3   Is this a dream*?

4 Do* I sleep*?

5   Master Ford, awake! awake, Master Ford ! †

6 There's* a hole made in your best coat*, Master Ford. †

7   This

   'tis to be married ! †

8   This 'tis to have ᴬlinen* , and ᴬbuck-

   baskets! †

9   Well, I will proclaim myself* what I am. †

10 I will now take the ᴬlecher*;   he* is at my house. †

11   He*

   cannot scape me ; 'tis impossible he* should ; he* can-

   not creep* into a half*ᵖpenny purse, nor into a ᴬpepper⁰

   ᴬbox* . †

12   But least the ᴬdevil* that guides him should

   aid* him, I will search impossible places. †

13   Though

   what I am I cannot avoid* ,yet to be what I would

   not shall not make me tame. †

14   If I have horns* to make

   one mad, let the proverb* go* with me : I'll be horn -

   mad.

First Folio

12/ Ford

1 Hum : ⁺ ha?

2   Is this a vision?

3   Is this a dreame?

4   Master Ford⁺ awake, ⁺ awake⁺ Master Ford : ⁺
   ther's a hole made in your best coate ₓ(Master Ford :)ₓ this
   'tis to be married ; ⁺ this 'tis to have Lynnen, and Buck-
   baskets: ⁺ Well, I will proclaime my selfe what I am :
   I will now take the Leacher : ₓ hee is at my house : hee
   cannot scape me ;ₓ 'tis impossible hee should :ₓ hee cannot creepe into a halfe-penny purse, nor into a Pepper-
   Boxe : But least the Divell that guides him,ₓ should
   aide him, I will search impossible places : though
   what I am,ₓ I cannot avoide ;ₓ yet to be what I would
   not,ₓ shall not make me tame : If I have hornes,ₓ to make
   one mad, let the proverbe goe with me, ⁺ Ile be horne-
   mad.

F's orthography and especially sentence structure reveals a much more disturbed and perhaps uncontrolled Ford than most modern texts put forth.

* though Ford's opening matches in both texts, and the first two very short sentences are unembellished, suggesting a great deal of control, it is only momentarily, for the short F #3 self-questioning 'Is this a dreame?' becomes highly emotional (0/3)

* and the painful answer becomes one enormous onrush, (which most modern texts split into a rational progression of ten grammatically correct sentences), with at least eleven surround phrases

* the opening call to awake is totally intellectual (4/0, F #4's first line), and then, not surprisingly, the resulting attack on himself becomes very passionate (5/4 the next three and a half lines), all burnt into his imagination via four successive surround phrases, especially the emotional (semicolon created) ': this 'tis to be married : this 'tis to have Lynnen, and Buck-baskets :'

* however, the picturing of Falstaffe at his house and how he, Ford, will turn the place upside down to find him, and search even 'impossible places' becomes highly emotional (5/10 in the next four lines)

* the vow to not accept being a Cuckold is trebly enhanced, being expressed in two surround lines, one both monosyllabic, unembellished and formed in part by an emotional semicolon ': though what I am, I cannot avoide ; yet to be what I would not, shall not make me tame :'

* however, springing from that vow, the final resolution to be 'mad' becomes very emotional (1/4)

#'s 13 - 14: FALSTAFFE'S FINAL DOWNFALL.

13/Falstaffe   The Windsor-bell hath stroke twelve :   between 5.5.1-21

Background: Incredibly, despite all that has happened, including a beating disguised as an old woman, Falstaffe still believes he has a chance with Mistris Ford. This time the women have tricked him to meet at midnight wearing, of all things, antlers on his head so as to follow their instruction to appear 'disguised like Herne with huge horns on his head'. Believing he will at last be successful, he shares his anticipation with the audience - little realising he is about to be exposed to everyone he has met in Windsor.

Style: initially solo, with the final two sentences to Mistris Ford

Where: at 'Herne the Hunter's Oake' in Windsor Forest   **To Whom:** direct audience address, and then Mistris Ford

# of Lines: 19   **Probable Timing: 1.00 minutes**

Modern Text

13/Falstaffe

1 The Windsor ° bell hath stroke twelve ;   the △mi-nute draws*°on. †

2   Now the hot-bloodied -△gods assist me !†
Remember, Jove, thou was't a △bull for thy Europa, △love set on thy horns* .

3 O powerful* △love, that in some respects makes a △beast a △man; in some* other, a △man a beast.

4 You were also, Jupiter, a △swan, for the love of Leda. †

5 O omnipotent △love, how near* the △god drew to the com-plexion of a △goose ! †

6 A fault done first in the form* of a beast (O Jove, a beastly fault !) and then another fault, in the semblance of a △fowl* - think* on't, Jove, a foul fault !

7 When △gods have hot backs*, what shall poor* men do?

8 For me, I am here* a Windsor △stag*, and the fattest, I think*, i'th △forest .

9 Send me a cool* rut-time, Jove, or who can blame me to piss* my △tallow?

10 Who comes here?*

11 My △doe with the black* △scut?

12 Let the sky*
rain* △potatoes; let it thunder to the tune of "Green-sleeves", hail°kissing △comfits, and snow △eringoes; △let there come a tempest of provocation, I will shelter me* here .

First Folio

13/Falstaffe

1 The Windsor-bell hath stroke twelve :   the Mi-nute drawes-on : Now the hot-bloodied -Gods assist me : + Remember+ Jove, thou was't a Bull for thy Europa, Love set on thy hornes .

2   O powerfull Love, that in some re-spects makes a Beast a Man: in som other, a Man a beast .

3 You were also x(Jupiter)x a Swan, for the love of Leda: O omnipotent Love, how nere the God drew to the com-plexion of a Goose : + a fault done first in the forme of a beast,x (O Jove, a beastly fault: +) and then another fault, in the semblance of a Fowle, thinke on't x(Jove)x a fowle-fault . +

4   When Gods have hot backes, what shall poore men do?

5   For me, I am heere a Windsor Stagge, and the fattest x(I thinke)x i'th Forrest.
Send me a coole rut-time

6   x(Jove)x or who can blame me to pisse my Tallow?
Who

7 comes heere?

8 My Doe,x with the blacke Scut?
Let the skie

9 raine Potatoes : x let it thunder,x to the tune of Greene-sleeves, haile-kissing Comfits, and snow Eringoes: x Let there come a tempest of provocation, I will shelter mee heere .

Amazingly, the speech opens extraordinarily intellectually (20/3, F #1-2, and the first two and a half lines of F #3, just seven and a half lines in all), so it seems that Falstaffe is almost willing the help of the hot-blooded Gods, especially the king of all (Jove/Jupiter), and holding on to his emotional self very tightly so as not to deflect his literally horny plea.

• despite the control, his need for success comes burning through both with the opening onrush (the two and a half sentences of F's intellectual opening being reset as seven by most modern texts) and the opening two lines of F #1, all of F #2, and the opening of F #3 being all surround phrases

• as ever, once Falstaffe starts to dream, so his passions or emotions come to the fore; and here is no exception, for as the lust begins to rise 'a fault done first the forme of a beast', so the remainder of the sentence turns passionate (4/4, the last three lines of F #3)

• and, as the short sentences continue the lust chat with the Gods, asking for a 'a coole rut-time' so that he doesn't 'pisse my Tallow', excusing himself for 'When Gods have hot backes, what shall poore men do?' (F #4-6), so the passions still run free (8/8 in just four lines)

• and as reality at last appears, so the passions disappear for a moment, with the two short sentences first becoming emotional ("Who comes heere?', 0/1) and then factual with his extremely vulgar acknowledgement of which lady has arrived ('My Doe, with the blacke Scut', 2/1)

• and then, as he realises his dreams might at last come true, the delighted celebratory yell for what were then believed to be aphrodisiacs ('Potatoes' and the sweetmeats known as 'Eringoes') and a love-song (which 'Greensleeves' was reckoned to be), so passions have their full sway once more (4/4 in the three and a half lines of F #9)

14/ Mistris Quickly   About, about : /Search Windsor Castle (Elves) within, and out .   5.5.55 - 75

Background: The elaborate plan to punish Falstaffe entails everyone except the Fords and Pages dressing as Fairies and pinching and burning Falstaffe with lighted tapers. To be successful they have to make him believe that they are Fairies, and this is Mistris Quickly's first speech as Queene of the Fairies designed to set the plot in action.

Style: public address

Where: at 'Herne the Hunter's Oake ' in Windsor Forest   **To Whom:** the assembled company of Pistoll, Evans and various children and young people, including Anne Page, Master Fenton, Slender and Caius all disguised as Fairies, the watching Pages and Fords, and all aimed to deceive Falstaffe

# of Lines: 22   Probable Timing: 1.10 minutes

Modern Text

14/ Mistris Quickly

1 About, about ;
Search Windsor Castle, △elves, within, and out .

2 Strew good luck*, △ouphes, on every sacred room* ,
That it may stand till the perpetual* doom*
In state as wholsome* as in state 'tis fit,
Worthy the △owner, and the △owner it.

3 The several* △chairs* of △order look* you scour*
With juice° of △balm and every precious flower*;
Each fair* △installment*, △coat*, and sev'ral* △crest,
With loyal* △blazon, evermore be blest !

4 And △nightly*°, meadow-△fairies, look° you sing
Like to the Garter's °△compass*, in a ring. †

5 Th'expressure that it bears*, △green* let it be,
More fertile-fresh [than] all the △field to see;
And, "Honi* °soit △qui △mal °y °△pense" write
In △em'rald ° tuffs°, △flowr's* purple, blue* , and white,
Like △sapphire*°, pearl*, and rich embroidery*,
Buckled below fair* △knight*hood's bending knee :
Fairies use △flow'rs* for their charactery*.

6 Away, disperse ! △but till 'tis one a'clock* ,
Our △dance of △custom*, round about the △oak*
Of Herne the △hunter, let us not forget .

First Folio

14/ Mistris Quickly

1 About, about : x
Search Windsor Castle x (Elves) x within, and out .

2 Strew good lucke x (Ouphes) x on every sacred roome ,
That it may stand till the perpetuall doome. x
In state as wholsome. x as in state 'tis fit,
Worthy the Owner, and the Owner it.

3 The severall Chaires of Order. x looke you scowre
With juyce of Balme ; and every precious flowre, +
Each faire Installment, Coate, and sev'rall Crest,
With loyall Blazon, evermore be blest . +

4 And Nightly +-meadow-Fairies, looke you sing
Like to the Garters-Compasse, in a ring,

5 Th'expressure that it beares : x Greene let it be,
More fertile-fresh [then] all the Field to see : x
And, Hony Soit Qui Mal-y-Pence, x write
In Emrold-tuffes, Flowres purple, blew, and white,
Like Saphire +-pearle, and rich embroiderie,
Buckled below faire Knight-hoods bending knee ; +
Fairies use Flowres for their characterie. .

6 Away, disperse : + But till 'tis one a clocke,
Our Dance of Custome, round about the Oke
Of Herne the Hunter, let us not forget .

This speech has been included because it gives the actress a chance to explore two things, the uncertainty of a woman not used to performing or actually be the centre of attention, and then the charm of the speech itself – the archaic quality encompassed in the rhyming couplets that make up the speech. Thus there is no doubt that the character is sincere, it's how successful Mistris Quickly might be in handling the speech is what gives the greatest sense of fun and exploration.

• F's orthography seems to suggest that, for a moment or two, Mistris Quickly's being centre stage in fooling Falstaffe runs away with her; for while she opens with some semblance of control (F #1, 3/0), very soon her passions are spilling all over the stage - though eventually she does manage to bring herself under control

• thus, as she starts issuing instructions, so she becomes much more passionate, moving from the general spreading of good luck (3/4 in F #2's four lines), to much more release as details of how they should 'scowre' the 'Chaires of Order' and all the emblems of state are impressed upon them (7/10 in just the four lines of F #3), the emotional semicolon separating the two tasks emphasising the importance of both

• the gardening instructions become more intellectual (16/7 in the nine lines of F #4), the ideas of ' : Greene let it be/More fertile-fresh then all the Field to see : ' and ' ; Fairies use Flowres for their charactere . ' being singled out as surround phrases

• and by the time of the final surround-phrase instruction, ' . Away, disperse : ' initially giving Falstaffe hope that he won't be discovered, only to be undercut by the supposedly sudden reminder that 'Our Dance of Custome' still has to be done exactly where Falstaffe is hiding 'round about the Oke/Of Herne the Hunter' - she has regained full control of self and situation (6/2, F #5)

#'s 15 - 18: A KEY SUB-PLOT, THE WOOING OF ANNE PAGE

15/ Evans　　There is also another device in my praine,　　between 1.1.43 - 57

Background: One of the first major speeches from the Welsh parson, also known as Doctor Hugh. As a marriage-making proposal it is self-explanatory.

Style: as part of a three-handed scene

Where: somewhere close to the Page's home　　**To Whom:** to Justice Shallow, the uncle of the proposed bridegroom, and the possible groom Abraham Slender

# of Lines: 11　　**Probable Timing: 0.40 minutes**

Modern Text	First Folio
15/ Evans	**15/ Evans**
1　{T}here is also another device in my prain*, which peradventure prings goot discretions with it: ◊ there is Anne Page, which is daughter to Master [George] Page, which is pretty virginity {,}	1　{T}here is also another device in my praine, which peradventure prings goot discretions with it.　　There is Anne Page, which is daughter to Master [Thomas][3] Page, which is pretty virginity{,}
┄┄┄┄┄┄┄┄	
{a}s just as	2　　　　　{a}s just as
you will desire, and seven hundred pounds of ᴬmoneys*, and ᴬgold, and ᴬsilver, is her ᴬgrandᵇsire upon his death's-bed. (Got deliver to a joyful* resurrectionsᴵ) give, when she is able to overtake seventeen* years* old.	you will desire, and seven hundred pounds of Moneyes, and Gold, and Silver, is her Grand-sire upon his deaths-bed. (Got deliver to a joyfull resurrections⁺) give, when she is able to overtake seventeene yeeres old.
It were a	3　　　　　　　It were a
2　goot motion if we leave our pribbles and prabbles, and desire a marriage between* Master Abraham and Mistress* Anne Page.	goot motion,ₓ if we leave our pribbles and prabbles, and desire a marriage betweene Master Abraham,ₓ and Mistris Anne Page.

It seems that Evans cannot keep his outward calm for very long, for after the very restrained opening mention of a 'device in my praine' (0/1, F #1), excitement takes over.

• the naming of names of the proposed marriage is stuffed full of facts, up to and including the Grand-sire's legacy (9/1, the first five lines of F #2), while the excitement of the legacy coming into effect now that Anne is 'seventeene yeeres old' turns into emotion (0/2, F #2's last line)

• the fact that F sets up the first mention of the names as a separate sentence (F #2, while modern texts fold it into their opening), gives even more weight to the proposal, especially since . . .

• . . . after a very careful unembellished appeal for calm by being calm, 'It were a goot motion, if we leave our pribbles and prabbles, and desire a marriage . . .', the naming of names is made once more, and once more is handled highly factually (5/1, the last one and a half-lines of F #3)

---

[3] as commentators point out, elsewhere in the play Page is referred to as George, not Thomas, though modern texts rarely alter the name here

16/ Slender   **I will marry her (Sir) at your request ; but . . .**   1.1.245 - 252

Background: The marriage-match proposed by Evans (speech #15 above) is of great interest to Justice Shallow, though Slender himself seems not to have quite the same fiscal sense, or dare it be said much grip on any reality, as either Evans or Shallow would like

Style: as part of a three-handed scene

Where: close to the Page's home   **To Whom:** to Justice Shallow and Evans

# of Lines: 7   **Probable Timing: 0.25 minutes**

Modern Text

16/ Slender

1 I will marry her, ᴬsir, at your request ; but if
there be* no great love in the beginning, yet ᴬheaven
may decrease it upon better acquaintance, when we*
are married and have more occasion to know one another. †

2   I hope, upon familiarity will grow more content . †

3 But if you say, "marry* °her," I will marry* °her ; that I am
freely dissolv'd, and dissolutely .

First Folio

16/ Slender

1 I will marry her ₓ(Sir)ₓ at your request ; but if
there bee no great love in the beginning, yet Heaven
may decrease it upon better acquaintance, when wee
are married,ₓ and have more occasion to know one another :   I hope⁺ upon familiarity will grow more content :
but if you say⁺ mary-her, I will mary-her, ⁺ that I am freely
dissolved, and dissolutely .

F's one sentence onrush, coupled with the emotional
semicolon in the first line, suggests that no matter how brave
the words, Slender may not be very comfortable with the idea
of marriage, especially coupled with . . .

a/ the three malapropisms of 'Heaven may decrease' their love 'upon
better acquaintance' plus the final surround phrases ' : I hope upon
familiarity will grow more content : but if you say mary-her, I will
mary-her, that I am freely dissolved, and dissolutely . '

b/ the short spelling of the word marry ('mary') the last two times it is
used

c/ and the fact that in the six and a half lines of the speech, the very
few releases (2/2) all disappear after the first three lines once the
(dreadful) phrase 'when wee are married' is voiced

17/ Evans   'Plesse my soule : how full of Collors I am,   3.1.11 - 26

Background: Caius, a French physician, is also interested in marrying Anne Page, and, mistaking Evans' intercession on behalf of Slender as genuine interest for himself, Caius has challenged Evans to a duel.   Evans is now nervously waiting for Caius and everyone else to arrive so the duel can begin, though everyone seems rather late, thereby increasing his nervous anticipation.

Style: solo
Where: a field in or near Frogmore, outside of Windsor   **To Whom:** self and audience

# of Lines: 10   **Probable Timing: 0.35 minutes**

Modern Text

17/ Evans

1 [Jeshu] 'pless* my soul*! how full of ^chollors* I am and trempling of mind*!†

2 me .†   I shall be glad if he have deceived

3 How melancholies I am!

4   I will knog his ^urinals* about his knave's costard, when I have good oportunities for the ork* .†

5   'Pless* my soul*! †

6 "To shallow ^rivers, to whose falls
Melodious Birds sings ^madrigals* ;
There will we make our* ^peds of ^roses,
And a thousand fragrant posies.

7   To shallow - "

8 Mercy* on me*! I have a great dispositions to cry .

9 "Melodious birds sing ^madrigals* -
When as I sat in Pabylon* -
And a thousand vagram ^posies.

10   To shallow, &c. "

First Folio

17/ Evans

1 [ ] 'Plesse my soule : + how full of Collors I am, x and trempling of minde : +   I shall be glad if he have deceived me : how melancholies I am? +

2   I will knog his Urinalls about his knaves costard, when I have good oportunities for the orke : 'Plesse my soule :+ *To shallow Rivers + to whose falls : + melodious Birds sings Madrigalls: x There will we make our Peds of Roses : x and a thousand fragrant posies .*
                              To shal-

3 *low.*

4 Mercie on mee, + I have a great dispositions to cry .

5 *Melodious birds sing Madrigalls : x ——— When as I sat in Pa- bilon : x and a thousand vagram Posies.*
                                  To shallow, &c.

The way the speech is composed of either so many surround phrases (F #1 completely shaped by four; F #2 ending with five; F #5 entirely made up of three) or short sentences (F #3, #4, and #6), shows that Evans' thoughts are very concentrated, and with the changes of topic almost phrase by phrase, not very rewarding.

• apart from those found in the song, the quiet unembellished lines all refer to the truth of his inner state, viz. ' : I shall be glad if he have deceived me : how melancholies I am ? ' : ', I have a great dispositions to cry . ', the first two enhanced by being surround phrases

• the first one and a half lines open emotionally (1/4), then close with the quiet hope that there will be no fight

• the vainglorious boast to 'knog his Urinalls' becomes passionate (1/2 the first two lines of F #2), while his attempt to sing to mask his worries becomes highly intellectual (7/2 in the remaining two and a half lines): the attempt is heightened by the five surround-phrases and the two short sentences that follow, their lack of embellishment and shortness (F #3-4, 0/1) suggesting the singing hasn't necessarily worked

• F #4's repeated surround-phrase attempt to sing is also highly factual (4/1)

• that F #6, the sentence attempting to continue the singing, is both short and unembellished again, might suggest that the second attempt to relax by singing might not have worked

18/ Host   Peace, I say, Gallia and Gaule, French & Welch,   between 3.1.97 -111

Background: Having finally brought Caius and the watchers to where Evans has been waiting, the Host explains why he has deceived them both.

Style: principally to two men, as part of a group address

Where: a field in or near Frogmore, outside of Windsor   **To Whom:** Caius and Evans, in front of Shallow, Slender, Master Page, Simple and Rugby (servant to Mistris Quickly and thus to Caius too)

# of Lines: 13   **Probable Timing: 0.45 minutes**

First Folio

18/ Host

1 Peace, I say, + Gallia and Gaule, French & Welch, Soule-Curer, and Body-Curer. +

2 Peace, I say: + heare mine Host of the Garter,

3 Am I politicke?

4 Am I subtle?   Am I a Machivell?

5 Shall I loose my Doctor?

6 No, hee gives me the Potions and the Motions.

7 Shall I loose my Parson? my Priest? my Sir Hugh? :x

8 No, he gives me the Proverbes, and the No-verbes.

9 [ ]
   Give me thy hand x(Celestiall) + so; Boyes of Art, I have deceiv'd you both: x I have directed you to wrong places: your hearts are mighty, your skinnes are whole, and let burn'd Sacke be the issue : Come, lay their swords to pawne: Follow me, [Lad] of peace, + follow, follow, follow.

F sets the (shaded) opening of the speech as verse, as if the Host has to work somewhat formally to get everyone's attention, allowing him to relax into prose once he has it. Most modern texts set the more casual prose right from the start.

- the speech starts with an interesting mix of
  a/ two unembellished appeals for calm 'Peace, I say', each time spoken without the modern texts' suggestion of a louder appeal by their addition of the exclamation mark
  b/ a tremendous intellectual name-gaming/tile-playing splurge (8/2 in the less than two lines of F #1, and first phrase of F #2)

- the speech then becomes passionate as he lists his own virtues (3/2, the remainder of F #2 through to F #4), his self-praise heightened by the short sentences, especially the last two

- and while the praise of Doctor Caius' physical gifts remains passionate (3/2, F #5-6), those of parson Evans' more moralistic ones start much more intellectually (4/1, F #7) and then finish equally passionately (2/2, F #8)

- and then it seems as if the short sentence attempts at self-control can no longer work, for as the joke on them both is revealed, so the Host finishes with a passionate onrush (F #9, 5/5) until the very last intellectual command to 'Follow' (2/0 the last line of F #9) – virtually all of F #9 being formed by at least six surround phrases: most modern texts remove this large shift by resetting F #9 as five sentences, starting the section with an extra sentence taken from the quarto, ' . Give me thy hand, (terrestrial): so. '

Modern Text

18/ Host

1 Peace, I say ! Gallia and Gaul*, French and Welsh*, soul*-△curer, and △body-△curer !

2 Peace, I say ! hear* mine △host of the Garter. †

3 Am I politic*?

4 Am I subtle?

5 Am I a Machivel*?

6 Shall I lose* my △doctor?

7 No, he* gives me the △potions and the △motions.

8 Shall I lose* my △parson? my △priest? my Sir Hugh?

9 No, he gives me the △proverbs*, and the △no-verbs* . †

10 [Give me thy hand (terrestrial); so] . †

11 Give me thy hand, △celestial*; so . †

12 △Boys* of △art, I have deceiv'd you both; I have directed you to wrong places . †

13 Your hearts are mighty, your skins* are whole, and let burnt △sack* be the issue . †

14 Come, lay their swords to pawn* . †

15 Follow me, [lads] of peace ; follow, follow, follow.

The Merry Wives of Windsor / 239

19/ Slender   Whoa hoe, hoe, Father Page.   between 5.5.177 - 193

Background: In a complex series of plottings to take place at the same time as the tricking of Falstaffe, Mistris Page arranged for daughter Anne to be dressed in one colour so Caius could recognise her and steal her away to be quickly married while, unbeknownst to his wife, Master Page has arranged for Anne to be in a different colour so Slender could recognise her and steal her away to be quickly married instead. As it turns out Anne manages to trick everyone and marry Fenton (of whom neither parent approves). Here the dismayed Slender tells of his embarrassing failure. One note: F#5/mt.#6 have been inserted here from later in the speech to allow Master Slender a more logical explanation.

Style: one on one in front of a larger group

Where: at 'Herne the Hunter's Oake' in Windsor Forest   **To Whom:** to Page, in front of Falstaffe, the assembled company of Mistris Quickly, Pistoll, Evans and various children and young people, all disguised as Fairies, the watching Fords and Mistris Page

# of Lines: 13   **Probable Timing: 0.45 minutes**

First Folio

19/ Slender

1   Whoa hoe, hoe, + Father Page .

2   {I am not d}ispatch'd{!}

3   Ile make the best in Glostershire
    know on't : would I were hang'd la, else . +

4   I came yonder at Eaton to marry Mistris Anne
    Page, and she's a great lubberly boy .

5   I went to her in [greene], + and cried Mum, and
    she cride budget, as Anne and I had appointed, and yet
    it was not Anne, but a Post-masters boy .

6   If it had not bene
    i'th Church, I would have swing'd him, or hee should
    have swing'd me .

7   If I did not thinke it had been Anne
    Page, would I might never stirre, + and 'tis a Post-masters
    Boy .

8   If I had bene married to him,
    (for all he was in womans apparrell) I would not have
    had him .

Modern Text

19/ Slender

1   Whoa ho* , ho*! ᐃfather Page .

2   {I am not d}ispatch'd{!}

3   I'll make the best in Gloucestershire*
    know on't . †

4   Would I were hang'd la, else !

5   I came yonder at Eton* to marry Mistress* Anne
    Page, and she's a great lubberly boy .

6   I went to her in [white], and cried "ᐃmum", and
    she cried* "budget", as Anne and I had appointed, and yet
    it was not Anne, but a ᐃpost°master's boy .

7   If it had not been*
    i'th ᐃchurch, I would have swing'd him, or he* should
    have swing'd me .

8   If I did not think* it had been Anne
    Page, would I might never stir*! and 'tis a ᐃpost°master's
    ᐃboy .

9   If I had been* married to him,
    (for all he was in woman's apparel*) I would not have
    had him .

19/ Slender

- after a wonderful opening running-on-stage verbal explosion (2/3, the short F #1), Slender, at least momentarily, manages to restore himself to a sense of dignity for the dreadful news for himself and Anne's father that he is not married (1/0, F #2-3)

- indeed, the further explanation of how the girl he thought he had married, despite being dressed in 'greene' and their exchanging the agreed upon pass-words 'Mum' and 'budget', has turned out to be a 'lubberly boy' (F #4-5) is a surprising mix of facts (8/1 in just five lines) and (including phrases from F #2-3 too) unembellished dignity preserving comments
    "I am not dispatch'd" plus "would I were hang'd la else"
    "and she's a great lubberly boy"

- and, for almost the first time in the play, he seems determined to take some sort of stand, for the whole of sentence two
    ". Ile make the best in Glostershire know on't : would I were hang'd la, else . "
    is made up of unembellished surround phrases

- but the control and intellect do not last, for informing all that it was only the discovery of the mistake being revealed in a church that prevented fisticuffs, followed by the fairly obvious statement that he wouldn't have married a 'Post-masters Boy' instead of Anne Page had he known, becomes passionate (5/5, F #6-7)

- while the final reassertion 'I would not have had him.' becomes almost self-controlled once more (just 0/1 in the two lines of F #8)

F 4 in the various colour confusions most modern texts set 'white', F = 'greene', Q1 = 'red'

AS YOU LIKE IT

SPEECHES IN ORDER

SPEECHES IN ORDER	TIME	PAGE
#'s 1 - 4: Orlando's Troubles		
1/ **Orlando** — As I remember Adam, it was upon this fashion	1.15	242
2/ **Charles** — I came to acquaint you with a matter :	0.45	244
3/ **Oliver** — Charles, I thanke thee for thy love to me,	1.00	245
4/ **Le Beu** — Good Sir, I do in friendship counsaile you	1.15	246
#'s 5 - 7: Rosalind's Troubles		
5/ **Celia** — I see thou lov'st mee not with the full	0.40	247
6/ **Le Beu** — You amaze me Ladies : I would have told	0.55	248
7/ **Duke Fredricke** — I Celia, we staid her for your sake,	0.45	249
#'s 8 - 10: Escape To Arden		
8/ **Celia** — O my poore Rosaline, whether wilt thou goe?	0.50	250
9/ **Orlando** — Speake you so gently? Pardon me I pray you,	0.45	251
10/ **Duke Senior** — True it is, that we have seene better dayes,	0.25	252
#'s 11 - 14: Orlando & Rosalind In Love		
11/ **Orlando** — Hang there my verse, in witnesse of my love,	0.35	252
12/ **Rosalind** — Good my complection, dost thou think though	0.30	253
13/ **Rosalind** — {Orlando?} Alas the day, what shall I do with my	0.20	254
14/ **Rosalind** — O coz, coz, coz : my pretty little coz,	0.40	255
#'s 15 - 17: Rosalind's (Self-Protective?) Thoughts On Love		
15/ **Rosalind** — There is none of my Unckles markes upon you :	0.35	256
16/ **Rosalind** — Love is meerely a madnesse, and I tel you,	1.10	257
17/ **Rosalind** — No faith, die by Attorney : the poore world . . .	0.45	258
#'s 18 - 20: Silvius' Thoughts On Love		
18/ **Silvius** — Oh Corin, that thou knew'st how I do love her.	0.50	259
19/ **Silvius** — Sweet Phebe doe not scorne me, do not Phebe	0.25	260
20/ **Silvius** — So holy, and so perfect is my love,	0.20	260
#'s 21 - 23: Phebe In Love		
21/ **Phebe** — I would not be thy executioner,	1.10	261
22/ **Rosalind** — And why I pray you? who might be your mother	1.40	262
23/ **Phebe** — Thinke not I love him, though I ask for him,	1.30	263

SPEECHES BY GENDER

Speech #(s)

SPEECHES FOR WOMEN (11)

Character	Description	Speech #(s)
Celia	Traditional & Today: young woman, usually slightly younger than Rosalind	#5, #8
Rosalind	Traditional & Today: young woman, usually slightly older than Celia	#12, #13, #14, #15, #16, #17, #22
Phebe	Traditional & Today: young woman	#21, #23

SPEECHES FOR EITHER GENDER (7)

Character	Description	Speech #(s)
Le Beau	Traditional: character male, any age Today: any gender, any age	#4, #6
Duke Fredericke	Traditional: older man of some authority Today: any age, and sometimes any gender	#7, #32, #33
1st. Lord	Traditional: male, usually young Today: any gender, any age	#29
Corin	Traditional: older character male Today: any gender, usually middle age up	#31

{see also Duke Senior & Jaques below}

SPEECHES FOR MEN (21)

Character	Description	Speech #(s)
Orlando	Traditional & Today: a young man, youngest of three brothers	#1, #9, #11
Charles	Traditional & Today: male character actor who can wrestle	#2
Oliver	Traditional & Today: a young man, oldest of three brothers	#3
Duke Senior	Traditional: older man of some authority, older than his brother Fredricke Today: any age (but older than Fredricke), and sometimes any gender	#10, #28
Silvius	Traditional: young male, would-be lover Today: as above, but sometimes older	#18, #19, #20
Clowne	Traditional: clown, male character actor, young to middle age Today: as above, but any age	#24, #25, #26, #27, #30
Jaques	Traditional: older male, usually close to the 'sixth' age of the 'seven ages' speech (#37 below) Today: sometimes younger (usually early middle age on), and sometimes any gender	#34, #35, #36, #37, #38, #39

#'s 24 - 27: The Clowne Touchstone On Love

24/	**Clowne**	I remember when I was in love,	0.35	265
25/	**Clowne**	That is another simple sinne in you, to bring the	0.30	266
26/	**Clowne**	Praised be the Gods, for thy foulnesse;	1.00	266
27/	**Clowne**	Wil {I} be married, {Sir}?	0.25	268

#'s 28 - 31: The Country Life As Seen By The Country And City Folk

28/	**Duke Senior**	Now my Coe-mates, and brothers in exile :	0.55	269
29/	**1st. Lord**	Indeed my Lord/The melancholy Jaques grieves at . .	1.55	270
30/	**Clowne**	Ah this shepherds life. Truely, in respect of	0.30	271
31/	**Corin**	I know the more one sickens, the worse at ease	0.45	272

#'s 32 - 33: Duke Fredricke's Anger

32/	**Duke Fredricke**	Can it be possible that no man saw them?	0.30	273
33/	**Duke Fredricke**	Not see him since? Sir, sir, that cannot be :	0.50	274

#'s 34 - 39: Jaques Observations and Longings

34/	**Jaques**	Well then, if ever I thanke any man, Ile thanke	0.20	275
35/	**Jaques**	A Foole, a foole : I met a foole i'th Forrest,	1.10	276
36/	**Jaques**	I am ambitious for a motley coat . /It is my onely	1.00	277
37/	**Jaques**	All the world's a stage,	1.30	278
38/	**Jaques**	I have neither the Schollers melancholy, ...	0.35	279
39/	**Jaques**	Sir, by your patience : if I heard you rightly,	0.50	280

AS YOU LIKE IT

#'s 1 - 4: ORLANDO'S TROUBLES

1/ Orlando   **As I remember Adam, it was upon this fashion**   1.1.1 -250

Background: The first speech of the play, explaining the appalling relationship between Orlando de Boys and Oliver, his oldest brother, the inheritor of the estate of their recently deceased father.   As such it is self explanatory.

Style: as part of a two-handed scene

Where: the orchard of the de Boys family   **To Whom:** Adam, the nearly eighty year old family retainer, loyal to Orlando

# of Lines: 24   **Probable Timing: 1.15 minutes**

Modern Text

1/ Orlando

1   As I remember, Adam, it was upon this fashion
bequeathed me by will but poor* a thousand
△crowns, and, as thou say'st, charged my brother, on his blessing, to breed me* well; and
there begins my sadness* . †

My brother Jacques he keeps*
at school*, and report speaks* goldenly of his profit . †

2

3   For my part, he keeps* me rustically at home, or (to speak
more properly) stays* me here* at home unkept; for call
you that keeping for a gentleman of my birth, that differs not from the stalling of an △ox*? †

His horses are bred

4   better, for besides that they are fair* with their feeding,
they are taught their manage*, and to that end △riders
dearly* hir'd; but I (his brother) gain* nothing under
him but growth, for the which his △animals on his
dunghills* are as much bound to him as I . †

Besides this no-

5   thing that he so plentifully gives me, the something that
nature gave me* his countenance seems* to take from
me. †

6   He* lets me* feed* with his hinds*, bars* me* the
place of a brother, and as much as in him lies, mines my
gentility with my education.

This is it, Adam, that

7   grieves me, and the spirit of my △father, which I think*
is within me*, begins to mutiny* against this servitude.

First Folio

1/ Orlando

1   As I remember+ Adam, it was upon this fashion
bequeathed me by will,x but poore a thousand
Crownes, and+ as thou saist, charged my bro-
ther+ on his blessing+ to breed mee well:x and
there begins my sadnesse : My brother Jacques he keepes
at schoole, and report speakes goldenly of his profit :
for my part, he keepes me rustically at home, or (to speak
more properly) staies me heere at home unkept:x for call
you that keeping for a gentleman of my birth, that differs not from the stalling of an Oxe? his horses are bred
better, for besides that they are faire with their feeding,
they are taught their mannage, and to that end Riders
deerely hir'd:x but I (his brother) gaine nothing under
him but growth, for the which his Animals on his
dunghils are as much bound to him as I : besides this nothing that he so plentifully gives me, the something that
nature gave mee,x his countenance seemes to take from
me : hee lets mee feede with his Hindes, barres mee the
place of a brother, and as much as in him lies, mines my
gentility with my education.   This is it+ Adam+ that
grieves me, and the spirit of my Father, which I thinke
is within mee, begins to mutinie against this servitude.

2

Though the structures match at the end of the speech, and though Orlando manages to reach a state of self-control by the time he's finished, the Folio & modern openings of the speech are totally different, with F's Orlando having one of the longest onrushed first sentences in Shakespeare – F's whole suggesting a gigantic outburst at the start of the play which he manages to control by speech's end.

• the opening of the speech, setting out the details of the will and how the middle brother Jacques is well taken care of by older brother and inheritor of the state Oliver, is, quite naturally, passionate (6/6 in the first six lines)

• as the surround phrases suggest, the root of the trouble stems from Oliver's refusal to carry out certain provisions of his father's will, at least as regards Orlando

" : and there begins my sadnesse : My brother Jacques he
keepes at schoole, and report speakes goldenly of his
profit : "

• and as Orlando goes on to detail his ill-treatment the speech turns emotional, at first under a fair amount of control (3/9 in ten lines) but, as he describes how he has to 'feede with his Hindes' (his brother's farm-labourers), he finally explodes (1/6 in just one line), and then he regains control for the last line and a half of F #1

• there is a moment of passion again (2/2, F #2) as he invokes the spirit of 'my Father' (2/2) to justify his possible 'mutinie against this servitude'

• thus, given the orthography of the opening to the speech, remarkably he manages to re-establish complete self-control for the last sentence

I will no longer endure it, though yet I know no wise remedy how to avoid it.

8

• throughout, the unembellished lines point to the uncomfortable details past, present, and even future that have and continue to give Orlando great difficulties in resolving

"it was upon this fashion bequeathed me by will,"

"for call you that keeping for a gentleman of my birth", i.e.

"besides this nothing that he so plentifully gives me",

"and as much as in him lies, mines my gentility with my education"

so that Orlando's spirit, shaped by that of his recently deceased father

"begins to mutinie against this servitude. I will no longer endure it, though yet I know no wise remedy how to avoid it."

3   I will no longer endure it, though yet I know no wise remedy how to avoid it.

2/ Charles **I came to acquaint you with a matter :** 1.1.122 - 136

Background: In a recent coup, Duke Fredericke has ousted the rightful Duke, his older brother, known simply as Duke Senior, who has fled to the Forest of Arden with his followers. Tomorrow, Charles, a wrestler, fights, perhaps for the first time, before the 'new' Duke, and, as the following explains, since Oliver's brother Orlando is one of his challengers, he is in a very difficult situation, and has thus come to Oliver for advice.

Style: as part of a two-handed scene

Where: the orchard of the de Boys family **To Whom:** Oliver, Orlando's eldest brother

# of Lines: 13 **Probable Timing:** 0.45 minutes

Modern Text

2/ Charles

1 {ψ}
     I came to acquaint you with a matter . †

2 I am given, sir, secretly to understand, that your younger* brother, Orlando, hath a disposition to come in disguis'd against me* to try a fall. †

3   Tomorrow, sir, I wrastle for my credit, and he* that escapes me without some broken limb* shall acquit him well. †

4   Your brother is but young and tender, and for your love I would be* loth to foil* him, as I must for my own* honor* if he* come in; therefore out of my love to you, I came hither to acquaint you withal*, that either you might stay him from his intendment, or brook* such disgrace well as he shall run* into, in that it is a thing of his own* search, and altogether against my will.

First Folio

2/ Charles

1 {ψ}
     I came to acquaint you with a matter : I am given⁺ sir⁺ secretly to understand, that your yonger⁺ brother⁺ Orlando⁺ hath a disposition to come in disguis'd against mee to try a fall : to morrow⁺ sir⁺ I wrastle for my credit, and hee that escapes me without some broken limbe, ⁺ shall acquit him well : your brother is but young and tender, and for your love I would bee loth to foyle him, as I must for my owne honour if hee come in : ₓ therefore out of my love to you, I came hither to acquaint you withall, that either you might stay him from his intendment, or brooke such disgrace well as he shall runne into, in that it is a thing of his owne search, and altogether against my will.

The tension in Charles can be seen in that, despite the onrush, much of the information is spoken in quite a restrained (unembellished) manner – as if while both the news and the class difference are sufficient to create nerves galore, Charles is doing his very best to handle them, at least at the start of the speech, as the occasional colon (four in the first eight lines, none in the last four and a half) also show.

• the unembellished lines illustrate how Charles would like to present the facts (the long-spelled 'mee' being the single – and very important – break)

 "I came to acquaint you with a matter : I am given sir secretly to understand, that your yonger brother … hath a disposition to come in disguis'd against mee to try a fall : to morrow sir I wrastle for my credit …"
 "your brother is but young and tender,"
 "therefore out of my love to you, I came hither …"
 "that either you might stay him from his intendment,"
 "and altogether against my will."

• the opening is very careful (1/1, the first three lines), and then becomes emotional as Charles explains he has to ensure there will be 'some broken limbe' (0/2)

• the most emotional moment is explaining to Oliver how he must beat Orlando (0/5 in just two and a half lines to the final colon), but Charles manages to regain some composure in the last four very rushed 'please do something' uncolored lines (0/4)

3/ Oliver   **Charles, I thanke thee for thy love to me,**   1.1.137 - 158

Background: Just before Charles' arrival, the two brothers came to blows, ending with Orlando nearly throttling Oliver and then demanding the small inheritance granted by his father's will. Oliver has essentially vowed revenge ('I will physicke your ranknesse'). Charles' news (speech #2 above) seems heaven sent, and thus Oliver begins to inflame Charles so that he will look forward to injuring Orlando in the ring.

Style: as part of a two-handed scene

Where: the orchard of the de Boys family   **To Whom:** Charles, the Duke's wrestler   **# of Lines: 19**   **Probable Timing: 1.00 minutes**

Modern Text

3/ Oliver

1 Charles, I thank* thee for thy love to me, which thou shalt find* I will most kindly requite . †
     I had my self* notice of my Brothers purpose herein*, and have by under°hand means* labor'd* to dissuade* him from it; but he is resolute.

2   I'll tell thee, Charles, it is the stubbornest young* fellow of France, full of ambition, an envious emulator of every man's good parts, a secret & villainous* contriver against me* his natural* brother; therefore use thy discretion - I had as lief* thou didst break* his neck* as his finger.

3   And thou wert best look* to't; for if thou dost him any slight disgrace, or if he* do* not mightily* grace himself* on thee, he* will practice against thee by poison*, entrap thee by some treacherous device*, and never leave thee till he hath ta'en thy life by some indirect means* or other; for I assure thee, (and almost with tears* I speak*) it) there is not one so young and so villanous* this day living.

4   I speak* but brotherly of him, but should I anatomize* him to thee as he* is, I must blush, and weep*, and thou must look* pale and wonder.

First Folio

3/ Oliver

1 Charles, I thanke thee for thy love to me, which thou shalt finde I will most kindly requite : I had my selfe notice of my Brothers purpose heerein, and have by under-hand meanes laboured to disswade him from it ; but he is resolute.
     Ile tell thee + Charles, it is the stubbornest yong fellow of France, full of ambition, an envious emulator of every mans good parts, a secret & villanous contriver against mee his naturall brother:ₓ therefore use thy discretion, I had as liefe thou didst breake his necke as his finger.

3   And thou wert best looke to't ; for if thou dost him any slight disgrace, or if hee doe not mightilie grace himselfe on thee, hee will practise against thee by poyson, entrap thee by some treacherous devise, and never leave thee till he hath tane thy life by some indirect meanes or other : ₓ for I assure thee, (and almost with teares I speake it) there is not one so young, and so villanous this day living.

4   I speake but brotherly of him, but should I anathomize him to thee, as hee is, I must blush, and weepe, and thou must looke pale and wonder.

Despite the high emotion of the speech (3/27 in just nineteen lines), Oliver seems to be exhibiting great skill in the manipulation of Charles - the quiet unembellished lines seem superbly designed to awake Charles' mistrust towards Orlando prior to the wrestling.

• from the opening emotional surround phrase
     " ; but he is resolute . "
     "full of ambition, an envious emulator of every mans good parts,"
     "therefore use thy discretion,"
     "entrap thee by some treacherous devise, and never leave thee till he hath tane thy life by some indirect . . ."
     "for I assure thee . . . there is not one so young, and so villanous this day living."

• while the few surround phrases underscore the seriousness of the danger, from the first '; but he is resolute . ' through to
     " ; therefore use thy discretion, I had as liefe thou didst breake his necke as his finger . / And thou wert best looke to't ; "

• as with the 'breake his necke' comment, Oliver's use of the long spelled words throughout seems to be released only at the appropriate times and designed for effect, often in short burst clusters - 'under-hand meanes labour'd to disswade', 'mee his naturall brother', 'teares I speake it' - as well as with the occasional single evocative word 'thanke', 'poyson', 'anathomize', and 'weepe'

• the only intellectual moment is probably the most telling of all, in the opening of F #2, the overall description of Orlando as a warning prelude of the dreadful things to come, 'Ile tell thee Charles, it is the stubbornest yong fellow of France', (2/0)

4/ Le Beu   Good Sir, I do in friendship counsaile you   between 1.2.261 - 285

Background: As the following explains, Le Beu, one of Duke Fredericke's retinue, seems to have been as 'enchanted' by Orlando as everyone else throughout the play, though, as he explains, Le Beu fears that the Duke has not been affected in the same way. One interesting note, this is the first time Le Beu has moved from the everyday world of speaking prose into the more heightened awareness of verse, which says much about his feelings in the current situation.

Style: as part of a two-handed scene

Where: in the grounds of the Ducal palace, the favourite spot where Celia and Rosalind often meet to be alone

To Whom: Orlando

# of Lines: 24   **Probable Timing:** 1.15 minutes

Modern Text

4/ Le Beau

1
Good Sir, I do in friendship counsel* you
To leave this place. †

2
     Albeit you have deserv'd
High commendation, true applause, and love ;
Yet such is now the Duke's condition
That he misconsters all that you have done . †

3
The Duke is humorous - what he is indeed*
More suits* you to conceive [than] I to speak* of.

4
{Which is the Duke's daughter that was here at the
        Δwrastling?}

5
Neither his daughter, if we judge by manners,
But yet indeed* the [smaller] is his daughter . †

6
The other is daughter to the banish'd Duke,
And here detain'd by her usurping Δuncle
To keep* his daughter company*, whose loves
Are dearer* [than] the natural* bond of Δsisters. †

7
But I can tell you, that of late this Duke
Hath ta'en displeasure 'gainst his gentle Δniece* ,
Grounded upon no other argument
But that the people praise her for her virtues,
And pity* her for her good Δfather's sake ;
And on my life his malice 'gainst the Δlady
Will suddenly* break* forth . †

8
     Sir, fare you well,
Hereafter, in a better world [than] this,
I shall desire more love and knowledge of you.

First Folio

4/ Le Beu

1
Good Sir, I do in friendship counsaile you
To leave this place ; Albeit you have deserv'd
High commendation, true applause, and love ;
Yet such is now the Dukes condition,ₓ
That he misconsters all that you have done :
The Duke is humorous, what he is indeede
More suites you to conceive,ₓ [then] I to speake of.

2
{Which is the Duke's daughter   { → }
That was here at the Wrastling?}

3
Neither his daughter, if we judge by manners,
But yet indeede the [taller] is his daughter,
The other is daughter to the banish'd Duke,
And here detain'd by her usurping Uncle
To keepe his daughter companie, whose loves
Are deerer [then] the naturall bond of Sisters :
But I can tell you, that of late this Duke
Hath tane displeasure 'gainst his gentle Neece,
Grounded upon no other argument,ₓ
But that the people praise her for her vertues,
And pittie her,ₓ for her good Fathers sake ;
And on my life his malice 'gainst the Lady
Will sodainly breake forth : Sir, fare you well,
Hereafter⁺ in a better world [then] this,
I shall desire more love and knowledge of you .

Given that this character is often played as an excessively flamboyant **pouter-pigeon stuffed with pride, this speech shows very little excess (just 13/8 in twenty-four lines) – and if this perfectly valid characterisation is followed through, then this is equally obviously a moment where all his natural tendencies have to be reined in (for fear of being overheard perhaps?)**

• the onrush of both sentences F #1 and especially F #3, are testimony to the pressure Le Beu is feeling, though the modern texts create a much more rational character throughout, splitting F # 1 into three sentences and F #3 into four

• the four extra breath-thoughts (marked ₓ) all seem to come as extra key information is being offered, such as adding the final doom-laden details, viz.
" ,ₓ /That he misconsters all that you have done : "
" ,ₓ then I to speake of . "
" ,ₓ But that the people praise her for her vertues,/And pittie her, ₓ for her good Fathers sake ; "

• the semicolon created emotional surround phrases point to the fears for both Orlando's safety
" Good Sir, I do in friendship counsaile you/To leave this place ;
Albeit you have deserv'd/High commendation, true applause, and love ; "
and for Rosalind, both stemming from the Duke's inner nature
" ; And on my life his malice 'gainst the Lady/Will sodainly breake forth : "

• as the single emotional cluster refers to the affection between the cousins Rosalind and Celia 'whose loves/Are deerer then the naturall bond of Sisters', it's quite fascinating to see that ten of Le Beu's thirteen capitals refer in one way or another to the relationships between the two young women and their respective fathers

#'s 5 - 7: ROSALIND'S TROUBLES

5/ Celia   I see thou lov'st mee not with the full   between 1.2.8 -23

Background: Celia's father, the new Duke, Fredericke, did not include Rosalind in the recent banishment of her father, Duke Senior, only because he knows that Celia and Rosalind, 'being ever from their Cradles bred together', are, in Celia's own words, inseparable as 'Juno's Swans'. Nevertheless, Celia is fearful for Rosalind's well-being: hence the following.

Style: as part of a two-handed scene

Where: unspecified, but presumably somewhere inside or outside the palace where the two cousins meet to be alone   **To Whom:** her cousin Rosalind

# of Lines: 12   Probable Timing: 0.40 minutes

Modern Text

5/ Celia

1   {ψ}   I see thou lov'st me* not with the full
weight that I love thee. †

2   If my △uncle, thy banished father,
had banished thy △uncle, the Duke my △father, so thou
hadst been* still with me* I could have taught my love
to take thy father for mine ; so wouldst thou, if the truth
of thy love to me were so righteously temper'd as mine
is to thee.
▨▨▨▨▨▨▨

3   You know my △father hath no child* but I, nor
none is like to have ; and truly* when he dies, thou shalt
be his heir*; for what he* hath taken away from thy father perforce, I will render thee again* in affection. †
                                                                        By

4   mine honour*, I will, and when I break* that oath, let me*
turn* monster. †

5   Therefore, my sweet Rose, my dear* Rose,
be merry.

First Folio

5/ Celia

1   I see thou lov'st mee not with the full
waight that I love thee ; if my Uncle + thy banished father +
had banished thy Uncle + the Duke my Father, so thou
hadst beene still with mee, I could have taught my love
to take thy father for mine ; so wouldst thou, if the truth
of thy love to me were so righteously temper'd,ₓ as mine
is to thee.
▨▨▨▨▨▨▨

2   You know my Father hath no childe,ₓ but I, nor
none is like to have ; and truely when he dies, thou shalt
be his heire ; for what hee hath taken away from thy father perforce, I will render thee againe in affection : by
mine honor + I will, and when I breake that oath, let mee
turne monster : therefore + my sweet Rose, my deare Rose,
be merry.

With four semicolons in this twelve-line speech, it seems
that Celia is in more than just a teasing mood.

* the fact that one or other of them (or both) may be in a fragile
state might be seen in the serious extended unembellished
passage that closes F #1. viz.

"I could have taught my love to take thy father for mine ; so
wouldst thou, if the truth of thy love to me were so
righteously temper'd, as mine is to thee."

* the speech opens passionately (4/3 the first three lines of F
#1), and continues with the unembellished ending of F #1, but it
seems Celia cannot maintain self-control any further, for in
offering to disinherit herself the speech becomes highly emotional
(1/8), though she does manage to close intellectually as she begs
her cousin to 'be merry' (2/1 the last line of F #2)

* the emotional surround phrases underscore her love for her
cousin

" . I see thou lov'st mee not with the full waight that I love
thee;"

" ; so wouldst thou, if the truth of thy love to me were so
righteously temper'd, as mine is to thee . "

to the extent of disinheriting herself as a future ruler of the
Dukedom

" . You know my Father hath no childe, but I, nor none is
like to have ; and truely when he dies, thou shalt be his
heire ; "

while the final logical (colon created) surround phrases stress the
integrity of her promise, as well as her love once more

" : by mine honor I will, and when I breake that oath, let
mee turne monster : therefore my sweet Rose, my deare
Rose, be merry."

6/ Le Beu   **You amaze me Ladies : I would have told**   between 1.2.109 - 146

Background: Initially their friend, the clown Touchstone, has been ordered to bring the two cousins to Duke Fredericke and the wrestling. Having been side-tracked, Le Beu has been dispatched to inform them that since they will not come to the wrestling the wrestling is about to come to them, invading their personal territory. Their obvious disinterest in the event leads to the following.

Style: as part of a four handed scene

Where: unspecified, but presumably somewhere inside or outside the palace where the two cousins meet to be alone   **To Whom:** Celia, Rosalind, and Touchstone

# of Lines: 17   **Probable Timing: 0.55 minutes**

Modern Text

6/ Le Beu

1   You amaze me, ᴬladies . †

        I would have told

2   you of good wrastling, which you have lost the sight of .

3   I will∗ tell you the beginning ;   and if it please
    your ᴬladyships∗, you may see the end, for the best is yet
    to do, and here∗ where you are, they are coming∗ to
    perform∗ it .

4   There comes an old man and his three sons - ◇
    {t}hree proper young∗ men, of excellent growth
    and presence .

5   The eldest of the three wrastled with Charles,
    the Duke's ᴬwrastler, which Charles in a moment threw
    him and broke three of his ribs∗ , that there is little
    hope of life in him . †

        So he serv'd the second, and so the

6   third . †

7   Yonder they lie, the poor∗ old man, their ᴬfather,
    making such pitiful∗ dole over them that all the behol-
    ders take his part with weeping .

        {You } shall {ψ} see

8   this wrastling {ψ}if you stay here∗, for here∗ is the
    place appointed {ψ}, and they are ready to
    perform∗ it .

First Folio

6/ Le Beu

1   You amaze me⁺ Ladies : I would have told
    you of good wrastling, which you have lost the sight of .

2   I wil tell you the beginning : ₓ and if it please
    your Ladiships, you may see the end, for the best is yet
    to doe, and heere where you are, they are comming to
    performe it .

3   There comes an old man,ₓ and his three sons .

4   Three proper yong men, of excellent growth
    and presence .

5   The eldest of the three,ₓ wrastled with Charles⁺
    the Dukes Wrastler, which Charles in a moment threw
    him,ₓ and broke three of his ribbes, that there is little
    hope of life in him : So he serv'd the second, and so the
    third : yonder they lie, the poore old man⁺ their Father,
    making such pittiful dole over them,ₓ that all the behol-
    ders take his part with weeping .

6   {You } shall {ψ} see
    this wrastling {ψ}if you stay heere, for heere is the
    place appointed {ψ}, and they are ready to
    performe it .

The fact of the early lines being unembellished or slightly intellectual suggests that Le Beu is taking great care to recover what little status he has left, especially since he has to inform Touchstone and the young women that the Duke is bringing the wrestling to the women whether they like it or not.

• thus the opening three surround phrases comprising F #1 and the opening two lines of F #2 (1/0), two of which are unembellished, could suggest a put-upon character taking great care not to offend further
   "You amaze me Ladies : I would have told you of good wrastling,
      which you have lost the sight of. I wil tell you the beginning :"
especially when followed by another almost unembellished line 'and if it please your Ladiships, you may see the end' (1/0)

• and following the suddenly exuberant release ending F #2, that the wrestling is coming (0/4), the ensuing short and unembellished sentences (F #3-4) suggest Le Beu is taking enormous care once more,
   "There comes an old man, and his three sons . Three proper yong
    men, of excellent growth and presence . The eldest of the three,"
though whether this is out of respect for his listeners or because of the strength of his own recollection of what has just taken place is up to each actor to explore

• as the facts are advanced of the crippling 'in a moment' defeat of the three brothers, emotions are held in check (5/1 in the four lines to the last colon of F #5), though the emphatic final surround phrase description of how Charles 'So he serv'd the second, and so the third', suggesting that some details are still fresh in his mind

• and then Le Beu's feelings finally break through (1/5) for both the description of the father's 'pittiful dole' and the repetition that 'heere is the place appointed' for the 'wrastling' (the last two lines of F #5 and all of F #6)

7/ Duke Fredericke   I Celia, we staid her for your sake,   between 1.3.67 - 89

Background: In addition to having banished her father, his brother, Fredricke has now banished his niece Rosalind too, and has been challenged publicly by his daughter Celia. His reasons, as explained below, might have been triggered by an incident at the wrestling, where, after Le Beu had indicated to Orlando that 'the Princesse cals for you', one of two unfortunate things took place: either Orlando did not address himself to Celia as he should have but addressed Rosalind instead, or Rosalind herself in her impetuosity asked the first question, as she would have done had she still been the rightful princess - either way it's possible Fredricke feels his daughter was publicly slighted.

Style: as part of a three-handed scene in front of others

Where: unspecified, but presumably somewhere inside or outside the palace where the two cousins meet to be alone   **To Whom:** Celia and then Rosalind in front of members of Fredricke's retinue

# of Lines: 13   **Probable Timing: 0.45 minutes**

Modern Text

7/ Duke Fredricke

1   Ay*, Celia, we stay'd her for your sake,
    Else had she with her ^father rang'd along.

2   She is too subtile for thee, and her smoothness*,
    Her very* silence and her patience
    Speak* to the people, and they pity* her . †

3   Thou art a fool*;   she robs thee of thy name,
    And thou wilt show more bright & seem more virtuous
    When she is gone. †

4   Then open not thy lips :
    Firm* and irrevocable is my doom*
    Which I have pass'd upon her ;   she is banish'd.

5   You, ^"niece*, provide yourself* ;
    If you out°stay the time, upon mine honor,
    And in the greatness* of my word, you die.

First Folio

7/ Duke Fredricke

1   I + Celia, we staid her for your sake,
    Else had she with her Father rang'd along.

2   She is too subtile for thee, and her smoothnes ; x
    Her verie silence, and her patience,x
    Speake to the people, and they pittie her :
    Thou art a foole, she robs thee of thy name,
    And thou wilt show more bright,x & seem more vertuous
    When she is gone : then open not thy lips +
    Firme,x and irrevocable is my doombe x
    Which I have past upon her, + she is banish'd.

3   {ψ}   You + Neice + provide your selfe, +
    If you out-stay the time, upon mine honor,
    And in the greatnesse of my word + you die.

Despite the proportionately large number of unembellished lines and accompanying relative lack of release, the onrushed mid-sentence F #2 and extra breath-thoughts (marked , x) suggest that Celia's father's apparent calm is only maintained with great difficulty.

• the one (unembellished) surround-phrase says it all
  ". She is too subtile for thee, and her smoothnes ; "
  especially when it is cut off in mid thought by the grammatically appalling F only emotional semicolon

• given their powerful content, the remaining unembellished lines could well suggest that no matter how misguided, her father is very sincere in his actions and really wants her to understand why he is banishing Rosalind,
  "Her verie silence, and her patience . . / . . robs thee of thy name, / And thou wilt show more bright, . . /When she is gone: then open not thy lips"
  his final words to Rosalind leaving no doubt how far he is prepared to go
  "If you out-stay the time, upon mine honor, . . . you die."

• the speech opens factually (2/0, F #1), while the onrushed F #2 shows just three emotional lines breaking the enforced calm (0/5 in eight lines), with emotion slightly outweighing facts in the final act of banishment (1/2, F #3)

#'s 8 - 10: ESCAPE TO ARDEN

8/ Celia   O my poore Rosaline, whether wilt thou goe?   between 1.3.90 - 107

Background: Despite Celia's protestations, even to the point of insisting 'Pronounce that sentence on me my Liege,/I cannot live out of her companie', her father has insisted on banishing Rosalind[1], finishing with the appalling final statement 'If you out-stay the time, upon mine honor,/And in the greatnesse of my word you die'. These are Celia's first words following Duke Fredricke's exit.

Style: as part of a two-handed scene

Where: unspecified, but presumably somewhere inside or outside the palace where the two cousins meet to be alone   **To Whom:** Rosalind

# of Lines: 15   **Probable Timing:** 0.50 minutes

Modern Text

8/ Celia

1 O my poor* Rosalind* , whether wilt thou go*? .

2 Wilt thou change Fathers? .

3   I will give thee mine . †

4 I charge thee be not thou more griev'd [than]I am. .

5 Prithee* be cheerful* . †

6   Know'st thou not the Duke
Hath banish'd me, his daughter? .

7 {Doth} Rosalind* {lack the} love
Which teacheth [me] that thou and I am one . †

8 Shall we be sund'red?   shall we part sweet* girl*? .

9 No, let my ^father seek* another heir* . †

10 Therefore devise with me how we may fly*,
Whether to go*, and what to bear* with us,
And do* not seek* to take [the charge] upon you,
To bear* your griefs* yourself*, and leave me out;
For by this heaven, now at our sorrows* pale,
Say what thou canst, I'll go* along with thee {,}
To seek* my ^uncle {thy ^father} in the ^forest* of Arden.

First Folio

8/ Celia

1 O my poore Rosaline, whether wilt thou goe?

2 Wilt thou change Fathers?

3   I will give thee mine :

4 I charge thee be not thou more griev'd [then] I am .

5 Prethee be cheerefull ; know'st thou not the Duke
Hath banish'd me + his daughter? .
          {Doth} Rosaline {lack the} love
Which teacheth [thee] that thou and I am one,
Shall we be sundred?   shall we part sweete girle?

6 No, let my Father seeke another heire:
Therefore devise with me how we may flie
Whether to goe, and what to beare with us,
And doe not seeke to take [your change] upon you,
To beare your griefes your selfe, and leave me out : ₓ
For by this heaven, now at our sorrowes pale,
Say what thou canst, Ile goe along with thee {,}
To seeke my Uncle {thy Father} in the Forrest of Arden.

Each slight F onrush (F #3 = mt. #3-4; F #4 = mt. #5-6; F #5 = mt. 6-7; F #6 = mt. #9-10) suggests that the powerful ideas are tumbling out of Celia slightly more unchecked than their modern counterpart, but in no way does this diminish the power and determination to save her beloved friend.

• thus the opening is a mixture of enforced (unembellished) calm and fierce passion (5/8, in the seven lines F #1-5)

• the unabashed denial of her father and choice to escape with Rosalind, made even stronger by being set as one sentence via a fast-link colon (the impact of which most modern texts reduce by creating two sentences, mt. #9-10), becomes highly emotional (1/11) until F #6's last line

• while the very last line, declaring that they will go look for Rosalind's father, is a triumph of a passionate (if youthful) spirit (4/2 in just eleven words)

• once more the unembellished lines underscore the determination already seen with her father, especially the surround phrases offering to 'change Fathers'

    "I will give thee mine : /I charge thee be not more griev'd then I am . "
then challenging whether Rosaline really does 'lacke the love'
    "Which teacheth thee that thou and I am one, /Shall we be sundred?"
    "Therefore devise with me how we may flie", vowing to "goe along with thee"
    "Say what thou canst"

• the emotionally (semicolon) created surround phrases point to the depths both of her feelings
    " . Prethee be cheerefull ; know'st thou not the Duke/Hath banish'd me his daughter?"
and her vows
    " : For by this heaven, now at our sorrowes pale ; "

[1] the First Folio also sets the character's name as Rosaline (as in this speech) and Rosalinde; for the sake of clarity, the commentary and background notes will continue to refer to her as 'Rosalind'

9/ Orlando   Speake you so gently ?   **Pardon me I pray you,**   2.7.106 - 119

Background: Because of Adam's frail condition, Orlando has been forced to become what he claimed he never would be and is attempting force 'with a base and boistrous sword enforce/A theevish living on the common rode' by threatening to rob from Duke Senior and his men, demanding 'Forbeare, and eate no more'. Mercifully, perhaps through Orlando's 'enchanting' powers, the Duke has recognised his worth and talked him out of his criminal intent by freely offering him the food, suggesting 'Your gentlenesse shall force, more then your force/move us to gentlenesse.'. Hence Orlando's reply.

Style: one on one in front of a larger group

Where: Duke Senior's encampment in the forest of Arden   **To Whom:** Duke Senior, in front of his followers including Jaques and Amyens

# of Lines: 14   **Probable Timing: 0.45 minutes**

Modern Text

9/ Orlando

1 Speak* you so gently?

2   Pardon me, I pray you . †

3 I thought that all things had been* savage here* ,
   And therefore put I on the countenance
   Of stern* command'ment.

4   But what e'er you are

   That in this desert inaccessible,
   Under the shade of melancholy* boughs* ,
   Loose, and neglect the creeping hours* of time :
   If ever you have look'd on better days* ,
   If ever been* where bells* have knoll'd to ᐃchurch,
   If ever sat* at any good man's feast,
   If ever from your eyeᵒlids wip'd a tear* ,
   And know what 'tis to pity* , and be pitied* ,
   Let gentleness* my strong enforcement be,
   In the which hope I blush, and hide my ᐃsword.

First Folio

9/ Orlando

1 Speake you so gently?

2   Pardon me + I pray you,
   I thought that all things had bin savage heere,
   And therefore put I on the countenance
   Of sterne command'ment.

3   But what ere you are   ˣ

   That in this desert inaccessible,
   Under the shade of melancholly boughes,
   Loose, and neglect the creeping houres of time :   ˣ
   If ever you have look'd on better dayes :   ˣ
   If ever beene where bels have knoll'd to Church :   ˣ
   If ever sate at any good mans feast :   ˣ
   If ever from your eye-lids wip'd a teare,
   And know what 'tis to pittie, and be pittied: ˣ
   Let gentlenesse my strong enforcement be,
   In the which hope,ₓ I blush, and hide my Sword.

• the short emotional sentence opening the speech points to Orlando's surprise at the Duke's response to his threats (F #1, 0/1), while the explanation that he had only 'put on' (that is pretended) 'the countenance/Of sterne command'ment' is also restrainedly emotional (0/2 in the three lines of F #2), while, after an unembellished line and a half, the request for forgiveness becomes somewhat more emotionally released (2/10 in the last nine lines of the speech)

• Orlando's honesty and amazement at having been saved at the last minute from disgracing himself comes shining through in the few unembellished lines
"Pardon me I pray you" &
"But what ere you are/That in this desert inaccessible,"

• while the three successive surround phrases (the first three of six pure pentameter lines – somewhat unusual for this stage of Shakespeare's writings) clearly show the innate chivalric principles by which he would like to live
" : If ever you have look'd on better dayes : / If ever beene where bels have knoll'd to Church :/ If ever sate at any good mans feast :"

• though used to describe the situation of those who have found him and appeal for their forgiveness, the two clusters of long spellings might well underscore what he feels his own life has been to date, first that he has
"Under the shade of melancholly boughes,/Loose and neglect the creeping houres of time :"   (lines three and four of F #3, 0/4)
"If ever from your eye-lids wiped a teare,/And know what 'tis to pittie, and be pittied : /Let gentlenesse my strong enforcement be" (lines seven to nine, F #3, 0/4)

10/ Duke Senior   True is it, that we have seene better dayes,   2.7.120 - 126

Background: Orlando's apology (speech #9 immediately above) draws the following response from Duke Senior (unusual in any Shakespeare play, in that it almost matches Orlando both in image and rhythmic pattern).

Style: one on one

Where: Duke Senior's encampment in the forest of Arden   **To Whom:** Orlando, in front of Duke Senior's followers including Jaques and Amyens

# of Lines: 7   Probable Timing: 0.25 minutes

Modern Text	First Folio
10/ Duke Senior	**10/ Duke Senior**
1 True it is that we have seen* better days* ,	1 True is it,ₓ that we have seene better dayes,
And have with holy bell been* knoll'd* to △church,	And have with holy bell bin knowld to Church,
And sat at good men's feasts, and wip'd our eyes*	And sat at good mens feasts, and wip'd our eies
Of drops, that sacred pity hath engend'red;	Of drops, that sacred pity hath engendred : ₓ
And therefore sit you down* in gentleness*	And therefore sit you downe in gentlenesse,
And take upon command, what help* we have	And take upon command, what helpe we have
That to your wanting may be minist'red.	That to your wanting may be ministred.

- in an equally restrained response to Orlando's apology (1/6 in the seven lines), the first of two emotional clusters comes as the Duke matches Orlando's appeal for understanding, i.e. that they have 'seene better dayes' (line one, 0/2), and been 'knowld to Church' (line two, 1/1), and then reinforces how Orlando has hoped he will be judged, 'therefore sit you downe in gentlenesse' (line five, 0/2) and he will be offered 'what helpe we have' (line six, 0/1)

- while the unembellished lines match Orlando's chivalric hopes, that they have indeed 'sat at good mens feasts, and wip'd our eies/Of drops, that sacred pity hath engendred'

#'s 11 - 14: ORLANDO & ROSALIND IN LOVE

11/ Orlando   Hang there my verse, in witnesse of my love,   3.2.1 - 10

Background: Now in spring, and being accepted as a member of Duke Senior's camp, Orlando's thoughts turn once more to Rosalind, and, as the following illustrates, is running round the forest of Arden hanging (or carving) on every available tree self-written poetry (rather bad poetry, as we later discover) in her praise.

Style: solo

Where: in the forest   **To Whom:** the verses, the goddess of chastity, the absent Rosalind, and himself

# of Lines: 10   Probable Timing: 0.35 minutes

Modern Text	First Folio
11/ Orlando	**11/ Orlando**
1 Hang there, my verse, in witness* of my love,	1 Hang there + my verse, in witnesse of my love,
And thou, thrice crowned △queen* of night, survey	And thou + thrice crowned Queene of night + survey
With thy chaste eye, from thy pale sphere* above,	With thy chaste eye, from thy pale spheare above +
Thy △huntress'* name that my full life doth sway.	Thy Huntresse name,ₓ that my full life doth sway.
2 O Rosalind, these △trees shall be my △books* ,	2 O Rosalind, these Trees shall be my Bookes,
And in their barks* my thoughts I'll character* ,	And in their barkes my thoughts Ile charracter,
That every* eye, which in this △forest* looks* ,	That everie eye, which in this Forrest lookes,
Shall see thy virtue witness'd every where.	Shall see thy vertue witnest every where.
3 Run, run Orlando, carve on every △tree	3 Run, run Orlando, carve on every Tree.ₓ
The fair* , the chaste, and unexpressive she* .	The faire, the chaste, and unexpressive shee.

- without the extra commas added by most modern texts (marked + in the Folio text), F Orlando's excitement bursts forth quite unchecked right from the start, and quite emotionally (2/4, F #1)

- however, with the mention of Rosalind's name in F #2's first line, he becomes determinedly intellectual (3/1 in the one line) but then rushes into unchecked emotion as he promises to blazon his love among the trees so 'That everie eye' will see 'thy vertue' – and, delightfully, the thought of her 'vertue' drives him into the only unembellished line in the short speech, ending F #2

- the heady mix of the struggle between intellect and emotion surfaces once more, with F #3's first line command to 'run' (an intellectual 2/0) immediately being swamped in the second line's emotional images of the 'faire . . . shee' (0/2)

12/ Rosalind　　Good my complection, dost thou think though　　3.2.194 - 203

Background: During their first meeting at the wrestling which eventually precipitated their flight, Rosalind was as equally smitten as Orlando, as Celia only too well knows, and the attraction has persisted even though Rosalind and Celia, together with the clown Touchstone whom they took with them to the forest, have now bought a small cottage, and have been living for some time pretending to be brother (Rosalind disguised as a man) and sister (Celia). The following is triggered by Celia having extensively tantalised Rosalind by first reading aloud one fairly appalling tree-hanging ode (see speech #11 immediately above), and then hinting that she knows who the author of the (dreadful, but whole-hearted) poetry may be, and that it's someone to whom Rosalind gave a 'chaine that you once wore' which he now wears 'about his necke'.

Style: as part of a two-handed scene

Where: the woods　　　　**To Whom:** Celia

# of Lines: 9　　　　**Probable Timing: 0.30 minutes**

Modern Text

12/ Rosalind

1　Good my complexion∗, dost thou think, though
　I am caparison'd like a man, I have a doublet and hose in
　my disposition?

2　　　　　One inch of delay more is a South°sea

3　[off] discoverie∗.　　I prithee∗ tell me who is it quickely∗, and
　speak∗ apace. †

4　　　　I would thou couldst stammer, that thou
　mightst pour∗ this conceal'd man out of thy mouth, as
　△wine comes out of a narrow-mouth'd bottle - either too
　much at once, or none at all.

5　　　　　　I prithee∗ take the △cork∗
　out of thy mouth that I may drink∗ thy tidings∗ .

First Folio

12/ Rosalind

1　Good my complection, dost thou think+ though
　I am caparison'd like a man, I have a doublet and hose in
　my disposition?

2　　　　　One inch of delay more, + is a South-sea

3　[of] discoverie.　　　　I pre'thee tell me,ₓ who is it quickely, and
　speake apace: I would thou couldst stammer, that thou
　might'st powre this conceal'd man out of thy mouth, as
　Wine comes out of a narrow-mouth'd bottle :ₓ either too
　much at once, or none at all.

4　　　　　　　I pre'thee take the Corke
　out of thy mouth,ₓ that I may drinke thy tydings.

Given the circumstances, Rosalind's enforced calm is very surprising (though whether it's done for her own benefit or to impress Celia is up to each actress to explore).

• thus the first sentence is completely unembellished, with the short second sentence only slightly intellectual (1/0)

• then, but only momentarily, the emotions make a brief appearance in the first surround line of the speech 'I pre'thee tell me, who is it quickely, and speake apace' (0/3, the first line of F #3), and then supposed calm returns once more with three more virtually unembellished lines to end the sentence (1/1)

• and then, at last, her self-control gives way in the (pleading? demanding?) one and a half line F #4 (1/3), the emotion enhanced by the extra breath-thought (marked , ₓ) that heralds the final wonderful (teasing? exasperated?) release of 'that I may drinke thy tydings'

13/ Rosalind   **{Orlando ?} Alas the day, what shall I do with my doublet & hose?**   3.2.218 - 224

Background: This is Rosalind's response when Celia finally admits that the someone (see background to speech #12 above) is in fact Rosalind's heart-throb Orlando.

Style: as part of a two-handed scene

Where: the woods   **To Whom:** Celia

# of Lines: 6   **Probable Timing: 0.20 minutes**

Whether folio or modern version is explored, essentially the speech is self-explanatory.

• because the speech is written in prose, and in Elizabethan/early Jacobean texts a capital letter following a question mark does not necessarily mean a new sentence has started, the first printing of this speech could be seen as anywhere between one and twelve sentences in length

• the shorter number of sentences chosen will mean Rosalind is in one heck of an onrushed state; the more sentences chosen would suggest that, for once, Rosalind's incredibly inventive mind and mouth (usually seen in the very long and witty sentences set for her) are stunned by the amazing news, and can only stammer out a series of very basic unadorned sentences

• that this latter may be the case is supported by the one thing of note in the F setting - given the circumstances there is very little release, and what little there is is all emotional (0/6 in six lines)

Modern Text

13/ Rosalind

1 {Orlando ?}

2   Alas the day, what shall I do with my doublet & hose?

3 What did he when thou saw'st him?

4   What said*

5 he? How look'd he?

6   Wherein went he?

7   What makes he*

8 here*? Did he ask* for me?

9   Where remains* he?

10   How

11 parted he with thee?

12   And when shalt thou see him a-

gain*?

12 Answer me in one word.

First Folio

13/ Rosalind

1 {Orlando ?}

2   Alas the day, what shall I do with my doublet &

hose?

3 What did he when thou saw'st him?

4   What sayde

he?

5 How look'd he?

6   Wherein went he?

7   What makes hee

heere?

8 Did he aske for me?

9   Where remaines he?

10   How

11 parted he with thee?

And when shalt thou see him a-

gaine?

12 Answer me in one word.

14/ Rosalind   **O coz, coz, coz :   my pretty little coz,**   between 4.1.205 - 217

Background: After a chance encounter with Orlando who does not see through their disguises, Rosalind has pushed her deception as a male to play the role of a saucy lackey and challenged Orlando to a series of meetings at their cottage where she can drive his love-sickness out of him (presumably in order to test his love and spend more time with him), all to Celia's dismay. After Orlando leaves following a second knife-edge and, to both he and Rosalind, disturbing exchange of wits and ideas, Rosalind reveals to Celia the enormous depths of her feelings. One note: Aliena is the name Celia that has adopted for herself to maintain her disguise of being a simple country girl.

Style: as part of a two-handed scene

Where: the woods close to their cottage   **To Whom:** Celia

# of Lines: 12   **Probable Timing: 0.40 minutes**

Modern Text	First Folio
14/ Rosalind	**14/ Rosalind**
1 O coz, coz, coz, my pretty little coz, that thou didst know how many fathom* deep* I am in love! † But	1 O coz, coz, coz : _x my pretty little coz, that thou didst know how many fathome deepe I am in love : + but it cannot bee sounded : _x my affection hath an unknowne bottome, like the Bay of Portugall.
2 it cannot be* sounded ; my affection hath an unknown* bottom*, like the ^Δbay of Portugal* .	
_ψ Or rather bottomless* -	_ψ Or rather bottomlesse -
3 that as fast as {one} pour{s}* affection in, [it] runs out.	2 that as fast as {one} poure{s} affection in, [in] runs out.
4 {O}, that same wicked ^Δbastard of Venus that was begot of thought, conceiv'd of spleen* , and born* of madness* , that blind* rascally boy, that abuses every ones eyes because his own* are out, let him be* judge, how deep* I am in love . †	3 {O}, that same wicked Bastard of Venus,_x that was begot of thought, conceiv'd of spleene, and borne of madnesse, that blinde rascally boy, that abuses every ones eyes,_x because his owne are out, let him bee judge, how deepe I am in love : ile tell thee + Aliena, I cannot be out of the sight of Orlando: Ile goe finde a shadow, and sigh till he come.
5 I'll tell thee, Aliena, I cannot be out of the sight of Orlando. †	
6 I'll go* find* a shadow, and sigh till he come.	

With Orlando's exit, F's onrush (F #1 = mt. #1-2, and especially F #3 = mt. #4-6) shows just how much release Rosalind has need of now that she can drop the male persona of the 'sawcy lackey' and be herself.

• the four surround phrases that completely form F #1 are sufficient testimony as to how truthfully she is speaking, while the only others, the two ending the speech, are so naked both as to her need (the unembellished opener) and inability to cope (the emotional 0/2 second)

" : ile tell thee Aliena, I cannot be out of sight of Orlando : Ile geo finde a shadow, and sigh till he come . "

• not surprisingly, overall the confession is highly emotional (6/17 in the eleven and a half lines of the speech); the two intellectual clusters refer to the depth of her love (the as yet unplumbed 'Bay of Portugall') and a sardonic dismissal of Cupid as the 'wicked Bastard of Venus'; the emotional clusters are either equally as rude about this 'Bastard', claiming he was 'conceiv'd of spleene, and borne of madnesse, that blinde rascally boy . . . ' (0/4), or refer once more to the depth of her love, i.e. to 'how many fathome deepe' she is in love (0/2), and Cupid can 'bee judge, how deepe I am in love' (0/2)

#'s 15 - 17: ROSALIND'S (SELF-PROTECTIVE?) THOUGHTS ON LOVE

15/ Rosalind   **There is none of my Unckles markes upon you :**   between 3.6.369 - 384

Background: In their first in-the-woods-encounter, Orlando, challenged by the disguised Rosalind's statement that she could cure the man that 'haunts the forrest, that abuses our yong plants by carving Rosalind on their barkes' and hangs love poetry on the trees, simply replies 'I am he that is so Love-shak'd, I pray you tel me your remedie'. However, Rosalind is apparently not prepared to accept the fact the he really is in love, as the following suggests.

Style: as part of a three-handed scene

Where: somewhere in the wood   **To Whom:** Orlando, in front of Celia

# of Lines: 14   **Probable Timing: 0.35 minutes**

Modern Text

15/ Rosalind

1   There is none of my ᐃuncle's* marks* upon you. †

He taught me how to know a man in love ;   in which cage of rushes I am sure you are not prisoner.

{They were}

2   a lean* cheek*, which you have not ;   a blue* eye* and sunken, which you have not ;   an unquestionable spirit, which you have not ;   a beard neglected, which you have not (but I pardon you for that, for simply your having [no] beard is a younger* brother's revenue*) ;   then your hose should be ungarter'd, your bonnet unbanded, your sleeve unbutton'd, your shoe* untied, and every* thing about you demonstrating a careless* desolation. †

3   But you are no such man ;   you are rather point-°device in your accoutrements* , as loving yourself* , [than] seeming the ᐃlover of any other.

First Folio

15/ Rosalind

1   There is none of my Unckles markes upon you :   he taught me how to know a man in love :   x   in which cage of rushes, I am sure you art not prisoner.

{They were}

2   a leane cheeke, which you have not :   x   a blew eie and sunken, which you have not :   x   an unquestionable spirit, which you have not :   x   a beard neglected, which you have not :   x   (but I pardon you for that, for simply your having [in] beard,   x   is a yonger brothers revennew) † then your hose should be ungarter'd, your bonnet unbanded, your sleeve unbutton'd, your shoo unti'de, and everie thing about you,   x   demonstrating a carelesse desolation :   but you are no such man ;   you are rather point device in your accoutrements, as loving your selfe, [then] seeming the Lover of any other.

While often played as an out and out joke/tease, the fact that F opens with seven surround phrases suggests that there may be quite a lot of bite accompanying Rosalind's bark.

• overall the speech seems fairly well contained (just 2/10 in the overall thirteen lines), yet there are a two sudden releases, each at the beginning of sentences, which might suggest that certain traditional signs of love which she does not find in Orlando are causing her some distress

• thus the forced calm of the unembellished ending of F #1 is preceded by attacking Orlando for having none of her 'Unckles markes' of love about him

• similarly, F #2 opens with the observation that there is no 'leane cheeke', no 'blew eie' before she can restore an apparent air of self-control for the next unembellished three and a half lines

• and the final, in part emotionally (semicolon) created, surround-phrase simply screams of her disappointment

" : but you are no such man ; "

16/ Rosalind — Love is meerely a madnesse, and I tel you, . . .
17/ Rosalind — No faith, die by Attorney : the poore world . . . .

between 3.2.400 - 427
4.1.94 - 108

Background: Speech #16: accidentally meeting Orlando in the woods, Rosalind embarks on the biggest bluff in her life in an attempt to see him more often.

Speech #17: having succeeded via speech #16 in persuading Orlando to come to the cottage where she and Celia dwell so that she could wash his 'Liver as cleane as a sound sheepes heart' and thus cure him of his love, she now lets loose with several quasi cynical statements as to love, though it's useful to remember that as far as she is concerned she has been abandoned twice by men who purported to love her – her father and her uncle.

Style: both, as part of a three-handed scene
Where: speech #16, somewhere in the woods; **To Whom:** both, Orlando in front of Celia

speech #16, # of Lines: 23   **Probable Timing: 1.10 minutes**
speech #17, # of Lines: 13   **Probable Timing: 0.45 minutes**

Modern Text

16/ Rosalind

1 Love is merely* a madness*, and I tell* you, de-serves as well* a dark* house and a whip* as madmen do; and the reason why they are not so punish'd and cured is, that the △lunacy* is so ordinary* that the whippers are in love too. †

2 {I cured one,} and in this manner.

3
4   He* was to ima-gine me his △love, his △mistress*; and I set him every* day to woo* me.

5   At which time would I, being but a moonish youth, grieve*, be effeminate, changeable, longing and liking, proud, fantastical, apish, shallow, inconstant, full* of tears*, full of smiles; for every passion something, and for no passion truly any thing, as boys* and women are for the most part, cattle of this color*; would now like him, now loathe* him; then entertain* him, then forswear him; now weep* for him, then spit at him; that I drave my △suitor* from his mad humor of love to a living humor of madness*, [which] was, to forswear* the full* stream of [the] world, and to live in a nook* merely* △monastic* . †
    And thus I cur'd him,

6 him, and this way will* I take upon me* to wash your △li-ver as clean* as a sound sheep's* heart, that there shall* not be one spot of △love in't.

First Folio

16/ Rosalind

1 Love is meerely a madnesse, and I tel you, de-serves as wel a darke house, and a whip,ₓ as madmen do ;ₓ and the reason why they are not so punish'd and cured,ₓ is⁺ that the Lunacie is so ordinarie,ₓ that the whippers are in love too : yet I professe curing it by counsel.

2 {I cured one,} and in this manner .

3   Hee was to ima-gine me his Love, his Mistris : ₓ and I set him everie day to woe me.

4   At which time would I, being but a moonish youth, greeve, be effeminate, changeable, longing,ₓ and liking, proud, fantastical, apish, shallow, inconstant, ful of teares, full of smiles ; for everie passion something, and for no passion truly any thing, as boyes and women are for the most part, cattle of this colour : ₓ would now like him, now loath him : ₓ then entertaine him, then forswear him : ₓ now weepe for him, then spit at him ; that I drave my Sutor from his mad humor of love,ₓ to a living humor of madnes, [w] was⁺ to forsweare the ful stream of [ÿ] world, and to live in a nooke meerly Monastick : and thus I cur'd him, and this way wil I take upon mee to wash your Li-ver as cleane as a sound sheepes heart, that there shal not be one spot of Love in't.

Interestingly, F's onrushed F #4 and its orthography **suggests that the idea of how Rosalind will deal with Orlando grows slowly, for it starts unembellished but ends full of passionate release – yet she might not be as confident as the words would suggest, for there are nearly twenty short spellings** (marked by the lowered* in the modern text).

• since the speech represents one of the most important actions in Rosalind's life, for if she succeeds she can see so much more of Orlando without revealing herself, it's not surprising that the opening (F #1-3) is triply highlighted

a/ by the four extra breath-thoughts (marked , ₓ), adding extra details as to how/why lovers are not 'punish'd and cured'

b/ the surround phrases emphasising how she has supposedly cured one other person in love, ' : yet I professe curing it by counsel, ' and the whole F #3, ' . Hee was to imagine me his Love, his Mistris : and I set him everie day to woe me . ', the first highly released (2/1) and the second overtly controlled with short spellings of 'everie' and 'woe'

c/ emphasised by the unembellished short sentence F #2, 'I cured one, and in this manner.'

• in the onrushed F #4, the emotional semicolons mark off three distinct stages of development/release

a/ the opening three lines, describing in general how she behaved (supposedly) as the ever changeable 'moonish youth' are unembellished with the exception of the one word 'teares'

b/ the next four lines (incorporating at least three surround phrases) describing the tremendous opposites she (supposedly) inflicted upon the (supposed) victim, start becoming emotional (0/4)

c/ and then the final summation, of how her 'Sutor' supposedly went to 'live in a nooke meerly Monastick'

{ctd. over}

Modern Text

17/ Rosalind

1 No, faith, die by △attorney. †

2 The poor° world is almost six thousand years° old, and in all this time there was not any° man died in his own° person, *videlicet*, in a love-°cause. †

3 Troilus° had his brains° dash'd out with a Grecian club, yet he did what he° could to die before, and he is one of the patterns° of love.

4 Leander, he would have liv'd many° a fair° year° though Hero had turn'd △nun, if it had not been° for a hot °midsummer° °night ; for, good youth, he went but forth to wash him in the Hel-lespont, and being taken with the cramp° was drown'd△; and the foolish △chroniclers° of that age found it was -

5 Hero of [Sestos].

But these are all lies : men have died from time to time, and worms° have eaten them, but not for love.

7 I would cure you, if you would but call me Rosa-lind, and come every° day to my △cote° and woo° me.

First Folio

17/ Rosalind

1 No⁺ faith, die by Attorney : the poore world is almost six thousand yeeres old, and in all this time there was not anie man died in his owne person $_x$(*videlicet*)$_x$ in a love cause : Troilous had his braines dash'd out with a Grecian club, yet he did what hee could to die before, and he is one of the patternes of love.

2 Leander, he would have liv'd manie a faire yeere though Hero had turn'd Nun; $_x$ if it had not bin for a hot Midsomer-night, ⁺ for⁺ $_x$ (good youth), he went but forth to wash him in the Hel-lespont, and being taken with the crampe, was drown'd, ⁺ and the foolish Chronoclers of that age,$_x$ found it was ⁺ Hero of [Cestos].

3 But these are all lies, ⁺ men have died from time to time, and wormes have eaten them, but not for love.

5 I would cure you, if you would but call me Rosa-lind, and come everie day to my Coat,$_x$ and woe me.

Fascinatingly, F suggests that here Rosalind goes directly against the conventional notion that a speech should start small and end big.

• with Rosalind's opening denial of any male dying for love (not even the traditional epitome 'Troilous'), the speech starts out powerfully (via the opening surround phrase) and emotionally (3/7 in F #1's five and a half lines)

• and then dismissing Leander, the other icon of supposed male fidelity, the speech becomes highly intellectual (8/4 in six and a half lines of F #2), though the dismissal of the accident of a 'hot Midsomer-night' is heralded by the only (emotional) semicolon in the speech, and the finish of the sentence is accompanied by two F only extra breath-thoughts (marked , $_x$) – as if she need the extra breaths to control her intellectual anger/defiance/scorn/amusement

• and then all energy seems leached out of her for the final summation of 'these are all lies', for Rosalind's final sentence is very quiet in comparison with what has gone on before (0/1, F #3)

and how she can do the same for Orlando, is offered via a pronounced and extended flourish (4/7 in the final six lines of F #4)

• and, again understandable given the enormity of the decision he is about to make in accepting or rejecting her offer, so her final 'I would cure you' is a wondrous mixture of controlled intellect (2/0, F #5), unembellished phrases, and a single extra-breath – the combination underlying and undermining her apparent outward calm

#'s 18 - 20: SILVIUS' THOUGHTS ON LOVE

18/ Silvius   Oh Corin, that thou knew'st how I do love her.   between 2.4.25 -43

Background: At his first on-stage appearance it's obvious that the shepherd Silvius has only thoughts for Phebe, the woman who 'scornes' him.

Style: as part of a two-handed scene in front of three hidden watchers

Where: unspecified, within the forest of Arden   **To Whom:** the older shepherd Corin, in front of the hidden Rosalind, Celia and Touchstone

# of Lines: 16   **Probable Timing: 0.50 minutes**

After the explosive two-word opening 'Oh Corin', the speech is startling in that there is hardly any excess, as if Silvius is being extraordinarily quiet in trying to explain his deepest feelings (an unquiet sense of quiet perhaps) (2/4 in the first seventeen lines of the eighteen line speech).

- that this may be a fine example of irrational rationality can be seen in what most modern texts regard as F's peculiar sentence structure, for though calm in utterance, the F speech suggests great stress in putting the thoughts together

- Silvius opens with a short 'nothing-more-to-be-said' declaration of love (F1, 1/1)

- which is followed by an onrushed second sentence denying Corin's ability, though once 'as true a lover', to understand what he, Silvius, is going through (0/3 in the seven lines of F #2)

- and then come what most modern texts regard as three ungrammatical sentences, each itemising different degrees of his own 'ridiculous' actions - remembering 'the slightest folly'; wearing listeners with his 'Mistris praise'; breaking 'from companie/Abruptly' – as Silvius is about to do: and the fact that these are set as separate sentences allows for each to have a much greater separate impact, much more than that allowed by most modern texts which reset all three sentences into one generalised whole (mt. #4)

- and the final short sentence, common to both sets of texts, suddenly allows Phebe's name to be mentioned for the first time in the speech, which Silvius does with fervent repetition (3/0, F #6)

First Folio

18/ Silvius

1   Oh Corin, that thou knew'st how I do love her. [+]

2   {But} , being old, thou canst not {ψ};
     Though in thy youth thou wast as true a lover
     As ever sigh'd upon a midnight pillow:
     But if thy love were ever like to mine,
     As sure I thinke did never man love so : [x]
     How many actions most ridiculous,[x]
     Hast thou beene drawne to by thy fantasie?

3   If thou remembrest not the slightest folly,[,x]
     That ever love did make thee run into,
     Thou hast not lov'd.

4   Or if thou hast not sat as I doe now,
     [Wearing] thy hearer in thy Mistris praise,
     Thou hast not lov'd.

5   Or if thou hast not broke from companie,[x]
     Abruptly[+] as my passion now makes me, [↑]
     Thou hast not lov'd.

6   O Phebe, Phebe, Phebe. [+]

Modern Text

18/ Silvius

1   Oh Corin, that thou knew'st how I do love her !:

2   {But} , being old, thou canst not {ψ};
     Though in thy youth thou wast as true a lover
     As ever sigh'd upon a midnight pillow. [†]
     But if thy love were like to mine -
     As sure I think* did never man love so -
     How many actions most ridiculous
     Hast thou been* drawn* to by thy fantasy*,?

3   If thou rememb'rest not the slightest folly
     That ever love did make thee run into,
     Thou hast not lov'd; ◊

4   Or if thou hast not sat as I do* now,
     [Wearing] thy hearer in thy ᴧmistress* praise,
     Thou hast not lov'd; ◊

5   Or if thou hast not broke from company*
     Abruptly, as my passion now makes me,
     Thou hast not lov'd.

6   O Phebe, Phebe, Phebe !

19/ Silvius — Sweet Phebe doe not scorne me, do not Phebe — 3.5.1‑7

Background: The love-wounded Silvius pleads with Phebe for some form of acknowledgment, presumably for the umpteenth time, though this is the first time it has been seen on-stage.

Style: as the opening to a two-handed scene

Where: somewhere in the woods, near the cottage of Rosalind and Celia

To Whom: Phebe

# of Lines: 7 **Probable Timing:** 0.25 minutes

First Folio

19/ Silvius

1 Sweet Phebe doe not scorne me, do not Phebe [+]
Say that you love me not, but say not so
In bitternesse ; the common executioner [+]
Whose heart th'accustom'd sight of death makes hard [+]
Falls not the axe upon the humbled neck,
But first begs pardon : will you sterner be
[Then] he that dies and lives by bloody drops?

19/ Silvius

As with the previous speech, it seems that Silvius is quiet in his expression of love, for yet again this short speech displays virtually no signs of extra release save for the mention of Phebe's name (twice) and the emotion behind the words 'doe not scorne me' and 'bitternesse': five of the seven lines remain unembellished, **especially notable is the extended four and a half line passage that ends the speech.**

• the emotional semicolon leads to one of the most disturbing of his continual doom-laden romantic images, 'the common executioner'

• the speech ending surround phrase expands this image ' : will you sterner be/Then he that dies and lives by bloody drops?'

Modern Text

19/ Silvius

1 Sweet Phebe do* not scorn* me, do not Phebe;
Say that you love me not, but say not so
In bitternesse* . [†]
The common executioner,
Whose heart th'accustom'd sight of death makes hard,
Falls not the axe upon the humbled neck
But first begs pardon. [†]
Will you sterner be

3 [Than] he that dies and lives by bloody drops?

20/ Silvius — So holy, and so perfect is my love, — 3.5.99‑104

Background: Phebe has fallen in love at first sight with 'Ganymede', the disguised-as-a-boy Rosalind, and since Silvius can talk so well about love, she decides to 'endure' his company and 'employ thee too', provided that Silvius realises he must not 'looke for further recompence/Then thine owne gladnesse, that thou art employed.'. This is his response.

Style: as part of a two-handed scene

Where: somewhere in the woods, near the cottage of Rosalind and Celia

To Whom: Phebe

# of Lines: 6 **Probable Timing:** 0.20 minutes

First Folio

20/ Silvius

1 So holy, [x] and so perfect is my love,
And I in such a poverty of grace,
That I shall thinke it a most plenteous crop
To gleane the broken eares after the man
That the maine harvest reapes : loose now and then
A scattred smile, and that Ile live upon.

Once more the quietness of Silvius underscores the absolute depth of his love, yet . . .

• . . . though the beauty of the first line of the speech, starting with the dismissive self-diminishing unembellished 'And I in such a poverty of grace,' should not be denied . . .

• . . . it is somewhat undermined by the dismissive self-diminishing unembellished 'And I in such a poverty of grace,' especially when this is in turn followed by the even more self-denying two and half line emotional reference to his being satisfied to 'gleane the broken eares' (0/5)

• and though the unembellished finale of his being content to live upon 'A scattred smile' is undoubtedly genuine, the continual self-abasement may be a little wearing to all who hear him

Modern Text

20/ Silvius

1 So holy and so perfect is my love,
And I in such a poverty of grace,
That I shall think* it a most plenteous crop
To glean* the broken ears* after the man
That the main* harvest reaps* . [†]
Loose now and then

2 A scatt'red smile, and that I'll live upon.

#'s 21 - 23: PHEBE IN LOVE

21/ Phebe   **I would not be thy executioner,**   between 3.58 - 34

Background: Until meeting the disguised Rosalind (speeches #22-3 immediately following) Phebe seems to have a healthy scepticsim whenever love is expressed in exaggerated hyperbole. Here is her factual response to Silvius' plea not to be sterner than an executioner (speech #19 above).

Style: as part of a two-handed scene

Where: somewhere in the woods, near the cottage of Rosalind and Celia   **To Whom:** Silvius

# of Lines: 23   **Probable Timing: 1.10 minutes**

Modern Text

21/ Phebe

1 I would not be thy executioner* ;
   I fly* thee for I would not injure thee . †

2 Thou tell'st me there is murder in mine eye :
   'Tis pretty, sure, and very probable,
   That eyes, that are the frail'st and softest things,
   Who shut their coward gates on atomies* ,
   Should be called tyrants, butchers, murtherers!

3 Now I do* frown* on thee with all my heart,
   And if mine eyes can wound, now let them kill thee . †

4 Now counterfeit to swound ;   why, now fall down* ,
   Or if thou canst not, ^O* , for shame,
   Lie* not, to say mine eyes are murtherers! †

5 Now show the wound mine eye hath made in thee,
   Scratch thee but with a pin, and there remains*
   Some scar* of it ;   ^lean* [but] upon a rush,
   The ^cicatrice and capable impressure
   Thy palm* some moment keeps* ;   but now mine eyes,
   Which I have darted at thee, hurt thee not,
   Nor I am sure there is no force in eyes
   That can doe[any] hurt .

6 Come not thou near* me ; and {if} that time {should come},
   Afflict me with thy mocks* , pity* me not,
   As till that time I shall not pity* thee.

First Folio

21/ Phebe

1 I would not be thy executioner, +
   I flye thee, for I would not injure thee :
   Thou tell'st me there is murder in mine eye +

2 'Tis pretty+ sure, and very probable,
   That eyes+ that are the frailst,x and softest things,
   Who shut their coward gates on atomyes,
   Should be called tyrants, butchers, murtherers . +

   Now I doe frowne on thee with all my heart,
   And if mine eyes can wound, now let them kill thee :
   Now counterfeit to swound,+ why+ now fall downe,
   Or if thou canst not, oh + for shame, for shame,
   Lye not, to say mine eyes are murtherers : +
   Now shew the wound mine eye hath made in thee,
   Scratch thee but with a pin, and there remaines
   Some scarre of it : x Leane [ ] ² upon a rush +
   The Cicatrice and capable impressure
   Thy palme some moment keepes ;x   but now mine eyes +
   Which I have darted at thee, hurt thee not,
   Nor I am sure there is no force in eyes
   That can doe [ ]hurt .

3 Come not thou neere me : x and {if} that time {should come},
   Afflict me with thy mockes, pitty me not,
   As till that time I shall not pitty thee.

It seems that most of the time Phebe can answer Silvius with relative ease, for though, in comparison to most modern texts, F's first two sentences are onrushed (F #1 usually being split into two, and F #2 in three), the dismissal of each of his points is handled by a very logical colon, with little or no extra release, save for a couple of ridiculing moments.

* thus, in her opening denial of being his 'executioner' and that eyes should be called 'tyrants, butchers, murtherers', she hardly breaks into a sweat (0/2 in the seven lines of F #1)

* mocking his idea of her being able to kill him because 'Now I doe frowne' releases some momentary emotion (0/2 the first line of F #2), and then she relaxes into a calm unembellished second line: calling him out as a liar if he cannot be so killed raises a little emotion once more (0/3 in the next four lines), though whether the emotions are amusement or annoyance is up to each actress to explore

* and then, as she demands to see 'the wound mine eye hath made in thee' since even the tiniest of things (a pin scratch or leaning on a rush will leave a 'scarre' or some 'impressure'), the releases become slightly more marked (2/5 in the next four and a half lines)

* but this momentary outburst subsides in the final all but unembellished three lines that end F #2, with only the final 'doe' in 'doe hurt' showing any release

* but, by her final monosyllabic surround phrase command ' . Come not thou neere me : ' and ensuing invitation for 'mockes', it seems as if something has given way, for in comparison to what has gone on before the whole sentence is quite emotional (0/4 in F #3's three lines)

---

² some modern texts add 'but', thus creating a ten syllable line, Ff do not set the extra word

22/ Rosalind   **And why I pray you?   who might be your mother**   between 3.5.35 - 80

Background: Perhaps on edge because she cannot reveal herself to her just-once-more-encountered heart-throb Orlando, and invited by Corin to see how dismissively Phebe responds to Sylvius' love vows, Rosalind, still disguised as the boy Ganymede, accepts his invitation, commenting that 'The sight of Lovers feedeth those in love'. However, once there she quickly interrupts the two country folk, unable to stop herself from being 'a busy actor in their play', presumably not being 'fed' particularly well.

Style: as part of a three handed scene with two others actively watching

Where: somewhere in the woods, near the cottage of Rosalind and Celia   **To Whom:** initially Phebe for Sylvius' benefit, and also Silvius in front of Celia and Corin

# of Lines: 34   **Probable Timing: 1.40 minutes**

Modern Text

22/ Rosalind

1 And why, I pray you? †

2   Who might be your mother,
That you insult, exult, and all at once,
Over the wretched? †

3   What though you have* no beauty -
As, by my faith, I see no more in you
[Than] without ᴬcandle may go* ᴅdark* to bed -
Must you be therefore proud and pitiless*?

4 Why, what means* this?   why do you look* on me?

5 I see no more in you [than] in the ordinary
Ofᴬnature's sale-work*?

6   ᴬOds my little life,
I think* she means* to tangle my eyes*, too! †

7 No, faith, proud ᴬmistress*, hope not after it . †

8 'Tis not your inky*, brows*, your black* silk* hair*,
Your bugle eye °balls, nor your cheek* of cream*
That can entame my spirits to your worship*. †

9 You foolish ᴬshepherd*, wherefore do you follow her,
Like foggy ᴬsouth, puffing with wind* and rain* . †

10 You are a thousand times a properer man
[Than] she a woman.

11   'Tis such fools* as you
That makes the world full of ill-favor'd* children. † ᵗ

12 'Tis not her glass*, but you that flatters her,
And out of you she sees herself* more proper
[Than] any of her lineaments can show her. †

13 But, ᴬmistress*, know yourself*, down* on your knees,
And thank* heaven, fasting, for a good mans love;
For I must tell you friendly in your ear*,

First Folio

22/ Rosalind

1 And why⁺ I pray you?   who might be your mother⁺
That you insult, exult, and all at once⁺
Over the wretched?   what though you hav no beauty⁺
As⁺ by my faith, I see no more in you
[Then] without Candle may goe darke to bed : ˣ
Must you be therefore prowd and pittilesse?

2 Why⁺ what meanes this?   why do you looke on me?

3 I see no more in you [then] in the ordinary
Of Natures sale-worke?

4   'ods my little life,
I thinke she meanes to tangle my eies too : ⁺
No⁺ faith⁺ proud Mistresse, hope not after it,
'Tis not your inkie browes, your blacke silke haire,
Your bugle eye-balls, nor your cheeke of creame
That can entame my spirits to your worship :
You foolish Shepheard, wherefore do you follow her⁺
Like foggy South, puffing with winde and raine,
You are a thousand times a properer man
[Then] she a woman.

5   'Tis such fooles as you
That makes the world full of ill-favourd children :
'Tis not her glasse, but you that flatters her,
And out of you she sees her selfe more proper
[Then] any of her lineaments can show her :
But⁺ Mistris, know your selfe, downe on your knees ⁺
And thanke heaven, fasting, for a good mans love ;
For I must tell you friendly in your eare,

While Rosalind seems to be verbally in charge throughout, there are moments (notably F #2 to the opening lines of F #4) where F's orthography and or sentence structure suggests that Rosalind may at times be quite disturbed, especially when unembellished calm quickly gives way to wholesale emotional release.

• surprisingly, Rosalind opens in a very controlled way, the first four lines (challenging Phebe as to her over-weaning sense of self-esteem) being completely unembellished: however, Rosalind may not be quite as calm as might appear, moving somewhat faster than most modern texts suggest with their added commas (marked ⁺) and opening with a short monosyllabic surround phrase

• and the calm certainly does not last, for F #1's ending two line attack on Phebe for being 'prowd' and 'pittilesse' (this enhanced by being set in a surround phrase) and an attack on her supposed dark hair and/or skin ('Than without Candle may goe darke to bed') is strongly emotional (1/4)

• from the short surround phrase and the release of emotion in F #2 through the first line and half of F #4 (1/5 in just four lines), it is clear that Phebe's sudden interest in the disguised Rosalind is a great surprise – though whether Rosalind handles it with amusement or with some difficulty is up to each actress to decide

• whatever the surprise, the dismissal of Phebe item by item ('browes', 'haire', 'eye-balls', 'cheeke') becomes strongly emotional – amused or genuine irritation is again a case of individual actress choice (1/7 in just four lines)

• the dismissal of Silvius as a 'foolish Shepheard' increases a notch, being abruptly passionate (2/3 in just two lines), though Rosalind does take a moment of unembellished self-control to praise him as a 'properer man' to end the sentence, though whether out of sympathy or to irk Phebe is again a matter of choice

• and then Rosalind's emotions take over yet again as she attacks initially both Phebe and Sylvius ('fooles as you', again via a surround phrase) and then Silvius for flattering her, finishing with yet another attack on Phebe for rejecting 'a good mans love' (1/8 the first seven and a half lines of F #5)

• yet the ultimate of insults to Phebe ('Sell when you can' and advice to take the 'offer' of Silvius) is completely unembellished, as if either this was spoken very quietly just for Phebe to hear (not really likely since all Rosalind's earlier

14 Sell when you can, you are not for all markets. †
15 Cry the man mercy, love him, take his offer;
Foul* is most foul*, being foul* to be a scoffer.
16 So take her to thee, △shepherd*. †
17 [Fare you well.]
18 Shepherd*, ply her hard. †
19 Come, Sister. †
20 Shepherdess*, look* on him better
And be not proud; though all the world could see,
None could be so abus'd in sight as he*.
21 Come, to our flock*. †

attacks have been so public) or it comes from a very personal place

- and then her emotions break through once more for the final instructions to both Silvius and Phebe (3/9 the last six lines of the speech)

- the setting of F #6-7 suggests that something awkward may be happening for Rosalind, and she doesn't escape scot-free: for though the opening surround phrase of F #6 ('. Shepheard ply her hard :') is only to be expected, the surround-phrase command ': Come Sister :' certainly is not, and the short monosyllabic F #7 ending the speech suggests that an escape may be necessary – given the following speech (#23) of the totally love-smitten Phebe, perhaps she has ignored Rosalind's harsh words and is still trying to 'entame' Rosalind's spirits and 'tangle' her 'eies' by her 'looke', as described so much earlier in the speech (F #4 and #2)

Sell when you can, you are not for all markets:
Cry the man mercy, love him, take his offer, +
Foule is most foule, being foule to be a scoffer.
So take her to thee + Shepheard, [fareyouwell.]
6 Shepheard + ply her hard:
Come + Sister: Shepheardesse, looke on him better
And be not proud, + though all the world could see,
None could be so abus'd in sight as hee.
7 Come, to our flocke, [3]

23/ Phebe **Thinke not I love him, though I ask for him,** 3.5.109 - 135

Background: Realising that Phebe is more than somewhat taken with her disguised self as the boy Ganymede, Rosalind has now fled the scene, followed by Celia and Corin. Phebe now tries to find out from Silvius just who this young 'man' might be, and it's obvious from the outset that though her first line is an order (presumably to prevent Silvius from afflicting her 'with thy mockes' as she offered should she ever fall in love - speech #21 above), it is also a lie.

Style: as part of a two-handed scene

Where: somewhere in the woods, near the cottage of Rosalind and Celia **To Whom:** Silvius

# of Lines: 27 **Probable Timing: 1.30 minutes**

Modern Text

23/ Phebe
1 Think* not I love him, though I ask for him;
'Tis but a peevish boy - yet he talks* well -
But what care I for words? †
2 Yet words do well
When he that speaks* them pleases those that hear*. †
3 It is a pretty youth - not very pretty* -
But sure he's* proud - and yet his pride becomes him. †
4 He'll* make a proper man. †
5 The best thing in him
Is his complexion; and faster [than] his tongue
Did make offense, his eye did heal* it up. †

Given the circumstances, it is not surprising that the speech is so emotional (4/20) nor the opening onrushed love-smitten assessment of the 'boy' (F #1 = mt. #1-6); and the onrushed speech ending decision to contact him again for the flimsiest of trumped up reasons (F #3 = mt. #9-11). And, as with several characters in the play (notably Jaques and Touchstone), it is the swing back and forth between two different styles of release which reveals the workings of her mind (rather than the mental quibbling in the case of Touchstone at least).

- the contrasting patterns seem to be between a released moment immediately followed by an unembellished one, as if she were trying either to recover from the embarrassment of the first or so taken with the ensuing image she has to stay calm to maintain some degree of public self-control, as with line six

"But sure hee's proud, and yet his pride becomes him"

or sometimes a quiet thought will lead to a sudden moment of excessive release, as if the followed up image is even more emotionally striking, as with

First Folio

23/ Phebe
1 Thinke not I love him, though I ask for him, +
'Tis but a peevish boy, yet he talkes well,
But what care I for words? yet words do well
When he that speakes them pleases those that heare:
It is a pretty youth, not very prettie,
But sure hee's proud, and yet his pride becomes him;
Hee'll make a proper man: the best thing in him
Is his complexion: x and faster [then] his tongue
Did make offence, his eye did heale it up:

{ctd. over}

[3] F1 - 2 set a comma (possibly as if Rosalind is in a great hurry to get away and doesn't finish her speech properly), F3/most modern texts print a period

6 He is not very tall - yet for his years* he's* tall ;
His leg is but so so - and yet 'tis well ;
There was a pretty redness* in his lip,
A little riper and more lusty* red
[Than]that mix'd in his cheek* ; 'twas just the difference
Betwixt the constant red and mingled ᴬdamask* .

7 There be some women, Silvius, had they mark'd him
In parcels* as I did, would have gone near*
To fall in love with him; but for my part
I love him not, nor hate him not; and yet
[I] ᴬhave more cause to hate him [than] to love him,
8 For what had he to do* to chide at me?

9 He said mine eyes were black and my hair* black* ,
And, now I am rememb'red, scorn'd at me. †

10 I marvel* why I answer'd not again* ,
But that's all one; omittance is no quittance . †

11 I'll write to him a very taunting* ᵃletter,
And thou shalt bear* it ; wilt thou, Silvius

---

line ten
"He is not very tall, yet for his yeeres hee's tall'
and the indignancy of F #3's opening line
"He said mine eyes were black, and my haire blacke"

• both sets of onrushed sentences (F #1 and #3) reveal a young lady capable both of very sustained thought, with an ability to build quite extended complex details for herself (the love imagery of F #1), as well as an ability to make very determined decisions for herself once her mind is set, as in F #3's quick last line adding Silvius into the mix of contacting Rosalind, with a fine sense of how to manipulate when needed, as the final gentle request (after so much earlier scorn) shows

• the onrushed F #1's surround phrases point to her besottedness with 'his' present and potential physicality, especially the emotional opening involved in
" ; Hee'll make a proper man : the best thing in him/Is his complexion : and faster then his tongue/Did make offence, his eye did heale it up : /He is not very tall, yet for his yeeres hee's tall : / His leg is but so so, and yet 'tis well :"

leading to the wonderful description of the 'rednesse in his lip' as the finest spun silk possible. viz.
" : 'twas just the difference/Betwixt the constant red, and mingled Damaske . "

• while the later surround phrases point to her attempt to save face, as with F #2's
" : but for my part/I love him not, nor hate him not :"
and F #3's response to his insults about her physical appearance
" : I marvell why I answer'd not againe,/But that's all one : omittance is no quittance :"

He is not very tall, yet for his yeeres hee's tall :
His leg is but so so, and yet 'tis well : ₓ
There was a pretty rednesse in his lip,
A little riper, and more lustie red
[Then]that mixt in his cheeke : ₓ 'twas just the difference
Betwixt the constant red,ₓ and mingled Damaske.

There be some women + Silvius, had they markt him
In parcells as I did, would have gone neere
To fall in love with him : but for my part
I love him not, nor hate him not : ₓ and yet

2 [ ] Have more cause to hate him [then] to love him,
For what had he to doe to chide at me?

3 He said mine eyes were black,ₓ and my haire blacke,
And + now I am remembred, scorn'd at me :
I marvell why I answer'd not againe,
But that's all one : ₓ omittance is no quittance :
Ile write to him a very tanting Letter,
And thou shalt beare it, + wilt thou + Silvius

#'s 24 - 27: The Clowne Touchstone On Love

24/ Clowne   I remember when I was in love,   2.4.46 - 56

Background: The first thing the three escapes from Duke Fredricke's court stumble across once they've reached the safety of the forest of Arden is the young shepherd Silvius expressing his love for Phebe to Corin (speech #18 above). This moves Rosalind to express her passion about her unreturned love, which in turn triggers this response from Touchstone, though whether he is in earnest or simply mocking both Rosalind and Silvius is up to each production to decide.

Style: as part of a three-handed scene, with a fourth person not overhearing also on stage

Where: somewhere in the forest of Arden   To Whom: Rosalind and Celia, with Corin also on-stage but unaware of their presence

# of Lines: 10   Probable Timing: 0.35 minutes

Modern Text

24/ Clowne

{ψ}

1   I remember when I was in love, I broke my sword upon a stone, and bid him take that for coming* a night to Jane Smile ;   and I remember the kis-sing* of her batler and the △cow's* dugs that her pretty* chopp'd* hands had milk'd ; and I remember the wooing of a peascod instead of her, from whom I took* two cods, and giving her them again* , said with weeping tears* , "△Wear* these for my sake" . †

2   We* that are true △lo-vers, run* into strange capers ; but as all is mortal* in nature, so is all nature in love mortal* in folly.

First Folio

24/ Clowne

{ψ}

1   I remember when I was in love, I broke my sword upon a stone, and bid him take that for comming a night to Jane Smile, + and I remember the kis-sing of her batler, and the Cowes dugs that her prettie chopt hands had milk'd ; and I remember the wooing of a peascod instead of her, from whom I tooke two cods, and giving her them againe, said with weeping teares, weare these for my sake : wee that are true Lo-vers, runne into strange capers ; but as all is mortall in nature, so is all nature in love,ₓ mortall in folly.

- whether mocking or no, Touchstone's only surround line " : wee that are true Lovers, runne into strange capers : " strangely echoes the love philosophy of the just departed Silvius

- Touchstone opens quite quietly with two unembellished phrases, which turns to passion at the first mention of 'Jane Smile' (3/2)

- following the first semicolon, the reverie of the 'peascod' (whether true or false) becomes purely emotional (0/4 the next three lines)

- which heightens in intensity for the final sententious maxim (1/4 the last two lines)

25/ Clowne — That is another simple sinne in you, to bring the — 3.2.78 - 85

Background: Wanting to talk but with very few lively minds available, Touchstone is forced to talk 'Philosophy' with the straightforward and honest 'shepheard', Corin, whose 'philosophy' (speech #31 below) is so uncomplicated as to leave Touchstone no choice but to tease him, especially after Corin's flurry of righteous self-definition ends with 'and the greatest of my pride, is to see my Ewes graze, & my Lambes sucke'. The following is in direct reply.

Style: as part of a two-handed scene

Where: somewhere in the woods near the cottage of Rosalind and Celia   **To Whom:** Corin

# of Lines: 8   **Probable Timing: 0.30 minutes**

Modern Text

25/ Clowne

1 That is another simple sin* in you, to bring the
△ewes and the △rams* together; and to offer to get your
living, by the copulation of △cattle ;   to be bawd to a △bel-
weather, and to betray a she*-△lamb* of a twelve△month
to a crooked-pated old* △cuckoldly △ram*, out of all
reasonable match.

2   If thou beest not damn'd for this, the
devil* himself* will have no shepherds ;   I cannot see else
how thou shouldst scape.

First Folio

25/ Clowne

1 That is another simple sinne in you, to bring the
Ewes and the Rammes together, and to offer to get your
living, by the copulation of Cattle, + to be bawd to a Bel-
weather, and to betray a shee-Lambe of a twelvemonth
to a crooked-pated olde Cuckoldly Ramme + out of all
reasonable match.

2   If thou bee'st not damn'd for this, the
divell himselfe will have no shepherds, + I cannot see else
how thou shouldst scape.

- Touchstone's description of Corin's 'simple sinne' shows no mercy in what, to Corin, must be a bewildering attack of both intellect and emotion (7/8 in the five lines of F #1)

- which is followed by an emotional summation (0/3, the first two phrases of F #2)

- and then, in the true manner of a fine tease by a splendid Clowne/Foole, the last phrase is almost thrown away in its unembellished nonchalance

---

26/ Clowne — Praised be the Gods, for thy foulnesse ; — between 3.3.40 - 63

Background: Touchstone too has fallen in love, though perhaps more accurately in lust, the object of his desires being Audrey the goat-girl, though it seems he's going to have to marry her to get what he wants. Having reassured Audrey that the marriage plans are in hand, the remainder of the to-be-heard-by-the-audience-only comments forms a traditional 'male debating the possibilities of being cuck-holded' (i.e. his wife being unfaithful to him) speech.

Style: initially as part of a two-handed scene, and then solo

Where: somewhere in the woods, near the cottage of Rosalind and Celia   **To Whom:** initially Audrey, and then the audience via direct address

# of Lines: 20   **Probable Timing: 1.00 minutes**

Modern Text

26/ Clowne

1 {ψ} Praised be the △gods for thy foulness*! slut-
tishness* may come hereafter* . {to Audrey}

2   But be it as it may be*,
I will* marry* thee ; and to that end I have been* with Sir
Oliver Mar*text, the △vicar of the next village, who hath
promis'd to meet* me in this place of the △forest* and to
couple us.

First Folio

26/ Clowne

1 {ψ}Praised be the Gods,ₓ for thy foulnesse; + slut-
tishnesse may come heereafter.

2   But be it,ₓ as it may bee,
I wil marrie thee :ₓ and to that end, I have bin with Sir
Oliver Mar-text, the Vicar of the next village, who hath
promis'd to meete me in this place of the Forrest,ₓ and to
couple us.

That Touchstone is more than somewhat disturbed can be seen in the struggle between emotional release and unembellished lines, with the use of so many surround phrases showing how deeply he is exploring his potential fate.

- after the opening emotional surround phrase delight that his erotic hopes may soon be satisfied (F #1, 1/3, the emotion heightened by the semicolon), most of the remaining surround phrases point more to Touchstone's fears of marriage and of being cuckolded therein, as with the short-spelled ending of

  ". But be it, as it may bee, I wil marrie thee : "

3 {aside} A man may, if he were of a fearful heart, stagger in this attempt; for here* we* have no △temple but the wood, no assembly but horn*-beasts.
4 But what though?
5 Courage!
6 As horns* are odious, they are necessary*.
7 It is said, "△Many a man knows* no end of his goods". †
8 Right! △many a man has good △horns*, and knows no end of them.
9 Well, that is the dowry* of his wife, 'tis none of his own* getting. †
10 Horns*? even so. †
11 Poor* men alone? †
12 No, no, the noblest △deer* hath them as huge as the △rascal*. †
13 Is the single man therefore bless'd*?
14 △town* is more worthier [than] a village, so is the forehead of a married man more honorable* [than] the bare brow of a △bachelor*; and by how much defense is better [than] no skill, by so much is a horn* more precious [than] to want.

". A man may if he were of a fearful heart, stagger in this attempt : "
". It is said, many a man knowes no end of his goods ; right :
Many a man has good Hornes, and knows no end of them. "
the first two phrases of the final set heightened by another emotional semicolon

• while the four surround phrases that compose F #8 illustrate his chop-logic attempts to make the best of things
"Well that is the dowrie of his wife, 'tis none of his owne getting ; hornes, even so poore men alone : No, no, the noblest Deere hath them as huge as the Rascall : Is the single man therefore blessed ?"

• while the three consecutive short sentences (F #4+5 unembellished, and F #6 almost so) point to his attempts to bolster himself to go through with the marriage
"But what though ? Courage. As hornes are odious, they are necessarie."

• after the opening emotion (1/3, F #1), the details of who will marry them, and when, becomes (rarely for Touchstone) essentially factual (5/2, F #2), his awkwardness heightened by the three extra breath thoughts (marked , x) that break up his explanation

• the exploration of 'hornes' is a mixture of unembellished and almost unembellished lines (fear perhaps) and emotion (3/9, F #3 to the first two lines of F #8)

• and the chop-logic correlation that since the 'noblest Deere hath' 'hornes', therefore to stay single is a blessing, leading to the extra (unnecessary if he were really convinced) reinforcement that 'the forehead of a married man' equates to the nobility of the 'wall'd Towne' becomes passionate (6/5, the last two lines of F #8 and F #9)

3 A man may+ if he were of a fearful heart, stagger in this attempt : x for heere wee have no Temple but the wood, no assembly but horne-beasts.
4 But what though?
5 Courage. +
6 As hornes are odious, they are necessarie.
7 It is said, many a man knowes no end of his goods; right : + Many a man has good Hornes, and knows no end of them.
8 Well + that is the dowrie of his wife, 'tis none of his owne getting; hornes, + even so poore men alone : No, no, the noblest Deere hath them as huge as the Rascall : Is the single man therefore blessed?
9 No, as a wall'd Towne is more worthier [then] a village, so is the forehead of a married man,x more honourable [then] the bare brow of a Batcheller : x and by how much defence is better [then] no skill, by so much is a horne more precious [then] to want.

27/ Clowne   **Wil {I} be married, {Sir}?**   between 3.3.78 - 94

Background: Jaques, one of Duke Senior's more worldly-wise and wearied followers, cannot believe that Touchstone intends to be married, especially by the dreadful hedgepriest that Touchstone has managed to dredge up (Sir Oliver Mar-text, whose name should explain all). Touchstone succinctly explains to Jaques the 'why's' of both marriage and especially by this particular cleric.

Style: as one-on-one in front of a small group who would be interested if they happened to hear

To Whom: Jaques, with Audrey and Sir Oliver Mar-text on-stage too, but not particularly close

Where: somewhere in the woods, probably near Duke Senior's camp

# of Lines: 7   **Probable Timing: 0.25 minutes**

Modern Text	First Folio
27/ Clowne	**27/ Clowne**
1 Will* {I} be married, {^sir}?	1 Wil {I} be married, {Sir}?
2 As the ^ox* hath his bow, sir, the horse his curb, and the ^falcon her bells*, so man hath his desires; and as ^pigeons bill, so wedlock* would be nibbling*.	2 As the Oxe hath his bow+ sir, the horse his curb, and the Falcon her bels, so man hath his desires, + and as Pigeons bill, so wedlocke would be nibling.
3 {And} I were better to be* married of him [than]of another, for he is not like to marry* me well*; and not being well* married, it will* be a good excuse for me hereafter* to leave my wife.	3 {And} I were better to bee married of him [then] of another, for he is not like to marrie me wel: x and not being wel married, it wil be a good excuse for me heereafter+ to leave my wife.

• given the shortness of the first sentence, it might be that Touchstone can hardly voice the possibility of marriage, while the occasional short spellings ('Wil', 'bels', 'marrie me wel', 'wel' and 'wil' suggest that Touchstone may be trying to speak quietly so Audrey – his 'intended' – does not hear

• the setting up of why he wishes to be (not 'wel') married is handled intellectually rather than emotionally (4/2, F #2)

• however, the final reasoning that later he will be able 'heereafter to leave my wife' is totally emotional (0/2, F #3)

• while the speech's only colon (penultimate line of F #3) leads to the wonderful chop-logic out of which so much of Touchstone's wit, as well as beliefs and actions, are born

As You Like It / 269

#'s 28 - 31: THE COUNTRY LIFE AS SEEN BY THE COUNTRY AND CITY FOLK

28/ Duke Senior   Now my Coe-mates, and brothers in exile :   2.1.1-17

Background: This is the first speech in the play for the exiled Duke Senior, spoken to some of his loyal followers who chose voluntary exile with him. Given that it is winter, the speech is self-explanatory. One note: the implication of 'Coe-mates', the compound noun in the opening line, suggests a social equality rarely seen in any other Shakespeare play save perhaps the 'Crispin-Crispian' speech of Henry V.

Style: group address

Where: at his encampment in the woods   **To Whom:** his followers, including Amyens

# of Lines: 17   **Probable Timing: 0.55 minutes**

Modern Text

28/ Duke Senior

1   Now, my △co*-mates and brothers in exile,
    Hath not old custom* made this life more sweet *
    [Than] that of painted pomp*?
                        Are not these woods

2   More free from peril* [than] the envious △court?

3   Here* feel* we not the penalty* of Adam,
    The season's difference, as the △icy* fang*
    And churlish chiding of the winter's wind*,
    Which when it bites and blows* upon my body
    Even till I shrink* with cold, I smile and say
    "This is no flattery: these are counsellors
    That feelingly persuade* me what I am." †

4   Sweet* are the uses of adversity*,
    Which like the toad, ugly* and venomous,
    Wears* yet a precious △jewel* in his head ;
    And this our life, exempt from public* haunt,
    Finds* tongues in trees, books* in the running brooks* ,
    Sermons in stones, and good in every thing.

First Folio

28/ Duke Senior

1   Now + my Coe-mates,ₓ and brothers in exile :   x
    Hath not old custome made this life more sweete
    [Then] that of painted pompe?
                        Are not these woods

2   More free from perill [then] the envious Court?

3   Heere feele we not the penaltie of Adam,
    The seasons difference, as the Icie phange
    And churlish chiding of the winters winde,
    Which when it bites and blowes upon my body
    Even till I shrinke with cold, I smile,ₓ and say
    This is no flattery: these are counsellors
    That feelingly perswade me what I am :
    Sweet are the uses of adversitie +
    Which like the toad, ougly and venemous,
    Weares yet a precious Jewell in his head :   x
    And this our life exempt + from publike haunt,
    Findes tongues in trees, bookes in the running brookes,
    Sermons in stones, and good in every thing.

Given that the Duke is often played as a quiet academic, the relative lack of intellectual release in the following (either capitals or colons) may be somewhat surprising (7/24), and could suggest a much more complete man than seen in many productions.

• given the enormously surprising non-hierarchical almost-communist-in its-equality content ('Coe-mates' and 'brothers'), it seems only right that the first line is both a surround line and intellectual, though, apart from the passion of F #2, this is virtually the only time intellect comes into any serious consideration throughout the speech

• the attempt to convince his followers of life in the woods being 'sweete' (despite it being winter!) is emotional (0/3, the last two lines of F #1)

• and, after the passionate question (or statement, given that the Elizabethan question mark could also function as a modern exclamation point) that at least the woods are less perilous than the 'envious Court' (1/1, F #2), the remaining justification that the hardships they are currently undergoing are 'Sweet' in their 'adversitie', and that in nature they find 'good in every thing' is almost completely emotional (3/13 in the thirteen lines of F #3)

• while the most telling point for the Duke may well be the only other surround phrase, as he tries to make good the 'churlish chiding' of the 'winters winde'

": these are counsellors/That feelingly perswade me what I am :"

29/ 1st. Lord   Indeed my Lord/The melancholy Jaques grieves at that,   between 2.1.25 - 63

Background: This is a response to Duke Senior's sad observation at having to 'kill us venison' for their food.

Style: one on one in front of a and for a larger group

Where: at Duke Senior's encampment in the woods

To Whom: Duke Senior and his followers

# of Lines: 37   **Probable Timing:** 1.55 minutes

Modern Text

29/ 1st. Lord

1 Indeed, my ᐃlord,
The melancholy Jaques grieves at that,
And in that kind* swears* you do* more usurp*
[Than] doth your brother that hath banish'd you. †
2 Today my Lord of Amiens and myself*
Did steal* behind* him as he lay along
Under an oak*, whose antic* root* peeps* out
Upon the brook* that brawls* along this wood,
To the which place a poor* sequest'red ᐃstag,
That from the ᐃhunter's aim* had ta'en a hurt,
Did come to languish ; and indeed, my ᐃlord,
The wretched animal* heav'd forth such groans*
That their discharge did stretch his leathern* coat
Almost to bursting, and the big round tears*
Cours'd one another down* his innocent nose
In piteous* chase ; and thus the hairy* fool*,
Much marked of the melancholy* Jaques,
Stood on th'extremest verge of the swift brook*,
Augmenting it with tears*.
3 {He did} moralize this spectacle into a thousand similes*.
4 First, for his weeping [in] the needless* stream*:
"Poor* ᐃdeer*," quoth he, "thou mak'st a testament
As worldlings do*, giving thy sum of more
To that which had too [much]." †
5   Then being there alone,
Left and abandoned of his velvet [friends]:
"'Tis right," quoth he, "thus misery* doth part
The ᐃflux* of company". †
6   Anon a careless* ᐃherd*,
Full of the pasture, jumps along by him
And never stays* to greet him. †

First Folio

29/ 1st. Lord

1 Indeed+ my Lord+
The melancholy Jaques grieves at that,
And in that kinde swears you doe more usurpe
[Then] doth your brother that hath banish'd you :
To day my Lord of Amiens,x and my selfe,x
Did steale behinde him as he lay along
Under an oake, whose anticke roote peepes out
Upon the brooke that brawles along this wood,
To the which place a poore sequestred Stag+
That from the Hunters aime had tane a hurt,
Did come to languish ; and indeed+ my Lord+
The wretched annimall heav'd forth such groanes
That their discharge did stretch his leatherne coat
Almost to bursting, and the big round teares
Cours'd one another downe his innocent nose
In pitteous chase : x and thus the hairie foole,
Much marked of the melancholie Jaques,
Stood on th'extremest verge of the swift brooke,
Augmenting it with teares.

2 {He did} moralize this spectacle into a thousand similies.

3 First, for his weeping [into]4 the needlesse streame ; +
Poore Deere+ quoth he, thou mak'st a testament
As worldlings doe, giving thy sum of more
To that which had too [must] :   then being there alone,
Left and abandoned of his velvet [friend] ; +
"Tis right+ quoth he, thus miserie doth part
The Fluxe of companie : anon a carelesse Heard+
Full of the pasture, jumps along by him
And never staies to greet him : [I] + quoth Jaques,

The 1st Lord's struggle between the desire to make a straightforward unemotional report of Jaques whereabouts and behaviour, and the feelings that are running within him, can be seen in the opening three and half lines (to the first colon): for it moves from an intellectual opening (2/0 the first line and a half), through to an enormous emotional outburst reporting Jaques' accusation that the Duke is a usurper (0/4, in the single line three), finishing with some form of (horrified?) control as he reports equating Duke Senior's behaviours to that of the real usurper, his evil brother Fredricke.

• overall, it would seem that from the start the 1st Lord tends to have sudden quick clusters of release, as if he cannot maintain full control of his feelings 'in that kinde sweares you doe more usurpe' (0/4); 'steale behinde' (0/2); 'an oake, whose anticke roote' (0/3); 'the brooke that brawles' (0/2); 'needlesse streame' '/Poore Deere' (0/4); 'carelesse Heard' (0/2)

• setting up the initial details of Amiens and himself finding Jaques talking to a wounded stag is more emotional than factual (4/8, in the six and half lines to the semicolon)

• but, heralded by that semicolon, the description of the 'wretched annimall' is almost totally emotional (1/10, in the eight lines ending F #1)

• given the overall lengthy sentence structure of the speech, the fact that F #2 is so short and unembellished suggests that the 1st Lord is amazed by (the audacity of) each of the moralizing points that Jaques was able to draw from the event

• and this seems to be the case throughout the again more emotional than intellectual F #3 (6/13), a sign that he still has been unable to return to straight reportage
": First, for his weeping into the needlesse streame ; "
": then being there alone,/Left and abandoned of his velvet friend ; /
"Tis right quoth he, thus miserie doth part/The Fluxe of companie : "
": anon a carelesse Heard/Full of the pasture, jumps along by him
: I quoth Jaques, / Sweepe on you fat and greazie Citizens,/'Tis just the fashion ; wherefore doe you looke/Upon that poore and broken bankrupt there ?"

---

4 Ff = 'into', some modern texts set 'in'; thus reducing the line to ten syllables

7

" [Ay]," quoth Jaques,
"Sweep* on you fat and greasy* Citizens,
'Tis just the fashion.†
Wherefore do* you look*

8

Upon that poor* and broken bankrupt there?"

9

Thus most invectively he pierceth through
The body of [the] △country*, △city*, △court,
Yea, and of this our life, swearing that we
Are mere* usurpers, tyrants, and what's worse,
To fright the △animals* and to kill them up
In their assign'd and native dwelling place.

First Folio

Sweepe on you fat and greazie Citizens,
'Tis just the fashion; wherefore doe you looke
Upon that poore and broken bankrupt there?

4

Thus most invectively he pierceth through
The body of [ ] Countrie, Citie, Court,
Yea, and of this our life, swearing that we
Are meere usurpers, tyrants, and whats worse+
To fright the Annimals,+ and to kill them up
In their assign'd and native dwelling place.

---

especially when so many of the surround phrases are in part created by emotional semicolons

• however, just for a moment the 1st Lord manages to regain some intellectual self-control as he summarises Jaques invective towards everything via two unembellished lines 'Countrie, Citie, Court,' (3/0 the first three lines of F #4, with the second line containing two short spellings), only to finish emotionally once more as he details what Jaques has called his fellows in exile, viz. 'usurpers, tyrants' (1/3 the last three lines of the speech)

30/ Clowne   **Ah this shepherds life.   Truely, in respect of it selfe, it is . . .**   3.2.11-21

Background: This is Touchstone's reply to Corin's question 'And how like you this shepherds life Mr Touchstone?'

Style: as part of a two-handed scene

Where: somewhere near the cottage of Rosalind and Celia   **To Whom:** Corin   **# of Lines:** 8   **Probable Timing:** 0.30 minutes

Modern Text

30/ Clowne

1

Ah this shepherds life {. * }

2

Truly* {ψ}, in respect of itself*, it is a
good life; but in respect that it is a shepherd's* life, it is
naught.

3

In respect that it is solitary, I like it very* well;
but in respect that it is private, it is a very vild life.
Now

4

in respect it is in the fields, it pleaseth me* well: but in
respect it is not in the △court, it is tedious.
As it is a spare

5

life (look* you) it fits my humor well; but as there is no
more plenty* in it, it goes much against my stomach* .

First Folio

30/ Clowne

1

Ah this shepherds life {. * }

2

Truely {ψ}, in respect of it selfe, it is a
good life; but in respect that it is a shepheards life, it is
naught.

3

In respect that it is solitary, I like it verie well :
but in respect that it is private, it is a very vild life.
Now

4

in respect it is in the fields, it pleaseth mee well : but in
respect it is not in the Court, it is tedious.
As it is a spare

5

life (looke you) it fits my humor well : x but as there is no
more plentie in it, it goes much against my stomacke.

The speech is a lovely simple build of opposites, both in terms of ideas and playing styles.

• the fun-filled opposites are set up by the easy method of dividing each proof sentence (F #2-5) into two parts by means of major punctuation; however, there is a possibility that the 'good life'/ 'naught' parallel may be close to the truth since the opposites are separated by the only emotional semicolon in the speech

• thus the short F #1 sets up an apparently calm unembellished start only to be immediately slapped down by an emotional tease (F #2, 0/2)

• similarly while the game playing around 'solitary'/'private' is similarly unembellished (F #3) the ease it suggests is quickly dissipated by both the 'fields/Court' dilemma (F #4, 1/1) and especially the emotionality of the 'spare life' going 'much against my stomacke' (F #5, 0/2)

31/ Corin   I know the more one sickens, the worse at ease he is :

Background: Corin's response to Touchstone's blatant question, 'Has't any Philosophie in thee shepheard?'.   3.2.23 - 31 plus 3.2.73 - 77   One note: sentence F #3 originally followed Touchstone's teasing suggestion that Corin may be 'damn'd' – in the context of this speech the sentence could be triggered by supposed laughter from Corin's scene partner.

Style: as part of a two-handed scene

Where: somewhere in the woods, near the cottage of Rosalind and Celia   **To Whom:** Touchstone

# of Lines: 13   Probable Timing: 0.45 minutes

Modern Text	First Folio

31/ Corin

1 {ψ}

    I know the more one sickens the worse at ease he is ;   and that he* that wants money, means* , and content is without three good friends* ; ◊ that the property* of rain* is to wet and fire to burn* ;   That good pasture makes fat sheep* ;   and that a great cause of the night is lack* of the Sun* ;   ᐃthat he* that hath learned no wit by ᐃnature, nor ᐃart, may complain* of good breeding, or comes of a very dull kindred.

2 {ψ} I am a true ᐃlaborer* : I earn* that I eat* , get that I wear* , owe no man hate, envy* no mans happiness* , glad of other men's good, content with my harm* , and the greatest of my pride, is to see my ᐃewes graze & my ᐃlambs* suck* .

31/ Corin

1 {ψ}

    I know the more one sickens,ₓ the worse at ease he is : ₓ and that hee that wants money, meanes, and content,ₓ is without three good frends.

2   That the propertie of raine is to wet,ₓ and fire to burne : That good pasture makes fat sheepe : ₓ and that a great cause of the night,ₓ is lacke of the Sunne : ₓ That hee that hath learned no wit by Nature, nor Art, may complaine of good breeding, or comes of a very dull kindred.

3 {ψ}   I am a true Labourer : [+] I earne that I eate : ₓ get that I weare ; ₓ owe no man hate, envie no mans happinesse ; ₓ glad of other mens good [+] content with my harme : ₓ and the greatest of my pride, is to see my Ewes graze,ₓ & my Lambes sucke.

- that perhaps Corin only eventually finds a way to triumph in his 'Philosophie' might be seen in the build - first F #1's quiet start with four of six phrases being unembellished ; then the growth first to emotion (0/5, F #1 and the first two lines of F #2) ; and then the moment of slight passion (1/1 in one line) over 'night' being caused by 'the lacke of the Sunne', which leads to his final much more passionate two line flourish with its sly dig at 'good breeding' (3/2 F #2)

- that this starts as hard work for him might be seen in the five surround phrases/lines that open the speech, and the two extra breath-thoughts (marked , ₓ) by which he strains to add the necessary extra detail to the point being made

- however, his strong self-definition of F #3 is a very different matter, with emotion flowing from the very start (1/6 in the first three lines), the emotion further heightened with three of the five surround phrases formed in part by the emotional semicolons

- thus it's interesting to see the (dignified?) ending as he describes his greatest pride (2/1, the last line and a half)

As You Like It / 273

#'s 32 - 33: DUKE FREDRICKE'S ANGER

32/ Duke Fredricke   Can it be possible that no man saw them?   between 2.21 - 21

Background: This is Duke Fredricke's response when told of his daughter's and Rosalind's disappearance. The first 'brother' refers to Orlando, the second 'Brother' to Oliver.

Style: general questioning of a small group   **To Whom:** members of his retinue

Where: somewhere in the palace   **# of Lines: 8**   **Probable Timing: 0.30 minutes**

Modern Text	First Folio
32/ Duke Fredricke	**32/ Duke Fredricke**
1 Can it be possible that no man saw them?	1 Can it be possible that no man saw them?
2 It cannot be . [†]	2 It cannot be, some villaines of my Court
Some villains* of my [△]court	Are of consent and sufferance in this.
3 Are of consent and sufferance in this.	3 Send to his brother, [+] fetch that gallant hither,
4 Send to his brother ; fetch that gallant hither . [†]	If he be absent, bring his Brother to me, [+]
5 If he be absent, bring his [△]brother to me ;	Ile make him finde him : do this sodainly ;
I'll make him find* him . [†]	And let not search and inquisition quaile, [x]
6 Do this suddenly*;	To bring againe these foolish runawaies.
And let not search and inquisition quail*	
To bring again* these foolish runaways*.	

- that Fredricke wastes neither words nor energy (2/4 in eight lines overall) can be seen in

  a/ the unembellished short opening question, being immediately answered by himself in . . . .

  b/ . . . the slightly onrushed F #2 (set as two sentences by most modern texts) in which he gets to the point very quickly, with just the right two key words highlighted, 'villaines' and 'Court'

  c/ and though F #3 (especially when compared to the three sentences it is split into by most modern texts) may seem onrushed again, it is entirely to the point, and suggests that this is a man who will not be deflected from any intention or argument once he has begun, the fast link-comma (marking mt. #4/5) and colon (marking mt. #5-6) simply adding to his sense of power

- the one surround phrase ' : do this sodainly ; ' is fascinating both in its brevity and suddenness (thus adding a powerful jolt to those who have to obey), and in the emotional semicolon that finishes it – perhaps suggesting a slight crack in the otherwise smooth self-presentation in the rest of the speech

33/ Duke Fredricke   Not see him since? Sir, sir, that cannot be :   between 3.1.1 - 18

Background: In response to speech #32 above, his retinue have found that Orlando has disappeared too, and thus have brought Oliver (Orlando's older brother) in for questioning. This speech, which starts the scene, suggests that Fredricke's questioning began somewhere offstage before the onstage scene started.

Style: one on one, in front of a small group

Where: somewhere in the palace   **To Whom:** Oliver, in front of members of his retinue

# of Lines: 15   **Probable Timing: 0.50 minutes**

Modern Text

33/ Duke Fredricke

1 Not see him since?

2   Sir, sir, that cannot be . †

3 But were I not the better part made mercy*,
   I should not seek* an absent argument
   Of my revenge, thou present. †

4   But look* to it :
   Find* out thy brother, wheresoe'er he is ;
   Seek* him with △candle ; bring him dead or living
   Within this twelvemonth, or turn* thou no more
   To seek a living in our △territory*.

5 Thy △lands and all things that thou dost call thine
   Worth seizure do we seize into our hands,
   Till thou canst quit thee by thy brother's mouth,
   Of what we think* against thee.

6   Well, push him out of doors* ,
   And let my officers of such a nature
   Make an extent upon his house and △lands. †

7 Do this expediently, and turn* him going.

First Folio

33/ Duke Fredricke

1 Not see him since?

2   Sir, sir, that cannot be :
   But were I not the better part made mercie,
   I should not seeke an absent argument
   Of my revenge, thou present : but looke to it, +
   Finde out thy brother + wheresoere he is, +

   Seeke him with Candle : x bring him dead, x or living
   Within this twelvemonth, or turne thou no more
   To seek a living in our Territorie.

3 Thy Lands and all things that thou dost call thine,
   Worth seizure, x do we seize into our hands,
   Till thou canst quit thee by thy brothers mouth,
   Of what we thinke against thee.

4   Well + push him out of dores
   And let my officers of such a nature
   Make an extent upon his house and Lands :
   Do this expediently, and turne him going.

That Duke Fredricke seems to deliberately employ a browbeating tactic of a sudden outburst in the sea of his usual calm is once more seen here, as is his tendency to employ as few sentences as possible to get his points across.

• the first three and a half lines, not only denying what Oliver might have said but threatening him too, are totally unembellished: yet the firmness of the denial is beyond question, beginning with a short (unembellished) monosyllabic sentence/question (F #1), which is then reinforced straightaway by an (unembellished) surround phrase (the opening of F #2)

• the calm is suddenly destroyed, but only momentarily, by the command to 'Finde out' Orlando (1/4 in just two lines), to be immediately followed by yet another unembellished line ferocious in its calmness ":bring him dead, x or living/Within this twelvemonth," enhanced by the extra breath-thought (marked , x)

• and then comes yet another small, this time factual, explosion (2/1) highlighting Oliver's potential banishment (the end of F #2) and the very definite and immediate seizure of all his property as a forfeit until successful (the first line of F #4) : again the extra breath-thoughts, rather than more excessive vocal releases, reinforce all the necessary details

• and the final six and a half lines of the speech, tidying-up the details and getting rid of Oliver, become relatively calm once more (just three of the lines showing any excess, 1/2)

#'s 34 - 39: JAQUES OBSERVATIONS AND LONGINGS

34/ Jaques   **Well then, if ever I thanke any man, Ile thanke . . . .**   2.5.25 - 30

Background: Jaques somewhat sardonic response to Amyens possible attempt to either please him, or, stretching the dialogue a little, make a modest demand for payment - for Amyens has said in response to Jaques demand for a song, 'More at your request, then to please my selfe.'

Style: one on one in front of a small group

Where: at Duke Senior's encampment   **To Whom:** Amyens

# of Lines: 6   Probable Timing: 0.20 minutes

Modern Text

34/ Jaques

1   Well then, if ever I thank* any man, I'll thank*
you ;   but that they call* compliment is like th'encounter
of two dog-△apes;   ◊ and when a man thanks* me heartily,
[methinks*] I have given him a penny*, and he renders me
the beggarly thanks*.

2   Come, sing ;   and you that will* not,

hold your tongues.

First Folio

34/ Jaques

1   Well then, if ever I thanke any man, Ile thanke
you : ₓ but that they cal complement is like th'encounter
of two dog-Apes.
                           And when a man thankes me hartily,
2   [me thinkes] I have given him a penie, and he renders me
the beggerly thankes.
                           Come⁺ sing ;   and you that wil not⁺

3   hold your tongues.

This **slightly emotional little speech (1/5) operates on opposites (somewhat like Touchstone at his best, see speeches #24-6 above).**

• thus the two surround lines of F #1 first giveth ('Ile thanke you') and then, after the colon, taketh away (the denigration of what he has just done, 'complement'), and the surround phrases of F #3 operate on the same 'charm then sting' principle, but this time (via the semicolon) somewhat more emotionally

• the intervening F #2 simply allows Jaques a slightly longer anti-'thankes' emotional discourse/diatribe (0/3)

• in such a short speech, the four short spellings ('cal', 'hartly', 'penie' and 'wil') possibly suggest moments of fatigue or melancholy

35/Jaques   A Foole, a foole :   I met a foole i'th Forrest,   2.7.12·34

Background: Jaques seems to be always looking for someone new to talk to, and is always eager, at least at the beginning of a scene (perhaps the high end of a bi-polar condition, a modern equivalency for the Elizabethan term 'melancholy'), for some form of intelligent disputive conversation. Here, having just met offstage the clown Touchstone, Jaques seems even more animated than usual (hence Duke Senior's seemingly amazed comment ('What, you look merrily').

Style: address to a group

Where: at Duke Senior's encampment   **To Whom:** Duke Senior, Amiens, and an undetermined number of Duke Senior's followers

# of Lines: 23   **Probable Timing: 1.10 minutes**

Modern Text

35/ Jaques

1 A Fool* , a fool*! †
2   I met a fool* i'th ^forest* ,
3 A motley ^fool* . †
4   (A miserable world!) †
5 As I do live by food* , I met a fool* ,
   Who laid him downe* , and bask'd him in the ^sun ,
   And rail'd on Lady Fortune in good terms* ,
   In good set termes* , and yet a motley fool* .
6 "Good morrow, fool* ," quoth I . †
7   "No, Sir'," quoth he,
   "Call me not fool* till heaven hath sent me fortune . " †
8 And then he drew a dial* from his poke*
   And looking on it, with lack*-lustre eye,
   Says* , very wisely, "it is ten a clock* ." †
9 "Thus we may see," quoth he, "how the world wags" . †
10 'Tis but an hour* ago* since it was nine,
   And after one hour* more 'twill be eleven,
   And so from hour* to hour* , we ripe and ripe,
   And then from hour* to hour* , we rot and rot ;
   And thereby hangs a tale" .
11   When I did hear*
   The motley ^fool* thus moral* on the time,
   My ^lungs began to crow like ^chanticleer* ,
   That ^fools* should be so deep* contemplative ;
   And I did laugh, sans intermission
   An hour* by his dial* .
12   O* noble fool*! †
13 A worthy fool*! †
14   Motley's the only* wear* .

First Folio

35/Jaques

1 A Foole, a foole : † I met a foole i'th Forrest,
   A motley Foole (a miserable world :) †
   As I do live by foode, I met a foole,
   Who laid him downe, and bask'd him in the Sun,
   And rail'd on Lady Fortune in good termes,
   In good set termes, and yet a motley foole.
2 Good morrow$^+$ foole$_x$(quoth I :)$_x$ no$^+$ Sir, quoth he,
   Call me not foole, till heaven hath sent me fortune,
   And then he drew a diall from his poake,
   And looking on it, with lacke-lustre eye,
   Sayes, very wisely, it is ten a clocke :
3 Thus we may see $_x$(quoth he)$_x$ how the world wagges :
   'Tis but an houre agoe$_x$, since it was nine,
   And after one houre more$_x$, 'twill be eleven,
   And so from houre to houre, we ripe, and ripe,
   And then from houre to houre, we rot,$_x$ and rot, $^+$
   And thereby hangs a tale.   When I did heare
   The motley Foole,$_x$ thus morall on the time,
   My Lungs began to crow like Chanticleere,
   That Fooles should be so deepe contemplative : $_x$
   And I did laugh, sans intermission
   An houre by his diall.
4   Oh noble foole, $^+$
   A worthy foole : $^+$ Motley's the onely weare.

The importance of his meeting Touchstone can be seen in the onrushed opening of the speech (split into five sentences by modern texts) starting with two highly passionate surround phrases, just in setting up the very briefest of the circumstances;   the new onrush of F #2's details of the meeting and conversation (reduced in impact by being split into five separate sentences by most modern texts); and the last two highly emotional surround phrases ending the speech (1/5), extolling the virtues of the 'worthy foole' and that essentially to be a 'foole' is the very best thing for the age ('Motley's the onely weare').

• the passion of the first two lines (3/5) is continued as Jaques describes in general how the 'foole' presented himself (3/6 the last four lines of F #1)

• and then, as the details are piled one on top of another in the long F #2, so emotion takes over completely - with the exception of the one capitalised word 'Sir' (1/13 in ten and a half lines)

• the description of Touchstone's sententious comments about life and time (the last five and a half lines) are suddenly punctuated by four extra breath-thoughts (marked , $_x$), though whether Jaques needs these for extra control to prevent himself from laughing, or simply to make sure he can get his amazed response over to his listeners is up to each actor to explore

• and then, as Jaques describes his own response to what Touchstone said, so passion returns (4/4 in the first three and a half lines of F #3)

• interestingly, the incredibly simple and short monosyllabic phrase testifying to his laughter ('And I did laugh') is one of the very few unembellished lines or phrases in the speech

• but, with the final praise of the 'foole', this quickly gives way to enormous emotion once more (1/7 in the last two lines of the speech)

36/ Jaques   **I am ambitious for a motley coat. /It is my onely suite,**   between 3.7 43 - 61

Background: The meeting with Touchstone seems to have triggered in Jaques an understanding of how he would like to conduct the remainder of his life. One note: the 'motley coat' was a multi-coloured, often patched, coat that licensed fools and jesters would wear as a symbol of their profession.

Style: one on one in front of a larger group

Where: at Duke Senior's encampment   **To Whom:** Duke Senior, in front of Amiens and an undetermined number of Duke Senior's followers

# of Lines: 19   **Probable Timing: 1.00 minutes**

Modern Text

36/ Jaques

1   I am ambitious for a motley coat.
━━━━━━━━━━━━━━━━━━━━━━
           It is my only* suit -
2   Provided that you weed your better judgments*
    Of all opinion that grows* rank* in them,
    That I am wise.
3   I must have liberty
    Withal*, as large a ^charter as the wind*,
    To blow on whom I please, for so fools* have ;
    And they that are most galled* with my folly,
    They most must laugh. †
4   And why, sir, must they so?
5   The why is plain* as way to ^parish ^church :
    He* that a ^fool* doth very wisely hit
    Doth very foolishly, although he smart,
    [Not to] ^seem* senseless* of the bob ; ◊ if not,
    The ^wise ° man's folly is anatomiz'd
    Even by the squand'ring glances of the fool*.
6   Invest me in my motley ;   ^give me leave
    To speak* my mind*, and I will through and through
    Cleanse the foul* body* of th'infected world,
    If they will patiently receive my medicine.

First Folio

36/ Jaques

1   I am ambitious for a motley coat .

2   It is my onely suite,
    Provided that you weed your better judgements
    Of all opinion that growes ranke in them,
    That I am wise.

3   I must have liberty
    Withall, as large a Charter as the winde,
    To blow on whom I please, for so fooles have : x
    And they that are most gauled with my folly,
    They most must laugh : And why + sir + must they so?

4   The why is plaine, x as way to Parish Church :
    Hee, x that a Foole doth very wisely hit, x
    Doth very foolishly, although he smart +
    [ ] Seeme senselesse of the bob.
                        If not,

5   The Wise-mans folly is anathomiz'd
    Even by the squandring glances of the foole .

6   Invest me in my motley : Give me leave
    To speake my minde, and I will through and through
    Cleanse the foule bodie of th'infected world,
    If they will patiently receive my medicine.

With Jaques' demonstrated ability to suddenly discover things about himself in the middle of conversations (see speech #38 below) it may be that, since the opening sentence is both short and unembellished, the realisation that he is 'ambitious for a motley coat' has either just struck him, or he is voicing it carefully and quietly to the Duke as a very serious proposition.

• as Jaques begins to explain the scope of what he wants, so he becomes emotional (1/8, F #2 and the first two and a half lines of F #3)

• and it looks as if Jaques has got either some specific targets in mind, or has great fancies as to what he might be able to do as a 'foole', for the introduction of 'And they that are most gauled with my folly,/They most must laugh' is unembellished and a surround phrase, and the embellishment of the idea continues the hard-working surround-phrase means of expression and becomes intellectual (3/1)

" . And why sir must they so ? / The why is plaine, as way to Parish Church : "

• then, as Jaques becomes more specific with 'Hee that a Foole . . .' he turns emotional once more (1/4, the last three lines of F #4)

• the idea of embarrassing even the 'Wise-man' simply by a look once more drives Jaques into an almost completely unembellished anticipation (1/1, F #5), leading to yet another unembellished surround phrase (demanding? pleading?) 'Invest me in my motley : ', leading again to emotion as to how to cleanse the 'foule bodie of th'infected world' (1/3, the next two and a half lines of the final sentence)

• however, the last line reverie/hope of what he might achieve 'If they will patiently receive my medicine' is once more spoken without embellishment (a dream or plea once more?)

37/Jaques   **All the world's a stage,**   2.7.139 - 166

Background: Following the calming of Orlando and the prevention of his attempted robbery (speeches #10-11 above), as Orlando leaves to fetch the exhausted Adam, Duke Senior has commented 'Thou seest, we are not all alone unhappie:/This wide and universall Theater/Presents more wofull Pageants then the Sceane/Wherein we play . . . .'. This is Jaques very famous reply.

Style: address to a group

Where: at Duke Senior's encampment   **To Whom:** Duke Senior, Amiens, and an undetermined number of Duke Senior's followers

# of Lines: 28   **Probable Timing: 1.30 minutes**

Modern Text

37/Jaques

1   All the world's a stage,
    And all the men and women, merely' △players;
    They have their △exits and their △entrances,
    And one man in his time plays* many parts,
    His △acts being seven ages.

              At first the △infant,
2   Mewling and puking in the △nurse's arms* . †
    Then the whining △school*△boy, with his △satchel
    And shining morning face, creeping like snail*
    Unwillingly to school*.

            And then the △lover,
4   Sighing like △furnace, with a woeful* ballad
    Made to his △mistress'* eye△brow.

              Then a △soldier,
5   Full of strange oaths, and bearded like the △pard,
    Jealous,* in honor, sudden*, and quick* in quarrel* ,
    Seeking the bubble △reputation
    Even in the △cannon's* mouth. †

              And then the △justice,
6   In fair* round belly with good △capon lin'd,
    With eyes severe and beard of formal* cut,
    Full of wise saws* and modern* instances,
    And so he plays* his part.

            The sixt age shifts
7   Into the lean* and slipper'd △pantaloon*,
    With spectacles on nose, and pouch on side,
    His youthful* hose, well sav'd, a world too wide
    For his shrunk* shank*, and his big* manly voice,
    Turning again* toward childish treble*, pipes
    And whistles in his sound.

First Folio

37/Jaques

1   All the world's a stage,
    And all the men and women, meerely Players ;
    They have their Exits and their Entrances,
    And one man in his time playes many parts,
    His Acts being seven ages.

              At first the Infant,
2   Mewling,x and puking in the Nurses armes :
    Then,x the whining Schoole-boy+ with his Satchell
    And shining morning face, creeping like snaile
    Unwillingly to schoole.

            And then the Lover,
3   Sighing like Furnace, with a wofull ballad
    Made to his Mistresse eye-brow.

              Then,x a Soldier,
4   Full of strange oaths, and bearded like the Pard,
    Jelous in honor, sodaine, and quicke in quarrell,
    Seeking the bubble Reputation
    Even in the Canons mouth :   And then,x the Justice+
    In faire round belly,x with good Capon lin'd,
    With eyes severe,x and beard of formall cut,
    Full of wise sawes,x and moderne instances,
    And so he playes his part.

            The sixt age shifts
5   Into the leane and slipper'd Pantaloone,
    With spectacles on nose, and pouch on side,
    His youthfull hose+ well sav'd, a world too wide,x
    For his shrunke shanke, and his bigge manly voice,
    Turning againe toward childish trebble+ pipes,x x
    And whistles in his sound.

Overall the speech falls into two parts - the first four ages being handled more intellectually than emotionally (17/12), as is the start of the fifth, but the conclusion of the fifth and the last two suddenly become far more emotional than intellectual (2/13): some commentators suggest that being not only is the character on the cusp between the fifth, the last of the energised ages, and the beginning of the inevitable decline into the last two, so the actor originating the part (supposedly Thomas Pope) was too. Certainly the idea that the character is approaching this age is highly viable, especially considering the addition of four extra breath-thoughts (marked, x) that suddenly appear in the four lines that make up the description of the age on the cusp, that of the Justice.

• in introducing the seven ages theme, the speech opens quite factually and calmly (3/1, F #1)

• the descriptions of all four strong and healthy ages (the 'Infant', the 'Schoole-boy', the 'Lover' and the 'Soldier') all seem passionate (11/10), yet on closer examination the pattern of opposites noted as part of Jaques' personal style speech #34 above) occurs again, for though most start either passionately or intellectually as each age is established, the punch-line/final description is always emotional

a/ the Infant is passionate throughout (2/1), while the Schoole-boy (2/2, the first line) starts passionately but his 'creeping/Unwilling'ly' is purely emotional (0/2)

b/ the Lover starts intellectually (2/0), while the 'wofull ballad' is dismissed more emotionally (1/2)

c/ the Soldier starts intellectually again (2/0), and then the death-risking attempt to make his 'Reputation' is handled intellectually once more (2/0)

• even establishing the Justice starts the same way (2/0), but the finish is totally emotional (0/4 in just two and a half lines)

• and the emotional roof caves in, both with 'leane and slipper'd Pantaloone' (1/6 in six lines) and the 'second childishnesse' (1/3): though, rather poignantly, the very last line itemising the 'meere oblivion' is totally unembellished, one of the very few in the speech

      "Sans teeth, sans eyes, sans taste, sans every thing."

Last ᐃscene of all,
That ends this strange eventful* history*,
Is second childishness*, and mere* oblivion,
Sans teeth, sans eyes, sans taste, sans every thing.

Last Scene of all,
That ends this strange eventfull historie,
Is second childishnesse, and meere oblivion,
Sans teeth, sans eyes, sans taste, sans every thing.

• one interesting side-bar: the fact that there are no surround phrases (save perhaps for the opening line and a half, formed in part by the emotional semicolon) could suggest that Jaques is more reflective in this speech than many productions give him credit for, or as some commentators suggest, since the overall theme is quite a common one in Elizabethan/Jacobean literature, Jaques could be quite casual in his story-telling/maxim creating address to the group

---

38/ Jaques   I have neither the Schollers melancholy, ...   4.1.10 - 20

Background: In his attempt to meet new people and learn new things, Jaques has fastened on the disguised Rosalind, much to her dismay, possibly because she is about to meet Orlando for another anti-love lesson and/or she finds Jaques' melancholy too much to deal with. Rosalind has dismissed Jaques' explanation 'Why, 'tis good to be sad and say nothing.' with the blunt 'Why then 'tis good to be a poste.', so Jaques explains himself further.

Style: as part of a three-handed scene
Where: somewhere in the woods, near Rosalind and Celia's cottage   **To Whom:** Rosalind, in front of Celia
# of Lines: 10   **Probable Timing: 0.35 minutes**

Modern Text

38/ Jaques

1 I have neither the ᐃscholar's* melancholy, which
is emulation ; nor the ᐃmusician's*, which is fantastical* ;
nor the ᐃcourtier's*, which is proud; nor the ᐃsoldier's*,
which is ambitious; nor the ᐃlawyer's*, which is politic* ;
nor the ᐃlover's, which
is all these: but it is a melancholy of mine own*, compounded of many simples, extracted from many objects,
and indeed the sundry* contemplation of my travels*, in
which [my] often rumination wraps me in a most humorous sadness* .

First Folio

38/ Jaques

1 I have neither the Schollers melancholy, which
is emulation: ₓ nor the Musitians, which is fantasticall ;
nor the Courtiers, which is proud: ₓ nor the Souldiers,
which is ambitious: ₓ nor the Lawiers, which is politick: ₓ
nor the Ladies, which is nice : ₓ nor the Lovers, which
is all these: but it is a melancholy of mine owne, compounded of many simples, extracted from many objects,
and indeed the sundrie contemplation of my travells, in
which [by] often rumination,ₓ wraps me in a most humorous sadnesse.

Though the structures of both speeches match, F's orthography **shows the speech splitting into two distinct parts, a highly released, highly self-revelatory opening, and an incredibly quiet self-contained finish.**

• thus the extended statement that his 'melancholy' is unlike anyone else's is very passionate (7/5 in just five and half lines), the enormity of its impact underscored by the whole being composed of seven successive short surround phrase hammer-blows of recognition/denial

• but as he defines what is unique to him, so all major punctuation and thus surround phrases disappear, and all he is left with is three emotional words in four and half lines which, when linked together, summarise how the 'melancholy' came about - 'owne', 'travells', and therefore 'sadnesse'

39/ Jaques   **Sir, by your patience :   if I heard you rightly,**   between 5.4.180 - 196

Background: The following is Jaques' reaction to the news of Duke Fredricke's miraculous conversion.

Style: various one on one addresses in front of a larger group

Where: near Duke Senior's encampment   **To Whom:** Duke Senior, Jaques, Touchstone and Audrey; Rosalind and Orlando, Celia and Oliver, the second de Boys brother also known as Jaques, Phebe and Silvius; perhaps Corin, Adam and William; Amiens and followers of the Duke. One note: names set within curly brackets in the modern text indicate the character Jaques is talking to next.

# of Lines: 15   **Probable Timing: 0.50 minutes**

Modern Text

39/ Jaques

1   Sir, by your patience. †

         If I heard you rightly,

2   The Duke hath put on a ^religious life,
     And thrown* into neglect the pompous ^court?
     ▪▪▪▪▪▪▪▪▪▪▪

3   To him will I. †

4   Out of these convertites
     There is much matter to be heard, and learn'd.

{Duke Senior}⁵

5   You to your former ^honor I bequeath,
     Your patience and your virtue well deserves it.

{Orlando}

6   You to a love, that your true faith doth merit;

{Oliver}   You to your land, and love, and great allies;

{Silvius}   You to a long, and well-deserved bed;

{Touchstone} And you to wrangling, for thy loving voyage
     Is but for two months* victuall'd. †

         So to your pleasures,

7   I am for other, [than] for dancing measures* .

8   To see no pastime I . †

         What you would have

9   I'll stay to know, at your abandon'd cave.

First Folio

39/ Jaques

1   Sir, by your patience :   if I heard you rightly,
     The Duke hath put on a Religious life,
     And throwne into neglect the pompous Court. +
     ▬▬▬▬▬▬▬▬▬▬▬
2   To him will I :   out of these convertites,ₓ
     There is much matter to be heard, and learn'd :
6   you to your former Honor,ₓ I bequeath⁺
     your patience,ₓ and your vertue,ₓ well deserves it.

3   you to a love, that your true faith doth merit : ₓ
     you to your land, and love, and great allies : ₓ
     you to a long, and well-deserved bed : ₓ
     And you to wrangling, for thy loving voyage
     Is but for two moneths victuall'd : So to your pleasures,
     I am for other, [then] for dancing meazures.
4   To see no pastime,ₓ I : what you would have,ₓ
     Ile stay to know, at your abandon'd cave.

The following is a very quiet and contemplative Jaques (5/4 in 15 lines).

- given the excitement and celebration of the surrounding scene, the speech starts amazingly quietly, with the first unembellished line supporting Jaques words of disbelief, especially the second phrase 'if I heard you rightly'

- this then leads to a hitherto unprecedented intellectual eagerness (3/1 the last two lines of F #1)

- it's almost as if Jaques believes that, with this news of the 'Religious' conversion of Duke Fredricke, his struggles throughout the play might be coming to an end, for the F #2 decision to join him is
  a/ totally unembellished and composed of two surround lines
  b/ out of which he rushes on via (to modern texts) an ungrammatical colon as he begins to make his farewells, first to the Duke

- in wishing the Duke well, apart from the onrush, Jaques' excitement/awkwardness can be seen in the three extra breath-thoughts (marked , ₓ) he needs just to get through these two lines, and in the unembellished quality, save for the well deserved word of praise 'Honor'

- the next four lines of farewell to Orlando, Oliver, Silvius (or perhaps Adam), and the start of farewell to Touchstone also seem to have a great impact on Jaques, for they are all unembellished and the first three are once more composed of surround phrases, though the final summary of Touchstone's marriage lasting only two months is emotional (0/2)

- initially the final summarising farewell is a little passionate (1/1 to end F #3), but then the (enforced?) calm of his unembellished surround phrases take over (all of F #4) as he reminds Duke Senior of what the original purpose of coming to the woods was supposed to be

---

⁵ for the next six lines, most modern texts indicate to whom Jaques is talking; to keep referring to this by footnote will split up the text far too much, so here the script will indicate with ornamental brackets and via a smaller font the character to whom the following remark is addressed (as suggested by most modern texts)

⁶ for this and the next four lines, the small 'y' of 'you or your' is as printed in F1, though the beginning of a verse line; F2/most modern texts set a capital each time

TWELFTH NIGHT

SPEECHES IN ORDER

SPEECHES IN ORDER	TIME	PAGE
#'s 1 - 2: Duke Orsino In Love		
1/ **Duke** If Musicke be the food of Love, play on,	0.55	282
2/ **Duke** Cesario,/Thou knowst no lesse, but all:	1.15	283
#'s 3 - 5: Viola In Love		
3/ **Viola** If I did love you in my masters flame,	0.45	284
4/ **Viola** I but I know.	0.45	285
5/ **Viola** By innocence I sweare, and by my youth,	0.25	286
#'s 6 - 7: Viola, What Is She? Woman, Boy, Or Eunuch		
6/ **Viola** There is a faire behaviour in thee Captaine,	0.50	287
7/ **Viola** I left no Ring with her: what meanes this Lady?	1.15	288
#'s 8 - 12: Olivia, In and Out Of Love		
8/ **Olivia** Have you any Commission from your Lord, to	0.40	289
9/ **Olivia** What is your Parentage?	0.50	290
10/ **Olivia** y'are servant to the Count Orsino youth.	1.00	291
11/ **Olivia** O what a deale of scorne, lookes beautifull?	0.40	292
12/ **Olivia** Hold Toby, on thy life I charge thee hold.	0.45	293
#'s 13 - 15: Andrew, A Fool In Love		
13/ **Andrew** Ile stay a moneth longer. I am a fellow oth. . . .	0.30	294
14/ **Fabian** This was a great argument of love in her. . . .	0.40	295
15/ **Toby** Build me thy fortunes upon the basis of . . .	1.45	296
#'s 16 - 19: Malvolio, In Love With . . . ?		
16/ **Maria** Sweet Sir Toby be patient for to night: Since	1.15	297
17/a **Malvolio** To be Count Malvolio.	1.10	299
/b **Malvolio** What employment have we heere?	1.30	300
18/ **Malvolio** Soft, here followes prose:	1.40	302
19/ **Malvolio** Oh ho, do you come neere me now: no worse	1.00	304
#'s 20 - 21: Sebastian		
20/ **Sebastian** I perceive in you so excellent a touch	1.10	305
21/ **Sebastian** This is the ayre, that is the glorious Sunne,	1.10	307
#'s 22 - 23: Eventual Resolution		
22/ **Antonio** Let me speake a little. This youth that you see	0.40	308
23/ **Sebastian** Do I stand there? I never had a brother:	0.30	309

SPEECHES BY GENDER

SPEECHES FOR WOMEN (11)

		Speech #(s)
Viola	**Traditional & Today:** a young woman, who disguises herself as the boy/eunuch Cesario	#3, #4, #5, #6, #7
Olivia	**Traditional:** young woman **Today:** sometimes a woman (slightly) older than Viola	#8, #9, #10, #11, #12
Maria	**Traditional & Today:** youngish (or, dependent upon the casting of Toby, middle-aged) woman	#16

SPEECHES FOR EITHER GENDER (2)

		Speech #(s)
Fabian	**Traditional:** male character actor, any age **Today:** any age, any gender	#14
Antonio	**Traditional:** male, usually young or early middle-age **Today:** sometimes any gender, usually young or early middle-age	#22

SPEECHES FOR MEN (11)

		Speech #(s)
Duke	**Traditional & Today:** younger or young-early middle age man	#1, #2
Andrew	**Traditional & Today:** a thin-faced character actor, usually young to young-middle age	#13
Toby	**Traditional:** older male, uncle to Olivia, brother to her deceased father **Today:** as above, though the age range is often ignored	#15
Malvolio	**Traditional:** an older male, of, at least in public, a puritanical demeanor **Today:** as above, but often the age range is more flexible	#17a, 17b, #18, #19
Sebastian	**Traditional & Today:** a young man, twin brother to Viola	#20, #21, #23

TWELFTH NIGHT

#'s 1 - 2: DUKE ORSINO IN LOVE

1/Duke   **If Musicke be the food of Love, play on,**   between 1.1.1 - 40

Background: This is one of Shakespeare's most famous opening speeches for character and play. If the actor keeps in mind that Orsino has been unsuccessfully wooing Olivia for quite some time, the speech is self-explanatory.

Style: general address to a small group

Where: somewhere in Orsino's palace   **To Whom:** an unspecified number of musicians and Lords, including Curio

# of Lines: 17   **Probable Timing: 0.55 minutes**

Modern Text

1/Duke

1 If △music* be the food of △love, play on,
   Give me excess* of it ; that surfeiting* ,
   The appetite may sicken,* and so die* .

2 That strain* again,* it had a dying fall ;
   O, it came o'er my ear* like the sweet sound
   That breaths* upon a bank* of △violets,
   Stealing and giving △odor* .
                    Enough, no more,

3 'Tis not so sweet now as it was before.

4 O spirit of △love, how quick* and fresh art thou,
   That notwithstanding thy capacity*
   Receiveth as the △sea, ◊△'nought enters there,
   Of what validity and pitch soe'er* ,
   But falls* into abatement and low price
   Even in a minute. †

5   So full of shapes is fancy* ,
   That it alone is high fantastical* .

6 Away before me to sweet beds of △flow'rs* ,
   Love-thoughts lie* rich when canopied* with bow'rs* .

First Folio

1/Duke

1 If Musicke be the food of Love, play on,
   Give me excesse of it : that surfetting,ₓ
   The appetite may sicken, and so dye.

2 That straine agen, it had a dying fall :ₓ
   O, it came ore my eare,ₓ like the sweet sound
   That breathes upon a banke of Violets;ₓ
   Stealing,ₓ and giving Odour.
                    Enough, no more,

3 'Tis not so sweet now,,as it was before.

4 O spirit of Love, how quicke and fresh art thou,
   That notwithstanding thy capacitie,ₓ
   Receiveth as the Sea.   Nought enters there,

5 Of what validity,ₓ and pitch so ere,
   But falles into abatement,ₓ and low price
   Even in a minute ; so full of shapes is fancie,
   That it alone,ₓ is high fantasticall.

6 Away before me,ₓ to sweet beds of Flowres,
   Love-thoughts lye rich,ₓ when canopy'd with bowres.

That Orsino's thoughts, breath and utterances are highly affected throughout can be seen in the ten extra breath-thoughts scattered throughout the speech (marked , x), especially noticeable when romantic analogies are being made, as with the end of F #2 (the scent of music); F #5 ('fancie' alone being 'high fantasticall'); and the final F #6's excess (of lying 'sweet beds of Flowres'), two of which are heralded by the emotional semicolon, viz. F #2's final surround phrase ' ; Stealing, and giving Odour. ' and F #5's ; ; so full of shapes is fancie'.

• after the passionate and factual insistence of the opening line (2/1), the first two sentences are splendidly emotional (2/7 in the remaining six lines of F #1-2)

• Orsino's need for the 'food of Love' is heightened by the rest of the passage being set as surround phrases, save for the middle two lines of F #2

• however, the disillusionment of F #3's 'no more' is totally contrasting in its quiet unembellishment, and not just a melodramatic calm perhaps for thereafter, though some releases do re-establish themselves for the rest of the speech, and though they are more emotional than intellectual, they are nowhere near as many as before (3/6 in the last eleven lines including these unembellished ones, as opposed to 4/8 in seven lines of the opening)

• thus the brief intellectual recognition of F #4, the 'spirit of Love' receiving all worship 'as the Sea' should be paid great attention, perhaps as a sudden realisation by Orsino: and the final emotional last line flourish of 'Love-thoughts lye rich, when canopy'd with bowres.' sings out for the actor's and reader's attention and enjoyment

2/ Duke   **Cesario,/Thou knowst no lesse, but all : I have unclasp'd**   between 1.4.12 - 40

Background: Having employed someone he believes to be the young 'lad' Cesario (in fact, Viola in disguise), he hopes that Cesario's youth will allow access to Olivia where the older 'wooers' have failed. Here Orsino instructs 'him' to break all the rules of normal behaviour, which, as Act One Scene 5 of the play shows, s/he does only too well.

Style: as part of a two-handed scene in front of another smaller group who may or may not be included

Where: somewhere in Orsino's palace   **To Whom:** Viola (disguised as Cesario), in front of a small group of attendants, including Valentine and Curio

# of Lines: 24   **Probable Timing: 1.15 minutes**

Modern Text	First Folio
2/ Duke	**2/ Duke**

Modern Text

2/ Duke

1 Cesario,
    Thou know'st no less* but all.†
                           I have unclasp'd†

2 To thee the book* even of my secret soul*.

3 Therefore, good youth, address* thy [gait] unto her,
    Be not denied* access*, stand at her doors*,
    And tell them, there thy fixed foot shall grow
    Till thou have audience.

4 Be clamorous, and leap* all civil* bounds,
    Rather [than] make unprofited return* .†

5 {U}nfold the passion of my love,
    Surprise* her with discourse of my dear* faith ;
    It shall become thee well to act my woes :
    She will attend it better in thy youth
    [Than] in a ^nuntio's of more grave aspect.

6 Dear* ^lad, believe* it ;
    For they shall yet belie* thy happy years* ,
    That say thou art a man .†

7   Diana's lip
    Is not more smooth and rubious : thy small pipe
    Is as the maiden's organ, shrill and sound,
    And all is semblative a woman's part.

8 I know thy constellation is right apt
    For this affair* .†

9   Some four* or five attend him -
    When least in company*. †

10   Prosper well in this,
    And thou shalt live as freely as thy ^lord,
    To call his fortunes thine.

First Folio

2/ Duke

1 Cesario,
    Thou knowst no lesse,x but all : I have unclasp'd
    To thee the booke even of my secret soule.

2 Therefore + good youth, addresse thy [gate] unto her,
    Be not deni'de accesse, stand at her doores,
    And tell them, there thy fixed foot shall grow
    Till thou have audience.

3 Be clamorous, and leape all civill bounds,
    Rather [then] make unprofited returne,

{ψ};
    Surprize her with discourse of my deere faith ;
    It shall become thee well to act my woes,x
    She will attend it better in thy youth,
    [Then] in a Nuntio's of more grave aspect.

4 Deere Lad, beleeve it ;
    For they shall yet belye thy happy yeeres,
    That say thou art a man : Dianas lip
    Is not more smooth,x and rubious : thy small pipe
    Is as the maidens organ, shrill,x and sound,
    And all is semblative a womans part.

5 I know thy constellation is right apt
    For this affayre : some foure or five attend him,
    All + if you will : x for I my selfe am best
    When least in companie : prosper well in this,
    And thou shalt live as freely as thy Lord,
    To call his fortunes thine.

Commentary

If F's onrushed (five sentences as opposed to most modern texts' ten) overall pattern of releases (4/17) were not enough to indicate Orsino's **emotional vulnerability, the surround phrases underscore just how raw he is.**

• from the opening
"Cesario, /Thou knowst no lesse, but all : I have unclasp'd /To thee the booke even of my secret soule."
through the partly emotional (thanks to the semicolon)
" ; It shall become thee well to act my woes : "
to the reassurance
" . Deare Lad, beleeve it ;
and the building up of an entourage to help 'Cesario'
" . I know thy constellation is right apt/For this affayre : some foure or five attend him,/All if you will :/For I my selfe am best/When least in companie : "

• though another small cluster of surround phrases suggests that Orsino has suddenly noticed something rather special about 'Cesario'
" ; For they shall yet belye thy happy yeeres,/That say thou art a man :
Dianas lip/Is not more smooth, and rubious : "
the impact more emotional than might be expected, thanks to the first semicolon

• the occasional unembellished line seems to underscore his vision of how the wooing should be conducted, as with
"And tell them, there thy fixed foot shall grow/Till thou have audience."
"unfold the passion of my love,/ ..../It shall become thee well to act my woes"
"prosper well in this"

• given the circumstance, the opening onrushed sentences understandably serve to support the notion of the depth of Orsino's love; however, F #5 (mt. #8-10) is a little more surprising, the jamming of his Garbo-like desire to be alone in between praise of Cesario and instructions for an entourage suggest that, all of a sudden, his emotions are too much to bear, and that social niceties and personal selfcontrol are nigh near impossible

#'s 3 - 5: VIOLA IN LOVE

3/ Viola   **If I did love you in my masters flame,**   between 1.5.264 - 276

Background: Though in love with Orsino (which of course she cannot proclaim since she is supposed to be a boy), Viola has committed herself to woo, on behalf of Orsino, one Olivia, who, as it turns out, is not interested in Orsino. The following is triggered by Olivia's dismissal of Orsino and his suite, even though she can appreciate his good qualities, with the final summation ' . . . But yet I cannot love him:/He might have tooke his answer long ago.'. This is Viola's response.

Style: as part of a two-handed scene

Where: somewhere in Olivia's palace   **To Whom:** Olivia   **# of Lines: 13**   **Probable Timing: 0.45 minutes**

Modern Text

3/ Viola

1   If I did love you in my master's flame,
With such a suff'ring, such a deadly life,
In your denial* I would find* no sense,
I would not understand it: {I would}
▬▬▬▬▬▬▬▬▬▬▬▬▬▬▬▬▬▬
Make me a willow △cabin* at your gate,
And call upon my soul* within the house ;
Write loyal* △cantons of contemned love,
And sing them loud* even in the dead of night ;
Hallow your name to the reverberate hills* ,
And make the babbling* △gossip of the air*
Cry out "Olivia" ! †

2   O, you should not rest
Between* the elements of air* and earth
But you should pity* me !

First Folio

3/ Viola

1   If I did love you in my masters flame,
With such a suffring, such a deadly life : x
In your deniall, x I would finde no sence,
I would not understand it: {I would}
▬▬▬▬▬▬▬▬▬▬▬▬▬▬▬▬▬▬
Make me a willow Cabine at your gate,
And call upon my soule within the house, †
Write loyall Cantons of contemned love,
And sing them lowd even in the dead of night : x
Hallow your name to the reverberate hilles,
And make the babling Gossip of the aire, x
Cry out Olivia : +   O+ you should not rest
Betweene the elements of ayre, x and earth, x
But you should pittie me. +

That three of the four opening lines are unembellished is a wonderful testament as to the deep personal place from which Viola begins to speak of love, and the fact that when they do come, the releases do come they are far more emotional than intellectual (5/10 in the other nine and a half lines) shows just how much she is affected.

• the finding no 'sence' in Olivia's 'deniall' is out and out emotional (0/2)

• not surprisingly, the beautiful and fulsome description of what Viola would do to show her love (build a 'willow Cabine'; write doomed-love poetry and sing verses 'in the dead of night'; echo Olivia's name in the 'reverberate hilles') is passionate (4/5)

• and the final declaration that Olivia would have no rest until she 'should pittie' Viola is emotional (1/3)

• and it's wonderful to see that at the end of the speech Viola needs three extra breath-thoughts (marked , x)to keep herself on track and in check, and it is these rather than the modern-text-added exclamation marks (ending both modern sentences), that go to the heart of the finish – an attempt at self-control rather than unchecked over-demonstrative exclamations

4/ Viola   I but I know.   between 2.4.103 - 218

Background: In a sort of locker-room man-to-man discussion (as Orsino believes) with 'Cesario' as to the differences in intensity between male and female love, Orsino suggests that men, especially he, feel things far more deeply than any woman could, dismissing women's love as mere 'appetite'. The following is Viola's response, and it's up to each actress to decide just how successfully Viola manages to maintain her male pose and poise throughout the speech.

Style: as part of a two-handed scene
Where: somewhere in Orsino's palace   **To Whom:** her unspoken love, Orsino
# of Lines: 14   **Probable Timing: 0.45 minutes**

Modern Text

4/ Viola

1 Ay*, but I know — ◊
   Too well what love women to men may owe* ;
   In faith, they are as true of heart, as we.

2 My △father had a daughter lov'd a man
   As it might be perhaps, were I a woman,
   I should your △lordship.

3   (ψ) She never told her love,
   But let concealment like a worm* i'th bud*
   Feed* on her damask* cheek* ; she pin'd in thought,
   And with a green* and yellow melancholy*
   She [sat]* like Patience on a △monument,
   Smiling at grief*.

4   Was not this love indeed*?

5 We men may say more, swear* more, but indeed
   Our shows* are more [than] will; for still we prove
   Much in our vows*, but little in our love.

First Folio

4/ Viola

1 I + but I know.

2 Too well what love women to men may owe : x
   In faith + they are as true of heart, as we.

3 My Father had a daughter lov'd a man
   As it might be perhaps, were I a woman +
   I should your Lordship.

4   (ψ) She never told her love,
   But let concealment like a worme i'th budde
   Feede on her damaske cheeke ; she pin'd in thought,
   And with a greene and yellow mellancholly, x
   She [sate] like Patience on a Monument,
   Smiling at greefe.

5   Was not this love indeede?

6 We men may say more, sweare more, but indeed
   Our shewes are more [then] will : x for still we prove
   Much in our vowes, but little in our love.

F's orthography clearly shows that, despite a very determined attempt to control her emotions, as the speech progresses, so Viola's emotions swamp what vestiges of the self-control she opened with.

• that F #1-2 are unembellished; F #2 is made up of two surround phrases; and F #3 is purely factual (2/), are all excellent indicators of her attempts at self-control - while the peculiar opening of a second ungrammatical sentence after the first four words of the speech suggests that she is struggling very hard to maintain the surface demeanor of objectivity

• but following the unembellished statement opening F #3 'She never told her love', as the 'concealment' is touched upon (her own of course, for she is the only daughter her father had), so emotion simply floods in (2/13 in just the eight lines that end the speech)

• the small clues of the very short sentence F #5, 'Was not this love indeede?' and two of the three surround phrases, first the unembellished statement that she knows
  " . Too well what love women to men may owe ; "
and second, in her disguised persona Cesario, how men usually behave
  " : for still we prove/Much in our vowes, but little in our love . "
again point to her love-wounded vulnerability

5/Viola　　　**By innocence I sweare, and by my youth,**　　　3.1.157 - 162

Background: Viola has played the role of Cesario far too well, and taken Orsino's advice ('Be clamorous, and leape all civill bounds, / Rather than make unprofited returne,'), to such extremes that Olivia has fallen in love with 'Cesario', and has overstepped all bounds of normal social behaviour to tell 'him' so. Since Viola has resolutely refused all of Olivia's advances and offers to date, Olivia has finally sworn her love 'By maid-hood, honor, truth and every thing', an absolutely enormously personally naked vulnerable means of expressing herself (see speech #11 below). Thus, presumably in an attempt to stop Olivia's unwarranted and embarrassing wooing once and for all, Viola is forced to reply in kind.

Style: as part of a two-handed scene　　　**To Whom:** Olivia

Where: the gardens of Olivia's home

# of Lines: 6　　　**Probable Timing: 0.25 minutes**

Modern Text

5/Viola

1　By innocence I swear*, and by my youth,
　I have one heart, one bosom*, and one truth,
　And that no woman has, nor never none
　Shall mistress* be of it, save I alone.

2　And so adieu, good △madam, never more,
　Will I my △master's tears* to you deplore.

First Folio

5/Viola

1　By innocence I sweare, and by my youth,
　I have one heart, one bosome, and one truth,
　And that no woman has, nor never none
　Shall mistris be of it, save I alone.

2　And so adieu+ good Madam, never more,
　Will I my Masters teares to you deplore.

- unlike speech #4 above, here Viola starts emotionally (0/2, F #1's opening two lines) as she swears by her 'innocence' she has just one 'truth': Viola then becomes very quiet as she unembellishedly explains that she will never give herself to a woman (0/0 for the last two lines of F #1); and then the attempt to leave for the last time becomes intellectual (2/1, F #2)

- the five releases in the speech are all key to her attempt to free herself from Olivia's attentions, hence the need to 'sweare'; she wants Olivia, as 'Madam' (and nothing more personal) to understand that Viola has just one 'bosome'; and Viola's predominant thought is of her 'Masters teares'

#'s 6 - 7: VIOLA, WHAT IS SHE? WOMAN, BOY, OR EUNUCH

6/ Viola   **There is a faire behaviour in thee Captaine,**   between 1.2:46 - 64

Background: Viola, travelling with her beloved twin-brother Sebastian, has been ship-wrecked, and believes (incorrectly as it turns out) that she alone was saved, and he drowned.   Having lost everything in the wreck, having no means to provide for herself, and learning that the gentle and generous sea-captain has brought her to Illyria, whose Duke (Orsino) her deceased father knew and spoke well of, Viola decides to disguise herself as a neutered male (a eunuch) and enter his service.

Style: one on one perhaps in front of a small group

Where: on the sea-shore of Illyria   **Whom:** the Sea-Captaine perhaps in front of a small group of sailors

# of Lines: 16   **Probable Timing: 0.50 minutes**

The enormity of what she is about to propose, and the personal risk she is taking, can be seen in the excessive releases of the first line of the speech (1/3): from then on the remaining (mainly emotional, 3/11) releases all enhance the idea she is exploring and/or the argument she is presenting:

- sometimes these come in clusters, as with her initially unembellished first thoughts (the first phrase of F #1) and her decision to trust the Captaine (0/5 the last two lines of F #1) "I [will] beleeve thou hast a minde that suites/With this thy faire and outward charracter."

- but mostly they come as a single key word in each phrase, as she uses the term 'prethee' to the Captaine, to 'ayde' her to 'conceale' her identity, and later explains she will 'speake' to the Duke via many forms of 'Musicke'

- the one moment of intellect in the speech comes as she realises that there may be a way out of her current dilemma, 'Ile serve this Duke' by disguising herself as an 'Eunuch' and make her way in his service by her ability in 'Musicke'

- given the enormity of the decisions within the speech, the very short unembellished monosyllabic final sentence 'Lead me on.', while often played as a triumphant conclusion, suggests rather that Viola may be attempting to enforce an appearance of calm which she may not necessarily be feeling

Modern Text

6/ Viola

1   There is a fair* behavior* in thee, △captain* ,
    And though that nature with a beauteous wall
    Doth oft close in pollution, yet of thee
    I [well] believe* thou hast a mind* that suits*
    With this thy fair* and outward character* .

2   I prithee (and I'll pay thee bounteously)
    Conceal* me what I am, and be my aid*
    For such disguise as haply shall become
    The form* of my intent.
                                    I'll serve this △duke ;
3   Thou shalt present me as an △eunuch to him,
    It may be worth thy pains* ; for I can sing*
    And speak* to him in many sorts of △music*
    That will allow me very worth his service.

4   What else may hap, to time I will commit,
    Only* shape thou thy silence to my wit.
    =================================
5   {ψ} Lead me on.

First Folio

6/ Viola

1   There is a faire behaviour in thee [+] Captaine,
    And though that nature, with a beauteous wall
    Doth oft close in pollution: [x] yet of thee
    I [will] beleeve thou hast a minde that suites [x]
    With this thy faire and outward charracter.

2   I prethee (and Ile pay thee bounteously)
    Conceale me what I am, and be my ayde, [x]
    For such disguise as haply shall become
    The forme of my intent.
                                    Ile serve this Duke, [+]
3   Thou shalt present me as an Eunuch to him,
    It may be worth thy paines : [x]   for I can sing, [x]
    And speake to him in many sorts of Musicke, [x]
    That will allow me very worth his service.

4   What else may hap, to time I will commit,
    Onely shape thou thy silence to my wit.
    =================================
5   {ψ} Lead me on.

7/Viola   **I left no Ring with her : what meanes this Lady?**   2.2.17 - 41

Background: Unfortunately, in following Orsino's instructions to the letter, Viola's outspoken behaviour as Cesario has caused Olivia to fall head over heels in love (describing love as a 'plague') with the supposed boy. Olivia's feelings are so passionate that, following their very first meeting, she has sent the 'boy' a ring, supposedly a male to female process (not vice versa) and only done after nine months of male-driven ardent wooing (not after half-an-hour). Not surprisingly, Viola, who, alone with the audience, can respond as a woman for once without fear of discovery or challenge, is astounded, especially when she realises she has created a rather tricky love triangle which will have to be sorted out, eventually, but not by her.

Style: solo

Where: somewhere in a street   **To Whom:** direct audience address   **# of Lines:** 25   **Probable Timing:** 1.15 minutes

Modern Text

7/Viola

1 I left no ᐃring with her . †
2   What means* this ᐃlady?
3 Fortune forbid my outºside have not charm'd her ! †
4 She made good view of me, indeed so much
   That [sure] [methought] her eyes had lost her tongue,
   For she did speak* in starts distractedly.
5 She loves me, sure ; the cunning of her passion
   Invites me in this churlish messenger . †
6 None of my ᐃlords ᐃring?
7   Why, he sent her none . †
8 I am the man ! †
9   If it be so, as 'tis,
   Poor* Lady, she were better love a dream* . †
10 Disguise, I see thou art a wickedness*
   Wherein the pregnant enemy*does much.
11 How easy*is it, for the proper-ºfalse
   In women's waxen hearts to set their forms* ! †
12 Alas, [our] frailty*is the cause, not we* ,
   For such as we are made [of], such we be* . †
13 How will this fadge?
14   My master loves her dearly* ,
   And I (poor* monster) fond as much on him;
   And she (mistaken) seems* to dote on me . †
15 What will become of this?

First Folio

7/Viola

1 I left no Ring with her : what meanes this Lady?
2 Fortune forbid my out-side have not charm'd her : +
   She made good view of me, indeed so much,ₓ
   That [ ] [me thought] her eyes had lost her tongue,
   For she did speake in starts distractedly.
3 She loves me+ sure,+ the cunning of her passion
   Invites me in this churlish messenger :
   None of my Lords Ring?
4   Why+ he sent her none ;
   I am the man,+ if it be so, as tis,
   Poore Lady, she were better love a dreame :
   Disguise, I see thou art a wickednesse,ₓ
   Wherein the pregnant enemie does much.
5 How easie is it, for the proper false
   In womens waxen hearts to set their formes : +
   Alas, [O] frailtie is the cause, not wee,
   For such as we are made,ₓ [if] + such we bee :
   How will this fadge?
6 And I (poore monster) fond as much on him :
   And she (mistaken) seemes to dote on me :ₓ
   What will become of this?

7/Viola

While F's onrush (eight sentences) shows a Viola in far less control than her much more rational modern counterpart (seventeen sentences), the large number of unembellished lines and surround phrases suggests that she is struggling to deal with the disturbing turn of events as well as she can.

• fascinatingly, unlike many other speeches, the opening of each F sentence contains the key theme underscoring both speech and situation

• thus the opening onrushed passionate short two surround phrase sentence (2/1) superbly sums up the situation both quickly and concisely

• F #2 opens with a key unembellished surround line expressing her fear

• F #3, without the added modern commas (marked + in the Folio text), moves so much faster in the (unfortunate? appalling? amused?) unembellished monosyllabic realisation that 'she loves me sure'

• F #4 is enormously potent, with the opening emotional unembellished monosyllabic surround phrase 'Why he sent her none:/I am the man'

• and, as Viola turns her attention to women's 'frailtie' in general in F #5, not only is the opening monosyllabic, it is also short spelled 'How easie is it'

• F #6's opening describing her own situation is expressed more emotionally than at the start of any of the earlier sentences (0/2)

• F #7's setting up the complications of her adopted male disguise becomes monosyllabic once more

• while F #8's handing over the solution to time opens with a completely unembellished first line

• among the unembellished lines and surround phrases, overall the speech starts out somewhat factually (4/2 in the first seven and half lines of F #1-3) as she establishes the 'Ring', the charm of her own 'out-side', and Olivia loving her 'sure'

• and then slowly the emotion begins to show

16
As I am man,
My state is desperate for my master's love ;
As I am woman (now alas the day ⁻)
What thriftlesse sighes shall poore Olivia breath?⁺

17
O time, thou must untangle this, not I,
It is too hard a knot for me t'unty .

a/ 1/3 in Viola's F ## four and a half line (fun? sympathetic?) realisation
'PooreLady, she were better love a dreame''
b/ 1/5 in her seven and a half line F #5-6 understanding of 'womens waxen
hearts', and applying, unsuccessfully, the understanding to her own situation
c/ 1/4 in the three and a half line F #7 attempt to balance the male and female
sides of the dilemma

• and then in abandoning herself to 'Time' for a solution, rather than herself, so a
(tired?) calmness with almost no releases appears (0/1)

#'s 8 - 12: OLIVIA, IN AND OUT OF LOVE

8/ Olivia   **Have you any Commission from your Lord, to**   between 1.5.231 - 249

Background: Though still in mourning for both her deceased father and brother, Olivia has been intrigued by the description of the rather handsome/pretty young man who has been haunting her doorstep and won't take 'no!' or 'go away!' for an answer. She is even more intrigued when Viola's wooing on Orsino's behalf, though somewhat clumsy, is so passionate, youthful, and breaks all the rules of normal courtship decorum. Enjoying teasing the would-be wooer, here she responds to Viola's 'Good Madam, let me see your face.', an unheard of demand from a servant-wooer for Olivia to unveil herself.

Style: as part of a two-handed scene
Where: somewhere in Olivia's palace   **To Whom:** Viola as Cesario
# of Lines: 12   **Probable Timing: 0.40 minutes**

First Folio

8/ Olivia

1 Have you any Commission from your Lord,ₓ to
negotiate with my face : you are now out of your Text : ₓ
but we will draw the Curtain, and shew you the picture.

2 Looke you ⁺ sir, such a one I was this present : Is't not
well done?

4 'Tis in graine⁺ sir, 'twill endure winde and weather.

5 {ψ}I will not be {ψ} hard-hearted : ₓ I will give
out divers scedules of my beautie.

6 It [shalbe] Inventoried ⁺
and every particle and utensile labell'd to my will : As,
Item⁺ two lippes⁺ indifferent redde,⁺ Item⁺ two grey eyes,
with lids to them : ₓ Item, one necke, one chin, & so forth.

7 Were you sent hither to praise me?

Though Olivia may start in full intellectual command, as the teasing of the apparent 'young man' develops along physical lines, a little emotion begins to creep into the picture.

• the opening two sentence reprimand/start of the tease is doubly incisive in that it is expressed via logical (colon only) surround phrases and is almost totally intellectual (5/1, four lines plus, F #1-2) – and it's lovely to note that the first long-spelled word is the command for Viola/Cesario to 'Looke', opening F #2

• and then, perhaps despite herself, emotion start to creep in with the final statement that her beauty is permanent, i.e. 'in graine' (0/2, F #4)

• and, after a more controlled suggestion that she will give out lists (scedules') of her 'beautie' (F #5) - though perhaps the control is established with some difficulty, since the sentence is made up of two unembellished surround phrases - as Olivia's actually begins to list her physical attributes the passions start to flow (5/4 in F #5's three and a half lines), so whether the passion is to tease 'Cesario' even more, or can be attributed to the fact that Olivia is turning herself on in being alone with a young (as she believes) man for the first time in twelve months is up to each actress to explore

• thus the final unembellished short sentence could be of great interest, a means of controlling herself as well as a genuine question perhaps

Modern Text

8/ Olivia

1 Have you any ᐃcommission from your ᐃlord to
negotiate with my face . †

2 You are now out of your ᐃtext ;
but we will draw the ᐃcurtain, and show you the picture.

3 Look* you, sir, such a one I was this present . †

4 Is't not
well done?

5 'Tis in grain* , sir, 'twill endure wind* and weather.

6 {ψ}I will not be {ψ} hard-hearted ; I will give
out divers schedules* of my beauty* .

7 It [shall* be] ᐃinventoried,
and every particle and utensil* labell'd to my will : ᐃas,
ᐃitem two lips* , indifferent red* ; ᐃitem, two grey eyes,
with lids to them ; ᐃitem, one neck*, one chin, & so forth.

8 Were you sent hither to praise me?

9/ Olivia   **What is your Parentage?**   between 1.5.289 - 311

Background: Viola's naked passion, spurred no doubt by her unspoken love for Orsino, proves too much for Olivia, who, quite obviously, is mightily smitten by the attractive 'boy' (Viola as Cesario) to the point of falling in love. When the opening question was originally asked, the answer was all-important, for if Cesario/Viola was of anything other than 'gentle' birth, Olivia could hold no hopes of any possible relationship, the social gap between them would have been far too big. However, Viola's response 'I am a Gentleman' was exactly what Olivia wanted to hear.

Style: solo

Where: somewhere in Olivia's palace   **To Whom:** self, and direct audience address

# of Lines: 15   **Probable Timing:** 0.50 minutes

Modern Text

9/ Olivia

1 "What is your △parentage?"

2 "Above my fortunes, yet my state is well :
   I am a △gentleman."

3   I'll be sworn* thou art ;
  Thy tongue, thy face, thy limbs*, actions, and spirit,
  Do give thee five ° fold blazon . †

4   Not too fast !   soft , soft ! †

5 Unless* the △master were the man.

6   How now?

7 Even so quickly may one catch the plague?

8 [Methinks*] I feel* this youth's perfections
  With an invisible, and subtle stealth
  To creep* in at mine eyes.

9   Well, let it be.

10 What ho* , Malvolio!

11 I do I know not what, and fear* to find*
   Mine eye too great a flatterer for my mind* . †

12 Fate, show thy force : our selves we do not owe ;
   What is decreed, must be ;   and be this so.

First Folio

9/ Olivia

1   What is your Parentage?

2   Above my fortunes, yet my state is well ; +
   I am a Gentleman.

3   Ile be sworne thou art, +
   Thy tongue, thy face, thy limbes, actions, and spirit,
   Do give thee five-fold blazon :   not too fast: + soft, soft, +
   Unlesse the Master were the man.   How now?

4

5   Even so quickly may one catch the plague?

6   [Me thinkes] I feele this youths perfections
   With an invisible, and subtle stealth
   To creepe in at mine eyes.   Well, let it be.

7

8   What hoa, Malvolio. +

9   I do I know not what, and feare to finde
   Mine eye too great a flatterer for my minde :
   Fate, shew thy force, + our selves we do not owe, +
   What is decreed, must be : x   and be this so.

The speech is a wonderful mix of short bursts of intellect, unembellished lines, and emotion – a sure sign that, for now, Olivia cannot keep herself in check.

• while the speech seems to open in control (2/0 the first two sentences), the fact that F #1 is so short, and F #2 made up of two emotional (thanks to the semicolon) surround phrases, suggests that the control may be difficult to establish, especially since the simple fact of F #2's ' . Above my fortunes, yet my state is well ; / I am a Gentleman.' means Olivia can in all good conscience chase after 'Cesario' since their difference in rank is not all that insurmountable

• dwelling on 'Cesario's' physical attributes, and wishing 'he' were wooing for 'himself' instead of for Orsino, emotions creep in (1/3, F #3) despite her strong admonition of caution to herself, via the unembellished monosyllabic surround phrase ' : not too fast : '

• and the (awful? joyous?) realisation that she has caught the 'plague' of love is also unembellished (F #5), as if the words can scarcely be uttered aloud

• and though Olivia's immediate response to her feeling (1 feele' rather than think) about 'the youths perfections' is emotional once more (0/2, F 6), the decision to 'Well, let it be.' is again very quiet, and triply weighted in being monosyllabic, unembellished, and a short sentence (F #8)

• her commitment to action, (calling in Malvolio via another very short sentence (F #8) is passionate, and though her immediate response to having done so is purely emotional (0/3, the first two lines of F #9), her handing herself over to 'Fate' is totally unembellished again, with the short monosyllabic surround-phrase ending the speech ' : and be this so : ' sounding remarkably like a prayer for success

10/ Olivia   y'are servant to the Count Orsino youth.   between 3.1.100 - 122

Background: Despite knowing of Olivia's feelings for her disguised persona as Cesario, Viola has had to return to Olivia, very unwillingly, to pursue Orsino's wooing. Olivia doesn't even know Viola's disguised self's name, and has thus asked the seemingly innocent question 'What is your name'. However, moments before Olivia has actually tried to touch Viola, under the guise of the request 'Give me your hand sir.', which of course, as a supposed servant, Viola/Cesario should never do except in carefully prescribed circumstances (helping on an awkward or dirty pathway for example). Thus, though seemingly answering Olivia's request as to his/her name, Viola takes great care in her reply 'Cesario is your servants name, faire Princesse' to remind Olivia of the servant-mistress gap between them. However, Olivia will have none of it, or of Orsino either.

Style: as part of a two-hander
Where: the gardens of Olivia's home   **To Whom:** Viola disguised as Cesario   **# of Lines: 19**   **Probable Timing: 1.00 minutes**

Modern Text

10/ Olivia

1 ^Y'are servant to the Count Orsino, youth .
2 For him, I think* not on him . †
       For his thoughts,
   Would they were blanks*, rather than fill'd with me .
3 {ψ} I {bid} you never speak* again* of him ;
   But would you undertake another suit* ,
   I had rather hear* you, to solicit that
   [Than] ^music* from the spheres* .
4 Give me leave, beseech you . †
       I did send,
5 After the last enchantment you did [here] ,
   A ^ring in chase of you ; ◊ so did I abuse
   Myself*, my servant, and I fear* me you . †
6 Under your hard construction must I sit,
   To force that on you in a shameful* cunning
   Which you knew none of yours .
       What might you think?
7 Have you not set mine ^honor at the stake,
8 And baited it with all th'unmuzzled* thoughts
   That tyrannous heart can think?
9   To one of your receiving
   Enough is shown* ; a ^cypress*, not a bosom* ,
   Hides my [poor] heart . †
10   So let me hear* you speak* .

First Folio

10/ Olivia

1 y'are servant to the Count Orsino+ youth .
2 For him, I thinke not on him.: for his thoughts,
   Would they were blankes, rather than fill'd with me .
3 {ψ} {I bid} you never speake againe of him ;
   But would you undertake another suite+
   I had rather heare you, to solicit that,x
   [Then] Musicke from the spheares .
4 Give me leave, beseech you : I did send,
   After the last enchantment you did [heare] ,
   A Ring in chace of you .
5   So did I abuse
   My selfe, my servant, and I feare me you :
   Under your hard construction must I sit,
   To force that on you in a shamefull cunning
   Which you knew none of yours .
6   What might you think?
7 Have you not set mine Honor at the stake,
   And baited it with all th'unmuzled thoughts
   That tyrannous heart can think?
8   To one of your receiving
   Enough is shewne, + a Cipresse, not a bosome,
   Hides my [ ] ^1 heart : so let me heare you speake.

F's orthography shows how and when Viola/Cesario fails to maintain self-control, especially when Viola/Cesario refuses to respond to any of her blandishments (and whether Olivia is genuine in her apologies or merely playing femme fatale is up to each actress to explore).

• the speech starts off intellectually with its opening rebuke (2/0, F #1) – and that's about the only time intellect has any part to play in it

• the denial of Orsino is completely emotional (0/2, F #2), and the emotions become even more apparent as Olivia suggests that Cesario woo for 'himself' (1/6 in just the four lines of F #3) – with both the final surround phrase denial of Orsino and her opening, the suggestion of Cesario undertaking 'another suite', heightened by the only emotional semicolon in the speech

• the fact that the high-ranking Olivia is abasing herself to whom she believes to be a lower status 'gentleman' is accentuated in that her request ' . Give me leave, beseech you : ' is doubly weighted by its being an unembellished surround-phrase: the calm thus indicated perhaps suggests Olivia is either unused to beseeching, or is deliberately trying to maintain an air of calm so as not to frighten/turn off Cesario any further - and certainly, in comparison with what came before the rest of this sentence, it is well under control (1/1, F #4)

• and after the somewhat emotional apology for abusing 'My selfe, my servant, and I feare me you ' is offered (0/2, line two of F #5), so the attempt to get some form of response from Cesario is very carefully voiced despite the extraordinarily powerful images used (1/1 the last three lines of F #5 through to F #7, five and a half lines in all) - though not particularly successfully, for even the careful short monosyllabic unembellished direct request for a reply 'What might you think?' (F #6) fails to elicit a reply

• finally, with no response to date, the emotional dam bursts and Olivia's last surround phrase ': so let me heare you speake . ' is the culmination of all caution seemingly thrown to the wind (1/5 in the two and a half lines of F #8)

---

w 1 most modern texts follow F1 and set this as a nine syllable line; a few follow F2 and create pentameter by adding 'poore'

11/ Olivia   O what a deale of scorne, lookes beautifull?   3.2.145 - 156

Background: The more vigorously Viola refuses Olivia's various enticements, the more inflamed Olivia becomes with the persona of the supposed Cesario. The following is triggered by Viola's blatant statement 'for now I am your foole'.

Style: as part of a two-hander

Where: the gardens of Olivia's home   **To Whom:** Viola disguised as Cesario

# of Lines: 12   **Probable Timing:** 0.40 minutes

Modern Text

11/ Olivia

1 O, what a deal* of scorn* looks* beautiful*
In the contempt and anger of his lip ! †

2 A murd'rous guilt shows* not itself* more soon*
[Than] love that would seem* hid : love's night, is noon * .

3 Cesario, by the △roses of the △spring,
By maid○hood, honor, truth, and every thing,
I love thee so, that maugre all thy pride,
Nor wit, nor reason, can my passion hide . †

4 Do not extort thy reasons from this clause,
For that I woo, thou therefore hast no cause ;
But rather reason thus, with reason fetter :
Love sought, is good, but given unsought is better.

First Folio

11/ Olivia

1 O ⁺ what a deale of scorne, ⁺ lookes beautifull? ₓ
In the contempt and anger of his lip, ⁺
A murdrous guilt shewes not it selfe more soone, ₓ
[Then] love that would seeme hid: Loves night, is noone

2 Cesario, by the Roses of the Spring,
By maid-hood, honor, truth, and every thing,
I love thee so, that maugre all thy pride,
Nor wit, nor reason, can my passion hide :
Do not extort thy reasons from this clause,
For that I woo, thou therefore hast no cause : ⁺
But rather reason thus, with reason fetter ; ⁺
Love sought, is good : ₓ but given unsought, ₓ is better.

The overall pattern of the speech is amazing in that, with the onrush, it starts highly emotionally yet ends very naked and straightforward, and thus offers a fascinating growth curve for any actress to explore.

• despite Cesario's total rejection of everything Olivia has offered, just the mere sight of the supposed boy is sufficient to cause Olivia to abandon any thoughts of immediate self-control (0/7, the first three and a half lines of F #1)

• however, the passion of the surround phrase ending of F #1 '. Loves night, is noone . ', spread into the opening declaration of F #2 ('Cesario, by the Roses of the Spring') seems to allow her to come to a state of quietness and control, for all seven lines of the woo-vow-oath are totally unembellished (rarely seen in any play, and here an amazing sense of control/self-worth/dignity considering the circumstances)

• the depth of her need can be seen in the three surround phrases that end the speech, in part emotionally created (via the semicolon)

12/ Olivia   **Hold Toby, on thy life I charge hold.**   between 4.1.45 - 59

Background: In the confusion of the twins being mistaken for one another, Sir Toby Belch has challenged whom he thinks is the cowardly boy Cesario (i.e. Viola) but is in fact Sebastian, Viola's twin-brother. Sharing Toby's mistake, Olivia rushes in to prevent any injury to her (mistakenly identified) beloved.

Style: one on one address in front of a small group   **To Whom:** directly to Toby, in front of Sir Andrew, Fabian, perhaps Feste - and the bemused Sebastian

Where: somewhere in a public street   **# of Lines: 14**   **Probable Timing: 0.45 minutes**

Modern Text	First Folio
12/ Olivia	**12/ Olivia**
1 Hold, Toby, on thy life I charge thee hold!	1 Hold + Toby, on thy life I charge thee hold. +
2 Will it be ever thus?	2 Will it be ever thus?
3 Ungracious wretch,	3 Ungracious wretch,
Fit for the ᐃmountains* and the barbarous ᐃcaves,	Fit for the Mountaines,ₓ and the barbarous Caves,
Where manners ne'er were preach'd! †	Where manners nere were preach'd.+
4 Out of my sight! †	out of my sight. +
5 Be not offended, dear* Cesario . †	4 Be not offended, deere Cesario :
6 Rudesby*, be gone!	Rudesbey+ be gone. +
7 I prithee* , gentle friend,	I prethee + gentle friend,
Let thy fair* wisdom* , not thy passion, sway	5 Let thy fayre wisedome, not thy passion + sway
In this uncivil* and unjust extent	In this uncivill,ₓ and unjust extent
Against thy peace.	Against thy peace.
8 Go with me to my house,	6 Go with me to my house,
And hear* thou there how many fruitless* pranks*	And heare thou there how many fruitlesse prankes
This ᐃruffian hath botch'd up, that thou thereby	This Ruffian hath botch'd up, that thou thereby
Mayst smile at this. †	Mayst smile at this : Thou shalt not choose but goe : ₓ
9 Thou shalt not choose but go* ;	Do not denie, beshrew his soule for mee,
Do not deny* . †	He started one poore heart of mine, in thee.
10 Beshrew his soul* for me* ,	
He started one poor* heart of mine, in thee.	

F's orthography suggests that, when the time for action presents itself, Olivia is very capable of taking charge.

- now that her beloved Cesario seems in danger, Olivia suddenly becomes much more decisive, with the few surround phrases showing she is perfectly capable of taking control of her own fate: her commands to Toby ' : out of my sight . ' and the even more direct ' . Rudesbey be gone . ' being matched in strength with her care towards Sebastian, whom she believes to be Cesario ' . Be not offended, deere Cesario: ' and ' : Thou shalt not choose but goe : ' ;

- that Olivia, in attempting to stop Toby, starts intellectually (F #1-3, 3/1) is also a sign of her new-found ability to maintain control

- however, as she finally loses her patience with Toby, emotions start to be released (1/2, F #4), and are then in full flow as she attempts to calm Sebastian/Cesario by appealing to his sense of 'fayre wisedome' (0/4 in the three lines of F #5)

- the appeal for her beloved to come with her ' And heare thou there how many fruitlesse prankes/This Ruffian . . . ' has been responsible for also emotional (1/3), and, following the last passionate surround phrase (1/1), Olivia's beseeching him to accept is also emotional (0/3 in the last two lines of the speech)

#'s 13 - 15: ANDREW, A FOOL IN LOVE

13/ Andrew   Ile stay a moneth longer. I am a fellow o'th strangest . . .   between 1.3.112 - 124

Background: Sir Toby, needing money and out of favour with his niece Olivia, is encouraging Sir Andrew ('a foolish knight'), whom he 'brought in one night', to woo Olivia so that he can have access to Andrew's money. Indeed, as Toby tells Fabian a little later in the play, 'I have been deere to him lad, some two thousand strong, or so'. Here Andrew, on the point of abandoning his wooing in favour of the Count Orsino, has been encouraged to stay by Toby's simple statement 'Shee'l none o'th Count . . . I have heard her swear't'.

Style: as part of a two-handed scene
Where: somewhere in Olivia's home   **To Whom:** Sir Toby

     # **of Lines: 9**   **Probable Timing: 0.30 minutes**

Modern Text

13/ Andrew

1   I'll stay a month* longer*.

2   I am a fellow o'th
strangest mind* i'th world*; I delight in △masques* and △re-
vels sometimes altogether*.

3   {I am as} good at these kick*°shawses {ψ}
{a}s any man in Illyria, whatsoever he be, under
the degree of my betters, & yet I will not compare with
an old man.

4   Faith, I can cut a caper {in a galliard}

   {a}nd I think* I have the back*-trick* simply as
strong as any man in Illyria.

First Folio

13/ Andrew

1   Ile stay a moneth longer.

2   I am a fellow o'th
strangest minde i'th world : ₓ I delight in Maskes and Revels sometimes altogether.

3   {I am as} good at these kicke-chawses {ψ}
{a}s any man in Illyria, whatsoever he be, under
the degree of my betters, & yet I will not compare with
an old man.

4   Faith, I can cut a caper {in a galliard}

   {a}nd I thinke I have the backe-tricke,ₓ simply as
strong as any man in Illyria.

Sir Andrew's F #2 surround phrase is a wonderful, if unwitting, description of himself, ' . I am a fellow o'th strangest minde i'th world : I delight in Maskes and Revels sometimes altogether .'

- and it seems that Andrew is incapable of hiding his enthusiasm (or seeing through deception), for in his short F #1 sentence his decision to stay, the time involved is emotionally embraced ('a moneth')

- for some reason, dancing seems very important to him - it is discussed either without any embellishment (as with the latter half of F #3 and the opening of F #4) or quite passionately (as with the opening of F #3, 1/2 in the first two lines, and the last line and a half of F #4, 1/3)

14/ Fabian   **This was a great argument of love in her toward you.**   between 3.2.11 - 29

Background: Andrew is on the point of abandoning his wooing of Olivia yet again, this time because of Olivia's obvious interest in Cesario/Viola. As Andrew tells Toby,
'Marry I saw your Neece do more favours to the Counts Serving-man, then ever she bestow'd upon mee: I saw't i'th'Orchard.'. Toby's henchman Fabian hastily attempts to
repair the damage.

Style: as part of a three-handed scene
Where: somewhere in Olivia's home or gardens   **To Whom:** Sir Andrew, in front of sir Toby

          # of Lines: 12   **Probable Timing: 0.40 minutes**

Modern Text

14/ Fabian

1 This was a great argument of love in her toward you.
━━━━━━━━━━━━━━━━

2 She* did shew favor* to the youth in your sight
only* to exasperate you, to awake your dormouse valor* ,
to put fire in your △heart, and brimstone in your △liver. †

3 You should then have accosted her, and with some excellent jests, fire-new from the mint, you should have bang'd
the youth into dumbness* . †

4   This was look'd for at your
hand, and this was balk'd* . †

5   The double gilt of this oppor-
tunity* you let time wash off, and you are now sail'd* into
the △north of my △lady's* opinion, where you will hang
like an icicle* on a Dutchman's beard, unless* you do redeem* it by some laudable attempt either of valor* or
policy* .

First Folio

14/ Fabian

1 This was a great argument of love in her toward you.
━━━━━━━━━━━━━━━━

2 Shee did shew favour to the youth in your sight,ₓ
onely to exasperate you, to awake your dormouse valour,
to put fire in your Heart, and brimstone in your Liver :
you should then have accosted her, and with some excellent jests, fire-new from the mint, you should have bangd
the youth into dumbenesse : this was look'd for at your
hand, and this was baulkt : the double gilt of this oppor-
tunitie you let time wash off, and you are now sayld into
the North of my Ladies opinion, where you will hang
like an ysickle on a Dutchmans beard, unlesse you do redeeme it,ₓ by some laudable attempt,ₓ either of valour or
policie.

- Fabian seems to have a very clever way of presenting fake bad
  news - as essentially with onrushed enthusiasm, and speaking it as
  simply as possible without any elaboration, as with both the short
  unembellished opening sentence

  "This was a great argument of love in her toward you."

  and the only surround phrase of the speech

  " : this was look'd for at your hand, and this was baulkt : "

- he also has a fine sense of when to play the emotional card and
  when to let the facts speak for themselves

- thus, as Fabian attempts to justify Olivia's behaviour with
  Cesario, the onrushed F #2 opens with emotion (0/4, the first two
  lines) to reinforce the facts that Andrew should, as a result, put 'fire
  in your Heart, and brimstone in your Liver (2/0 in jus one line)

- and then his ability to add extra uneasiness by calm talk comes
  into play once more with the two and a half 'unembellished' line
  suggestion of how Andrew should have 'accosted' Olivia with 'jests'
  and then banged Cesario into 'dumbnesse' (the only released word
  in the passage)

- only then do intellect and emotion join, as he impresses on
  Andrew how desperate the situation now is (3/5 the last five lines of
  the speech)

15 / Toby **Build me thy fortunes upon the basis of valour.** between 3.2.35 – 50 and 3.4.184 – 196 (with an insert from 3.2.58 – 63)

Background: In a direct follow up to Fabian's speech to revitalise Sir Andrew's flagging hopes (speech #14 above), Toby builds on the image of Andrew proving his manhood, only revealing his secret agenda (F #7/mt.#13 to the end of the speech) once Andrew leaves the stage.

Style: initially as part of a three-handed scene

Where: somewhere in Olivia's home or gardens   **To Whom:** Sir Andrew, in front of Fabian, then Fabian alone

# of Lines: 36   **Probable Timing: 1.45 minutes**

Modern Text

15 / Toby

1 {ψ B}uild me thy fortunes upon the basis of valor*.

2 Challenge the Count's youth to fight with him, hurt him in eleven places - my △niece* shall take note of it, and assure thyself*, there is no love-△broker in the world can more prevail* in man's commendation with woman [than] report of valor*.

3 Go, write it in a martial hand, be curst and brief* . †

4 It is no matter how witty*, so it be* eloquent and full of invention. †

5 Taunt him with the license of △ink* . †

6 If thou thou'st him some thrice, it shall not be amiss*; and as many △lies* as will lie* in thy sheet* of paper, although the sheet* were big* enough for the bed* of Ware in England, set 'em down* . †

7 Go about it.

8 Let there be* gall* enough in thy ink*, though thou write with a △goose-pen, no matter. †

9 About it.

10 Go, sir Andrew, scout me* for him at the corner of the △orchard like a bum○△baily*. †

11 So soon* as ever thou seest him, draw, and as thou draw'st, swear* horrible; for it comes to pass* off that a terrible oath, with a swaggering accent sharply* twang'd off, gives manhood* more approbation, [than] ever proof* itself* would have earn'd him.

12 Away!

First Folio

15 / Toby

1 {ψ B}uild me thy fortunes upon the basis of valour.

2 Challenge me the Counts youth to fight with him +, hurt him in eleven places, my Neece shall take note of it, and assure thy selfe, there is no love-Broker in the world,ₓ can more prevaile in mans commendation with woman,ₓ [then] report of valour.

3 Go, write it in a martial hand, be curst and briefe: it is no matter how wittie, so it bee eloquent, and full of invention: taunt him with the license of Inke: if thou thou'st him some thrice, it shall not be amisse, + and as many Lyes,ₓ as will lye in thy sheete of paper, although the sheete were bigge enough for the beddle of Ware in England, set 'em downe, go about it.

4 Let there bee gaulle enough in thy inke, though thou write with a Goose-pen, no matter: about it.

5 Go + sir Andrew: ₓ scout mee for him at the corner of the Orchard like a bum-Baylie: so soone as ever thou seest him, draw, and as thou draw'st, sweare horrible: for it comes to passe oft,ₓ that a terrible oath, with a swaggering accent sharpely twang'd off, gives manhoode more approbation, [then] ever proofe it selfe would have earn'd him.

6 Away. +

Two sides of Toby seem to be revealed here, the game-playing manipulator, and the genuine man – for once Andrew has left (post F #6), Toby's style changes completely from the earlier part of the speech – almost as if, now that **the deception of Andrew has succeeded, he is free to talk as openly as he likes.**

• the first of very few unembellished phrases goes straight to the heart of Toby's manipulations

"Go write it in a martial hand, be curst . . . and full of invention"

• and while the first surround phrases add encouragement and flesh out some of the details as to how

" : taunt him with the license of Inke : " & " : about it . "

" . Go sir Andrew : scout mee for him at the corner of the Orchard like a bum-Baylie : so soone as ever thou seest him, draw, and as thou draw'st, sweare horrible : "

the later ones suggest that Toby has his own agenda in mind

"Now will I not deliver his Letter : for the behaviour of the yong Gentleman, gives him out to be of good capacity, and breeding : his employment betweene his Lord and my Neece, confirmes no lesse."

" . : he will finde it comes from a Clodde-pole . "

" . But sir, I will deliver his Challenge by word of mouth ; "

• the speech opens carefully, with just one key extended image ('valour') breaking through an otherwise unembellished short sentence start (0/1, F #1), and then moves into passion, urging Andrew to 'Challenge me the Counts youth' (3/4, F #2)

• encouraging Andrew by adding detail upon detail as to how to write the challenge, Toby becomes emotional (5/13 F #3-4) though whether the emotion is for Andrew's benefit or his own is up to each actor to decide

• the initial suggestion as to where and how Andrew should search for youth is factual (3/1, the first one and a half surround phrase lines opening F #5), but Toby's emotions spring through once more as he adds extra details swearing 'horrible' by an oath 'terrible' (0/7, the remainder of F #5)

7 Now will not I deliver his Letter: ₓ for the behavi-our of the yong Gentleman,ₓ gives him out to be of good capacity, and breeding: ₓ his employment betweene his Lord and my Neece,ₓ confirmes no lesse.
Therefore, this

8 Letter⁺ being so excellently ignorant, will breed no terror in the youth: ₓ he will finde it comes from a Clodde-pole.

9 **insert** {I thinke Oxen and waine-ropes cannot hale them together.}

10 For Andrew, if he were open'd and you finde so much blood in his Liver,ₓ as will clog the foote of a flea, Ile eate the rest of th'anatomy. }

11 But⁺ sir, I will deliver his Challenge by word of mouth; ₓ set upon Ague-cheeke a notable report of valor, and drive the Gentleman (as I know his youth will aptly receive it) into a most hideous opinion of his rage, skill, furie, and impetuositie.

12 This will so fright them both, that they wil kill one another by the looke, like Cockatrices.

• once Andrew has left, Toby's style changes completely: his initial announcement that he will not deliver the letter is intellectual (2/1, the first two and a half lines of F #7), while his explanation as to why not becomes passionate (4/6, the last line of F #7 and F #8)

• the belief that as it currently stands Andrew and Cesario will never fight is passionate (5/7, F #8-10)

• however, the statement that he will deliver the 'Challenge by word of mouth' suggests that Toby may have some serious reason for frightening Cesario/Viola, for while the idea of inflating Andrew's reputation is handled intellectually (3/1, the first two and a half lines of F #11), the last two lines, referring to 'the Gentleman', are icily calm (the rarity in this speech plus the length of this unembellished passage make it well worthy of exploration)

• the speech finishes with a small moment of intellectual and emotional release (1/1, F #12), the relative lack of release possibly suggesting that the remarks are more for himself than for Fabian

---

13 Now will not I deliver his △letter; for the behavi-or* of the young* △gentleman gives him out to be of good capacity, and breeding; his employment between* his △lord and my △niece* confirmes* no lesse*.
Therefore, this

14 △letter, being so excellently ignorant, will breed no terror in the youth; he will find* it comes from a △clod°pole.

15 **insert** {I think* △oxen and wain*°ropes cannot hale them together.}

16 For Andrew, if he were open'd and you find* so much blood in his △liver as will clog the foote* of a flea, I'll eat* the rest of th'anatomy. }

17 But, sir, I will deliver his △challenge by word of mouth, set upon Ague°cheeke* a notable report of valor, and drive the △gentleman (as I know his youth will aptly receive it) into a most hideous opinion of his rage, skill, fury*, and impetuosity*.

18 This will so fright them both, that they will kill one another by the look*, like △cockatrices.

#'s 16 - 19: MALVOLIO, IN LOVE WITH . . . ?

16/Maria   **Sweet Sir Toby be patient for to night : Since**   between 2.3.131 - 176

Background: In a speech of reprimand breaking up a late-night boisterous sing-along, Malvolio not only threatened Toby, Andrew, and Feste (Olivia's Foole), he made the mistake of threatening Maria, (Toby's eventual sweetheart) , chief lady-in-waiting, and companion (as well as perhaps house chatelaine) to Olivia. Maria, one of the feistiest women Shakespeare ever created, is determined to have her revenge, hence the following.

Style: as part of a four-handed scene
Where: somewhere in the house or gardens of Olivia's home   **To Whom:** Toby and Andrew and a very silent Feste
# of Lines: 26   **Probable Timing: 1.15 minutes**

Modern Text	First Folio

16/ Maria
1 Sweet Sir Toby, be patient for tonight. †
2 Since
the youth of the Count's was today with my △lady, she is much out of quiet.

16/ Maria
1 Sweet Sir Toby⁺ be patient for to night : Since
the youth of the Counts was to day with my Lady, she is much out of quiet.

With the onrushed nature of the speech throughout, the virtual lack of unembellished phrases and the sudden flurry of surround phrases ending the speech, F's orthography points to a very determined lady who is convinced that she can pull down their mutual enemy by playing on his vanity and over-weaning ambition.

• the early surround phrases are testimony to a lady who is shrewd and practical, as her following advice and observations clearly show

{ctd. over}

For Monsieur Malvolio, let me alone

2 with him : If I do not gull him into an ayword, and make him a common recreation, do not thinke I have witte e-nough to lye straight in my bed : I know I can do it.

3 {ψ} Hee is, {ψ} a time-pleaser, an affection'd Asse, that cons State without booke, and utters it by great swarths.

4 The best perswaded of himselfe : so cram'd (as he thinkes) with excellencies, that it is his grounds of faith, that all that looke on him, love him:_x and on that vice in him, wil my revenge finde notable cause to worke.

5 I will drop in his way some obscure Epistles of love, wherein by the colour of his beard, the shape of his legge, the manner of his [gate], the expressure of his eye, forehead, and complection, he shall finde himselfe most feelingly personated.

6 I can write very like my Ladie your Neece, + on a forgotten matter wee can hardly make distinction of our hands.

7 {ψ} He shall thinke by the Letters that {I} wilt drop that they come from my {Lady}, and that shee's in love with him.

8 {ψ} O twill be {ψ} sport royall + I warrant you : I know my Phy-sicke will worke with him, I will plant you two, and let the Foole make a third, where he shall finde the Letter : x observe his construction of it : For this night + to bed, and dreame on the event : Farewell.

"Sweet Sir Toby be patient for to night : Since the youth of the Counts was to day with my Lady, she is much out of quiet.
For Monsieur Malvolio, let me alone with him : . . . : I know I can do it."
especially as to Malvolio

" . The best perswaded of himselfe : "

" : and on that vice in him, will my revenge finde notable cause to worke. "

• and that her belief that the end result will be 'sport royall' is deep seated can be seen in that the final sentence contains at least four surround phrases, three anticipating the event
" . O twill be sport royall I warrant you : . . . observe his construction of it : For this night to bed, and dreame on the event : Farewell. "

• though Maria starts strongly factual, both about Olivia's 'out of quiet' and her own determination to deal with Malvolio (7/0, F #1 and the first line of F #2), as she confidentially states that she will 'gull' him, so her underlying emotion springs through (0/3, between F #2's two colons), followed by an icy unembellished monosyllabic surround phrase concluding assertion ': I know I can do it . '

• at first her denigration of Malvolio as a time-pleasing know-nothing is passionate (2/3, F #3), but very quickly, as she elaborates further just how she will work upon his weakness (his sense of his own importance) by a fake love-letter, her emotions are given full rein (1/9, F #4-5)

• and, as she reveals that the letter would supposedly come from Olivia, and thus Malvolio will undoubtedly believe Olivia is in love with him, both intellect and emotion flow on unchecked (9/10, the remaining eight and half lines ending the speech, F #6-8)

For Monsieur Malvolio, let me alone

3 with him . †

4 If I do not gull him into an ayword, and make him a common recreation, do not think* I have wit* e-nough to lie* straight in my bed . †

5 I know I can do it .

6 {ψ} He* is, {ψ} a time-pleaser, an affection'd △ass*, that cons △state without book* and utters it by great swarths; ◊ the best persuaded* of himself* so cramm'd* (as he thinks*) with excellencies, that it is his grounds of faith, that all that look* on him love him; and on that vice in him will my revenge find* notable cause to work* .

7 I will drop in his way some obscure △epistles of love, wherein by the color* of his beard, the shape of his leg*, the manner of his [gait], the expressure of his eye, forehead, and complexion*, he shall find* himself* most feelingly personated.

8 I can write very like my △lady* niece*; on a forgotten matter we* can hardly make distinction of our hands.

9 {ψ} He shall think* by the △letters that {I} wilt drop that they come from my {Lady}, and that she's* in love with him.

10 {ψ} O 'twill be {ψ} sport royal*, I warrant you . †

11 I know my △phy-sic* will work* with him . †

12 I will plant you two, and let the △fool* make a third, where he shall find* the △letter; observe his construction of it . †

13 For this night, to bed, and dream* on the event . †

14 Farewell.

17a/ Malvolio   To be Count Malvolio.   between 2.5.35 - 80

Background: Maria has dropped the Malvolio-enticing letter, written in exact copy of Olivia's handwriting, and he is about to discover it. Believing he is alone he indulges in his, presumably favourite, fantasy. In fact Toby, Andrew and Fabian (not Feste as originally suggested) are hidden in the box-trees watching his every move, listening to his every word. One note, the speech is constructed by removing all the *sotto voce* asides between Toby, Andrew, and Fabian.

Style: solo, in front of three very interested eaves-droppers
Where: somewhere in Olivia's gardens   **To Whom:** self, and audience, in front of the hidden Toby, Andrew and Fabian
# of Lines: 22   **Probable Timing: 1.10 minutes**

First Folio

17a/ Malvolio

1 To be Count Malvolio. +{ψ}

2 There is example for't : ₓ The Lady of the Stra-chy, married the yeoman of the wardrobe. {ψ}

3 Having beene three moneths married to her, sitting in my state. {ψ}

4 Calling my Officers about me, in my branch'd Velvet gowne :ₓ having come from a day bedde, where I have left Olivia sleeping. {ψ}

5 And then to have the humor of state : ₓ   and after a demure [travaile] of regard:ₓ telling them I knowe my place,ₓ as I would they should doe theirs : ₓ to aske for my kinsman Toby. {ψ}

6 Seaven of my people with an obedient start, make out for him : I frowne the while, and perchance winde up my watch, or play with my+ some rich Jewell : Toby approaches; curtsies there to me. {ψ}

7 I extend my hand to him thus :ₓ quenching my familiar smile with an austere regard of controll. {ψ}

8 Saying, Cosine Toby, my Fortunes + having cast me on your Neece, give me this prerogative of speech.;{ψ}

9 You must amend your drunkennesse. {ψ}

10 Besides + you waste the treasure of your time, with a foolish knight. {ψ}

11 One sir Andrew. {ψ}

Modern Text

17a/ Malvolio

1 To be Count Malvolio !{ψ}

2 There is example for't ; ᐃthe Lady of the Stra-chy, married the yeoman of the wardrobe. {ψ}

3 Having been* three months* married to her, sitting in my state - {ψ}

4 Calling my ᐃofficers about me, in my branch'd ᐃvelvet gown* ; having come from a day-bed*, where I have left Olivia sleeping - {ψ}

5 And then to have the humor of state ;   and after a demure [travel] of regard - telling them I know* my place as I would they should do* theirs - to ask* for my kinsman Toby - {ψ}

6 Seven* of my people with an obedient start, make out for him. †

7   I frown* the while, and perchance wind* up my watch, or play with my - some rich ᐃjewell*.†

8 Toby approaches; curtsies there to me - ◊ {ψ}

9 I extend my hand to him thus, quenching my familiar smile with an austere regard of control* - {ψ}

10 Saying, "Cousin* Toby, my ᐃfortunes, having cast me on your ᐃniece, give me this prerogative of speech"-{ψ}

11 "You must amend your drunkenness* .{ψ}

12 "Besides, you waste the treasure of your time, with a foolish knight - {ψ}

13 One ᐃSir Andrew." {ψ}

That the hopes of marrying Olivia are such an essential part of Malvolio's psyche can be seen in the short sentences that open and, especially, close the speech; the fact that there is no consistency in release from one sentence to the next; and the content of the surround phrases.

• F #2's first surround phrase focuses on his need to find a parallel on which he can build his hopes

" There is example for't : The Lady of the Strachy, married the yeoman of the wardrobe "

heightened by the first phrase being monosyllabic and unembellished, and the second (naturally with the naming of names, 3/0) deeply factual

• and then, startlingly, in one of the most extended sequences of such phrases in the canon, the next eleven imagination lines reeking of images of power and eroticism are formed by twelve successive surround phrases (F #4-7), the most powerful of all seeming to be the humiliation of Toby, as the semicolon created surround phrases show

" : Toby approaches ; curtsies there to me . "

• Malvolio starts out highly intellectually (5/0, F #1-2), the opening short sentence shows where the dream is focused - not on Olivia herself, but on the status marrying her will give him, though the idea of three months married to her is momentarily emotional (0/2, F #3)

• and, as the dreams of 'Calling my Officers about me' (F #4) and the later extension into 'Seaven of my people' to get Toby (F #6) takes shape (and note the long-spelling of 'Seaven'), so the passions flow (3/2 and 2/3, respectively), while the scolding of them (F #5) is splendidly emotional (1/5)

• however, the scolding of Toby, after a moment of emotion (F #7, 0/1, delight perhaps), is initially highly intellectual (4/1, F #8)

• and then it seems some sort of mask drops, and Malvolio ends much more directly with two short sentences out of three, Toby's 'drunkennesse' handled emotionally (0/1) while Andrew is initially icily dismissed (the unembellished F #10) and then factually (1/0, F #11), the little regard Malvolio has for him shown in the fact that Andrew's title is not capitalised

17b/ Malvolio   **What employment have we heere?**   between 2.5,82 - 141

Background: And now Malvolio finds the letter (see speech #16 and background to speech #17a above).

Style: solo, in front of three very interested eaves-droppers

Where: somewhere in Olivia's gardens   **To Whom:** self, and audience, in front of the hidden Toby, Andrew, and Fabian

# of Lines: 29   **Probable Timing: 1.30 minutes**

Modern Text

17b/ Malvolio

1 What employment have we here*? {ψ}

2 By my life, this is my ᴬlady's* hand. †

3   These be* her
very ᴬc's, her ᴬu's, and her ᴬt's; and thus makes she* her
great ᴬp's.

4   It is, in contempt of question, her hand. {ψ}

5 "To the unknown* belov'd, this, and my good ᴬwishes" :
- her very ᴬphrases! †

6   By your leave, wax.

7   Soft ! †

8   And the im-
pressure her Lucrece, with which she uses to seal* . †

9 ᴬlady . †   'Tis my

10   To whom should this be? {ψ}

11 "Jove knows* I love,
But who ?
Lips do not move* ;
No man must know . "

12 "No man must know."   What follows* ? †

13

14 The numbers alter'd ! †

15   "No man must know . " †

16 If this should be thee Malvolio? {ψ}

17 "I may command where I adore,
But silence, like a Lucrece* knife,
With bloodless* stroke my heart doth gore,
M.O.A.I. doth sway my life." {ψ}

18 "M.O.A.I. doth sway my life."
             Nay, but first

19 Let me see, let me see, let me see. {ψ}

First Folio

17b/ Malvolio

1 What employment have we heere? {ψ}

2 By my life + this is my Ladies hand : these bee her
very *C*'s, her *U*'s, and her *T*'s; and thus makes shee her
great *P*'s.

3   It is + in contempt of question + her hand . {ψ}

4 *To the unknowne belov'd, this, and my good Wishes :*
Her very Phrases : + By your leave + wax.

5   Soft, + and the im-
pressure her Lucrece, with which she uses to seale : 'tis my
Lady : To whom should this be? {ψ}

6 *Jove knowes I love, but who, + Lips do not moove, + no
man must know .*

7   No man must know .

8   What followes?

9 The numbers alter'd : +   No man must know, +
If this should be thee Malvolio? {ψ}

10 *I may command where I adore, but silence + like a Lu-
cresse knife +*
*With bloodlesse stroke my heart doth gore, M.O.A.I. doth
sway my life .* x

11 *M.O.A.I. doth sway my life.*

12   let me see, let me see, let me see .   Nay + but first

Though the speech most definitely points to a man whose mind is working overtime (42/14 overall), there are pulses of released energy suddenly interrupted by moments of enforced unembellished calm.

• the unembellished lines show just how well Maria's plot has taken, and how Malvolio is doing everything in his power to make his over-weaning dreams come true
"It is in contempt of question her hand."
"Jove knows I love, but who . . . , no man must know."
"No man must know."
"I may command where I adore,"
"Nay but first let me see, let me see, let me see."
"There is no obstruction in this, and the end: . . . if I could
     make that resemble something in me?"
"This simulation is not as the former: and yet to crush this a
little, it would bow to . . ."
this last suddenly broken by the over-extended 'mee'!

• while the short sentences (#1, #3, #7-8, #11, #12, #14, #16-18 and #20-1) mainly mark the next step Malvolio undertakes, as with F #1's 'What employment have we heere?', or #8's 'What followes?', or end a conclusion just undertaken as with #14's 'Why this is evident to any formall capacitie.'

• the surround phrases, especially those completely making up F sentences #2, #4, #5, #9, #13, point to the enormous number of explosive (false and self-deluding) realisations Malvolio is currently undergoing

• given the interruptions of some tiny emotion in Malvolio's first noticing the fake love-letter (F #1, 0/1) and the unembellished self-deceiving belief that it is from Olivia (F #3), the speech starts very intellectually (12/5, F #1-5)

• at the sight of the first phrase of the fake love-letter, Malvolio's passions momentarily break free (3/2, F #6-8), and then, as he begins to try to force the letter to mean him, as his intellect runs almost into overload (12/2 in the five lines F #9-11)

• and then comes another moment of enforced unembellished monosyllabic calm ('Nay but first, let me see, let me see, let me see.'), the need for calm heightened by being set in a short sentence (F #12)

13   *I may command,* ₓ *where I adore:* Why⁺ shee may
command me: I serve her, she is my Ladie.
14   Why⁺ this is
evident to any formall capacitie.
15   There is no obstruction
in this, and the end: ₓ What should that Alphabeticall position portend, ⁺ if I could make that resemble something
in me? ⁺
16   Softly, *M.O.A.I.* {ψ}
17 *M.*
18 *Malvolio, M.* why⁺ that begins my name.   {ψ}
18 *M.*
19   But then there is no consonancy in the sequell⁺
that suffers under probation: *A.* should follow, but *O.*
does. {ψ}
20   And then *I.* comes behind. {ψ}
21   *M, O, A, I.*
22 This simulation is not as the former: ₓ
and yet⁺ to crush this a little, it would bow to mee. for e-
very one of these Letters are in my name.

• which leads to the passionate belief that he really is the intended recipient of 'Olivia's' love (4/3, in the five lines F #12-15)

• and then, as he finishes the speech by attempting to force the letters M.O.A.I to resemble his name, once more his mind is put to work extraordinarily hard (13/2 in the final seven and a half lines, F #16-22)

---

20 "I may command where I adore." †
21   Why, she* may
command me: I serve her, she is my ᴬlady*.
22   Why, this is
evident to any formal* capacity*, ◊ there is no obstruction
in this. †
24   And the end - ᴬwhat should that ᴬalphabetical* position portend? †
25   If I could make that resemble something
in me!
26   Softly, M.O.A.I. - {ψ}
27 M. - ◊ Malvolio,; M - why, that begins my name.   {ψ}
29 M. - †ᴬbut then there is no consonancy in the sequel* ;
that suffers under probation: A. should follow, but O.
does. {ψ}
30   And then I. comes behind. {ψ}
31   M, O, A, I.
32 This simulation is not as the former ;
and yet, to crush this a little, it would bow to me*, for e-
very one of these ᴬletters are in my name.

18/ Malvolio   **Soft, here followes prose :**   2.5.142 - 179

Background: Having opened the letter (see speech #16, and background to speech #17 above), Malvolio has desperately attempted to see if his name could fit the mysterious single letters signifying Olivia's supposed 'unknowne belov'd', and so far hasn't been able to do so. But now he discovers more hidden in the letter, and . . .

Style: solo, in front of three very interested eaves-droppers

Where: somewhere in Olivia's gardens   **To Whom**: self, and audience, in front of the hidden Toby, Andrew and Fabian

# of Lines: 34   **Probable Timing: 1.40 minutes**

The three moments of onrush, F #1, #2, and especially the longer #6 (split into two, two, and nine sentences respectively by most modern texts) show where Malvolio's feverish imagination is running away with him, substituting haste and the occasional jumbling together of somewhat unrelated topics for his usual careful grammatical niceties.

• the surround phrases show what a tremendous impact his self-deluded decoding of the fake love-letter is having upon him, first as to the identity of the sender

". In my stars I am above thee, but be not affraid of greatnesse :" and then as to the new (foolish) behaviour that is expected of him, the last ('the tricke of singularitie' i.e. eccentric even to the point of being quarrelsome) seeming especially welcome emotionally, as suggested by the emotional semicolon that precedes him

": cast thy humble slough, and appeare fresh. Be opposite with a kinsman, surly with servants: Let thy tongue tang arguments of state ; put thy selfe into the tricke of singularitie."

as well as an occasional tempting reminder

": I say remember, goe too, thou art made if thou desir'st to be so:"

all of which leads to the (incorrect) joyous conclusion

". I doe not now foole my selfe, to let my imagination jade mee ; for every reason excites to this, that my Lady loves me. "
this last (chop-)logically accentuated with the phrase-ending colon

". I thanke my starres, I am happy: "

• and the unembellished phrases seem to mark his deliberately trying to calm himself as he zooms in on what to him is very important (to the observer very foolish) instruction, or piece of information, starting with the letter's surround phrase instructions

". : If this fall into thy hand, revolve. " and

". Be opposite with a kinsman, surly with servants : "

". Remember who commended thy yellow stockings, and wish'd to see thee ever crosse garter'd : "

" I will be point devise, the very man."

". She did commend my yellow stockings of late,"

Modern Text

18/ Malvolio

1   Soft, here fol-
lows* prose . †

2   "If this fall into thy hand, revolve . *

    In my stars
3   I am above thee, but be not afraid* of greatnesse* . †   Some
4   are [born] great, some [achieve] greatnesse* , and some
have greatnesse* thrust upon* 'em.

    Thy ᐃFates open their*
5   hands, let thy blood and spirit embrace them, and to in-
ure thyself* to what thou art like to be, cast thy humble
slough and appear* fresh.

    Be opposite with a kinsman,
6   surly with servants; ᐃlet thy tongue tang arguments of
state ;   put thyself* into the trick* of singularity* .   She*

7   thus advises thee, that sighs* for thee.

    Remember who
8   commended thy yellow stockings, and wish'd to see thee
ever cross*-°garter'd: I say remember . †

    Go* to*, thou art
9   made if thou desir'st to be so; ᐃif not, let me see thee a steward still, the fellow of servants, and not [worth*] to
touch Fortune's fingers . †

    Farewell . †

    She* that would alter
10
11   services with thee,

12   [The] ᐃFortunate ᐃUnhappy . " .

First Folio

18/ Malvolio

1   Soft, here fol-
lowes prose : *If this fall into thy hand, revolve* .

    In my stars
2   I am above thee, but be not affraid of greatnesse : Some
are [become] great, some [atcheeves] greatnesse, and some
have greatnesse thrust uppon em.

    Thy fates open theyr
3   hands, let thy blood and spirit embrace them, and to in-
ure thy selfe to what thou art like to be : ₓ cast thy humble
slough, and appeare fresh.

    Be opposite with a kinsman,
4   surly with servants : ₓ   Let thy tongue tang arguments of
state ;   put thy selfe into the tricke of singularitie.

    Shee
5   thus advises thee, that sighes for thee.

    Remember who
6   commended thy yellow stockings, and wish'd to see thee
ever crosse garter'd : I say remember, goe too, thou art
made if thou desir'st to be so: ₓ If not, let me see thee a steward still, the fellow of servants, and not [woorthie] to
touch Fortunes fingers .² Farewell, Shee that would alter
services with thee, [that] fortunate unhappy.³ daylight and

---

² Ff set no punctuation, as if Malvolio's excitement runs away with him; most modern texts set a period   ³ here all modern texts indicate that the letter is finished and that Malvolio is speaking/gabbling his own thoughts

champian discovers not more : This is open, I will bee
proud, I will reade polliticke Authours, I will baffle Sir
Toby, I will wash off grosse acquaintance, I will be point
devise, the very man.

7   I do not now foole my selfe, to let
imagination jade mee ; for every reason excites to this,
that my Lady loves me.

8   She did commend my yellow
stockings of late, shee did praise my legge being crosse-
garter'd, and in this she manifests her selfe to my love, &
with a kinde of injunction drives mee to these habites of
her liking.

9   I thanke my starres, I am happy : I will bee
strange, stout, in yellow stockings, and crosse Garter'd,
even with the swiftnesse of putting on.

10   Jove,ₓ and my
starres be praised. +

11   Heere is yet a postscript.

12   *Thou canst*

13   *not choose but know who I am.*

14   *If thou entertainst my love, let*
it appeare in thy smiling,⁺ thy smiles become thee well.
There-

15   *fore in my presence still smile, [deero] my sweete, I prethee.*
Jove

I thanke thee, I will smile, I wil do every thing that thou
wilt have me.

---

with the final two more heightened by being unembellished

> *"Thou canst not choose but know: who I am. If thou entertainst my
> love . . . thy smiles become thee well. Therefore in my presence
> still smile,"*
> *"I wil do every thing that thou wilt have me."*

• understandably the speech opens very emotionally (3/14, F # 1-5),
but from the F #6 enforced quiet opening moment of his deluded (and
false) recollection of Olivia's praising his 'crosse garter'd' yellow
stockings (actually a style and colour she abhors) his releases change,
momentarily

• for as he reads the stern admonition that if he doesn't take action he
should remain 'a steward still', the fellow of servants' his passions are
released (8/8 in the eight lines from the first colon of F #6 on)

• and in accepting that Olivia really does love him, so his emotions flow
almost unchecked (1/10, the eight lines of F #7-9),

• F #10's offering praise to 'Jove' (i.e. God) heralds a series of short
sentences, and this and the discovery of an extra series of hints and
instructions in the letter's postscript seem to calm him down somewhat
(or else he is extraordinarily tired after all he has been through), for
while the emotional releases still predominate, proportionately they are
not quite as plentiful as before (0/6, the six lines of F #10-15)

---

13   Daylight and
champian discovers not more . †

14   This is open . †

15   I will be*
proud . †

16   I will read* politic* ᵃauthors*, I will baffle Sir
Toby, I will wash off gross* acquaintance, I will be point-ᵒ
devise, the very man.

17   I do not now fool* myself*, to let
imagination jade me* ; for every reason excites to this,
that my ᵃlady loves me.

18   She* did commend my yellow
stockings of late, she* did praise my leg* being cross*-
garter'd, and in this she manifests herself* to my love, &
with a kind* of injunction drives me* to these habits* of
her liking.

19   I thank* my stars*, I am happy* . †

20   I will be*
Jove and my

21   stars* be praised !

22   Here* is yet a postscript.
"Thou canst

23   not choose but know who I am.

24   If thou entertain'st my love, let
it appear* in thy smiling ; thy smiles become thee well.
Therefore

25   in my presence still smile, [dear] my sweet*, I prithee* ."
Jove

26   I thank* thee . †

27   I will smile, I will* do every* thing that thou
wilt have me.

19/Malvolio   Oh ho, do you come neere me now : no worse   3.4.64 - 83

Background: Malvolio has done everything the letter has commanded (see speech #18 above), to excess, and of course Olivia now doubts his sanity. Unfortunately Olivia's sfinal words as she makes a hasty exit to meet with Cesario once more, 'Where's my Cosine Toby, let some of my people have a speciall care of him, I would not have him miscarrie for the halfe of my Dowry' - the 'him' referring to Malvolio - only seems to convince him of the veracity of the letter, and inflame him even more.

Style: solo
Where: somewhere in Olivia's home   **To Whom:** direct audience address   **# of Lines:** 19   **Probable Timing:** 1.00 minutes

Modern Text

19/Malvolio

1 O* ho, do you come near* me now? †
2   No worse
man [than] ^Sir Toby to look* to me! †
3   This concurs* direct-
ly with the ^letter :   she sends him on purpose, that I may
appear* stubborn* to him;   for she incites me to that in
the ^letter.
4   "Cast thy humble slough," says* she;   be opposite with a ^kinsman, surly with servants;   let thy tongue
[tang] with arguments of state;   put thyself* into the
trick* of singularity";   and consequently sets* down* the
manner how :   as a sad face, a reverend carriage, a slow
tongue, in the habit* of some ^sir of note, and so forth* .
5 I have lim'd* her, but it is Jove's doing, and Jove make me
thankful*!
6   And when she went away now, "^Let this ^fel-
low be look'd too";   "^fellow"! not "^Malvolio", nor after my
degree, but "^fellow".
7   Why, every thing adheres together*,
that no dram* of a scruple, no scruple of a scruple, no
obstacle, no incredulous or unsafe circumstance - What
can be said*?
8   Nothing that can be, can come between*
me, and the full prospect of my hopes.
9   Well, Jove, not I,
is the doer of this, and he is to be thank'd.

First Folio

19/Malvolio

1 Oh ho, do you come neere me now : no worse
man [then] ſir Toby to looke to me. +
2   This concurres direct-
ly with the Letter, + she sends him on purpose, that I may
appeare stubborne to him : for she incites me to that in
the Letter.
3   Cast thy humble slough + sayes she : be opposite with a Kinsman, surly with servants, + let thy tongue
[langer] with arguments of state, + put thy selfe into the
tricke of singularity : x and consequently setts downe the
manner how : as a sad face, a reverend carriage, a slow
tongue, in the habite of some Sir of note, and so foorth.
4 I have lymde her, but it is Joves doing, and Jove make me
thankfull. +
5   And when she went away now, let this Fellow be look'd too : x Fellow?+ not Malvolio, nor after my
degree, but Fellow.
6   Why+ every thing adheres together,
that no dramme of a scruple, no scruple of a scruple, no
obstacle, no incredulous or unsafe circumstance : x What
can be saide?
7   Nothing that can be, can come betweene
me, and the full prospect of my hopes.
8   Well + Jove, not I,
is the doer of this, and he is to be thanked.

• once more the surround phrases highlight the most fervent of Malvolio's hopes

" .. Oh ho, do you come neere me now : no worse man then ſir Toby to looke to me . "
" : for she incites me to that in the Letter. Cast thy humble slough sayes she : "
" : and consequently setts downe the manner how : "
" : And when she went away now, let this Fellow be look'd too :
Fellow? not Malvolio, nor after my degree, but Fellow. "
" : What can be saide ? "

• with his new 'tricke of singularity' seeming to have worked better than he could have hoped, the speech starts emotionally (1/3, F #1)

• that this agrees with the 'Letter' (capitalised twice) becomes passionate (F #2, 2/3), and as Malvolio continues to remind himself of what the letter told him to do, he becomes emotional once more (2/7, F #3)

• with the notion that he has 'lymde her' having to be swiftly turned into 'Jove'/God's doing and not his, his passions come to the fore (2/2, the short F #4)

• the determination to turn anything into proof positive of Olivia's love has him transpose the rather dismissive 'Fellow' into something worthwhile and has his mind working to the exclusion of all else (4/0, F #5)

• and after this, as with the previous speech, though still essentially emotional as he realises 'every thing adheres together' and again thanks 'Jove', his energy, or at least his releases, seem to diminish once more (1/3, the five lines ending the speech, F #6-8)

#'s 20 - 21: SEBASTIAN

20/ Sebastian   I perceive in you so excellent a touch   between 2.1.12 - 43

Background: At the top of the play, Sebastian believes he alone was saved from the ship-wreck and that his twin-sister Viola was drowned. Arriving in Illyria, having spent three months in the company of the man who saved him (Antonio), Sebastian (who for some reason has not yet revealed his true identity or life story) decides to strike out on his own, to Antonio's dismay, who wants to know at the very least where the young man is bound. Sebastian at last unburdens himself.

Style: as part of a two-handed scene

Where: unspecified, perhaps at the dock in Illyria   **To Whom:** his rescuer Antonio

# of Lines: 22   **Probable Timing: 1.10 minutes**

Modern Text

20/ Sebastian

1   {ψ} I perceive in you so excellent a touch
of modesty,* that you will not extort from me what I am
willing to keep* in ;   therefore it charges me in manners
the rather to express* myself* . †

2   You must know of me*
then, Antonio, my name is Sebastian, which I call'd Rodorigo;   my father was that Sebastian of Messaline, whom I
know you have heard of.

3   He left behind* him myself*
and a sister, both born* in an hour* . †

4   If the ᵃheavens had
been* pleas'd, would we had so ended.

5   But you, sir, al-
ter'd that, for some hour* before you took* me from the
breach of the sea was my sister drown'd.

6   A ᵃlady, sir, though it was said she* much resem-
bled me, was yet of many accounted beautiful; but though*
I could not with such estimable wonder over-ᵛfar* believe* that, yet thus far* I will boldly publish her :   she*

7   She* is
drown'd already, sir, with salt water, though I seem* to
drown* her remembrance again* with more.

═══════════

First Folio

20/ Sebastian

1   {ψ} I perceive in you so excellent a touch
of modestie, that you will not extort from me,ₓ what I am
willing to keepe in: ₓ   therefore it charges me in manners,ₓ
the rather to expresse my selfe : you must know of mee
then⁺ Antonio, my name is Sebastianₓ (which I call'd Rodorigo) ⁺ my father was that Sebastian of Messaline, whom I
know you have heard of.

2   He left behinde him,ₓ my selfe,ₓ
and a sister, both borne in an houre : if the Heavens had
beene pleas'd, would we had so ended.

3   But you⁺ sir, al-
ter'd that, for some houre before you tooke me from the
breach of the sea,ₓ was my sister drown'd.

4   A Lady⁺ sir, though it was said shee much resem-
bled me, was yet of many accounted beautiful: ₓ but thogh
I could not with such estimable wonder over-farre beleeve that, yet thus farre I will boldly publish her, ⁺ shee
bore a mind that envy could not but call faire :   Shee is
drown'd already⁺ sir⁺ with salt water, though I seeme to
drowne her remembrance againe with more.

• the opening starts very carefully, the first two unembellished
phrases leading to the surround phrase which sums the essential
chivalric honor by which he (seems to wish to) conducts himself
": therefore it charges me in manners, the rather to expresse my
selfe:"
and then the information that he wishes Antonio to have is handled as
factually as possible (5/1, the last three lines of F #1)

• the facts of his sister's death are seemingly emotionally burned in
his brain, as the surround phrases of F #2 (1/4) show
" . He left behinde him, my selfe, and a sister, both borne in an
houre: if the Heavens had beene pleas'd, would we had so
ended."

• the recollection that he rather than his sister has been saved is,
naturally, emotional (0/2, F #3), and though it seems that he tries to
contain himself as he describes her to Anthonio (1/1, the first two lines
of F #4), as he recalls the beauty of her mind, joining this via the fast-
link ungrammatical colon (the last in F #4) to her drowning (the
drowning set as a separate sentence by most modern texts), the
emotional floodgates open (1/8, in the remaining five lines of the
onrushed F #4)

F's onrush (five sentences as opposed to most modern texts'
ten) shows that, almost throughout, **Sebastian is not in full
control of his feelings, initially presumably because at last he
has to confess to have misrepresented himself for the last
three months, and then, as F's orthography shows, the
memory of his (supposedly) dead sister adds even more to his
inability to handle himself as tidily as most modern texts
would have the actor believe.**

{ctd. over}

8
                    Fare
ye well at once ; my bosom* is full of kindness* , and I
am yet so near* the manners of my mother, that upon the
least occasion more mine eyes will tell tales of me . †
                              I am
9
bound to the Count Orsino's Court . †
10   Farewell.

• the attempted farewell stays emotional (0/3, the first three lines of F #5), and it seems very clear that his claim to be close to tears is very genuine, as the (rare in this speech) unembellished line
    "that upon the least occasion more, mine eyes will tell tales of me"
will testify

• the final doubly ungrammatical moment of the facts as to where he is going (3/0, the last line of the speech), his final word of 'farewell', plus the claim of trying to avoid tears being tacked together as one sentence (via first a fast link colon, and then a fastlink comma) suggests that Sebastian has still not managed to regain self-control – unlike his modern counterpart who is given two separate sentences (mt. #9-10) to make a more tidy departure

                    Fare
ye well at once, + my bosome is full of kindnesse, and I
am yet so neere the manners of my mother, that upon the
least occasion more,x mine eyes will tell tales of me : I am
5
bound to the Count Orsino's Court, farewell.

21/ Sebastian   **This is the ayre, that is the glorious Sunne,**   4.3. 1-21

Background: Mistaken by Olivia for Cesario, the public male persona disguise of his twin sister Viola, Sebastian has been vigorously wooed by Olivia (see speech #12 above): and fallen under her spell. This is his first time alone since her all out sensual love-driven onslaught.

Style: solo

Where: somewhere in house or gardens   **To Whom:** self and direct audience address

# of Lines: 21   **Probable Timing: 1.10 minutes**

Modern Text

21/ Sebastian

1 This is the air*, that is the glorious sun*,
   This pearl* she gave me, I do feel't and see't,
   And though 'tis wonder that enwraps me thus,
   Yet 'tis not madnesse*.
                    Where's Antonio* then? †

2 I could not find* him at the Elephant,
   Yet there he was, and there I found this credit*,
   That he did range the town* to seek* me out . †

3 His counsel* now might do me golden service,
   For though my soul* disputes well with my sence*,
   That this may be some error, but no madness* ,
   Yet doth this accident and flood of Δfortune
   So far* exceed all instance, all discourse,
   That I am ready* to distrust mine eyes,
   And wrangle with my reason that persuades* me
   To any other trust but that I am mad,
   Or else the Δlady's* mad ; yet if 'twere so,
   She could not sway her house, command her followers,
   Take, and give back* affairs*, and their dispatch,
   With such a smooth, discreet, and stable bearing
   As I perceive she do's. †

4 There's something in't

5 That is deceivable*.

6   But here* the Δlady comes.

First Folio

21/ Sebastian

1 This is the ayre, that is the glorious Sunne,
   This pearle she gave me, I do feel't,ₓ and see't,
   And though tis wonder that enwraps me thus,
   Yet 'tis not madnesse.
                    Where's Anthonio then, †

2 I could not finde him at the Elephant,
   Yet there he was, and there I found this credite,
   That he did range the towne to seeke me out,
   His councell now might do me golden service,
   For though my soule disputes well with my sence,
   That this may be some error, but no madnesse,
   Yet doth this accident and flood of Fortune,ₓ
   So farre exceed all instance, all discourse,
   That I am readie to distrust mine eyes,
   And wrangle with my reason that perswades me
   To any other trust,ₓ but that I am mad,
   Or else the Ladies mad ; yet if 'twere so,
   She could not sway her house, command her followers,
   Take, and give backe affayres, and their dispatch,
   With such a smooth, discreet, and stable bearing
   As I perceive she do's : there's something in't
   That is deceiveable.

3   But heere the Lady comes.

21/ Sebastian

Though the first sentences match, according to F's onrushed second sentence Sebastian's apparent self-control quickly disappears once the troubling thoughts of possible insanity get in the way of his opening reverie, especially since he cannot seek **Antonio's advice.**

• the tug of opposites of mad versus not mad are often expressed by very quiet unembellished lines, as if Sebastian must restrain himself lest the dream disappear altogether: thus the 'not mad' sequences include, first about the ring
   "I do feel't, and see't"
   and the denial of Olivia's 'madnesse' for
   " ; yet if 'twere so,/She could not sway her house, command her followers,/ . . ./With such a smooth, discreet, and stable bearing/As I perceive she do's"
   while, the unembellished possibly mad sequences include
   " . . . this may be some error,/ . . ./Yet doth this accident. . ./ . . . exceed all instance, all discourse,/That I am readie to distrust mine eyes,/And wrangle with my reason . . ./ . . . but that I am mad,"

• the only surround phrase wonderfully sums up the whole problem
   " : there's something in't/That is deceiveable. "
   thus matching Viola and Olivia who earlier also believed they could not solve their dilemmas (speeches #7 and #9 above, respectively)

• thus the speech opens full of (joyful) emotion (1/4, F #1)

• the inability to locate Antonio is at first handled passionately (2/2, the first two lines of F #2), then quickly turns to emotion as Sebastian realises how much he needs Antonio's advice (0/6, the next five lines)

• as a result of all the unembellished phrases discussed above, the possibility of madness in either himself or Olivia 'yet doth this accident . . .' is handled very gingerly (an occasional factual release, 2/1 the first five and a half lines to the semicolon), and then his losing himself in how Olivia conducts herself becomes slightly emotional (0/3 the remaining five lines of F #2), which turns to passion (0/1 in the very short F #3) as she joins him on-stage

#'s 22 - 23: EVENTUAL RESOLUTION

22/ Antonio   Let me speake a little.   This youth that you see heere,   between 3.4.359 - 373

Background: Believing that he has saved Sebastian from a duel with Sir Andrew Aguecheek, Antonio has been arrested for brawling in the street - in fact he has saved Viola (her disguise as Cesario fooling him as everyone else). In the first speech, having lent Sebastian his purse, Antonio asks Viola/Cesario for its return, which of course she cannot do though she is willing to share what little money she has on her. From her refusal, Antonio believes Sebastian has rejected him in his hour of need, and in his second part of the speech vehemently denounces the Cesario/Viola persona believing it to be Sebastian.

Style: one on one address in front of a larger group

Where: a public street   To Whom: the arresting officers, plus Toby, Andrew, and Fabian in front of and about Viola/Cesario

# of Lines: 12   Probable Timing: 0.40 minutes

Modern Text

22/ Antonio

1   Let me speak* a little.
2   This youth that you see here*
     I snatch'd one-° half* out of the jaws* of death,
     Reliev'd* him with such sanctity* of love,
     And to his image, which [methought] did promise
     Most venerable worth, did I devotion.

3   But ᐃO*, how vild* an idol* proves this ᐃgod ! †

4   Thou hast, Sebastian, done good feature, shame.

5   In ᐃnature, there's no blemish but the mind* ;
     None can be call'd deform'd but the unkind* .

6   Virtue is beauty, but the beauteous evil*
     Are empty trunks* o'er-flourish'd by the devil* .

7   Lead* me on.

First Folio

22/ Antonio

1   Let me speake a little.
2   This youth that you see heere,ₓ
     I snatch'd one halfe out of the jawes of death,
     Releev'd him with such sanctitie of love ; ₓ
     And to his image, which [me thought] did promise
     Most venerable worth, did I devotion.

3   But oh, how vilde an idoll proves this God : ⁺
     Thou hast ⁺ Sebastian ⁺ done good feature, shame.

4   In Nature, there's no blemish but the minde : ₓ
     None can be call'd deform'd,ₓ but the unkinde.

5   Vertue is beauty, but the beauteous evill
     Are empty trunkes,ₓ ore-flourish'd by the devill.

6   Leade me on.

• the surround phrases suggest the honesty from which Antonio's seemingly justified anger stems, is coming from a very moral place, as, reversing the order in which the two sentences are set, F #4 and #3 show
    " . In Nature, there's no blemish but the minde : ./None can be call'd deform'd, but the unkinde. "   (F #4)
    " . But oh, how vilde an idoll proves this God : ./Thou hast Sebastian done good feature, shame. "   (F #3)

• the speech starts emotionally (0/4, the first three lines of the speech), with the need to speak heightened by the very short opening sentence

• then the ensuing (emotional) semicolon points to how upset Antonio is, yet F #2's last two unembellished lines expressing his own foolishness in worshipping outward appearances, show that no matter how painful the images may be, he still manages to maintain his dignity, at least for a moment

• for then comes the passionate explosion as Antonio publicly denounces Sebastian for doing 'good feature, shame' (2/3 the two lines of F #3), and while there is a modicum of intellect retained during the first maxim (1/2, F #4), the final maxim becomes emotional once more (0/3, the two lines of F #5)

• and just as the short sentence emotional opening seemed awkward and demanding, so too the very short final instruction 'Leade me on.' (0/1, F #6)

Twelfth Night / 309

23/ Sebastian   **Do I stand there? I never had a brother :**   between 5.1.224 - 241

Background: The twins finally face each other, three months after each believed the other had been drowned.

Style: initially public questioning, and then one on one in front of a larger group

Where: a public street   **To Whom:** Viola as Cesario, and Orsino and his followers, Olivia and hers, the Priest, Antonio and his guards

# of Lines: 9   **Probable Timing: 0.30 minutes**

Modern Text

23/ Sebastian

1 Do I stand there?

2   I never had a brother ;
   Nor can there be that ᐃdeity in my nature
   Of here* and every where.

3   I had a sister,
   Whom the blind* waves and surges have devour'd. †

4 Of charity, what kin* are you to me?

5 What ᐃcountryman*?

6   What name?

7   What ᐃparentage?

8 Were you a woman, as the rest goes even,
   I should my tears* let fall upon your cheek*,
   And say, "Thrice welcome, drowned Viola." "

First Folio

23/ Sebastian

1 Do I stand there?

2   I never had a brother : ₓ
   Nor can there be that Deity in my nature
   Of heere,ₓ and every where.

3   I had a sister,
   Whom the blinde waves and surges have devour'd:

4 Of charity, what kinne are you to me?

5 What Countreyman?

6   What name?

7   What Parentage?

8 Were you a woman, as the rest goes even,
   I should my teares let fall upon your cheeke,
   And say, thrice welcome⁺ drowned Viola.

F's sentence structure and orthography reinforces the enormity of the reconciliation, its greatest gift being to show when Sebastian is in control and when not. **The style is essentially one of great control with sudden quick small bursts of emotion or intellect.**

• F #1's quiet opening is triply illustrated by being unembellished, monosyllabic, and short, to be followed by an unembellished surround phrase

• then the sequence (of hope?) turns into a brief moment of intellect and emotion (the last line and a half of F #2), and the subsequent questioning of Viola is fully emotional (F #3, 0/2), F #3's last line question (1/1) enhanced by being a surround phrase

• then come three very short identification demanding questions adding to a moment of passion (2/1, the one verse line containing the three sentences F #4-6)

• the hope that the creature standing before him is female is stunningly withheld via the unembellished 'Were you a woman, as the rest goes even,' with the one line admission of the potential for 'teares' naturally turning emotional (0/2) and the final line factual in the naming of her name (1/0)

SPEECHES IN ORDER	TIME	PAGE
MEASURE FOR MEASURE		
# 1: The Driven Duke		
1/ **Duke** No: holy Father, throw away that thought,	2.00	311
#'s 2 - 3: Angelo's First Taste of Power		
2/ **Angelo** We must not make a scar-crow of the Law,	1.10	313
3/ **Angelo** Condemne the fault, and not the actor of it,	1.00	314
#'s 4 - 8: Isabella Powerless, and The Tempation of Angelo		
4/ **Isabella** So you must be ÿ first that gives this sentence,	0.55	315
5/ **Angelo** From thee: even from thy vertue.	1.15	316
6/ **Angelo** When I would pray, & think, I thinke, and pray	1.30	317
7/ **Angelo** Who will beleeve thee Isabell?	0.55	319
8/ **Isabella** To whom should I complaine? Did I tell this,	0.55	320
#'s 9 - 10: The Powerlessness of The Duke and Claudio		
9/ **Duke** Be absolute for death: either death or life	1.55	321
10/ **Claudio** Oh Isabell/Death is a fearefull thing.	0.50	323
#'s 11 - 12: The Duke Challenged By The Real World		
11/ **Lucio** What newes Frier of the Duke?	1.55	324
12/ **Duke** He who the sword of Heaven will beare,	1.10	326
# 13: The Duke Takes Back His Power		
13/ **Mariana** Oh my most gracious Lord,	0.45	327
# 14: The Real World		
14/ **Clowne** I am as well acquainted heere, as I was in . . .	0.55	328

SPEECHES BY GENDER	Speech #(s)
SPEECHES FOR WOMEN (3)	
Isabella Traditional & Today: a young woman, and a novitiate	#4, #8
Mariana Traditional & Today: dependent upon the age of Angelo, young or youngish middle-age woman	#13
SPEECHES FOR EITHER GENDER (0)	
SPEECHES FOR MEN (11)	
Duke Traditional: older male of some authority Today: as above, though age range much more flexible	#1, #9, #12
Angelo Traditional & Today: young to youngish middle-age man	#2, #3, #5, #6, #7
Claudio Traditional & Today: a young man, brother to Isabella	#10
Lucio Traditional & Today: a young or youngish-middle aged man	#11
Clowne Traditional: older character male **Today:** usually male, any age	#14

MEASURE FOR MEASURE

1: THE DRIVEN DUKE

1/ Duke   **No : holy Father, throw away that thought,**   between 1.3.1- 54

Background: The Duke of Vienna has announced that he will be leaving the city, placing his deputy Angelo in charge in his place. However, unbeknownst to any in the Duke's retinue he will not be leaving. Instead, he wishes to disguise himself as a member of a religious group (assuming the guise of a Frier referred to by others as Frier Lodowick) and see the effect his absence has, especially on Angelo. The Duke explains not just why he is pretending to leave, but also his own culpability for the current state of moral and legal laxity within Vienna, as well as his concerns about Angelo.

Style: as part of a two-handed scene

Where: unspecified, perhaps in Frier Thomas' monastery   **To Whom:** Frier Thomas

    # of Lines: 42   **Probable Timing: 2.00 minutes**

Modern Text

1/ Duke

1   No; holy △father, throw away that thought ;
   Believe* not that the dribbling* dart of △love
   Can pierce a complete* bosom* . †
          Why, I desire thee

2   To give me secret harbor*, hath a purpose
   More grave and wrinkled [than] the aims* and ends
   Of burning youth.

3   My holy △sir, none better knows* [than] you
   How I have ever lov'd the life removed,
   And held in idle price, to haunt assemblies
   Where youth, and cost, witless* bravery keeps* .

4   We have strict △statutes, and most biting △laws,
   (The needful* bits and curbs* to headstrong weeds*,)
   Which for this fourteen* years* we have let slip,
   Even like an o'er-grown* △lion* in a △cave
   That goes not out to prey. †

5   Now, as fond △fathers,
   Having bound up the threat'ning twigs of birch,
   Only* to stick* it in their children's sight
   For terror, not to use, in time the rod
   [Becomes] more mock'd, [than] fear'd; so our △decrees,
   Dead to infliction, to themselves are dead,
   And liberty* plucks △justice by the nose;
   The △baby beates the △nurse, and quite athwart
   Goes all decorum.

First Folio

1/ Duke

1   No :x   holy Father, throw away that thought, +
   Beleeve not that the dribling dart of Love
   Can pierce a compleat bosome :   why, I desire thee +
   To give me secret harbour, hath a purpose
   More grave,x and wrinkled, x [then] the aimes,x and ends
   Of burning youth.

2   My holy Sir, none better knowes [then] you
   How I have ever lov'd the life removed +
   And held in idle price, to haunt assemblies
   Where youth, and cost, witlesse bravery keepes .

3   We have strict Statutes, and most biting Laws,
   (The needfull bits and curbes to headstrong weedes,)
   Which for this fourteene yeares, x we have let slip,
   Even like an ore-growne Lyon in a Cave
   That goes not out to prey :   Now, as fond Fathers,
   Having bound up the threating twigs of birch,
   Onely to sticke it in their childrens sight,x
   For terror, not to use :   in time the rod
   [ ] More mock'd, [then] fear'd : x   so our Decrees,
   Dead to infliction, to themselves are dead,
   And libertie, x plucks Justice by the nose;
   The Baby beates the Nurse, and quite athwart
   Goes all decorum.

That the Duke may not be in full self-control can be seen in the nine onrushed sentences (F's four being reset as nine by most modern texts), especially F #4; in the extra breath-thoughts (marked , x) he uses at critical points to ensure the finer points of his argument are driven home; in the constant switches in released energy; and in the fact that the last six and a half lines of the speech are made up entirely of surround-phrases.

• his (perhaps out of touch) need for privacy can be seen in several of the unembellished passages
   "How I have ever lov'd the life removed/And held in idle price, to
      haunt assemblies"
that the State's 'Decrees' are now
   "Dead to infliction, to themselves are dead"
and his dilemma
   "Sith twas my fault, to give the people scope,/'Twould be my tirrany
      to strike and gall them"
are equally quietly explained (guilt?   acceptance of responsibility?)

• the opening denial of love causing his supposed withdrawal from Venice is stronger than might be expected, with the very first word ' . No : ' being among the mere handful of one-word surround-phrases to be found in Shakespeare

• and the suggestion that the Duke is not in complete control of his thoughts can be seen in what modern texts regard as an untidy onrush, for what they set as mt. #2, the reason for his absence being graver than 'ends/Of burning youth' is set as an onrushed continuation of the opening denial

• the constant switches in styles is seen from the outset, with the first two lines establishing the denial being intellectual (2/0), and then the ensuing explanation/justification of himself becoming fully emotional (1/7 in the remainder of F # 1 and all of F #2, seven lines in all)

{ctd. over}

4

Sith 'twas my fault, to give the people scope,
'T would be my tirrany to strike and gall them,
For what I bid them doe: x   For, we bid this be done x
When evill deedes have their permissive passe,
And not the punishment: therefore indeede x (my father)x
I have on Angelo impos'd the office,
Who may+ in th'ambush of my name, strike home,
And yet,x my nature never in the fight
To do in slander: And to behold his sway
I will, as 'twere a brother of your Order, x
Visit both Prince, and People: x   Therefore I pre'thee
Supply me with the habit, and instruct me
How I may formally in person beare
Like a true Frier: Moe reasons for this action
At our more leysure, shall I render you; +
Onely, this one: Lord Angelo is precise, +
Stands at a guard with Envie: x   scarce confesses
That his blood flowes: x   or that his appetite
Is more to bread [then] stone: hence shall we see
If power change purpose: what our Seemers be.

• the first surround phrase of onrushed F #3 ' : in time the rod/More mock'd then fear'd : ' goes much towards explaining why the lapse of 'strict Statutes' over the last 'fourteene yeares' creates so much passion in him (6/8, the first seven and a half lines of F #3), and though the four lines of explanation that end the sentence may be intellectual (4/1), the sentence ending second surround phrase

' '; The Baby beates the Nurse, and quite athwart/Goes all decorum . " suggests (via the emotional semicolon) the probable emotional strain that lies just underneath the surface

• even though in F #4's first eight and half lines he does attempt to speak with as little release as possible (2/5, the opening two lines unembellished), with the Duke facing up to his own part in the mess, F sets F #4 as the longest onrushed sentence of the speech (which most modern texts split into four): thus both the admission of responsibility and the measures proposed to correct the problem (the appointment of Angelo as his Deputy), come tumbling out of him, once more suggesting a lack of self-control

• and perhaps the Duke is aware of this, for suddenly, in his request that Frier Thomas disguise and instruct him as a member of the Order to enable him to watch Angelo 'And to behold his sway', he becomes strongly factual (8/2, the next seven lines to the semicolon)

• and whether intellectually controlled or not, once Angelo is mentioned three unusual occurrences take place – first, the topic of the Duke's hitherto unmentioned hidden agenda of testing Angelo to see 'if power change purpose' comes out of the blue, tacked on to the end of a seemingly totally unrelated passage/sentence; then, all points about Angelo are expressed via a sudden flurry of surround phrases; and then, though the first definition of Angelo is factual (' : Lord Angelo is precise,/Stands at a guard with Envie : '), the speech's final three and half lines of explanation are almost unembellished, with just two words significantly singled out, whether Angelo's blood 'flowes' and whether he might be a 'Seemer' rather than for real

6

Sith 'twas my fault, to give the people scope,
'T would be my tyrrany* to strike and gall them,
For what I bid them do*; △for, we bid this be done,
When evil* deeds* have their permissive pass*,
And not the punishment. †
            Therefore indeed*, my father,
I have on Angelo impos'd the office,
Who may, in th'ambush of my name, strike home,
And yet my nature never in the fight
To do in slander . †

7
            And to behold his sway
I will, as 'twere a brother of your △order,
Visit both △prince, and △people; △therefore I prithee*
Supply me with the habit, and instruct me
How I may formally in person bear*
Like a true △friar . †

8
            Moe reasons for this action
At our more leisure*, shall I render you ;
Onely*, this one: Lord Angelo is precise ;
Stands at a guard with △envy,*; scarce confesses
That his blood flows*; or that his appetite
Is more to bread [than] stone: hence shall we see
If power change purpose: what our △seemers be.

9

#'S 2 - 3: ANGELO'S FIRST TASTE OF POWER

2/ Angelo   We must not make a scar-crow of the Law,   between 2.1.1 - 36

Background: Among the lapsed laws concerning the Duke, one deals with the propriety of sexual behaviour: in theory, two forms of marriage ritual had to occur before full conjugal relationships could be established, one civil, one religious. For years, in absence of application of the law, a simple civil ceremony has proven to be enough, which Claudio and his betrothed Juliet have undergone, and she is now pregnant. Technically this is illegal, and, with Angelo's reinforcing of the law demanding both rituals, Claudio has been sentenced to death. Escalus, a second administrator appointed by the Duke, has been arguing for clemency. Angelo rejects Escalus' argument, setting out some very clear principles.

Style: as part of a two-handed scene

Where: unspecified, presumably somewhere where judicial proceedings are about to begin   **To Whom:** Escalus

# of Lines: 23   **Probable Timing:** 1.10 minutes

Modern Text

2/ Angelo

1 We must not make a scare°crow of the ᐃlaw,
   Setting it up to fear* the ᐃbirds of prey,
   And let it keep* one shape, till custom* make it
   Their perch* and not their terror.

2 'Tis one thing to be tempted, Escalus,
   Another thing to fall . †

3   I not deny
   The ᐃjury, passing on the ᐃprisoner's life,
   May in the sworn*° twelve have a thief* or two
   Guiltier [than] him they try. †
          What's open made to ᐃjustice.

4 That ᐃjustice seizes. †

5   What knows* the ᐃlaws*
   That thieves* do pass* on thieves*?

6   'Tis very pregnant,
   The ᐃjewel* that we find*, we stoop* and take't
   Because we see it, but what we do* not see
   We tread upon, and never think* of it.

7 You may not so extenuate his offense
   For I have had such faults; but rather tell me,
   When I, that censure him, do so offend,
   Let mine own* ᐃjudgment* pattern* out my death,
   And nothing come in partial*.

8   Sir, he must die* .

9 See that Claudio
   Be executed by nine to morrow morning. †

10 Bring him his ᐃconfessor, let him be prepar'd,
   For that's the utmost of his pilgrimage.

First Folio

2/ Angelo

1 We must not make a scar-crow of the Law,
   Setting it up to feare the Birds of prey,
   And let it keepe one shape, till custome make it
   Their perch, [+] and not their terror.

2 'Tis one thing to be tempted [x] (Escalus)[x]
   Another thing to fall: I not deny
   The Jury [+] passing on the Prisoners life [x]
   May in the sworne-twelve have a thiefe, [x] or two
   Guiltier [then] him they try; what's open made to Justice,
   That Justice ceizes; What knowes the Lawes
   That theeves do passe on theeves?

3   'Tis very pregnant,
   The Jewell that we finde, we stoope, and take't [x]
   Because we see it; [x] but what we doe not see,[x]
   We tread upon, and never thinke of it.

4 You may not so extenuate his offence,[x]
   For I have had such faults; but rather tell me [+]
   When I, that censure him, do so offend,
   Let mine owne Judgement patterne out my death,
   And nothing come in partiall.

5   Sir, he must dye.

6 See that Claudio
   Be executed by nine to morrow morning,
   Bring him his Confessor, let him be prepar'd,
   For that's the utmost of his pilgrimage.

Though Angelo seems secure in his argument and strong presentation of self, F's orthography suggests there may be cracks in this facade - most notably in

a/ four of the five pieces of major punctuation are the emotional semicolons,

b/ in turn creating four emotionally tinged surround lines/ideas, suggesting a great deal of personal involvement is at stake

c/ the large-scale switches between logic and emotion

d/ and the small flurry of extra breath-thoughts (marked , x) in the somewhat dense philosophical utterance of F #3.

- though intellect is found in the speech's first two lines, Angelo's opening need-for-the-Law-to-be-strong statement is essentially emotional (2/4, F #1)

- and while it seems that the start to the 'tempted' versus the 'fall' argument in the somewhat onrushed F #2 is factual and logical (5/2 in the four and a half lines till the first semicolon), even though the surround phrase upholding of Justice (' ; what's open made to Justice,/That Justice ceizes ; ') still maintains a logical appearance (2/1), the semicolons are sufficient to suggest that Angelo is becoming more personally involved than might be expected

- and then suddenly, with the mere mention of 'theeves', emotions break through almost unchecked (1/10, the last line and a half of F #2 and all of F #3)

- and it does seem that Angelo may be aware of this somewhat unusual breach in self-presentation, for, in beginning F #4's argument that Claudio cannot be excused simply because others have had such thoughts, Angelo becomes icy calm, with three unembellished lines opening F #4, but the emotional vehemence of his belief in his own moral righteousness sweeps through to end the sentence (1/4 , F #4's last line and a half)

- whatever the effect of the sentencing of Claudio to death may have on Angelo, the decision is expressed in an exceedingly short sentence (F #5), and whether the brevity is intended to end all further discussion or simply because Angelo finds the sentence awkward or distasteful is for each actor to decide

- whatever the reason, the way the final detailed instructions are handled (2/0, F #6) suggests that Angelo is, or wishes to give the impression that he is, back in control of himself

3/ Angelo   **Condemne the fault, and not the actor of it,**   between 2.2.37 - 99

Background: At Claudio's request Lucio, a skeptic, scoffer, and wit, came to an Abbey to persuade Claudio's sister Isabella to help Claudio, even if it means temporarily postponing her full entry into the religious order (full entry would mean she would not be allowed conversation with anyone from the secular world), an entry due that very day. He succeeds. Isabella removes herself from the religious world and, accompanied by Lucio, enters the very seat of political and judicial power, Angelo's office/chambers, to appeal for her brother Claudio's life, even though she abhors the 'vice' for which Claudio has been condemned. In response, Angelo explains and expands the principles established with Escalus in speech #2, immediately above.

Style: as one on one in front of two silent observers

Where: presumably Angelo's office or chambers   **To Whom:** Isabella, in front of Claudio's friend Lucio and the Provost, who, though responsible for supervising imprisonment and execution, has also expressed sympathy for Claudio

# of Lines: 20   **Probable Timing: 1.00 minutes**

As with speech #2 above, though Angelo's argument appears sound, the onrush of F #1-3 suggests that he may not possess as much equanimity as most modern texts (which reset these three sentences as seven) would like.

- after a slightly emotional opening line, Angelo seems to settle comfortably into his argument (5/1), though again the setting up of himself as the centre of the event (lines three through five) and oblique reinforcement of Claudio's death sentence are both added to the opening premise as one sentence, to the dismay of most modern texts which set each of the topics as a separate sentence: however, F's onrush may undermine the rational appearance Angelo would like to present

- and while the sentence ending announcement ': he must die to morrow . ', is an icily calm surround phrase, the preamble leading to it is somewhat emotional (1/2, F #3)

- while F #3's opening attempt to further justify the decision "The law hath not bin dead, thogh it hath slept" is both monosyllabic and unembellished, and set in a relatively unreleased sentence (1/2, the four lines of F#3), the calm this suggests is immediately undone by the lack of punctuation ending the line, implying that he plunges into the next step of the argument without any syntactical help, something regarded as totally ungrammatical by most modern texts which often set a period here and thus start a logical and correct new sentence thereafter, completely undoing the lack of control F seems to show

- the apparent control does not last much longer, for after a slightly intellectual line and a half (1/0, the start of F #4), the thought of 'future evils' seems to arouse Angelo's emotions for there is a sudden flurry of release (0/6) in the next four lines, the once again rather dense explanation needing two extra breath-thoughts (marked , [x]) from him in order to ensure that he is clearly understood

---

Modern Text

3/ Angelo

1 Condemn* the fault, and not the actor of it ? †
   Why, every fault's condemn'd ere it be done. †
   Mine were the very* △cipher of a △function
   To fine the faults, whose fine stands in record,
   And let go* by the △actor . †

~~~~~~~~~~

4 Your △brother is a forfeit of the △law,
   And you but waste your words.

~~~~~~~~~~

3 It is the △law, not I, [condemns]* your brother . †

5 Were he my kinsman, brother, or my son* ,
   It should be thus with him: he must die tomorrow.

~~~~~~~~~~

6 The △law hath not been* dead, though* it hath slept.†

7 Those many had not dar'd to do* that evil*
   If [but]the first that did th'△edict infringe
   Had answer'd for his deed.

8   Now 'tis awake,
   and like a △prophet
   Looks* in a glass* that shows* what future evils
   Either now, or by remissness* new conceiv'd,
   And so in progress* to be hatc'hd and born* ,
   Are now to have no successive degrees,
   But here they live, to end.

First Folio

3/ Angelo

1 Condemne the fault, and not the actor of it,
   Why[x] every fault's condemnd ere it be done:
   Mine were the verie Cipher of a Function
   To fine the faults, whose fine stands in record,
   And let goe by the Actor :

~~~~~~~~~~

2 Your Brother is a forfeit of the Law,
   And you but waste your words.

~~~~~~~~~~

3 It is the Law, not I, [condemne] your brother,
   Were he my kinsman, brother, or my sonne,
   It should be thus with him : he must die to morrow.

4 The Law hath not bin dead, thogh it hath slept
   Those many had not dar'd to doe that evill
   If [ ] the first,[x] [1] that did th' Edict infringe
   Had answer'd for his deed.
        Now 'tis awake,
   Takes note of what is done, and like a Prophet
   Lookes in a glasse that shewes what future evils
   Either now, or by remissenesse[x] new conceiv'd,
   And so in progresse to be hatc'hd, and borne,
   Are now to have no successive degrees,
   But here they live [+] to end.

---

[1] many commentators have been unhappy with this nine syllable line and have sought to alter the first phrase both for clarification and to establish a pentameter line: some alter F's 'If the first' to 'If but the first', 'If that the first', or 'If he the first', others replace the phrase with 'If the first he'

#'s 4 - 8: ISABELLA POWERLESS, AND THE TEMPTATION OF ANGELO

4/ Isabella   **So you must be ÿ first that gives this sentence,**   between 2.2. 105 - 123

Background: In speech #3 above Angelo has rejected Isabella's plea for Claudio's life, justifying it with statements including the iron-clad 'the Law hath not bin dead, thogh it hath slept . . . Now 'tis awake', and ending with 'Be satisfied:/Your Brother dies to morrow; be content', which triggers the following.

Style: as one on one in front of two silent observers

Where: presumably Angelo's office or chambers   **To Whom:** Angelo, in front of Lucio and the Provost

# of Lines: 17   **Probable Timing: 0.55 minutes**

Modern Text

4/ Isabella

1 So you must be [the] first that gives this sentence,
And he*, that suffers. †
           O*, it is excellent

2 To have a △giant's strength; but it is tyrannous
To use it like a △giant.

           Could great men thunder

3 As Jove himself* does*, Jove would never be quiet,
For every pelting petty △officer
Would use his heaven for thunder, nothing but thunder!†
Merciful* heaven,
Thou rather with thy sharp* and sulphurous bolt
Splits the un‛wedgeable* and gnarled △oak*
[Than] the soft △myrtle*; △but man, proud man,
Dress'd in a little brief* authority*,
Most ignorant of what he's most assur'd
(His glassy* △essence), like an angry △ape
Plays* such fantastic* tricks before high heaven
As makes the △angels weep*; who, with our spleens* ,
Would all themselves laugh mortal* .

First Folio

4/ Isabella

1 So you must be [ÿ] first that gives this sentence,
And hee, that suffers: Oh, it is excellent
To have a Giants strength : but it is tyrannous
To use it like a Giant.

                  Could great men thunder

As Jove himselfe do's, Jove would never be quiet,
For every pelting petty Officer
Would use his heaven for thunder; x
Nothing but thunder: + Mercifull heaven,
Thou rather with thy sharpe and sulpherous bolt
Splits the un-wedgable and gnarled Oke,x
[Then] the soft Mertill : x But man, proud man,
Drest in a little briefe authoritie,
Most ignorant of what he's most assur'd,x
(His glassie Essence) x like an angry Ape
Plaies such phantastique tricks before high heaven,x
As makes the Angels weepe:x who+ with our spleenes,
Would all themselves laugh mortall.

2

F's orthography clearly shows Isabella's struggles first between intellect and passion, and then, possibly more disturbing for a novitiate nun, intellect and emotion, while F's two onrush sentences suggest, despite surface appearances, how difficult it is for her to maintain control at any time in the speech.

• her humanitarian argument is beautifully encapsulated in the surround phrases ending her first sentence
": Oh, it is excellent/To have a Giants strength : but it is tyrannous
     To use it like a Giant. "

• the emotional power (scorn?) of her accusation of those in Angelo's position who do ' ; Nothing but thunder ; ' is clearly heightened via the emotional semicolon that establishes the unembellished surround phrase

• after a slightly emotional summation of the situation (0/1, the first line and a half of the speech), Isabella settles into a strongly intellectual response (6/2, the remainder of F #1 and the first four lines of F #2), reinforced by the two surround phrases already mentioned above

• but her argument that heaven reserves its attack for a worthy opponent ('the gnarled Oke') releases her passions, at least for three lines (3/4 between the two colons of F #3), and the sudden loss of intellectual control is marked by what most modern texts regard as F's ungrammatical onrush, which they correct by setting this argument as a rational new sentence (mt. #4), instead of leaving Isabella's momentary loss of debating skills as is

• there is a brief recovery, as she refers to 'proud man' resembling an 'angry Ape' (3/1, the next three and half lines), but then, with the reference to such a man's acts being enough to make 'the Angels weepe', her intellect gives way to emotion for the first time in the speech (1/4, the last three lines of F #2)

5 / Angelo   From thee : even from thy vertue.   2.2.161 - 186

Background: Unfortunately, at least in this case, as with many other younger men in Shakespeare's comedies, Angelo, despite himself, seems to have fallen in love at the very first meeting with Isabella.   The following is triggered by her parting salutation 'Save your honour.'

Style: solo

Where: presumably Angelo's office or chambers   **To Whom:** self, and possibly some direct audience address

# of Lines: 26   **Probable Timing: 1.15 minutes**

Modern Text

5 / Angelo

1   From thee, even from thy virtue!

2   What's this? what's this? †

3   Is this her fault, or mine? †

4   The ᴬtempter, or the ᴬtempted, who sins most, ha?

5   Not she; nor doth she tempt; but it is I
    That, lying by the ᴬviolet in the ᴬsun*,
    Do* as the ᴬcarrion does*, not as the flow'r*,
    Corrupt with virtuous season. †

6   Can it be
    That ᴬmodesty may more betray our ᴬsense
    [Than] woman's lightness*? †

7   Having waste ground enough,
    Shall we desire to raze the ᴬsanctuary
    And pitch our evils there? †

8   O* fie, fie, fie!

9   What dost thou? or what art thou, Angelo?

10 Dost thou desire her foully* for those things
    That make her good? †

11   O*, let her brother live!

12 Thieves* for their robbery have authority
    When ᴬjudges steal* themselves. †

         What, do* I love her,
    That I desire to hear* her speak* again*? †

         What is't I dream* on? †

13 O* cunning enemy; that to catch a ᴬsaint,
    With ᴬsaints dost bait thy hook*†.†

14   Most dangerous
    Is that temptation that doth goad us on
    To sin* in loving vertue. †

It is obvious not only from Angelo's words that Isabella has had an enormous impact on him, but from his phrasing too – especially the occasional short surround phrases at the top of the speech; the **extra breath-thoughts** scattered throughout (marked , x), usually cropping up as he poses a very awkward question for himself; **and the placing of the unembellished surround phrases** often at the beginning or ending of a sentence, as if he is posing thoughts or **making discoveries which really should not be named.**

• thus the opening four lines are all made up of at least nine surround phrases, seven of which are unembellished (as if even from the very outset he can barely dare give voice to his thoughts), and six of those are monosyllabic, all suggesting that Angelo is reeling within a self generated brain-storm of questions and (unwelcome) revelations

• but within this maelstrom it seems that his mind is still capable of holding it's own, for the first three sentences, ending with three more demanding and condemning unembellished surround phrases ('. . . ? oh fie, fie, fie. /What dost thou? or what art thou Angelo ? '), are profoundly emotion controlled and therefore intellectually dominant (10/5 in twelve lines)

• yet as soon as 'desire' is mentioned, especially in the context of 'fowly', emotion just sweeps all semblance of intellectual control away (1/9, F #4), the sentence again ending in an unembellished surround phrase in the last line, '? /And feast upon her eyes ? '

• naturally, the blaming of the devil, the first three and a half lines of F #5, together with the self-serving assertion that he is a 'Saint' (as well as Isabella) is passionate (2/3)

• and yet, surprisingly, the speech ends with him in full intellectual control as he realises the extent of his predicament (5/0 the last four and a half lines of the speech), though the final realisation of how smitten he is, acknowledging that he can now no longer claim not to understand being totally absorbed by a woman, though

     " : Ever till now/When men were fond, I smild, and wondred how . "
is spoken once more without any embellishment and as a surround phrase, a personally profound conclusion perhaps

First Folio

5 / Angelo

1   From thee : x even from thy vertue. +

2   What's this? what's this?   is this her fault, or mine?
    The Tempter, or the Tempted, who sins most.? ha?

3   Not she : x nor doth she tempt : x but it is I, x
    That, lying by the Violet in the Sunne,
    Doe as the Carrion do's, not as the flowre,
    Corrupt with vertuous season :   Can it be, x
    That Modesty may more betray our Sence
    [Then] womans lightnesse? having waste ground enough,
    Shall we desire to raze the Sanctuary
    And pitch our evils there?   oh fie, fie, fie : +
    What dost thou? or what art thou+ Angelo?

4   Dost thou desire her fowly, x for those things
    That make her good? oh, let her brother live : +
    Theeves for their robbery have authority, x
    When Judges steale themselves : what, doe I love her,
    That I desire to heare her speake againe?
    And feast upon her eyes? what is't I dreame on?

5   Oh cunning enemy, that to catch a Saint,
    With Saints dost bait thy hooke : x most dangerous
    Is that temptation, that doth goad us on
    To sinne, x in loving vertue : never could the Strumpet x

Never could the △strumpet,
With all her double vigor, △art, and △nature,
Once stir my temper ; but this virtuous △maid
Subdues me quite . †
Ever till now
When men were fond, I smil'd and wond'red how .

16

With all her double vigor, Art, and Nature +
Once stir my temper : but this vertuous Maid
Subdues me quite : Ever till now
When men were fond, I smild, [x] and wondred how .

16

6/ Angelo   When I would pray, & think, I thinke, and pray   between 2.4.1-30

Background: Just before his second meeting with Isabella, Angelo, the 'precise', continues the struggle between his conscience and his loins (see speech #5 above).

Style: solo

Where: presumably Angelo's office or chambers   **To Whom:** self, and possibly some direct audience address

# of Lines: 28   **Probable Timing: 1.30 minutes**

Modern Text

6/ Angelo

1 When I would pray & think, I think* and pray
   To several* subjects . †
2   Heaven hath my empty words,
   Whilst my △invention, hearing not my △tongue,
   Anchors on Isabel* ; [God] in my mouth,
   As if I did but only* chew his name,
   And in my heart the strong and swelling evil*
   Of my conception . †
3   The state, whereon I studied,
   Is like a good thing, being often read,
   Grown* [sere] and tedious ; yea, my △gravity*,
   Wherein (let no man hear* me) I take pride,
   Could I, with boot*, change for an idle plume,
   Which the air* beats for vain* . †
4   △O* place, △O* form* ,
   How often dost thou with thy case, thy habit,
   Wrench awe from fools*, and tie* the wiser souls*
   To thy false seeming!
5   Blood, thou art [but] blood :
   Let's write "good △angel*" on the △devil's* horn* ,
   'Tis not the △devil's* crest.
6   How now? who's there?

First Folio

6/ Angelo

1 When I would pray, & think, I thinke, [x] and pray
   To severall subjects : heaven hath my empty words,
   Whilst my Invention, hearing not my Tongue,
   Anchors on Isabell : [x] [heaven] in my mouth,
   As if I did but onely chew his name,
   And in my heart the strong and swelling evill
   Of my conception : the state + whereon I studied +
   Is like a good thing, being often read +
   Growne [feard], and tedious : [x] yea, my Gravitie +
   Wherein (let no man heare me) I take pride,
   Could I, with boote, change for an idle plume +
   Which the ayre beats for vaine : oh place, oh forme,
   How often dost thou with thy case, thy habit [x]
   Wrench awe from fooles, and tye the wiser soules
   To thy false seeming? +

2   Blood, thou art[] blood . ²
   Let's write good Angell on the Devills horne +
   'Tis not the Devills Crest : how now? who's there?

{ctd. over}

Given the circumstances, it's only natural that the speech should be onrushed and emotional (10/30 overall). What F's orthography and sentence structure seems to add is that in the longest onrush (the fourteen and a half line opening F #1, which most modern texts split into four) there is little consistency, starting with small varied releases until a concentrated cluster of emotional releases flow (especially after he admits **he would willingly change his 'Gravitie' for 'an idle plume'**).

• facsinatingly, the only two surround phrases deal with the possibility of his being overheard, first the unembellished monosyllabic ' : how now? who's there ? ', and then the final monosyllabic ' : how now faire Maid . '; this latter interesting in that F sets it as a statement and not a question

• and the one moment of pure intellect comes following the (appalled?) unembellished recognition that 'heaven hath my empty words'
" : Whilst my Invention, hearing not my Tongue,/Anchors on Isabell : " (3/0)
and this concern that his will knows no bounds leads to the only other burst of intellect, again preceded by a very quiet unembellished recognition of man's inner nature, 'Blood, thou art blood,' the ensuing intellect accompanied this time by an equally powerful emotional rush
" Let's write good Angell on the Devills horne,/'Tis not the Devills Crest ," (4/4)

• the opening eight and a half lines of F #1 are highly inconsistent
a/ the praying to 'severall subjects' is emotional (0/2 in the first line and a half
b/ then comes the intellectual acknowledgement of being fixated on Isabell (3/1)
c/ followed by an emotional admission that in his heart lies the 'evill/Of my conception' (0/2) as is the shocking. (presumably to him), though more carefully spoken, awareness that his interest in the state is now 'tedious' (0/1)

---

2 since this FfF line is only nine syllables long (suggesting a quite justified tiny hesitation as Angelo battles with his conscience), some modern texts attempt to create pentameter by changing the last phrase 'thou art blood' into either 'thou art but blood' or 'thou still art blood'

7 Oh heavens! †
8 Why does my blood thus muster to my heart,
Making both it unable for itself*,
And dispossessing all my other parts
Of necessary fitness*?
9 So play the foolish throngs with one that swounds,
Come all to help him, and so stop the air*
By which he* should revive; and even so
The general* subject to a well*-wish'd △king
Quit their own* part, and in obsequious fondness*
Crowd to his presence, where their un°taught love
Must needs appear offense.
10 How now, faire Maid.

• and then in F #1's last six lines, admitting and elaborating his willingness to change his 'Gravitie' for an 'idle plume', emotions flow free (1/10), with the major concentration at the end of the sentence

• this in turn leads to the passionate understanding (and given what follows, not necessarily self-justification) of 'Blood, thou art blood' (4/4, F #2) • and then, as the intellectual abstract reasoning of much of the speech to date gives way to a much more personal exploration ('Why doe's my bloud thus muster to my heart,'), emotion flows relatively unchecked (0/5, F #3)

• and even though the other-people comparison/exploration/justification returns once more (F #4) this exploration still remains emotional (2/6)

3 Oh heavens x
Why doe's my bloud thus muster to my heart,
Making both it unable for it selfe,
And dispossessing all my other parts
Of necessary fitnesse?
4 So play the foolish throngs with one that swounds,
Come all to help him, and so stop the ayre
By which hee should revive: x and even so
The generall subject to a wel-wisht King
Quit their owne part, and in obsequious fondnesse
Crowd to his presence, where their un-taught love
Must needs appear offence: how now+ faire Maid.

7/ Angelo   **Who will beleeve thee Isabell?**   2.4.154 – 170

Background: For the first time alone with Isabella, Angelo's enormously difficult inner struggle (as expressed in speeches #5-6 directly above) is finally resolved, in favour of his loins - and as he says in the following (as must be the case for many in-lust-for-the-first-time men), 'I have begun./And now I give my sensuall race, the reine,'.

Style: as part of a two-hander

Where: presumably Angelo's office or chambers   **To Whom:** Isabella

# of Lines: 17   **Probable Timing:** 0.55 minutes

Modern Text

7/ Angelo

1 Who will believe* thee, Isabel*?

2 My unsoil'd name, th'austerenes* of my life,
   My vouch against you, and my place i'th △state,
   Will so your accusation over°weigh,
   That you shall stifle in your own* report,
   And smell of calumny*.

3   I have begun,
   And now I give my sensual* race the rein.*

4 Fit thy consent to my sharp* appetite,
   Lay by all nicety* and prolixious blushes
   That banish what they sue for . †

5   Redeem* thy brother,
   By yielding* up thy body* to my will,
   Or else he must not only* die the death,
   But thy unkindness* shall his death draw out
   To ling'ring sufferance. †

6   Answer me tomorrow,
   Or by the affection that now guides me most,
   I'll prove a △tyrant* to him.

7   As for you,
   Say what you can: my false, o'er°weighs your true.

First Folio

7/ Angelo

1 Who will beleeve thee + Isabell?

2 My unsoild name, th'austeerenesse of my life,
   My vouch against you, and my place i'th State,
   Will so your accusation over-weigh,
   That you shall stifle in your owne report,
   And smell of calumnie.

3   I have begun,
   And now I give my sensuall race,ₓ the reine,
   Fit thy consent to my sharpe appetite,
   Lay by all nicetie,ₓ and prolixious blushes
   That banish what they sue for : Redeeme thy brother,
   By yeelding up thy bodie to my will,
   Or else he must not onelie die the death,
   But thy unkindnesse shall his death draw out
   To lingring sufferance: Answer me to morrow,
   Or by the affection that now guides me most,
   Ile prove a Tirant to him.

4   As for you, + my false, ore-weighs your true.
   Say what you can;

Two moments in F's sentence structure, and its orthography, could suggest an Angelo lost in the ways of the world, rather than an arch-villain.

a/ given the usual length of Angelo's pronouncements, the emotional, short, speedy (less punctuated than most modern texts) opening sentence suggests that he is being more direct than ever before

b/ and as he begins to let loose his 'sensual race', the long onrushed F #3 gives clear evidence how new this is to him, running over all the debate/rational presentation niceties most modern texts think he should still be able to command: however, F's onrush may be Angelo's saving grace, a man unused to his sensual side: by splitting F #3 into four separate sentences most modern texts have created a far more despicable creature who is fully in control of both self and situation, a far cry from F's Angelo

• not surprisingly, most of the speech is emotional (3/10): however, the last three and a half lines show an interesting switch . . .

• first there is the intellectual demand that Isabell must 'Answer me to morrow' (2/0, the last two lines of F 3)

• and then the speech ends in what seems to be the ultimate of all threats " As for you,/Say what you can ; my false, ore-weighs your true. " and while the words taken at face value are horrific, there may be a saving grace for the character in the orthography, for the sentence is monosyllabic, totally unembellished, and formed by surround phrases linked by the only emotional semicolon in the speech – all of which suggests that Angelo may be having great difficulty in controlling himself as he says what he says: if this is the case, the difficulty here plus the onrushed F #3 could indicate a man way out of his depth, rather than the arch-villain so many modern productions seem to present

8/ Isabella   To whom should I complaine? Did I tell this,   2.4.171 - 187

Background: Despite Angelo's intellectual stand justifying Claudio's death sentence (speeches #2-3 above), in speech #7 immediately above Angelo demands that, to save Claudio, Isabella must submit to exactly the same offence, otherwise, as Angelo unequivocally states 'Ile prove a Tirant to him'. And if this weren't enough, before exiting he finishes with the appalling 'As for you,/Say what you can; my false, ore-weighs your true', which triggers the following.

Style: solo

Where: presumably Angelo's office or chambers   **To Whom:** self, and direct audience address

# of Lines: 17   **Probable Timing: 0.55 minutes**

Modern Text

8/ Isabella

1 To whom should I complain*?

2   Did I tell this,

  Who would believe* me?

3   O perilous mouths* ,

That bear* in them one and the self*-same tongue,
Either of condemnation, or approof*,
Bidding the △law make curtsy* to their will,
Hooking both right and wrong to th'appetite,
To follow as it draws*! †

4   I'll to my brother . †

5 Though he hath fall'n* by prompture of the blood,
Yet hath he in him such a mind* of △honor*,
That had he twenty* heads to tender down*
On twenty* bloody* blocks*, he'ld* yield* them up,
Before his sister should her body* stoop*
To such abhor'd* pollution.

6 Then, Isabel*, live chaste, and brother, die;
More [than] our △brother is our △chastity*.

7 I'll tell him yet of Angelo's request,
And fit his mind* to death, for his soul's* rest.

First Folio

8/ Isabella

1 To whom should I complaine?

2   Did I tell this,

  Who would beleeve me?

3   O perilous mouthes +

That beare in them, $_x$ one and the selfesame tongue,
Either of condemnation, $_x$ or approofe,
Bidding the Law make curtsie to their will,
Hooking both right and wrong to th'appetite,
To follow as it drawes . +

4   Ile to my brother,

Though he hath falne by prompture of the blood,
Yet hath he in him such a minde of Honor,
That had he twentie heads to tender downe
On twentie bloodie blockes, hee'ld yeeld them up,
Before his sister should her bodie stoope
To such abhord pollution.

5 Then, $_x$ Isabell $_x$ live chaste, and brother, $_x$ die;
More [then] our Brother, + is our Chastitie.

6 Ile tell him yet of Angelo's request,
And fit his minde to death, for his soules rest.

The natural shocked response to what has just occurred is magnified by F's lack of colons throughout (very unusual in major speeches in this play); by the opening two short sentences; and by the initial emotional realisation of her helplessness, especially when one and the same person has the power of 'condemnation, or approofe' (0/6, the first four lines of the speech) . . .

• . . . F then suggests her power of resilience, for in her final elaboration of this theme she becomes much more controlled - balancing intellect, emotional and unembellished thoughts (1/1, the last two and a half lines of F #3)

• and this resiliency initially gives way to emotion in her belief that since her brother has a 'minde of Honor', he will do the right thing (1/3, the first two and half lines of F #4), though the onrush via the fast-link comma at the end of the first line suggests need rather than total conviction, and the (romantic? child-like?) envisioning of 'hee'ld yeeld' as many heads as necessary to save her from shame is unabashedly emotional (0/5 the next three lines of F #4)

• and again, perhaps child-like, her vision of surrendering her virginity to save him ('such abhord pollution') is unembellished, as if she can hardly bring herself to say the words – and in F #4's last three and a half lines there are at least five short spellings ('twentie' twice; 'bloodie'; 'bodie' and 'abhord') that might well reinforce her verbal awkwardness

• her F #5 maxim/decision that Claudio should die to save 'our Chastitie' is made even more fervent by being created by two surround phrases, themselves linked by an emotional semicolon, the whole expressed intellectually (3/1 in two lines)

• though, while the first line of 'Ile tell him' is still intellectual, the fact that she must prepare him for death, the last line of the speech, quickly turns emotional once more (0/2) – the awful human cost of what she is about to ask/do hitting home perhaps

#'s 9 - 10: THE POWERLESSNESS OF THE DUKE AND CLAUDIO

9/ Duke   **Be absolute for death : either death or life**   3.1.5 - 41

Background: Following Claudio's apparently well-balanced assessment that 'I have hope to live, and am prepar'd to die ' (a position Claudio totally rejects a few moments later when alone with Isabella, speech #10 immediately below) the Duke, in the guise of Frier Lodowick, is sufficiently encouraged to prepare Claudio for the inevitable.

Style: as part of a two-handed scene
Where: the prison   **To Whom:** Claudio   **# of Lines: 37**   **Probable Timing: 1.55 minutes**

Modern Text	First Folio
9/ Duke	**9/ Duke**
1 Be absolute for death : either death or life	1 Be absolute for death : either death or life
Shall thereby be the sweeter.	Shall thereby be the sweeter.
Reason thus with life :	Reason thus with life :
2 If I do lose* thee, I do lose* a thing	2 If I do loose thee, I do loose a thing
That none but fooles* would keep'st * . †	That none but fooles would keepe : a breath thou art,
A breath thou art,	Servile to all the skyie-influences,
3 Servile to all the skyey-°influences,	That dost this habitation where thou keepst
That dost this habitation where thou keep'st	Hourely afflict : Meerely, thou art deaths foole,
Hourly* afflict . †	For him thou labours by thy flight to shun,
4 Merely* , thou art death's fool* ,	And yet runst toward him still.
For him thou labor'st* by thy flight to shun,	3 Thou art not noble,
And yet run'st toward him still.	For all th'accommodations that thou bearst,
Thou art not noble,	Are nurst by basenesse: Thou'rt by no meanes valiant,
5 For all th'accommodations that thou bear'st,	For thou dost feare the soft and tender forke
Are nurs'd by baseness* . †	Of a poore worme : thy best of rest is sleepe,
Thou'rt by no means* valiant,	And that thou oft provoakst, yet grosselie fearst
6 For thou dost fear* the soft and tender fork*	Thy death, which is no more.
Of a poor* worm* . †	4 Thou art not thy selfe,
7 Thy best of rest is sleep* ,	For thou exists on manie a thousand graines
And that thou oft provok'st* , yet grossly* fear'st*	That issue out of dust.
Thy death, which is no more.	5 Happie thou art not,
8 Thou art not thyself* ,	For what thou hast not, still thou striv'st to get,
For thou exists on many* a thousand grains*	And what thou hast + forgetst.
That issue out of dust.	
9 Happy* thou art not,	
For what thou hast not, still thou striv'st to get,	
And what thou hast, forget'st.	

With their fifteen sentences, most modern texts offer quite a rational character, a far different figure from the nine counseling Duke the original F text shows. **This may well be the first counseling the Duke has had to perform in his disguise as 'Frier', and from the outset it may be seen as somewhat daunting for him and even beyond him, for there is a continual pattern of unembellished lines suddenly being broken, first by emotional outbursts (initially quite short, and then increasing in intensity) and then, as he gets into his stride, outbursts of passion.**

• thus the opening two lines of advice, starting with the stark '. Be absolute for death : ' are created by unembellished surround-phrases, which are then broken into by the suddenly emotional (and rather strange) surround phrase suggestion that only 'fooles' would be upset about losing life (1/4, the one and half lines between the first two colons of F #2)

• whether embarrassed by the outburst (at revealing his own beliefs) or concerned at Claudio's reaction, the Duke quickly returns to a sense of (enforced?) calm for F #2's next two and a half lines describing man's life as one of servility, only for the sentence to finish emotionally (1/3) as he describes Claudio as 'deaths foole'

• the calm returns again at the top of F #3's equally disconcerting suggestion to his looking-for-comfort-listener that 'Thou art not noble', but this only holds for a line and a half, for the rest of the sentence (trying to equate death as merely another form of sleep) is highly emotional (1/8), and F #4's denial of the 'selfe' as a separate entity is equally non-intellectual (0/2)

• and yet again the Duke returns to unembellished calm in trying to put forward F #5's complex dense logic (suggesting Claudio cannot be 'Happie')

• the continuation of stripping Claudio's understanding of the values of life (there is no certainty in his personal make-up - the 'complexion' referred to; the paradox of being rich means he is really poor because he has/will have no friends; and that his body will eventually let him down) suddenly becomes passionate for the first time in the speech (8/11), making the reader wonder if these are the problems of the (older?) Duke rather than those of the younger Claudio

{ctd. over}

6
Thou art not certaine,
For thy complexion shifts to strange effects,
After the Moone: If thou art rich, thou'rt poore,
For like an Asse, whose backe with Ingots bowes; x
Thou bearst thy heavie riches but a journie,
And death unloads thee; Friend hast thou none.

7
For thine owne bowels which do call thee, [fire] +
The meere effusion of thy proper loines x
Do curse the Gowt, [Sapego], and the Rheume
For ending thee no sooner.

8
Thou hast nor youth, x nor age +
But as it were an after-dinners sleepe +
Dreaming on both, for all thy blessed youth
Becomes as aged, and doth begge the almes
Of palsied-Eld: x and when thou art old, x and rich +
Thou hast neither heate, affection, limbe, nor beautie x
To make thy riches pleasant: what's yet in this
That beares the name of life?

9
Yet in this life
Lie hid moe thousand deaths; yet death we feare
That makes these oddes, x all even.

• interestingly, it is here that the emotional semicolons make their impact, appearing for the first time in the speech, and forming surround phrases over one of the loneliest images in the piece, viz.
": Thou bearst thy heavie riches but a journie,/And death unloads thee ."
Friend hast thou none ."

• this may well be supported by the fact that, while in the opening of F #8 the dismissal of youth is only mildly emotional (1/3, the first four lines), the description of the disaffections of old age are much stronger (1/5, the last four lines of F #8)

• and the final emotional semicolon surround-phrase sentence again seems to have relevance for both of them, both in the opening unembellished
": Yet in this life/Lie hid moe thousand deaths ;"
and the final, almost world-weary
"; yet death we feare/That makes these oddes , x all even . "
these last words heightened by the F only extra breath thought (marked , x), and perhaps by being monosyllabic (which it would be if 'even' were to be counted as a single syllable word – 'ev'n' - as it often is in poetry/scansion)

10
Thou art not certain*,
For thy complexion shifts to strange effects,
After the Moon*. †

11
If thou art rich, thou'rt poor*,
For like an △ass*, whose back* with △ingots bows*,
Thou bear'st thy heavy* riches but a journey*,
And death unloads thee. †

12
Friend hast thou none, ◊
For thine owne bowels which do call thee [sire],
The mere* effusion of thy proper loins* ,
Do curse the △gout*, △[serpigo], and the △rheum*
For ending thee no sooner.

13
Thou hast nor youth nor age
But as it were an after-dinner's sleep*,
Dreaming on both, for all thy blessed youth
Becomes as aged, and doth beg* the alms*
Of palsied ○△eld ; and when thou art old and rich,
Thou hast neither heat*, affection, limb* , nor beauty*,
To make thy riches pleasant. †

14
What's yet in this
That bears* the name of life?

15
Yet in this life
Lie hid moe thousand deaths; yet death we fear*
That makes these odds* all even.

10/ Claudio   Oh Isabell/Death is a fearefull thing.   between 3.1.115-131

Background: Initially, as with the disguised Duke, believing there is no hope of reprieve, Claudio can hold firm in the face of death, assuring Isabella 'If I must die,/I will encounter darknesse as a bride,/And hugge it in mine armes.' However, once Claudio learns he would be spared if Isabella will sacrifice her virginity to Angelo, no matter how indignant his first response to Angelo's duplicity may be, Claudio has enormous second doubts.

Style: as part of a two-handed scene

Where: the prison   **To Whom:** Isabel

# of Lines: 16   **Probable Timing: 0.50 minutes**

Modern Text

10/ Claudio

1 O* Isabel*!

2   Death is a fearful* thing.

3(ψ)To die, and go we know not where;
To lie in cold obstruction, and to rot;
This sensible warm* motion to become
A kneaded clod;   ᴬand the delighted spirit
To bathe* in fiery* floods, or to reside
In thrilling ᴬregion of thick*-ribbed ᴬice;
To be imprison'd in the viewless* winds*
And blown* with restless* violence round about
The pendant world;   or to be worse [than] worst
Of those that lawless* and incertain* [thoughts]
Imagine howling - 'tis too horrible!

4 The weariest, and most loathed worldly life
That ᴬage, ᴬache, [penury],   and imprisonment
Can lay on nature, is a ᴬparadise
To what we fear* of death.

First Folio

10/ Claudio

1 Oh Isabell. +

2   Death is a fearefull thing.

3 (ψ)To die, and go we know not where, +
To lie in cold obstruction, and to rot,ₓ
This sensible warme motion,ₓ to become
A kneaded clod;   And the delighted spirit +
To bath in fierie floods, or to recide
In thrilling Region of thicke-ribbed Ice, +
To be imprison'd in the viewlesse windes
And blowne with restlesse violence round about
The pendant world: ₓ or to be worse [then] worst
Of those,ₓ that lawlesse and incertaine [thought],ₓ
Imagine howling, 'tis too horrible. +

4 The weariest, and most loathed worldly life
That Age, Ache, [perjury], and imprisonment
Can lay on nature, is a Paradise
To what we feare of death.

Though to the romantic or morally superior, Claudio's request to live may seem a sign of weakness, F's orthography portrays quite clearly the struggles of a young man trying to come to terms with the situation, showing that the request is not just the preamble to one concerted self-centered bleat for help, but more a conscious attempt to come to some form of understanding.

• just how taken aback he is can be seen in the two opening short sentences followed straightway by the starkly unembellished key dilemma facing all men
"To die, and go we know not where,/To lie in cold obstruction, and to rot"
and this quiet opening F #3 is matched by its close, extending the horrors associated with death, 'Imagine howling, 'tis too horrible.'

• the speech starts strongly emotional (1/3, in the seven words forming F #1-2), and, after the unembellished opening to F #3, stays slightly emotional, considering how the 'warme' body will become a 'kneaded clod' (0/1, the next one and a half lines to the semicolon)

• there is a moment of intellect (3/1, the next two and a half lines) marking where the 'delighted spirit' (or 'delinquent' as some modern texts would have it) might go, to be followed by a sudden emotional flood in the possibility of the horrors that may ensue (0/6, the remainder of F #3, the last half line being unembellished)

• and then, in seeing the most 'loathed wordly life' as a 'Paradise' compared to death, Claudio's intellect takes over once more (3/1, F #4)

#'s 11 - 12:   THE DUKE CHALLENGED BY THE REAL WORLD

11/ Lucio   What newes Frier of the Duke?

Background: Retreating from the political world into the supposedly monastic does not save the Duke from a series of shocks, both personal and communal. Here the scoffer and libertine Lucio, thinking he is shocking a Frier (not realising he is in fact talking to the Duke) dismisses Angelo as, literally, a very cold fish, and suggests that the Duke himself is known to be something of a libertine.

Style: as part of a two-handed scene

Where: unspecified, presumably somewhere where judicial proceedings have just finished   **To Whom:** the Duke, disguised as Frier Ludowick

between 3.2.86 - 184   # of Lines: 37   **Probable Timing:** 1.55 minutes

First Folio

11/ Lucio

1   What newes⁺ Frier ⁺ of the Duke?

2   It was a mad fantasticall tricke of him to steale from the State, and usurpe the beggerie hee was never borne to: Lord Angelo Dukes it well in his absence: ₓ he puts transgression too't.. ᵩ}

3   A little more lenitie to Lecherie would doe no harme in him: Something too crabbed that way .

4   They say this Angelo was not made by Man and Woman,ₓ after this downe-right way of Creation:

5   Some report, a Sea-maid spawn'd him .   Some, that he was begot betweene two Stock-fishes.

6

7   But it is certaine,ₓ that when he makes water,ₓ his Urine is congeal'd ice, that I know to bee true: ₓ and he is a motion [generative], that's infallible.

8   Why, what a ruthlesse thing is this in him, for the rebellion of a Cod-peece, to take away the life of a man?⁺

9   Would the Duke that is absent have done this?

10   Ere he would have hang'd a man for the getting a hundred Bastards, he would have paide for the Nursing a thousand.

                                                                    He had some feeling of the sport, ⁺ hee knew the service, and that instructed him to mercie.

Modern Text

11/ Lucio

1   What news*, ᐃfriar*, of the Duke?

2   It was a mad fantastical* trick* of him to steal* from the ᐃstate, and usurp* the beggary* he* was never born* to. †

3   Lord Angelo ᐃdukes it well in his absence; he puts transgression too't. ᵩ}

4   A little more lenity* to ᐃlechery* would do* no harm* in him. †

5   They say this Angelo was not made by ᐃman and ᐃwoman after this down'right way of ᐃcreation. †

6   Some report, a ᐃsea-maid spawn'd him ; ◊ some, that he was begot between* two ᐃstock°fishes.

7   But it is certain* that when he makes water his ᐃurine is congeal'd ice, that I know to be* true; and he is a motion [ungenerative], that's infallible.

8   Why, what a ruthless* thing is this in him, for the rebellion of a ᐃcod°piece*, to take away the life of a man! †

9   Would the Duke that is absent have done this?

10   Ere he would have hang'd a man for the getting a hundred ᐃbastards, he would have paid* for the ᐃnursing a thousand.

11   He had some feeling of the sport; he* knew the service, and that instructed him to mercy*.

(commentary column)

Lucio is akin to a gad-fly the way his style keeps shifting in his put-downs of Angelo (an inventive mind, perhaps coupled with being a little concerned about the consequences of speaking out of turn, for often the first phrases of denunciation are full of release, while the follow-ups are far more circumspect, see F #2-3).   **However, once he raises the matter of Claudio's impending death he settles down, somewhat.**

• thus, though F #1's faster opening (without the extra punctuation, marked ⁺ in the Folio text) is basically factual (2/1, with 'newes' probably being the important word here), the criticism of the Duke's self-imposed absence is, surprisingly, highly emotional (1/6 in just two and half lines to the first colon of F #2)

• the first mention of Angelo is cynically intellectual, with the wonderful creation of the (capitalised) verb 'Dukes' heightened by the surround phrase ' ; Lord Angelo Dukes it well in his absence : ' (3/0 in just the one phrase), followed by the very careful unembellished surround phrase assessment of how Angelo 'Dukes' it, i.e. ' : he puts transgression too't .'

• indeed, Angelo seems to be a great irritant to Lucio, for the next four sentences of scornful description are all somewhat out of the ordinary
a/ the passionate F #3 (2/2) attack on Angelo's 'crabbed' attitude towards 'Lecherie' is created by two surround phrases
b/ his outrageous suggestion that Angelo was not conceived in any normal way is heavily intellectual (6/2, F #4+5)
c/ while the wonderful suggestion of Angelo's 'Urine' being 'congeal'd ice' starts slightly emotionally (1/2, the first phrase of F #6), needs two extra breath-thoughts (marked ,) to get the points across, and then once more he reins himself in with unembellished care 'and he is a motion [un]generative', that's infallible', the modern texts' gloss of 'ungenerative' suggesting Angelo cannot reproduce!
d/ F #7's final attack on Angelo for proposing to execute Claudio for his 'rebellion of a Cod-peece' becomes emotional once more (1/2)

• and then, as Lucio turns his somewhat (mischievous? jaundiced?) eye to the Duke (while the sexual put-downs continue, they are at least proactive), he becomes more relaxed, the comments mainly intellectual

12 Yes, your beggar of fifty;
and his use was, to put a ducat* in her △clack-dish. †
The

13 Duke had Crochets in him.

14 But no more of this. †

15 Claudio die{s} to morrow,
{f}or filling a bottle with a △tun -dish. †

16 I would the Duke we talk* of were return'd again* . †
This

17 ungenitur'd △agent will un°people the △province with △continency.

18 Sparrows* must not build in his house-
eaves*, because they are lecherous. †

19 The Duke yet would
have dark* deeds darkly* answered, he* would never
bring them to light. †

20 Would he* were return'd!

21 Marry*,
this Claudio is condemned for untrussing.

22 Farewell*, good
△friar . †

23 I prithee* pray for me. †

24 The Duke (I say to thee
again*) would eat* △mutton on Fridays*.

25 He's now past

26 it, yet (and I say to thee) he* would mouth with a beggar, though she smelt brown*° bread and △garlic* . †
Say

27 that I said so. †
Farewell.

(6/2, F 8-11), finishing with a three surround phrase all-praising
flourish, the last two emotionally created by the only semicolon in the
speech
". Yes, your beggar of fifty : and his use was , to put a ducket in her
Clack-dish : the Duke had Crotchets in him . "

• while the disconcerting wit still surfaces occasionally, as Lucio raises
the topic of Claudio's death 'to morrow', so matters become much
more serious, with the next three sentences all bearing the hallmarks
of serious concern

a/ according to most modern texts F #12 is far too onrushed,
lumping together Claudio's impending execution; the reason
why; the wish for the Duke's return; and once more a put
down of Angelo – the intellectual and emotional whole (6/3)
expressed totally via four surround phrases: most modern texts
reduce this intensity by splitting F #12 in three

b/ the onrushed F #13, the continued attack on Angelo and wish
for the Duke's return (again reduced in effect by being split in
three by most modern texts), becomes suddenly very emotional
(2/6), the effect heightened by also being totally created by (this
time three) surround phrases

c/ while the final summation comes via a short, virtually
unembellished (thus calm except for Claudio's name) F #14
(1/0)

• the farewell to the 'Frier' and the mocking appreciation of the Duke
starts totally intellectual (5/0, F #15), while the final assessment (the
age-ist put-down of 'He's now past it') is led into by a moment of
emotion (1/3) and completed by two surround-phrases, the first
seeming to really accept responsibility for all he has said (' : say that I
said so : ') in that the phrase is also unembellished and monosyllabic

---

11 Yes, your beggar of fifty: x
and his use was, to put a ducket in her Clack-dish ; the
Duke had Crochets in him.

12 But no more of this : {.} Claudio die{s} to morrow,
{f}or filling a bottle with a Tunne-dish :
I would the Duke we talke of were return'd againe : this
ungenitur'd Agent will un-people the Province with
Continencie.

13 Sparrowes must not build in his house-
eeves, because they are lecherous: The Duke yet would
have darke deeds darkelie answered, hee would never
bring them to light: would hee were return'd . x

14 Marrie +
this Claudio is condemned for untrussing.

15 Farewell + good
Friar, I prethee pray for me: The Duke (I say to thee
againe) would eate Mutton on Fridaies.

16 He's now past
it, yet (and I say to thee) hee would mouth with a beggar, though she smelt browne-bread and Garlicke: say
that I said so: Farewell.

12/ Duke   **He who the sword of Heaven will beare,**   3.2.261 - 282

Background: For some reason the Duke's speech pattern changes mightily for the following sequence, moving into the ritual often associated with magic or incantation (indicated by the bolding in the First Folio text). [3] Could it be that the shock of Lucio's calumnies (speech # 11 above) together with the appalling news of Angelo's cynical proposal of exchanging Isabella's chastity for Claudio's life, (thus proving the Duke's worst fears about Angelo's inner nature, speech #1 above) has shocked the Duke to a new understanding of the world, and what he has to do (both as a man and as head of state) to correct things. For details of how 'with Angelo to night shall lye/His old betroathed' see the background to speech #13 below.

Style: solo

Where: unspecified, presumably somewhere where judicial proceedings have just finished   **To Whom:** self, and partial audience address

# of Lines: 22   **Probable Timing: 1.10 minutes**

Modern Text

12/ Duke

1   He who the sword of Heaven will bear*
    Should be as holy, as severe*;
    Pattern* in himself* to know,
    Grace to stand, and ᐃvirtue, go :
    More nor less* to others paying
    [Than] by self*-offenses weighing .

2   Shame to him, whose cruel* striking
    Kills* for faults of his own* liking ! †

3   Twice treble* shame on Angelo,
    To weed* my vice, and let hisgrow!

4   O*, what may ᐃman within him hide,
    Though ᐃangel on the outward side!

5   How may likeness* made in crimes,
    Making practice on the ᐃtimes,
    To draw with idle*ᐃspiders'strings
    Most ponderous and substantial* things!

6   Craft against vice, I must apply*.

7   With Angelo to night shall lie*
    His old betrothed* (but despised) ;
    So disguise shall by th'disguised
    Pay with falsehood, false exacting,
    And perform* an old* contracting .

First Folio

12/ Duke [4]

1   He who the sword of Heaven will beare,ₓ
    Should be as holy, as seveare : ₓ
    Patterne in himselfe to know,
    Grace to stand, and Vertue ⁺ **go:**
    More,ₓ nor lesse to others paying,ₓ
    [Then] by selfe-offences weighing .

2   **Shame to him, whose cruell striking,**ₓ
    Kils for faults of his owne liking: ⁺

3   Twice trebble shame on Angelo,
    To weede my vice, and let his grow . ⁺

4   Oh, what may Man within him hide,
    Though Angel on the outward side? ⁺

5   **How may likenesse made in crimes,**
    Making practise on the Times, [5]
    To draw with ydle Spiders strings
    Most ponderous and substantiall things?⁺

6   Craft against vice, I must applie.

7   With Angelo to night shall lye
    His old betroathed (but despised:)ₓ
    So disguise shall by th'disguised
    Pay with falshood, false exacting,
    And performe an olde contracting .

In addition to the unusual language pattern (an eight syllable rather than ten syllable metric pattern), the Duke's intensity can be seen in the four extra breath-thoughts (marked , x) that he seems to need at the start of the speech. One note about the bolded (magic) text; it seems to appear when matters become absolutely clear to the Duke, while the more normal (non-bolded) lines usually accompany initial or subsequent exploration and/or commentary.

• the depths of his struggle can be seen in the first sentence, for, while the two key concepts that should apply to all human endeavour are capitalised ('Heaven' and 'Vertue'), the overall exploration is emotional (2/6, F #1)

• and the emotion continues even more unabated in his assessment of 'Twice trebble shame on Angelo,' (1/4, F #2)

• fascinatingly, the only sign of any intellectual control in the speech occurs in the perennial question of what may lie within a man though he seems an 'Angel' on the outside (2/1, the two lines of F #3), which in turn leads to a moment of passion as he realises how people often attempt to establish their greatest crimes by making 'practise on the Times' (2/3, F #4)

• having explored every angle, in coming to a determination as to how he is going to have to behave, the Duke becomes very quiet, the unembellished short sentence F #5
    ' "Craft against vice, I must applie."
leading to the equally unembellished lines three and four of the last sentence, hoping that
    "So disguise shall by th'disguised/Pay with falshood, false exacting,"

• not surprisingly, the bed-trick by which he hopes to bring Angelo to justice for all his offences (substituting the woman who should be Angelo's wife, Mariana, for Isabella) is also emotional in two separate bursts (1/4, the first two and the final of the five lines of F #6)

---

[3] see Appendix 3

[4] once alone, the Duke again moves into verse, but of a very peculiar kind: the utterance is hardly ever in iambic pentameter, and on several occasions the speaking patterns shift into the style used when characters in *The Tempest*, *Macbeth*, and *A Midsommer Nights Dreame* are using the language of ritual and/or magic (though not done so in F, this speech will bold these 'ritual' lines for easier recognition): it seems that the ritual/magic lines are reserved for the general maxim, the non-ritual for the current situation: whatever has occurred (or is occurring), the Duke is having great difficulty in maintaining his self-control as he faces the two sides of the (self-)debate

[5] several commentators have suggested that there is a couplet missing at this point: others suggest that the problem can be easily solved by altering 'Making practice on the times' to 'Make my practice on the times'

13: THE DUKE TAKES BACK HIS POWER

13/ Mariana **Oh my most gracious Lord,** between 5.1.416 - 442

Background: The way that the Duke proposed solving Angelo's sexual demands was to pull one of Shakespeare's famous bed-tricks, that is, having Mariana, Angelo's one-time betrothed, take Isabella's place, which would not only protect Isabella and save Claudio, it would also solve an earlier wrong committed by Angelo, abandoning Mariana, the woman he was already civilly betrothed to, because she could not provide an adequate dowry. The bed-trick works, but to everyone's horror, once his lust has been satiated, Angelo breaks his promise and insists that Claudio's execution go ahead (which is forestalled by the presentation of the head of a just deceased prisoner instead of Claudio's). The Duke thus returns determined to apply justice in its utmost rigid form, which means he forces Angelo to formally marry Mariana, and then condemns the just-married Angelo to death. Here Angelo's new bride Mariana pleads on his behalf.

Style: public address to two different people in front of a larger group

Where: the gates of the city   **To Whom:** initially the Duke, no longer in his guise as Frier Ludowick, then Isabella, in front of Lucio. the Provost, Claudio, Escalus, Angelo, Varrius, Lords, Citizens

# of Lines: 13   **Probable Timing: 0.45 minutes**

Modern Text

13/ Mariana

1 O* my most gracious Lord,
   I hope you will not mock* me with a husband! †

2 I crave no other, nor no better man.

3 Gentle my ᐃliege - ◊

4 {S}weet Isabel*, take my part ! †

5 Lend me your knees, and all my life to come
   I'll lend you all my life to do* you service.

6 Isabel* ! †

7 Sweet Isabel, do* yet but kneel* by me,
   Hold up your hands, say nothing; I'll speak* all.

8 They say best men are molded* out of faults,
   And for the most, become much more the better
   For being a little bad; ᐃso may my husband.

9 O* Isabel ! will you not lend a knee?

First Folio

13/ Mariana

1 Oh my most gracious Lord,
   I hope you will not mocke me with a husband? +

2 I crave no other, nor no better man.

3 Gentle my Liege.

4 {S}weet Isabell, take my part, +
   Lend me your knees, and all my life to come, ₓ
   I'll lend you all my life to doe you service.

5 Isabell: +

   Sweet Isabel, doe yet but kneele by me,
   Hold up your hands, say nothing: ₓ I'll speake all.

6 They say best men are moulded out of faults,
   And for the most, become much more the better
   For being a little bad: ₓ So may my husband.

7 Oh Isabel: + will you not lend a knee?

The unembellished phrases speak both to her own need and the need for the help of others, the quietness perhaps suggesting that even though she is expressing very private needs in a very public place, she is still attempting to preserve her dignity. Thus the releases in the speech tend to balance out (6/8 in the fourteen lines overall).

• the short sentence 'I crave no other, nor no better man.', followed by the ungrammatical (to modern eyes) three word F #3 'Gentle my Liege.', in turn followed by yet another unembellished appeal to 'Sweet Isabell'

 "Lend me your knees, and all my life to come,/I'll lend you all my life . . ." are clear indications of how she has cut through any unnecessary verbiage to deal as directly with the situation as she possibly can

• when this doesn't seem to have an immediate effect, so her appeal to Isabel intensifies, with 'Hold up your hands, say nothing.', and the incredible hope that Angelo can become good since the 'best men' supposedly

 ". . . for the most, become much more the better/For being a little bad:" both also unembellished

• and this in turn leads to the only three surround phrases of the speech, that end the speech

': So may my husband . /Oh Isabel : will you not lend a knee ?"
the final plea heightened by being both monosyllabic and unembellished

14: The Real World

14/ Clowne   I am as well acquainted heere, as I was in . . .   4.3.1-19

Background: Having been imprisoned for being a pimp, the Clowne (known as Pompey Bum) finds, to his delight, that he knows many of his fellow prisoners.

Style: solo

Where: prison   **To Whom:** direct audience address

# of Lines: 18   **Probable Timing:** 0.55 minutes

Modern Text

14/ Clowne

1   I am as well acquainted here* as I was in our house of profession.*†

2   One would think* it were Mistress* Over°done's* own* house, for here* be many* of her old* △customers.

3   First, here's young* [Master] Rash, he's* in for a commodity* of brown* paper and old*△ginger, nine score and seventeen* pounds, of which he* made five △marks* ready* money.*†

4   Marry*, then,△ ginger was not much in request, for the old*△ women were all dead.

5   Then is there here* one [Master] Caper, at the suite of Master Three-△pile the △mercer, for some four* suits* of △peach-color'd*△satin, which now peaches him a beggar.

6   Then have we here*, young* Dizzy*, and young* [Master] Deep*-vow, and [Master] Copperspur*, and Mr Starve-△lackey the △rapier and dagger man, and young* Drop-[hair] that kill'd* lusty* Pudding, and [Master] Forthright] the tilter, and brave [Master Shoe*-tie]* the great △traveller, and wild* Half*-△can* that stabb'd Pots, and I think* forty* more, all great doers in our △trade, and are now "for the Lord's sake".

First Folio

14/ Clowne

1   I am as well acquainted heere, as I was in our house of profession: one would thinke it were Mistris Over-dons owne house, for heere be manie of her olde Customers.

2   First, here's yong [Mr] Rash, hee's in for a commoditie of browne paper, and olde Ginger, nine score and seventeene pounds, of which hee made five Markes readie money: marrie then, Ginger was not much in request, for the olde Women were all dead.

3   Then is there heere one [Mr] Caper, at the suite of Master Three-Pile the Mercer, for some foure suites of Peach-colour'd Satten, which now peaches him a beggar.

4   Then have we heere, yong Dizie, and yong [Mr] Deepe-vow, and [Mr] Copperspurre, and Mr Starve-Lackey the Rapier and dagger man, and yong Drop-[heire] that kild lustie Pudding, and [Mr Forthlight] the tilter; and brave [Mr Shootie] the great Traveller, and wilde Halfe-Canne that stabb'd Pots, and I thinke fortie more, all great doers in our Trade, and are now for the Lords sake. [6]

While the opening of the speech dwells on the **emotional side of passionate (9/12, F #1-2)** suggesting great excitement at the top of the speech, the listing of most of those he recognises as customers of Mrs. Overdone's house of ill-repute moves (relaxes?) into a **form of intellectual delight as he reels them all off together with their various crimes.**

• extending the size of a surround-phrase, it seems that Pompey's joy at being where he is knows no bounds, for F #1 can be seen as two surround phrases, the first (almost unbelievingly?) slightly emotional (0/1), the second splendidly passionate as he describes how familiar he is with his fellow inmates (3/4)

• the admiration of Mr. Rash is just as passionate (6/7, F #2)

• while the recognition and explanation why Mr. Caper is incarcerated becomes a little more factual (8/5, F #3)

• and the listing of all the inmates continues the intellectual trend (21/9)

• a final point of interest: there are many short spellings (almost twenty if Mr. is accounted as such), so a key question is why? (fear of being overheard perhaps and his joy at the familiarity somehow being curtailed perhaps?)

---

[6] some modern texts put the phrase 'for the Lords sake' in inverted commas, suggesting it was a familiar cry used by prisoners begging from their windows (see *The Arden Shakespeare Measure for Measure*, page 122, footnotes to lines 19 - 20)

SPEECHES IN ORDER	TIME	PAGE	SPEECHES BY GENDER	Speech #(s)
ALL'S WELL THAT ENDS WELL				
#'s 1 – 5: Hellen and the Vagaries of Love				
1/ **Parrolles** Are you meditating on virginitie?	0.55	330		
2/ **Parrolles** Virginitie breedes mites, much like a Cheese,	0.55	331	**SPEECHES FOR WOMEN (7)**	
3/ **Hellen** Not my virginity yet:	1.00	332		
4/ **Old Countesse** Even so it was with me when I was yong:	0.30	333	**Hellen** **Traditional & Today:** a young woman	#3, #5, #9
5/ **Hellen** Then I confesse/Here on my knee, ...	1.15	334	**Old Countesse** **Traditional & Today:** older woman, mother of Bertram, often referred to in the text as 'Old Lady'	#4, #10
#: 6: The Braggart				
6/ **Parrolles** Ten a clocke: Within these three houres 'twill	1.15	335	**Diana** **Traditional & Today:** young chaste woman	#11, #12
#: 7: Hellen, The King and Bertram				
7/ **King** 'Tis onely title thou disdainst in her,	2.20	337	**SPEECHES FOR EITHER GENDER (0)**	
#'s 8 – 10: Bertram's Escape From His New Wife Hellen				
8/ **Parrolles** France is a dog-hole, and it no more merits,	0.35	339	**SPEECHES FOR MEN (7)**	
9/ **Hellen** *Till I have no wife I have nothing in France.*	1.30	340	**Parrolles** **Traditional & Today:** young to middle aged male, a blow-hard 'miles gloriosus'	#1, #2, #6, #8
10/ **Countesse** Alas! and would you take the letter of her:	2.00	342		
#'s 11 – 12: Diana's Practical View of Love and Life				
11/ **Diana** I so you serve us	0.45	344	**King** **Traditional & Today:** older male of some authority	#7
12/ **Diana** When midnight comes, knocke at my chamber . . .	1.00	345	**Clowne** **Traditional:** male character actor, usually young or middle age	#13, #14
#'s 13 – 14: Clowne's Cynical View of Love and Life				**Today:** male of any age
13/ **Clowne** I hope to have friends for my wives sake,	0.55	346		
14/ **Clowne** Why sir, if I cannot serve you, I can serve	0.45	347		

ALL'S WELL THAT ENDS WELL

#'s 1 - 5: HELLEN AND THE VAGARIES OF LOVE

1/ Parrolles	Are you meditating on virginitie?	between 1.1.110 -138
2/ Parrolles	Virginitie breedes mites, much like a Cheese,	between 1.1.141 - 164

Background: Hellen's recently deceased father, a physician of great renown, was doctor to the house of Rossillion, where he and Hellen lived. Hellen has fallen in love with Bertram who has just become the head of the family, and thus the Count, following the death of his father, a long-time friend of the King. In her eyes, marriage with Bertram would be totally impossible because of the differences in their social standing, and also because he is totally unaware of her feelings. Bertram is about to leave Rossillion for the French Court in Paris, guided by Lafew (an elderly friend of his father's and the king's) and accompanied by Parrolles (a blow-hard 'miles gloriosus'). Unaware that Hellen knows him for what he is ('a notorious Liar', 'great way foole', and 'solie a coward'), Parrolles tries his wit (and luck?) with her in a very risqué conversation. Speech #1 opens the conversation in general, while in speech #2 Parrolles attempts to press his point home.

Style: both, as part of a two handed scene

Where: somewhere in the house or grounds of Rossillion   **To Whom:** Hellen

speech #1, # of Lines: 17   **Probable Timing: 0.55 minutes**
speech #2, # of Lines: 18   **Probable Timing: 0.55 minutes**

Modern Text

1/ Parrolles

1 Are you meditating on virginity*? {ψ}

2 Man is enemy* to Virginity*; {ψ}
and {your} virginity* though valiant, in the defense
yet is weak• .{ψ}

3 Man, setting down* before you, will
undermine you and blow you up• . {ψ}

4 There {is} no ᴬmilitary policy how ᴬvirgins might blow up men{.}

5 {Yet} ᴬvirginity being* blown* down* , ᴬman will
quicklier be blown* up• . {ψ}

6 It is not politic* in the ᴬcommon•wealth of
ᴬnature to preserve virginity•.   Loss* of ᴬvirginity*, is

7 rational* increase, and there was never ᴬvirgin [got] till
virginity* was first lost.

8 That you were made of is mettall to make ᴬVirgins.

9 Virginity*, by being* once lost,
may be ten times found; by being ever kept, it is ever
lost. †

'Tis too cold a companion; ᴬaway with't ! !

First Folio

1/ Parrolles

1 Are you meditating on virginitie? {ψ}

2 Man is enemie to virginitie, ⁺{ψ}
and {your} virginitie though valiant, in the defence
yet is weak• .{ψ}

3 Man ⁺ setting downe before you, will
undermine you,ₓ and blow you up. {ψ}

4 There {is} no Military policy how Virgins might blow up men{.}

5 {Yet} Virginity beeing blowne downe, Man will
quicklier be blowne up. {ψ}

6 It is not politicke,ₓ in the Common-wealth of
Nature,ₓ to preserve virginity.

7 Losse of Virginitie, is
rationall encrease, and there was never Virgin[goe],⁺ till
virginitie was first lost.

8 That you were made of,ₓ is mettall to make Virgins.

9 Virginitie, by beeing once lost,
may be ten times found: by being ever kept, it is ever
lost: 'tis too cold a companion :ₓ Away with't. ⁺

1/ Parrolles

- the speech starts very carefully with two unembellished sentences when even the topic, 'virginitie', is presented in its short spelling form - either a sound seduction tactic or, admittedly less likely, a sign of a man not too sure of how to begin

- the first off-colour image, of a man 'setting downe before you', is the first time emotion makes an appearance (F #3, 0/1), with the possibility that Parrolles is not quite as in control as he would wish to be evidenced by the first extra breath-thought that appears (marked ,ₓ), as if he needs to control himself before offering the rather graphic monosyllabic/unembellished image 'and blow you up,'

- for the next off-colour sequence, though the suggestion that women cannot 'blow up men' starts intellectually (2/0, F #4), the follow through is much more passionately emotional (2/4, F #5)

- as F #6's argument not to 'preserve virginity' is advanced, while it and the following general chop-logic suggestion that loss of (now capitalised) 'Virginitie' will only serve to breed more virgins (F #7-8) stays passionate (5/6), it seems that Parrolles might be somewhat excited by his own logic, for three more extra breath-thoughts suddenly appear in F #6 and #8

- then, for some reason it seems that Parrolles feels he needs to change his approach, for though the images remain essentially the same, F #9's build to his blatant urging of Hellen ' : Away with it .' is completely made up of four surround phrases

'' . Virginitie, by beeing once lost, may be ten times found : by being ever kept, it is ever lost: 'tis too cold a companion : Away with't .'' the second and third unembellished, as if to speak any louder might break the mood

10   'Tis against the

rule of Nature.

11   To speake on the part of virginitie,ₓ is
to accuse your Mothers :ₓ which is most infallible disobedience.

First Folio

2/ Parrolles

1   Virginitie breedes mites, much like a
Cheese, consumes it selfe to the very payring, and so
dies with feeding his owne stomacke.

2   Besides, Virgini-
tie is peevish, proud, ydle, made of selfe-love, which
is the most inhibited sinne in the Cannon.

3   Keepe it not,
you cannot choose but loose by't.

4   Out with't :⁺ within
[ten] yeare it will make it selfe two, which is a goodly increase, and the principall it selfe not much the worse.

5   Away with't.⁺

6   The longer kept, the lesse worth : Off with't while 'tis
vendible.

7   Answer the time of request, Virginitie⁺ like
an olde Courtier, weares her cap out of fashion, richly
suited, but unsuteable, just like the brooch & the tooth-
pick, which [were] not now : your Date is better in your
Pye and your Porredge,ₓ [then] in your cheeke:;and your
virginity, your old virginity, is like one of our French
wither'd peares, it lookes ill, it eates drily, marry 'tis a
wither'd peare :   it was formerly better, marry yet 'tis a
wither'd peare : Will you any thing with it?

• Parrolles' F #10 attempt to sum up, though seemingly relaxed (1/0), is via a very short sentence, suggesting that in his desire to seduce, no more can be said, yet obviously there must be, for the F #11 'Mothers' argument (unnecessary if he had been successful) is again composed of surround lines, starting with passion (1/1), and ending in an (enforced?) unembellished calm which may belie what is going on underneath

Whereas in the first speech intellect and emotion virtually matched (12/10), in this follow-up speech emotions are given much more sway (11/26 overall), perhaps another sign that Parrolles' seduction efforts are not proceeding according to plan.

• the return to chop-logic, arguing kept virginity consumes itself, is highly emotional (1/5, F #1)

• and F #2's moral attack on the concept of virginity (as being 'peevish, proud, ydle, made of selfe-love') and F #3's repeated-from-the-first-speech-urging to 'Keepe it not' continue the emotional drive (2/7, F #2-3)

• it seems that Hellen gives him neither response nor encouragement, for this is immediately followed up by yet another change in style, a very short monosyllabic unembellished surround phrase opening F #4 '. Out with't : .' – again an attempt at a confidential invitation perhaps

• that this doesn't work or is not deemed enough can be seen in that Parrolles then switches to pure emotion once more (F #4, 0/4) to argue yet again lose-your-virginity-now-so-as-to-make-more, which had little or no effect in speech #1

• and once more the F #5 urging 'Away with't.', though seemingly calm, is offered via a very short unembellished sentence, as if the appearance of calm was all that was needed to succeed

• however, what ensues is certainly not calm, for the 'longer kept, the lesse worth' argument is made via a passionate short two surround-phrase sentence (F #6, 1/1), and the suggestion/demand/bleat 'Answer the time of request' that opens F #7 becomes passionate (2/3 in the first three and a half lines)

• and the passion intensifies in the age-is-better-elsewhere argument, (3/3 in the one colon – implying logic rather than emotion - created surround line ' : your Date is better in your Pye and your Porredge, [then] in your cheeke :)

• and the whole finishes (desperately? humourously?) emotionally (2/5, the end of the argument formulated once more by two surround phrases of somewhat less than salubrious imagery ' : it was formerly better, marry yet 'tis a wither'd peare : Will you any thing with it? . '

---

10   'Tis against the

rule of △nature.

11   To speak* on the part of virginity* is
to accuse your △mothers*, which is most infallible disobedience.

Modern Text

2/ Parrolles

1   Virginity* breeds* mites, much like a
△cheese, consumes itself* to the very paring*, and so
dies with feeding his own* stomach*.

2   Besides, △virgini-
ty* is peevish, proud, idle*, made of self*-love, which
is the most inhibited sin* in the △canon*.

3   Keep* it not,
you cannot choose but lose* by't.

4   Out with't !†

5   Within
[t'one] year* it will make itself* two, which is a goodly increase, and the principal* itself* not much the worse.

6   Away with't!

7   The longer kept, the less* worth.†

8   Off with't while 'tis
vendible ; ◊ answer the time of request .†

9   Virginity*, like
an old* △courtier, wears* her cap out of fashion, richly
suited*, but unsuitable* - just like the brooch & the tooth-
pick, which [wear] not now.†

10   Your △date is better in your
△pie* and your △porridge* [than] in your cheek*; and your
virginity, your old virginity, is like one of our French
wither'd pears*, it looks* ill, it eats* drily, marry 'tis a
wither'd pear*; it was formerly better, marry yet 'tis a
wither'd pear*.†

11   Will you any thing with it?

3/ Hellen   **Not my virginity yet :**   between 1.1.165 - 186

Background: A direct response to Parrolles' somewhat startlingly bold approach (speeches #1-2 above).

Style: as part of a two handed scene

Where: somewhere in the house or grounds of Rossillion   **To Whom:** Parrolles

# of Lines: 20   **Probable Timing: 1.00 minutes**

Modern Text

3/ Hellen

1 Not my virginity yet :
   There shall your ᐃmaster have a thousand loves,
   A ᐃmother, and a ᐃmistress* , and a friend,
   A ᐃphoenix∗, ᐃcaptain* , and an enemy,
   A guide, a ᐃgoddess* , and a ᐃsovereign* ,
   A ᐃcounsellor, a ᐃtraitress* , and a ᐃdear* ;
   His humble ambition, proud humility ;
   His jarring, concord, and his discord, dulcet;
   His faith, his sweet disaster;   with a world
   Of pretty fond adoptious christendoms*
   That blinking Cupid gossips.
                            Now shall he -
2 I know not what he shall - God send him well !
3 The ᐃcourt's a learning place, and he is one -
   ▭▭▭▭▭▭▭▭▭▭▭
   That I wish well .   'Tis pity* -
4 That wishing well had not a body in't,
   Which might be felt, that we, the poorer born* ,
   Whose baser stars* do shut us up in wishes,
   Might with effects of them follow our friends,
   And show what we alone must think* , which never
   Returns* us thanks* .

First Folio

3/ Hellen

1 Not my virginity yet :
   There shall your Master have a thousand loves,
   A Mother, and a Mistresse, and a friend,
   A Phenix, Captaine, and an enemy,
   A guide, a Goddesse, and a Soveraigne,
   A Counsellor, a Traitoresse, and a Deare : x
   His humble ambition, proud humility : x
   His jarring, concord : x and his discord, dulcet : x
   His faith, his sweet disaster : x   with a world
   Of pretty fond adoptious christendomes
   That blinking Cupid gossips.
                            Now shall he : x
2 I know not what he shall, God send him well, +
   The Courts a learning place, and he is one,
   That I wish well .   'Tis pitty,
3 That wishing well had not a body in't,
   Which might be felt, that we + the poorer borne,
   Whose baser starres do shut us up in wishes,
   Might with effects of them follow our friends,
   And shew what we alone must thinke, which never
   Returnes us thankes.

When Hellen's refusal of Parrolles' rather obvious enticements comes, it comes with complete finality, the speech starting with the unembellished surround phrase ' . Not my virginity yet : ' .

- however, the thought(s) of Bertram becoming her first lover moves her into an entirely different mood

a/ first intellectual, as she lists in the next six lines all the different aspects of her femininity she could present him (10/6)

b/ and this then moves her into five consecutive surround phrases as she imagines what effect this would have on him and how he would respond, the reverie being incredibly quiet for the first four unembellished surround phrases, as if she didn't want to break the magic of the dream she is weaving, with only the last finally breaking into a little passion (1/1, the last two lines of F #1)

- the slightly onrushed F #2 points to the probable awkwardness she experiences when her Bertram-reverie finally breaks, for after what seems to build to yet another wonderful moment of imagination (the opening unembellished surround phrase of F #2, ' . Now shall he : '), her attempt at some form of intellectual recovery (2/0, the remainder of F #2) is more than somewhat undermined by both the ensuing content and the ungrammatical fast-link comma ending F #2's second line (this attempts to connect two totally different ideas, the already peculiar non-sequitur of 'I know not' coupled with her good wishes for Bertram, being tacked onto an irrelevant comment about 'The Courts a learning place', with one more peculiar illogical - and unfinished - switch back to Bertram 'and he is one')

- her final attempt to explain to the presumably now totally befuddled (yet perhaps even more aroused) Parrolles that it would be nice if wishes could become reality, is, for the first time in the speech, totally emotional (0/6) – (personal embarrassment at how much of herself she has revealed in the earlier part of the speech perhaps?)

4/ Old Countesse   **Even so it was with me when I was yong:**   1.3.128 - 136

Background: The Countesse has been informed by Rynaldo, her loyal Steward, that he has overheard Hellen confess her love for Bertram. She is very fond of Hellen, remarking later 'You know Hellen I am a mother to you.'. Here, unobserved, she watches Hellen for confirmation of Rynaldo's information.

Style: solo

Where: somewhere in the house or grounds of Rossillion

To Whom: self and audience address

# of Lines: 9   **Probable Timing: 0.30 minutes**

Modern Text

4/ {Countesse as} **Old Countesse**

1 Even so it was with me when I was young* : :
   If ever we are nature's, these are ours. †
                         This thorn*

2 Doth to our Rose of youth [rightly*] belong ;
   Our blood* to us, this to our blood is born* . †

3 It is the show and seal* of nature's truth,
   Where love's strong passion is impress'd* in youth . †

4 By our remembrances of days* forgone*,
   Such were our faults, or then we thought them none . †

5 Her eye* is sick* on't;   I observe her now.

First Folio

4/ {Countesse as} **Old Countesse**

1 Even so it was with me when I was yong :
   If ever we are natures, these are ours, this thorne
   Doth to our Rose of youth [righlie] belong +
   Our bloud to us, this to our blood is borne,
   It is the show,ₓ and seale of natures truth,
   Where loves strong passion is imprest in youth,
   By our remembrances of daies forgon,
   Such were our faults, or then we thought them none,
   Her eie is sicke on't, + I observe her now .

The couplet rhyming scheme of lines five through eight ('truth'/'youth' and 'forgon'/'none') suggests that observing Hellen and the resultant memories this evokes has enormous impact on the Countesse. Thus, the fact of F's single onrushed sentence adds great weight to the idea that the Countesse is highly moved by what is taking place. Unfortunately, most modern texts wipe out this second clue by resetting the speech as five separate rational sentences.

• the first line is so nakedly vulnerable, being an unembellished surround phrase, and, if 'Even' is scanned metrically as a single syllable (Ev'n') as it should be here, the line is even further weighted by being monosyllabic too

• and this vulnerability continues throughout the speech, with what little release, there is being almost totally emotional (1/5 in nine lines overall)

• as the original prefix (the 'Old Countesse') suggests, the quality of the speech is a reminiscence of an older person of their younger days: as such it is underscored by at least four short spellings, the very interesting 'daies forgon', 'righ{t}lie', and 'eie'

5/ Hellen   **Then I confesse/Here on my knee, high and you,**   1.3.191-217

Background: Pushed very hard by the Countesse, Hellen at last tells the Countesse of her impossible love for the Countesse's son, Bertram.

Style: as part of a two handed scene

Where: somewhere in the house of Rossillion   **To Whom:** Bertram's mother, the Countesse

# of Lines: 26   **Probable Timing: 1.15 minutes**

Modern Text

5/ Hellen

1 Then I confesse*
Here on my knee, before high heaven and you,
That before you, and next unto high heaven,
    I love your son* . †

2 My friends were poor*, but honest, so's my love. †

3 Be not offended, for it hurts not him
That he is lov'd of me ; I follow him not
By any token of presumptuous suit*,
Nor would I have him till I do* deserve him,
Yet never know how that desert should be. †

4 I know I love in vain*, strive against hope ;
Yet in this captious, and [untenable] ᐃsieve* ◊
I still pour* in the waters of my love
And lack* not to lose* still . †
                    Thus Indian-ᵒlike,

5 Religious in mine error, I adore
The ᐃsun* , that looks* upon his worshipper,
But knows* of him no more.
                    My dearest* ᐃmadam,

6 Let not your hate encounter with my love
For loving where you do* ; but if yourself*,
Whose aged honor cites a virtuous youth,
Did ever, in so true a flame of liking
Wish chastely*, and love dearly*, that your Dian
Was both herself* and love, O then give pity*
To her whose state is such, that cannot choose
But lend and give where she is sure to lose* ;
That seeks* not to find* that her search implies,
But riddle like lives sweetly* where she dies.

First Folio

5/ Hellen

1 Then I confesse
Here on my knee, before high heaven and you,
That before you, and next unto high heaven, I love your
    Sonne:

My friends were poore⁺ but honest, so's my love :
Be not offended, for it hurts not him
That he is lov'd of me ; I follow him not
By any token of presumptuous suite,
Nor would I have him,ₓ till I doe deserve him,
Yet never know how that desert should be:
I know I love in vaine, strive against hope : ₓ
Yet in this captious, and [intemible] Sive. ₓ

2 I still poure in the waters of my love
And lacke not to loose still ; thus Indian like⁺
Religious in mine error, I adore
The Sunne⁺ that lookes upon his worshipper,
But knowes of him no more.
                    My deerest Madam,

3 Let not your hate incounter with my love,ₓ
For loving where you doe ; but if your selfe,
Whose aged honor cites a vertuous youth,
Did ever, in so true a flame of liking,ₓ
Wish chastly, and love dearely, that your Dian
Was both her selfe and love, O then give pittie
To her whose state is such, that cannot choose
But lend and give where she is sure to loose ;
That seekes not to finde that,ₓ her search implies,
But riddle like,ₓ lives sweetly where she dies.

F's sentence structure suggests that, though Hellen may be uncomfortable at the top of the speech, especially with the onrush of F #1 and the very ungrammatical period that ends it, she manages to harness her thinking, if not her emotions, to a more rational flow by the speech's end. **And though she attempts to start carefully, the four semicolons scattered through the speech suggests that there are times where the strength of her love for Bertram almost runs away with her.**

• after the release of 'confesse' in the opening line (the key to the whole speech), her attempt to control the, to her, awful confirmation of aiming above her station by loving the Countesse's son, lasts for almost two unembellished lines – the attempt blown apart by the second line being fourteen syllables long, and the veritable explosion of the final admission of whom she loves, 'your Sonne'.

• the very few surround phrases point to the emotional tug of war Hellen is suffering – first as to her own worth

then as to her chances of success
" : My friends were poore but honest, so's my love : "
" : I know I love in vaine, strive against hope : /Yet in this captious, and intemible Sive ./I still poure in the waters of my love/And lacke not to loose still ; "

and the depth of feeling here is underscored by what most modern texts regard as a dreadful period after 'Sive', and they remove all punctuation on to allow the idea to flow on unchecked: however, F's totally ungrammatical period allows Hellen a long moment of recovery from the appalling image of her never-ending loss before continuing with F #2 – and indeed this moment seems to mark where the nature of her speech markedly changes

• overall, the speech has opened somewhat emotionally (2/6, the first ten lines of F #1, to this ungrammatical point), but after the seemingly much needed (yet modern texts denied) period, the releases start to flow much more heavily

• F #2's opening imagery of her still pouring in 'the waters of my love' is out and out emotional (0/3 in one and a half lines), followed by passion as she describes her behaviour as 'Religious in mine error' (2/3, the remaining three and a half lines of F #2) – and the last long flowing sentence appealing for empathy and understanding is again almost completely emotional (3/10 in F #3's ten and a half lines)

6: THE BRAGGART

6/ Parrolles   Ten a clocke :   Within these three houres 'twill   between 4.1.24 - 64

Background: Now in Florence, and already under suspicion by his fellow soldiers including Lords G. & E. and Bertram, Parrolles has publicly bragged once too often and been caught out and challenged. Their regimental drum having been captured by the enemy (at most, a symbolic defeat), Parrolles, after sounding off about the disgrace so earned, has offered to get it back before morning - an offer eagerly accepted by his fellows, who are determined once and for all to prove him a coward and a blow-hard. One note, most modern texts are content to explain that Parrolles has muddled his biblical references, see *The Arden Shakespeare All's Well That Ends Well*, op. cit. page 98. footnote 4.1.42. Some commentators have suggested changing his F #9 allusion to 'Bajazeth's Mule' to the correct 'Balaam's Ass', but this assumes his erudite quotes are always correct (and, as with so many other Shakespeare blow-hards, this may not necessarily be so.)

Style: solo

Where: unspecified, presumably somewhere near the battlefield   **To Whom:** self and direct audience address

# of Lines: 25   **Probable Timing: 1.15 minutes**

Modern Text

6/ Parrolles

1 Δwithin these three hours* 'twill be time enough to go* home.

2   What shall I say I have done?

3   It must be* a very plausive invention that carries it.

4   They begin* to smoke* me*, and disgraces have of late knock'd too often at my door* .†

5   I find* my tongue is too fool*hardy*, but my heart hath the fear* of Mars before it, and of his creatures, not daring the reports of my tongue.

6   What the devil* should move me* to undertake the recovery* of this drum*, being not ignorant of the impossibility, and knowing I had no such purpose?

7   I must give myself* some hurts, and say I got them in exploit.†

8   Yet slight ones will not carry* it.

9   They will say,

10   "Came you off with so little?"   And great ones I dare not give ; wherefore what's the instance.

11   Tongue, I must put you into a Δbutter-woman's mouth, and buy myself* another of Bajazeth's Δmule, if you prattle me* into these perilles* .

First Folio

6/ Parrolles

1 Ten a clocke : Within these three houres 'twill be time enough to goe home.

2   What shall I say I have done?

3   It must bee a very plausive invention that carries it.

4   They beginne to smoake mee, and disgraces have of late,x knock'd too often at my doore : I finde my tongue is too foole-hardie, but my heart hath the feare of Mars before it, and of his creatures, not daring the reports of my tongue.

5   What the divell should move mee to undertake the recoverie of this drumme, being not ignorant of the impossibility, and knowing I had no such purpose?   I must give my selfe some hurts, and say I got them in exploit : yet slight ones will not carrie it.

6

7   They will say,   And great ones I dare not

8   came you off with so little?

9 give, + wherefore what's the instance.   Tongue, I must put you into a Butter-womans mouth, and buy my selfe another of Bajazeths Mule, if you prattle mee into these perilles.

{ctd. over}

- the unembellished lines point to Parrolles' understanding of the enormous self-created difficulties he is now facing, the quietness showing that there is now no reason for his usual bravado and fine extravagant words and images (see speech # 8 below)
"What shall I say I have done?"
especially since 'disgraces have of late' piled up on him, and now his tongue really has run away with him in promising to rescue the regimental drum, stupidly so since he and his tongue
"being not ignorant of the impossibility, and knowing I had no such purpose?"
so, to get out of the dilemma, he could possibly mutilate himself
": yet slight ones will not carrie it. They will say, came you off with so little? And great ones I dare not give, wherefore what's the instance."
and this does seem to be a fearful point, for the quote immediately above is formed either by a surround phrase or short sentence: obviously there is no time for (self)-deception through language games or flourishes

- but, being too fearful even to hurt himself a little, Parrolles then thinks that he could do something drastic to his general appearance, including
"Or the baring of my beard, and to say it was in stratagem."
or getting rid of his clothes, 'and say I was stript.'

- thus the speech starts emotionally (1/3, F #1) as he realises when he might safely return, only to become very quiet as the short sentences pose the question of just how he is going to get out of the mess his bragging has landed him in (0/1, F #2-3)

- not surprisingly, the acknowledgement both that his fellows are about to call his bluff and that 'too often' recently he has suffered 'disgraces', and his cursing out of himself for being so foolish is highly emotional (1/10, F #4-5)

- while the idea of the self-inflicted wounds as a way out is almost totally unembellished (0/1, F #6-8), the fear/queasiness of self-inflicted pain getting to him perhaps

12 I would the cutting of my garments would* serve the turn*, or the breaking of my Spanish sword.

13 Or the baring of my beard, and to say it was in stratagem.

14 Or to drown* my clothes*, and say I was stripp'd*.

15 Though I swore I leapt from the window of the △citadel* -

    thirty fadom* .

16 I would I had any drum* of the enemy's*.† I

17 would swear* I recover'd it.

A drum* now of the enemy's* -

• and then in the second go-round of blaming his tongue for his faults Parrolles becomes passionate (3/3, F #9)

• as with the earlier idea of more serious self-harm, the new idea of damaging just the outward show of himself (his 'garments' or his 'sword' or 'beard') becomes very quiet 1/1, F #10-11), which seems to allow him to build to some emotional dream-of-successful-excuse small climax, enhanced by being expressed by three short sentences (F #12-14, 1/4)

• and emotions continue, but presumably in an entirely different vein, first as he wishes for another way out via a 'drumme of the enemies' (F #15, 0/2), and then, to his (shocked?) surprise, as the emotional final short sentence attests, comes 'A drumme now of the enemies.' (0/1)

10 I would the cutting of my garments wold serve the turne, or the breaking of my Spanish sword.

11 Or the baring of my beard, and to say it was in stratagem.

12 Or to drowne my cloathes, and say I was stript.

13 Though I swore I leapt from the window of the Citadell. x

14   Thirty fadome.

15 I would I had any drumme of the enemies, I would sweare I recover'd it.

16 A drumme now of the enemies. x

7: HELLEN, THE KING, AND BERTRAM

7/ King   'Tis onely title thou disdainst in her, …   between 2.3.117 - 166

Background: To everyone's amazement, Hellen has succeeded in curing the King of a malady he and his doctors regarded as fatal. In return he has agreed that she may ask for the hand of anyone in his court, her own stipulation being that she will not choose anyone of royal blood. She has chosen Bertram, who, arguing class differences between them, has refused - and the King is not used to having his agreements flouted by those in his charge. The speech deals first with Bertram's class-riddled response and Hellen's worth, and then moves into a much more personal 'My Honor's at the stake' and 'Obey our will' approach.

Style: one on one public address in front of a large and very interested group

Where: the French Court   **To Whom:** to Bertram, in front of the whole Court, including Lafew, Parrolles, other noble young men Hellen has passed over in favour of Betram, and Attendants

# of Lines: 48   **Probable Timing: 2.20 minutes**

Modern Text

7/ King

1 'Tis only* title thou disdain'st in her, the which
   I can build up. †

2   Strange is it that our bloods,
   Of color*, weight, and heat, pour'd all together,
   Would quite confound distinction, yet stands off
   In differences so mighty*.

3   If she be*
   All that is virtuous - save what thou dislik'st,
   A poor*△ physician's* daughter - thou dislik'st
   Of virtue for the name. †

4   But do* not so. †

5   From lowest place, [when] virtuous things proceed,
   The place is dignified by th'doers deed*.

6   Where great additions swell's, and virtue none,
   It is a dropsied honour.

7   Good alone
   Is good, without a name; ◊ vileness* is so :
   The property* by what [it] is, should go,
   Not by the title.

8   She* is young, wise, fair*,
   In these, to Nature she's* immediate heir* ;
   And these breed honor*. †

9   That is honor's* scorn* ,
   Which challenges itself* as honor's* born* ,
   And is not like the fire. †

10   Honor's* thrive,
   When rather from our acts we them derive
   [Than] our fore*goers. †

First Folio

7/ King

1 'Tis onely title thou disdainst in her, the which
   I can build up. [+]
   Of colour, waight, and heat, pour'd all together,
   Would quite confound distinction: [x] yet stands off
   In differences so mightie.

2   If she bee
   All that is vertuous [x] (save what thou dislik'st)[x]
   A poore Phisitians daughter, thou dislik'st
   Of vertue for the name: but doe not so:
   From lowest place, [whence] vertuous things proceed,
   The place is dignified by th'doers deede.

3   Where great additions swell's, and vertue none,
   It is a dropsied honour.

4   Good alone,[x]

5   Vilenesse is so :
   The propertie by what [is] is, should go,
   Not by the title.

6   Shee is young, wise, faire,

   In these, to Nature shee's immediate heire : [x]
   And these breed honour : that is honours scorne,
   Which challenges it selfe as honours borne,
   And is not like the fire : Honours thrive,
   When rather from our acts we them derive
   [Then] our fore-goers : the meere words,[x] a slave

{ctd. over}

The King's attempts to maintain self-control can be seen in the opening and especially in the closing of the speech, where the last five sentences match in both texts: fascinatingly, the final control is established when the King is talking about himself and his reputation and 'Honor'. However, the start of the speech, all concentrating on Hellen, quickly moves from the minor onrush of F #1-2 to a much greater loss of control once he lists her virtues (two F only shorter sentences, F #4-5, set as one by most modern texts, followed by an onrushed, highly emotional, surround phrase dominated F #6), especially her 'honour' - an interesting concentration considering the later emphasis he places on his own 'Honor' too.

• despite the mild onrush, the speech opens very carefully but slightly emotionally (0/2, F #1), with the latter of the two surround phrases unembellished and the first almost so

" 'Tis onely title thou disdainst in her, the which/I can build up : … . "
the intervening phrase arguing that while blood from those of different social standing is indistinguishable,, people themselves
" … : yet stands off/In differences so mightie . "

• the argument becomes a little more emotional (1/4, F #2), as the King, believing Bertram's disapproval of Hellen stems for her lack of social standing, counters again with a very terse monosyllabic surround phrase ' : but doe not so : '

• and as the King argues that people should not be judged by their title, though emotional control is re-established in the virtually unembellished passage, with, interestingly, 'Vilenesse' being the only released word (0/1, F #4-5) the shortness of the sentences and the surround phrase attack on good names hiding bad things
' . Vilenesse is so : ' suggests that control may be difficult

• which proves to be so, for in listing Hellen's virtues and dwelling upon the honour due to her the King suddenly becomes extraordinarily emotional (4/16 in nine and a half lines) in what most modern texts regard as a highly ungrammatical sentence (splitting F #6 in four): yet the original setting, containing at least five surround lines, marks an enormous change in the King's

Folio version

7
Debosh'd on everie tombe, on everie grave :$_x$
A lying Trophee, and as oft is dumbe,$_x$
Where dust, and damn'd oblivion is the Tombe.
Of honour'd bones indeed, what should be saide?

8
If thou canst like this creature,$_x$ as a maide,
I can create the rest: Vertue,$_x$ and shee
Is her owne dower:$_x$ Honour and wealth,$_x$ from mee.

9
Thou wrong'st thy selfe, if thou shold'st strive
to choose.

10
My Honor's at the stake, which to defeate⁺
I must produce my power.

11
                    Heere, take her hand,
Proud scornfull boy, unworthie this good gift,
That dost in vile misprision shackle up
My love, and her desert :$_x$ that canst not dreame,
We poizing us in her defective scale,
Shall weigh thee to the beame:$_x$ That wilt not know,$_x$
It is in Us to plant thine Honour,$_x$ where
We please to have it grow.

12
                    Checke thy contempt :$_x$
Obey Our will, which travailes in thy good:$_x$
Beleeve not thy disdaine, but presentlie
Do thine owne fortunes that obedient right
Which both thy dutie owes,$_x$ and Our power claimes,
Or I will throw thee from my care for ever
Into the staggers,$_x$ and the carelesse lapse
Of youth and ignorance :$_x$ both my revenge and hate
Loosing upon thee, in the name of justice,
Without all termes of pittie.

13
                    Speake, thine answer.

Commentary

self-control, which is very important given the public nature of the occasion (and whether this is a deliberate loss-of-control-tactic to shame Bertram, or is genuine, the King being upset at the shame publicly heaped on Hellen – implying a very deep bond between the old man and the young woman who has saved his life - is up to each actor to decide)

• modern texts also alter the end of F #6, setting no punctuation at the end of the third line from the finish, viz. 'on everie grave:/A lying Trophee', even though F as set gives the King's passion so much more weight: they also move what they (and the second Folio of 1632) regard as a peculiar period ending F #6, though the original setting and resulting short emotional demanding F #7 (0/2) make sense as set

• in promising direct intervention to provide title and wealth for Hellen, though F #8 still remains emotional (2/5), the three surround phrases which totally make up the onrushed sentence, plus the three extra breath-thoughts (marked ,$_x$) underscore how hard the King is working to both control himself and get his argument clearly understood, which is spelled out even more clearly in the short monosyllabic F #9 that follows

• the emotion persists as the King decides to 'produce my power' and orders the 'proud scornfull boy' to 'take her hand' (1/5, the first five lines of F #11)

• which turns to passion as he demeans Bertram for not recognising the King's authority, and orders him 'Checke thy contempt' (4/3, the last two lines of F #11 and the first line and a half of F #12)

• the speech ends emotionally but not so heavily as before (1/8, the last eight lines), with the King's last words ordering for Bertram to respond contained in a very short demanding sentence 'Speake, thine answer.' (F #13)

Modern version

11
          The mere* words a slave
Debosh'd on every* tomb*, on every* grave
A lying △trophy*, and as oft is dumb*
Where dust and damn'd oblivion is the △tomb*, ◊
Of honoured* bones indeed . †
                    What should be said*?.

12
If thou canst like this creature as a maid* ,
I can create the rest. †

13
          Virtue and she*
Is her own* dower*; △honor* and wealth from me* .

14
Thou wrong'st thyself* , if thou shold'st strive
to choose.

15
My △honor's at the stake, which to defeat* ,
I must produce my power.

16
          Here* , take her hand,

17
Proud scornful* boy, unworthy* this good gift,
That dost in vile misprision shackle up
My love, and her desert* ;   that canst not dream* ,
We poising* us in her defective scale,
Shall weigh thee to the beam* ;   △that wilt not know
It is in △us to plant thine △honor* where
We please to have it grow.

18
          Check* thy contempt;
Obey △our will, which travails* in thy good;
Believe* not thy disdain* , but presently*
Do thine own* fortunes that obedient right
Which both thy duty* owes and △our power claims* ,
Or I will throw thee from my care for ever
Into the staggers and the careless* lapse
Of youth and ignorance;   both my revenge and hate
Loosing upon thee, in the name of justice,
Without all terms* of pity* .

19
          Speak* , thine answer.

#'s 8 - 10: BERTRAM'S ESCAPE FROM HIS NEW WIFE HELLEN

8/ Parrolles   **France is a dog-hole, and it no more merits,**   between 2.3.274 - 285

Background: In accordance with the King's agreement with Hellen (see background to speech #7 immediately above) the King has forced Bertram to marry her, but Bertram plans not only to never consummate the marriage but also to send Hellen away from Paris and the King back to his mother the Countesse. In the following, Parrolles counsels Bertram to join the other French lords in the Florentine wars.

Style: as part of a two-handed scene

Where: somewhere in the French court   **To Whom:** Bertram

# of Lines: 10   **Probable Timing: 0.35 minutes**

Modern Text	First Folio
8/ Parrolles	**8/ Parrolles**
1 France is a dog-hole, and it no more merits, The tread of a man's foot . † To*'th' wars* !	1 France is a dog-hole, and it no more merits, The tread of a mans foot : too'th warres . +
2 To* 'th' wars* my boy, to*'th' wars* ! †	2 too'th warrs my boy, too'th warres ; +
3	He weares his honor in a boxe vnseene,
4 He wears* his honor in a box* unseen* , That hugs* his kicky*-°wicky* here* at home, Spending his manly* marrow in her arms* , Which should sustain* the bound and high curvet Of Mars's fiery* steed . †	That hugges his kickie wickie heare at home, Spending his manlie marrow in her armes Which should sustaine the bound and high curvet Of Marses fierie steed : to other Regions, + France is a stable, wee that dwell in't Jades,
5 To other °regions! †	Therefore to th'war !
6 France is a stable, we* that dwell in't °jades, Therefore to th'war !	

Given the overall exuberance of the speech, and especially the onrush (most modern texts' six sentences presenting a far more in control rational character than F's two), it seems that Parrolles may have his own reasons for leaving France (being called a fraud to his face by one of the King's closest friends, Lafew, perhaps).

• thus, the deceptive calm of the opening is very surprising; while F#1 is composed of two surround phrases, the fact of the opening phrase anti-French derogatory sentiments being unembellished (in style a reminder of how Parrolles began his unsuccessful seduction of Hellen, see speech #1 above), it might suggest that Parrolles is being very careful not to be overheard by some passing royal functionary

• however, F #1's final surround phrase ': too'th warres . 'leads to a second much more emotional surround phrase repetition opening F #2 'Too'th warrs my boy, too'th warrs', the 0/4 release in the one line merely a part of the total emotional exuberant encouragement to leave France (0/14 in just six lines from the last phrase of F #1 to the last colon of F #2), and while the final two line urging on is both passionate (2/1) and ended with a very rare (for the original texts) exclamation mark, suggesting an even greater release

9/ Hellen   *Till I have no wife I have nothing in France .*   3.2.99 - 129

Background: Though nominally married, Hellen has been sent back to Rossillion with a letter from Bertram which, quoted as the first line of this speech, explains very clearly that Bertram will not pursue conjugal relationships with her, but if she can get the Rossillion family ring from his finger and 'shew mee a childe begotten of thy bodie that I am father too' he will then acknowledge her as his wife, but until then 'Never'. It is this letter which leads to the following reasoning

Style: solo

Where: somewhere in the palace of Rossillion   **To Whom:** self

# of Lines: 31   **Probable Timing: 1.30 minutes**

Modern Text

9/ Hellen

1 "Till I have no wife, I have nothing in France ."

2 Nothing in France until* he has no wife ! †

3 Thou shalt have none, Rossillion, none in France ;
   Then hast thou all again* . †

          Poor* △lord, is't I †

4 That chase thee from thy △country*; and expose
   Those tender limbs* of thine, to the event
   Of the none-sparing war*?

          And is it I

5 That drive thee from the sportive △court, where thou
   Was't shot at with fair* eyes, to be the mark*
   Of smoky* △muskets?

6   O you leaden messengers,
   That ride upon the violent speed* of fire,
   Fly with false aim* , move the still-[piercing] air*
   That sings with piercing, do not touch my △lord. †

7 Whoever shoots at him, I set him there; ◇
   Whoever charges on his forward breast*,
   I am the △caitiff* that do hold him to't*;
   And though I kill him not, I am the cause
   His death was so effected. †

8   Better 'twere

9 I met the ravin* △lion* when he roar'd
   With sharp* constraint of hunger; better 'twere,
   That all the miseries which nature owes
   Were mine at once.

10   No, come thou home, Rossillion,
   Whence honor but of danger wins* a scar* ,
   As oft it loses* all.

First Folio

9/ Hellen

1 *Till I have no wife* † *I have nothing in France .*

2 Nothing in France untill he has no wife: †
   Thou shalt have none + Rossillion, none in France , +
   Then hast thou all againe : poore Lord, is't I
   That chase thee from thy Countrie, and expose
   Those tender limbes of thine, to the event
   Of the none-sparing warre?

3   And is it I, ₓ
   That drive thee from the sportive Court, where thou
   Was't shot at with faire eyes, to be the marke
   Of smoakie Muskets?

4   O you leaden messengers,
   That ride upon the violent speede of fire,
   Fly with false ayme, move the still-[peering] aire
   That sings with piercing, do not touch my Lord :
   Who ever shoots at him, I set him there.

5 Who ever charges on his forward brest +
   I am the Caitiffe that do hold him too't, +
   And though I kill him not, I am the cause
   His death was so effected: Better 'twere
   I met the ravine Lyon when he roar'd
   With sharpe constraint of hunger : better 'twere,
   That all the miseries which nature owes
   Were mine at once.

6   No + come thou home + Rossillion,
   Whence honor but of danger winnes a scarre,
   As oft it looses all.

In responding to the guilt-ridden (and essentially inaccurate) belief that she is responsible for sending Bertram to his possible warrior death and her subsequent exploration as to what to do to rectify the situation, she begins an amazingly quiet sense of analysis, with very little release until she decides to leave the ancestral seat of Rossillion, the only place she has known as home.

• thus the quiet unembellished moments include
   " : Who ever shoots at him, I set him there ."
   the horror of this underscored by being a monosyllabic surround phrase, and
   "Who ever charges on his forward brest"
   "And though I kill him not, I am the cause/His death was so effected"
   therefore
   "better 'twere,/That all the miseries which nature owes/Were mine at once ."

• and the pain of his rejection of her via the letter can be seen in the unembellished short sentence quote from it with which Hellen starts the speech (F #1), heightened by the surround phrase almost word for word repetition of it that opens F #2

• yet, and a great tribute to her strength of character, despite this, the first five lines of the speech are essentially intellectual (6/3), until the realisation that she may be responsible for exposing his tender 'limbes' to the 'warre' (0/2, the last line and a half of F #2)

• her acknowledgement that she is also responsible for driving him from the possible amours of the 'sportive Court' becomes passionate (2/2, F #3)

• her prayer that the bullets 'do not touch my Lord' becomes emotional (1/3, F #4, till the final unembellished line)

• for the second time the self-blame, now for being the 'cause' that his possible 'death' might be 'so effected' becomes passionate (3/4, F #5 - within the framework of opening and closing unembellished lines)

• and, in making the unembellished monosyllabic surround phrase decision to leave Rossillion (': I will be gone : '), the floodgates open, for the remainder of the speech becomes almost totally emotional (3/14, in the last ten lines, F #6-9)

7
      I will be gone :
My being heere it is, that holds thee hence,
Shall I stay heere to doo't?
           No, no, although

8 The ayre of Paradise did fan the house,
And [Angles] offic'd all : I will be gone,
That pittifull rumour may report my flight
To consolate thine eare.

9   Come night, end day, +
For with the darke ₓ(poore theefe)ₓ Ile steale away.

• interestingly, most of the releases come in clusters, as if perhaps she is still trying to control herself, but occasionally failing, as with the idea of 'danger winnes a scarre'; 'Shall I stay heere to doo't'; 'That pittifull rumour may report 'her flight; and the highly emotional last line

    "For with the darke (poore theefe) Ile steale away."

11
      I will be gone. †
My being here* it is, that holds thee hence. †
Shall I stay here* to do't*?
           No, no, although

12 The air* of ^paradise did fan the house,
And [^angels] offic'd all. †

13   I will be gone,
That pitiful* rumor* may report my flight
To consolate thine ear*.

14   Come night, end day! †

15 For with the dark*, poor* thief*, I'll steal* away.

10/ Countesse as Lady   Alas! and would you take the letter of her :

between 3.4.1 - 42

Background: As a result of speech #9 immediately above, Hellen has left a letter to the Countesse explaining the reasoning behind her becoming a pilgrim going to 'S. Jaques'[1].
This is the Countesse's response to Rynaldo, her trusted Steward, who handed her the letter she has just finished reading. One note: in the play itself, she asks someone else (presumably Rynaldo) to read the letter aloud.

Style: as part of a two-handed scene

Where: somewhere in the palace at Rossillion   **To Whom:** Rynaldo, the steward

# of Lines: 39   **Probable Timing: 2.00 minutes**

Modern Text

10/ {Countesse as} **Lady**

1 Alas! and would you take the letter of her ? †

2 Might you not know she would do, as she has done,
   By sending me a ^letter ?

3   {Let me} read* it again* . †

Letter

4 "I am Saint Jaques' Pilgrim, thither gone . †

5 Ambitious love hath so in me offended,
   That barefoot plod I the cold ground upon
   With sainted vow my faults to have amended.

6 Write, write, that from the bloody* course of war* ,
   My dearest* ^master, your dear* son* , may hie . †

7 Bless* him at home in peace, ◊ whilst I from far* ,
   His name with zealous fervor* sanctifie*. †

8 His taken labors* bid him me forgive;
   I, his despiteful* Juno, sent him forth
   From Courtly friends, with *camping foes to live,
   Where death and danger dogs' the heels* of worth .

9 He is too good and faire for death and me* ,
   Whom I myself* embrace to set him free . "

10 Ah, what sharp* stings are in her mildest words! †

11 Rinaldo*, you did never lack* advice so much
    As letting her pass* so . †

12   Had I spoke with her,
    I could have well diverted her intents,
    Which thus she hath prevented.

First Folio

10/ {Countesse as} **Lady**

1 Alas! and would you take the letter of her :
   Might you not know she would do, as she has done,
   By sending me a Letter . +

2   {Let me} reade it agen .

Letter

3 I am S. Jaques Pilgrim, thither gone:
   Ambitious love hath so in me offended,
   That bare-foot plod I the cold ground upon
   With sainted vow my faults to have amended. +

4 Write, write, that from the bloodie course of warre, ₓ
   My deerest Master+ your deare sonne, may hie,
   Blesse him at home in peace.

5   Whilst I from farre,
   His name with zealous fervour sanctifie:
   His taken labours bid him me forgive:ₓ
   I+ his despightfull Juno+ sent him forth,ₓ
   From Courtly friends, with Camping foes to live,
   Where death and danger dogges the beeles of worth.

6 He is too good and faire for death, and mee,
   Whom I my selfe embrace,ₓ to set him free.

7 Ah+ what sharpe stings are in her mildest words?+

8 Rynaldo, you did never lacke advice so much,ₓ
   As letting her passe so : had I spoke with her,
   I could have well diverted her intents,
   Which thus she hath prevented.

As with speech #4 above, the Countesse opens with great self-control - at least as regards release, though, given the circumstance, it's not surprising that F's orthography clearly shows her strain in maintaining such control.

• the strain can be seen from

a/ the first line of F #1 is formed by two surround phrases

b/ followed by a very short F #2 (which, when spoken in the play itself to the offending Rynaldo, might be seen as a reprimand?)

c/ the subsequent letter starting out with yet another surround phrase line

d/ and an unembellished three-line reading of Hellen's self-blaming preamble

• but once the moment Hellen's letter explains she has left so that her 'deerest Master' can return home 'in peace', so the letter and/or the reader (here the Countesse) becomes highly emotional (1/8, F #4, and the first two and half lines of F #5), with both Hellen's never-ending love and her apologies to Bertram for causing him such 'labours' heightened by being expressed in F #5's opening surround phrases

     " . Whilst I from farre,/His name with zealous fervour sanctifie: /His taken labours bid him me forgive :"

• the further details of the letter are written/read rather more emotionally than intellectually (3/5, the last three lines of F #5, and F #6, five lines in all)

• the rebuke of Rynaldo (the short F #7 and the first line and a half of F #8) is purely emotional (0/4 in just two and a half lines), while the self-rebuke that had the Countesse herself spoken with Hellen 'I could have well diverted her intents' becomes totally unembellished (perhaps the calmness of simply recognising the inevitable? or a somewhat deeper calm of bleak tiredness? or despair?)

---

[1] the most famous shrine to this Saint is at Compostella in north-western Spain, so, as *The Riverside Shakespeare* dryly remarks, 'it is never made clear why Helena's route should in III.v bring her to Florence' (fn. to 3.4.4)

                         What Angell shall
9 Blesse this unworthy husband, he cannot thrive,
   Unlesse her prayers, whom heaven delights to [beare]
   And loves to grant, repreeve him from the wrath
   Of greatest Justice.
                         Write, write Rynaldo,
10 To this unworthy husband of his wife,
   Let everie word waigh heavie of her worth,
   That he does waigh too light : my greatest greefe,
   Though little he do feele it, set downe sharpely.
11 Dispatch the most convenient messenger,
   When haply he shall heare that she is gone,
   He will returne, and hope I may that shee
   Hearing so much, will speede her foote againe,
   Led hither by pure love : which of them both
   Is deerest to me, I have no skill in sence
   To make distinction : provide this Messenger :
   My heart is heavie, and mine age is weake, +
   Greefe would have teares, and sorrow bids me speake.

• but the calm does not last, for her evocation of possible religious intervention ('Angell' 'Blesse' and 'prayers') to save her son is emotional (2/5, F #9)

• the depth of her disgust with her son can be seen in that her F #10's assessment of and desire to punish Bertram
"To this unworthy husband of his wife,/Let everie word waigh heavie of her worth,/That he does waigh too light"
is not just unembellished, several words ('everie', 'waigh' – twice – and 'heavie') are set as short-spellings, perhaps suggesting that she is having difficulty in voicing what must be very painful thoughts about her own child

• and then the mixture of 'my greatest greefe' (the end of F #10), the hope that Bertram will 'returne' so as to 'speede' Hellen's 'foote againe' back to Rossillion (the first four and a half lines of F #11), seems almost too much to bear, for it is totally and highly emotional (0/10 in just six lines), an unusually heavy release for the Countesse, especially in such a concentrated passage

• and though she does once more attempt to control herself (1/1 in the next two and a half lines), her confusion is compressed into the somewhat lengthy first surround phrase, and the terse surround phrase order that follows it
" : which of them both/Is deerest to me, I have no skill in sence/To make distinction : provide this Messenger : "

• the words of her final 'Greefe' and 'teares' and 'weake' age are underscored by both the emotion that accompanies them (0/4, the last two lines of F #11) and the couplet rhyming scheme in which they are set
"My heart is heavie, and mine age is weake, /Greefe would have teares, and sorrow bids me speake."

                              What ^angel* shall
13 Bless* this unworthy husband ? †
                              He cannot thrive,
14 Unless* her prayers, whom heaven delights to [hear]
   And loves to grant, reprieve* him from the wrath
   Of greatest ^justice.
                              Write, write Rinaldo*, †
15 To this unworthy husband of his wife. †
16 Let every* word weigh heavy* of her worth,
   That he does weigh too light. †
                              My greatest grief*,
17 Though little he do feel* it, set down* sharply*. †
18 Dispatch the most convenient messenger. †
19 When haply he shall hear* that she is gone,
   He will return*, and hope I may that she*
   Hearing so much, will speed* her foot* again*,
   Led hither by pure love. †
                              Which of them both
20 Is dearest* to me, I have no skill in sense
   To make distinction. †
21   Provide this ^messenger. †
22 My heart is heavy*, and mine age is weak* ;
   Grief* would have tears*, and sorrow bids me speak*.

#'s 11 - 12: DIANA'S PRACTICAL VIEW OF LOVE AND LIFE

11/ Diana   **I so you serve us**   between 4.2.17 - 31

Background: Considering himself not to be married, which may be true in the legal sense (see background to speeches #8-9 above) Bertram, before returning to France, is making a serious attempt to bed a chaste young woman of Florence, Diana (named after the goddess who is a symbol both for chastity and the hunt). In a series of coincidences Hellen has lodged with Diana and her mother, and persuaded Diana verbally to agree to Bertam's pleadings, but then allow Hellen to change places with her in bed so as to achieve the conditions Bertram has laid out for Hellen if he is to consider her to be his wife (see background to speech #9 above). The following is triggered by Bertram's words of never-ending devotion ' . . . and will for ever/Do thee rights of service.'

Style: as part of a two-handed scene

Where: unspecified, but presumably somewhere in or near Diana's home   **To Whom:** Bertram

# of Lines: 14   **Probable Timing: 0.45 minutes**

As befits a character named after the goddess of chastity and the hunt, F's orthography shows that, when she chooses, Diana can easily strip Bertram of all his flawed logic in his attempts to seduce her.

- thus the opening very frank and brutally simple to-the-point cold-water denial of his words of 'ever' lasting devotion is triply heightened by being unembellished, monosyllabic, and a surround phrase '. I so you serve us/Till we serve you : ' (followed by a very heady analysis of men's usual sexual exploitation of women ' . . . : But when you have our Roses')

- and her demand for him to answer the key question that she is about to pose ' : then pray you tell me. ' is equally powerfully unembellished, and this pattern of proffering her final point in each powerful argument as an irrefutable unembellished statement is seen at the end of F #3 and #5 as well as here in F #2

- this is not to say that she is a cold fish, for amidst the moments of unembellished self-control come sudden floods of emotional release - as with the accusation of the traditional male abandonment of women once men are satisfied (0/4, the last two lines of F #1); the dismissal of men's oaths (1/8, the six and a half lines of F #2-3); and the final denial of Bertram's 'oathes' as 'words and poore conditions' (0/4, F #4-5)

Modern Text

11/ Diana

1 Ay*, so you serve us
Till we serve you ; ᐃbut when you have our ᐃroses,
You barely leave our thorns* to prick* our selves,
And mock* us with our bareness* .

2 'Tis not the many oaths* that makes the truth,
But the plain* single vow, that is vow'd true . †

3 What is not holy*, that we swear* not by,
But take the ᐃHigh'st to witness* . †

4   Then pray you tell me , ◇

If I should swear* by Jove's great attributes
I lov'd you dearly*, would you believe* my oaths* ;
When I did love you ill?

5   This has no holding,
To swear* by ᐃHim whom I protest to love
That I will work* against him ; ◇ therefore your oaths*
Are words and poor* conditions, but unseal'd –
At least* in my opinion.

First Folio

11/ Diana

1 I + so you serve us
Till we serve you : ₓ   But when you have our Roses,
You barely leave our thornes to pricke our selves,
And mocke us with our barenesse.

2 'Tis not the many oathes that makes the truth,
But the plaine single vow, that is vow'd true :
What is not holie, that we sweare not by,
But take the high'st to witnesse : then pray you tell me.

3 If I should sweare by Joves great attributes,ₓ
I lov'd you deerely, would you beleeve my oathes,ₓ
When I did love you ill?

4   This ha's no holding +
To sweare by him whom I protest to love
That I will worke against him.

5   Therefore your oathes
Are words and poore conditions, but unseal'd +
At lest in my opinion.

12/ Diana   **When midnight comes, knocke at my chamber window:**   between 4.254 · 76

Background: As a continuation of the background to speech #11 immediately above, Diana appears to acquiesce to Bertram's seductive pleadings, though once he leaves she makes it very clear just what has been going on (a definite victory for the chaste huntress it would seem).

Style: intitially as part of a two-handed scene, and then solo

Where: unspecified, but presumably somewhere in or near Diana's home   **To Whom:** Bertram, and then direct audience address

# of Lines: 20   **Probable Timing: 1.00 minutes**

Modern Text

12/ Diana

1 When midnight comes, knock* at my cham-
      ber window ;
   I'll order take my mother shall not hear* .

2 Now will I charge you in the band of truth,
   When you have conquered my yet-°maiden ° bed,
   Remain* there but an hour*, nor speak* to me* . †

3 My reasons are most strong, and you shall know them
   When back* again* this △ring shall be deliver'd ;
   And on your finger in the night, I'll put
   Another △ring, that what in time proceeds
   May token to the future, our past deeds.

4 Adieu till then, then fail* not . †
                              You have won*

5   She says* , all men
   As if she sate in's heart.

6 My mother told me just how he would woo,
   Have the like oaths* . †

7 When his wife's dead ;   therefore* I'll lie* with him
   When I am buried.

8 Since Frenchmen are so braid* ,

9 Marry that will, I live and die a △maid . †

10 Only* in this disguise I think't no sin*
   To cozen* him that would unjustly win .

First Folio

12/ Diana

1 When midnight comes, knocke at my cham-
      ber window : x
   Ile order take, x my mother shall not heare .

2 Now will I charge you in the band of truth,
   When you have conquer'd my yet maiden-bed,
   Remaine there but an houre, nor speake to mee :
   My reasons are most strong, and you shall know them, x
   When backe againe this Ring shall be deliver'd : x
   And on your finger in the night, Ile put
   Another Ring, that what in time proceeds, x
   May token to the future, our past deeds.

3 Adieu till then, then faile not : you have wonne
   A wife of me, though there my hope be done.

4 My mother told me just how he would woo,
   As if she sate in's heart.

5   She saves, all men

   Have the like oathes : He [had] sworne to marrie me
   When his wife's dead : x therfore Ile lye with him
   When I am buried.

6   Since Frenchmen are so braide,
   Marry that will, I live and die a Maid :
   Onely in this disguise, x I think't no sinne, x
   To cosen him that would unjustly winne.

Once more Diana's skilful use of calmness is evident, this time as a stunning seduction technique, as is the long tantalising sexual build-up of onrushed F # 2.

• thus the opening assignation time-setting 'When midnight comes' is unembellished, as is the strength of the suggestion that they will not be disturbed 'Ile order take', which leads to the two line unembellished enticement
   "Now will I charge you in the band of truth,/When you have conquer'd my
   yet maiden-bed,"

• the clever unembellished suggestion of games within games, that she'll put a 'Ring'
   "And on your finger in the night, . . . that what in time proceeds, /May
      token to the future, our past deeds."
is brilliantly understated, in that at one and the same time it ensures the bed-trick will actually work, for Bertram will have given up his own ring which the actual bed-partner Hellen will need as part of his challenge to her that she must obtain before he will acknowledge her as his wife, while at the same time fooling Bertram into concentrating on the physicality of the evening's forthcoming pleasures

• while Diana's unembellished build to her final begulement
   ". . Adieu till then, then faile not : you have wonne/A wife of me, though there
      my hope be done . "
is utterly brilliant, its enticements heightened by being made up of two surround phrases too

• as with the previous speech, small bursts of emotion do shake Diana's outward calm at times, as with the instructions to "remaine there but an houre, nor speake to mee' (0/4 in one line); that supposedly his own ring will be returned 'backe againe' (which it won't); the rhyme of the speech ending justification of deceiving him, 'sinne'/'winne'

• once the besotted and aroused Bertram leaves, the enormous depth of her convictions are shown by the only remaining unembellished line 'My mother told me just how he would woo" and by the three final dismissive surround phrases totally forming F #5

• thus it's not surprising that overall, amid the moments of needed and skilful self-control, Diana's releases in the speech are essentially emotional (5/19 in twenty lines)

#'s 13 - 14: CLOWNE'S CYNICAL VIEW OF LOVE AND LIFE

13/ Clowne   **I hope to have friends for my wives sake,**   between 13, 39 - 63

Background: The Countesse has kept on Lavatch, a clown belonging to her late husband. Blessed with a mordant wit, here he offers a somewhat cynical view of marriage, and the apparent benefits in having a wife who may cheat on him.

Style: as part of a two-handed scene

Where: somewhere in the palace of Rossillion   **To Whom:** the Countesse

# of Lines: 17   **Probable Timing:** 0.55 minutes

Modern Text

13/ Clowne

1   I hope to have friends for my wive's sake ,

for the
knaves come to do* that for me which I am a weary* of . †

2   He that ears* my △land spares my team* , and gives me*
leave to △inn* the crop . †

3   If I be his cuckold he's* my
drudge . †

4   He that comforts my wife is the cherisher of
my flesh and blood ; he* that cherishes my flesh and
blood loves my flesh and blood ; he that loves my flesh
and blood is my friend ; *ergo*, he that kisses my wife is my
friend . †

5   If men could be contented to be what they are,
there were no fear* in marriage, for young* Charbon the
△papist, how some* er* their △religion, their heads are both one ;
hearts are sever'd in △religion, their heads are both one :
they may jowl* horns together like any △deer* i'th'herd.

---

6   A △prophet I, (ψ)and I speak* the truth, (ψ)
     For I the △ballad will repeat*
     Which men full true shall find*:
     Your marriage comes by destiny,
     Your △cuckoo* sings by kind* .

First Folio

13/ Clowne

1   I hope to have friends for my wives sake ,

for the
knaves come to doe that for me which I am a wearie of :
he that eres my Land,ₓ spares my teame, and gives mee
leave to Inne the crop : if I be his cuckold hee's my
drudge ; he that comforts my wife,ₓ is the cherisher of
my flesh and blood ; hee that cherishes my flesh and
blood,ₓ loves my flesh and blood ; he that kisses my wife is my
friend : if men could be contented to be what they are,
there were no feare in marriage, for yong Charbon² the
Puritan,ₓ and old Poysam the Papist, how somere their
hearts are sever'd in Religion, their heads are both one, ⁺
they may joule horns together like any Deare i'th Herd.

2   A Prophet I, (ψ)and I speake the truth, (ψ)
for I the Ballad will repeate, which men full
true shall finde, ⁺ your marriage comes by destinie, your
Cuckow sings by kinde.

While most modern texts set up a highly rational six sentence character, thus implying that Lavatch's wit is well under control, and that he finishes neatly and tidily with a ballad. However, F's two onrushed sentences plus his speaking in rhyme rather than singing it suggests a much more challenged, challenging, and sardonic character. Compared to the following speech, it seems Lavatch finds either the subject of marriage, or amusing the Countesse, one of his more difficult tasks.

• as with several of Shakespeare's Clowne/Foole's (notably Touchstone), Lavatch begins deceptively calmly in setting up the premise from which the ensuing wit games will stem (0/1 the first two lines)

• and then begins a series of mildly emotional chop-logic embellishments on the theme of a man's wife's infidelity having its own rewards (2/5, in the seven and a half lines till the final colon of the speech), here highly overworked in being set as six consecutive surround phrases, with the most highly cynical points within the argument underscored by three successive emotional semicolons, viz.
" : if I be his cuckold hee's my drudge ; he that comforts my wife, is the cherisher of my flesh and blood : hee that cherishes my flesh and blood, loves my flesh and blood ; he that loves my flesh and blood is my friend : "

• and once the foolishness of the final surround phrase ' : *ergo*, he that kisses my wife is my friend : ' is over, so Lavatch becomes highly intellectual in the put down of both Protestants and Catholics alike (7/3, the last five lines of F #1)

• and the F spoken rather than sung jaundiced maxim that ends the speech (as shown by the shaded lines) becomes emotionally passionate (3/5, F #2) thus matching the surround phrase elaborations offered earlier

---

² because of the inherent pun in the first name 'Charbon', (sounding both like the French word for flesh, 'char', thus implying the Puritan is rather well fleshed, and the English description 'chair-borne, i.e. carried), some modern texts alter Ff's Poysam to the French word for fish, Poisson, also a wonderful dig at the Friday diet of the Papist

14/ Clowne   **Why sir, if I cannot serve you, I can serve . . . .**   between 4.5.36 - 55

Background: The King and his entourage are staying with the Countess at Rossillion, for the King plans to make peace with Bertram, and, believing Hellen to have died, as everyone now does, is intending to arrange a new marriage between Bertram and Lafew's daughter.   Lafew, in accompanying the King, has had some private words with the Countesse, and then attempts to exchange wits with Lavatch, who (whether seriously or no) counters with the following once Lafew has refused Lavatch's original offer to be 'At your service' with a resounding 'No, no, no.'

Style: as part of a three-handed scene

Where: somewhere in the palace or grounds of Rossillion   **To Whom:** Lafew, in front of the Countesse

# of Lines: 13   **Probable Timing: 0.45 minutes**

Modern Text	First Folio
14/ Clowne	**14/ Clowne**
1 Why, sir, if I cannot serve you, I can serve as great a prince as you are.	1 Why⁺ sir, if I cannot serve you, I can serve as great a prince as you are.
2 'A has an English [name], but his fisnomy* is more hotter in France [than] there.	2 'A has an English [maine], but his fisnomie is more hotter in France [then] there.
3 The black* prince, sir, alias the prince of darkness* , alias the devil*.	3 The blacke prince⁺ sir, alias the prince of darkenesse, alias the divell.
4 I am a woodland fellow, sir, that always* lov'd* a great fire, and the master I speak* of ever keeps a good fire. †	4 I am a woodland fellow⁺ sir, that alwaies loved a great fire, and the master I speake of ever keeps a good fire, but sure he is the Prince of the world,⁺ let his No-bilitie remaine in's Court.
5 But sure he is the ⁴prince of the world ; let his ⁴no-bility* remain* in's ᐃcourt.	5 I am for the house with the narrow gate, which I take to be too little for pompe to enter : some that humble themselves may, but the ma-nie will be too chill and tender; and theyle bee for the flowrie way that leads to the broad gate,ₓ and the great fire.
6 I am for the house with the narrow gate, which I take to be too little for pomp* to enter. †	
7 Some that humble themselves may, but the ma-ny* will be too chill and tender; and they'll* be* for the flow'ry* way that leads to the broad gate and the great fire.	

As with the previous speech, Lavatch starts quietly. However, **whereas the previous speech was quite heavily released (12/14 in sixteen and a half lines), the discussion of his relationship with the dark forces is handled more carefully (5/9 in thirteen lines).**

• after the unembellished premise as set up in F #1, Lavatch's first clue as to whom the 'great a prince' might be is slightly factual (2/1, F #2), and, as befits the entertainer, the naming of the 'divell' is accompanied by a total (and presumably surprising) change in style (0/3 in the short F #3)

• his self-description, and thus why he has a relationship with such a 'master', becomes passionate (3/2, F #4)

• and then, surprisingly, his further self-definition as being the entry presumably to heaven 'for the house with the narrow gate' (after all the supposed worship of the devil) and why, becomes very calm, suggesting an ease not seen in the previous speech, an admission of his true self perhaps (0/3, the four and a half lines of F #5), with two of the three releases (joyfully perhaps?) clustered together (viz. 'theyle bee') for those whose pride and self-deception ensures that they will go to hell

THE WINTER'S TALE

SPEECHES IN ORDER

SPEECHES IN ORDER	TIME	PAGE
#'s 1 – 4: Leontes and the Effects Of Jealousy		
1/ **Hermione** What? have I twice said well? when was't before?	0.50	349
2/ **Leontes** Too hot, too hot:	1.55	350
3/ **Leontes** To your owne bents dispose you: you'le be found,	1.30	352
4/ **Antigonus** Come, poore babe;	2.10	354
#'s 5 – 10: Hermione's Dignity, Leontes' Punishment & Eventual Salvation		
5/ **Hermione** There's some ill Planet raignes:	1.00	356
6/ **Hermione** Since what I am to say, must be but that	1.40	357
7/ **Hermione** Sir, spare your Threats:	1.15	358
8/ **Paulina** Woe the while: /O cut my Lace, least	1.30	360
9/ **Paulina** I am sorry (Sir) I have thus farre stir'd you: but	1.10	362
10/ **Leontes** Her naturall Posture.	1.00	364
#'s 11 – 15: Young Love Crossed and Triumphant		
11/ **Florizell** Thou deer'st Perdita,	0.50	365
12/ **Florizell** What you do,/Still betters what is done.	0.40	366
13/ **Perdita** Sir, welcome: / It is my Fathers will,	0.50	367
14/ **Perdita** Now (my fairst Friend) I would I had some Flowres	1.15	368
15/ **Polixenes** Marke your divorce (yong sir)	1.15	369
#'s 16 – 17: Perdita's Adoptive Family		
16/ **Old Shepherd** I would there were no age betweene ten. . .	1.00	371
17/ **Clowne** I have seene two such sights, by Sea & by Land:	1.00	372
#'s 18 – 20: The Triumphs and Come-Uppance of a Rogue		
18/ **Autolicus** Ha, ha, what a Foole Honestie is? and Trust (his	1.10	373
19/ **Autolicus** Whether it like me, or no, I am a Courtier.	0.30	374
20/ **Clowne** You are well met (Sir:) you deny'd to fight	0.45	375
# 21: A Theatrical Link		
21/ **Time** I that please some, try all: both joy and terror	1.35	376

SPEECHES BY GENDER

		Speech #(s)
SPEECHES FOR WOMEN (8)		
Hermione	**Traditional & Today:** married woman with young child	#1, #5, #6, #7
Paulina	**Traditional:** older married woman **Today:** woman of any age	#8, #9
Perdita	**Traditional & Today:** a young woman	#13, #14
SPEECHES FOR EITHER GENDER (2)		
Old Shepheard	**Traditional:** older male character with a son of marriageable age **Today:** as above, any gender	#16
Time	**Traditional:** male, often cast as 'Father Time' **Today:** any gender, any age	#21
SPEECHES FOR MEN (11)		
Leontes	**Traditional & Today:** married male (often middle-aged) with young child	#2, #3, #10
Antigonus	**Traditional & Today:** middle aged or older male	#4
Florizell	**Traditional & Today:** a young man	#11, #12
Polixenes	**Traditional & Today:** middle aged man, with marriageable aged son	#15
Clowne	**Traditional & Today:** a young man of marriageable age	#17, #20
Autolicus	**Traditional & Today:** singing/acting male of any age	#18, #19

THE WINTER'S TALE

#'s 1 - 4: LEONTES AND THE EFFECTS OF JEALOUSY

1/ Hermione   What? have I twice said well? when was't before?   between 1.2.90 - 106

Background: Daughter of the 'Emperor of Russia', married to Leontes King of Sicilia, has publicly and with no difficulty whatsoever very quickly managed to persuade Polixenes, King of Bohemia, a close boyhood friend of her husband, to stay at the Sicilian court a week longer, even though Leontes had been unable to do so. The following is her response to Leontes 'thou never spoak'st/To better purpose.', which he has immediately modified with his further 'Never, but once'.

Style: one on one in front of a small group, and perhaps a larger group in the background

Where: somewhere in the palace of Sicilia   **To Whom:** her husband Leontes, in front of Polixenes, Camillo (Leontes' key advisor), Mamillius (her son), and perhaps members of both courts

Probable Timing: 0.50 minutes   **# of Lines: 15**

First Folio

1/ Hermione

1   What? have I twice said well? when was't before?

2   I prethee tell me : ₓ cram's with prayse, and make's
     As fat as tame things : One good deed, dying tonguelesse,ₓ
     Slaughters a thousand, wayting upon that.

3   Our prayses are our Wages.

                                        You may ride's

4   With one soft Kisse a thousand Furlongs,ₓ ere
     With Spur we heat an Acre.

                                        But to th'Goale :

5   My last good deed, was to entreat his stay. ₓ

6   What was my first? it ha's an elder Sister,
     Or I mistake you : O, would her Name were Grace. ⁺

7   But once before I spoke to th'purpose? when?

8   Nay, let me have't : ₓ I long.

9   Why lo-you now ; ⁺ I have spoke to th'purpose twice :
     The one, for ever earn'd a Royall Husband ;
     Th'other, for some while a Friend.

Modern Text

1/ Hermione

1   What? have I twice said well? †

2   When was't before?

3   I prithee tell me ; cram's with praise *, and make's
     As fat as tame things . †

4   One good deed, dying tongueless*

5   Slaughters a thousand, waiting* upon that.

6   Our praises* are our ᐃwages.

                              You may ride's

7   With one soft ᐃkiss* a thousand ᐃfurlongs ere
     With ᐃspur we heat an ᐃacre.

                              But to th'ᐃgoal* : ◇

8   My last good deed, was to entreat his stay. †
     What was my first? †

9   It has an elder ᐃsister,

10 Or I mistake you . †

11   O, would her ᐃname were Grace !

12 But once before I spoke to th'purpose? when?

13 Nay, let me have't ; I long.

     Why lo ° you now ! †

            I have spoke to th'purpose twice :
     The one, for ever earn'd a ᐃroyal* ᐃhusband ;
     Th'other, for some while a ᐃfriend.

In such a pleasant social situation, the plethora of surround phrases seem to suggest a character who is enjoying herself thoroughly in teasing and challenging all around her, especially her husband Leontes.

- Hermione's lively mind and spirit can be seen throughout
  a/ from the easy unembellished but persistent surround phrase opening of F #1 and the first phrase of F #2 leading to ' I prethee tell me : '
  b/ through the logical unembellished surround phrases of F #5-6 starting with '. But to th'Goale : '
  c/ to the (delighted?) finale of F #9 including '; I have spoke to th'purpose twice : '

- while the speech starts fairly easily (0/1, the first two and a half lines), Hermione soon allows releases to begin, enjoying herself perhaps?. (1/2, the one and a half lines ending F #2)

- the shortness of F #3's 'Our prayses are our Wages.' suggests that she really does enjoy public approval, for the explanation of a 'Kisse' being better encouragement than a 'Spur' is splendidly intellectual (4/1, F #4)

- once she embarks on her mission to discover when was the first time she 'said well', emotions seem to have no place, for in her single-mindedness the remainder of the speech becomes a mixture of short sentences (F #7 and #8) unembellished phrases (ten), surround phrases (eleven), and intellect (8/2 in eight and a half lines, F #5-9)

- and though there is one emotional release in the final stage (the accurate and yet lovely assessment of her husband as 'Royall'), the s of the final sentence suggest that there is a great deal of pleasure in her pursuit

| 2/ Leontes | Too hot, too hot : | between 1.2.108 - 146 |

Background: Unfortunately, Hermione's success (see background to speech #1 above) and ensuing friendly behaviour with Polixenes gives Leontes serious doubts and fears.

Style: solo

Where: somewhere in the palace of Sicilia   **To Whom:** self, and direct audience address

# of Lines: 38   **Probable Timing:** 1.55 minutes

Modern Text

2/ Leontes

1 Too hot, too hot! †

2 To mingle friendship far* is mingling bloods.

3 I have *tremor △cordis* on me; my heart dances* ,
  But not for joy; not joy.

4   This △entertainment
May a free face put on, derive a △liberty*
From △heartiness* , from △bounty* , fertile △bosom*
And well become the △agent; 't may - I grant* . †

5 But to be paddling* △palms* and pinching △fingers,
As now they are, and making practic'd △smiles,
As in a △looking-△glass* ; and [than] to sigh, as 'twere
The △mort o'th'△deer* - O* , that is entertainment
My △bosom* likes not, nor my △brows*!

6   Mamillius,

I'fecks! †

7 Why, that's my △bawcock. †

8   What? has't smutch'd thy △nose?

9 They say it is a △copy* out of mine.

10   Come, △captain* ,
We must be neat; not neat, but cleanly, △captain :
And yet the △steer* , the [△heifer*] , and the △calf* ,
Are all call'd △neat.

11   Still △virginalling
Upon his △palm* ?

12   How now, you wanton △calf* ,
Art thou my △calf* ?

13 Thou want'st a rough pash & the shoots that I have,
To be full like me; yet they say we are
Almost as like as △eggs* ; △women say so -
(That will say any thing.)

First Folio

2/ Leontes

1 Too hot, too hot : +
  To mingle friendship farre, is mingling bloods.

2 I have *Tremor Cordis* on me: x my heart daunces,
  But not for joy; not joy.

3   This Entertainment
May a free face put on: x   derive a Libertie
From Heartinesse, from Bountie, fertile Bosome,
And well become the Agent: x 't may; x I graunt:
But to be padling Palmes, x and pinching Fingers,
As now they are, and making practis'd Smiles +
As in a Looking-Glasse; and [then] to sigh, as 'twere
The Mort o'th'Deere: x oh, that is entertainment
My Bosome likes not, nor my Browes. +

4   Mamillius,

I'fecks: +

Why + that's my Bawcock: what? ha'st smutch'd thy Nose?

5 They say it is a Coppy out of mine.

6   Come + Captaine,
We must be neat; not neat, but cleanly, Captaine:
And yet the Steere, the [Heycfer], and the Calfe,
Are all call'd Neat.

7   Still Virginalling
Upon his Palme?

8   How now, x (you wanton Calfe)x
Art thou my Calfe?

9 Thou want'st a rough pash, x & the shoots that I have +
To be full, x like me: x yet they say we are
Almost as like as Egges; Women say so,
(That will say any thing.)

Though overall the speech is intellectual (50/30), the fact that there are so many releases in the speech (eighty in just thirty-six lines) and twenty pieces of major punctuation (seven of which are s) shows a veritable brain-storm of information and release. It's thus fascinating to see most modern texts regard the speech as essentially grammatical, save for two onrushed sentences dealing with the legitimacy of his son, (F #11-12) which most modern texts reset as six.

• sadly, in this speech all Leontes' ed surround phrases seem to relate to disturbing images, as F #2's ": my heart daunces,/But not for joy ; not joy. ", and F #3's prelude to his suspicion that Hermione and Polixenes have been 'padling Palmes'': 't may ; I graunt : ', while the later jaundiced view of women's actions, as
": and then to sigh, as 'twere/The Mort o'th'Deere : "
", Women say so,/(That will say any thing .)"
and the doubts, even if women do say his Mamillius looks like him
". But were they false/As o're-dy'd Blacks, as Wind, as Waters ; . . ./yet were it true,/To say this Boy were like me . "

• the one possibly happy ed pleasure (though in view of what else is going on in the speech it too may be tinged with melancholy) is with his son
". Come Captaine,/We must be neat ; not neat, but cleanly, Captaine : "

• the suspicion that Hermione and Polixenes are too close starts off deceptively calmly (0/1, F #1), and then surges between intellect/emotion and enforced calm all in one and a half lines (F #2) – the ferocious internal struggles that mar all his actions until the fateful middle of the play are already in place

• the violent mood swings continue, with an attempt at self-control as he tries to persuade himself that their friendship could indeed be innocent ('May a free face put on:'), the first three lines of F #3 being quite intellectual (6/2) – but then his control gives way as he sees them 'padling Palmes' and 'pinching Fingers' and is replaced by passionate suspicion (9/7 the remaining five and half lines of F #3), suspecting them of 'practis'd Smiles'

• and then, alone with his young son Mamillius, the four surround phrases of F #4 suggests that Leontes is making strenuous attempts to assert self-control, especially considering emotion is momentarily suppressed (2/0)

• but this cannot last, and though seemingly focused on Mamillius (F #5-8), the interruption of the very short F #7 ('Still Virginalling/Upon his Palme?') shows him still highly aware of the closeness of his wife and supposed friend;

10
But were they false
As o're-dy'd Blacks, as Wind, as Waters; false
As Dice are to be wish'd,ₓ by one that fixes
No borne 'twixt his and mine; ₓ yet were it true.ₓ
To say this Boy were like me.
                    Comeₓ (Sir Page)ₓ

11
Looke on me with your Welkin eye: sweet Villaine,⁺
Most dear'st,⁺ my Collop:⁺ Can thy Dam, may't be ⁺¹
Affection?⁺ thy Intention stabs the Center.

12
Thou do'st make possible things not so held,
Communicat'st with Dreames (how can this be?)⁺
With what's unreall:ₓ thou coactive art,ₓ
And fellow'st nothing.

13
          Then 'tis very credent,
Thou may'st co-joyne with something, and thou do'st,ₓ
(And that beyond Commission)ₓ and I find it,
(And that to the infection of my Braines,ₓ
And hardning of my Browes.)

---

thus it's not surprising that this passage of attempted cheerfulness, reassurance, and doubt is again highly passionate (11/9 in just five and half lines)

• and after the voicing of F #8's terrifying question for any father, 'Art thou my Calfe?', coming as it does at the end of an apparently joyful start to the sentence, as if the thought has only just hit him, so most emotional release seems to disappear from him, whether deliberately by a great deal of self-control, or from simple exhaustion is up to each actor to decide

• thus the food reference of the boy's growing up ('rough pash', 'full, like me') is both monosyllabic and unembellished (remarkable in that there are hardly any unembellished phrases in the speech), followed by a highly intellectual expression of his distrust of women's words, especially about his son looking like him (7/1, the last two lines of F #9 and F #10)

• as the doubts whether Hermione has been or could now be unfaithful to him become voiced (F #11), so his relatively calm intellectual analysis grows even stronger (9/2 in just three and a half lines) with his burning love for his son underscored by the sudden surround line ': sweet Villaine,/Most dear'st, my Collop :'

• and in comparison to most of the rest of the speech, the question of what might be 'Dreames' and 'unreal' is very quietly explored (1/2, F #12)

• however, the final belief that it is possible 'Affection' could give him cause to believe there are grounds for his suspicions releases both his intellect and emotion once more (3/3, F #13)

14
But were they false
As o're-dy'd △blacks, as △wind, as △waters, false
As △dice are to be wish'd by one that fixes
No bourn* 'twixt his and mine, yet were it true
To say this △boy were like me.
                    Come, △sir △page,

15
Look* on me with your △welkin eye . ⁺
                    Sweet △villain*!⁺

16

17 Most dear'st! my △collop!⁺
18   Can thy △dam?- may't be - ?
19 Affection! thy △intention stabs the △centre*.
20 Thou do'st make possible things not so held,
Communicat'st with △dreams* (how can this be?),
With what's unreal*, thou co-△active art
And fellow'st nothing.
21   Then 'tis very credent,
Thou may'st co-join* with something, and thou dost
(And that beyond △commission), and I find it,
(And that to the infection of my △brains*
And hard'ning of my △brows* .)

---

¹ dramatically, this whole section shows Leontes under great stress, and Ff set the punctuation accordingly: however, both here and at the end of the next sentence most modern texts rationalise the punctuation more, setting a question mark here, and replacing the colon with a comma

3/ Leontes   **To your owne bents dispose you : you'le be found,**   1.2.179 - 207

Background: Even though the behaviour of his wife and Polixenes seems perfectly proper, and despite their concern for his well-being {Polixenes, 'What cheere? how is't with you, best brother?' and Hermione's 'You look as if you held a Brow of much distraction:/Are you mov'd (my Lord?)'}, Leontes is still convinced he, like so many men, is being deceived and that they are lovers.

Style: solo

Where: somewhere in the palace of Sicilia   **To Whom:** self, and direct audience address, in front of a presumably initially close and watchful Mamillius

# of Lines: 29   **Probable Timing: 1.30 minutes**

Modern Text

3/ Leontes

1 To your own* bents dispose you ;   you'll* be found,
   Be you beneath the ᐃsky . †

2   I am angling now,
   (Though you perceive me not how I give ᐃline*) . †

3 Go* to*, go* to*!

4 How she holds up the ᐃneb!   the ᐃbill* to him!
   And arms* her with the boldnesse* of a ᐃwife
   To her allowing ᐃhusband.

5   Gone already ! †

6 Inch* -thick, knee-deep* , o'er head and ears* a fork'd one!

7 Go* play, ᐃboy, play . †

8   Thy ᐃmother plays*, and I
   Play too, but so disgrac'd a part, whose issue
   Will hiss* me to my ᐃgrave: ᐃcontempt and ᐃclamor
   Will be my ᐃknell.

9   Go* play, ᐃboy, play . †

10   There have been
    (Or I am much deceiv'd) ᐃcuckolds ere now,
    And many a man there is (even at this present,
    Now, while I speak* this) holds his ᐃwife by th'ᐃarm*,
    That little thinks* she has been sluic'd* in's absence,
    And his ᐃpond fish'd by his next ᐃneighbor - by
    Sir Smile, his ᐃneighbor . †

11   Nay, there's comfort in't,
    Whiles other men have ᐃgates, and those ᐃgates open'd,
    As mine, against their will.   Should all despair*

12 That have revolted ᐃwives, the tenth of ᐃmankind
    Would hang themselves.

First Folio

3/ Leontes

1 To your owne bents dispose you :   you'le be found,
   Be you beneath the Sky: I am angling now,
   (Though you perceive me not how I give Lyne)
   Goe too, goe too. +

2 How she holds up the Neb? + the Byll to him? +
   And armes her with the boldnesse of a Wife
   To her allowing Husband.

3   Gone already, +

   Ynch-thick, knee-deepe; x ore head and eares a fork'd one. +

4 Goe play x (Boy) x play: thy Mother playes, and I
   Play too; x but so disgrac'd a part, whose issue
   Will hisse me to my Grave: Contempt and Clamor
   Will be my Knell.

5   Goe play x (Boy) x play, there have been
   (Or I am much deceiv'd) Cuckolds ere now,
   And many a man there is (even at this present,
   Now, while I speake this) holds his Wife by th'Arme,
   That little thinkes she ha's been sluyc'd in's absence,
   And his Pond fish'd by his next Neighbor x (by
   Sir Smile, his Neighbor:) x nay, there's comfort in't,
   Whiles other men have Gates, and those Gates open'd +
   x (As mine) x against their will.

6   Should all despaire
   That have revolted Wives, the tenth of Mankind
   Would hang themselves.

As with the previous speech, Leontes' mind is still working in overdrive (34/26 in just twenty-nine lines, and at least eleven surround phrases) , however, this time there are far fewer s (just three) and the surround phrases seem to come in short bursts, suggesting that whatever fixation Leontes may be growing into, at least it is beginning to stabilize . . .

• . . . but not at the start, for the F #1 dismissal of both Hermione and Polixenes is highly emotional (2/7) and made up of at least two surround phrases

• once they have left him, Leontes' drawing the wrong facts from their behaviour, turns passionate (4/3, F #2), but then becomes emotional - for the second time in the speech - as he envisages their physical closeness ' , Ynch-thick, knee-deepe : ', the though enhanced by being set, in part, as an emotional ed surround phrase (0/4, F #3's one and half lines)

• and the surround phrase brain storm (more factually than intellectually - 6/3) continues unabated into F #4's voicing of the behaviour and gossip that will result if his beliefs are proved correct

• in attempting to console himself with the thought that many men are Cuckolds without knowing it, the passion continues (4/5, the first four and half lines of F #5) though the surround phrases temporarily disappear, perhaps suggesting that this cynical belief is actually comforting him, for as he admits he finds 'comfort in t' so he becomes almost totally factual (9/1, the last three and half lines of F #5, and F #6)

• and in F #7, developing further the universality of this, five successive surround phrases sweep back in (a sign of the overburdened mind once again?), the most important thoughts heightened by the
  " : It is a bawdy Planet, that will strike/Where 'tis predominant ; and 'tis powrefull : "
and while the gloomy realisation that 'Physicke for't, there's none' starts the assertion emotionally, the 'comfort' is essentially intellectual (9/3, F #7-8), though his final surround phrase words on the subject
  " : many thousand on s/Have the Disease, and feele't not . "
have the same emotional tinge as at the start

13   Physic* for't, there's none. †

14 It is a bawdy △planet, that will strike
Where 'tis predominant; and 'tis powr'ful* - think* it -
From △east, △west, △north, and △south. †   Be it concluded,

15 No △barricado for a △belly.   Know't,

16 It will let in and out the △enemy,
With bag and baggage. †

17   Many thousand on's
Have the △disease, and feel't not.

18   How now △boy?

• despite the concentration on infidelity, Leontes seems to make a very quick recovery, at least in style, as he greets Mamillius with the very short monosyllabic F #9 greeting 'How now Boy?' – the shortness perhaps suggesting that the boy's arrival has startled him: Mamillius has evidently not gone to 'play' as commanded in F #4, but is suddenly noticed by his father (how long the child has been watching is up to each production to decide)

      Physick for't, there's none:

7 It is a bawdy Planet, that will strike
Where 'tis predominant; and 'tis powrefull: [x] thinke it: [x]
From East, West, North, and South, be it concluded,
No Barricado for a Belly.

      Know't,

8 It will let in and out the Enemy,
With bag and baggage: many thousand on's
Have the Disease, and feele't not.

9   How now Boy?

4/ Antigonus   Come, poore babe ;   3.3.15 - 58

Background: Leontes jealous suspicions have now extended to the baby-daughter Hermione has just borne him. Believing it to be Polixenes' child and not his, Leontes has commanded that it be taken 'To some remote and desart place, quite out/Of our Dominions; and there thou leave it/(Without more mercy) to it own protection,/And favour of the Climate'. The person so ordered is Antigonus, another of the counsellors who has offended Leontes not only by protesting Hermione's innocence, but by being married to Leontes' fiercest vocal opponent in this matter, Paulina, the closest friend Hermione has. Here Antigonus has come to the 'Desarts of Bohemia', and, with a fierce storm brewing which has the Marriners fearful for their lives (correctly as it turns out, see speech #17 below), Antigonus prepares to abandon the child. One note: the end of the speech from 'A savage clamor?' refers to the fact a bear has come across him and the child - hence one of the most famous scene-ending stage directions in all of Shakespeare, 'Exit pursued by a Beare', which in fact kills him (again, see speech #17 below.)

Style: address to a silent partner

Where: somewhere on the shores of Bohemia (a famous Shakespearean geographical error, since in reality Bohemia is land-locked)

To Whom: Hermione and Leontes' baby-daughter, soon to be named Perdita by the Old Shepherd who finds her (speech #16 below)

# of Lines: 44   **Probable Timing: 2.10 minutes**

Modern Text

4/ Antigonus

1   Come, poor* babe . †

2   I have heard (but not believ'd*) the ᐃspirits o'th'dead
    May walk* again* . †

3   If such thing be, thy ᐃmother
    Appear'd to me last night;   for ne'er was dream*
    So like a waking.

4   To me comes a creature,
    Sometimes her head on one side, some another -
    I never saw a vessel* of like sorrow,
    So fill'd, and so becomming ;   in pure white ᐃrobes,
    Like very sanctity, she did approach
    Myᐃcabin* where I lay ; ◇ thrice bow'd before me,
    And (gasping to begin some speech) her eyes
    Became two spouts ;   the fury* spent, anon
    Did this break* from her : † "Good Antigonus,
    Since ᐃfate (against thy better disposition)
    Hath made thy person for the ᐃthrower-out
    Of my poor* babe, according to thine oath,
    Places remote enough are in Bohemia,
    There weep* and leave it crying ;   and for the babe
    Is counted lost for ever, Perdita
    I prithee* call't . †

5   For this ungentle business* ,
    Put on thee by my ᐃlord, thou ne'er shalt see
    Thy ᐃwife Paulina more ." †

First Folio

4/ Antigonus

1   Come, poore babe ;
    I have heard (but not beleev'd) the Spirits o'th'dead
    May walke againe : if such thing be, thy Mother
    Appear'd to me last night : ₓ for ne're was dreame
    So like a waking.

2   To me comes a creature,
    Sometimes her head on one side, some another,
    I never saw a vessell of like sorrow⁺
    So fill'd, and so becomming : ₓ in pure white Robes ⁺
    Like very sanctity⁺ she did approach
    My Cabine where I lay : ₓ thrice bow'd before me,
    And (gasping to begin some speech) her eyes
    Became two spouts ;   the furie spent, anon
    Did this breake from her.   Good Antigonus,

3   Since Fate (against thy better disposition)
    Hath made thy person for the Thrower-out
    Of my poore babe, according to thine oath,
    Places remote enough are in Bohemia,
    There weepe,ₓ and leave it crying : ₓ and for the babe
    Is counted lost for ever, Perdita
    I prethee call't :   For this ungentle businesse ⁺
    Put on thee, by my Lord, thou ne're shalt see
    Thy Wife Paulina more :   and so, with shriekes ⁺

- the three emotional surround phrases, set in part by the s, point to what has concerned/worried Antigonus the most
  "Come, poore babe ; /I have heard (but not beleev'd) the Spirits o'th'dead/May walke againe :"
  and about the warning the vision of Hermione gave him
  " : the furie spent, anon/Did this breake from her ."

- the most memorable details of what has occurred seem to be spoken very quietly, without embellishment, possibly suggesting that he is exercising great control in recounting them
  "To me comes a creature,/Sometimes her head on one side, some another,"
  who, the following enhanced by being essentially set as a long surround line,
  " : thrice bow'd before me,/And (gasping to begin some speech) her eyes Became two spouts ;"
  therefore
  " . Affrighted much, /I did in time collect my selfe, and thought/This was so, and no slumber : . . ./Yet for this once, yea superstitiously, /I will be squar'd by this."

and as the speech ends with the storm about to break, both literally and figuratively, first comes the concern for the child, again heightened both by being spoken with such control and being set as surround phrases
  " : thou'rt like to have/A lullabie too rough : I never saw/The heavens so dim, by day . "
  which immediately turns into his sighting the bear that is to kill him
  " . A savage clamor? / . . . : This is the Chace, /I am gone for ever . "
  with one interpretation of 'This is the Chace' being that he is drawing attention to himself by calling out to the bear, thus diverting its attention away from the child even if it means his own death: again, this last section is heightened by being not only unembellished but also by being set as monosyllabic surround phrase/lines too

[Folio text]

She melted into Ayre.
Affrighted much,
I did in time collect my selfe,ₓ and thought
This was so, and no slumber : Dreames,ₓ are toyes,
Yet for this once, yea⁺ superstitiously,
I will be squar'd by this.
I do beleeve

4

Hermione hath suffer'd death, and that
Apollo would (this being indeede the issue
Of King Polixenes) it should heere be laide⁺
ₓ(Either for life,ₓ or death)ₓ upon the earth
Of it's right Father.
Blossome, speed thee well,⁺

5

There lye, and there thy charracter : ₓ there these,
Which may if Fortune please, both breed thee ₓ(pretty)ₓ
And still rest thine.
The storme beginnes, poore wretch,

6

That for thy mothers fault,ₓ art thus expos'd
To losse, and what may follow. ⁺
Weepe I cannot,

7

But my heart bleedes : ₓ and most accurst am I
To be by oath enjoyn'd to this.
Farewell,⁺

8

9

The day frownes more and more : ₓ thou'rt like to have
A lullabie too rough : I never saw
The heavens so dim, by day.
A savage clamor?⁺

10

Well may I get a-boord : ⁺ This is the Chace,⁺
I am gone for ever.

[Commentary]

• F #1's sympathy for the 'Babe' and recalling of the 'dreame/So like waking' is very strong, being passionately emotional (2/4) and expressed via four surround phrases, the opening two heightened in part by the emotional which separates them

• F #2's elaboration of how Hermione appeared and behaved before speaking is a mixture of unembellished quiet (the first line and a half, and all of the last three and a half lines save for one word) with the description of how she was dressed, approached him, and 'thrice bow'd before' him being passionate (3/2 in three and a half lines), the key details expressed yet again in a long logical surround phrase
" : in pure white Robes/Like very sanctity she did approach/My Cabine where I lay :."

• here F creates a new sentence (#3), as if to mark the difference between Hermione's actions and her words, and thus emphasises the importance of both, unlike most modern texts which often set both actions and words as one long sentence (mt. #4), which, at least according to F's orthography, does Antigonus a great disservice . . . .

• . . . for now he seems to control himself, with F #3's reporting of what Hermione said becoming straightforwardly factual (9/3, the first nine lines), the naming of the child heightened by being set as a surround phrase
" : and for the babe/Is counted lost for ever, Perdita/I prethee call't : "

• but, in ending the sentence with the description of how 'with shriekes/She melted into Ayre', he becomes emotional once more (1/2 in the last eight words), the description heightened by being set as yet another surround phrase

• save for one phrase 'Dreames, are toyes,' F #4's four lines (Antigonus' reporting his fright) are unembellished

• and then releases begin to flood in: his belief that Hermione has died is passionate (4/4, F #5), and the eight line farewell to the child ('Blossome') is almost completely emotional (1/9 F #6-7, and the first line of F #8) – the only capitalized word being a wonderful appeal to 'Fortune' to 'breed thee' (pretty)

• his virtually unembellished response to the double danger of storm and bear would suggest that he has no energy to spare in trying to deal with both, the strength of his attempts highlighted by the surround phrases in which they are set: thus the sudden outburst (and the possible bravery) of 'This is the Chace' is well worth further exploration

---

[Modern text]

6

And so, with shrieks* ,
She melted into ᐃair* .
Affrighted much,

7

I did in time collect myself* and thought
This was so, and no slumber* . †
Dreams* are toys* ,

8

Yet for this once, yea, superstitiously,
I will be squar'd by this.
I do believe*

9

Hermione hath suffer'd death, and that
Apollo would (this being indeed* the issue
Of King Polixenes) it should here* be laid* ,
Either for life or death, upon the earth
Of it's right ᐃfather.
Blossom* , speed thee well* ! †

10

There lie* , and there thy character* ; there these,
Which may if Fortune please, both breed thee, pretty,
And still rest thine.

11

Poor* wretch,
That for thy mother's fault art thus expos'd
To loss* , and what may follow !

12

Weep* I cannot,

13

The storm* begins* . †

14

But my heart bleeds* ; and most accurs'd am I
To be by oath enjoyn'd to this.
Farewell ! †

15

16

The day frowns* more and more; thou'rt like to have
A lullaby* too rough. †
I never saw

17

The heavens so dim, by day.

18

A savage clamor !
This is the ᐃchase* ;

19

I am gone for ever.

#'s 5 - 10: HERMIONE'S DIGNITY, LEONTES' PUNISHMENT & EVENTUAL SALVATION

5/ Hermione   There's some ill Planet raignes :   between 2.1.105 - 124

Background: The first indication Hermione has of Leontes' (groundless) suspicions is when he bursts into her chamber accompanied by some Lords, and, after some inflammatory accusations, orders, pregnant as she is (the 'plight' referred to in F #3), 'Away with her, to Prison'. The following is her immediate response.

Style: public address

Where: Hermione's chambers within the palace   **To Whom:** specifically not to Leontes, but those of both their retinues, in front of their son Mamillius

# of Lines: 20   **Probable Timing: 1.00 minutes**

Modern Text

5/ Hermione

1   There's some ill ᐃplanet reigns* ;
   I must be patient, till the ᐃheavens look*
   With an aspect more favorable.
             Good my ᐃlords,

2   I am not prone to weeping, as our ᐃsex
   Commonly are, the want of which vain* dew
   Perchance shall dry your pities* ;   but I have
   That honorable ᐃgrief* lodg'd here which burns*
   Worse [than] ᐃtears* drown* .

3   'Beseech you all, my ᐃlords,
   With thoughts so qualified as your ᐃcharities
   Shall best instruct you, measure me ;   and so
   The King's will be perform'd !

4   Who is't that goes with me? †

5   'Beseech your ᐃHighness*
   My ᐃwomen may be with me, for you see
   My plight requires it.

6   Do* not weep* , good ᐃfools* ,
   There is no cause . †

7   When you shall know your ᐃmistress*
   Has deserv'd ᐃprison, then abound in ᐃtears*
   As I come out ;   this ᐃaction I now go* on
   Is for my better grace.

8   Adieu, my ᐃlord,
   I never wish'd to see you sorry, now
   I trust I shall . †

9   My ᐃwomen, come, you have leave.

First Folio

5/ Hermione

1   There's some ill Planet raignes :   x
   I must be patient, till the Heavens looke
   With an aspect more favorable.
               Good my Lords,

2   I am not prone to weeping ₓ(as our Sex
   Commonly are)ₓ the want of which vaine dew
   Perchance shall dry your pitties : ₓ   but I have
   That honorable Griefe lodg'd here,ₓ which burnes
   Worse [then] Teares drowne :   'beseech you all ₓ(my Lords)ₓ
   With thoughts so qualified,ₓ as your Charities
   Shall best instruct you, measure me ;   and so
   The Kings will be perform'd . +

3   Who is't that goes with me? 'beseech your Highnes
   My Women may be with me, for you see
   My plight requires it.

4   Doe not weepe ₓ(good Fooles)ₓ
   There is no cause :   When you shall know your Mistris
   Ha's deserv'd Prison, then abound in Teares,ₓ
   As I come out ;   this Action I now goe on,ₓ
   Is for my better grace.

5   Adieu ₓ(my Lord)ₓ
   I never wish'd to see you sorry, now
   I trust I shall :   my Women + come, you have leave.

- fascinatingly, here the two emotional ( ) surround phrases – ending F #3 and #4 - each underscore a moment of her sense of 'noblesse oblige', to Leontes' will (not as husband but as King) and to public decorum

- the more logical (colon created) surround phrases first seem to reinforce her belief that the innate goodness of life will eventually win out, even with the opening '. There's some ill Planet raignes : '

- and thus she makes great efforts to encourage her women with
" : but I have/That honorable Griefe lodg'd here, which burnes/Worse then Teares drowne : ", and
" . Doe not weepe (good Fooles)/There is no cause : "
and protecting them till the very end, ' : my Women come, you have leave . '

- the occasional small monosyllabic phrase gives testament to her inner calm belief in her self and her strength 'I must be patient' ; 'I am not prone to weeping' ; and the quiet calm of her questioning 'Who is't that goes with me ? . . . for you see my plight requires it' and her last words in the speech to Leontes 'I never wish'd to see you sorry, now/I trust I shall'

- yet despite the calm, at times releases burst through – as with

a/ the opening, ascribing the unfortunate events to 'ill' planetary influences (2/2, the first two lines of F #1), only immediately to regain control by an unembellished end to the sentence

b/ the opening factual line and a half of F #2 (2/0), asking for the understanding of those Lords accompanying Leontes, suddenly being swamped with emotion as she explains her 'Griefe' is 'honorable' (2/6)

c/ while the renewal of her appeal for the Lords to judge her well plus her request to know how she will be accompanied (the last three lines of F #2 and F #3) is totally intellectual once again (5/0)

d/ the most concentrated and passionate release (6/5, F #4's four lines) comes as she attempts to stop her women from crying, some difficulty perhaps indicated by the appearance of two extra breath-thoughts (marked , ₓ)

- in finishing, she finds intellectual calm (for public consumption?, 2/0, F #5)

6/ Hermione   **Since what I am to say, must be but that**   3.2.22 - 54

Background: Though just having given birth, 'The Child-bed priviledge' has been denied her, and she has been 'hurried . . . i'th'open air' to be tried for High Treason. This is her first, personal, and very well argued, statement of defence.

Style: public address, sometimes to one person, at other times to the larger group

Where: in open court   **To Whom:** sometimes directly to Leontes, at others to all present - Lords, Officers, Ladies, and the general public

# of Lines: 33   **Probable Timing: 1.40 minutes**

Modern Text

6/ Hermione

1 Since what I am to say must be but that
Which contradicts my △accusation, and
The testimony* on my part no other
But what comes from myself*, it shall scarce boot me
To say, "Not guilty*." †
      Mine △integrity*,
2 Being counted △falsehood, shall (as I express* it)
Be so receiv'd.
3   But thus, if △power's* △divine
Behold our human* △actions (as they do*)
I doubt not then but △innocence shall make
False △accusation blush, and △tyranny*
Tremble at △patience.
4   You, my △lord, best know
[Who] least will seem* to do* so) my past life
Hath been* as continent, as chaste, as true,
As I am now unhappy*; which is more
[Than] △history* can pattern*, though devis'd
And play'd to take △spectators.
                 For behold me,
5 A △fellow of the △royal* △bed, which owe
A △moi'ty* of the △throne, a great △king's* △daughter,
The △mother to a hopeful* △prince, here standing
To prate and talk* for △life and △honor 'fore
Who please to come, and hear*.
          For △life, I prize it
6 As I weigh △grief*, which I would spare;   △for △honor,
'Tis a derivative from me to mine,
And only* that I stand for.

First Folio

6/ Hermione

1 Since what I am to say,$_x$ must be but that
Which contradicts my Accusation, and
The testimonie on my part,$_x$ no other
But what comes from my selfe, it shall scarce boot me
To say, Not guiltie: mine Integritie⁺
Being counted Falsehood, shall (as I expresse it)
Be so receiv'd.
2   But thus, if Powres Divine
Behold our humane Actions (as they doe)
I doubt not then,$_x$ but Innocence shall make
False Accusation blush, and Tyrannie
Tremble at Patience.
3   You$_x$ (my Lord)$_x$ best know
([Whom] least will seeme to doe so) my past life
Hath beene as continent, as chaste, as true,
As I am now unhappy; which is more
[Then] Historie can patterne, though devis'd,$_x$
And play'd,⁺ to take Spectators.
                 For behold me,
4 A Fellow of the Royall Bed, which owe
A Moitie of the Throne: $_x$ a great Kings Daughter,
The Mother to a hopefull Prince, here standing
To prate and talke for Life,$_x$ and Honor,$_x$ fore
Who please to come, and heare.
          For Life, I prize it
5 As I weigh Griefe $_x$(which I would spare: $_x$)$_x$ For Honor,
'Tis a derivative from me to mine,
And onely that I stand for.

Alongside the evidence of Hermione's superb debate/intellectual skills under the most trying of circumstances, the eight extra breath-thoughts scattered throughout (marked , $_x$) show not only where she is taking great care to ensure a key point in her argument is clearly understood, but also, as in F #1, where she needs an extra breath simply to steady herself before continuing.   The fact that there are essentially no surround phrases/ lines in this speech might suggest that here, unlike the following speech, the argument is perhaps more spontaneous than planned, and certainly not as nakedly revelatory.

• that the opening may be difficult for her can be seen in the very few releases in the first four lines (1/1) and the syntactically peculiar yet emotionally perfectly understandable mid-line extra breath-thoughts in lines one and three

• but as she considers the futility of her plea (the last two and half lines of F #1) and begins to defend herself (F #2), so her intellect kicks in (10/4)

• her F #3 appeal to Leontes (as husband rather than as judge) is carefully intellectual (3) and slightly emotional (4), a total of just seven releases in five lines, the two F only bracketed phrases interrupting the main thread of her argument, perhaps suggesting that this particular line of reasoning may be awkward (embarrassing?) for her

• and following F #3's final image of their domestic drama being 'play'd, to take Spectators', so F #4's magnificently clear public defining of her worthy self generates her greatest set of releases in the speech (11/4 in just five lines)

• presumably, having gained the attention of Leontes, Court officials, and 'Spectators' alike, so her terse explanation of what 'Life' and 'Honor' mean to her continues intellectually (4/1, the first line and half of F #5), but tails off to light emotion in the consideration of 'Honor' (0/1, F #5's two lines)

{ctd. over}

7

I appeal*
To your own* △conscience, △sir, before Polixenes
Came to your △court, how I was in your grace,
How merited to be so; △since he came,
With what encounter so uncurrent I
Have strain'd t'△appear* thus; if one jot beyond
The bound of △honor, or in act or will
That way inclining, hard'ned be the hearts
Of all that hear* me, and my neer'st* of △kin
Cry fie upon my △grave !

6

I appeale
To your owne Conscience_x(Sir)_x before Polixenes
Came to your Court, how I was in your grace,
How merited to be so: _x Since he came,
With what encounter so uncurrant,_x I
Have strayn'd t'appeare thus; if one jot beyond
The bound of Honor, or in act,_x or will
That way enclining, hardned be the hearts
Of all that heare me, and my neer'st of Kin
Cry fie upon my Grave. +

• and then perhaps the strain of the situation, (imprisonment, recent child-birth, and public trial) seem to hit her, for while the opening appeal of F #6 for Leontes to recall her deserved state of grace in his eyes ('before Polixenes/Came to your Court') is factual (5/2, the first three and half lines), it momentarily slips as she demands that he give evidence of how she may have 'strayn'd t'appeare' thus (the single emotional cluster in the speech), only to return to intellect once more in the final challenge that if he can do so, then, and only then, could her 'neer'st of Kin/Cry fie upon my Grave.'

7/ Hermione   **Sir, spare your Threats :**   3.2.91 - 116

Background: As the court battle reaches its climax, the following is Hermione's direct response to Leontes, triggered by his unequivocal final remark, 'so thou/Shalt feele our Justice; in whose easiest passage,/Looke for no lesse then death'.

Style: essentially one on one, via public address until the last sentence, which is directed towards the larger group

Where: in open court   **To Whom:** Leontes, in front of the full assembly - with all present being addressed in the final sentence

# of Lines: 26   **Probable Timing: 1.15 minutes**

First Folio

7/ Hermione

1   Sir, spare your Threats :
     The Bugge which you would fright me with, I seeke :
     To me can Life be no commoditie ;
     The crowne and comfort of my Life _x (your Favor)_x
     I doe give lost, for I doe feele it gone,
     But know not how it went.

2   My second Joy,
     And first Fruits of my body, from his presence
     I am bar'd, like one infectious.

3   My third comfort
     (Star'd most unluckily) is from my breast
     (The innocent milke in it most innocent mouth)
     Hal'd out to murther.

4   My selfe on every Post
     Proclaym'd a Strumpet : _x With immodest hatred
     The Child-bed priviledge deny'd, which longs
     To Women of all fashion.

7/ Hermione

1   Sir, spare your △threats . †
2   The △bug* which you would fright me with, I seek* †
3   To me can △life be no commoditie* ;
     The crown* and comfort of my △life, your △favor,
     I do* give lost, for I do* feel* it gone,
     But know not how it went.
4   My second △joy,
     And first △fruits of my body, from his presence
     I am bar'd*, like one infectious.
5   My third comfort
     (Starr'd* most unluckily) is from my breast
     (The innocent milk* in it most innocent mouth)
     Hal'd out to murther; ◇ myself* on every △post
     Proclaim'd a △strumpet ; △with immodest hatred
     The △child-◇bed privilege* denied*, which 'longs
     To △women of all fashion; ◇ lastly, hurried

A wonderful indication of Hermione's nobility and strength of character is the way that she handles her personal grief in such a quiet unembellished manner, the needed facts for all to understand not giving way to unseemly emotion. And that the listing of her third discomfort leads to two further separate sentences spelling all that has happened to her (F #4-5) instead of being lumped in as part of her third grief (mt. #5) suggests a **formidable intellect at work despite the pain.**

• though onrushed, Hermione's opening put-down of Leontes' less than rational response is superbly absolute; passionate (3/2, the first three lines of F #1); driven home by three successive surround phrases; though there is obviously some emotion lurking underneath, the last surround phrase finishing with a

• of the unembellished phrases, the first gives stark recognition to the grief that her acknowledged loss of what were her three greatest 'comforts' are causing her,
a/ from the first mention of the loss of her husband's love, via the monosyllabic end of F #1, 'But know not how it went.'
b/ then as regards her beloved son
  " . . from his presence/I am bar'd, like one infectious."
c/ and the loss of her new-born baby daughter
  "My third comfort/(Star'd most unluckily) is from my breast/ . . /Hal'd out to murther"
and then she turns to her physical state
  "Lastly, hurried/Here, to this place . . . before/I have got strength of limit."

6
Here to this place, i'th'open air*, before
I have got strength of limit.
            Now, my △liege,
Tell me what blessings I have here alive,
That I should fear* to die?
            Therefore proceed. †

7

8
But yet hear* this - mistake me not; no △life,
(I prize it not a straw) but for mine △honor,
Which I would free - if I shall be condemn'd
Upon surmises* (all proofs* sleeping else
But what your △jealousies awake), I tell you
'Tis △rigor and not △law.
            Your △honors all,

9
I do* refer* me to the △oracle:
Apollo be my △judge!

---

followed by the direct public challenge to her husband/judge
"Now . . ./Tell me what blessings I have here alive, . . .'Therefore proceed:"

• but in the midst of her personal grief she never loses sight of what is essential, as the surround phrase strength with which she so firmly points out to the assembled crowd how badly her reputation has been impugned testifies
". . My selfe on every Post/Proclaym'd a Strumpet : "

• and the remaining surround phrases are equally strong, though they don't appear till her demand that the trial proceed (the four that open F #7), and the final demand that she be judged not by the assembled 'Honors all' but rather by the Gods in the person of 'Apollo' (the whole of F #8)

• the speech is a mixture of unembellished lines with intellect usually dominating emotion (22/18 overall), with the only emotional passage the public acknowledgement of the loss of Leontes' love (2/4, the last three lines of F #1), and the only moment of almost matched intellectual and emotional release in F #4's delineation of how badly she has been treated both in reputation, being 'Proclaym'd a Strumpet', and in having her 'Child-bed priviledge deny'd' (5/4)

• apart from the passionate opening (3/2, the first three lines), the strongest intellectual release is seen in the try-rme challenge of F #7-8 (9/4, the last eight lines)

            Lastly, hurried

5
Here,x to this place, i'th'open ayre, before
I have got strength of limit.
            Now x(my Liege)x

6
Tell me what blessings I have here alive,
That I should feare to die?
            Therefore proceed:

7
But yet heare this: x mistake me not: x no Life,
(I prize it not a straw) but for mine Honor,
Which I would free: x if I shall be condemn'd
Upon surmizes (all proofes sleeping else.x
But what your Jealousies awake)+ I tell you
'Tis Rigor and not Law.

8
            Your Honors all,
I doe referre me to the Oracle:
Apollo be my Judge. +

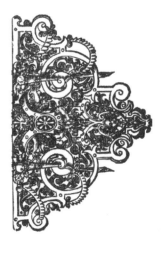

8/ Paulina   Woe the while : /O cut my Lace, least my heart (cracking it)   between 3.2.172 - 202

Background: To establish the truth once and for all, Leontes has sent to the sacred Oracle at Delphos for judgement to back up his own court proceedings. The Oracle has unequivocally stated 'Hermione is chast, Polixenes blameless, Camillo a true subject, Leontes a jealous Tyrant, his innocent Babe truly begotten'. Leontes is prepared to accept none of this, stating to everyone's consternation 'There is no truth at all i'th'Oracle:/The Sessions shall proceed', for which he is immediately punished by the news of the death of his beloved son and heir Mamillius, who feared for his mother's safety. Hermione has fainted and been taken off by her women and Paulina. Though Paulina is wife to one of Leontes' leading counsellors, Antigonus, in the question of Hermione's reputation and honour she refuses to bow to any man's authority, least of all that of Leontes or her husband. A publicly outspoken critic of Leontes' behaviour throughout, she now returns with the news that Hermione too is dead: (in fact Hermione may not be dead, but whether Paulina knows this and is deliberately punishing Leontes, or is speaking from a genuine belief, is up to each production to decide).

Style: both one on one and public address
Where: in open court   **To Whom:** Leontes, in front of the full assembly
# of Lines: 30   **Probable Timing: 1.30 minutes**

First Folio

8/ Paulina

1   Woe the while : +
    O+ cut my Lace, least my heart x(cracking it)x
    Breake too. +

2   What studied torments+ x(Tyrant)x hast for me?

3   What Wheeles?

4   Racks?

5   Fires?

6   What flaying? boyling?

7   In Leadsx, or Oyles?   What old, or newer Torture

    Must I receive?x whose every word deserves
    To taste of thy most worst. +

8   Thy Tyranny+
    x(Together working with thy Jealousies,
    Fancies too weake for Boyes, too greene and idle
    For Girles of Nine) O thinke what they have done,
    And then run mad indeed: x starke-mad: + for all
    Thy by-gone fooleries were but spices of it.

9   That thou betrayed'st Polixenes, 'twas nothing,
    (xThat did but shew thee, of a Foole, inconstant,
    And damnable ingratefull: x) x   Nor was't much. 2

Modern Text

8/ Paulina

1   Woe the while!

2   O, cut my ᴬlace, least my heart, cracking it,
    Break* too!

3   What studied torments, ᴬtyrant, hast for me?

4   What ᴬwheels*? ◇ ᴬracks? ◇ ᴬfires?

5   What flaying? boiling*?

6   In ᴬleads or ᴬoils*?
                What old, or newer ᴬtorture

7   Must I receive, whose every word deserves
    To taste of thy most worst?

                     Thy ᴬtyranny,
    Together working with thy ᴬjealousies -
    Fancies too weak* for ᴬboys*, too green* and idle
    For ᴬgirls* of ᴬnine - O think* what they have done,
    And then run mad indeed - stark*° mad! for all
    Thy by-gone fooleries were but spices of it.

8   That thou betrayedst Polixenes, 'twas nothing -
    That did but shew thee, of a ᴬfool*, inconstant,
    And damnable ingrateful* ; ᴬnor was't much ◇

That just four of the thirteen surround phrases appear in the first fourteen lines of the speech, and the remaining nine in the last fifteen, is a sure sign that it takes a while before Paulina's formidable debating skills recover from the shock of the death of young Mamillius and the resultant (apparent?) subsequent death of Hermione. Indeed, the sequence of five very short sentences (F #2-6) are not only evidence of a mind not bothering with the subtler niceties of debate, they also are most unusual for Paulina anywhere in the play.

• that from the outset (the opening surround phrase cry of 'Woe the while' notwithstanding) Paulina is struggling to maintain her self-control, can be seen in the opening (pain-filled? sarcastic?) challenge to Leontes, with most of the challenging images capitalised rather than long-spelled (F# 1 1/1; 4/1, the very short F #2-5)

• and while her emotions sweep in temporarily during F #6's more savage of the suggested sarcastic tortures of 'boyling' and 'Oyles' (2/2), she quickly recovers to quietly inform him that her 'every word deserves' the worst 'Torture' he can devise, F #7 being virtually unembellished (1/0)

• and then her passions finally get the better of her, for in F #8's build-up to the surround phrase demand that the run : starke-mad: , the accusation that his 'Jealousies' are worse than those of children is given enormous release (6/5, F #8's first four lines) — yet she still remains in control for F #8's last line of denunciation 'for all/Thy by-gone fooleries were but spices of it' is once more determinedly unembellished

---

2 by setting a period. F shows this phrase as a strong summation of what Paulina has just said: most modern texts omit punctuation altogether, thus setting it as a (probably weaker) start to the next stage of the argument

Thou would'st have poison'd* good Camillo's ᴬhonor,
To have him kill a ᴬking - poor*ᴬtrespasses,
More monstrous standing by ;   whereof I reckon
The casting forth to ᴬcrows* thy ᴮbaby ° daughter,
To be or none, or little - though a ᴬdevil*
Would have shed water out of fire, ere done't*⸴;
Nor is't directly laid* to thee, the death
Of the young Prince, whose honorable thoughts
(Thoughts high for one so tender) cleft the heart
That could conceive a gross* and foolish ᴬsire
Blemish'd his gracious ᴬdam;   this is not, no,
Laid* to thy answer* : but the last - O ᴬlords,
When I have said, cry "ᴬWoe! †" : the Queen*, the Queen*,
The sweet'st, dear'st creature's dead,& vengeance for't
Not dropp'd* down* yet.

• the attack on Leontes' betrayal of Polixenes remains passionate (3/2, F #9), and then comes what most modern texts regard as a totally ungrammatical period; they usually remove any punctuation, thus attaching the phrase 'Nor was't much' to the description of his mistreatment of his one-time advisor Camillo, rather than leaving it as a very difficult assessment of everything that has gone on before: however, F's syntactic peculiarity seems to show how difficult it is for Paulina to maintain self-control at this moment

• and then the public destruction of all that Leontes has done becomes initially intellectual (his dealing with Camillo and the abandoning of his new-born daughter, 7/4 the first six lines of F #10), driven home by four surround phrases, but this turns to passion, moderate at first (2/2, the four and a half lines dealing with the sadness of Mamillius' death)

• but, in leading up to the news of Hermione's death (whether true or not), both the surround phrases (five consecutive) and passion (4/6 in the final four lines) spring forth more densely than before

10 Thou would'st have poyson'd good Camillo's Honor,
    To have him kill a King:: x   poore Trespasses,
    More monstrous standing by: x   whereof I reckon
    The casting forth to Crowes,x thy Baby-daughter,
    To be or none, or little; x   though a Devill
    Would have shed water out of fire, ere don't: x
    Nor is't directly layd to thee, the death
    Of the young Prince, whose honorable thoughts
    (Thoughts high for one so tender) cleft the heart
    That could conceive a grosse and foolish Sire
    Blemish'd his gracious Dam: x   this is not, no,
    Layd to thy answere: but the last: x   O Lords,
    When I have said, cry woe: + the Queene, the Queene,
    The sweet'st, deer'st creature's dead:.x & vengeance for't
    Not drop'd downe yet.

9/ Paulina   **I am sorry (Sir) I have thus farre stir'd you : but**   between 5.3.74 - 109

Background: In view of the reconciliation between Leontes and Polixenes and the discovery of Hermione and Leontes' daughter, Perdita, Paulina tells all concerned that she has a statue of Hermione, which she is prepared to show them. Leontes, who came to his senses the minute Hermione's supposed death was announced more than fifteen years ago, is incredibly moved at the sight (see speech #10 immediately below) - and Paulina is now prepared to reveal the truth by bringing the 'statue', which could be Hermione herself, 'back to life'.

Style: general address, at times to different individuals within the group

Where: in Paulina's art gallery   **To Whom:** at different times Leontes, Musicians, and the 'statue', as well as the larger group comprising Camillo, Perdita, Florizell, Polixines, and accompanying Lords

# of Lines: 23   **Probable Timing: 1.10 minutes**

Modern Text

9/ Paulina

1 I am sorry, Sir, I have thus far* stirr'd* you ; but
I could afflict you farther.

2 Either forbear*,
Quit presently the △chapel*, or resolve you
For more amazement . †

3   If you can behold it, descend,
And take you by the △hand ; but then you'll* think*
(Which I protest against) I am assisted
By wicked △powers.

4 It is requir'd
You do* awake your △faith . †

5   Then, all stand still . †

6 On ; those that think* it is unlawful* △business*
I am about, let them depart.

7 Music* ! awake her ! △strike ! †

8 'Tis time ; descend ; be △stone no more ; approach ;
Strike all that look* upon with marvel* . †
                Come ;

9 I'll fill your △grave up . †

10   Stir* ; nay, come away ; for from him
Bequeath to △death your numbness ;
Dear* △life redeems* you . †

11   You perceive she stirs* .

12 Start not ; her △actions shall be holy, as
You hear* my △spell is lawful* . †

First Folio

9/ Paulina

1 I am sorry,x(Sir), I have thus farre stir'd you : x but
I could afflict you farther.

2 Either forbeare,
Quit presently the Chappell, or resolve you
For more amazement : if you can behold it, x descend,
And take you by the hand : x but then you'le thinke
(Which I protest against) I am assisted
By wicked Powers.

3 It is requir'd
You doe awake your Faith : then, all stand still :
On : x those that thinke it is unlawfull Businesse
I am about, let them depart.

4 Musick ; + awake her : + Strike : +
'Tis time ;x descend ;x be Stone no more ;x approach :x
Strike all that looke upon with mervaile : Come :x
Ile fill your Grave up : stirre : x nay, come away : x
Bequeath to Death your numnesse : x x (for from him,x
Deare Life redeemes you)x you perceive she stirres :
Start not : x her Actions shall be holy, as
You heare my Spell is lawfull : doe not shun her,x

Though the first sentences match, thereafter most modern texts regard F as enormously onrushed, reworking F's three remaining sentences into fourteen. However, Paulina's late F #4 urging that 'my Spell is lawfull' suggests that this may not be a piece of fanciful imagery, and that she is in fact performing magic – hence the serious warning that opens F #2, 'Either forbeare,/Quit presently the Chappell, or resolve you/For more amazement :', and the essential F #3 demand that 'It is requir'd/You doe awake your faith' as well as the suggestion 'those that thinke it is unlawfull Businesse/I am about, let them depart.'

• thus the enormous number of twenty-one surround phrases that comprise the whole of F #4, joining together in one long arc the command for 'Musick'; the instructions/spell for Hermione to 'be Stone no more'; and that Leontes 'doe not shun her' but 'present your Hand' could well be indicative of Hermione's extended concentration to keep the magic going without break or interference till the spell has been successful in every respect – the final essential that just as Leontes once publicly rejected Hermione, so now he must accept her for the spell to be complete

• with just four intellectual and five emotional releases in the first seven and a half lines (F #1-2) suggesting that the opening of the speech is fairly withheld, the earnestness within Paulina's five surround phrases (containing both an apology to Leontes and warnings to all who have accompanied him) are more than enough to convince everyone of the seriousness of the moment without her wasting her energy (which is going to be needed shortly for the spell)

• but by the time of F #3's final request for 'Faith' or 'depart', emotion momentarily dominates (2/4), which is only natural given what is to follow

• the opening three and a half lines of F #4's 'spell' are passionate (4/4) up to and including the amazing monosyllabic 'Ile fill your Grave up:' and then, following hushed unembellished monosyllabic instruction 'nay, come away', so emotional releases increase (2/4) to the moment 'she stirres'

13   Do* not shun her
Until* you see her die* again* , for then
You kill her double . †
14   Nay, present your △hand . †
15 When she was young, you woo'd her ; now, in age,
Is she become the △suitor?

• the climax of the event is accompanied by three quick and highly revelatory switches in release: thus the appeal for all to believe her 'Spell is lawfull' is passionate (2/2); her urging on of Leontes ' : doe not shun her,/Untill you see her dye againe ; ' is remarkably emotional (0/4 in just ten words, plus the surround phrase ending in a semicolon); which is followed by yet another hushed unembellished moment springing out of the same emotional ' ; for then/You kill her double:'

• and the unusual intellectual quality of the final urging for *Leontes* to offer *Hermione* his hand (3/0, the last two lines of the speech) might well suggest that any superfluous emotion at this extremely delicate moment could ruin the spell completely

Untill you see her dye againe; x for then
You kill her double: Nay, present your Hand:
When she was young, you woo'd her : x now, in age,
Is she become the Suitor?

10/ Leontes   **Her naturall Posture.**   between 5.3.23 - 73

Background: Leontes first response to the sight of Hermione as 'statue', even before Paulina brings 'it' to 'life'.

Style: as part of a four-handed scene in front of a larger group

Where: in Paulina's art gallery   **To Whom:** the statue, Paulina and Polixines, in front of the larger group comprising Camillo, Perdita, Florizell, and accompanying Lords and Musicians

# of Lines: 20   **Probable Timing: 1.00 minutes**

Modern Text

10/ Leontes

1 Her natural* △posture !

2 Chide me, dear* △stone, that I may say indeed
   Thou art Hermione ; or rather, thou art she
   In thy not chiding ; for she was as tender
   As △infancy* and △grace.

3   O*, thus she stood,
   Even with such △life of △majesty* (warm* △life,
   As now it coldly stands), when first I woo'd her !

4 I am asham'd ; does* not the △stone rebuke me
   For being more* △stone [than] it?

5   O* △'royal* △piece* ,
   There's △magic* in thy △majesty*, which has
   My △evils conjur'd to remembrance, and
   From thy admiring △daughter took* the △spirits,
   Standing like △stone with thee.

6 Do* not draw the △Curtain* .

7 Let be, let be. †

8 Would I were dead, but that [methinks*] already* - ◇
   (What was he that did make it?)

9   See*, my △lord,

10 Would you not deem* it breath'd? and that those veins*
   Did verily bear* blood?

11 The [fixture] of her △eye has motion in't,
   As we are mock'd with △art.

11   Let't alone.

First Folio

10/ Leontes

1 Her naturall Posture. +

2 Chide me ₓ(deare Stone)ₓ that I may say indeed
   Thou art Hermione ; or rather, thou art she,ₓ
   In thy not chiding : ₓ for she was as tender
   As Infancie,ₓ and Grace.

3   Oh, thus she stood,
   Even with such Life of Majestie (warme Life,
   As now it coldly stands) ₓ when first I woo'd her. +

4 I am asham'd : ₓ Do's not the Stone rebuke me,ₓ
   For being more Stone [then] it?

5   Oh Royall Peece : ₓ
   There's Magick in thy Majestie, which ha's
   My Evils conjur'd to remembrance ; ₓ and
   From thy admiring Daughter tooke the Spirits,
   Standing like Stone with thee.

6 Doe not draw the Curtaine.

7 Let be, let be:

8 Would I were dead, but that [me thinkes]alreadie.
   (What was he that did make it?)

9   See ₓ(my Lord)ₓ

10 Would you not deeme it breath'd? and that those veines
   Did verily beare blood?

11 The [fixture] of her Eye ha's motion in't,
   As we are mock'd with Art.

11   Let't alone.

The confusion in Leontes is seen not merely in the contradictory request of F #2, but also in the opening orthography – for the shortness of F #1, the three surround phrases completely forming F #2, and F #2's two extra breath-thoughts (marked , ₓ) all speak to a mind having difficulty in coping. Thus it's also interesting to note that proportionately there are far more releases in the first fourteen lines (21/11) up to and including the order 'Doe not draw the Curtaine', than in the last six (4/4), **when he is assured that he can gaze his fill.**

• even so, the speech starts highly intellectually(13/3, F 1-4), suggesting a certainty of both how closely the statue resembles his memory of Hermione, and of his own guilt – the latter underscored by the unembellished surround phrase opening F #4, ' . I am asham'd : '

• framing F #5's praise to the 'Magicke in thy Majestie' come two of only three emotional clusters in the speech, the opening 'Oh Royall Peece' (2/3 in three words!), and the short sentence plea of F #6's 'Doe not draw the Curtaine.' (1/2)

• with the 'Curtaine' staying open, so Leontes begins to quieten, his ironic comment about him in essence being dead almost unembellished (0/1, F #7), suggesting that quite a truth has been uttered, followed by the unembellished request to know the sculptor's identity (F #8)

• as Leontes becomes aware of the others accompanying him for, it would seem, the first time in the speech, he becomes emotional in asking at least one of them (probably Polixenes) to comment upon the life-like quality of the 'statue' (1/3), while his own proof via the 'fixture of her Eye' becomes intellectual once more

• and in the last moment of the speech he seems wrapped in wonder, with F #11's incredibly short unembellished 'Let't alone' being all he can finally say

#'s 11 - 15: YOUNG LOVE CROSSED AND TRIUMPHANT

11/ Florizell   **Thou deer'st Perdita,**   between 4.4.40 - 54

Background: By accident Florizell, son to Polixenes, King of Bohemia, met Perdita, a young woman reared from birth as daughter to the old Shepheard , in reality the abandoned daughter of Hermine and Leontes (see speech #16 below) and they have fallen in love. To prevent parental interference based on class distinctions, they have hidden their love from his father, and pretended to those who have reared her that he is merely a land-owner with a 'worthy-feeding's named Doricles. This is Florizell's response to Perdita's fear that his father will find out all and end their relationship.

Style: as part of a two-handed scene, with a larger group on-stage, not attempting to listen

Where: Bohemia, outdoors, where the sheep-shearing festival is to be held   **To Whom:** Perdita, in front of a larger group finishing preparations for the sheep-shearing festival

# of Lines: 15   **Probable Timing: 0.50 minutes**

Modern Text	First Folio
11/ Florizell	**11/ Florizell**

1 Thou dear'st* Perdita,
   With these forc'd thoughts I prithee* darken not
   The ^Δmirth o'th'^Δfeast . [†]
	1 Thou deer'st Perdita,
	    With these forc'd thoughts, I prethee darken not
	    The Mirth o'th'Feast : Or Ile be thine_x (my Faire)_x

Or I'll be thine, my ^Δfair* ,	

2 Or not my ^Δfather's; ◊ for I cannot be
   Mine own*, nor any thing to any, if
   I be not thine.
	2 For I cannot be
	    Mine owne, nor any thing to any, if
	    I be not thine.

3 To this I am most constant,	3 To this I am most constant,
Though destiny say no.	Though destiny say no.
4 Be merry, ^Δgentle! [†]	4 Be merry (_xGentle) ⁺

Strangle such thoughts as these with any thing
   That you behold the while.
	Strangle such thoughts as these,_x with any thing
	    That you behold the while.

5 Your guests are coming*:	5 Your guests are comming:

Lift up your countenance, as it were the day
   Of celebration of that nuptial*, which
   We two have sworn* shall come.
	Lift up your countenance, as it were the day
	    Of celebration of that nuptiall, which
	    We two have sworne shall come.

6 See, your ^Δguests approach,
   Address* yourself* to entertain* them sprightly,
   And let's be red with mirth.
	6 See, your Guests approach,
	    Addresse your selfe to entertaine them sprightly,
	    And let's be red with mirth.

Florizell's attempt to assuage Perdita's fears start out determinedly intellectual (6/3, F #1), **the first of only two surround phrases in the speech ' : Or Ile be thine (my Faire)/Or not my Fathers . ' making it as plain as he possibly can how devoted he is.**

• and it looks as if this hard-working reassurance may quietly take effect, for there are very few further releases within the speech, and those there are, are essentially emotional (2/6 in the final ten lines, as compared to 6/2 in the first three)

• thus the next three sentences of reassurance as to his being nothing 'if/I be not thine', unequivocally stating 'To this I am most constant' and that she should thus 'Strangle' the negative thoughts she is currently bedeviled by, are almost completely unembellished (1/1 in the five lines F #2-4), his calm hopefully calming her down

• and while his reminder that she must 'entertaine' the 'Guests' who 'are comming' for the sheep-shearing (of which, as her father later describes her, she is the presiding ceremonial 'Hostesse of the meeting') is emotional (1/6, F #5-6) there are still some very gentle unembellished personal comments, as

"Lift up your countenance, as it were the day/Of celebration . . ."

of their eventual wedding, and the charming suggestion that if she is 'red' (i.e. blushing – presumably at the thought of their 'nuptiall') then it might be better that

"And let's be red with mirth."

12/ Florizell   **What you do,/Still betters what is done.**   4.4.135 - 146

Background: Called to task by her 'father', the old Shepherd, for not attending to her duties as 'Hostesse of the meeting', Perdita has deftly responded with a series of graceful and witty greetings to the first guests (speech #13), including a very sensual one to Florizell (speech #14). This is Florizell's admiring reply.

Style: as part of a two-handed scene, with a larger group on-stage, not attempting to listen

Where: Bohemia, outdoors, where the sheep-shearing festival is to be held   **To Whom:** Perdita, in front of a larger group on-stage but not particpating in the scene, including the Old Shepherd, her 'brother' the young Shepherd, the shepherdesses Mopsa and Dorcas, the disguised Polixines and Camillo, and various servants and guests

# of Lines: 12   **Probable Timing: 0.40 minutes**

Modern Text

12/ Florizell

1 What you do
Still betters what is done.

2   When you speak* , △sweet,
△when you sing,
I'd* have you do it ever ; △when you sing,
I'd* have you buy, and sell so; so give △alms* ,
Pray so; and for the ord'ring your △affairs* ,
To sing them too.

3   When you do dance, I wish you
A wave o'th △sea, that you might ever do
Nothing but that; move still, still so,
And own* no other function.

4   Each your doing
(So singular in each particular)
Crowns* what you are doing, in the present deeds,
That all your △acts* are △queens* .

First Folio

12/ Florizell

1 What you do,x
Still betters what is done.

2   When you speake,x (Sweet)x
When you sing,
I'ld have you do it ever : x When you sing,
I'ld have you buy, and sell so: x so give Almes,
Pray so: x and for the ord'ring your Affayres,
To sing them too.

3   When you do dance, I wish you
A wave o'th Sea, that you might ever do
Nothing but that: x move still, still so: x
And owne no other function.

4   Each your doing,x
(So singular,x in each particular)
Crownes what you are doing, in the present deeds,
That all your Actes,x are Queenes.

This unabashed love speech is a wonderful mix of unembellished (delighted? amazed? confidential?) quiet, suddenly broken by excesses of passion, noticeably F #2, in praise of her voice (4/3) and especially the last line and a half of the speech, suggesting all her 'Actes' are 'Queenes' (2/3).

• Florizell's besottedness is apparent in the many unembellished lines he uses to describe virtually everything she does, from the whole of the short F #1 "What you do, /Still betters what is done." to the totally surround phrase created if she should 'speake' "I'ld have you do it ever : When you sing,/I'ld have you buy, and sell so: . . . /Pray so : " and as for her prayers "To sing them too." and not only her voice entrances him, but her movements too, for as he explains - with the addition of one capitalised word "When you do dance, I wish you/A wave o'th Sea, that you might ever do/ Nothing but that : move still, still so : " so that in fact everything about her seems wondrous, again with one released word, the emotional 'Crownes', a wonderful release given the circumstances "Each your doing, /(So singular, in each particular)/Crownes what you are doing, in the present deeds, . . ."

13/ Perdita   **Sir, welcome : It is my Fathers will,**   between 4.4.70 - 112

Background: Fearing that Perdita is not attending to her duties as 'Hostesse of the meeting', her 'father', the Old Shepheard who rescued her as an abandoned baby (see speech #16 below), calls her to task. In response to her father's rebuke, Perdita begins the formal welcomes to the feast, starting with the two strangers, little realising they are her beloved Florizell's father, King Polixines, and his key advisor, Camillo, in disguise.

Style: as part of a three handed scene via public address in front of a larger group

Where: Bohemia, outdoors, where the sheep-shearing festival is to be held   **To Whom:** the disguised Polixines and Camillo, in front of a larger group, including Florizell, her 'brother' the young Shepherd. the Old Shepherd, the shepherdesses Mopsa and Dorcas, and various servants and guests

# of Lines: 16   **Probable Timing: 0.50 minutes**

First Folio

13/ Perdita

1   Sir, welcome :
It is my Fathers will,ₓ I should take on mee
The Hostesseship o'th'day : you're welcome⁺ sir .

2   Give me those Flowres thereₓ(Dorcas)ₓ .

3   Reverend Sirs,
For you,ₓ there's Rosemary, and Rue, these keepe
Seeming,ₓ and savour all the Winter long:
Grace,ₓ and Remembrance be to you both,
And welcome to our Shearing . ⁺

4   Here's flowres for you :
Hot Lavender, Mints, Savory, Marjorum,
The Mary-gold, that goes to bed with 'Sun,
And with him rises,ₓ weeping : These are flowres
Of middle summer, and I thinke they are given
To men of middle age .

5   Y'are very welcome .

6   {Do not} leave grasing, {ψ} and onely live by gazing .

7   Out alas : ⁺
You'ld be so leane, that blasts of January
Would blow you through and through .

---

* at the start of her 'Hostesse' duties Perdita seems to be working rather hard, for the first sentence is made up of three surround phrases; F #2's command to her friend Dorcas is quite short, and F #3 contains three extra breath-thoughts (marked , ₓ) enhancing and expanding the meaning of the first gift of herbs

* her mind seems to be working overtime during these opening greetings, and continues throughout most of the gift of flowers that follows (6/2 in this small section -16/5, F #1 through the ten lines in all to the colon of F #4)

* and once the formalities of herb and flower giving are essentially done with, it seems that she can relax at last, for the six lines ending the greetings and enjoying a gentle tease are very calm by comparison (1/2, the last two lines of F #4 through to the end of #6)

* given the orthography, the teasing of the 'men of middle age' seems quite charmingly done, for the whole of F #6's 'Do not leave grasing, and onely live by gazing. ' because the cold winters wind 'Would blow you through and through. ' is almost unembellished, suggesting a lovely decorum throughout

Modern Text

13/ Perdita

1   Sir, welcome . †

2   It is my ᐃfather's will I should take on me*
The ᐃhostess-'ship o'th'day . †
                    You're welcome, sir . †

3   Give me those flow'rs there, Dorcas.

4   Reverend ᐃsirs,

5   For you there's ᐃrosemary, and ᐃrue, these keep*
Seeming and savor* all the ᐃwinter long . †

6   Grace and ᐃremembrance be to you both,
And welcome to our ᐃshearing !

7   Here's flow'rs for you :
Hot ᐃlavender, ᐃmints, ᐃsavory, ᐃmarjorum,
The ᐃmariᵒgold*, that goes to bed wi'th' ᐃsun,
And with him rises weeping . †

8   These are flow'rs
Of middle summer, and I think* they are given
To men of middle age .

9   Y'are very welcome .

10   {Do not} leave grazing*, {ψ} and only* live by gazing .

11   Out alas ! †

12   You'ld be so lean*, that blasts of January
Would blow you through and through .

14/ Perdita Now (my fairst Friend), I would I had some Flowres 4.4.112 - 134

Background: Moving on from speech #13 above, Perdita now turns her attention to her friends Mopsa and Dorcas (momentarily) and then concentrates on her beloved Florizell.

Style: initially as part of a four handed scene, and then one on one, all with a larger group in the background going about their own business

Where: Bohemia, outdoors, where the sheep-shearing festival is to be held **To Whom:** initially Florizell and the shepherdesses Mopsa and Dorcas, and then Florizell alone, the larger group (her 'brother' & 'father' - i.e. young and Old Shepherds, the disguised Polixines & Camillo, and various servants and guests) not part of the action

# of Lines: 24 Probable Timing: 1.15 minutes

First Folio

14/ Perdita

1
    Now ₓ (my fairst Friend,
I would I had some Flowres o'th Spring,ₓ that might
Become your time of day : ₓ and yours, and yours,
That weare upon your Virgin-branches yet
Your Maiden-heads growing : O Proserpina
For the Flowres now, that ₓ (frighted)ₓ thou let'st fall
From Dysses Waggon : ⁺ Daffadils,
That come before the Swallow dares, and take
The windes of March with beauty : Violets ₓ (dim,
But sweeter [then] the lids of Juno's eyes,
Or Cytherea's breath) ⁺ pale Prime-roses,
That dye unmarried, ere they can behold
Bright Phœbus in his strength (a Maladie
Most incident to Maids) : ₓ bold Oxlips, and
The Crowne Imperiall : ₓ Lillies of all kinds,
(The Flowre-de-Luce being one.)

2
                 O, these I lacke,
To make you Garlands of,ₓ and my sweet friend,
To strew him o're,ₓ and ore. ⁺

3
                  {Not} like a Coarse{,}
{But} like a banke, for Love to lye, and play on : ₓ
Not like a Coarse : ₓ or if : not to be buried,
But quicke,ₓ and in mine armes.

4
                    Come, take your flours,
[Me thinkes] I play as I have seene them do
In Whitson-Pastorals : Sure this Robe of mine
Do's change my disposition : ⁺

Modern Text

14/ Perdita

1
    Now, my fair'st △friend,
I would I had some flow'rs o'th' △spring that might
Become your time of day - ³ and yours, and yours,
That weare upon your △virgin ° branches yet
Your △maiden°heads growing . ⁺

2
           O Proserpina,
For the flow'rs now, that, frighted, thou let'st fall
From Dis's* △waggon ! △daffadils,
That come before the △swallow dares, and take
The winds* of March with beauty ; △violets, dim,
But sweeter [than] the lids of Juno's eyes,
Or Cytherea's breath ; pale △prime°roses,
That die △ unmarried, ere they can behold
Bright Phœbus in his strength (a △malady*
Most incident to △maids) ; bold △oxlips, and
The △crown* △imperial* ; △lilies* of all kinds,
(The △flow'r-△de-△luce being one.)

3
              O, these I lack*
To make you △garlands of, and my sweet friend,
To strew him o'er and o'er !

4
            {Not} like a △corse*{,}
{But} like a bank*, for △love to lie*, and play on ;
Not like a △corse ; or if - not to be buried,
But quick* and in mine arms*.

5
           Come, take your flow'rs . ⁺

6
[Methinks*] I play as I have seen* them do
In Whitsun °△pastorals . ⁺

7
    Sure this △robe of mine

    Does* change my disposition .

- the opening greeting (presumably to Florizell as the 'fairst Friend' is purely factual (3/0, to F #1's first colon), and initially the virginal quality of the references to the flowers she gives to her closest female friends Mopsa and Dorcas is also intellectual (10/3, the next six lines up to the image of 'Violets')

- then, as the images become more than a little sensual (Cytherea´ is another name for Venus, the goddess of love, and the idea of Phœbus in his strength' is quite a strong male image), so even less emotion is released (7/1 in the five lines up to 'Most incident to Maids'), a sign of self control perhaps

- but with the sentence ending references to the tall thin flowers 'Oxlips' and 'Lillies', again a probable male image, so emotion begins to creep in a little more (a very powerful 6/3 in just two lines), which in turn leads to a mild apology for not having such flowers with her (1/1 in F #2's first two lines)

- and then there is a remarkable moment of unembellished self-control as she turns her attention to Florizell once more, including him in F #2's apology 'and my sweet friend/To strew him o're,ₓ and ore.' - the extra comma perhaps suggesting how quickly focused her attention on him becomes

- it looks as if the more naughty aspects of the flower giving, which started with the 'Venus' image midway through F #1, has finally got to her, for talking of the flowers that might be placed upon him, her images of 'like a banke, for Love to lye, and play on:' and so that he would be 'in mine armes' are emotionally released for the first time in the speech (3/6, F #3), the power of her thoughts heightened by at least three surround phrases that end the images

- Perdita's invitation for them all to play as they do at 'Whitson-Pastorals' is passionate (2/2 in F #4's first two lines)

- and then it seems that she suddenly realises just how much love-thoughts have run away with her, for in addition to her attempt to explain her 'change' of 'disposition' becoming emotional (1/4), she finishes not only with a surround phrase but also with one of the rare instances where a speech ends with something other than a period (here a colon), perhaps suggesting she doesn't complete her thoughts but tails off in somewhat embarrassed silence

---

WHO ³ most modern texts indicate this is spoken to Mopsa and Dorcas

15/ Polixenes   **Marke your divorce (yong sir)**

Background: Having struck up a conversation with Florizell (who still does not realise the stranger is his disguised father) about his intentions towards Perdita, and having failed to persuade his son to let his father know of his intentions, Polixines finally throws off his disguise and, as the following clearly shows, his anger knows no bounds.

Style: a four-hander in front of a larger group

Where: Bohemia, outdoors, where the sheep-shearing festival is to be held   **To Whom:** variously at times to his son Florizell, the Old Shepherd, and Perdita, in front of Camillo and whomever of the guests has remained on stage

between 4.4.417- 441

# of Lines: 25   **Probable Timing: 1.15 minutes**

Modern Text

15/ Polixenes

1 Mark* your divorce, young* sir, †
   Whom son* I dare not call. †
                    Thou art too base

2 To be acknowledg'd.
           Thou, a △sceptre's heir* ,
3 That thus affects a sheep*-hook*!
                    Thou, old △traitor,

4 I am sorry, that by hanging thee, I can
   But shorten thy life one week* .
                    And thou, fresh piece*

5 Of excellent △witchcraft, [who] of force must know
   The royal* △fool* thou cop'st* with- ◊
   I'll have thy beauty scratch'd with briers & made
   More homely [than] thy state.

6   For thee, fond boy,
   If I may ever know thou dost but sigh
   That thou no more shalt [ ] see this knack* (as never
   I mean* thou shalt), we'll* bar* thee from succession,
   Not hold thee of our blood, no, not our △kin,
   Far* [than] Deucalion off. †
                    Mark* thou my words . †

7 Follow us to the △court.
                    Thou, △churl*, for this time,

8 Though full of our displeasure, yet we free thee
9 From the dead blow of it.

First Folio

15/ Polixenes

1 Marke your divorce x(yong sir)x
   Whom sonne I dare not call : Thou art too base
   To be acknowledged. †
                    Thou + a Scepters heire,
2 That thus affects a sheepe-hooke?+
3 I am sorry, that by hanging thee, I can
                    Thou, old Traitor,
   But shorten thy life one weeke.
                    And thou, fresh peece
4 Of excellent Witchcraft, [whom] of force must know
   The royall Foole thou coap'st with.
5 Ile have thy beauty scratcht with briers & made
   More homely [then] thy state.
6   For thee x(fond boy)x
   If I may ever know thou dost but sigh x
   That thou no more shalt [never] see this knacke (as
   never
   I meane thou shalt) + wee'l barre thee from succession,
   Not hold thee of our blood, no+ not our Kin,
   Farre [then] Deucalion off: x(marke thou my words) +
   Follow us to the Court.
                    Thou + Churle, for this time +
7 x(Though full of our displeasure)x yet we free thee
   From the dead blow of it.

Polixenes' quietness when making his most disturbing threats and judgments suggests a man who is very used to (as only befits a king), thus it's very interesting to see that most of the releases are directed, when they do come, towards his son primarily (especially when threatening to bar him from succession), and only rarely towards Perdita or her father.

- the opening series of attacks on each of them (F #1-4) is emotional (4/10 in the first eight lines of the speech)

- the second round of attacks on Perdita and then Florizell is unembellished (F #5 and the first two and half lines of F #6), suggesting that Polixines controls his anger, at least for four lines, but he then explodes emotionally once more as he threatens Florizell that he will 'barre thee from succession' (3/6, the last four lines of F #6)

- the second attack on her father and then the start of the third attack on Perdita, are both passionate (4/3, F #7-8), and though the words of his final threat to Perdita are very real (F #9), the extra breath-thoughts (marked x) and the relative lack of release (1/2 in four lines) suggest that it appears he is trying to re-establish some form of self-control

- the icy unembellished attacks on his son start with the statement that he is
"too base/To be acknowledged."
followed later with
"For thee (fond boy)/If I may ever know thou dost but sigh,/That thou no more shalt never see this . . ."

- and though the initial attack on Perdita's father leaves no room for doubt, the last word 'weeke' the only thing to break the quietness
"I am sorry, that by hanging thee, I can/But shorten thy life one weeke"
Polixines soon softens towards him, if only a little
"(Though full of our displeasure) yet we free thee/From the dead blow of it"

- while the attack on Perdita is very clear
"Ile have thy beauty scratcht with briers & made/More homely then thy state."
warning her later that should she
"to his entrance open, or [hope] his body more, with thy embraces,/I will devise a death, . . ."

{ctd. over}

8   And you⁺ Enchantment,
Worthy enough a Heardsman: ₓ yea⁺ him too,
That makes himselfe (but for our Honor therein)
Unworthy thee.
9   If ever⁺ henceforth, thou
These rurall Latches,ₓ to his entrance open,
Or [hope] his body more, with thy embraces,
I will devise a death, as cruell for thee
As thou art tender to't.

10   And you, △enchantment -
Worthy enough a △herdsman* , yea, him too,
That makes himself- ◊ if ever, henceforth, thou
Unworthy thee- ◊ if ever, henceforth, thou
These rural* △latches to his entrance open,
Or [hoop] his body more with thy embraces,
I will devise a death, as cruel* for thee
As thou art tender to't.

#'s 16 - 17: PERDITA'S ADOPTIVE FAMILY

16/ Old Shepheard   I would there were no age betweene ten and . . .   3.3.59-78

Background: Close to the spot where Antigonus abandoned the daughter of Leontes and Hermione, this is the first speech for the character, and as such it is self-explanatory.

Style: solo

Where: somewhere on the shores of Bohemia   **To Whom:** self, and direct audience address   **# of Lines:** 19   **Probable Timing:** 1.00 minutes

---

The Old Shepheard seems to have an interesting style when **something important occurs to him, for he often seems to conclue an idea, or push forward the start of a new one by means of surround phrases – as with his fury with the 'boylde-braines' young men whose hunting caused his sheep to stray (ending F #1); the knowledge of where his sheep might be (ending F #2) – possibly a pleasant realisation since it begins with an emotional ; F #5's discovery of the child; the fact that the child is not dressed warmly enough (the end of F #6); and the need for the advice of his son (all of F #7).**

• given the releases that come later in the speech, the relative calm in the first two lines (0/1) is surprising, and might suggest that the character is exhausted from looking for his missing sheep

• but then comes the (traditional-old-man-complaining-about-the-young) emotional explosion at the young idiots who have caused two of his sheep to go missing (1/6, the last five lines of F #1)

• and though the facts of what has occurred and where he may find them then get added in, he still remains highly emotional (4/7, F #2)

• the initial discovery of what turns out to be the child is heightened by being both emotional (0/2, F #3) and set as the first of three successive short sentences, which then turns to passion (3/3, F #4+5) as he realises that what he has found is a baby – which seems to push him into a state of great calm (perhaps trying not to wake the child) for the first two unembellished closer examination phrases of F #6

• and then, as he comes to believe that the child is a result of a 'Scape' by some 'Waiting-Gentlewoman', so he becomes intellectual (4/1, lines two and three of F #6), but this quickly turns into emotion as he elaborates on the 'behinde-doore worke' in the child's conception, and its lack of warm clothing (2/10 in the three lines ending F #6)

• after all the bluster, his decision to protect the child is very quietly taken (0/1, F #7), though F ##8's apparent yell to his son may wake the baby up!

Modern Text

16/ Old Shepheard

1 I would there were no age between* ten and
three and twenty, or that youth would sleep out the rest;
for there is nothing (in the between*) but getting wenches with child*, wronging the ^ancientry*, stealing,
fighting - hark* you now !†

2   Would any but these boil'd-
brains* of nineteen* and two and twenty hunt this weather?

3   They have scar'd* away two of my best ^sheep*,
which I fear* the ^wolf* will sooner find* [than] the ^ma-
ster* .†

4   If any where I have them, 'tis by the sea°side, brow-
ing* of ivy.

5   Good ° luck*, and't be thy will !†

6   What have
we here*?

7   Mercy on's, a ^barne?

8   A very pretty barne! †

9   A
boy, or a ^child*, I wonder?

10   A pretty one, a very* pretty*
one : sure some ^scape .†

11   Though I am not bookish, yet I
can read* ^waiting-^gentlewoman in the scape .†

12   This has
been* some stair*-work*, some ^trunk*-work*, some
behind*-door* work* .†

13   They were warmer that got this,
[than] the poor* ^thing is here*.

14   I'll take it up for pity, yet
I'll tarry till my son* come*; he hallow'd but even now.

15 Whoa-ho-hoa.

First Folio

16/ Old Shepheard

1 I would there were no age betweene ten and
three and twenty, or that youth would sleep out the rest: x
for there is nothing (xin the betweene)x but getting wenches with childe, wronging the Auncientry, stealing,
fighting, hearke you now: + would any but these boylde-
braines of nineteene, x and two and twenty hunt this weather?

2   They have scar'd away two of my best Sheepe,
which I feare the Wolfe will sooner finde [then] the Maister; if any where I have them, 'tis by the sea-side, brou-
zing of Ivy.

3   Good-lucke x (and't be thy will) + what have
we heere?

4   Mercy on's, a Barne?

5   A very pretty barne; + A
boy, or a Childe + I wonder?

6   x(A pretty one, a verie prettie
one) + sure some Scape; Though I am not bookish, yet I
can reade Waiting-Gentlewoman in the scape: this has
beene some staire-worke, some Trunke-worke, some
behinde-doore worke: they were warmer that got this,
[then] the poore Thing is heere.

7   Ile take it up for pity, yet
Ile tarry till my sonne come: x he hallow'd but even now.

8   Whoa-ho-hoa.

17/ Clowne   **I have seene two such sights, by Sea & by Land :**   between 3.3.80 - 103

Background: As with his father (speech #16 above) the first speech for the character also known as the Young Shepheard is virtually self-explanatory. The ship wrecked is the one that brought Antigonus and Hermione's about-to-be-abandoned baby-daughter to Bohemia (see speech #4 above), the 'poore Gentleman' torn apart by the bear is, as the Clowne explains, Antigonus.

Style: as part of a two-handed scene

Where: somewhere on the shores of Bohemia   **To Whom:** his father, the Old Shepherd

# of Lines: 19   **Probable Timing: 1.00 minutes**

Modern Text

17/ Clowne

1 I have seen* two such sights, by △sea & by △land ! †

2 But I am not to say it is a △sea, for it is now the sky*, be-twixt the △firmament and it you cannot thrust a bodkin's point.

3 I would you did but see how it chafes, how it ra-ges, how it takes up the shore! †

4 But that's not to the point . †

5 O*, the most piteous* cry of the poor* souls*! †

6 Sometimes to see 'em, and not to see 'em; △now the △ship* boring* the △moon* with her main* mast, and anon swallow'd with yest and froth, as you'ld thrust a △cork* into a hogs° head.

7 And then for the △land-service, to see how the △bear* tore out his shoulder-bone, how he cried* to me* for help*, and said his name was Antigonus, a △nobleman. †

8 But to make an end of the △ship, to see how the △sea flap-dragon'd it; but, first, how the poor* souls* roar'd*, and, the sea mock'd them; and how the poor* △gentleman roar'd*, and the △bear* mock'd him, both roaring louder* [than] the sea or weather.

9 (ψ) I have not wink'd since I saw these sights. †

10 The men are not yet cold under water, nor the △bear* half* din'd on the △gentleman . †

11 He's at it now.

First Folio

17/ Clowne

1 I have seene two such sights, by Sea & by Land : + but I am not to say it is a Sea, for it is now the skie, be-twixt the Firmament and it,x you cannot thrust a bodkins point.

2 I would you did but see how it chafes, how it ra-ges, how it takes up the shore, + but that's not to the point : Oh, the most pitteous cry of the poore soules, + sometimes to see 'em, and not to see 'em;x Now the Shippe boaring the Moone with her maine Mast, and anon swallowed with yest and froth, as you'ld thrust a Corke into a hogs-head.

3 And then for the Land-service, to see how the Beare tore out his shoulder-bone, how he cride to mee for helpe, and said his name was Antigonus, a Nobleman : But to make an end of the Ship, to see how the Sea flap-dragon'd it: x but+ first, how the poore soules roared, and, the sea mock'd them : x and how the poore Gentleman roared, and the Beare mock'd him, both roaring lowder [then] the sea,x or weather.

4 (ψ) I have not wink'd since I saw these sights: the men are not yet cold under water, nor the Beare halfe din'd on the Gentleman : he's at it now.

• unlike his father, the Clowne's few surround phrases are not a character style, but highlight the most painful of the sights he has just seen, from the opening

" . I have seene two such sights, by Sea & Land ; "

with the sounds as equally disturbing as what he saw

" : Oh, the most pitteous cry of the poore soules, sometimes to see 'em, and not see 'em : "

as the emotional opening (1/4, the first two phrases), and sudden unembellished quiet of the last two show, echoed later by the recollection

" : but first how the poore soules roared, and, the sea mock'd them : "

and the speech ends with the details seemingly burned in his brain, as all three surround phrases that make up the final F #4 show

• the speech starts intellectually (4/1, F #1)

• then, fascinatingly, his first recollection of the storm being so violent that he cannot distinguish between the sea and the sky

"you cannot thrust a bodkins point . I would you did but see how it chafes, how it rages, how it takes up the shore, but that's not to the point:"

is completely unembellished; perhaps even he is surprised by it's ferocity

• and while the 'Oh, the most pitteous cry of the poore soules' is remembered emotionally (1/4), his visual memory of what he saw at sea turns passionate (5/5 in F #2's last two and half lines), as is the memory of Antigonus and the bear (4/4, the first three lines of F #3)

• then, as one thought piles on top of the other, so the accompanying styles change too, returning to the idea of the ship is intellectual (3/0); the sound of the 'poore soules' emotional once more (0/2); and the 'poore Gentleman' both (2/3) - a lovely tug of war for the actor to explore

• the effect on him seems profound, for the start of F #4 'I have not wink'd since I saw these sights : the men are not yet cold under water' forces him into unembellished quiet once more, though the action of the 'Beare' still seems disturbing (2/2 in just eight words)

The Winter's Tale / 373

#'s 18 - 20: The Triumphs and Come-Uppance of a Rogue

18/ Autolicus — Ha, ha, what a Foole Honestie is? and Trust (his

Background: Following Polixines' public explosion at Florizell, Perdita, and the Old Shepheard (speech #15 above) and subsequent abrupt finish to the festival, Autolicus, a charmingly seductive, itinerant peddler and expert pick-pocket, shares a moment's summation of his achievements on this very profitable (for him) day.

Style: solo
Where: Bohemia, outdoors, where the sheep-shearing festival is breaking up   **To Whom:** direct audience address

4.4.595 - 618

# of Lines: 23   **Probable Timing: 1.10 minutes**

Modern Text

18/ Autolicus

1 Ha, ha, what a △fool* Honesty* is! and Trust, his sworn* brother, a very simple △gentleman!

      I have sold

2 all my △trumpery*; not a counterfeit △stone, not a △ribbon, △glass*, △pomander, △brooch*, △table-book*, △ballad, △knife, △tape, △glove, △shoe*-tie, △bracelet, △horn*-△ring, to keep* my △pack from fasting.* †

3   They throng who should buy first, as if my △trinkets had been* hallow'd and brought a be-nediction to the buyer ; by which means* I saw whose △purse was best in △picture, and what I saw, to my good use I remember'd.

4   My △clown* (who wants but some-thing to be a reasonable man) grew so in love with the △wenches' △song, that he* would not stir* his △petti*rtoes, till he had both △tune and △words, which so drew the rest of the △herd* to me that all their other △senses stuck* in △ears* . †

5   You might have pinch'd a △placket, it was sense-less ; 'twas nothing to geld* a △cod*piece* of a △purse; I would have filed* △keys* of that hung in △chains* . †

6   No

hearing, no feeling, but my △sir's △song, and admiring the △nothing of it.

7   So that in this time of △lethargy* I pick'd and cut most of their △festival* △purses; △and had not the old ° man come in with a △whoo°bub against his △daugh-ter, and the King's son*, and scar'd my △choughs* from the △chaff*, I had not left a △purse alive in the whole △army.

First Folio

18/ Autolicus

1 Ha, ha, what a Foole Honestie is? and Trust_x(his sworne brother)_x a very simple Gentleman. +

      I have sold

2 all my Tromperie : x not a counterfeit Stone, not a Ribbon, Glasse, Pomander, Browch, Table-booke, Ballad, Knife, Tape, Glove, Shooe-tye, Bracelet, Horne-Ring, to keepe my Pack from fasting : they throng who should buy first, as if my Trinkets had beene hallowed,_x and brought a be-nediction to the buyer : by which meanes,_x I saw whose Purse was best in Picture ; x and what I saw, to my good use,_x I remembred.

3   My Clowne (who wants but some-thing to be a reasonable man) grew so in love with the Wenches Song, that hee would not stirre his Petty-toes, till he had both Tune and Words, which so drew the rest of the Heard to me,_x that all their other Sences stucke in Eares : you might have pinch'd a Placket, it was sence-lesse ; 'twas nothing to gueld a Cod-peece of a Purse : x I would have fill'd Keyes of that hung in Chaynes : no hearing, no feeling, but my Sirs Song, and admiring the Nothing of it.

4   So that in this time of Lethargie,_x I pickd and cut most of their Festivall Purses : x And had not the old-man come in with a Whoo-bub against his Daugh-ter, and the Kings Sonne, and scar'd my Chowghes from the Chaffe, I had not left a Purse alive in the whole Army.

• Autolicus is rarely at rest, thus the two small unembellished moments, the first heightened by being an emotional () surround phrase

    " ; and what I saw, to my good use, I remembred . "

followed almost straightway by the less than flattering description of the young Clowne (the Old Shepheard's son)

    " (who wants but something to be a reasonable man)"

should be relished as moments when Autolicus is at his most confidentially quiet

• the pinnacle of his success seems to be underscored by the successive surround phrases, heralded first with F #1's start

    " . Ha, ha, what a Foole Honestie is? and Trust (his sworne brother) a very simple Gentleman . "

• followed by F #2's

    " : by which meanes, I saw whose Purse was best in Picture ; and what I saw, to my good use, I remembred . "

in turn followed by the end of F #3/beginning of F #4

    " : you might have pinch'd a Placket, it was sencelesse : 'twas nothing to gueld a Cod-peece of a Purse : I would have nothing to gueld a Cod-peece of a Purse : no hearing, no feeling, but my Sirs Song, and admiring the Nothing of it . So that in this time of Lethargie, I pickd and cut most of their Festivall Purses :"

• overall the speech is highly factual/intellectual (51/26 in twenty-three - presumably celebratory - lines), with many of the emotional releases coming in small clusters, as with the description of what he has sold, 'Glasse, …, Browch, Table-booke, …, Shooe-tye, …, Horne-Ring'; the foolishness of prospective purchasers enticed by the Clowne's reaction to Autolicus' singing which drew the others, described as 'the Heard to me, that all their Sences stucke in Eares'; the joy of filching, as 'gueld a Cod-peece of a Purse : I would have fill'd Keyes of that hung in Chaynes'; and the final 'Whoo-bub' about Perdita and Florizell which 'scar'd my Chowghes from the Chaffe'

19/ Autolicus   **Whether it like me, or no, I am a Courtier.**   4.4.730 - 738

Background: To save the love-birds Florizell and Perdita, Camillo is helping them flee to Leontes for help. They have come across Autolicus, and in an attempt to disguise Florizell they have paid Autolicus to change clothes with him. Since both the Old Shepherd and thus possibly his son, the Clowne, are in trouble, they have gathered the secret documents that Antigonus included in Perdita's cradle when he abandoned her (speech #4 above) and are attempting to find a way to show the irate King she is not really a member of their family. They meet Autolicus, whom they don't recognise thanks to his fine new clothes. The three are equally interested in each other - Autolicus because he wants to know, and get his hands on, what's in the box; the two rustics because, if he is a Courtier, perhaps he can help them. The following is Autolicus' response to the Old Shepherd's question, 'Are you a Courtier, and't like you Sir?'

Style: as part of a three-handed scene

Where: Bohemia, somewhere close to where the abortive festival took place   **To Whom:** Old Shepherd and his son, the Clowne

# of Lines: 9   **Probable Timing: 0.30 minutes**

Modern Text

19/ Autolicus

1 Whether it like me or no, I am a △courtier.
                                        Seest
2 thou not the air* of the △court in these △enfoldings?
                                                   Hath
3 not my [gait] in it the measure of the △court?
                                     Receives not
4 thy △nose °court °△odor* from me?
                              Reflect I not on thy
5 △baseness* , △court-△Contempt?
                  Think'st thou, for that I
6 insinuate, [that] toze* from thee thy △business* , I am
   therefore no △courtier?
7   I am △courtier △cap-a-pe, and one that
   will either* push ° on or pluck ° back thy △business* there;
   whereupon I command thee to open thy △affair* .

First Folio

19/ Autolicus

1 Whether it like me,ₓ or no, I am a Courtier.
                                          Seest
2 thou not the ayre of the Court,ₓ in these enfoldings?
                                                      Hath
3 not my [gate] in it,ₓ the measure of the Court?
                                       Receives not
4 thy Nose Court-Odour from me?
                                  Reflect I not on thy
5 Basenesse, Court-Contempt?
                    Think'st thou, for that I
6 insinuate, [at] toaze from thee thy Businesse, I am therefore no Courtier?
7   I am Courtier Cap-a-pe ; ₓ and one that
   will eyther push-on,ₓ or pluck-back,ₓ thy Businesse there :ₓ
   whereupon I command thee to open thy Affaire.

• Autolicus starts out quite quietly, the extra breath-thoughts (marked,ₓ) in the first three sentences doing the work of impressing the country-folk rather than excessive imagery or unnecessary emotional flourishes

• thus the first three sentences are short, and intellectually to the point (3/1, the first three lines of the speech)

• but inevitably Autolicus' joy of being the centre of attention begins to take over, and as he browbeats them further, with the idea of his 'Court-Odour' reflecting on their 'Basenesse' so his intellectual flourish begins to assert itself (6/2, the two lines of the short sentences F #4-5)

• and, as he attempts to push home the final proof that he is a 'Courtier Cap-a-pe' in an effort to 'command thee to open thy Affaire' (i.e. box), he resorts to passion (6/5, F #6-7), the final sentence requiring three complete surround phrases, the threat that he can stop their life-saving approach to Polixines being introduced via the only emotional semicolon in the speech

20/ Clowne   **You are well met (Sir :) you deny'd to fight**   between 5.2.128 - 145

Background: Far from the awful doom prophesied by Autolicus for the Old Shepherd and the Clowne, once Leontes learned from the documents produced by the Old Shepherd that Perdita was Leontes' own daughter, he promptly granted the Old Shepherd and the Clowne the rank of Gentlemen, and provided them clothing and status accordingly, as the Clowne is only to eager to point out.

Style: as part of a three-handed scene

Where: somewhere in the palace of Sicilia   **To Whom:** Autolicus, in front of the Old Shepherd

# of Lines: 14   **Probable Timing: 0.45 minutes**

First Folio

20/ Clowne

1 You are well met ₓ(Sir :)ₓ you deny'd to fight with mee this other day, because I was no Gentleman borne.

2   See you these Clothes? say you see them not, ₓ and thinke me still no Gentleman borne : You were best say these Robes are not Gentleman borne.

3   Give me the Lye : ₓ   doe : ₓ   and try whether I am not now a Gentleman borne.

4 {For I} have been so any time these foure houres.

5   {Ψ}   {And} I was a Gentleman borne before my Father : ₓ for the Kings Sonne tooke me by the hand, and call'd mee Brother : ₓ   and then the two Kings call'd my Father Brother : ₓ and then the Prince ₓ(my Brother,) and the Princesse ₓ(my Sister)ₓ call'd my Father, Father, and so wee wept : ₓ and there was the first Gentleman-like teares that ever we shed.

Modern Text

20/ Clowne

1 You are well met, ᐃsir . †

2   You denied* to fight with me* this other day, because I was no ᐃgentleman born* .

3   See you these ᐃclothes? †

4   Say you see them not ᐃ me still no ᐃgentleman borne . †

5   You were best say these ᐃrobes are not ᐃgentlemen born* .

6   Give me the ᐃlie* , do;   and try whether I am not now a ᐃgentleman born.

7 {For I} have been so any time these four* hours* .

8   {Ψ}   {And} I was a ᐃgentleman born* before my ᐃfather;   for the King's ᐃson* took* me by the hand, and call'd me* ᐃbrother ;   and then the two ᐃkings call'd my ᐃfather ᐃbrother ;   and then the Prince, my ᐃbrother; and the Princess* , my ᐃsister, call'd my ᐃfather, ᐃfather; and so we* wept;   and there was the first ᐃgentleman ° like tears* that ever we shed.

With his new promotion to the rank of gentleman the Clowne shows **virtually no self-control, either in vocal release (24/18), or in surround phrases (at least ten) in just thirteen lines overall.**

- the Clowne's excitement is almost tangible, both with the opening surround phrase monosyllabic challenge, and the passion that fills the first four lines (4/5)

- then, as with so many foolish Shakespeare characters, the next stage of his proof that he is a 'Gentleman' becomes based on his outward appearance, a somewhat intellectual attachment to his clothing (2/1, the last line of F #2) is pushed even harder, with passion (2/3) and three surround phrases completely forming F #3

- the sweet if foolish brag that he has been a gentleman 'these foure houres' is pushed emotionally (0/2), the shortness of F #4 perhaps suggesting that he is still somewhat stunned by the whole idea

- and then the recalling of the joyous events that took place with both Kings swamps him completely, starting with the passionate description of how the 'Kings Sonne . . . call'd mee Brother' (5/4, the first two lines of F #5), and the vastly intellectual releases of the new inter-family naming of names (9/1, the next two and half lines)

- while the final recollection of 'so wee wept' becomes almost too much to bear, for not only is it emotional (1/2), the recollection is formed by two surround phrases, the first heightened by the only emotional in the speech

21: A THEATRICAL LINK

21/Time   I that please some, try all: both joy and terror   4.1.1-32

Background: A self-explanatory speech, linking the opening scenes in Sicilia and the sixteen year gap [4] before the scenes in Bohemia begin.

Style: solo

Where: the theatre as a theatre   To Whom: direct audience address   # of Lines: 32   Probable Timing: 1.35 minutes

Modern Text		First Folio

Modern Text

21/Time

1
I, that please some, try all, both joy and terror
Of good, and bad, that makes and unfolds error,
Now take upon me, in the name of Time,
To use my wings . †
    Impute it not a crime

2
To me, or my swift passage, that I slide
O'er sixteen* years* and leave the growth untried*
Of that wide gap, since it is in my pow'r
To o'erthrow ^law, and in one self*-born* hour*
To plant and o'er'whelm* ^custom* .
    Let me pass*

3
The same I am, ere ancient'st ^order was,
Or what is now receiv'd.

4
    I witness* to
The times that brought them in ; so shall I do
To th'freshest things now reigning, and make stale
The glistering of this present, as my ^tale
Now seems* to it . †
    Your patience this allowing,

5
I turn* my glass*, and give my ^scene such growing
As you had slept between* . †
    Leontes leaving -

6
Th'effects of his fond jealousies so grieving*
That he shuts up himself* - ◊ imagine me,
Gentle ^spectators*, that I now may be
In fair* Bohemia, and remember well,
I mentioned a son* o'th'King's, which Florizel*
I now name to you ; and with speed so pace
To speak* of Perdita, now grown* in grace
Equal* with wond'ring.

Here F's orthography reveals the art of the story-teller throughout, rather than psychological character development.

• thus the surround phrases serve to grab the audience's attention, as with the three that open F #1
" I that please some, try all : both joy and terror/Of good, and bad : that makes, and unfolds error,/Now take upon me (in the name of Time)/To use my wings :"
and tantalising the audience as to the new character Perdita
". What of her issues/I list not prophesie : but let Times newes/Be knowne when 'tis brought forth. "
plus the inevitable final curtying of favour with the audience (as with Rumour in Henry Four Part Two, the Chorus in Henry the Fifth, and Pucke/Robin in A Midsummer Night's Dream)
"': of this allow,/If ever you have spent time worse, ere now : /If never, yet that Time himselfe doth say,/He wishes earnestly, you never may . "

• as with good story tellers, the capitals point to the new topic the audience needs to consider/be guided to, as, amongst others, the abstracts of 'Time', 'Law', and 'Custome' in F #1 and 'Order' in F #2; the theatricality of what is taking place, 'Tale' and 'Scene' in F #3, and 'Spectators' of F #4; and people, 'Leontes', 'Florizell', and 'Perdita' or places involved, 'Bohemia'

• the emotional clusters suddenly underscore the point being made, as with the passage of time that he is covering, 'sixteene yeeres'; and his ability to transpose time, 'in one selfe-borne howre . . ore-whelme Custome', since he can 'turne my glasse'

• and, unlike the other narrators listed above, Time's shifts in stylistics relate more to the story being told - knowing when to grab the audience's attention and when to relax a little – rather than to personal response and/or involvement

• surround phrases are deemed enough to start the speech (1/0, the first three and half lines), moving then via the intriguing phrase 'Impute it not a crime' to a rousing emotional finish explaining that he can vanquish the laws of time and 'ore-whelme Custome' (3/9, the remainder of F #1)

First Folio

21/Time

1
I+ that please some, try all : x both joy and terror
Of good, and bad : x that makes, and unfolds error,
Now take upon me, x(in the name of Time)x
To use my wings : Impute it not a crime
To me, or my swift passage, that I slide
Ore sixteene yeeres, x and leave the growth untride
Of that wide gap, since it is in my powre
To orethrow Law, and in one selfe-borne howre
To plant, x and ore-whelme Custome.
    Let me passe

2
The same I am, ere ancient'st Order was,
Or what is now receiv'd.

3
    I witnesse to
The times that brought them in, + so shall I do
To th'freshest things now reigning, and make stale
The glistering of this present, as my Tale
Now seemes to it : your patience this allowing,
I turne my glasse, and give my Scene such growing
As you had slept betweene : Leontes leaving +
Th'effects of his fond jealousies, x so greeving
That he shuts up himselfe.

4
    Imagine me +
x(Gentle Spectators)x that I now may be
In faire Bohemia, and remember well,
I mentioned a sonne o'th'Kings, which Florizell
I now name to you : x and with speed so pace
To speake of Perdita, now growne in grace
Equall with wond'ring.

---

4 or perhaps just fifteen years, if the timing in a later speech from Camillo to Polixenes is preferred

5

What of her issues
I list not prophesie: ₓ but let Times newes
Be knowne when 'tis brought forth.
            A shepherds daughter⁺

6

And what to her adheres, which followes after,
Is th'argument of Time: of this allow,
If ever you have spent time worse, ere now: ₓ
If never, yet that Time himselfe doth say,
He wishes earnestly,ᵥₓ you never may.

• and (presumably) having intrigued the audience enough, so Time relaxes as he promises to do 'th'freshest things' (2/3, the two lines of F #2, and the first four of F #3), and then he turns up the emotion once more (2/5 the last four lines of F #3) as he promises to 'turne the glasse' as if 'you had slept betweene'

• as he instructs the audience to join him in Bohemia to meet Florizell he returns to passion (4/3, F #4's first four lines), though, as might befit a good storyteller turning to the heroine, the introduction of Perdita becomes emotional (2/5, the last two lines of F #4, plus F #5)

• however, the final plot line/audience seduction becomes moderately passionate (2/2 in the five and a half lines of F #6), moderate perhaps to settle the audience down for what is to follow

7

What of her ensues*
I list not prophesy*; but let Time's news*
Be known* when 'tis brought forth.

8

            A shepherd's daughter,
And what to her adheres, which follows* after,
Is th'argument of Time . †

9

        Of this allow,
If ever you have spent time worse, ere now;
If never, yet that Time himself* doth say,
He wishes earnestly you never may.

THE TEMPEST

SPEECHES IN ORDER	TIME	PAGE
#'s 1 - 4: Prospero's Revenge and Repentance		
1/ **Prospero** — I pray thee marke mee:	2.00	379
2/ **Prospero** — I had forgot that foule conspiracy	1.15	381
3/ **Prospero** — Ye Elves of hils, brooks, stading lakes & groves,	1.15	383
4/ **Prospero** — Now my charmes are all ore-throwne,	1.00	384
#'s 5 - 6: Prospero's Attempts To Control His Spirits		
5/ **Ariel** — To every Article.	1.00	385
6/ **Caliban** — All the infections that the Sunne suckes up	0.55	386
#'s 7 - 9: Milan's Sinners and Honest Men		
7/ **Anthonio**{*} — {I} did supplant {my} Brother Prospero.	1.10	387
8/ **Ariel** — You are three men of sinne, whom destiny	1.30	388
9/ **Gonzalo** — Had I plantation of this Isle my Lord,	1.00	390
#'s 10 - 14: A Strange Conspiracy: Cailban, Trinculo, And Stephano		
10/ **Trinculo** — Here's neither bush, nor shrub to beare off any	1.15	391
11/ **Caliban** — I have seene thee in [the Moone} : and I	0.50	393
12/ **Caliban** — As I told thee before, I am subject to a Tirant,	1.10	394
13/ **Caliban** — Be not affeard, the Isle is full of noyses,	0.30	395
14/ **Stephano** — Monster, your Fairy, w you say is a harmles Fairy,	0.45	396
#'s 15 - 21: Two Young People Fall In Love		
15/ **Miranda** — If by your Art (my deerest father) you have	0.45	397
16/ **Miranda** — Abhorred Slave, /Which any print of goodnesse . . .	0.40	398
17/ **Ferdinand** — Where shold this Musicke be?	0.40	399
18/ **Ferdinand** — There be some Sports are painfull ; & their labor	0.50	400
19/ **Miranda** — Alas, now pray you/Worke not so hard:	0.40	401
20/ **Ferdinand** — Noble Mistris, {*} I do beseech you	1.30	402
21/ **Miranda** — I do not know/One of my sexe ; no womans face	1.10	404

	Speech #(s)
SPEECHES FOR WOMEN (4)	
Miranda — Traditional & Today: a young (teenage) woman	#15, #16, #19, #21
SPEECHES FOR EITHER GENDER (2)	
Ariel — Traditional & Today: any age and gender that can convey the (presumed) mercurial spirit of the character {see also **Prospero, Anthonio, and Gonzalo below**}	#5, #8
SPEECHES FOR MEN (15)	
Prospero — Traditional: older male Today: occasionally either gender	#1, #2, #3, #4
Caliban — Traditional & Today: male character actor of any age, often young	#6, #11, #12, #13
Anthonio — Traditional: the younger brother of Prospero middle aged man and upwards Today: sometimes either gender	#7
Gonzalo — Traditional: older male character actor Today: sometimes any gender, usually maintaining the age proviso	#9
Trinculo — Traditional & Today: male character, any age	#10
Stephano — Traditional & Today: male character, any age	#14
Ferdinand — Traditional & Today: a young man of marriageable age	#17, #18, #20

THE TEMPEST

#'s 1 - 4: Prospero's Revenge and Repentance

1/ Prospero **I pray thee marke me :** between 1.2.88 - 148

Background: Faced with the prospect of dealing face to face with antagonists both past and present, Prospero begins to acquaint his daughter Miranda with the full details of how they have come to spend their last twelve years alone on the island they call home. In many ways she has demanded this, for the storm which Prospero has had to create to achieve his aims has disturbed her greatly (see speech #15 below).

Style: part of a two handed scene

Where: unspecified, but somewhere close to their cell and close to Caliban's cave **To Whom:** his daughter Miranda

# of Lines: 42 **Probable Timing: 2.00 minutes**

Modern Text

1/ Prospero

1 I pray thee mark* me. †

2 I, thus neglecting worldly ends, all dedicated
To closeness$_*$, and the bettering of my mind
With that which, but by being so retir'd,
O'er-priz'd all popular rate, in my false brother
Awak'd an evil* nature, and my trust,
Like a good parent, did beget of him
A falsehood in it's contrary$_*$, as great
As my trust was, which had indeed* no limit,
A confidence sans bound.

3 He being thus $^{\Delta}$lorded,
Not only* with what my revenue* yielded*,
But what my power might else$_*$ exact- ◊ $^{\Delta}$like one
Who having into truth, by telling of it,
Made such a sinner* of his memory$_*$
To credit* his own* lie - he did believe*
He was indeed the Duke, out o'th' $^{\Delta}$substitution,
And executing th'outward face of $^{\Delta}$royalty$_*$
With all prerogative. †

4 Hence his $^{\Delta}$ambition growing -
Dost thou hear*?

5 To have no $^{\Delta}$screen* between this part he play'd$_*$
And him he play'd$_*$ it for, he needs* will be
Absolute Milan* - $^{\Delta}$me (poor* man) my $^{\Delta}$library$_*$
Was $^{\Delta}$dukedom* large enough: of temporal* royalties
He thinks me now incapable; ◊ $^{\Delta}$confederates

That Prospero cannot deal with events objectively can be seen in the two ungrammatical periods (ending F #2 and #4); the way several sentences start out reported either calmly or intellectually and then move into emotion or passion; and the surround phrases urging Miranda to 'marke' and 'heare' him.

- it seems that the opening monosyllabic surround phrase ' . I pray thee marke me : ' has a great impact on Miranda (or perhaps himself, in confessing his negligence to his daughter), for the remainder of F #1's nine lines, dealing with how an 'evill nature' awoke in his brother, are almost totally unembellished, establishing one of the longest calm passages in the later Shakespeare plays (0/2)

- however, as F #2's expansion of his brother 'being thus Lorded' is touched upon, so his control begins to slip, both emotionally (1/3), and in the thinking process, for F adds a very strange ungrammatical period to end the thought, even though F #3 continues on with a much greater elaboration of Anthonio's growing beliefs and 'Ambition', - a period never set by modern texts

- and though ungrammatical, the period seems to mark a change with enormous implications for Prospero for the elaboration shifts from the emotion of F #2 to passion in F #3 (4/5), the ending turning towards surround phrases once more, enhancing both the notion of ' : hence his Ambition growing : ' and the monosyllabic reinforcement of the need for Miranda to understand everything, ' : Do'st thou heare ? '

- the expansion of Anthonio's 'Ambition' becomes even more passionate (5/6 in the four and half lines of F #4), and equally troublesome to his logical presentation, for F #4 ends with yet another period most modern texts regard as ungrammatical – yet F's setting provides Prospero with a second break before he manages to establish some form of mental discipline in describing how Anthonio became 'Confederates' with the 'King of Naples' (F #5, 9/5): the needed break between F#4 and #5 coming with the (upsetting?) surround phrase of how Anthonio ' : of temporall royalties/He thinks me now incapable . '

First Folio

1/ Prospero

1 I pray thee marke me:
I$^+$ thus neglecting worldly ends, all dedicated
To closenes, and the bettering of my mind
with that,$_x$ which$^+$ but by being so retir'd$^+$
Ore-priz'd all popular rate: $_x$ in my false brother
Awak'd an evill nature, and my trust$^+$
Like a good parent, did beget of him
A falsehood in it's contrarie, as great
As my trust was, which had indeede no limit,
A confidence sans bound.

2 He being thus Lorded,
Not onely with what my revenew yeelded,
But what my power might els exact.

3 Like one
Who having into truth, by telling of it,
Made such a synner of his memorie
To credite his owne lie, he did beleeve
He was indeed the Duke, out o'th' Substitution$^+$
And executing th'outward face of Roialtie
With all prerogative: hence his Ambition growing: $_x$
Do'st thou heare?

4 To have no Schreene between this part he plaid,$_x$
And him he plaid it for, he needes will be
Absolute Millaine, Me (poore man) my Librarie
Was Dukedome large enough: of temporall royalties
He thinks me now incapable.

{ctd. over}

(So dry* he was for △sway) [wi'th'] King of Naples
To give him △annual* tribute, do* him homage,
Subject his △coronet, to his △crown*, and bend
The △dukedom yet unbow'd (alas, poor* Milan*!)
To most ignoble stooping.

6 Mark* his condition, and th'event, then tell me
If this might be a brother.

7 This King of Naples, being an △enemy
To me inveterate, hearkens my △brother's suit,

△ whereon

8 A treacherous △army* levied, one mid△night
Fated to th'purpose, did Antonio* open
The gates of Milan*, and i'th' dead of darkness*
The ministers for th'purpose hurried thence
Me and thy crying self*.

9 In few, they hurried us a△board a △bark*,
Bore us some △leagues to △sea, where they prepared
A rotten carcass* of a △butt, not rigg'd,
Nor tackle, sail* , nor mast, the very rats
Instinctively have quit it. †

- once more an instruction to Miranda, this time to 'Marke his condition' i.e. his brother's, is handled quite quietly (0/1, F #6), and, as before, at first he seems to be able to establish intellectual control, for F #7's first four line description of his brother opening 'The gates of Millaine' to 'The King of Naples' an 'Enemy/To me inveterate' is strongly intellectual (7/1)

- and then F #7's final two line recollection of himself and Miranda being hurried away 'ith' dead of darkenesse' becomes emotional (0/2)

- the final description of the 'rotten carkasse of a Butt' on to which they were hurried becomes passionate again (4/3, F #8) – though the last horrific recollection that the ship's condition was so bad 'the very rats/Instinctively have quit it is unembellished, perhaps suggesting that the memory is almost too painful to talk about

---

Confederates

5 (so drie he was for Sway) [with] King of Naples
To give him Annuall tribute, doe him homage +
Subject his Coronet, to his Crowne + and bend
The Dukedom yet unbow'd (alas+ poore Millaine) +
To most ignoble stooping.

6 Marke his condition, and th'event, then tell me
If this might be a brother.

7 This King of Naples + being an Enemy
To me inveterate, hearkens my Brothers suit : +

Whereon

A treacherous Armie levied, one mid-night
Fated to th'purpose, did Anthonio open
The gates of Millaine, and ith' dead of darkenesse
The ministers for th'purpose hurried thence
Me,x and thy crying selfe.

8 In few, they hurried us a-boord a Barke,
Bore us some Leagues to Sea, where they prepared
A rotten carkasse of a Butt, not rigg'd,
Nor tackle, sayle, nor mast, the very rats
Instinctively have quit it.

2/ Prospero   I had forgot that foule conspiracy   between 4.1.139 - 166

Background: With two of three matters of concern in hand if not completely resolved (the betrothal of Miranda and Alonso's son, Ferdinand - see speeches #15-21 below - and the controlling of his old Milanese and Neapolitan adversaries (see speeches #7-8), there is still one major concern outstanding, which causes Prospero to interrupt the glorious musical and visual Masque being offered by Ariel and the spirits to celebrate the betrothal.

Style: intially as a group interruption, then as part of a three-handed scene, finally as a two-handed scene   **To Whom:** initially the group as a whole, spirits including Ariel, Juno, Ceres and Iris, and the

Where: wherever on the island the betrothal celebration Masque is being held   humans Miranda and Ferdinand;   then just the two humans; finally Ariel alone

# of Lines: 24   **Probable Timing: 1.15 minutes**

First Folio

2/ Prospero

1
I had forgot that foule conspiracy
Of the beast Calliban,$_x$ and his confederates
Against my life: the minute of their plot
Is almost come: Well done, avoid: $_x$ no more.

2
You doe looke $_x$(my son)$_x$ in a mov'd sort,
As if you were dismaid: $_x$ be cheerefull⁺ Sir,
Our Revels now are ended: These our actors,$_x$
(As I foretold you) were all Spirits, and
Are melted into Ayre, into thin Ayre,
And like the baselesse fabricke of this vision⁺
And Clowd-capt Towres, the gorgeous Pallaces,
The solemne Temples, the great Globe it selfe,
Yea, all which it inherit, shall dissolve,
And like this insubstantiall Pageant faded
Leave not a racke behinde: we are such stuffe
As dreames are made on; and our little life
Is rounded with a sleepe: Sir, I am vext,⁺
Beare with my weakenesse, my old braine is troubled:
Be not disturb'd with my infirmitie,
If you be pleas'd, retire into my Cell,
And there repose, a turne or two,$_x$ Ile walke
To still my beating minde.

Commentary

• the urgent thought that has interrupted him is highlighted by the final surround phrases of F #1
" : the minute of their plot/Is almost come : Well done, avoid : no more."
and those of F #3-4 that end the speech
" . Come with a thought : I thank thee Ariell : come . /Spirit : We must prepare to meet with Caliban."

• noticing the shock that his interruption has given to Ferdinand (if not Miranda too) he comments in another surround phrase
" . : be cheerfull Sir,/Our Revels now are ended . "

• while both his philosophy and confusion are highlighted in a third passage of three successive surround phrases, the opening philosophy heightened by being expressed in part via the only (emotional) semicolon in the speech
" . : we are such stuffe/As dreames are made on ; and our little life/Is rounded with a sleepe : Sir, I am vext, /Beare with my weakenesse, my old braine is troubled:"
followed by the very quiet (plea?), unembellished
"Be not disturb'd with my infirmitie,'
which, coupled with the later comment in Act Five of 'Every third thought shall be my grave', may have more significance for Prospero than his listeners may comprehend

• the speech opens powerfully (1/2, the first one and a half lines), and then, via the surround phrases, Prospero evinces some momentary control (1/0 to the end of F #1)

• the attempt to calm Ferdinand and the explanation of how 'Our Revels now are ended' which opens F#2's first six lines are passionate (5/7), and, while the initial description of the edifices continues passionately (5/4 the next two lines), so as the 'Globe it selfe' is mentioned there comes the hushed 'Yea, all which it inherit, shall dissolve' before an emotional conclusion covering both the thought 'we are such stuffe/As dreames are made on' and the admission that his 'braine' is 'troubled' (2/9 the next five lines to the final colon of F #2)

Modern Text

2/ Prospero

1
I had forgot that foul* conspiracy
Of the beast Caliban* and his confederates
Against my life. †
       The minute of their plot

2
Is almost come. †
       Well done, avoid; no more.

3
You do* look*, my son, in a mov'd sort,
As if you were dismay'd*; be cheerful*, △sir. †

       These our actors

4
Our △revels now are ended . †

5
(As I foretold you) were all △spirits, and
Are melted into △air*, into thin △air*,
And like the baseless* fabric* of this vision,
And △cloud-capp'd* △tow'rs, the gorgeous △palaces*,
The solemn* △temples, the great △globe itself*,
Yea, all which it inherit, shall dissolve,

6
And like this insubstantial* △pageant faded
Leave not a rack* behind . †

7
       We are such stuff*
As dreams* are made on; and our little life
Is rounded with a sleep* . †

8
       Sir, I am vex'd ;
Bear* with my weakness*, my old brain* is troubled:
Be not disturb'd with my infirmity* . †

9
If you be pleas'd, retire into my △cell,
And there repose . †

10
       A turn* or two I'll walk*
To still my beating mind* .

{ctd. over}

11 Come with a thought.†
12 I thank thee.†
13 Ariel*! come.

[Enter Ariell]

14 Spirit,
We must prepare to meet with Caliban.

• and he may be tired (hardly surprising, considering the magic he has initiated already throughout the play) for apart from the emotional idea that 'a turne or two, Ile walke/To still my beating minde', the remaining six lines of the speech are passionate but quieter (4/3), though the F #3-4 surround phrases that end the speech underscore that he very clearly understands how much he has left to do

3 Come with a thought: I thank thee Ariell: + come.

[Enter Ariell]

4 Spirit: x We must prepare to meet with Caliban.

3/ Prospero   Ye Elves of hils, brooks, stãding lakes & groves,   5.1.33 - 57

Background: Though his former enemies are in his power, Prospero still has to meet them face to face, and, judging by the enormous power of which he boasts in the following speech, and Miranda's concern as expressed earlier to Ferdinand 'Never till this day/Saw I him touch'd with anger, so distemper'd', he has not yet resolved whether to free or destroy them. Here, he is gathering his strength for this, as he judges it, his final major task.

Style: ostensibly solo, yet directed towards a series of highly detailed personal visions

Where: unspecified, but somewhere close to his cell

To Whom: all the spirits from which he draws his power

# of Lines: 25   **Probable Timing: 1.15 minutes**

First Folio

3/ Prospero

1 Ye Elves of hils, brooks, [stãding] lakes + & groves,
And ye,ₓ that on the sands with printlesse foote
Doe chase the ebbing-Neptune, and doe flie him
When he comes backe :ₓ you demy-Puppets,ₓ that
By Moone-shine doe the greene sowre Ringlets make,
Whereof the Ewe not bites :ₓ and you,+ whose pastime
Is to make midnight-Mushrumps, that rejoyce
To heare the solemne Curfewe,+ by whose ayde
(Weake Masters though ye be) I have bedymn'd
The Noone-tide Sun, call'd forth the mutenous windes,
And twixt the greene Sea, and the azur'd vault
Set roaring warre :ₓ To the dread ratling Thunder
Have I given fire, and rifted Joves stowt Oke
With his owne Bolt :ₓ The strong bass'd promontorie
Have I made shake, and by the spurs pluckt up
The Pyne,ₓ and Cedar.

2   **Graves at my command**
Have wak'd their sleepers, op'd+ and let 'em forth
By my so potent Art.

3   But this rough Magicke
I heere abjure :ₓ and when I have requir'd
Some heavenly Musicke (which even now I do)
To worke mine end upon their Sences,ₓ that
This Ayrie-charme is for, I'le breake my staffe,
Bury it certaine [fadomes] in the earth,
And deeper [then] did ever Plummet sound
Ile drowne my booke.

Modern Text

3/ Prospero

1 Ye △elves of hills*, brooks*, [standing] lakes*, & groves,
And ye that on the sands with printless* foot*
Do* chase the ebbing ○△Neptune, and do* fly* him
When he comes back* ; you demi-△puppets that
By △moon*○shine do* the green* sour* △ringlets make,
Whereof the △ewe not bites ; and you whose pastime
Is to make midnight ○△mushrumps, that rejoice*
To hear* the solemn* △curfew* : by whose aid*
(Weak* △masters though ye be) I have bedimm'd
The △noon*○tide △sun, call'd forth the mutinous winds* ,
And 'twixt the green* △sea and the azur'd vault
Set roaring war* ; △ to the dread rattling* △thunder
Have I given fire, and rifted Jove's stout* △oak*
With his own* △bolt; △the strong bass'd promontory*
Have I made shake, and by the spurs pluck'd up
The △pine* and △cedar.

2   **Graves at my command**
Have wak'd their sleepers, op'd, and let 'em forth
By my so potent △art.

3   But this rough △magic*
I there* abjure ; and when I have requir'd
Some heavenly Music* (which even now I do)
To work* mine end upon their △senses that
This △airy, ○ charm* is for, I'll break* my staff* ,
Bury it certain* [fathoms*] in the earth,
And deeper [than] did ever △plummet sound
I'll drown* my book* .

In this speech the releases often seem more attached to specific images rather than a concentrated passage of one particular form of release: apart from single releases scattered throughout there are occasional clusters, which would include

a/ **intellectually**, the 'Noone-tide Sun'; 'Joves stowt Oke'; the 'Pyne and Cedar'

b/ **emotionally**, with 'printlesse foote/Doe chase'; 'that rejoyce/To heare the solemne Curfewe'; 'this rough Magicke/I heere abjure'; 'I'le breake my staffe'; 'Ile drowne my booke'

• Prospero's opening appeal to the 'Elves' is emotional (2/5, the first three and a half lines); and then he becomes passionate as he next calls upon the 'demy-Puppets' (4/3), and those 'whose pastime /Is to make midnight-Mushrumps' (2/4), in which vein he stays as he recalls how he has striven with nature - the 'Noone-tide Sun', the 'mutenous windes', the 'greene Sea' (4/7)

• but, as he recalls challenging Jove, and uprooting trees, and even opening graves, so his intellect begins to assert itself (8/3), though interestingly each image declines in intensity, from the powerful surround phrase of
a/ ". To the dread ratling Thunder/Have I given fire, and rifted Joves stowt Oke/With his owne Bolt : " (5/2)

b/ through to the uprooting of trees (3/1)

c/ to the almost hushed two line F #2 image of graves letting forth their sleepers (1/0), suggesting either diminishing energy (see the previous speech) or that he becomes quieter as he realises the enormity of what he dared to achieve – yet the magical pattern of the (bolded) opening [1] suggests an enormous sense of power (and even danger?) within the recollection – the calm perhaps suggesting that he is struggling to contain the enormously dangerous thoughts the image triggers/contains

• thus the enormity of the vow that opens F #3 is doubly enhanced, first by being set as a surround phrase
". But this rough Magicke/I heere abjure : "
and in turn by being part of a highly emotional sentence (5/11) containing both his quest for 'Some heavenly Musicke' to achieve what must be done with Alonso, Sebastian, and above all brother Anthonio, and his promise to 'breake my staffe' and 'drowne my booke', i.e to end his magical powers once and for all

---

1 See Appendix 3 for a more detailed explanation of the patterns of magic

4/ Prospero as EPILOGUE   Now my charmes are all ore-throwne,   Epilogue 1 - 20

Background: With all outstanding matters resolved, with his Dukedom restored, his daughter and Ferdinand about to be married, Ariel and his fellow spirits released as promised, Caliban seeking for 'grace' 'heereafter', and a reconciliation made with Alonso, Prospero asks the audience to release him so that he may journey back to Milan (where, rather ominously, 'Every third thought shall be my grave'). Since scholars pinpoint *The Tempest* to be the last play written by Shakespeare without collaboration, romantics tend to regard this speech as his personal farewell to the theatre. One note: bolding in the First Folio text suggests magic — see the commentary and Appendix 3.

Style: solo

Where: both the island and the theatre   **To Whom:** direct audience address

# of Lines: 20   **Probable Timing: 1.00 minutes**

Modern Text	First Folio
4/ EPILOGUE: SPOKEN BY PROSPERO	4/ EPILOGUE: SPOKEN BY PROSPERO
1 Now my △charms* are all o'er'thrown*, And what strength I have's mine own*, ◇ Which is most faint. †	1 **Now my Charmes are all ore-throwne,** **And what strength I have's mine owne.** Which is most faint: now 'tis true + I must be heere confinde by you, Or sent to Naples, Let me not +
2 Now 'tis true, I must be here* confin'd* by you, Or sent to Naples. † Let me not, Since I have my △dukedom* got, And pardon'd the deceiver, dwell In this bare △island, by your △spell. But release me from my bands With the help* of your good hands. †	**Since I have my Dukedome got,** And pardon'd the deceiver, dwell In this bare Island, by your Spell, **But release me from my bands** **With the helpe of your good hands:**
4 Gentle breath of yours my △sails* Must fill, or else my project fails*, Which was to please. †	**Gentle breath of yours,ₓ my Sailes** Must fill, or else my project failes, Which was to please: Now I want **Spirits to enforce :** ₓ Art to inchant, **And my ending is despaire,** Unlesse I be reliev'd by praier+
5 Now I want Spirits to enforce, △art to enchant*, And my ending is despair* , Unless₂ I be reliev'd by prayer*, Which pierces so, that it assaults Mercy itself*, and frees all faults.	Which pierces so, that it assaults Mercy it selfe, and frees all faults.
6 As you from crimes would pardon'd be, Let your △indulgence set me free.	3 As you from crimes would pardon'd be, Let your Indulgence set me free.

The six sentences most modern texts present show a very rational Prospero, a far cry from what was first set, where an ungrammatical period puts an early end to F #1, and the onrushed F #2 is usually split into three. However, in human terms the 'incorrect' period is very important, allowing Prospero a much needed personal break following his admission he no longer has magical powers. Quite fascinatingly, though he says he has no more magic left, much of the speech, as shown by the bolded text, shows him still using the spoken patterns of magic and incantation [2] (it seems he cannot let go, at least unconsciously).

And the onrushed F #2 - which joins as one his need for the audience's help; his admission for a second time that he lacks 'Art to inchant', and the realisation that only 'praier' can relieve him — suggests that now perhaps exhausted (see the previous two speeches and in this speech the F #2 opening 'Which is most faint' and add in the earlier statement 'Every third thought shall be my grave'), his ability to present himself and his needs with complete clarity is somewhat impaired.

- one of the very few unembellished lines sums up the speech completely, "But release me from my bands" and such an appeal to the audience from a man so used to power throughout the play must be both difficult and humbling, no wonder it's spoken so quietly

- the first four lines of the speech expressing his lack of 'Charmes' and thus he may be 'confinde' (either on the island or in the theatre is up to each actor to decide) are emotional (1/5)

- the first words after the ungrammatical F #1 ending period are set as an unembellished monosyllabic surround phrase which suggests the acknowledgement of being 'faint' is both difficult to admit and may well be very accurate

- yet the idea of being 'sent to Naples' as the alternative to being 'confinde' is voiced intellectually (5/1 the next four lines), but after the unembellished line discussed above the speech becomes somewhat quieter, his fear of his 'project' failing culminating in the sad surround phrase repetition of ': Now I want/Spirits to enforce : Art to inchant . . . ': only slightly passionate (3/2 in five lines), the sentence end of his 'despaire' being relieved by 'praier' becoming emotional once more

- and, possibly with tiredness claiming him once more, the speech ends quietly intellectually with a plea for the audience's 'Indulgence' (1/0, F #3)

#'s 5 - 6: PROSPERO'S ATTEMPTS TO CONTROL HIS SPIRITS

5/ Ariel   **To every Article.**   between 1.2.195 - 215

Background: Prospero created the opening tempest (see speech #15 below) in order to both frighten and separate the various parties on-board so as to deal with them more easily.

Ariel, Prospero's main confidant and chief controller of all the other spirits at Prospero's command, had some very specific tasks to perform without which Prospero's plans cannot come to fruition. The following is a response to Prospero's direct question 'Hast thou, Spirit,/Perform'd to point, the Tempest that I bad thee'.

Style: as part of a two-handed scene, with a third person sleeping on-stage

Where: unspecified, but somewhere close to Prospero's cell and close to Caliban's cave

To Whom: Prospero, in front of the sleeping Miranda

# of Lines: 19   **Probable Timing: 1.00 minutes**

Modern Text

5/ Ariel

1   To every ᐃarticle .

2   I boarded* the King's ship; now on the ᐃbeak*,
Now in the [*waist*], the ᐃdeck*, in every ᐃcabin ,
I flam'd amazement . †

3   Sometime I'd* divide,
And burn* in many places; on the ᐃtop°mast,
The ᐃyards and ᐃbore°sprit*, would I flame distinctly,
Then meet* and join* .

4   Jove's ᐃlightning, the precursors
O'th'dreadful* ᐃthunder-claps, more momentary*
And sight-outrunning were not; the fire and cracks
Of sulphurous roaring, the most mighty Neptune
Seem* to besiege, and make his bold waves tremble,
Yea, his dread ᐃtrident shake.

5   Not a soul*
But felt a ᐃfever* of the mad*, and play'd*
Some tricks of desperation. †

6   All but ᐃmariners
Plung'd in the foaming brine*, and quit the vessel* ;
Then all afire with me, the King's son*, Ferdinand,
With hair* up-staring (then like reeds, not hair*),
Was the first man that leapt; cried*, "ᐃHell is empty,
And all the ᐃdevils* are here*" .

First Folio

5/ Ariel

1   To every Article.

2   I boorded the Kings ship: ₓ now on the Beake,
Now in the [Waste], the Decke, in every Cabyn,
I flam'd amazement, sometime I'll divide ⁺
And burne in many places; on the Top-mast,
The Yards and Bore-spritt, would I flame distinctly,
Then meete,ₓ and joyne.

3   Joves Lightning, the precursers
O'th dreadfull Thunder-claps⁺ more momentarie
And sight out-running were not; the fire,ₓ and cracks
Of sulphurous roaring, the most mighty Neptune
Seeme to besiege, and make his bold waves tremble,
Yea, his dread Trident shake. {→}
════════════════════

4   Not a soule
But felt a Feaver of the madde, and plaid
Some tricks of desperation; all but Mariners
Plung'd in the foaming bryne, and quit the vessell ;
Then all a fire with me⁺ the Kings sonne⁺ Ferdinand ⁺
With haire up-staring (then like reeds, not haire)⁺
Was the first man that leapt; cride⁺ hell is empty,
And all the Divels are heere.

That Ariel is more a spirit of instant response and emotion rather than considered intellectual logic can be seen not simply in the releases throughout the speech, but also that, within the major punctuation, there are five emotional semicolons to just one colon, and just three surround phrases.

• after the very careful short F#1 reassuring Prospero he has done exactly as commanded (1/0), Ariel's reporting of the overall details is very passionate (8/10 in F #2's five and half lines . . .

• . . . while the vainglorious comparison of his own appearances to that of 'Jove's Lightning' is somewhat more restrained, and slightly more intellectual than emotional (4/2, five and half lines of F #3)

• the surround phrases seem those of a triumphant (child-like?) story-teller - the first of which opens F # 2 (logical thanks to the colon), announcing success ' . I boorded the Kings ship : '; the second is emotional (thanks to the semicolon), explaining how he kept safe the minor characters with no part to play in the ensuing unfolding of events, ' ; all but Mariners/Plung'd in the foaming bryne, and quit the vessell ; '; the last, that ends the speech, deals with the successful separation of Ferdinand, who '; cride hell is empty,/And all the Divels are heere . ', from those who are to be punished

• thus it's not surprising that the F #4 build-up to all but 'Mariners' quitting the vessel because they all 'felt a Feaver of the madde' is emotional (2/5), enhanced by two closely set emotional semicolons, and the description of Ferdinand's separation, one of the prime objectives he had to perform, also remains emotional (3/5, the last three and a half lines of the speech)

6/ Caliban   **All the infections that the Sunne suckes up**   2.2.1-17

Background: Now gathering the wood as Prospero charged, and alone, Caliban gives vent to his feelings, presumably in part trying to win the audience to his side.

Style: solo

Where: somewhere uninhabited on the island, possibly near the shore   **To Whom:** direct audience address

# of Lines: 17   **Probable Timing: 0.55 minutes**

Modern Text

6/ Caliban

1 All the infections that the △sun* sucks* up
From △bogs, △fens, △flats, on Prospero fall, and make him
By inch*-meal* a disease ! †

        His △spirits hear* me,
And yet I needs* must curse.

2

                But they'll nor pinch,
3 Fright me with △urchin*-shows*, pitch me i'th mire,
Nor lead me, like a fire°brand, in the dark*
Out of my way, unless* he bid'em; but
For every trifle are they set upon me,
Sometime like △apes that mow* and chatter at me,
And after bite me ; then like △hedge*°hogs which
Lie* tumbling in my bare°foot°* way, and mount
Their pricks at my foot°fall; sometime am I
All wound with △adders, who with cloven tongues
Do* hiss* me into madness* . †

[Enter Trinculo]

                Lo, now △lo,
4 Here comes a △spirit of his, and to torment me
For bringing wood in slowly. †

                I'll fall flat,
5 Perchance he will not mind* me.

First Folio

6/ Caliban

1 All the infections that the Sunne suckes up
From Bogs, Fens, Flats, on Prospero fall, and make him
By ynch-meale a disease : + his Spirits heare me,
And yet I needes must curse.

2

                But they'll nor pinch,
Fright me with Urchyn-shewes, pitch me i'th mire,
Nor lead me + like a fire-brand, in the darke
Out of my way, unlesse he bid'em; but
For every trifle,ₓ are they set upon me,
Sometime like Apes,ₓ that moe and chatter at me,
And after bite me : ₓ then like Hedg-hogs,ₓ which
Lye tumbling in my bare-foote way, and mount
Their pricks at my foot-fall : ₓ sometime am I
All wound with Adders, who with cloven tongues
Doe hisse me into madnesse :

[Enter Trinculo]

                Lo, now Lo,
Here comes a Spirit of his, and to torment me
For bringing wood in slowly : I'le fall flat,
Perchance he will not minde me.

Even though the first sentences match, thereafter F's single onrushed sentence shows a far more disturbed character than do the five sentences most modern texts split it into: and F's orthography shows an interesting pattern in that after the opening passionate explosion (6/6), despite the onrushed F #2, Caliban begins to calm down and establish some form of self control.

• that Caliban can never be in full control is summed up in the surround phrase that ends F #1, ': his Spirits heare me./And yet I needes must curse. ', while the somewhat longer surround phrases that end the speech sum up both his fears and his response to danger

    ": then like Hedg-hogs, which/Lye tumbling in my bare-foote way, and
    mount/Their pricks at my foot-fall : sometime am I/All wound with
    Adders, who with cloven tongues/Doe hisse me into madnesse : Lo,
    now Lo,/Here comes a Spirit of his, and to torment me /For bringing
    wood in slowly : I'le fall flat,/Perchance he will not minde me."

• Caliban seems to want to present himself as a calm character, only to have this mask suddenly destroyed by bursts of release as with the emotional 'Sunne suckes up' and the intellectual 'Bogs, Fens, Flats, on Prosper fall' all in the first sentence; or the emotional 'Doe hisse me into madnesse' and the intellectual ': Lo, now Lo,/Here comes a Spirit of his,' in the second sentence

• the explosion of the first sentence (6/6 in just three and a half lines) becomes more controlled, that is, proportionately less releases (just 4/9 in F #2's first ten lines) but nevertheless emotional rather than intellectual in describing what Prospero's 'Spirits' do to him – an attempt at gaining the audience's empathy/sympathy perhaps?

• the (mistaken) realisation that Prospero has sent another 'Spirit' to torment him (in fact the character entering is the very human Trinculo, jester to Alonso) is intellectual (3/0), while the plan to avoid detection by falling 'flat' is spoken very quietly (0/1), perhaps as if not to give himself away

#'s 7 - 9: MILAN'S SINNERS AND HONEST MEN

7/ Anthonio {I} did supplant {my} Brother Prospero, between 2.1.269 - 296

Background: Whatever his own agenda (probably to stop paying tribute to Alonso for his help in supplanting Prospero), Anthonio seems hell-bent on persuading Sebastian, Alonso's younger brother, to oust Alonso as King of Naples, just as he, Anthonio, usurped Prospero's throne. One note: line 17's 'Sir Prudence' is a belittling term for Gonzalo.

Style: as part of a two-handed scene in front of a larger sleeping group
Where: unspecified, somewhere on the island   **To Whom:** Sebastian, in front of the sleeping Alonso, Gonzalo, Adrian, Francisco, and unspecified 'others'
# of Lines: 22   **Probable Timing: 1.10 minutes**

Modern Text

7/ Anthonio

1 {ψ} {I} did supplant {my} △brother Prospero {,}
And look* how well my △garments sit upon me,
Much feater [than] before. †

2 My △brother's servants
Were then my fellows*, now they are my men.

3 {ψ} {As for my} conscience {,}
{ψ}Ay*, △sir ; where lies that?

4 If 'twere a kibe* ,
This △deity in my bosom* . †

5 Twenty* conscences,
That stand 'twixt me and Milan* , candied be they,
And melt ere they molest*! †

6 Here* lies your △brother,
No better [than] the earth he lies upon,
If he were that which now he's* like - that's dead,
Whom I with this obedient steel* , three inches of it,
Can lay to bed for ever ; whiles you, doing thus,
To the perpetual* wink* for aye might put
This ancient morsel* , this Sir Prudence, who
Should not upbraid our course. †

7   For all the rest,
They'll* take suggestion as a △cat laps milk* ;
They'll* tell the clock*, to any business* that
We say befits the hour*.

8 Draw together ;
And when I rear* my hand, do you the like,
To fall it on Gonzalo.

First Folio

7/ Anthonio

1 {ψ} {I} did supplant {my} Brother Prospero {,}
And looke how well my Garments sit upon me,
Much feater [then] before: My Brothers servants
Were then my fellowes, now they are my men.

2 {ψ} {As for my} conscience {,}

3 {ψ}I+ Sir : x where lies that?
                                    If 'twere a kybe+
'Twould put me to my slipper : x But I feele not
This Deity in my bosome: 'Twentie consciences+
That stand 'twixt me,x and Millaine, candied be they,
And melt ere they mollest:+ Heere lies your Brother,
No better [then] the earth he lies upon,
If he were that which now hee's like x(that's dead)x
Whom I with this obedient steele x(three inches of it)x
Can lay to bed for ever : x whiles you+ doing thus,
To the perpetuall winke for aye might put
This ancient morsell: x this Sir Prudence, who
Should not upbraid our course: for all the rest+
They'l take suggestion,x as a Cat laps milke,+
They'l tell the clocke, to any businesse that
We say befits the houre.   {↑→}

4 Draw together : x
And when I reare my hand, do you the like+
To fall it on Gonzalo.

Here Anthonio presents a very interesting method of persuasive attack to get **what he needs - a sudden flurry of surround phrases to introduce or fortify the point he wants accepted, and then he relaxes somewhat so the other person can seemingly make their own decision.**

• thus, at the end of F #1 through to the third line of F #3, five successive surround phrases/lines convey the idea that conscience need not get in the way of absolute power

": My Brothers servants/Were then my fellowes, now they are my men. As for my conscience, I Sir : where lies that ? If 'twere a kybe 'Twould put me to my slipper : But I feele not/This Deity in my bosome : "

• and in F #3, two more phrases to his need to get rid of Gonzalo

": whiles you doing thus,/To the perpetuall winke for aye might put/This ancient morsell : this Sir Prudence, who/Should not upbraid our course : "

• in his attempt to seduce Sebastian, Anthonio gets straight to the point with a highly intellectual description of seizing and enjoying power (5/2, F #1)

• F #2's dismissal of 'conscience' starts a little more carefully, via a careful short sentence (1/0) composed of surround phrases; but having begun to put aside Sebastian's possible objection and potential fear, Anthonio swiftly moves into overwhelm mode as he disavows any possibility of such an abstract notion standing 'twixt me, and Millaine,' passionate intellect and emotion hard at work for F #3's first four and half lines (6/4)

• introducing the idea of killing both King Alonso (Sebastian's brother) and his advisor Gonzalo ('This ancient morsell'), Anthonio becomes totally emotional (0/5 the next five and half lines), though his further scornful description of Gonzalo as 'Sir Prudence' becomes momentarily intellectual (2/0)

• while his dismissal of the remainder as taking 'suggestion, as a Cat laps milke' turns emotional once more (1/4, the last three lines of F #3)

• and, apparently having succeeded in moving Sebastian to action, the last sentence becomes careful (1/1, F #4), the first phrase containing a moment of emotional encouragement to strike (via the word 'reare'), the second one of specific fact (directing Sebastian's murderous act towards 'Gonzalo')

8/ Ariel   You are three men of sinne, whom destiny   3.3.53 - 82

Background: In accordance with Prospero's ever-more urgent needs, Ariel takes to task the three sinners in Alonso's party - taking the shape of a Harpy (a mythical beast of terrifying appearance and voice) in order to frighten them even more. One note: in line 8, after 'Their proper selves', most modern texts add variations of the stage direction 'Alonso, Sebastian and Anthonio (attempt to) draw their swords'.

Style: full public address, specifically to three people in front of others

Where: unspecified, somewhere on the island   **To Whom:** Alonso, Anthonio & Sebastian, in front of Gonzalo, Adrian, Francisco, and unspecified 'others'

# of Lines: 30   **Probable Timing: 1.30 minutes**

Modern Text

8/ Ariel

1 You are three men of sin*, whom ᐃDestiny,
That hath to instrument this lower world
And what is in't, the never surfeited ᐃsea
Hath caus'd to belch up you; and on this ᐃisland
Where man doth not inhabit - you 'mongst men
Being most unfit to live. †
    I have made you mad;

2 And even with such like valor* men hang, and drown*
Their proper selves . †
    You fools*! †
    I and my fellows*

3   I and my fellows* .†

4 Are ministers of Fate. . †
    The ᐃelements,

5 Of whom your swords are temper'd, may as well
Wound the loud winds*, or with bemock'd-at °ᐃstabs
Kill the still closing waters, as diminish
One dowle that's in my plume* . †

6   My fellow ministers

7 Are like ° invulnerable . †
    If you could hurt,

8 Your swords are now too massy* for your strengths,
And will not be uplifted. †
    But remember

(For that's my business* to you) that you three
From Milan* did supplant good Prospero,
Expos'd unto the ᐃsea (which hath requit it)
Him, and his innocent child*; for which foul* deed
The ᐃpow'rs, delaying (not forgetting), have
Incens'd the ᐃseas and ᐃshores - yea, all the ᐃcreatures,
Against your peace. †

First Folio

8/ Ariel

1 You are three men of sinne, whom destiny[+]
That hath to instrument this lower world[x]
And what is in't: [x] the never surfeited Sea.[x]
Hath caus'd to belch up you; and on this Island,[x]
Where man doth not inhabit, you 'mongst men,[x]
Being most unfit to live: I have made you mad;
And even with such like valour,[x] men hang, and drowne
Their proper selves: you fooles: [+] I and my fellowes
Are ministers of Fate, the Elements[+]
Of whom your swords are temper'd, may as well
Wound the loud windes, or with bemockt-at-Stabs
Kill the still closing waters, as diminish
One dowle that's in my plumbe: My fellow ministers
Are like-invulnerable: if you could hurt,
Your swords are now too massie for your strengths,
And will not be uplifted: But remember
(For that's my businesse to you) that you three
From Millaine did supplant good Prospero,
Expos'd unto the Sea (which hath requit it)
Him, and his innocent childe: [x] for which foule deed,[x]
The Powres, delaying (not forgetting)[x] have
Incens'd the Seas,[x] and Shores;[x] yea, all the Creatures[+]
Against your peace: Thee of thy Sonne, Alonso[+]

Considering that F sets the speech as just one onrushed sentence which most modern texts split into nine, it is that suggested the reader explore the stepping stones of the modern text first before trying to put F's onrush together. However, since Ariel's task is to madden Alonso, Sebastian, and Anthonio by the end of the speech, F's one sentence can do much to create the continual relentless build needed to achieve such a result. Interestingly, to prevent overplaying, the speech is very careful to intersperse several extended unembellished lines amongst a text which is rarely over-melodramatic, at least as far as releases are concerned.

• thus, after a slightly emotional first phrase precisely pinpointing their guilt as 'men of sinne', (0/1) come the first two unembellished lines suggesting that the fates are judging them

"whom destiny/That hath to instrument this lower world, /And what is in't"
and after a line and a half of intellectual reminder (2/0) that they now belong to the whim of nature ('the never surfeited Sea', and 'on this Island') comes the terrifying (to them)

"Where man doth not inhabit, you 'mongst men, /Being most unfit to live : 1
    have made you mad ."

the emotional caper following suggests that they should commit suicide (0/2)

• their attempt to draw their swords is easily foiled, and then mocked emotionally and intellectually (3/4, the next six lines), finishing with the calm statement that

": if you could hurt,/Your swords are now too massie for your strengths,/And will not be uplifted :"

• the stark reminder that what they did to Prospero 'and his innocent childe' has caused the 'Powres' to work against their peace is now more intellectual than emotional (8/4), as pronouncing the punishment for Alonso, the losse 'of thy Sonne' (3/1)

9
       Thee of thy △son*, Alonso,
They have bereft; and do* pronounce by me
Ling'ring perdition (worse [than] any death
Can be at once) shall step, by step attend
You and your ways*, whose wraths to guard you from -
Which here, in this most desolate △isle, else falls
Upon your heads - is nothing but heart's △ sorrow,
And a clear* life ensuing.

• and then, Ariel finishes quite calmly, perhaps ensuring that they clearly understand their punishment to come, perhaps also signifying his mission is almost accomplished, for the final six lines are only slightly emotionally released (1/3), the final sets of unembellished lines establishing a terrible fate
"Ling'ring perdition (worse then any death/Can be at once) shall step, by step attend/You,"
"else fals/Upon your heads, is nothing but hearts-sorrow"

• and Ariel's surround phrases seem to stress the powerlessness of the human party to withstand the supernatural forces opposing them
" : the never surfeited Sea,/Hath caus'd to belch up you ; "
" : I have made you mad ; /And even with such like valour, men hang, and drowne/Their proper selves : "
" : My fellow ministers/Are like-invulnerable : "
" ; yea, all the Creatures/Against your peace : Thee of thy Sonne, Alonso/ They have bereft ; "
all but my 'fellow ministers' enhanced by being formed in part by the emotional semicolon

They have bereft ; and doe pronounce by me
Lingring perdition (worse [then] any death
Can be at once) shall step, by step attend
You,$_x$ and your wayes, whose wraths to guard you from,
Which here, in this most desolate Isle, else fals
Upon your heads, is nothing but hearts-sorrow,
And a cleere life ensuing.

9/ Gonzalo   **Had I plantation of this Isle my Lord,**   between 2.1.144 - 168

Background: Described by Prospero both as a 'Noble Neopolitan' and 'Holy Gonzalo', Gonzalo is doing anything he can to bring Alonso, the King of Naples, distraught at the apparent drowning death of his son Ferdinand, back into a sense of current reality and responsibility so as to unite the increasingly bickering fragmented group (the two factions being the darker forces of Anthonio and Sebastian on the one hand, and the leaderless remainder, including 'good' Gonzalo, on the other).

Style: one on one address in front of a larger group

Where: unspecified, somewhere on the island   **To Whom:** Alonso, in front of Sebastian, Anthonio, Adrian and Francisco, and an unspecified number of 'others'

# of Lines: 19   **Probable Timing: 1.00 minutes**

Modern Text	First Folio
9/ Gonzalo	**9/ Gonzalo**
1 Had I plantation of this △isle my △lord -	1 Had I plantation of this Isle my Lord {,}
And were the △king on't, what would I do?	And were the King on't, what would I do?
2 I'th' △commonwealth I would, by contraries,	2 I'th'Commonwealth I would x (by contraries)x
Execute all things ; △ for no kind* of △traffic*	Execute all things : x For no kinde of Trafficke
Would I admit ; △ no name of △magistrate ;	Would I admit : x No name of Magistrate : x
Letters should not be known* ; △ riches, poverty,	Letters should not be knowne : x Riches, poverty,
And use of service, none ; △contract, △succession,	And use of service, none : x Contract, Succession,
[Bourn]* , bound of △land, △tilth, △vineyard none ;	[Borne], bound of Land, Tilth, Vineyard none : x
No use of △metal* , △corn* , or △wine, or △oil* ;	No use of Mettall, Corne, or Wine, or Oyle : x
No occupation, all men idle, all ;	No occupation, all men idle, all : x
And △women too, but innocent and pure ;	And Women too, but innocent and pure : x
No △sovereignty- ◊	No Soveraignty.
All things in common △nature should produce	All things in common Nature should produce
Without sweat or endeavor* : △ treason, felony* ,	Without sweat or endevour : Treason, fellony,
Sword, △pike, △knife, △gun, or need* of any △engine,	Sword, Pike, Knife, Gun, or neede of any Engine +
Would I not have ; but △nature should bring forth,	Would I not have : x but Nature should bring forth +
Of it own* kind* , all foison* , all abundance,	Of it owne kinde, all foyzon, all abundance +
To feed my innocent people.	To feed my innocent people.
3 I would with such perfection govern* , Sir,	4 I would with such perfection governe + Sir : x
T'△excel* the △golden △age.	T'Excell the Golden Age.

This sequence is often played as one long boring blab, yet F's orthography clearly shows a key difference in conception and realisation between (the discoveries of) F #2 and (the resultant reverie of F #3).

1

• in trying to get Alonso's attention, Gonzalo opens quite intellectually (4/0, F #1 and the first line and half of F #2), but once the idea of ruling by 'contraries' is voiced, so his pattern completely changes

2

• the lengthy F #2 itemising how this would work is composed entirely of ten surround phrases, and whether this is an attempt to get through to the distracted Alonso, or is indicative of his own mind running rampant with the somewhat revolutionary ideas (though modern editors suggest that this passage is meant as a criticism of the rather startling propositions of the French philosopher Montaigne) is up to each actor to decide

• the first explorations in the denial-of-status-distinction ideas from 'For no kinde of Trafficke/Would I admit' through to 'And use of service, none', is passionate (4/3 in just three lines), and then moving into concerns of business and the impact of the new order on human beings becomes intellectual (11/3, the last five lines of F #2)

3

• and with F #3's utopian overview, the surround phrases, if such still can be said to exist, become much longer, and though the suggestion that 'Nature' should be allowed to develop without 'sweat or endevour' still remains intellectual (6/3, the first three and half lines of F #3), the shift into the idealistic hope that 'Nature should bring forth/Of it owne kinde' becomes (delightedly?) emotional (1/3)

4

• F #4's intellectual, surpassing the 'Golden Age', finale (4/2) is heightened by being expressed once again via two surround phrases

#'s 10 - 14: A STRANGE CONPIRACY; CALIBAN, TRINCULO, AND STEPHANO

10/ Trinculo   Here's neither bush, nor shrub to beare off any   2.2.18–41

Background: The first speech for one of the shipwrecked Neapolitans, Trinculo, jester to Alonso, who has just 'swom ashore like a Ducke'.   Keeping in mind that the second sentence marks his discovery of the inadequately camouflaged Caliban, the speech is self-explanatory.   Considering that F sets the speech as just two sentences which most modern texts split into seventeen, it is suggested that the reader explore the stepping stones of the modern text first before trying to put F's onrush together, and even then, as an intermediary step, it might be worthwhile considering redividing F to match the modern text sentence structure as follows; mt. #1-5, the impending storm; #6-8, a man or a fish?; #9-11, how much money I could make in England; #12-14, the decision that this is 'an Islander'; #15-16, what to do now the storm's here; #17, the finale.

Style: solo

Where: on an open part of the island   **To Whom:** direct audience address

# of Lines: 25   **Probable Timing: 1.15 minutes**

Modern Text	First Folio

10/ Trinculo

1 Here's neither bush nor shrub to bear* off any weather at all. †

2 And another △storm* brewing, I hear* it sing i'th' wind*. †

3 Yond same black* cloud, yond huge one, looks* like a foul* bumbard that would shed his liquor*. †

4 If it should thunder as it did before, I know not where to hide my head. †

5 Yond same cloud cannot choose but fall by pail*°fuls.

6 What have we here? a man, or a fish? dead or alive? †

7 A fish, he° smells* like a fish; a very ancient and fish-like smell; a kind* of, not of the newest poor*-John. †

8 A strange fish ! †

9 Were I in England now (as once I was) and had but this fish painted, not a holiday △°fool* there but would give a piece* of silver. †

10 There would this △monster, make a man; any strange beast there makes a man. †

11 When they will not give a doit to relieve a lame △beggar*, they will lay out ten to see a dead Indian. †

12 Legg'd* like a man; and his △fins* like △arms*! †

13 Warm* , o'my troth ! †

10/ Trinculo

1 Here's neither bush,ₓ nor shrub to beare off any weather at all: and another Storme brewing, I heare it sing ith' winde: yond same blacke cloud, yond huge one, lookes like a foule bumbard that would shed his liquor: if it should thunder,ₓ as it did before, I know not where to hide my head: yond same cloud cannot choose but fall by paile-fuls.

2   What have we here, + a man, or a fish? dead or alive? a fish, hee smels like a fish: a very ancient and fish-like smell: ₓ a kinde of, not of the newest poore-john: a strange fish: + were I in England now (as once I was) and had but this fish painted;ₓ not a holiday-foole there but would give a peece of silver: would this Monster, make a man: any strange beast there,ₓ makes a man: when they will not give a doit to relieve a lame Begger, they will lay out ten to see a dead Indian: Leg'd like a man; and his Finnes like Armes: + warme + o'my troth: + I doe now let loose my

That the onrushed speech is composed almost entirely of surround phrases (at least twenty-four) suggests a character who is working very hard to accommodate himself to the strangeness of his new surroundings, and it is not surprising that here Trinculo is more emotional than intellectual, having made his way from the shipwreck to the island, as he describes it later because he 'swom ashore . . . like a Ducke'.

• accordingly, the fact of the storm coming (the modern texts' first three sentences) is emotional (1/8, the first four lines of the speech), especially marked by the two surround phrases that open the speech

• and it may be that Trinculo is afraid of 'thunder', for the remaining two and half lines of F #1 are completely unembellished save for the last word anticipating the awful amount of rain that is bounds to fall, 'paile-fuls'

• he may also be frightened by the discovery of Caliban 'What have we here, a man or a fish? dead or alive ? ' for not only is this opening of F #2 also unembellished and monosyllabic, as with F #1 it starts with two surround phrases

• Caliban's smell (mt. #7) is responded to emotionally (1/3 in two lines), while the thought of having such a fish in England, leading to riches, becomes somewhat intellectual for the first time in the speech (4/2, the six lines equal to mt. 9-11)

{ctd. over}

14   I do* now let loose my
opinion, hold it no longer: this is no fish, but an ᵃislan-
der, that hath lately suffered by a ᵃthunderbolt. †
                                        Alas,
the storm* is come again*! †
15
16   My best way is to creep* under his ᵃgaberdine; there is no other shelter hereabout. †
17   Misery acquaints a man with strange bedfel-
lows*; I will here shroud* till the dregs* of the storm*
be past.

• the final conjecture that Caliban might be 'an Islander' felled by a 'Thunderbolt', is passionate (5/4, the three line equivalent of mt. #12-14), though approaching Caliban to make this assessment may be somewhat disturbing for Trinculo, since there are three emotional semicolons set within the passage; affecting four of the six surround phrases the discovery/decision is couched in

• again, the approaching storm seems to disturb him, for the surround phrase- ': Alas, the storme is come againe : 'has three releases in six words (1/2)

• and while the initial decision, smell not withstanding, to 'creepe under his Gaberdine' for shelter/safety is passionate, the idea (and/or smell) may be repugnant to him for the immediate follow-up is the unembellished surround phrase ': there is no other shelter hereabout :', in turn succeeded by a somewhat heartfelt and released surround phrase maxim (1/1) ': Misery acquaints a man with strange bedfellowes :'

• the very last (surround) monosyllabic phrase becomes highly emotional ': I will here shrowd till the dregges of the storme be past.' (0/3), though whether this signifies fear (of the storm), joy (at being partly sheltered), or disgust (at the smell) is up to each actor to decide

opinion; ₓ hold it no longer; ⁺ this is no fish, but an Islander, that hath lately suffered by a Thunderbolt : Alas,
the storme is come againe :⁺ my best way is to creepe under his Gaberdine : ₓ there is no other shelter hereabout : Misery acquaints a man with strange bedfellowes : ₓ I will here shrowd till the dregges of the storme
be past.

11/ Caliban   I have seene thee in {the Moone} : and I doe adore thee: between 2.2.139 - 172

Background: Apart from Miranda and Prospero, these are the only humans Caliban has met, and, dressed in their finery, Caliban believes them to 'be fine things', and if they be not sprights', and having drunk from Stephano's bottle is already favouring Stephano, remarking in an aside 'that's a brave god, and beares Celestiall liquor: I will kneele to him'. The following is Caliban's serious full-belief response to Stephano's assurance that he has stepped from heaven, 'Out o'th Moone I doe assure thee. I was the/Man ith'Moone when time was'.

Style: as part of a three-handed scene

Where: on an open part of the island   **To Whom:** Stephano in front of Trinculo

# of Lines: 15   **Probable Timing: 0.50 minutes**

Modern Text

11/ Caliban

1 I haveseen*theein {the △moon*}, and I do*adorethee.†
        My
2 △mistress*, show'd me thee, and thy △dog, and thy △bush.

3 I'll show thee every fertile* inch* o'th △island - and I will kiss* thy foot*. †

        I prithee* be my god.
4

5 I'll show thee the best △springs; I'll pluck* thee △berries; I'll fish for thee, and get thee wood enough.

6 A plague upon the △tyrant that I serve! †

7 I'll bear* him no more △sticks*, but follow thee, Thou wondrous man.

8 I prithee* let me bring thee where △crabs grow; And I with my long nails* will dig* thee pig-nuts, Show thee a △jay's* nest, and instruct thee how To snare the nimble △marmazet. †

               I'll bring thee
9
               I'll get thee
10 To clust'ring △filberts*, and sometimes I'll get thee Young △scamels from the △rock*. †

               Wilt thou go* with me?

First Folio

11/ Caliban

1 I have seene thee in {the Moone} :+ and I doe adore thee:+ My Mistris shew'd me thee, and thy Dog, and thy Bush.

2 Ile shew thee every fertill ynch 'oth Island: x and I will kisse thy foote: I prethee be my god.

3 I'le shew thee the best Springs: x I'le plucke thee Berries: x and get thee wood enough.

4 A plague upon the Tyrant that I serve;+ I'le beare him no more Stickes, but follow thee, thou wondrous man.

5 I'prethee let me bring thee where Crabs grow; and I with my long nayles will digge thee pig-nuts; x show thee a Jayes nest, and instruct thee how to snare the nimble Marmazet: I'le bring thee to clustring Philbirts, and sometimes I'le get thee young Scamels from the Rocke: Wilt thou goe with me?

The overall onrush, the quick stylistic switches in the first four sentences, the large number of colons (and surround phrases) opening the speech turning into semicolons after about a third of the way through, all reinforce the idea of a Caliban overwhelmed by the thought of meeting a 'God' that can free him. Also, F's setting shows Caliban starting in verse (shaded text) and finishing in prose (as his excitement gets the better of him, perhaps?): most modern texts set the last six sentences as verse .

• thus, breaking down the surround-phrase sentences F #1 - start of F #5

a/ F #1, line one is highly emotional (1/3), line two intellectual (3/0)

b/ F #2, the first line and a half very emotional (1/4), the slightly embellished last phrase which really sums the whole speech ': I prethee be my god .'

c/ F #3, the first line and half passionate (2/1), the last two unembellished phrases promising 'god'': I'le fish for thee; and get thee wood enough .'

d/ F #4's cursing of the 'Tyrant' (Prospero) is passionate (2/2), intensified by the emotional (semicolon created) surround phrase, the worship of Stephano heightened by ending the sentence 'but follow thee, thou wondrous man' totally unembellished

e/ F #5's details of what Caliban will obtain for Stephano start carefully, ('Crabs', line one 1/1), become emotional ('pig-nuts', 0/2, line two), then passionate ('Jayes nest' and 'Marmazet', line three and half, 2/1): however, with the best saved for the last ('Philbirts' and 'Scamels') the next two lines are intellectual (3/1)

• and quite naturally, the final five word surround phrase plea ': Wilt thou goe with me ?' is passionate (1/1)

12/ Caliban   **As I told thee before, I am subject to a Tirant,**   between 3.2.42 – 105

Background: Caliban's attempt to seek the human's aid in wreaking the fullest possible revenge on Prospero has been frustratingly delayed by their continued drinking. Here he tries yet again, moving the scene from the casualness of prose that preceded this speech into the earnestness of verse.

Style: as part of a three-handed scene

Where: somewhere on the island   **To Whom:** Stephano and Trinculo

# of Lines: 21   **Probable Timing: 1.10 minutes**

Modern Text

12/ Caliban

1 As I told thee before, I am subject to a △tyrant*,
   A △sorcerer, that by his cunning hath
   Cheated me of the △island.

2 (ψ) As I told thee, 'tis a custom* with him,
   I'th afternoon* to sleep*.

3   There thou mayst brain* him,
   Having first seiz'd his bookes*; △ or with a log*
   Batter his skull, or paunch him with a stake,
   Or cut his wezand with thy knife.

4   Remember
   First to possess* his △books*; for without them
   He's* but a △sot, as I am; nor hath not
   One △spirit to command: they all do hate him
   As rootedly as I.

5   Burn* but his △books* . †

6 He has brave △utensils (for so he calls* them)
   Which, when he has a house, he'll* deck* withall* .

7 And that most deeply to consider, is
   The beauty* of his daughter. †   He himself*

8 Calls* her a non°pareil* . †

9   I never saw a woman,
   But only* Sycorax my △dam, and she;
   But she as far* surpasseth Sycorax
   As great'st does* least.

10 (ψ) She will become thy bed, I warrant,
   And bring thee forth brave brood.

Commentary

12/ Caliban

• F #1's background reminder is handled swiftly and factually (3/0)

• however, the new details of when and how Prospero can be killed are highly emotional, with the speech's first surround phrase making Caliban's intentions very clear
  " : there thou maist braine him,/Having first seiz'd his bookes : "

• the importance of the 'Bookes' is emphasised both by the second set of surround phrases, encompassed in a passionate surround phrase opening (3/3, F #3's first three lines), underscored by three of the four surround phrases being in part created by emotional semicolons
  " : Remember/First to possesse his Bookes; for without them/Hee's but a Sot, as I am; nor hath not/One Spirit to command: they all do hate him/As rootedly as I. "
  the comment about his fellow Spirits hating Prospero being totally unembellished (as if concerned that they may overhear him perhaps, see speech #6 above)

• this quickly turns into the highly emotional F #4 (2/6), which once more concentrates on where Caliban believes Prospero's power lies, starting with the terrifying phrase 'Burne but his Bookes'

• that he is still fixated on Prospero's daughter Miranda, whom, before the play opened, he attempted to ravish (see the background to speech #16), can be seen in the build of F #5-6, which deals solely with her, - from an unembellished line and half opening tribute to her 'beautie', through the surround phrase full of emotion (0/2) as he builds the enticement with a quote from Prospero
  "he himselfe/Cals her a non-pareill : "
  the passionate finish to the sentence (3/2, the last three lines) opening with the emotional surround phrase
  " : I never saw a woman/But onely Sycorax my Dam, and she; "

• and then, amazingly, in tempting Stephano with bedding Miranda, so Caliban turns to complete quiet, the whole of F #6 being unembellished, the last line 'And bring thee forth brave brood' further heightened by being monosyllabic – (it seems Caliban knows not only which buttons to press, but how – for anything excessive might just break the dream he hopes will finally move Stephano to action)

First Folio

12/ Caliban

1 As I told thee before, I am subject to a Tirant,
   A Sorcerer, that by his cunning hath cheated me
   Of the Island.

2 (ψ) As I told thee, 'tis a custome with him +
   I'th afternoone to sleepe: there thou maist braine him,
   Having first seiz'd his bookes : x Or with a logge
   Batter his skull, or paunch him with a stake,
   Or cut his wezand with thy knife.

                    Remember

3 First to possesse his Bookes; for without them
   Hee's but a Sot, as I am; nor hath not
   One Spirit to command: they all do hate him
   As rootedly as I.

4   Burne but his Bookes,
   He ha's brave Utensils (for so he calles them)
   Which + when he ha's a house, hee'l decke withall.

5 And that most deeply to consider, is
   The beautie of his daughter: he himselfe
   Cals her a non-pareill: I never saw a woman +
   But onely Sycorax my Dam, and she;
   But she as farre surpasseth Sycorax, x
   As great'st do's least.

6 (ψ)   She will become thy bed, I warrant,
   And bring thee forth brave brood.

13/ Caliban   Be not affeard, the Isle is full of noyses,   3.2.135 - 143

Background: Unbeknownst to the conspirators, Ariel has been listening to Caliban's attempt to enlist Stephano and Trinculo in his plot to kill Prospero. Trying to distract them, Ariel starts to play back to them the tune of the aggressive catch of attack that they have been singing in celebration. Since he is invisible, Trinculo and Stephano become very alarmed, and thus, in the following, Caliban tries to reassure them.

Style: as part of a three-handed scene

Where: somewhere on the island   **To Whom:** Stephano and Trinculo, in front of the invisible Ariel

# of Lines: 9   **Probable Timing: 0.30 minutes**

Modern Text

13/ Caliban

1 Be not afeard*; the ᐃisle is full of noises*,
Sounds and sweet airs*, that give delight and hurt not.†

2 Sometimes a thousand twangling ᐃinstruments
Will hum about mine ears*; and sometime voices,
That, if I then had wak'd after long sleep*,
Will make me sleep* again*: and then, in dreaming,
The clouds methought would open and show riches
Ready to drop upon me, that, when I wak'd,
I cried* to dream* again*.

First Folio

13/ Caliban

1 Be not affeard,⁺ the Isle is full of noyses,
Sounds,ₓ and sweet aires, that give delight and hurt not:
Sometimes a thousand twangling Instruments
Will hum about mine eares; and sometime voices,
That⁺ if I then had wak'd after long sleepe,
Will make me sleepe againe,⁺ and then⁺ in dreaming,
The clouds methought would open,ₓ and shew riches
Ready to drop upon me, that⁺ when I wak'd⁺
I cri'de to dreame againe.

With modern texts splitting F's onrushed single sentence in two, their speech becomes a matter of explanation: the original F setting allows Caliban to be caught up in his reverie from the start, the two extra breath thoughts (marked ₓ) allowing for extra details of delight.

• the opening overall description is passionate (2/4 the first three and a half lines) and then Caliban become emotional as the longing between waking and dreaming is expanded upon (0/6, the last five lines)

• the surround phrase ‘ : Sometimes a thousand twangling Instruments/Will hum about mine eares ; ’ created in part by the emotional semicolon, seems to point to the most wondrous of what the isle has to offer

• generally the few releases tend to come in small clusters, as ‘the Isle is full of noyses’ (1/1); ‘Will make me sleepe againe’ (0/2); and ‘I cri'de to dreame againe’ (0/3)

14/ Stephano Monster, your Fairy, {which} you say is a harmles Fairy, between 4.1.196 - 214

Background: In a further attempt to lead the conspirators astray and thus prevent them from attacking Prospero (see speech #12, and background to speech #13 above) Ariel has coaxed them, 'red-hot with drinking' as they are, to chase him through 'Tooth'd briars, sharpe firzes, pricking gosse, & thorns' until he left them 'I'th'filthy mantled poole beyond your Cell./There dancing up to th'chins, that the fowle Lake/Ore-stunck their foot'. The following is an outraged litany of complaints here assigned to Stephano, though the speech is in fact a construct compiled from eight separate speeches originally assigned to both Stephano and Trinculo.

Style: as part of a three-handed scene

Where: close to Prospero's cell   **To Whom:** Caliban in front of Trinculo

# of Lines: 13   **Probable Timing: 0.45 minutes**

Modern Text

14/ Stephano

1 Monster, your ᐃfairy, [which] you say is a harmless∗ ᐃfairy, has done little better [than] play'd∗ the Jack∗ with us.

2{ψ}   I do smell all horse-piss∗ ; at which my nose is in great indignation.

3 Do you hear∗ , ᐃmonster ? †

4   If I should take a displeasure against you, ᐃlook∗ you {,}

{ψ} thou wert but a lost ᐃmonster.

5{ψ}To loose our bottles in the ᐃpool∗ - there is not onely∗ disgrace and dishonor in that, monster, but an infinite loss{,} that's more

{ψ} to me [than] my wetting;   yet this is your harmless∗ ᐃfairy, ᐃmonster.

6   I will fetch off my bottle, though I be o'er ears∗ for my labor∗ .

First Folio

14/ Stephano

1 Monster, your Fairy, [w] you say is a harmles Fairy, Has done little better [then] plaid the Jacke with us.

2 {ψ}   I do smell all horse-pisse, + at which My nose is in great indignation.

3 Do you heare + Monster : + If I should Take a displeasure against you : x Looke you {,}

{ψ} Thou wert but a lost Monster.

4{ψ}To loose our bottles in the Poole {,}

    There is not onely disgrace and dishonor in that +
    Monster, but an infinite loss{,}

{ψ} That's more to me [then] my wetting: x
    Yet this is your harmlesse Fairy, Monster.

5 I will fetch off my bottle,
    Though I be o're eares for my labour.

Most modern texts set this passage as prose: however, F's verse suggests a Stephano vainly attempting to balance anger and drunkenness with the appearance of poise, equilibrium, and authority.

• the opening is deceptively intellectual (3/1, F #1), while the reference to smelling 'all horse-pisse' is similarly deceptively withheld, with just a slight tinge of emotion (F #2, 0/1)

• and then, as the scolding of Caliban begins, all decorum and most control disappear in the passionate F #3 (4/2, in just two and half lines) heightened by the three surround phrases through which the displeasure is expressed

• and, for the drinkers, it is the loss of 'our bottles in the Poole' that seems to cause the most distress, for F #4 starts emotionally (1/2) and then becomes unembellished for the truthfulness of the two mournful lines ' . . an infinite loss,/That's more to me than my wetting', which springs into the surround phrase explosion of

" : Yet this is your harmlesse Fairy, Monster . "

• so it's not surprising that the final decision of the speech to go and search for their lost drink ends totally emotionally 'Though I be o're eares for my labour.' (F #5, 0/2)

#'s 15 - 21: Two Young People Fall In Love

15/ Miranda   **If by your Art (my deerest father) you have**   1.2.1-13

Background: As her first speech in the play, chiding her father for creating such a dreadful tempest (see Ariel's speech #5 above), it is self-explanatory.

Style: as the opening speech of a two-handed scene

Where: unspecified, but somewhere close to her father's cell and close to Caliban's cave   **To Whom:** her father Prospero

# of Lines: 13   **Probable Timing:** 0.45 minutes

Modern Text

15/ Miranda

1 If by your ᐃart, my dearest* father, you have
   Put the wild waters in this ᐃroar*, allay* them. †
2 The sky* it seems* would pour* down stinking pitch,
   But that the ᐃsea, mounting to th' welkin's cheek* ,
   Dashes the fire out.
3   Oh!
4   I have suffered
   With those that I saw suffer. †
5   A brave vessel*
   (Who had, no doubt, some noble creature in her)
   Dash'd all to pieces*! †
6   O, the cry did knock*
   Against my very heart. †
7   Poor* souls* , they perish'd.
8 Had I been* any ᐃgod of power, I would
   Have sunk* the ᐃsea within the ᐃearth or ere
   It should the good ᐃship so have swallow'd, and
   The fraughting ᐃsouls* within her.

First Folio

15/ Miranda

1 If by your Art ₓ(my deerest father)ₓ you have
   Put the wild waters in this Rore;ₓ alay them:
   The skye it seemes would powre down stinking pitch,
   But that the Sea, mounting to th' welkins cheeke,
   Dashes the fire out.
2   Oh!
3   I have suffered
   With those that I saw suffer: A brave vessel
   (Who had ⁺ no doubt ⁺ some noble creature in her)
   Dash'd all to peeces: ⁺ O ⁺ the cry did knocke
   Against my very heart: poore soules, they perish'd.
4 Had I byn any God of power, I would
   Have suncke the Sea within the Earth,ₓ or ere
   It should the good Ship so have swallow'd, and
   The fraughting Soules within her.

Initially, F's onrushed #1 and especially #3 would suggest a much less rational character than that which most modern texts present (all in all eight sentences to F's four). However, F's orthography shows Miranda growing before our eyes, moving through emotional concerns to a fine intellectual moral judgement – an essential and necessary step before her father will expose her to the good of life (Ferdinand) after the bad (Caliban).

- it seems throughout the play that Miranda never masks her feelings, thus the opening two line surround phrases show her ability to stand up to her father for what she believes is right, and though the first line is passionate (1/1), she has sufficient self-control to not cloud the key second descriptive line and command, (although the semicolon in ' ; alay them : ' suggests that emotions are not too far from the surface)

- however, after the command, she becomes highly emotional (1/4, the next two and a half lines of F #1-2) ending with a rare (for F) exclamation mark

- that the opening of F #3 may not be just teenage hyperbole can be seen in the fact that her suffering is expressed as an unembellished surround phrase, and that the remaining three surround phrases which complete the sentence are filled with emotion (2/5, F #3's remaining three and a half lines)

- and then, through the pain, her intellect finally takes over as she takes a firm moral stand, preferring to destroy nature rather than sacrifice human life (5/3, F #4)

16/ Miranda   **Abhorred Slave, /Which any print of goodnesse wilt not take,**   1.2.351-362

Background: Prospero has so engineered matters that Miranda is forced to deal with the truth about Caliban (the potential dark side of life) before introducing her to the potential goodness of Ferdinand, even though Ferdinand is the son of his avowed enemy, Alonso. The following is triggered by Caliban's unrepentant response to her father's reminding him of his almost successful rape of Miranda 'Oh ho, oh ho, would't had been done:/ . . . I had peopel'd else/This Isle with Calibans'. One note: for some inexplicable reason quite a few commentators and even editors insist on re-assigning this speech to Prospero.

Style: as part of a three-handed scene

Where: unspecified, but somewhere close to her and her father's cell and close to Caliban's cave   **To Whom:** Caliban, in front of Prospero

# of Lines: 12   **Probable Timing: 0.40 minutes**

First Folio

16/ Miranda

1
    Abhorred Slave,
Which any print of goodnesse wilt not take,
Being capable of all ill: + I pittied thee,
Took pains to make thee speak, taught thee each houre
One thing or other: when thou didst not $_x$(Savage)$_x$
Know thine owne meaning;$_x$ but wouldst gabble,$_x$ like
A thing most brutish, I endow'd thy purposes
With words that made them knowne: But thy [vild] race +
('Tho thou didst learn) had that in't,$_x$ which good natures
Could not abide to be with: therefore wast thou
Deservedly confin'd into this Rocke, who hadst
Deserv'd more [then] a prison.

Modern Text

16/ Miranda

1
    Abhorred $^{\Delta}$slave,
Which any print of goodness* wilt not take,
Being capable of all ill! †
2
    I pitied* thee,
Took pains to make thee speak, taught thee each hour*
One thing or other. †
3
    When thou didst not, $^{\Delta}$savage,
Know thine own* meaning, but wouldst gabble like
A thing most brutish, I endow'd thy purposes
With words that made them known* · †
4
    But thy [vile] race,
(Though* thou didst learn) had that in't which good natures
Could not abide to be with; therefore wast thou
Deservedly confin'd into this $^{\Delta}$rock* ,
Who hadst deserv'd more [than] a prison.

Given the unpleasant circumstances this speech touches upon, though the speech is totally onrushed (just a single sentence compared to most modern texts' four), the tremendous self control Miranda displays (just ten excesses in eleven lines) and the balance between intellect and emotion (4/6) is startling for anyone, let alone someone so young – only the slight shifts between different styles mark the major signs of the difficulties she is undergoing.

• instead, the occasional releases stress specific points she wishes to drive home, including intellectually 'Slave', 'Savage', and 'Rocke', and emotionally 'goodnesse', 'pitied'

• thus the two line opening definition of Caliban as a 'Slave' . . . capable of all ill' is quite careful (1/1); how she responded to him and taught him becomes emotional (0/2): the surround phrase emphasis on Caliban's ignorance (; when thou didst not (Savage),/Know thine owne meaning ; ') is passionate (1/1); and then the last six lines of assessment and judgement (thus passing the second Prospero imposed test) are essentially a careful expression of almost completely unembellished lines, with only two of the last six phrases showing any signs of release (2/2)

17/ Ferdinand   Where shold this Musick be?   between 1.2.388 -408

Background: As part of the plan to allow Miranda and Ferdinand to meet, Prospero, through Ariel, has separated Ferdinand from his father and the rest of his party, both sides believing the other to be drowned. Ferdinand has been brought close to the cell where Prospero will soon allow Miranda to see and meet him, the first young human man she will have encountered since infancy.   The following are the first words from Ferdinand in the play, and as such are self explanatory.

Style: solo, unbeknownst to him in front of others
Where: unspecified, but somewhere close to Prospero & Miranda's cell and close to Caliban's cave   **To Whom:** self and audience address, led on by the invisible Ariel, in front of the hidden Prospero & Miranda

Probable Timing: 0.40 minutes

# of Lines: 12

Modern Text

17/ Ferdinand

1 Where should* this ^music* be?
         I'th'air* , or th'earth?

2

3 It sounds no more; and sure it waits* upon
   Some ^god o'^th'^island.*. †

4   Sitting on a bank*,
   Weeping again* the King my ^father's wrack* , ◊
   This ^music* crept by me upon the waters,
   Allaying both their fury and my passion
   With it's sweet ^air* ; thence I have follow'd it,
   (Or it hath drawn* me rather) . †
              But 'tis gone.

5 No, it begins again* .

6

7 The ^ditty does* remember my drown'd father . †

8 This is no mortal* business*, nor no sound
   That the earth owes. †

9   I hear* it now above me.

First Folio

17/ Ferdinand

1 Where shold this Musick be?
              I'th aire, or th'earth?

2

3 It sounds no more: ₓ and sure it waytes upon
   Some God' oth'lland,³ sitting on a banke,
   Weeping againe the King my Fathers wracke.

4 This Musicke crept by me upon the waters,
   Allaying both their fury,ₓ and my passion
   With it's sweet ayre: ₓ thence I have follow'd it ⁺
   (Or it hath drawne me rather) but 'tis gone.

5 No, it begins againe.

6 The Ditty do's remember my drown'd father,
   This is no mortall busines, nor no sound
   That the earth owes: I heare it now above me.

The disorientation suggested by F's orthography is discussed in detail in the footnote below. This, plus the first two very short sentences (a half line each) and F #3's opening with a short unembellished monosyllabic surround phrase suggest that, as yet, Ferdinand has difficulty in formulating complex ideas.

• in attempting to pin-point the 'Musicke', both as to place and to whom it belongs, the speech starts passionately (5/4, F #1-3), only to come up short against a totally ungrammatical period at the end of F #3, syntactically incorrect perhaps but in human terms an essential marker for Ferdinand, allowing him time to recover before continuing

• in describing how he first encountered the 'Musicke' and how 'it hath drawne me rather', though 'Musicke' is released as are the key words 'ayre' and 'drawne' in the last two lines, its impact both upon him ('Allaying both their fury, and my passion . . .') and his actions ('thence I have follow'd it/ . . . but 'tis gone.') is made even stronger by being unembellished

• as the music begins once more the short emotional F #5 (0/1) suggests for a moment Ferdinand returns to the somewhat inarticulate state he was in at the start of the speech

• and, as his faculties slowly return, so the releases move from the factual 'Ditty' through the emotional struggle 'no mortall busines' (with the long-spelled 'mortall' fighting against the short-spelled 'busines'), and the speech ends with the (slightly emotional) surround phrase at last pin-pointing where the music is coming from (0/1)

PCT ₃ most modern texts 'normalise' the punctuation of the passage as follows
        It sounds no more; and sure it waits upon
        Some god' oth'island.
            Sitting on a bank,
        Weeping again the King my father's wrack,
        This music crept by me upon the waters,
        It sounds no more: and sure it waytes upon
        Some God' oth'lland, sitting on a banke,
        Weeping againe the King my Fathers wracke.
        This Musicke crept by me upon the waters,
thus showing, at his first entry since the 'wreck', a Ferdinand much more rational than the original text offers: F's punctuation irregularities suggest a great deal of initial disorientation for him, viz.
with the comma after 'iland' suggesting that he is hurrying through to the next memory, and the non-grammatical period after 'wracke' giving him a much needed moment of silent gathering himself together at the recollection of his father's supposed death

18/ Ferdinand   There be some Sports are painfull ; & their labor   3.1.1-15

Background: To test Ferdinand and Miranda's strength of affection for each other, Prospero has forced him, a prince unused to manual labour, to tidy up the wood that Caliban has brought. As such the speech is self-explanatory.

Style: solo

Where: near to Prospero's cell   **To Whom:** direct audience address   **# of Lines:** 16

Probable Timing: 0.50 minutes

Modern Text

18/ Ferdinand

1 There be some △sports are painful* , & their labor
Delight in them [sets] off; △ some kinds* of baseness*
Are nobly undergone*; and most poor* matters
Point to rich ends. †

2   This my mean* △task*
Would be as heavy to me as odious, but
The △mistress* which I serve quickens what's dead,
And makes my labors* pleasures. †

3   O, △she is
Ten times more gentle [than] her △father's crabbed;
And he's compos'd of harshness* .

4   I must remove
Some thousands of these △logs, and pile them up,
Upon a sore injunction. †

5   My sweet △mistress*
Weeps* when she sees me work* , & says* such baseness*
Had never like △executor . †

6   I forget;
But these sweet thoughts, do* even refresh my labors* ,
Most [busil'est] when I do* it.

First Folio

18/ Ferdinand

1 There be some Sports are painfull;,x   & their labor
Delight in them [set] off: x   Some kindes of basenesse
Are nobly undergon; and most poore matters
Point to rich ends: this my meane Taske
Would be as heavy to me,x as odious, but
The Mistris which I serve,x quickens what's dead,
And makes my labours,x pleasures: O+ She is
Ten times more gentle,x [then] her Father's crabbed;
And he's compos'd of harshnesse .

2   I must remove
Some thousands of these Logs, and pile them up.
Upon a sore injunction; my sweet Mistris
Weepes when she sees me worke, & saies,x such basenes
Had never like Executor : I forget: x
But these sweet thoughts, doe even refresh my labours,
Most [busie lest],x when I doe it.

Within the onrushed F #1, the four pieces of major punctuation in the first four lines and the four extra breath-thoughts that quickly follow (marked, x) all seem to mark just where Ferdinand's (probable) handling the first menial task in his life requires extra effort, with the semicoloned moments perhaps requiring more effort than the others.

• and the occasional small cluster of unembellished words in the somewhat emotional (2/4) first three and half lines (' ; & their labor/Delight in them sets off :; 'Are nobly undergon'; 'Point to rich ends'; 'Would be as heavy to me, as odious'; 'quickens what's dead') could well suggest a moment of rest before beginning the physical heavy work once again

• it's possible that he stops the work to condemn 'this my meane Taske' making his 'labours, pleasures', for these next three lines are not interrupted by major punctuation and are also passionate (2/3)

• then the comparison of Miranda ('ten times more gentle') to her father ('crabbed') is intellectual (3/1, F#1's last two lines), and highlighted by being set as emotional (semicolon created) surround phrases

• the relative care of F #2's first two lines (1/0) and the subject matter suggest that Ferdinand may have started his labours once more

• however, recalling his 'Mistris' tears and words move him to passion once more (2/2), and in finishing with the fact that he can 'refresh' himself from 'these sweet thoughts', so he becomes totally emotional (0/3 the last two lines of the speech)

19/ Miranda   Alas, now pray you/Worke not so hard :   I would the lightning had   between 3.1.15 - 32

Background: Defying her father's orders, Miranda has come to help Ferdinand.   Unbeknownst to her, Prospero is watching over them both, and is secretly delighted.

Style: as part of a two-handed scene

Where: near to Prospero's cell   **To Whom:** Ferdinand, unaware that Prospero is watching

# of Lines: 12   **Probable Timing: 0.40 minutes**

Modern Text

19/ Miranda

1 Alas, now pray you
   Work* not so hard . †

        I would the lightning had

2 Burnt up those ⁴logs that you are enjoin'd* to pile. †

3 Pray set it down*, and rest you . †

4   When this burns* ,

               My ⁴father
5 "Twill weep* for having wearied you . †

   Is hard at study ; pray now rest your self* ,
   He's* safe for these three hours* .

                    If you'll* sit down* ,
6
                         Pray give me that,

7 I'll bear* your ⁴logs* the while . †

   I'll carry it to the pile.

               It would become me

   As well as it do's you ; and I should do it
   With much more ease, for my good will is to it,
   And yours it is against {,}

               {for y}ou look* wearily.

First Folio

19/ Miranda

1 Alas, now pray you
   Worke not so hard :   I would the lightning had
   Burnt up those Logs that you are enjoynd to pile :
   Pray set it downe, and rest you :   when this burnes +
   'Twill weepe for having wearied you :   my Father
   Is hard at study ; pray now rest your selfe,
   Hee's safe for these three houres .

                         If you'l sit downe +
2 Ile beare your Logges the while :   pray give me that,
   Ile carry it to the pile.

                    It would become me
3
   As well as it do's you ;   and I should do it
   With much more ease ;   for my good will is to it,
   And yours it is against {.}   x
4
                              {for y}ou looke wearily.

Given that this is her first first teenage love situation, it's not surprising that the **speech is emotional overall (3/12 in eleven and a half lines).   What is startling is that all but the last phrase can be described as surround phrases.   Also the eight pieces of major punctuation not only mark where she wants to make her thoughts absolutely clear (compare speeches #15-16 above), they also seem to set up moments where she's almost tongue-tied and not quite sure what to say next - especially at each point where the semicolons mark where she almost says much too much.**

• the first sentence is carefully emotional (2/8) with essentially just one heightened word per phrase, and this together with the monosyllabic opening 'Alas, now pray you/Worke not so hard:' suggests Miranda is very vulnerable both in words and feelings

• thus the two phrases with double releases, about the 'Logs' ('when this burnes/'Twill weepe for having wearied you') and her father ("Hee's safe for these three houres.'), probably carry extra weight as far as she (and may be Ferdinand) is concerned

• the move from talking to him to actually physically helping him, F #2's '. If you'l sit downe/Ile beare your Logges the while : ' is very strong, set as it is as a passionate monosyllabic surround phrase (1/3), so it's strange that the surround phrase that follows is unembellished - unless she either realises that she may have said too much or perhaps even come too close to him physically

• whatever the reason, it has had a great impact on her - for the final three and half line sentence is also totally unembellished, and it seems the calmness is very carefully enforced, for bubbling underneath her explanation is the two surround phrase start (created by the emotional semicolon), the second also monosyllabic

20/ Ferdinand   Noble Mistris, {ψ} I do beseech you   between 3.1.33 - 76

Background: This is Ferdinand's response to Miranda's suggestion 'You looke wearily', in which, upon at last learning her name, he starts his wooing by (perhaps rather clumsily) playing formal word games based upon her name, which he quickly abandons for straightforward honesty.

Style: as part of a two-handed scene

Where: near to Prospero's cell   **To Whom:** Miranda, unaware that Prospero is watching

# of Lines: 28   **Probable Timing: 1.30 minutes**

Modern Text

20/ Ferdinand

1
{ψ} Noble △mistress*, {ψ} I do beseech you
Chiefly* that I might set it in my prayers -
What is your name?

2
        Admir'd Miranda,
Indeed* the top of △admiration ! worth
What's dearest* to the world! †
                    Full many a △lady
I have ey'd with best regard, and many a time
Th'harmony of their tongues hath into bondage
Brought my too diligent ear* . †

3
            For several* virtues
Have I lik'd several* women, never any
With so full soul* but some defect in her
Did quarrel* with the noblest grace she ow'd,
And put it to the foil* .

4
        But you, O you,
So perfect and so peerless* , are created
Of every* Creatures best !

5
        I am, in my condition,
A △prince, Miranda; I do think* , a △king
(I would, not so !), and would no more endure
This wooden* slavery* [than] to suffer
The flesh-fly* blow my mouth. †
        Hear* my soul* speak* .

6
The very* instant that I saw you, did
My heart fly* to your service, there resides
To make me slave to it, and for your sake
Am I this patient △log*-man.

First Folio

20/ Ferdinand

1
{ψ} Noble Mistris, {ψ} I do beseech you
Cheefely, that I might set it in my prayers,
What is your name?

2
        Admir'd Miranda,
Indeede the top of Admiration : + worth
What's deerest to the world: + full many a Lady
I have ey'd with best regard, and many a time
Th'harmony of their tongues, hath into bondage
Brought my too diligent eare: for severall vertues
Have I lik'd severall women, never any
With so full soule,ₓ but some defect in her
Did quarrell with the noblest grace she ow'd,
And put it to the foile.

3
        But you, O you,
So perfect, and so peerelesse, are created
Of everie Creatures best. +

4
        I am, in my condition +
A Prince ₓ (Miranda) + I do thinke + a King
(I would + not so+)+ and would no more endure
This wodden slaverie,ₓ [then] to suffer
The flesh-flie blow my mouth: heare my soule speake.

5
The verie instant that I saw you, did
My heart flie to your service, there resides
To make me slave to it, and for your sake
Am I this patient Logge-man.

This is another fine example of a teenager in love, and what is remarkable about it is that after the opening flailing (9/15 in the eighteen lines of F #1-4), the moment he speaks of 'The verie instant that I saw you', five of the final ten lines are unembellished, in part suggesting that his attempted rhetorical game playing and embarrassment are over – but his feelings are not, for the remaining six lines are full of emotional release (0/6).

• thus Ferdinand starts very carefully, with the beginning of the first and second lines each showing a little release, and then finding some self-control for the remainder of each line, and the monosyllabic unembellished key question 'What is your name?' – so far having only been able to refer to her as his 'Mistris'

• learning her name allows him to spring into a small series of passionate dreadful word games (3/2, the first four lines of F #2), though he becomes (enforced calm?) very quiet as he offers the word sound match of 'full many a Lady/I have ey'd'

• and then, whether he is immediately conscious of it, expanding his earlier mention of 'full many a Lady' to stating he has admired 'severall women' arouses emotion in him (0/5 the five and a half lines ending the sentence)

• and, as he turns his attention to 'you, O you', he becomes passionate (2/1, F #3)

• his intellectual definition (3/1, the first line that opens F #4) of himself as 'King', quickly undercut by the unembellished sad oblique reference to the presumed death of his father ('I would not so'), then turns to emotion (0/4, the last three lines of F #4) as the sentence ends with his emotional monosyllabic surround phrase plea to ':heare my soule speake. ')

• then comes an unembellished passage of nearly four lines as he explains it is only because 'My heart flie to your service' that he is putting up with being a 'Logge-man' (the only words that break the calm, F #5, 1/1)

6　O heaven;ₓ　O earth, beare witnes to this sound,
　And crowne what I professe with kinde event
　If I speake true:⁺ if hollowly, invert
　What best is boaded me,ₓ to mischiefe:⁺ I,
　Beyond all limit of what else i'th world⁺
　Do love, prize, honor you.
　　　　　　　　　　　Wherefore weepe you?

7

9　O heaven, O earth, bear* witness* to this sound,
　And crown* what I profess* with kind* event
　If I speak* true*! if hollowly* invert
　What best is boded* me to mischief*!⁺ †
　　　　　　　　　　　　　I,

10　Beyond all limit of what else i'th'world,
　Do love, prize, honor you.
　　　　　　　　　Wherefore weep* you?

11　　　　　　　　　　　

• not surprisingly his appeal for 'heaven' and 'earth' to 'witnes' what he is about to say is highly emotional (1/7, F #6's first four lines), while, quite charmingly, the final two line declaration that 'I . . . love, prize, honor you' is completely unembellished

• and then comes the wonderful, and again charming, teenage lack of understanding as he innocently poses the last very short question, 'Wherefore weepe you?' (F #7, 0/1)

21/ Miranda   I do not know/One of my sexe ;   no womans face remember,   between 3.1.48 - 86

Background: And this is Miranda's response to Ferdinand's love declaration (speech #20 immediately above). Since she has had no experience of playing coy (compare Juliet's lovely admission to Romeo, 'I should have beene more strange, I must confesse'), she is as innocently open, direct, and honest as she is elsewhere in the play.

Style: as part of a two-handed scene

Where: near to Prospero's cell   **To Whom:** Ferdinand unaware that Prospero is watching

# of Lines: 21   **Probable Timing: 1.10 minutes**

Modern Text

21/ Miranda

1   I do not know
     One of my sex* ; no woman's face remember,
     Save, from my glass*, mine own* ; △ nor have I seen*
     More that I may call men [than] you, good friend,
     And my dear* △father* . †

          How features are abroad

2   I am skilless* of; but by my modesty*
     (The jewel* in my dower), I would not wish
     Any △companion in the world but you;
     Nor can imagination form* a shape,
     Besides your self*, to like of. †

                    But I prattle
     Something too wildly* , and my △father's precepts
     I therein do forget.

3   I am a fool*
     To weep* at what I am glad of.

4   {And I weep* }
     At mine unworthiness*, that dare not offer
     What I desire to give, and much less* take
     What I shall die to want. †

                    But this is trifling;
     And all the more it seeks* to hide itself*;
     The bigger bulk* it shows*.

5   Hence, bashful* cunning!
     And prompt me, plain* and holy innocence !

6   I am your wife, if you will marry* me;
     If not, I'll die your maid . †

                    To be your fellow

7   You may deny*, me ; but I'll be your servant,
     Whether you will or no.

First Folio

21/ Miranda

1   I do not know
     One of my sexe; no womans face remember,
     Save + from my glasse, mine owne: x   Nor have I seene
     More that I may call men, x [then] you + good friend,
     And my deere Father: how features are abroad
     I am skillesse of; but by my modestie
     (The jewell in my dower) + I would not wish
     Any Companion in the world but you : x
     Nor can imagination forme a shape +
     Besides your selfe, to like of: but I prattle
     Something too wildely; and my Fathers precepts
     I therein do forget.

2   I am a foole
     To weepe at what I am glad of.

3   {And I weepe }
     At mine unworthinesse, that dare not offer
     What I desire to give; x and much lesse take
     What I shall die to want: But this is trifling; +
     And all the more it seekes to hide it selfe,
     The bigger bulke it shewes.

4   Hence + bashfull cunning, +
     And prompt me + plaine and holy innocence. +

5   I am your wife, if you will marrie me;
     If not, Ile die your maid: to be your fellow
     You may denie me, but Ile be your servant +
     Whether you will or no.

In comparison to most modern texts' rational nine sentences, F's five sentences seem to present a character with **much less self-control – yet by speech's end, F's orthography has marked Miranda's wonderful growth from awkwardness to maturity – a far more interesting and truthful human reality for a young adolescent in love than the self-controlled young woman the modern reworking seems to present.**

* as with speech #19 above, that Miranda finds her I-don't-know-what-men-and-women-are-like opening quite awkward can be seen in that
  a/ F sets the confession as one onrushed sentence
  b/ there are four pieces of major punctuation in the first five lines
  c/ three of the four surround phrases so created are emotional, formed in part by semicolons
  d/ the whole is quite emotional (2/6)

* and, as she asserts by the 'jewell' of her 'modestie' she 'would not wish/Any Companion in the world but you', she seems to establish self-control, for in the ensuing four lines only three operative words are singled out for release, (as already seen 'jewell' and 'Companion', accompanied by 'your selfe'), all three vital to her own declaration of love, the latter heightened by being set in a surround phrase

* and, as charmingly as with Ferdinand's awkwardness, her confession that she prattles 'Something too wildely' is also set as a surround phrase where emotion and intellect both break into her self-control (1/1, the last two lines of F #1)

* and then her emotions take over a she voices thoughts of her own 'unworthinesse' and acknowledges her tears (1/9, F #2-3) – especially noticeable in the only (emotional) surround phrase in the sentence, ':'and much lesse take/What I shall die to want;' - its pain heightened by being monosyllabic

* yet, a great testament to her inner fortitude, following her emotional rejection of 'bashfull cunning' and her plea for the help of 'holy innocence' (F #4, 0/2), the final three and half line declaration of complete love is totally unembellished, the first declarations once more formed by two emotional surround phrases

BIBLIOGRAPHY

The most easily accessible general information is to be found under the citations of *Campbell*, and of *Halliday*. The finest summation of matters academic is to be found within the all-encompassing *A Textual Companion*, listed below in the first part of the bibliography under *Wells, Stanley and Taylor, Gary* (eds.)

Individual modern editions consulted are listed below under the separate headings 'The Complete Works in Compendium Format' and 'The Complete Works in Separate Individual Volumes,' from which the modern text audition speeches have been collated and compiled.

All modern act, scene, and/or line numbers refer the reader to *The Riverside Shakespeare*, in my opinion still the best of the complete works, despite the excellent compendiums that have been published since.

The F/Q material is taken from a variety of already published sources, including not only all the texts listed in the 'Photostatted Reproductions in Compendium Format' below, but also earlier individually printed volumes, such as the twentieth century editions published under the collective title *The Facsimiles of Plays from The First Folio of Shakespeare* by Faber & Gwyer, and the nineteenth century editions published on behalf of The New Shakespere Society.

The heading 'Single Volumes of Special Interest' is offered to newcomers to Shakespeare in the hope that the books may add useful knowledge about the background and craft of this most fascinating of theatrical figures.

PHOTOSTATTED REPRODUCTIONS OF THE ORIGINAL TEXTS IN COMPENDIUM FORMAT

Allen, M.J.B. and K. Muir, (eds.). *Shakespeare's Plays in Quarto.* Berkeley: University of California Press, 1981.

Blaney, Peter (ed.). *The Norton Facsimile (The First Folio of Shakespeare).* New York: W.W.Norton & Company, Inc., 1996 (see also Hinman, below).

Brewer D.S. (ed.). *Mr. William Shakespeare's Comedies, Histories & Tragedies, The Second/Third/Fourth Folio Reproduced in Facsimile.* (3 vols.), 1983.

Hinman, Charlton (ed.). *The Norton Facsimile (The First Folio of Shakespeare).* New York: W.W.Norton & Company, Inc., 1968.

Kökeritz, Helge (ed.). *Mr. William Shakespeare's Comedies, Histories & Tragedies.* New Haven: Yale University Press, 1954.

Moston, Doug (ed.). *Mr. William Shakespeare's Comedies, Histories, and Tragedies.* New York: Routledge, 1998.

MODERN TYPE VERSION OF THE FIRST FOLIO IN COMPENDIUM FORMAT

Freeman, Neil. (ed.). *The Applause First Folio Of Shakespeare In Modern Type.* New York & London: Applause Books, 2001.

MODERN TEXT VERSIONS OF THE COMPLETE WORKS IN COMPENDIUM FORMAT

Craig, H. and D. Bevington (eds.). *The Complete Works of Shakespeare.* Glenview: Scott, Foresman and Company, 1973.

Evans, G.B. (ed.). *The Riverside Shakespeare.* Boston: Houghton Mifflin Company, 1974.

Wells, Stanley and Gary Taylor (eds.). *The Oxford Shakespeare, William Shakespeare, the Complete Works, Original Spelling Edition,* Oxford: The Clarendon Press, 1986.

Wells, Stanley and Gary Taylor (eds.). *The Oxford Shakespeare, William Shakespeare, The Complete Works, Modern Spelling Edition.* Oxford: The Clarendon Press, 1986.

MODERN TEXT VERSIONS OF THE COMPLETE WORKS IN SEPARATE INDIVIDUAL VOLUMES

The Arden Shakespeare. London: Methuen & Co. Ltd., Various dates, editions, and editors.

Folio Texts. Freeman, Neil H. M. (ed.) Applause First Folio Editions, 1997, and following.

The New Cambridge Shakespeare. Cambridge: Cambridge University Press. Various dates, editions, and editors.

New Variorum Editions of Shakespeare. Furness, Horace Howard (original editor.). New York: 1880. Various reprints. All these volumes have been in a state of re-editing and reprinting since they first appeared in 1880. Various dates, editions, and editors.

The Oxford Shakespeare. Wells, Stanley (general editor). Oxford: Oxford University Press, Various dates and editors.

The New Penguin Shakespeare. Harmondsworth, Middlesex: Penguin Books, Various dates and editors.

The Shakespeare Globe Acting Edition. Tucker, Patrick and Holden, Michael. (eds.). London: M.H.Publications, Various dates.

SINGLE VOLUMES OF SPECIAL INTEREST

Baldwin, T.W. *William Shakespeare's Petty School.* 1943.

Baldwin, T.W. *William Shakespeare's Small Latin and Lesse Greeke.* (2 vols.) 1944.

Barton, John. *Playing Shakespeare.* 1984.

Beckerman, Bernard. *Shakespeare at the Globe, 1599-1609.* 1962.

Berryman, John. *Berryman's Shakespeare.* 1999.

Bloom, Harold. *Shakespeare: The Invention of the Human.* 1998.

Booth, Stephen (ed.). *Shakespeare's Sonnets.* 1977.

Briggs, Katharine. *An Encyclopedia of Fairies.* 1976.

Campbell, Oscar James, and Edward G. Quinn (eds.). *The Reader's Encyclopedia OF Shakespeare.* 1966.

Crystal, David, and Ben Crystal. *Shakespeare's Words: A Glossary & Language Companion.* 2002.

Flatter, Richard. *Shakespeare's Producing Hand.* 1948 (reprint).

Ford, Boris. (ed.). *The Age of Shakespeare.* 1955.

Freeman, Neil H.M. *Shakespeare's First Texts.* 1994.

Greg, W.W. *The Editorial Problem in Shakespeare: A Survey of the Foundations of the Text.* 1954 (3rd. edition).

Gurr, Andrew. *Playgoing in Shakespeare's London.* 1987.

Gurr, Andrew. *The Shakespearean Stage, 1574-1642.* 1987.

Halliday, F.E. *A Shakespeare Companion.* 1952.

Harbage, Alfred. *Shakespeare's Audience.* 1941.

Harrison, G.B. (ed.). *The Elizabethan Journals.* 1965 (revised, 2 vols.).

Harrison, G.B. (ed.). *A Jacobean Journal.* 1941.

Harrison, G.B. (ed.). *A Second Jacobean Journal.* 1958.

Hinman, Charlton. *The Printing and Proof Reading of the First Folio of Shakespeare.* 1963 (2 vols.).

Joseph, Bertram. *Acting Shakespeare.* 1960.

Joseph, Miriam (Sister). *Shakespeare's Use of The Arts of Language.* 1947.

King, T.J. *Casting Shakespeare's Plays.* 1992.

Lee, Sidney and C.T. Onions. *Shakespeare's England: An Account Of The Life And Manners Of His Age.* (2 vols.) 1916.

Linklater, Kristin. *Freeing Shakespeare's Voice.* 1992.

Mahood, M.M. *Shakespeare's Wordplay.* 1957.

O'Connor, Gary. *William Shakespeare: A Popular Life.* 2000.

Ordish, T.F. *Early London Theatres.* 1894. (1971 reprint).

Rodenberg, Patsy. *Speaking Shakespeare.* 2002.

Schoenbaum. S. *William Shakespeare: A Documentary Life.* 1975.

Shapiro, Michael. *Children of the Revels.* 1977.

Simpson, Percy. *Shakespeare's Punctuation.* 1969 (reprint).

Smith, Irwin. *Shakespeare's Blackfriars Playhouse.* 1964.

Southern, Richard. *The Staging of Plays Before Shakespeare.* 1973.

Spevack, M. *A Complete and Systematic Concordance to the Works Of Shakespeare.* 1968–1980 (9 vols.).

Tillyard, E.M.W. *The Elizabethan World Picture.* 1942.

Trevelyan, G.M. (ed.). *Illustrated English Social History.* 1942.

Vendler, Helen. *The Art of Shakespeare's Sonnets.* 1999.

Walker, Alice F. *Textual Problems of the First Folio.* 1953.

Walton, J.K. *The Quarto Copy of the First Folio.* 1971.

Warren, Michael. *William Shakespeare, The Parallel King Lear 1608–1623.*

Wells, Stanley and Taylor, Gary (eds.). *Modernising Shakespeare's Spelling, with Three Studies in The Text of Henry V.* 1975.

Wells, Stanley. *Re-Editing Shakespeare for the Modern Reader.* 1984.

Wells, Stanley and Gary Taylor (eds.). *William Shakespeare: A Textual Companion.* 1987.

Wright, George T. *Shakespeare's Metrical Art.* 1988.

HISTORICAL DOCUMENTS

Daniel, Samuel. *The Fowre Bookes of the Civile Warres Between The Howses Of Lancaster and Yorke.* 1595.

Holinshed, Raphael. *Chronicles of England, Scotland and Ireland.* 1587 (2nd. edition).

Halle, Edward. *The Union of the Two Noble and Illustre Famelies of Lancastre And Yorke.* 1548 (2nd. edition).

Henslowe, Philip: Foakes, R.A. and Rickert (eds.). *Henslowe's Diary.* 1961.

Plutarch: North, Sir Thomas (translation of a work in French prepared by Jacques Amyots). *The Lives of The Noble Grecians and Romanes.* 1579.

APPENDIX 1:
GUIDE TO THE PHOTOSTATS OF THE EARLY TEXTS

A QUARTO (Q)

A single text, so called because of the book size resulting from a particular method of printing. Eighteen of Shakespeare's plays were published in this format by different publishers at various dates between 1594–1622, prior to the appearance of the 1623 Folio. An extremely useful collection of them is to be found in: Allen, Michael J.B., and Kenneth Muir (eds.), *Shakespeare's Plays In Quarto*, Berkeley: University of California Press. 1981.

THE FIRST FOLIO (F1) [1]

Thirty-six of Shakespeare's plays (excluding *Pericles* and *Two Noble Kinsmen*, in which he had a hand) appeared in one volume, published in 1623. All books of this size were termed Folios, again because of the sheet size and printing method, hence this volume is referred to as the First Folio. For publishing details see Bibliography, 'Photostated Reproductions of the Original Texts.'

THE SECOND FOLIO (F2)

Scholars suggest that the Second Folio, dated 1632 but perhaps not published until 1640, has little authority, especially since it created hundreds of new problematic readings of its own. Nevertheless more than 800 modern text readings can be attributed to it. The most recent reproduction is Brewer, D.S. (ed.). *Mr. William Shakespeare's Comedies, Histories & Tragedies, the Second Folio Reproduced in Facsimile.* Dover. Boydell & Brewer Ltd., 1985.

The Third Folio (1664) and the Fourth Folio (1685) have even less authority, and are rarely consulted except in cases of extreme difficulty.

THE THIRD FOLIO (F3)

The Third Folio, carefully proofed (though apparently not against the previous edition), takes great pains to correct anomalies in punctuation ending speeches and in expanding abbreviations. It also introduced seven new plays supposedly written by Shakespeare, only one of which, Pericles, has been established as such. The most recent reproduction is, Brewer, D.S. (ed.). *Mr. William Shakespeare's Comedies, Histories & Tragedies, The Third Folio Reproduced in Facsimile*, Dover. Boydell & Brewer Ltd.. 1985.

THE FOURTH FOLIO (F4)

Paradoxically, while the Fourth Folio was the most carefully edited of all, its concentration on grammatical clarity and ease of comprehension by its readers at the expense of faithful reproduction of F1 renders it the least useful for those interested in the setting down on paper of Elizabethan theatre texts. The most recent reproduction is, Brewer, D.S. (ed.). *Mr. William Shakespeare's Comedies, Histories & Tragedies, The Fourth Folio Reproduced in Facsimile.* Dover. Boydell & Brewer Ltd., 1985.

---

[1] for a full overview of the First Folio see the monumental two volume work by Charlton Hinman, *The Printing And Proof Reading Of The First Folio Of Shakespeare.* (2 volumes). Oxford: Clarendon Press. 1963.. and W.W Greg. *The Editorial Problem In Shakespeare: A Survey Of The Foundations Of The Text.* Oxford: Clarendon Press. 1954 (3rd. edition).: for a brief summary, see the forty-six page publication from, Peter W.M. Blayney, *The First Folio Of Shakespeare:* Washington, D.C: Folger Library Publications. 1991.

APPENDIX 2:
WORD, WORDS, WORDS

PART ONE: VERBAL CONVENTIONS (and how they will be set in the Folio Text column)

"THEN" AND "THAN"

These two words, though their neutral vowels sound different to modern ears, were almost identical to Elizabethan speakers and readers, despite their different meanings. F and Q make little distinction between them, setting them interchangeably. The original setting will be used, and the modern reader should soon get used to substituting one for the other as necessary.

"I," "AY," AND "AYE"

F/Q often print the personal pronoun "I" and the word of agreement "aye" simply as "I." Again, the modern reader should quickly get used to this and make the substitution when necessary. The reader should also be aware that very occasionally either word could be used and the phrase make perfect sense, even though different meanings would be implied.

"MY SELFE/HIM SELFE/HER SELFE" VERSUS "MYSELF/HIMSELF/HERSELF"

Generally F/Q separate the two parts of the word, "my selfe" while most modern texts set the single word "myself." The difference is vital, based on Elizabethan philosophy. Elizabethans regarded themselves as composed of two parts, the corporeal "I," and the more spiritual part, the "self." Thus, when an Elizabethan character refers to "my selfe," he or she is often referring to what is to all intents and purposes a separate being, even if that being is a particular part of him- or herself. Thus soliloquies can be thought of as a debate between the "I" and "my selfe," and, in such speeches, even though there may be only one character on-stage, it's as if there were two distinct entities present.

UNUSUAL SPELLING OF REAL NAMES, BOTH OF PEOPLE AND PLACES

Real names, both of people and places, and foreign languages are often reworked for modern understanding. For example, the French town often set in F1 as "Callice" is usually reset as "Calais." F will be set as is.

NON-GRAMMATICAL USES OF VERBS IN BOTH TENSE AND APPLICATION

Modern texts 'correct' the occasional Elizabethan practice of setting a singular noun with plural verb (and vice versa), as well as the infrequent use of the past tense of a verb to describe a current situation. The F reading will be set as is, without annotation.

ALTERNATIVE SETTINGS OF A WORD WHERE DIFFERENT SPELLINGS MAINTAIN THE SAME MEANING

F/Q occasionally set what appears to modern eyes as an archaic spelling of a word for which there is a more common modern alternative, for example "murther" for murder, "burthen" for burden, "moe" for more, "vilde" for vile. Though some modern texts set the F1 (or alternative Q) setting, others modernise. F1 will be set as is with no annotation.

ALTERNATIVE SETTINGS OF A WORD WHERE DIFFERENT SPELLINGS SUGGEST DIFFERENT MEANINGS

Far more complicated is the situation where, while an Elizabethan could substitute one word formation for another and still imply the same thing, to modern eyes the substituted word has a entirely different meaning to the one it has replaced. The following is by no means an exclusive list of the more common dual-spelling, dual-meaning words

anticke-antique	mad-made	sprite-spirit
borne-borne	metal-mettle	sun-sonne
hart-heart	mote-moth	travel-travaill
human-humane	pour-(powre)-power	through-thorough
lest-least	reverent-reverend	troth-truth
lose-loose	right-rite	whether-whither

Some of these doubles offer a metrical problem too, for example "sprite," a one syllable word, versus "spirit." A potential problem occurs in *A Midsummer Nights Dream*, where the modern texts set Q1's "thorough," and thus the scansion pattern of elegant magic can be established, whereas F1's more plebeian "through" sets up a much more awkward and clumsy moment.

The F reading will be set in the Folio Text, as will the modern texts' substitution of a different word formation in the Modern Text column. If the modern text substitution has the potential to alter the meaning (and sometimes scansion) of the line, it will be noted accordingly.

PART TWO: WORD FORMATIONS COUNTED AS EQUIVALENTS FOR THE FOLLOWING SPEECHES

Often the spelling differences between the original and modern texts are quite obvious, as with "she"/"shee". And sometimes Folio text passages are so flooded with longer (and sometimes shorter) spellings that, as described in the General Introduction, it would seem that vocally something unusual is taking place as the character speaks.

However, there are some words where the spelling differences are so marginal that they need not be explored any further. The following is by no means an exclusive list of words that in the main will not be taken into account when discussing emotional moments ("Russian" or "Volcanic" Shakespeare) in the various commentaries accompanying the audition speeches.

(modern text spelling shown first)

and - &	murder - murther	tabor - taber
apparent - apparant	mutinous - mutenous	ta'en - tane
briars - briers	naught - nought	than - then
choice - choise	obey - obay	theater - theatre
defense - defence	o'er - o're	then - than
debtor - debter	offense - offence	
enchant - inchant	quaint - queint	uncurrant - uncurrent
endurance - indurance	reside - recide	
ere - e'er		venomous - venemous
expense - expence	Saint - S.	virtue - vertue
has - ha's	sense - sence	weight - waight
heinous - hainous	sepulchre - sepulcher	
	show - shew	
I''ll - Ile	solicitor - soliciter	
increase - encrease	sugar - suger	

APPENDIX 3:
THE PATTERN OF MAGIC, RITUAL & INCANTATION

THE PATTERNS OF "NORMAL" CONVERSATION

The normal pattern of a regular Shakespearean verse line is akin to five pairs of human heart beats, with ten syllables being arranged in five pairs of beats, each pair alternating a pattern of a weak stress followed by a strong stress. Thus, a normal ten syllable heartbeat line (with the emphasis on the capitalised words) would read as

weak - STRONG, weak - STRONG, weak - STRONG, weak - STRONG, weak - STRONG
(shall   I   com——PARE thee TO   a   SUMM——ers   DAY)

Breaks would either be in length (under or over ten syllables) or in rhythm (any combinations of stresses other than the five pairs of weak-strong as shown above), or both together.

THE PATTERNS OF MAGIC, RITUAL, AND INCANTATION

Whenever magic is used in the Shakespeare plays the form of the spoken verse changes markedly in two ways. The length is usually reduced from ten to just seven syllables, and the pattern of stresses is completely reversed, as if the heartbeat was being forced either by the circumstances of the scene or by the need of the speaker to completely change direction. Thus in comparison to the normal line shown above, or even the occasional minor break, the more tortured and even dangerous magic or ritual line would read as

STRONG - weak, STRONG - weak, STRONG - weak, STRONG
(WHEN   shall   WE   three   MEET   a——GAINE)

The strain would be even more severely felt in an extended passage, as when the three weyward Sisters begin the potion that will fetch Macbeth to them. Again, the spoken emphasis is on the capitalised words and the effort of, and/or fixed determination in, speaking can clearly be felt.

THRICE the BRINDed CAT hath MEW"D
THRICE and ONCE the HEDGE-Pigge WHIN"D
HARPier CRIES, 'tis TIME, 'tis TIME.

UNUSUAL ASPECTS OF MAGIC

It's not always easy for the characters to maintain it (as with Pucke in *A Midsummer Nights Dream*, speech #34, and especially Prospero in *The Tempest*, speech #4). And the magic doesn't always come when the character expects it (as with the Duke in *Measure For Measure*, speech #12, or Prospero in *The Tempest*, speech #3). What is even more interesting is that while the pattern is found a lot in the Comedies, it is usually in much gentler situations, often in songs (*Two Gentlemen of Verona, Merry Wives of Windsor, Much Ado About Nothing, Twelfth Night, The Winters Tale*) and/or simplistic poetry (*Loves Labours Lost* and *As You Like It*), as well as the casket sequence in *The Merchant of Venice*.

It's too easy to dismiss these settings as inferior poetry known as doggerel. But this may be doing the moment and the character a great disservice. The language may be simplistic, but the passion and the magical/ritual intent behind it is wonderfully sincere. It's not just a matter of magic for the sake of magic, as with Pucke and Oberon enchanting mortals and Titania; or Prospero controlling the elements; or the weyward Sisters; or even Macbeth attempting to control the denizens of the 'half' and spirit worlds. It's a matter of the human heart's desires too.

And though none of the following speeches are included in these volumes, no wonder magic is used by, among others: Dumaine, the youngest Navarre lover in *Loves Labours Lost*, in his poetry when worshipping a lady for whom Jove himself would deny his godhood and turn 'mortall for thy Love'; Phebe in *As You Like It*, wondering whether Ganymede, the disguised Rosalind, is a 'god, to Shepherd turn'd?'; and Orlando, also in *As You Like It*, when writing paons of praise to Rosalind suggesting that she is composed of the best parts of the mythical heroines because

THEREfore HEAven NAture CHARG'D
THAT one BODie SHOULD be FILL"D
WITH all GRACes WIDE enLARG"D

And what could be better than Autolycus (*The Winters Tale*) using magic in his opening song as an extra enticement to trap the unwary into buying all his peddler's goods, ballads, and trinkets.

To help the reader, most magic/ritual lines will be bolded in the Folio text version of the speeches.